Legal Terminology

Fifth Edition

Gordon W. Brown, J.D.
Member of the Massachusetts and Federal Bars
Professor Emeritus
North Shore Community College
Danvers, Massachusetts

Upper Saddle River, New Jersey 07458

Library of Congress Cataloging in Publication Data

Brown, Gordon W.

Legal terminology / Gordon W. Brown.—5th ed.

p. cm.

Includes index.

ISBN-13 978-0-13-156804-4

ISBN-10 0-13-156804-3

1. Law—United States—Terminology. I. Title.

KF156.B725 2008

349.73'01'4—dc22 2007004604

Editor-in-Chief: Vernon R. Anthony
Senior Acquisitions Editor: Gary Bauer
Developmental Editor: Linda Cupp
Editorial Assistant: Dan Trudden
Marketing Manager: Leigh Ann Sims
Marketing Coordinator: Alicia Dysert
Managing Editor—Production: Mary Carnis
Manufacturing Buyer: Ilene Sanford
Production Liaison: Denise Brown
Full-Service Production and Composition: Jessica Balch/Pine Tree Composition
Media Production Project Manager: Lisa Rinaldi
Senior Design Coordinator: Christopher Weigand
Cover Design: Wanda España
Cover Image: Corbis Images
Printer/Binder: R.R. Donnelley, Willard, OH
Cover Printer: Phoenix Color Corp.

Pearson Education LTD.
Pearson Education Singapore, Pte. Ltd
Pearson Education, Canada, Ltd
Pearson Education–Japan
Pearson Education Australia PTY, Limited
Pearson Education North Asia Ltd
Pearson Educación de Mexico, S.A. de C.V.
Pearson Education Malaysia, Pte. Ltd
Pearson Education, Upper Saddle River, NJ

10 9 8 7 6 5
ISBN-13: 978-0-13-156804-4
ISBN-10: 0-13-156804-3

Dedication

It is with love, joy, and gratitude that I dedicate this distinctive book filled with weird and wonderful terms to:

1. *My lineal descendants to whom I am related by consanguinity and their spouses (who are not my kindred but whom I love just the same): Steven, Linda, Joshua, Kaleigh, Christopher, Matthew, Jan, Ryan, Corey, Emily, Deborah, Michael, Patrick, Connor, Camden, Melonie, Jennifer, Harbir, Millin, Kurrin, Timothy, Celeste, Nicholas, and David.*
2. *My collateral kindred and their spouses:*

   Siblings—*Alan, Lois, Natalie, Robert, and Jacqueline;*

   Nieces and Nephews—*Mary Ann, Robert, William, James, Christopher, Ruth, Bruce, David, and Cheryl;*

   Grand Nieces and Nephews—*Thomas, Meire, Joshua, Timothy, Dereck, Desteny, Kevin, Brian, and Justin;*

   Great Grand Nieces—*Olivia and Isabella;*

   First Cousins—*Eva and Lois;*

   First Cousins Once Removed—*Carol Lee, Alan, Suzanne, James, Mary Ann, and Robert;*

   First Cousins Twice Removed—*Christine, Gregory, Heather, Thomas, and Meire;*

   First Cousins Thrice Removed—*Trevor, Spencer, Parker, Olivia, and Isabella;*

   Second Cousins—*Virginia, Suzanne, Bob, Wendy, and Mark;*

   Second Cousins Once Removed—*Kathleen, Danny, Stephanie, and Alison;*

   Second Cousin Twice Removed—*Robert*
3. *Those to whom I am related by affinity and their spouses: Myra, Brian, Meredith, Stephen, Heidi, Patrick, Holly, Hannah, Melisa, Borge, Borge Connor, Rowen, Marsha, Robert, Michael, Jeffery, Karlyn, Lisa, Michelle, Christopher, Elizabeth, Kristina, Jeffrey, Macey, Greyson, Thomas, and Uncle Louis's nephew Robert.*
4. *My legal associates and special friends: Charlie, Carl, Sylvia, Claudia, John, Judy, Peter, Paul, Susan, Jennifer, Cynthia, Dick, Betsy, Beth, Ralph, June, Sue, Darrel, Thomas, Jodie, Jamie, Taylor, Abbie, Bruce, Madeleine, Sam, and Terrie.*
5. *The most important person in my life for half a century, my Janie.*

Dedication

[illegible]

[illegible] Wonderful grandchildren [illegible]

[illegible]

[illegible]

[illegible]

[illegible]

[illegible]

[illegible]

[illegible]

[illegible]

[illegible]

[illegible]

[illegible]

[illegible]

[illegible]

[illegible]

[illegible]

Contents

Preface

Legal Terminology, Fifth Edition, has been written with your best interests in mind. Emphasis is placed on your developing an understanding of legal terminology through the study of law itself and on using legal terminology in many different ways rather than relying solely on rote memory. The short, easy-to-understand chapters are written in a lively manner to hold your attention and capture your interest in the law. Amusing cartoons and other graphics catch your attention and highlight various legal concepts. "Word Wise," "Web Wise," and "Constitution Wise" boxes have been updated and remain popular features of the text.

Each chapter begins with a question labeled "Ante Interrogatory" intended to whet your appetite by testing you on the meaning of a legal term or concept before you study the chapter. This is followed by a chapter outline and a list of the key legal terms in the chapter with their phonetic pronunciations. The comprehensive "Glossary of Legal Terms" at the end of the text provides the same phonetic pronunciations. At the end of each chapter, you will answer questions about the subject matter in the section entitled "Reviewing What You Learned." A segment called "Understanding Legal Concepts" allows you to check your understanding of legal theory. Next, you can confirm your knowledge by completing a "Checking Terminology" assignment, followed by a project in "Using Legal Language." Finally, for reinforcement, you can "Puzzle Over What You Learned" by completing a crossword puzzle of legal terms presented in the chapter.

New Features

- The **order of presentation** has been revised in response to user comments to begin with more basic and general terms related to the court system and the Law.
- A **Chapter Outline** at the beginning of each chapter provides an overview of what lies ahead.
- ***Unraveling Legalese*** is a new exercise in which students rewrite a legal statute quote into simple, non-legal language that a layperson would be able to understand.
- ***Sharpen Your Latin Skills*** provides an opportunity within the chapters for the students to practice defining relevant Latin legal terminology.
- ***Court Systems and Jurisdictions,*** a new chapter 1, examines selection of a court and alternative dispute resolution.
- ***Criminal Trial Procedure*** and ***Civil Trial Procedure*** are now separate chapters.

- **Over 100 new terms** have been added, including the principal sources of law in the U.S., the federal and state court systems, class actions, standing to sue, default judgment, burden of proof, summary judgment, cybercrime and cyberlaw, illegal profiling, sexual assault, anti-sodomy laws, revised drug-abuse penalties, cybertorts, conditions precedent, quid pro quo, amended patent law, medical power of attorney, lineal and collateral descendants, origin of real property law, leasehold estates, sealed instruments, the acknowledgment, marriage, civil union, equitable distribution laws, the Check 21 Act, substitute checks, Uniform Partnership Act (UPA), Revised Uniform Partnership Act (RUPA), limited liability limited partnership (LLLP), derivative action, and amended bankruptcy law.

Student Supplements

- **VangoNotes for *Legal Terminology*, fifth edition:** Study by listening to the following for each chapter of your textbook:
  - **Big Ideas:** Your "need to know" for each chapter
  - **Practice Test:** A gut check for the Big Ideas—tells you if you need to keep studying
  - **Key Term Review**
  - **Rapid Review:** A quick drill session—use it right before your test
- **Companion Website:** ***http://www.prenhall.com/brown***. Use this book-specific website to prepare for tests.
  - **Learning Objectives**
  - **Chapter Summary**
  - **Flashcards for Legal Terms**
  - **Quizzes**

Instructor Supplements

- The **Online Instructor's Manual** provides answers to Reviewing What You Learned, Understanding Legal Concepts, Checking Terminology, Unraveling Legalese, Using Legal Language, and Puzzling Over What You Learned. A complete **Test Item File** is also included.
- **Online TestGenerator:** this computerized test generation system gives you maximum flexibility in preparing tests. It can create custom tests and print scambled versions of a test at one time, as well as build tests randomly by chapter, level of difficulty, or question type. The software also allows online testing and record-keeping and the ability to add problems to the database.
- **PowerPoint Lecture Presentation:** Lecture presentation screens for each chapter are available online.

OneKey Distance Learning

Ready-made **WebCT** and **Blackboard** online courses are available and include **Research Navigator,** a premium online research tool.

ACKNOWLEDGMENTS

Special thanks to the following reviewers: Pam Cummings, Minnesota State Community and Technical College; Leslie Ratliff, Griffin Technical College; Paula Witt, Houston Community College; Linda Cupick, Daytona Beach Community College; Jody L. Cooper, Blackhawk Technical College; and Claudine Dulaney, International Institute of the Americas.

My hope is that this book helps you do well in all of your Legal Terminology reading and comprehension tests.

Gordon W. Brown

ACKNOWLEDGMENTS

[illegible]

1

PART ONE

TERMS USED IN PRACTICE AND PROCEDURE

Whether you work as a court reporter, an office technician, a legal assistant, or a business executive, knowledge of the procedures involved in taking a case to court is important. Indeed, people outside the legal field also have an interest in court procedure, stemming either from their own personal experiences or from reading about trials, and watching them in movies and on television. After differentiating between the federal and state court systems, Chapter 1 examines the subject of selecting the court, including the matters of jurisdiction and venue. This chapter also explores alternative dispute resolutions for those who wish to settle disputes outside of court. Chapter 2 explains criminal trial procedure beginning with the arrest, preliminary hearing, indictment, and arraignment, followed by sentencing and defendants' rights. Chapter 3 discusses civil trial procedure including court selection, pleadings, service of process, and attachments. Chapter 4 explains defensive pleadings including the demurrer, five commonly used motions, the defendant's answer, the counterclaim, the cross-claim, and the cross-complaint. Methods of discovery, including bills of particular, interrogatories, and depositions, are examined in Chapter 5. The process of impaneling the jury, including the examination and challenging of jurors, is explained in Chapter 6, and the steps in a trial are outlined in Chapter 7.

1

CHAPTER 1
Court Systems and Jurisdiction

ANTE INTERROGATORY

The power of two or more courts to decide a particular case is called (A) original jurisdiction, (B) appellate jurisdiction, (C) exclusive jurisdiction, and (D) concurrent jurisdiction.

CHAPTER OUTLINE

Federal Courts
- *U.S. District Courts*
- *U.S. Courts of Appeals*
- *U.S. Supreme Court*

State Courts
- *State Trial Courts*
- *State Intermediate Appellate Courts*
- *State Supreme Courts*

Jurisdiction and Venue
- *In Rem Action*
- *Quasi in Rem Action*
- *In Personam Action*
- *Venue*

Alternative Dispute Resolutions

KEY TERMS

admiralty *(AD·mer·ul·tee)*
alternative dispute resolutions *(al·TERN·a·tiv dis·PYOOT res·o·LOO·shuns)*
appeal *(a·PEEL)*
appellate courts *(a·PEL·et)*
appellate jurisdiction *(a·PEL·et joo·res·DIK·shen)*
arbitration *(ar·be·TRAY·shun)*
arbitrator *(AR·be·tray·tor)*
binding arbitration *(BINE·ding ar·be·TRAY·shun)*
cert. den. (certiorari denied) *(ser·sho·RARE·ee dee·NIDE)*
change of venue *(VEN·yoo)*
circuits *(SER·kits)*
code *(KOHD)*
compulsory arbitration *(kom·PUL·so·ree ar·be·TRAY·shun)*
conciliation *(kon·sil·ee·AY·shun)*
conciliator *(kon·SIL·ee·ay·tor)*
concurrent jurisdiction *(kon·KER·ent joo·res·DIK·shen)*
court *(KORT)*
courts of appeal *(a·PEEL)*
diversity of citizenship *(dy·VER·sit·ee ov SIT·e·sen·ship)*
exclusive jurisdiction *(eks·KLOO·siv joo·res·DIK·shen)*
federal question *(FED·er·ul KWES·chen)*
forum non conveniens *(FOR·em non kon·VEEN·yenz)*
in personam action *(in per·SOH·nem AK·shun)*
in personam jurisdiction *(per·SOH·nem joo·res·DIK·shen)*
in rem action *(in rem AK·shun)*
jurisdiction *(joo·res·DIK·shen)*
justice *(JUSS·tis)*
local action *(LO·kal AK·shun)*
long-arm statutes *(STAT·shoots)*
mandatory arbitration *(MAN·da·tor·ee ar·be·TRAY·shun)*
maritime *(MER·i·tym)*
mediation *(mee·dee·AY·shun)*

mediator *(MEE·dee·ay·tor)*
mini-trial *(tryl)*
nonbinding arbitration *(non·BINE·ding ar·be·TRAY·shun)*
original jurisdiction *(o·RIJ·i·nel joo·res·DIK·shen)*
plenary jurisdiction *(PLEN·e·ree joo·res·DIK·shen)*
quasi in rem action *(KWAY·zi in rem AK·shun)*
res *(reyz)*
statute *(STAT·shoot)*
transitory action *(TRAN·zi·tore·ee AK·shun)*
venue *(VEN·yoo)*
writ of certiorari *(ser·sho·RARE·ee)*

A **court** is a body of government organized to administer justice. There are two court systems in the United States—the federal court system and state court systems.

FEDERAL COURTS

The federal court system, established by Article III of the U.S. Constitution, includes the U.S. district courts, the U.S. courts of appeals, and the U.S. Supreme Court. Those courts hear cases that raise a **federal question**—a matter that involves the U.S. Constitution, acts of Congress, or treason. Federal courts also decide cases that involve **diversity of citizenship**—a term used to describe cases between persons from different states, and between citizens of the United States and a foreign government, and between citizens of the United States and citizens of a foreign country. Diversity cases must exceed the sum of $75,000. In addition, federal courts hear bankruptcy cases, patent and copyright cases, and **admiralty** or **maritime** cases—those pertaining to the sea.

U.S. District Courts

U.S. district courts hear most federal cases when they originally go to court; that is, before there is an appeal. Each state and territory and the District of Columbia has at least one U.S. district court within its boundary. They are often referred to as **federal district courts.**

Sources of Law

There are five principal sources of law in the United States:

1. Federal and state constitutions
2. English common law
3. Federal and state **statutes** (laws passed by a legislature)
4. Court decisions
5. Administrative regulations

The federal government and many state governments consolidate their statutes, administrative regulations, and other laws into a systematic collection called a **code.** The United States Code, and the California Civil Code are examples.

U.S. Courts of Appeals

U.S. courts of appeals decide cases that have been appealed from federal district courts. The United States is divided into thirteen judicial districts called **circuits.** Each circuit has several U.S. district courts but only one U.S. court of appeals. A group of three judges decide most cases that are appealed to this court.

WORD WISE

Different Meanings for "Court"

The court officer announced, "The court is now in session!" Used in this way, the term "court" means a body, including judge and jury, organized to administer justice. Lawyers are officers of the court.

"May it please the court" is a sentence often used by lawyers when addressing a judge. The term "court," as used here, means "judge."

"I'll see you in court," the attorney said to her fellow attorney. Here, the term "court" probably refers to the courthouse building.

U.S. Supreme Court

The U.S. Supreme Court is the highest court in the land. It hears appeals from both the U.S. courts of Appeals and the highest state courts when federal questions are involved. Coming from the Latin word *supremus* (the last), the term *supreme* means "superior to all other things."

In the U.S. Supreme Court, appeals are heard when four out of the nine **Justices** (the title given to appellate court judges) believe the case is important enough to be heard. When it agrees to hear a case on appeal, the U.S. Supreme Court issues a **writ of certiorari,** which is an order from a higher court to a lower court to deliver its records to the higher court for review. When the Court decides not to hear an appeal, as it does with most cases, the Court denies issuing the writ of certiorari by writing the abbreviation "**cert. den.**" on the court record. Most state courts have discontinued using certiorari, considering it an outdated common law practice.

State Courts

Each state in the United States has its own court structure that is separate from the executive and legislative branches of state government. Like the federal courts, state courts are divided into three broad categories—trial courts, intermediate appellate courts, and supreme courts.

State Trial Courts

State trial courts have general authority to hear cases involving activity that occurred in a particular state. Called **superior courts, circuit courts,** or **courts of common pleas,** they are typically arranged so that there is one in each county. Major civil and criminal cases, both jury and non-jury, are tried in these county courts.

In addition, somewhat lesser courts with limited authority are located throughout each county, including district or municipal courts, juvenile courts, traffic courts, housing courts, and land courts. Each county also has special courts that handle such matters as adoption, divorce, and the settlement of estates.

State Intermediate Appellate Courts

Following a court's decision, either party may file an **appeal**—that is, a request to a higher court to review the decision of a lower court. Courts that review the decisions of lower courts are called **courts of appeal,** or **appellate courts.** Many states have intermediate appellate courts where appeals must be taken and heard by a three-judge panel before being eligible to go to the state's supreme court.

State Supreme Court

Each state has a court of last resort—a state supreme court. Parties aggrieved by lower state court decisions may appeal to their state's supreme court, which is usually the final decision. Appeals from this court may be made to the U.S. Supreme Court only when a federal or U.S. constitutional question is raised.

JURISDICTION AND VENUE

Jurisdiction is the power or authority that a court has to hear a particular case. Such power is given to the court either by the federal or state constitution or by a federal or state statute. If, by chance, a court should hear a particular case and make a decision without having jurisdiction, the decision would be meaningless.

Some courts have **original jurisdiction** over certain cases, which means that they have the power to hear the case originally—when it first goes to court. Other courts have **appellate jurisdiction,** which means that they have the power to hear a case when it is appealed. When one court only has the power to hear a particular case, to the exclusion of all other courts, the court is said to have **exclusive jurisdiction.** When two or more courts have the power to hear a case, they have **concurrent jurisdiction.** A court with concurrent jurisdiction has the right, under a doctrine called **forum non conveniens,** to refuse to hear a case if it believes that justice would be better served if the trial were held in a different court. Some courts have exclusive original jurisdiction or exclusive appellate jurisdiction over particular cases. Similarly, some courts have concurrent original jurisdiction or concurrent appellate jurisdiction over certain cases.

When considering the question of jurisdiction, one of the first points that must be determined is whether the case is an in rem, quasi in rem, or in personam action.

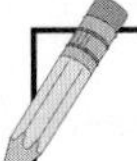

WORD WISE

To Speak

"Dic," "dict," and "dit," whether used as prefixes or suffixes, mean "to say" or "to speak," as in these words:

verdict *(VER·dikt)*
jurisdiction *(joo·res·DIK·shen)*
edict *(E·dikt)*
indictment *(in·DITE·ment)*
dictation *(dik·TAY·shun)*
dictator *(DIK·tay·ter)*
contradict *(kon·tra·DIKT)*

In Rem Action

An **in rem action** is a lawsuit that is directed against property rather than against a particular person. The action usually concerns title to real property and, if so, is called a **local action.** It seeks to settle some questions about the property, and the court's decision is effective to everyone in the world, not merely to the defendant in the case. For a court to have jurisdiction over an action in rem, the property (called the **res**) must be located in the state (and usually in the county) where the court sits. In addition, some kind of notice must be given to people who may have an interest in the proceeding.

Quasi in Rem Action

If a defendant owns real property in one state and lives in another, the court where the real property is located has jurisdiction over the property only, not the person. If suit is brought in that court and the out-of-state defendant does not appear, the plaintiff's recovery will be limited to an amount up to the value of the property located in that state. Such a lawsuit is called a **quasi in rem action.** In such a case, the court has jurisdiction over the defendant's property but not over the defendant's person; therefore, the most the defendant can lose is the out-of-state real property. Usually, when this type of jurisdiction exists, the dispute that the court is asked to settle has nothing to do with title to the property.

In Personam Action

In an **in personam action** (personal action), the plaintiff must select a court that has jurisdiction over not only the subject matter but also over the parties involved in the case. **In personam jurisdiction** means jurisdiction over the person. A court automatically has personam jurisdiction over the plaintiff because the plaintiff chooses the court where the action is brought. In contrast, only the court where the defendant lives or has a place of business has jurisdiction over the defendant. An exception is that state courts will obtain personam jurisdiction over anyone who is served by process while inside the state's boundaries. Service of process is explained in Chapter 2.

Some so-called **long-arm statutes** allow one state court to reach out (with its long arm) to obtain personam jurisdiction over a person in another state if that person does much business in the state where the court is located. The term **plenary jurisdiction** refers to the situation in which a court has complete jurisdiction over the plaintiff, the defendant, and the subject matter of a lawsuit.

An action that does not concern land is called a **transitory action** and may be brought in more than one place as long as the court in which it is heard has proper jurisdiction.

Venue

The place where the trial is held is called the **venue.** Each state has established rules of venue for the purpose of providing convenient places for trials. Such rules state exactly where particular actions may be brought. If the plaintiff's attorney begins an action in a court of improper venue, the defendant's attorney may have the case transferred or dismissed by filing a motion for that purpose or by raising that issue in the defendant's answer (a document discussed in Chapter 18). If the defendant's attorney does not raise the question of improper venue, the court may hear the case as long as it has jurisdiction. The difference between venue and jurisdiction is that jurisdiction relates to the power of

Figure 1-1 The place where the trial is held is known as the *venue*. An action brought in a court of improper venue may be dismissed by filing a motion for that purpose or by raising the issue in the defendant's answer.

the court to hear a case, whereas venue relates to the geographic location where the action should be tried.

Sometimes, for the sake of justice, one of the parties will ask the court to change the place of the trial. The court, in some cases, has the power to order a change of venue. A **change of venue** is the removal of a suit begun in one county or district to another county or district for trial.

ALTERNATIVE DISPUTE RESOLUTIONS

In civil cases, rather than take their disputes to court, some people prefer to use quicker, less complicated, and less expensive methods to resolve disputes. Procedures for settling disputes by means other than litigation are called **alternative dispute resolutions.** They include mediation, arbitration, and mini-trials. **Mediation,** sometimes called **conciliation** is an informal process in which a neutral third person, called a **mediator** or **conciliator,** listens to both sides and makes suggestions for reaching a solution. The mediator tries to persuade the parties to compromise and settle their differences.

In contrast, **arbitration** is a method of settling disputes in which a neutral third party, called an **arbitrator,** makes a decision after hearing the arguments on both sides. If the parties agree in advance to **binding arbitration,** the decision of the arbitrator will prevail and must be followed. If, instead, the parties agree to **nonbinding arbitration,** the arbitrator's decision is simply a recommendation and need not be complied with. Arbitration that is required by agreement or by law is called **compulsory** or **mandatory arbitration.**

An increasingly popular method of settling disputes is an informal trial, sometimes referred to as a **mini-trial,** run by a private organization established for the purpose of settling disputes out of court. Retired judges and lawyers are often used to hear the disputes, and the parties agree to be bound by the decision.

REVIEWING WHAT YOU LEARNED

After studying the text, write the answers to each of the following questions.

1. What types of cases are heard by federal courts?

____

____

____

____

2. When may appeals be made from a state supreme court to the U.S. Supreme Court? __________

____

____

____

____

3. What cases do U.S. courts of appeals decide?

____

____

____

____

4. For a court to have jurisdiction over an in rem action, where must the property be located?

____

____

____

____

5. If a defendant owns real property in one state and lives in another, which court has jurisdiction?

____

____

____

____

____

6. In a situation such as that described in question 5, if suit is brought against the defendant in the state where the property is located and the out-of-state defendant does not appear, the plaintiff's recovery will be limited to what? __________

____

____

____

____

____

7. To bring a lawsuit against a person and hold that person personally liable, what kind of action must be brought? __________

____

____

____

____

____

8. If the plaintiff's attorney begins an action in a court of improper venue, what may the defendant's attorney do? ______________________

____

____

____

____

____

9. What may the court do if the defendant's attorney does not raise the question of improper venue?

____

____

10. What is the difference between jurisdiction and venue? ______________________

____

____

UNDERSTANDING LEGAL CONCEPTS

Indicate whether each statement is true or false. Then, change the italicized word or phrase of each *false* statement to make it true.

Answers

______________ **1.** Cases heard by the U.S. courts of appeals are decided by *three* judges.

______________ **2.** The U.S. Supreme Court hears appeals when *five* out of the nine justices believe the case is important enough to be heard.

______________ **3.** If, by chance, a court should hear a particular case and make a decision without having *jurisdiction,* the decision would be meaningless.

______________ **4.** Some courts have *exclusive original jurisdiction* or exclusive appellate jurisdiction over particular cases.

______________ **5.** Courts *never* have concurrent original jurisdiction over certain cases.

______________ **6.** An action in rem is a lawsuit that is directed against *a particular person.*

______________ **7.** For a court to have jurisdiction over an *in rem action,* the property must be located in the state (and usually in the county) where the court lies.

______________ **8.** If a defendant owns real property in one state and lives in another, the court with jurisdiction where the real property is located has jurisdiction over the *person* and not the *property.*

______________ **9.** The court where the *plaintiff* lives has jurisdiction over the defendant.

______________ **10.** When parties agree in advance to binding arbitration, the decision of the arbitrator *must be followed.*

CHECKING TERMINOLOGY (PART A)

From the list of legal terms that follows, select the one that matches each definition.

Answers

a. admiralty
b. appellate courts
c. appellate jurisdiction
d. cert. den.
e. circuits
f. concurrent jurisdiction
g. court
h. courts of appeal
i. diversity of citizenship
j. exclusive jurisdiction
k. federal question
l. forum non conveniens
m. in personam action
n. in rem action
o. justice
p. local action
q. maritime
r. original jurisdiction
s. plenary jurisdiction
t. quasi in rem action
u. transitory action
v. writ of certiorari

____ **1.** The power of two or more courts to hear a particular case.
____ **2.** The power to hear a case when it first goes to court.
____ **3.** A lawsuit that is directed against property rather than against a particular person.
____ **4.** The right of a court to refuse to hear a case if it believes that justice would be better served if the trial were held in a different court.
____ **5.** A lawsuit that can occur only in one place.
____ **6.** Complete jurisdiction.
____ **7.** A lawsuit in which the court has jurisdiction over the defendant's property but not over the defendant's person.
____ **8.** A lawsuit that may be brought in more than one place as long as the court in which it is heard has proper jurisdiction.
____ **9.** A matter that involves the U.S. Constitution, acts of Congress, or treason.
____ **10.** Pertaining to the sea (select two answers).
____ **11.** Name given to the division of U.S. district courts.
____ **12.** Title given to an appellate court judge.
____ **13.** An order from a higher court to a lower court to deliver its records to the higher court for review.
____ **14.** A phrase used in connection with the jurisdiction of the federal courts.
____ **15.** The power of one court only to hear a particular case to the exclusion of all other courts.
____ **16.** A lawsuit in which the court has jurisdiction over the person.
____ **17.** The power to hear a case when it is appealed.
____ **18.** Courts that review the decision of lower courts (select two answers).

CHECKING TERMINOLOGY (PART B)

From the list of legal terms that follows, select the one that matches each definition.

Answers

a. alternative dispute resolutions
b. appeal
c. arbitration
d. arbitrator
e. binding arbitration
f. change of venue

____ **1.** Arbitration that is required by agreement or by law (select two answers).
____ **2.** Arbitration in which the decision of the arbitrator will prevail and must be followed.
____ **3.** An informal process in which a neutral third person listens to both sides and makes suggestions for reaching a solution (select two answers).
____ **4.** The removal of a suit begun in one county or district to another county or district for trial.

g. code
h. compulsory arbitration
i. conciliation
j. conciliator
k. in personam jurisdiction
l. jurisdiction
m. long-arm statutes
n. mandatory arbitration
o. mediation
p. mediator
q. mini-trial
r. nonbinding arbitration
s. res
t. statute
u. venue

____ **5.** The power or authority that a court has to hear a case.
____ **6.** The property; the thing.
____ **7.** Statutes that allow one state to reach out and obtain personal jurisdiction over a person in another state.
____ **8.** An informal trial run by a private organization established for the purpose of settling disputes out of court.
____ **9.** Procedures for settling disputes by means other than litigation.
____ **10.** A method of settling disputes in which a neutral third party makes a decision after hearing the arguments on both sides.
____ **11.** A neutral third person in an arbitration session who listens to both sides and who makes a decision with regard to the dispute.
____ **12.** Arbitration in which the arbitrator's decision is simply a recommendation and need not be complied with.
____ **13.** A systematic collection of statutes, administrative regulations, and other laws.
____ **14.** The place where a trial is held.
____ **15.** A request to a higher court to review the decision of a lower court.
____ **16.** A law passed by a legislature.
____ **17.** A neutral third person in a conciliation session who listens to both sides and who makes suggestions for reaching a solution (select two answers).
____ **18.** Jurisdiction over the person.

UNRAVELING LEGALESE

Use simple, non-legal language, with the help of the glossary, to rewrite this quote in the space below so that it is shorter and can be understood by a layperson without losing its meaning.

> The Appellants argue that Congress's use of the permissive "may" instead of obligatory "must" demonstrates an intention to sustain concurrent jurisdiction. While it is true that some courts have found concurrent jurisdiction because of the use of the permissive "may," the statutes at issue in such cases did not contain the more potent language contained in this statute: "original exclusive jurisdiction." That difference makes the analysis in those cases inapplicable.

USING LEGAL LANGUAGE

Read the following story and fill in the blank lines with legal terms taken from the list of terms at the beginning of this chapter.

To settle a dispute by means other than litigation over who owned the lot next to her, Susan tried to get Conrad to participate in a(n) ____________________ resolution. She wanted to use ____________________ (also called ____________________)—an informal process in which a neutral third person listens to both sides and makes suggestions for reaching a solution. This case was not one involving a defendant who owned land in one state and lived in another; therefore, it was not a(n) ____________________ action. The ____________________ for the trial was Salem because the disputed land was located there, and the court in that city had ____________________ over the case. Because the case involved title to land, the trial had to be held in the county where the ____________________ was located, and because the suit was directed against property, it was a(n) ____________________ action, not a(n) ____________________ action. The suit was a(n) ____________________ action rather than a(n) ____________________ action, because it could be brought only in one place. In addition, because the Salem court was the only one that had the power to hear the case, it had ____________________ rather than ____________________. Owing to the fact that the case was being tried for the first time, the court had ____________________, not ____________________.

PUZZLING OVER WHAT YOU LEARNED

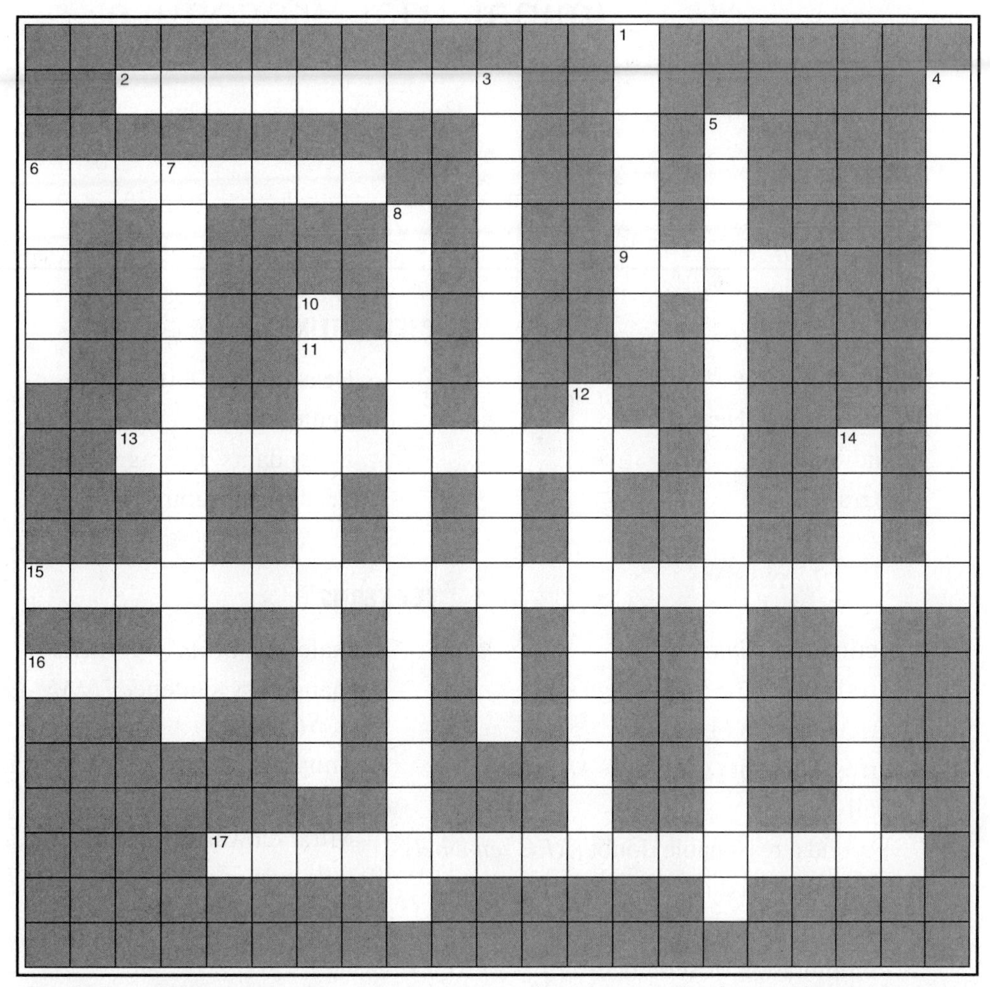

Caveat: Do not allow squares for spaces between words and punctuation (apostrophes, hyphens, etc.) when filling in crossword.

Across

2. An informal trial run by a private organization established for the purpose of settling disputes out of court.
6. Name given to the division of U.S. courts.
9. A systematic collection of statutes, administrative regulations, and other laws.
11. The property; the thing.
13. An informal process in which a neutral third person listens to both sides and makes suggestions for reaching a resolution.
15. The power to hear a case when it is appealed.
16. The place where a trial is held.
17. An order from a higher court to a lower court to deliver its records to the higher court for review.

Down

1. Title given to an appellate court judge.
3. Statutes that allow one state to reach out and obtain personal jurisdiction over a person in another state.
4. The power or authority that a court has to hear a case.
5. Arbitration in which the decision of the arbitrator will prevail and must be followed.
6. A body of government organized to administer justice.
7. The removal of a suit begun in one county or district to another county or district for trial.
8. A lawsuit in which the court has jurisdiction over the defendant's property, but not over the defendant's person.
10. A method of settling disputes in which a neutral third party makes a decision after hearing the arguments on both sides.
12. A neutral third person in a conciliation session who listens to both sides and makes suggestions for reaching a solution.
14. A neutral third person in an arbitration session who listens to both sides and makes a decision with regard to the dispute.

1

CHAPTER 2
Criminal Trial Procedure

ANTE INTERROGATORY

A formal written charge of a crime made by a grand jury is called (A) an arraignment, (B) nolo contendere, (C) probable cause, (D) an indictment.

CHAPTER OUTLINE

Arrest
Preliminary Hearing
Indictment
Arraignment
Reasonable Doubt
Sentencing
Defendants' Rights
Trial Separation

KEY TERMS

action *(AK·shun)*
arraignment *(a·RAIN·ment)*
arrest *(a·REST)*
arrest warrant *(a·REST WAR·ent)*
bail
beyond a reasonable doubt *(REE·zen·e·bel)*
bifurcated trial *(BY·fer·kay·ted tryl)*
citation *(sy·TAY·shun)*
commutation of sentence *(kom·yoo·TAY·shun ov SEN·tense)*
concurrent sentences *(kon·KER·ent SEN·ten·sez)*
consecutive sentences *(kon·SEK·yoo·tiv SEN·ten·sez)*
crime *(krym)*
criminal complaint *(KRIM·in·el kom·PLAYNT)*
cumulative sentences *(KYOOM·yoo·la·tiv SEN·ten·sez)*
defendant *(de·FEN·dent)*
fact finder *(fakt FINE·der)*
grand jury *(JOOR·ee)*
guilty *(GILL·tee)*
inadmissible *(in·ad·MISS·i·bel)*
indictment *(in·DITE·ment)*
information *(in·for·MA·shun)*
malefactor *(mal·e·FAK·ter)*
mandatory sentence *(MAN·da·tor·ee SEN·tense)*
minimum sentence *(MIN·i·mum SEN·tense)*
Miranda warnings *(mer·AN·da)*
nolo contendere *(NO·lo kon·TEN·de·ray)*
pardon *(PAR·den)*
parole *(pa·ROLE)*
parole board
parole commission *(ke·MISH·en)*
parolee *(pa·role·EE)*
personal recognizance *(PER·son·al re·KOG·ni·zense)*
plaintiff *(PLAIN·tif)*
plea bargaining *(plee BAR·gen·ing)*
preliminary hearing *(pre·LIM·i·ner·ee HEER·ing)*
probable cause *(PROB·a·bel kawz)*
probable cause hearing *(PROB·a·bel kawz HEER·ing)*
prosecute *(PROS·e·kyoot)*
prosecution *(pros·e·KYOO·shun)*
reasonable doubt *(REE·zen·e·bel dowt)*
rendition *(ren·DI·shun)*

rules of criminal procedure *(KRIM·i·nel pro·SEED·jer)*
sentence *(SEN·tense)*
severance of actions *(SEV·er·ense ov AK·shuns)*
suspended sentence *(sus·PEN·ded SEN·tense)*
victim's impact statement *(VIK·tems IM·pakt)*

The process of taking a criminal case to court is governed by rules that have been adopted by federal and state governments. The federal **rules of criminal procedure** govern criminal actions brought in federal courts. These rules are available on the Internet. Individual states have also adopted rules of procedure that must be followed when bringing criminal actions in those states.

A **crime** is an offense against the public at large. It is a wrong against all of society, not merely against the individual victim. For that reason, the **plaintiff**—that is, the one who **prosecutes** (brings the action)— in a criminal case is always the federal, state, or local government, which has the burden of proving its case. The one against whom the action is brought is known as the **defendant.** A person found guilty of a crime is known as a **malefactor.**

ARREST

A criminal **action** (lawsuit or court proceeding), known as a **prosecution,** begins with the issuance of an **arrest warrant,** which is a written order of the court commanding law enforcement officers to arrest a person and bring him or her before the court. To **arrest** means to deprive a person of his or her liberty. Suspects can be arrested without a warrant when there is **probable cause**—that is, reasonable grounds for belief that an offense has been committed.

A process known as **rendition** permits the return of fugitives to the state where they are accused of having committed a crime by the governor of the state to which they have fled.

For minor offenses, such as traffic violations, a citation is issued instead of an arrest warrant. A **citation** is a written order by a judge (or by a police officer) commanding a person to appear in court for a particular purpose.

Miranda Warnings*

When arrested, suspects must be told, before being questioned, that they have the following constitutional rights:

1. They have the right to remain silent.
2. Any statements made by them may be used against them to gain conviction.
3. They have the right to consult with a lawyer and to have a lawyer present during questioning.
4. A lawyer will be provided without cost for indigent defendants.

Any statements made by the accused that were obtained in violation of this rule are **inadmissible** (cannot be received) as evidence in court.

**Miranda v. Arizona,* 384 U.S. 436 (1966).

PRELIMINARY HEARING

After the arrest, a **criminal complaint** (a written statement of the essential facts making up the offense charged) is drafted by the arresting authorities. Next, the suspect is brought before the court for a **preliminary hearing,** also called a **probable cause hearing,** which is a hearing before a judge to determine whether there is sufficient evidence to believe that the person has committed a crime. If the court finds probable cause, the defendant is either kept in jail or released on **bail** (money or property left with the court to assure that the person will return to stand trial) or on **personal recognizance** (a personal obligation to return to stand trial).

INDICTMENT

In misdemeanor cases, a date is set for a trial. In felony cases, formal charges must be brought either by an **indictment** (a formal written charge of a crime made by a grand jury) or, if waived in some states, by **information** (a formal written charge of a crime made by a public official rather than by a grand jury). A **grand jury** is a jury consisting of not more than 23 people who listen to evidence and decide whether or not to charge someone with the commission of a crime.

ARRAIGNMENT

Following the indictment or information, the person charged with the crime must face **arraignment,** which is the act of calling a prisoner before the court to answer an indictment or information. The charge is read to the person, and he or she is asked to plead **"guilty"** (having committed the crime), **"not guilty,"** or, when permitted, **"nolo contendere"** (a plea in which the defendant neither admits nor denies the charges). If the person pleads guilty or nolo contendere, he or she is sentenced by the court. Sometimes the prosecution and defense will work out a mutually satisfactory disposition of the case through a process known as **plea bargaining.** The defendant will often plead guilty to a lesser offense in exchange for a lighter sentence. Any such arrangement must be approved by the court. A date is set for a trial when a person pleads not guilty.

REASONABLE DOUBT

To convict someone of a crime, the prosecution must prove beyond a reasonable doubt that the illegal act occurred. **Beyond a reasonable doubt** means that the **fact finder** (the jury, or the judge in a nonjury trial) is fully persuaded that the accused has committed the crime. If there is a **reasonable doubt**—that is, doubt based on reason—the accused must be acquitted.

SENTENCING

When the defendant is found guilty in a criminal case, the judgment of the court imposing punishment is called a **sentence.** At the time of sentencing, most states allow victims' impact statements to be made. A **victim's impact statement** is a statement to the court, at the time of sentencing, relative to the impact that the crime had on the victim or

WEB WISE

- For overviews of criminal and civil procedure, go to the Legal Information Institute (LII) at **www.law.cornell.edu.** When there, put your curser on "Law about . . ." and double click "All topics alphabetically." On the list that follows, click "civil procedure" and "criminal procedure."
- In addition to the website mentioned above, the federal procedural rules can be found at **www.findlaw.com.** At that site, click "Federal Resources." Then key in "Rules of Civil Procedure" or "Rules of Criminal Procedure."
- Find out about *Internet jurisdiction* by going to **www.findlaw.com** and keying in "jurisdiction."

on the victim's family. Depending on state law, impact statements are made before or after sentencing and are often preserved for use at a later time by a **parole board** or **parole commission** (a group of people authorized to grant parole). **Parole** is a conditional release from prison allowing the **parolee** (person placed on parole) to serve the remainder of a sentence outside of prison under specific terms.

When two or more sentences are imposed on a defendant to be served one after the other, they are called **consecutive** or **cumulative sentences.** If they are to be served at the same time, they are called **concurrent sentences.** A **suspended sentence** is a sentence that is given formally, but not actually served. Suspended sentences are sometimes given during the good behavior of the defendant while in society. A **mandatory sentence** is a fixed sentence that must be imposed with no room for discretion. A **minimum sentence** refers to the smallest amount of time that a prisoner must serve before being released or placed on parole.

The president of the United States, in federal cases, and state governors, in state cases, have the power to change sentences, making them less severe. When a sentence is changed to one that is less severe, it is known as **commutation of sentence.** A **pardon,** on the other hand, is a setting aside of punishment altogether by a government official.

Figure 2-1 Concurrent sentences are two or more sentences served at the same time. Consecutive sentences are two or more sentences served one after the other.

DEFENDANTS' RIGHTS

In addition to being told of certain rights when arrested (see the Miranda Warnings box on p. 15), defendants in criminal cases have the following rights:

1. The right to be free from any unreasonable search and seizure.
2. The right to a speedy trial.
3. The right to plead not guilty.
4. The right to be represented by an attorney.
5. The right to a court-appointed attorney if the defendant cannot afford one.
6. The right to summon witnesses and require their attendance.
7. The right to confront and cross-examine witnesses.
8. The right to be presumed innocent until proven guilty by a judge or jury beyond a reasonable doubt.

TRIAL SEPARATION

Sometimes trials are divided into separate parts. A **bifurcated trial** is a trial that is divided into two parts, providing separate hearings for different issues in the same lawsuit. For example, in criminal cases, one hearing may be held to determine the guilt or innocence of the defendant, followed by a separate hearing, if necessary, to determine sanity or punishment. In non-criminal, personal-injury cases, separate hearings are sometimes held on the questions of liability and damages.

A different kind of trial separation, called **severance of actions,** occurs when a court separates lawsuits or prosecutions involving multiple parties into separate, independent cases, resulting in separate, final judgments.

REVIEWING WHAT YOU LEARNED

After studying the text, write the answers to each of the following questions.

1. Who brings the action in a criminal case?
____
____
____

2. When does a criminal action begin? ________
____
____
____

3. What happens to the defendant if the court finds probable cause that he or she committed a crime?
____
____
____

4. How many people serve on a grand jury and what is the jury's function? ______________
____
____

5. How does an indictment differ from an arraignment? ______________________
____
____

6. What must occur if the judge or jury finds there is a reasonable doubt that the defendant committed the crime? ______________
____
____

7. When arrested, what must a suspect be told before being questioned? ____________________

____

8. For what reason do you believe victims' impact statements are often preserved for later use by a parole board? ____________________

____

9. How does a commutation of a sentence differ from a pardon? ____________________

____

10. What is the difference between a bifurcated trial and a severance of action? ____________________

____

UNDERSTANDING LEGAL CONCEPTS

Indicate whether each statement is true or false. Then, change the italicized word or phrase of each *false* statement to make it true.

Answers

____________________ 1. A crime is an offense against *the individual victim alone.* It *is not* a wrong against all of society.

____________________ 2. The one who brings an action in a criminal case is *usually* the federal, state, or local government.

____________________ 3. A grand jury is a jury consisting of *not more than* 23 people.

____________________ 4. An indictment is a formal written charge of a crime made by a grand jury.

____________________ 5. Nolo contendere is a plea in which the *plaintiff* neither admits nor denies the charges.

____________________ 6. To convict someone of a crime, the prosecution must prove *beyond a reasonable doubt* that the illegal act occurred.

____________________ 7. A *pardon* is a conditional release from prison allowing the person to serve the remainder of a sentence outside of prison under specific terms.

____________________ 8. A *suspended* sentence is a sentence that is given formally but not actually served.

____________________ 9. Two or more sentences imposed on a defendant to be served at the same time are *consecutive* sentences.

____________________ 10. A *severance of action* is a trial that is divided into two parts, providing separate hearings for different issues in the same lawsuit.

CHECKING TERMINOLOGY (PART A)

From the list of legal terms that follows, select the one that matches each definition.

- **a.** action
- **b.** arraignment
- **c.** arrest
- **d.** arrest warrant
- **e.** bail
- **f.** beyond a reasonable doubt
- **g.** bifurcated trial
- **h.** citation
- **i.** commutation of sentence
- **j.** concurrent sentences
- **k.** consecutive sentences
- **l.** crime
- **m.** criminal complaint
- **n.** cumulative sentences
- **o.** defendant
- **p.** fact finder
- **q.** grand jury
- **r.** guilty
- **s.** inadmissible
- **t.** indictment
- **u.** information
- **v.** plaintiff

Answers

____ **1.** A written order by a judge or by a police officer commanding a person to appear in court for a particular purpose.

____ **2.** An offense against the public at large.

____ **3.** A person against whom a legal action is brought.

____ **4.** A lawsuit or court proceeding.

____ **5.** A written order of the court commanding law enforcement officers to arrest a person and to bring him or her before the court.

____ **6.** The act of calling a prisoner before the court to answer an indictment or information.

____ **7.** A written statement of the essential facts making up an offense charged in a criminal action.

____ **8.** Money or property left with the court to ensure that a person will return to stand trial.

____ **9.** To deprive a person of his or her liberty.

____**10.** A formal written change of a crime made by a grand jury.

____**11.** The fact finder who is fully persuaded that the accused has committed a crime.

____**12.** The jury in a jury trial or the judge in a nonjury trial.

____**13.** A trial that is divided into two parts, providing separate hearings for different issues in the same lawsuit.

____**14.** Two or more sentences imposed on a defendant to be served one after the other (select two answers).

____**15.** Having committed a crime.

____**16.** A formal written charge of a crime made by a public official rather than by a grand jury.

____**17.** Two or more sentences imposed on a defendant to be served at the same time.

____**18.** The changing of a sentence to one that is less severe.

CHECKING TERMINOLOGY (PART B)

From the list of legal terms that follows, select the one that matches each definition.

- **a.** malefactor
- **b.** mandatory sentence
- **c.** minimum sentence
- **d.** Miranda warnings
- **e.** nolo contendere
- **f.** pardon
- **g.** parole

Answers

____ **1.** The judgment of the court imposing punishment when the defendant is found guilty in a criminal case.

____ **2.** A person placed on parole.

____ **3.** Reasonable grounds for belief that an offense has been committed.

____ **4.** A person found guilty of a crime.

____ **5.** The party by whom criminal proceedings are started or conducted; the state.

h. parole board
i. parole commission
j. parolee
k. personal recognizance
l. plea bargaining
m. preliminary hearing
n. probable cause
o. probable cause hearing
p. prosecute
q. prosecution
r. reasonable doubt
s. rendition
t. rules of criminal procedure
u. sentence
v. severance of actions
w. suspended sentence
x. victims' impact statements

____ **6.** A plea in which the defendant neither admits nor denies the charges.

____ **7.** A hearing before a judge to determine whether there is sufficient evidence to believe that the person has committed a crime (select two answers).

____ **8.** A fixed sentence that must be imposed with no room for discretion.

____ **9.** A personal obligation by a person to return to stand trial.

____ **10.** The smallest amount of time that a prisoner must serve before being released or placed on parole.

____ **11.** A group of people authorized to grant parole (select two answers).

____ **12.** A setting aside of punishment altogether by a government official.

____ **13.** A statement to the court, at the time of sentencing, relative to the impact that the crime had on the victim or on the victim's family.

____ **14.** A sentence that is given formally but not actually served.

____ **15.** A conditional release from prison allowing the person to serve the remainder of a sentence outside of prison under specific terms.

____ **16.** Regulations that govern the proceedings in criminal cases.

____ **17.** The working out of a mutually satisfactory disposition of a case by the prosecution and by the defense.

____ **18.** The separation of lawsuits or prosecutions involving multiple parties into separate, independent cases, resulting in separate, final judgments.

____ **19.** Doubt based on reason.

____ **20.** To proceed against a person criminally.

UNRAVELING LEGALESE

Use simple, non-legal language, with the help of the glossary, to rewrite this case quote in the space below so that it is shorter and can be understood by a layperson without losing its meaning.

> The parties must disclose the plea agreement in open court when the plea is offered, unless the court for good cause allows the parties to disclose the plea agreement in camera.

USING LEGAL LANGUAGE

Read the following story and fill in the blank lines with legal terms taken from the list of terms at the beginning of this chapter.

Alphonse, high on drugs and carrying a handgun, broke into Krista's apartment one evening, unaware that Krista and her dog, Lilly, were present. Lilly lunged at the surprised Alphonse, causing him to shoot himself in the foot. Krista disarmed the bleeding Alphonse and called 911. When the police arrived, Alphonse was placed under ______________________; that is, deprived of his liberty. He was also told about his rights, called ______________________. The next morning, Alphonse went before the court for a(n) ______________________ hearing, which is also called a(n) ______________________ hearing. The judge set a high ______________________ to ensure Alphonse's return to stand trial. The district attorney presented the case to a(n) ______________________ jury, which issued a(n) ______________________—a formal written charge of a crime. This was followed by a court appearance called a(n) ______________________ at which Alphonse pleaded ______________________, denying that he had committed the crime. The trial that followed was governed by regulations known as ______________________. The state brought the action, that is, ______________________, against Alphonse who was the ______________________. To find Alphonse guilty, the jury, that is, the ______________________, was required to find beyond ______________________ that Alphonse committed the crime. At the time of sentencing, Krista was able to give a(n) ______________________ pointing out the effect the crime had on her life. Alphonse was given a(n) ______________________ sentence—one that is fixed with no room for discretion.

PUZZLING OVER WHAT YOU LEARNED

1

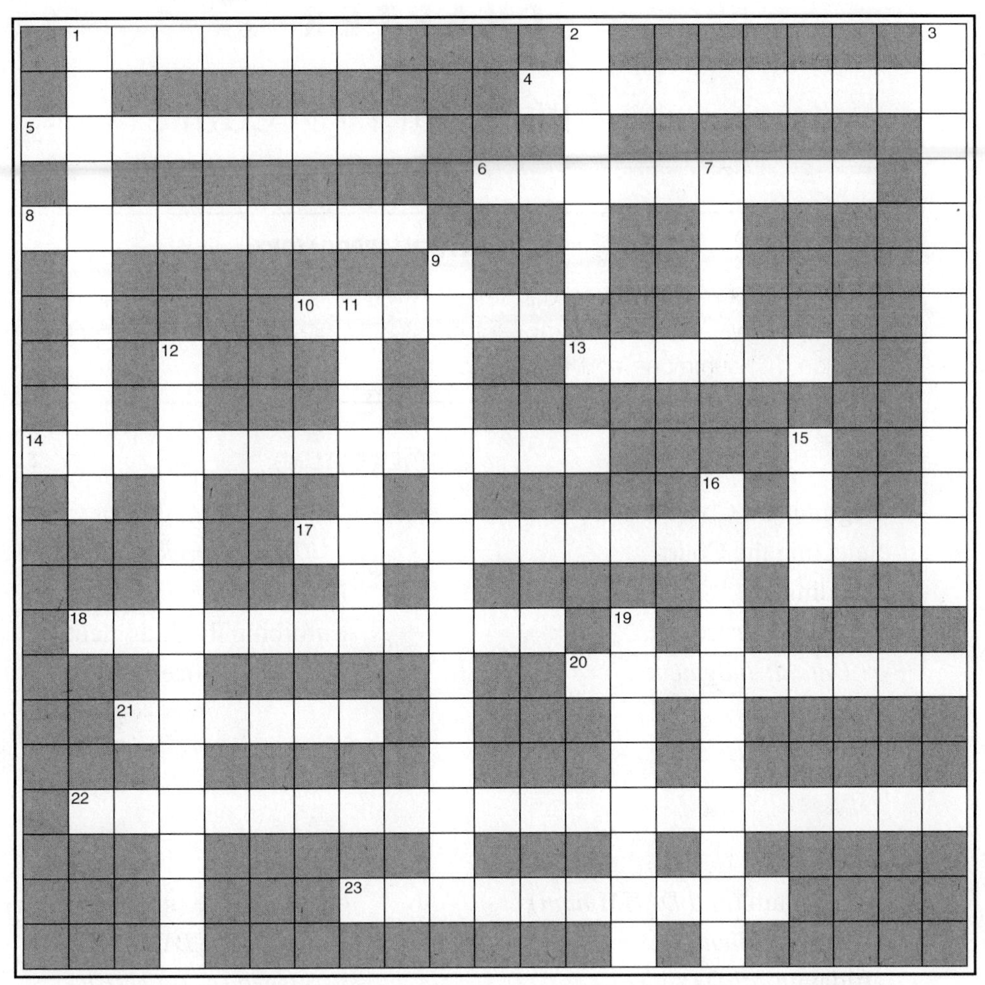

Caveat: Do not allow squares for spaces between words and punctuation (apostrophes, hyphens, etc.) when filling in crossword.

Across

1. A person placed on parole.
4. The jury in a jury trial or the judge in a nonjury trial.
5. A jury consisting of not more than 23 people who listen to evidence and decide whether or not to charge someone with the commission of a crime.
6. To proceed against a person criminally.
8. A person who brings legal action against another.
10. A lawsuit or court proceeding.
13. To deprive a person of his or her liberty.
14. A written order of the court commanding law enforcement officers to arrest a person and bring him or her before the court.
17. The constitutional right given to people when they are arrested to be told before being questioned of certain rights.
18. The act of calling a prisoner before the court to answer an indictment or information.
20. A person against whom legal action is brought.
21. A setting aside of punishment altogether by a government official.
22. Two or more sentences imposed on a defendant to be served one after the other.
23. A person found guilty of a crime.

Down

1. A group of people authorized to grant parole.
2. A conditional release from prison allowing the person to serve the remainder of a sentence outside of a prison under specific terms.
3. Reasonable grounds for belief that an offense has been committed.
7. A wrong against society.
9. A trial that is divided into two parts, providing separate hearings for different issues in the same lawsuit.
11. A written order by a judge or police officer commanding a person to appear in court for a particular purpose.
12. The working out of a mutually satisfactory disposition of a case by the prosecution and the defense.
15. Money or property left with the court to assure that a person will return to stand trial.
16. The party by whom criminal proceedings are started or conducted; the state.
19. The judgment of the court imposing punishment when the defendant is found guilty in a criminal case.

1

CHAPTER 3
Civil Trial Procedure

ANTE INTERROGATORY

A formal notice to the defendant that a lawsuit has begun and that the defendant must file an answer within the number of days set by state law is a (A) complaint, (B) declaration, (C) summons, and (D) verification.

CHAPTER OUTLINE

KEY TERMS

ad damnum *(ahd DAHM·num)*
affiant *(a·FY·ent)*
affidavit *(a·fi·DAY·vit)*
allege *(a·LEJ)*
allegation *(al·e·GAY·shun)*
attachment *(a·TACH·ment)*
aver *(a·VER)*
averments *(a·VER·ments)*
cause of action *(AK·shun)*
civil action *(SIV·el AK·shun)*
class action *(klas AK·shun)*
complaint *(kom·PLAYNT)*
constructive service *(kon·STRUK·tiv SER·viss)*
declaration *(dek·la·RAY·shun)*
default judgment *(de·FAWLT JUJ·ment)*
deponent *(de·PONE·ent)*
docket *(DOK·et)*
docket number *(DOK·et NUM·ber)*
Doe defendants *(de·FEN·dents)*
encumbrance *(en·KUM·brens)*
ex parte *(eks PAR·tay)*
garnishee *(gar·nish·EE)*
garnishment *(GAR·nish·ment)*
gravamen *(GRAH·va·men)*
justiciable *(jus·TISH·e·bel)*
legal issues *(LEE·gul ISH·oos)*
lien *(leen)*
lis pendens *(lis PEN denz)*
litigant *(LIT·i·gant)*
litigation *(lit·i·GAY·shun)*
personal service *(PER·son·al SER·viss)*
petition *(pe·TI·shun)*
pleadings *(PLEED·ings)*
preponderance of evidence *(pre·PON·der·ens ov EVI·dens)*
process *(PROSS·ess)*
process server *(PROSS·ess SERV·er)*
ripeness doctrine *(RIPE·ness DOK·trin)*
rules of civil procedure *(SIV·el pro·SEED·jer)*

service of process *(SER·viss ov PROCESS·ess)*
standing to sue *(STANDing to SOO)*
substituted service *(SUB·sti·tew·ted SER·viss)*
summary proceeding *(SUM·e·ree pro·SEED·ing)*
summons *(SUM·ens)*
trial docket *(tryl DOK·et)*
trial list *(tryl list)*
trustee *(trus·TEE)*
trustee process *(trus·TEE PROSS·ess)*
verification *(ver·i·fi·KAY·shun)*
writ
writ of attachment *(a·TACH·ment)*
writ of execution *(ek·se·kyoo·shen)*
writ of garnishment *(GAR·nish·ment)*

A **civil action**—that is, a lawsuit other than a criminal one—comes about when two or more people become involved in a dispute that they are unable to settle by themselves. One of them seeks to have a third party, the court, settle the dispute for them. To do this, a court action, known as **litigation** (a suit at law) must be brought. The parties to a lawsuit are called **litigants.** The person who brings the suit is called the **plaintiff.** The person against whom the suit is brought is called the **defendant.** A **class action** is a lawsuit brought, with the court's permission, by one or more persons on behalf of a very large group of people who have the same interest in the matter.

Under the **ripeness doctrine,** a court will not hear a case unless there is an actual, present controversy for the court to decide. Judges will not decide cases that are hypothetical or speculative. To be brought to court, potential cases must be **justiciable**—appropriate for court assessment.

The federal **rules of civil procedure** govern civil cases brought in federal courts. These rules can be found on the Internet. Individual states have also adopted rules of civil procedure that apply to cases brought in their state courts.

BEGINNING A CIVIL ACTION

To begin a civil lawsuit, the plaintiff usually makes an appointment with an attorney and tells the attorney the facts of the dispute as he or she understands them. The attorney, after listening to the client's version of the facts, determines the **legal issues** (questions of law) that are involved in the case. The attorney then tells the client about the law as it applies to the legal issues and gives the client an opinion as to how successful a lawsuit might be. The client, with the advice of the attorney, then decides whether or not to bring the lawsuit.

An important consideration is whether the client has standing to sue. **Standing to sue** means that a party has a tangible, legally protected interest at stake in a lawsuit. For example, you could not bring suit against someone who breached your friend's contract because you were not a party to that contract. You would not have "standing."

If the client decides to bring suit, the attorney usually writes a letter to the defendant, saying that he or she represents the plaintiff and has been authorized to bring suit against the defendant. In the letter, the attorney often makes an attempt to settle the case out of court and gives the defendant a few days to answer the letter. If no settlement can be reached, the plaintiff's attorney will begin the lawsuit.

SELECTING THE COURT

The attorney's first task in bringing suit is to select the court in which to bring the action. In choosing a court, the attorney must determine which court has jurisdiction over both the person who is being sued and the subject matter of the case as discussed in Chapter 1.

PLEADINGS

Civil suits are begun and defended at the outset by the use of papers known as pleadings. **Pleadings** are the written statements of claims and defenses used by the parties in the lawsuit. Pleadings serve the purpose of giving notice to all parties of the claims and defenses in the suit and, in addition, narrow the issues for trial so that both parties and the court know the legal issues that must be decided.

To begin a civil suit, the plaintiff's attorney files a complaint with the clerk of the court, which is the plaintiff's first pleading. A **complaint** (called a **declaration** at common law) is a formal document containing a short and plain statement of the claim indicating that the plaintiff is entitled to relief and containing a demand for the relief sought. The complaint sets forth the plaintiff's **cause of action,** which is the ground on which the suit is maintained. The essential basis or gist of the complaint is known as the **gravamen** of the lawsuit. The complaint contains **allegations** (also called **averments**), which are claims that the party making it expects to prove. To **allege** or to **aver** means to make an allegation; to assert positively. The clause in the complaint stating the damages claimed by the plaintiff is called the **ad damnum.** In some states, a complaint must be accompanied by a verification signed by the plaintiff. A **verification** is a written statement under oath confirming the correctness, truth, or authenticity of a pleading. In some states, especially in courts of equity (see Chapter 7), civil suits are begun by the filing of a **petition**—a written application for a court order.

The lawsuit begins when the complaint or petition is filed with the court. The plaintiff's attorney either mails (registered or certified) or hand delivers the complaint to the court with the proper filing fee. The clerk of court keeps a record, called a **docket,** of cases

Figure 3-1 To allege means to assert positively a claim that one expects to prove, made before proving it.

that are filed and assigns a **docket number** to each case. The term **trial docket** or **trial list** refers to the calendar of cases that are ready for trial.

Once the complaint is filed with the court, the defendant is notified of the suit by a method known as process. **Process** is defined as the means of compelling the defendant in an action to appear in court.

WORD WISE

Truth

The root "ver-" used in the term "verification" is from the Latin word for "truth," *veritas*. Other words with the same root are:

Word	*Meaning*
verdict [*ver* (truth) + *dict* (to say)]	Decision of the jury (see Chapter 20)
verify [*ver* (truth) + *facere* (to make)]	To prove to be true

Even that most familiar word, "very," which means "truly" or "really," comes from "ver-."

SERVICE OF PROCESS

A summons is used to notify the defendant of the lawsuit. A **summons** is a formal notice to the defendant that a lawsuit has begun and that the defendant must file an answer within the number of days set by state law or lose the case by default. **Service of process** is the delivering of summonses or other legal documents to the people who are required to receive them. A summons is obtained from the court, filled out, and given, along with a copy of the complaint, to a **process server** (a person who carries out service of process). The process server delivers copies of the summons and the complaint to the defendant and then fills in the back of the summons indicating when and how service was made. The summons is then returned to the court.

The process server may serve process by delivering a copy of the summons and complaint to the defendant personally, which is known as **personal service.** Service that is not personal service is called **constructive service** when the summons and complaint are left at the defendant's last and usual place of abode and **substituted service** when they are delivered to the defendant's agent or mailed or published in a newspaper. If the defendant is a corporation, process may be served on an officer of the corporation, on a registered agent of the corporation, or on the person in charge of the corporation's principal place of business. When the defendant's whereabouts is unknown, process may be served by publication in a newspaper. In some states, service may be made by mail.

When names of defendants are unknown, summonses and complaints refer to people as **Doe defendants,** such as First Doe, Second Doe, John Doe, and Jane Doe.

Default Judgment

When a defendant fails to file an answer or other pleading in response to a summons and complaint, he or she may lose the case by default. A **default judgment** is a court decision entered against a party who has failed to plead or defend a lawsuit.

DIFFERENCES BETWEEN CRIMINAL AND CIVIL ACTIONS

	Criminal Action	Civil Action
1. **Who brings the action?**	The government	The injured party
2. **What is the plaintiff's burden of proof?**	Prove guilt beyond a reasonable doubt	Prove preponderance of evidence
3. **What can be the result for a losing defendant?**	Prison, fine, or both; restitution	Pay money to the winning party; do or refrain from doing a particular act

ATTACHMENTS

At times, plaintiffs need the assurance that if they obtain a judgment against the defendant (that is, win the lawsuit), money will be available from the defendant to pay the amount of the judgment. This assurance is accomplished by attaching the defendant's property at the beginning of the action. An **attachment** is the act of taking a person's property and bringing it into the custody of the law so that it may be applied toward the defendant's debt if the plaintiff wins the suit.

The method of obtaining an attachment varies somewhat from state to state. Under a typical state law, the plaintiff's attorney files a motion for attachment with the court at the same time the complaint is filed. The plaintiff's attorney must also file an affidavit signed by the plaintiff, stating facts that would warrant a judgment for the plaintiff. An **affidavit** is a written statement sworn to under oath before a notary public as being true to the affiant's own knowledge, information, and belief. An **affiant** (also called a **deponent**) is a person who signs an affidavit. The motion, affidavit, summons, and complaint together with a notice of hearing are sent to the process server, who serves them on the defendant. A hearing is then held by the court to determine whether or not to allow the attachment. The court may allow the attachment if it finds that a reasonable likelihood exists that the plaintiff will recover a judgment against the defendant for the amount of the attachment over and above any insurance coverage that the defendant has.

Ex Parte Hearing

Sometimes, the plaintiff's attorney wishes to attach the defendant's property but does not want to notify the defendant in advance that an attachment is going to occur. In such cases, the plaintiff's attorney attends an ex parte session of the court. **Ex parte** means that the hearing is attended by one party only. The plaintiff's attorney asks the court to allow the attachment without notifying the defendant beforehand. The court may allow the attachment without notifying the defendant if it finds (1) that the defendant is not within its jurisdiction (but the defendant's property is, thereby giving it quasi in rem jurisdiction), or (2) that a danger exists that the defendant will conceal the property or sell it or remove it from the state, or (3) that a danger exists that the defendant will damage or destroy the property.

Writ of Attachment

A **writ** is a written order of a court, returnable to the same, commanding the performance or nonperformance of an act. If the court allows an attachment, the judge signs a paper called a **writ of attachment.** This written order is to the sheriff, commanding the sheriff to attach the real or personal property of the defendant up to an amount approved by the court.

When real property is attached, the writ of attachment or a notice of **lis pendens** (pending suit) is recorded at the registry of deeds in the county where the property is located. This procedure has the effect of putting a lien on the property until the lawsuit is completed. A **lien** (also called an **encumbrance**) is a claim that one has against the property of another. The claim attaches to the property until the lawsuit is completed. If the plaintiff obtains a judgment against the defendant, an officer of the court, such as a sheriff, can sell the property under the court's direction and obtain the money to satisfy the judgment.

If personal property is attached, the court officer may take possession of it, or, in some circumstances, place a keeper over it, or sell it immediately, as in the case of perishable property. With variations from state to state, certain items are exempt from attachment such as necessary wearing apparel, furniture and books up to a particular value, tools necessary to carry on a trade, and materials and stock up to a specified value. Other technical restrictions on the attachment of personal property exist.

Trustee Process and Garnishment

Sometimes it is necessary to attach property of the defendant that is being held by another person. This is most commonly done to attach money that the defendant has in a bank account or wages or other money that has been earned by the defendant but not yet paid.

The procedure for attaching the defendant's property that is in the hands of a third person is called **trustee process** in some states and **garnishment** in others. To begin trustee process, the plaintiff's attorney obtains a trustee process summons or a **writ of garnishment** from the court, fills it out, and files it with the court together with the complaint, a motion for approval of attachment on trustee process, and a supporting affidavit. The defendant is notified (unless the attachment is on an ex parte basis), and a hearing is held by the court to determine if the trustee process attachment should be allowed. If it is allowed, the summons is sent to the process server, who serves it on the **trustee** or **garnishee** (the one holding the defendant's property). The summons orders the trustee to file within a prescribed number of days after service a disclosure under oath of the goods, effects, or credits, if any, of the defendant that are in the possession of the trustee at the time of service.

In some states, trustee process cannot be used in actions for malicious prosecution, slander, libel, assault and battery, and specific recovery of goods. Certain other actions are also exempt from trustee process. With some exceptions, the plaintiff must file a bond with the court before trustee process can be used. The bond is for the purpose of paying the defendant's court costs and damages in the event the attachment was wrongfully brought by the plaintiff.

BURDEN OF PROOF

Recall that in criminal cases, the prosecution must *prove beyond a reasonable doubt* that the defendant committed the crime. In civil cases, the burden of proof is different. To win a civil case, the plaintiff must prove the case by a **preponderance of evidence**–evidence of the greatest weight. This is the degree of proof that is more probable than not.

ENFORCING THE JUDGEMENT

If the losing party is ordered to pay money over to the winning party and does not do so, the winning party must ask the court for a **writ of execution.** This process is used to enforce a judgment for the payment of money. The writ orders the sheriff to enforce the judgment.

SUMMARY PROCEEDINGS

Lengthy and complicated trials are expensive for the parties and the governmental agencies administering them. Whenever possible, it is beneficial to hold a trial quickly, in a simple manner. A **summary proceeding** is the name given to a short and simple trial. Proceedings held in small-claims courts are examples of summary proceedings.

REVIEWING WHAT YOU LEARNED

After studying the text, write the answers to each of the following questions:

1. How does the plaintiff's attorney begin a civil suit? ____________________

2. What two purposes do pleadings serve? ____________________

3. How is the defendant notified that a lawsuit has been brought against him or her? ____________________

4. Describe three ways that process may be served on the defendant. ____________________

5. In what ways may process be served if the defendant is a corporation? ____________________

6. How can plaintiffs be assured that money will be available from defendants if they win a lawsuit? ____________________

7. Under a typical state law, what two documents must the plaintiff's attorney file with the court to obtain an attachment? ____________________

8. How is the defendant notified of the plaintiff's motion for attachment? ____________________

9. The court may allow an attachment if it finds what? ______________________________
____
____
____

10. On what three occasions may the court allow an attachment without notifying the defendant beforehand? ______________________________
____
____
____
____

11. What is done with the writ of attachment or notice of lis pendens when real property is attached? ______________________________
____
____
____
____

12. What is another name for trustee process?
____
____
____
____

UNDERSTANDING LEGAL CONCEPTS

Indicate whether each statement is true or false. Then, change the italicized word or phrase of each *false* statement to make it true.

Answers

______________ 1. To begin a lawsuit, the plaintiff's attorney files a *summons* with the clerk of the court.

______________ 2. *Pleadings* help to narrow the issues for trial so that both parties and the court know what legal issues must be decided.

______________ 3. A *complaint* is a formal notice to the defendant that a lawsuit has begun and that the defendant must file an answer within the number of days set by state law or lose the case by default.

______________ 4. To obtain an attachment, under a typical state law, the plaintiff's attorney files a motion for attachment with the court *at the same time that* the complaint is filed.

______________ 5. An affiant is also known as a *deponent.*

______________ 6. An ex parte session of the court is attended by *both parties* to the suit.

______________ 7. A *writ of attachment* is a written order to the sheriff to attach the property of the defendant.

______________ 8. When real property is attached, the writ of attachment is recorded at the *city or town hall* where the property is located.

______________ 9. The procedure for attaching the defendant's property that is in the hands of a third person is called *a writ of encumbrance* in some states.

______________ 10. A trustee process *summons* orders the trustee to file within a prescribed number of days a disclosure under oath of the goods, effects, or credits of the defendant that are in the possession of the trustee.

1

CHECKING TERMINOLOGY (PART A)

From the list of legal terms that follows, select the one that matches each definition.

- **a.** ad damnum
- **b.** affiant
- **c.** affidavit
- **d.** allegation
- **e.** allege
- **f.** attachment
- **g.** aver
- **h.** averment
- **i.** cause of action
- **j.** civil action
- **k.** class action
- **l.** complaint
- **m.** constructive service
- **n.** declaration
- **o.** default judgment
- **p.** deponent
- **q.** docket
- **r.** docket number
- **s.** Doe defendants
- **t.** encumbrance
- **u.** ex parte
- **v.** garnishment
- **w.** gravamen
- **x.** justiciable
- **y.** legal issues
- **z.** lien
- **aa.** lis pendens

Answers

____ **1.** A record of cases that are filed with the court.

____ **2.** A formal document containing a short and plain statement of the claim indicating that the plaintiff is entitled to relief and containing a demand for the relief sought (select two answers).

____ **3.** The act of taking a person's property and bringing it into the custody of the law so that it may be applied toward the defendant's debt if the plaintiff wins the case.

____ **4.** A person who signs an affidavit (select two answers).

____ **5.** On one side only.

____ **6.** A claim that one has against the property of another (select two answers).

____ **7.** A procedure for attaching the defendant's property that is in the hands of a third person.

____ **8.** The ground on which a suit is maintained.

____ **9.** A number assigned to each case by the clerk of court.

____ **10.** A written statement sworn to under oath before a notary public as being true to the affiant's own knowledge, information, and belief.

____ **11.** A type of service in which the summons and complaint are left at the defendant's last and usual place of abode.

____ **12.** References to defendants whose names are unknown.

____ **13.** The clause in the complaint stating the damages claimed by the plaintiff.

____ **14.** A court decision entered against a party who has failed to plead or defend a lawsuit.

____ **15.** The essential basis or gist of a complaint filed in a lawsuit.

____ **16.** Appropriate for court assessment.

____ **17.** Questions of law to be decided by the court in a lawsuit.

____ **18.** A pending suit.

____ **19.** Claims that the party making it expects to prove (select two answers).

____ **20.** To make an allegation; to assert positively (select two answers).

CHECKING TERMINOLOGY (PART B)

From the list of legal terms that follows, select the one that matches each definition.

a. litigant
b. litigation
c. personal service
d. petition
e. pleadings
f. preponderance of evidence
g. process
h. process server
i. ripeness doctrine
j. rules of civil procedure
k. service of process
l. standing to sue
m. substituted service
n. summary proceeding
o. summons
p. trial docket
q. trial list
r. trustee
s. trustee process
t. verification
u. writ
v. writ of attachment
w. writ of execution

Answers

____ 1. A written application for a court order.

____ 2. A party that has a tangible, legally protected interest at stake in a lawsuit.

____ 3. Parties to a lawsuit.

____ 4. Evidence of the greater weight.

____ 5. Regulations that govern the proceedings in civil cases.

____ 6. A suit at law.

____ 7. A principal under which the court will not hear a case unless there is an actual, present controversy for the court to decide.

____ 8. A short and simple trial.

____ 9. A written order to the sheriff, commanding the sheriff to enforce a judgment of the court.

____ 10. The written statements of claims and defenses used by the parties in the lawsuit.

____ 11. A formal notice to the defendant that a lawsuit has begun and that the defendant must file an answer within the number of days set by state law or lose the case by default.

____ 12. The calendar of cases that are ready for trial (select two answers).

____ 13. A written order to the sheriff commanding the sheriff to attach the real or personal property of the defendant.

____ 14. A person who holds legal title to property in trust for another.

____ 15. A written statement under oath confirming the correctness, truth, or authenticity of a pleading.

____ 16. The means of compelling the defendant in an action to appear in court.

____ 17. The delivering of summonses or other legal documents to the people who are required to receive them.

____ 18. A person who carries out service of process.

____ 19. Delivering a copy of the summons and complaint to the defendant personally.

____ 20. A written order of a court, returnable to the same, commanding the performance or nonperformance of an act.

____ 21. A type of service in which the summons and complaint are delivered to the defendant's agent or mailed or published in a newspaper.

1

UNRAVELING LEGALESE

Use simple, non-legal language, with the help of the glossary, to rewrite this quote in the space below so that it is shorter and can be understood by a layperson without losing its meaning.

> Averments in a pleading to which a responsive pleading is required, other than those as to the amount of damage, are admitted when not denied in the responsive pleading. [Rule 8(d) Federal Rules of Civil Procedure]

USING LEGAL LANGUAGE

Read the following story and fill in the blank lines with legal terms taken from the list of terms at the beginning of this chapter:

> The attorney began the lawsuit by filing the ______________________, which is the plaintiff's first ______________________ with the clerk of the court, who assigned a(n) ______________________ to the case to identify it. The attorney then had the ______________________ serve copies of the ______________________ and complaint on the defendant, who was called a(n) ______________________ because of an unknown name. Because of the fact that ______________________—that is, the means for compelling the defendant to appear in court—occurred by leaving the papers at the defendant's last and usual place of abode, it was not ______________________ service; instead, it was called ______________________. The attorney also filed a motion for a(n) ______________________ at a(n) ______________________ session of the court to place a(n) ______________________, which is also called a(n) ______________________ on the defendant's real property without the defendant being notified beforehand. Along with the motion, the attorney was required to file a(n) ______________________, which was signed under oath by the client who was called the ______________________ or ______________________. The attachment was allowed by the court, and the ______________________ was recorded at the Registry of Deeds. Because this did not involve the attachment of property in the hands of a third party, ______________________, which is also called ______________________, was not used. When the case was ready for trial, it was placed on the ______________________, which is sometimes referred to as the ______________________.

PUZZLING OVER WHAT YOU LEARNED

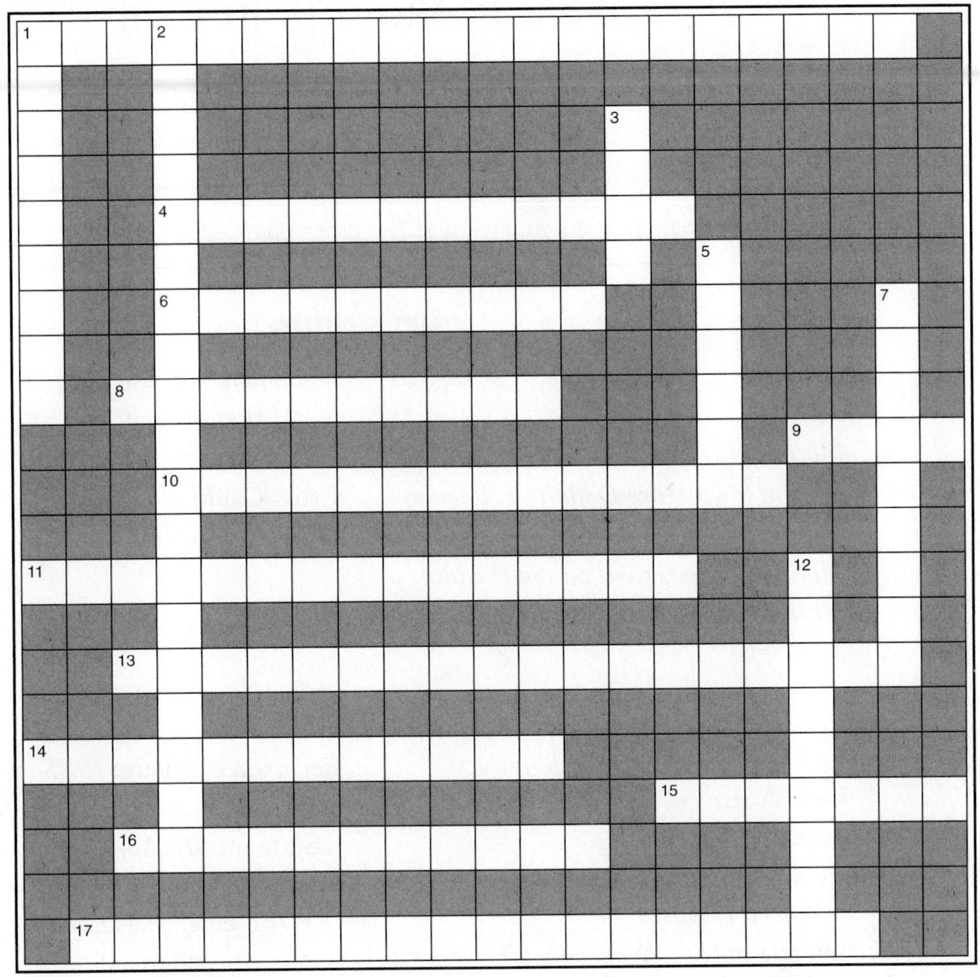

Caveat: Do not allow squares for spaces between words and punctuation (apostrophes, hyphens, etc.) when filling in crossword.

Across

1. Service in which papers are left at defendant's last and usual place of abode.
4. Calender of cases that are ready for trial.
6. Another name for trial docket.
8. Act of bringing a person's property into the custody of the law.
9. Written order of the court commanding the performance of an act.
10. Defendants whose names are unknown.
11. Ground on which a suit is maintained.
13. Written order to a sheriff commanding the attachment of property.
14. Written statement under oath confirming the correctness of a pleading.
15. Person who signs an affidavit.
16. The common law name for a complaint.
17. The delivering of summonses or other legal documents.

Down

1. Formal document containing short statement of the plaintiff's claim.
2. Service in which summons and complaints are delivered to an agent or mailed.
3. Claim that one has against the property of another.
5. Record of cases that are filed with the clerk of court.
7. Written statement sworn to under oath.
12. Written statements of claims and defenses used in a lawsuit.

CHAPTER 4

Defensive Pleadings in Civil Trials

ANTE INTERROGATORY

A statement or claim that the party making it expects to prove is a(n) (A) affirmative defense, (B) allegation, (C) demurrer, and (D) cross-complaint.

CHAPTER OUTLINE

Demurrer
Motions
Motion to Dismiss
Motion for a More Definite Statement
Motion to Strike
Motion for Judgment on the Pleadings
Motion for Summary Judgment
Defendant's Answer
Affirmative Defenses
Counterclaim
Cross Claim
Cross Complaint

KEY TERMS

affirmative defense *(a·FERM·a·tiv de·FENSE)*
answer *(AN·ser)*
confession and avoidance *(kon·FESH·en and a·VOY·dense)*
counterclaim *(KOWN·ter·klame)*
cross-claim *(kross klame)*
cross-complaint *(kross kom·PLAYNT)*
default judgment *(de·FAWLT JUJ·ment)*
demurrer *(de·MER·er)*
dismissal *(dis·MISS·el)*
dismissal without prejudice *(PREJ·e·diss)*
dismissal with prejudice
establishment clause *(es·TAB·lish·ment)*
freedom of assembly *(FREE·dum ov a·SEM·blee)*
freedom of speech *(FREE·dum)*
freedom of the press *(FREE·dum)*
free exercise clause *(EKS·er·size)*
misnomer *(mis·NO·mer)*
motion *(MOH·shun)*
motion for a more definite statement *(DEF·e·net STATE·ment)*
motion for judgment on the pleadings *(JUJ·ment on the PLEED·ings)*
motion for summary judgment *(MOH·shun for SUM·er·ee JUJ·ment)*
motion for recusal *(re·KYOO·zel)*
motion to dismiss *(dis·MISS)*
motion to strike
nonsuit *(NON·soot)*
overrule *(o·ver·ROOL)*
recuse *(re·KYOOZ)*
reply *(re·PLY)*
summary judgment *(SUM·er·ee JUJ·ment)*
sustain *(sus·TANE)*

After a civil action has begun and the summons and complaint have been served on the defendant, it is necessary for the defendant to file one or more defensive pleadings within a certain number of days from the date of service of the summons. The number of days within which this filing must be done varies from state to state. In Massachusetts, a defensive pleading must be filed within 20 days; in California, 30 days. If a defensive pleading is not filed within the time period, the defendant will lose the case by default unless an exception is made by the court.

DEMURRER

A defensive pleading used at common law and still used in some states is the demurrer. A **demurrer** is a pleading available to the defendant to attack the plaintiff's complaint by raising a point of law, such as the failure of the complaint to state a cause of action on which relief can be granted. In effect, a demurrer points out that even if the plaintiff's allegations are true, no cause of action exists. Some grounds for using a demurrer follow:

1. The complaint does not state facts sufficient to constitute a cause of action.
2. The court has no jurisdiction over the subject matter of the case.
3. The plaintiff has no legal capacity to sue.
4. Another action is pending between the same parties for the same cause.
5. A defect or misjoinder of the parties in the suit exists.

If the court **sustains** (supports) the demurrer, the case will end by a nonsuit unless the court allows the plaintiff to amend the complaint. A **nonsuit** is the termination of an action that did not adjudicate issues on the merits. If the demurrer is **overruled** (annulled, made void, or not sustained), the defendant is given a certain number of days to file an answer (discussed later).

The federal courts and many states have done away with the demurrer, replacing it with one or more of the motions discussed subsequently.

MOTIONS

A **motion** is a written or oral request made to a court for certain action to be taken. For example, when an attorney believes that the sitting judge is biased or prejudiced against a client, the attorney might make a **motion for recusal.** This is a request that the judge **recuse** (disqualify) himself or herself from the case because of the unfairness.

Motions are made for many different reasons and can be made by either party to a suit. Some of the important defensive motions follow:

1. Motion to dismiss
2. Motion for a more definite statement
3. Motion to strike
4. Motion for judgment on the pleadings
5. Motion for summary judgment

Motion to Dismiss

In some cases, the plaintiff will do something that will give the defendant grounds to have the case dismissed. When this happens, the defendant may make a **motion to dismiss** the case. **Dismissal** is an order disposing of an action without trial of the issues. The motion must be made within a prescribed number of days after the defendant received service of process.

After a motion to dismiss is filed with the court and mailed to the opposing attorney, the attorney for the defendant marks the motion up to be heard by the court during one of its motion sessions. At this session, the attorneys for the parties argue their viewpoints as to the merits of the motion. The clients usually do not attend the motion session. The judge then makes a decision to either allow or deny the motion. If the motion to dismiss is allowed by an order for **dismissal without prejudice,** the plaintiff is allowed to correct the error and bring another action on the same claim. In contrast, if the order is a **dismissal with prejudice,** the plaintiff is barred from bringing another action on the same claim. If the motion to dismiss is denied, the defendant is given a certain number of days to file an answer.

The defendant may make a motion to dismiss for any of the following reasons:

1. Lack of jurisdiction over the subject matter of the case
2. Lack of jurisdiction over the defendant personally
3. Improper venue
4. Insufficiency of process (such as a defective summons)
5. Insufficiency of service of process (as when service of process is made on someone not authorized to accept service)
6. Failure to state a claim on which relief can be granted
7. Failure to join a necessary party
8. **Misnomer** (mistake in name) of a party
9. Pendency of a prior action in a court of the same state

Motion for a More Definite Statement

If a pleading is so vague that the other party cannot properly respond to it, a **motion for a more definite statement** may be made. If the motion is allowed, the other party must file the more definite statement within a prescribed number of days (usually 10). The one who brought the motion then has 10 more days to answer the more definite statement. If the motion is denied, the answer must be filed within 10 days after notice of the court's denial.

Motion to Strike

A **motion to strike** may be used by either party to have stricken from any pleading any insufficient defense or any redundant, immaterial, impertinent, or scandalous matter.

Motion for Judgment on the Pleadings

A **motion for judgment on the pleadings** may be made by either the defendant or the plaintiff. It may be made only after both the plaintiff's complaint and the defendant's answer have been filed. The plaintiff might make the motion on the ground that the defendant's answer does not set forth a legally sufficient defense. The defendant might make the motion on the ground that the plaintiff's complaint does not state a claim on which relief can be granted. This motion and the motion to dismiss replace the demurrer in many states.

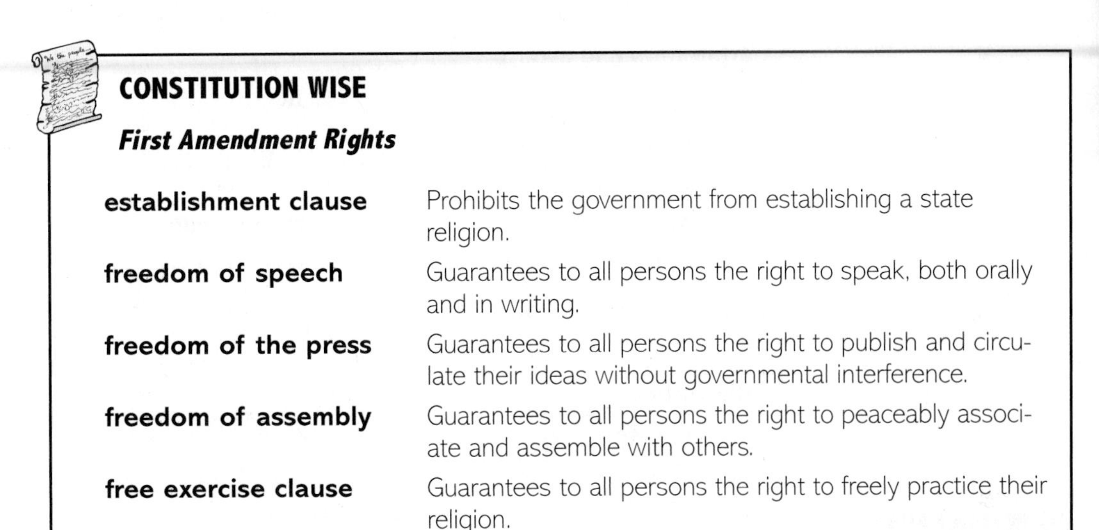

CONSTITUTION WISE

First Amendment Rights

establishment clause	Prohibits the government from establishing a state religion.
freedom of speech	Guarantees to all persons the right to speak, both orally and in writing.
freedom of the press	Guarantees to all persons the right to publish and circulate their ideas without governmental interference.
freedom of assembly	Guarantees to all persons the right to peaceably associate and assemble with others.
free exercise clause	Guarantees to all persons the right to freely practice their religion.

Motion for Summary Judgment

A **motion for summary judgment** may be made when all of the papers filed in a case show that there is no genuine issue of fact and that the party making the motion will win the case as a matter of law. A **summary judgment** is an immediate decision by the court without going to trial based on the papers filed by the parties.

Defendant's Answer

Unless the case is dismissed by the allowance of a motion to dismiss, the defendant must file a written **answer** within a prescribed number of days after service of process. The defendant's answer must state in short and plain terms the defenses he or she wishes to assert. In addition, each of the claims made by the plaintiff must be admitted or denied. If the defendant is without knowledge or information sufficient to form a belief as to the truth of an allegation, he or she may so state, which has the effect of a denial. If an allegation is partly true and partly false, the defendant may admit part and deny part of the allegation. If the defendant fails to deny an allegation made in the plaintiff's complaint, it is automatically admitted.

Failure to file an answer will cause a **default judgment** to enter. This judgment is entered on failure of a party to appear or plead at the proper time.

Affirmative Defenses

Many times the defendant will have done the act for which he or she is being sued but will have some other reason that will stop the plaintiff from winning the case, which is called an **affirmative defense** (a **confession and avoidance** under the common law). The defendant admits the plaintiff's allegation but introduces something new that constitutes a defense to it. When an affirmative defense is used in federal and in many state courts, it must be stated in the defendant's answer. If it is omitted from the answer, the defense is lost and cannot be used later.

The affirmative defenses are:

accord and satisfaction
arbitration and award
assumption of risk
contributory negligence
discharge in bankruptcy
duress
estoppel
failure of consideration
fraud
illegality
injury by fellow servant
laches
license
payment
release
res judicata
statute of frauds
statute of limitations
waiver

COUNTERCLAIM

If the defendant (after receiving the summons and complaint) wishes to bring a suit against the plaintiff, he or she will file a counterclaim. A **counterclaim** is a claim that the defendant has against the plaintiff. It is made a part of the defendant's answer. The counterclaim is compulsory if the defendant wishes to bring a claim that arises out of the same transaction or occurrence as that of the plaintiff's suit and the venue is correct and the court has jurisdiction. The plaintiff is required to file a reply to the defendant's counterclaim within a prescribed number of days after receiving the counterclaim. The **reply** is the legal name given to the answer to the counterclaim.

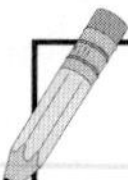

WORD WISE

Compound Words

In addition to words made up of prefixes, suffixes, and roots, English has many words made by compounding—that is, joining two or more words already in usage to create a new word with a new meaning. The term "counterclaim," introduced in this chapter, is such a word. Almost any combination of the parts of speech may be used to create a compound word. The following methods are the most common: noun with adjective (heartsick, airtight); adjective with noun (blackberry, hothouse); adverb with noun (overhead, downfall); verb with adverb (dugout, kickoff).

CROSS-CLAIM

Sometimes a suit will be brought against two defendants, and one of those defendants will wish to bring a claim against the other defendant. A claim brought by one defendant against another defendant in the same suit is called a **cross-claim.** The subject matter of the cross claim must arise out of the same transaction or occurrence as that of the original suit. A cross-claim must be answered within a prescribed number of days after it is received.

CROSS-COMPLAINT

The State of California uses a pleading known as a **cross-complaint** in place of a counterclaim and a cross claim. The California cross complaint may be used to file a claim by a defendant (1) against another defendant, (2) against a third party, and (3) against the plaintiff in the same action.

REVIEWING WHAT YOU LEARNED

After studying the text, write the answers to each of the following questions.

1. What must the defendant do after he or she has been served with a summons and a complaint? What will happen if this is not done? ________

2. What is one ground for using a demurrer? ________

3. Who usually attends the hearing for the demurrer to be heard by the court? ________

4. Name four important defensive motions. ________

5. Who attends a motion session? What happens at such a session? ________

6. What must the defendant do if the motion to dismiss is denied? ________

7. List three grounds for a motion to dismiss. ________

8. What may the opposing party do if a pleading is so vague that the party cannot respond to it? ________

9. What may the opposing party do if a pleading contains an insufficient defense or any redundant, immaterial, impertinent, or scandalous matter? ________

10. On what ground might a plaintiff make a motion for judgment on the pleadings? On what ground might a defendant make such a motion? _____

11. What must the defendant's answer state? ____

12. What will be the result if the defendant fails to deny any allegation made in the plaintiff's complaint? ____

13. What will be the result if an affirmative defense is omitted from the defendant's answer? _____

14. List three affirmative defenses. ____

15. What may the defendant do if he or she wishes to bring a suit against the plaintiff? In what way is this related to the defendant's answer? _____

16. How must the plaintiff respond to a defendant's counterclaim? ____

17. Who are the parties to a cross-claim? Out of what must the subject matter of a cross-claim arise?

UNDERSTANDING LEGAL CONCEPTS

Indicate whether each statement is true or false. Then, change the italicized word or phrase of each *false* statement to make it true.

Answers

______ **1.** After an action has begun, it is necessary for the defendant to file one or more defensive pleadings within *20 days* from the date of service of the summons in California.

______ **2.** If the court *sustains* a demurrer, the defendant is given a certain number of days to file an answer.

______ **3.** A motion to dismiss *may be* allowed for failure to state a claim for which relief can be granted.

______ **4.** A motion to dismiss may be allowed for *misnomer* of a party.

______ **5.** A motion for judgment on the pleadings may be made by *the defendant only.*

______ **6.** The plaintiff might make a motion for judgment on the pleadings on the ground that the *defendant's answer* does not set forth a legally sufficient defense.

______ **7.** Unless the case is dismissed by the allowance of a motion to dismiss, the defendant must file *a written* answer within a prescribed number of days after service of process.

______ **8.** If the defendant fails to deny an allegation made in the plaintiff's complaint, it is *automatically admitted.*

______ **9.** When an affirmative defense is used, the defendant *denies* the plaintiff's allegation.

______ **10.** A *cross-claim* is a claim that the defendant has against the plaintiff.

CHECKING TERMINOLOGY

From the list of legal terms that follows, select the one that matches each definition.

a. affirmative defense
b. answer
c. confession and avoidance
d. counterclaim
e. cross claim
f. cross complaint
g. default judgment
h. demurrer
i. dismissal
j. dismissal without prejudice
k. dismissal with prejudice
l. establishment clause
m. freedom of assembly
n. freedom of speech
o. freedom of the press
p. free exercise clause
q. misnomer
r. motion
s. motion for a more definite statement
t. motion for judgment on the pleadings
u. motion for summary judgment
v. motion for recusal
w. motion to dismiss
x. motion to strike
y. nonsuit
z. overrule
aa. recuse
bb. reply
cc. summary judgment
dd. sustain

Answers

____ **1.** A clause in the U.S. Constitution that guarantees to all persons the right to peaceably associate and assemble with others.
____ **2.** Mistake in name.
____ **3.** A dismissal in which the plaintiff is allowed to correct the error and to bring another action on the same claim.
____ **4.** A claim that the defendant has against the plaintiff.
____ **5.** To support.
____ **6.** A motion made by the defendant asking the court to dismiss the case.
____ **7.** A clause in the U.S. Constitution that prohibits the government from establishing a state religion.
____ **8.** An order disposing of an action without trial of the issues.
____ **9.** A claim brought by one defendant against another defendant in the same suit.
____ **10.** The termination of an action that did not adjudicate issues on the merits.
____ **11.** A defense that admits the plaintiff's allegations but introduces another factor that avoids liability (select two answers).
____ **12.** A motion asking the court to order the other party to remove from a pleading any insufficient defense or any redundant, immaterial, impertinent, or scandalous matter.
____ **13.** A motion by a party, when a pleading is vague, asking the court to order the other party to make a more definite statement.
____ **14.** A pleading used in California by a defendant to file a claim against another defendant, a third party, and the plaintiff in the same action.
____ **15.** A clause in the U.S. Constitution that guarantees to all persons the right to publish and circulate their ideas without governmental interference.
____ **16.** The main pleading filed by the defendant in a lawsuit in response to the plaintiff's complaint.
____ **17.** To annul, make void, or refuse to sustain.
____ **18.** A dismissal in which the plaintiff is barred from bringing another action on the same claim.
____ **19.** The plaintiff's answer to the defendant's counterclaim.
____ **20.** A motion by either party for a judgment in that party's favor based solely on information contained in the pleadings.
____ **21.** A clause in the U.S. Constitution that guarantees to all persons the right to freely practice their religion.
____ **22.** Disqualify.
____ **23.** A judgment entered on failure of a party to appear or plead at the proper time.
____ **24.** A written or oral request made to a court for certain action to be taken.
____ **25.** A request that a judge disqualify himself or herself from a case because of bias or prejudice.

UNRAVELING LEGALESE

Use simple, non-legal language, with the help of the glossary, to rewrite this quote in the space below so that it is shorter and can be understood by a layperson without losing its meaning.

> A party against whom a claim, counterclaim, or cross claim is asserted or a declaratory judgment is sought may, at any time, move with or without supporting affidavits for a summary judgment in the party's favor as to all or any part thereof. [Rule 56(b) Federal Rules of Civil Procedure]

SHARPENING YOUR LATIN SKILLS

In the space provided, write the definition of each of the following legal terms, referring to the glossary when necessary.

ad damnum ______________________________

ex parte ______________________________

in personam ______________________________

in rem ______________________________

lis pendens ______________________________

nolo contendere ______________________________

quasi in rem ______________________________

USING LEGAL LANGUAGE

Read the following story and fill in the blank lines with legal terms taken from the list of terms at the beginning of this chapter.

After reading the allegations in the plaintiff's complaint and determining that they were not vague, the attorney for the defendant decided not to file a motion ____________________. Similarly, because the complaint contained nothing that was redundant, immaterial, impertinent, or scandalous, the attorney for the defendant did not file a(n) ____________________. The attorney did, however, file a motion ____________________ on the ground of ____________________ (mistake in name) of a party. A(n) ____________________ is an order disposing of an action without trial of the issues. When the defendant's motion was disallowed by the court, the defendant's attorney filed a(n) ____________________ within the prescribed time, which contained the ____________________ defense (called a(n) ____________________ under the common law) of the statute of frauds. Neither party filed a(n) ____________________, which may be filed only after the plaintiff's complaint and defendant's answer have been filed and which replaces the older ____________________. The defendant's attorney also filed a(n) ____________________ to bring a claim against the plaintiff, which arose out of the same transaction. In answer to this claim, the plaintiff filed a(n) ____________________. Because the case did not have two defendants, no ____________________ was filed.

PUZZLING OVER WHAT YOU LEARNED

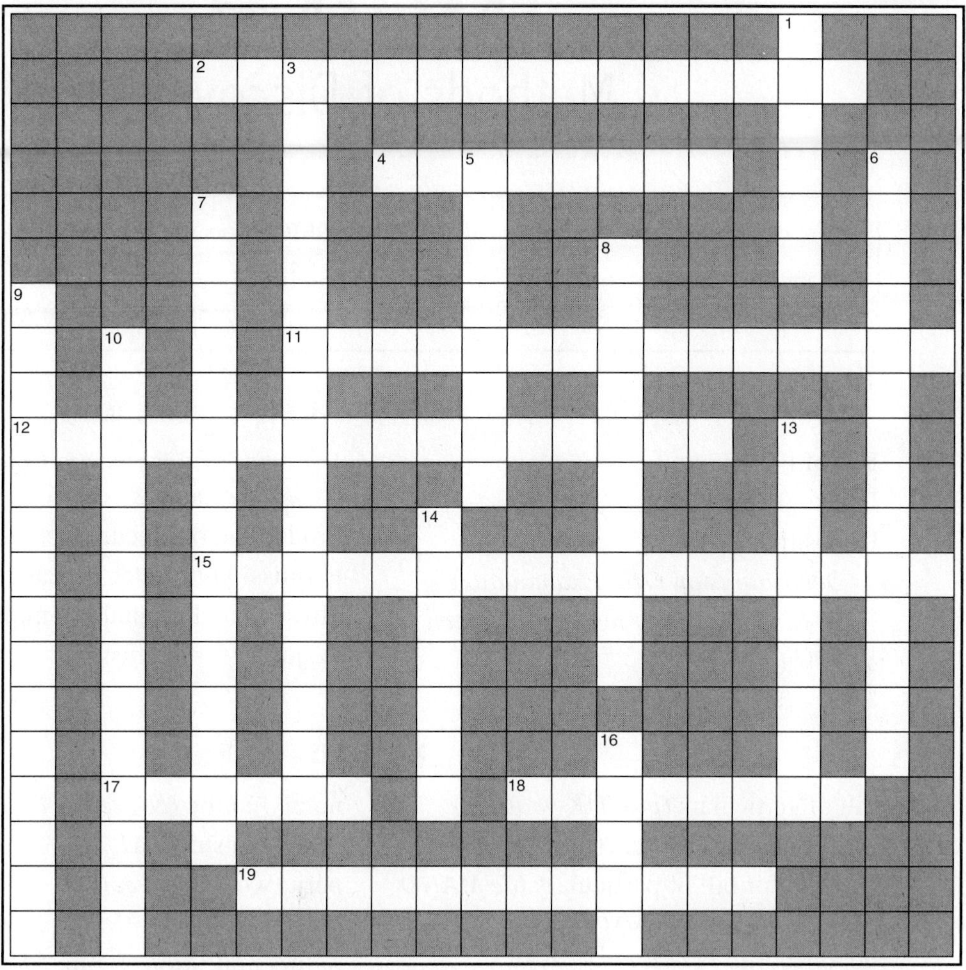

Caveat: Do not allow squares for spaces between words and punctuation (apostrophes, hyphens, etc.) when filling in crossword.

Across

2. A judgment entered on failure of a party to appear or plead at the proper time.
4. A pleading used by the defendant to attack the plaintiff's complaint by raising a point of law.
11. A motion made by the defendant asking the court to dismiss the case.
12. A request that a judge be disqualified from a case because of bias or prejudice.
15. A clause in the U.S. Constitution that guarantees to all persons the right to peaceably associate and assemble with others.
17. Disqualify.
18. To annul, make void, or refuse to sustain.
19. A claim that the defendant has against the plaintiff.

Down

1. The main pleading filed by the defendant in a lawsuit in response to the plaintiff's compl
3. A clause in the U.S. Constitution that guarante to all persons the right to publish and circulate their ideas without government interference.
5. Mistake in name.
6. A pleading used in California by a defendant to file a claim against another defendant, a third party, and the plaintiff in the same action.
7. A clause in the U.S. Constitution that guarantees to all persons the right to speak, both orally and in writing.
8. A claim brought by one defendant against another defendant in the same suit.
9. An immediate decision by the court without goi to trial based on the papers filed by the parties
10. A motion asking the court to order the other party to remove from a pleading any insufficient defense or any redundant, immaterial, impertinent, or scandalous matter.
13. An order disposing of an action without trial of the issues.
14. The termination of an action that did not adjudicate issues on the merits.
16. The plaintiff's answer to the defendant's counterclaim.

1

CHAPTER 5
Methods of Discovery

ANTE INTERROGATORY

An agreement between the parties to an action regulating any matter relative to the proceedings is a(n) (A) deposition, (B) interrogatory, (C) subpoena, and (D) stipulation.

CHAPTER OUTLINE

Bill of Particulars
Interrogatories
Depositions
Depositions on Oral Examination
Depositions of Witnesses on Written Questions
Use of Depositions in Court Proceedings
Production of Documents and Things
Permission to Enter on Land
Physical and Mental Examination
Requests for Admission

KEY TERMS

bill of particulars *(par·TIK·yoo·lars)*
cross questions *(kross KWES·chens)*
demand for bill of particulars *(de·MAND for bill ov par·TIK·yoo·lars)*
deponent *(de·PONE·ent)*
deposition *(dep·e·ZISH·en)*
deposition on oral examination *(eg·zam·in·AY·shun)*
deposition on written questions *(KWES·chens)*
discovery *(dis·KUV·e·ree)*
impeach *(im·PEECH)*
interrogatories *(in·te·RAW·ga·tore·rees)*
motion for order compelling discovery *(com·PEL·ing dis·KUV·e·ree)*
notary public *(NO·te·ree PUB·lik)*
party to a suit *(PAR·tee)*
perjury *(PER·jer·ee)*
recross questions *(RE·kross KWES·chens)*
redirect questions *(re·de·REKT KWES·chens)*
stipulate *(STIP·yoo·late)*
stipulation *(stip·yoo·LA·shun)*
subpoena *(suh·PEEN·a)*
subpoena ad testificandum *(suh·PEEN·a ad tes·te·fe·KAN·dem)*
subpoena duces tecum *(suh·PEEN·a DOO·sess TEK·um)*
verbatim *(ver·BATE·im)*

In the past, it was considered good legal practice for one party to a lawsuit to give the other party as little information as possible about the case before the trial. Today, the opposite is true. Attorneys will often enter into agreements, called stipulations, about different aspects of the case. They may for example, **stipulate** (agree) to extend the time for pleading, to waive objections, to admit certain facts, or to continue the case to a later date. A **stipulation** is an agreement between the parties to an action regulating any matter relative to the proceedings.

Several methods, called methods of **discovery,** have been established that allow each party to obtain information from the other party and from witnesses about the case before going to trial. In this way, the real issues in the case are exposed earlier, and much less time is wasted. The most common methods of discovery follow:

1. Bill of particulars
2. Interrogatories
3. Depositions
4. Production of documents and things
5. Permission to enter on land
6. Physical and mental examinations
7. Requests for admission

BILL OF PARTICULARS

In some states, including California, the plaintiff is not required to set forth in the complaint the details of the amount due on a contract for the sale of goods. All that is required by the plaintiff is to set forth the total amount owed. If the defendant files a pleading, called a **demand for bill of particulars,** within a prescribed time period (10 days after service of process in California), the plaintiff must deliver to the defendant details of the amount owed in the form of a bill of particulars. A **bill of particulars** is a written statement of the particulars of a complaint showing the details of the amount owed. In California, the bill of particulars must include a verification if the complaint contains a verification.

INTERROGATORIES

After an action has begun, any **party to a suit** (any plaintiff and any defendant) may ask written questions (up to 30 in Massachusetts) of any other party to the suit. The written questions are called **interrogatories.** They may be served on any defendant along with the summons and complaint or at a later time. They may be served on the plaintiff at any time after the action has begun. If not sent along with the summons and complaint, interrogatories are usually served by mailing a copy to the opposing attorney, and the original copy is filed with the court.

Interrogatories must be answered in writing and signed by the client answering them under the penalties of **perjury**—that is, the giving of false testimony under oath. Each interrogatory must be answered separately and fully unless it is objected to, in which event the reasons for objections must be stated. The party interrogated has from 30 to 45 days, depending on state law, to file the answers to the interrogatories with the court and to mail a copy of the answers to the interrogating party. In California, interrogatories and answers to interrogatories are not filed with the court unless the court orders them to be filed.

Rules governing the failure of a party to answer interrogatories vary from state to state. For example, California law provides for the interrogating party to file a motion to compel interrogatories when necessary. Massachusetts law provides that if the party interrogated fails to file the answers within 45 days, the interrogating party may file an application for a request for final judgment (against the defendant) or a request for a dismissal (against the plaintiff), whichever is appropriate. The clerk of court will then notify all parties that a final judgment or a dismissal will be entered unless the answers are filed within 30 days. If 30 days elapse without an answer to the interrogatories being filed, the interrogator may reapply for a final judgment or a dismissal, and it will be allowed by the court if the answers are not then on file.

DEPOSITIONS

An important method of discovery before the trial occurs is the **deposition,** which is the testimony of a witness given under oath but not in open court. The witness who gives the testimony is known as a **deponent** (one who gives testimony under oath). Two principal types of depositions are (1) depositions on oral examination and (2) depositions of witnesses on written questions.

Depositions on Oral Examination

After an action begins, any party may take the testimony of any person, including a party, by **deposition on oral examination.** In this deposition, lawyers orally examine and cross-examine a witness. With a few exceptions, permission of the court is not required for this deposition. Witnesses may be compelled to attend by **subpoena,** sometimes called a **subpoena testificandum** (an order commanding a person to appear and testify in a legal action).

A party desiring to take the deposition must give a prescribed number of day's written notice to every other party to the action. The notice must state the time and place for taking the deposition and the name and address of each person to be examined. A **subpoena duces tecum** is an order commanding a person to appear and bring certain papers or other materials that are pertinent to the legal action. Accountants and record keepers are often subpoenaed this way. If a subpoena duces tecum is to be served on the person to be examined, the materials to be produced must be listed on the notice.

Depositions are taken before a person authorized to administer oaths, such as a **notary public.** Lawyers for each side examine and cross-examine the witnesses. The testimony is taken down by a stenographer, unless the court authorizes some other method of recording it. Usually, the stenographer is also a notary public and performs both functions of administering the oath and taking down the testimony. Instead of participating in the oral examination, parties may, if they wish, submit written questions to be answered by the witness under oath. The questions and answers are taken down **verbatim** (word for word) by the stenographer.

After the testimony is transcribed by the stenographer, it is either read or shown to the witness whose testimony it is. Any changes that the witness desires to make are written on the deposition by the officer who administered the oath with reasons given by the witness for making the changes. The deposition is signed by the witness or a reason is noted for the witness's failure to sign. It is then hand delivered to the court or mailed to the court by registered or certified mail. Some states no longer require a deposition to be filed with the court.

Depositions of Witnesses on Written Questions

After an action begins, any party may take the testimony of any person, including a party, by **deposition on written questions.** In this type of deposition, lawyers examine and cross-examine a witness who has received in advance written questions to be answered.

Witnesses may be compelled to attend by subpoena. A party desiring to take such a deposition must serve the written questions on all parties to the action together with the name and address of the person who is to answer them and the name and address of the officer before whom the deposition is to be taken. In some states, after the questions are served, a party may serve **cross questions** (questions asked by a deponent in response to questions asked at a deposition) on any other party. The party receiving the cross questions may serve **redirect questions** (further questions in response to cross questions) on all other parties. In addition, after being served with redirect questions, a party may serve **recross questions** (further questions asked in response to redirect questions) on all other parties.

The depositions of witnesses on written questions are handled by the stenographer and filed with the court in the same manner that depositions on oral examinations are handled, as explained earlier.

Use of Depositions in Court Proceedings

When the case goes to court, the depositions may be used to contradict or **impeach** (call in to question) any contrary testimony of a witness. The deposition may also be used at the trial if the witness is dead; is at a distance greater than 100 miles from the place of the trial; or is unable to testify because of age, sickness, infirmity, or imprisonment; or if other exceptional circumstances make it desirable that the deposition be used.

PRODUCTION OF DOCUMENTS AND THINGS

Any party may serve on any other party a request for permission to inspect and copy documents (including writings, drawings, graphs, charts, photographs, and other data compilations) or to inspect and copy, test, or sample any tangible things.

The party on whom the request is made must serve a written response within a prescribed number of days after the service of the request stating that the request will be permitted or that it is objected to, with reasons given for any objection. If an objection occurs, the party submitting the request may make a **motion for order compelling discovery.** After a hearing, the court may allow or disallow the motion.

WORD WISE

Time Prefixes

Prefix	*Meaning*	*Examples*
re-	again	reapply, rediscover, reorganization, rebuttal, recross questions, redirect questions, republish
post-	after	postpone, postgraduate, postmortem
pre-	before	preadolescence, prearrange, predecease, premarital, premeditated, prenuptial

PERMISSION TO ENTER ON LAND

Any party may serve on any other party a request to permit entry on land or other property in the possession or control of the party on whom the request is served. The entry may be for the purpose of inspecting, measuring, surveying, photographing, testing, or sampling the property. The party to whom the request is made must respond in the manner described in the preceding paragraph.

PHYSICAL AND MENTAL EXAMINATIONS

When the mental or physical condition of a party is in controversy, the court in which the action is pending may order the party to submit to a physical or mental examination. The order may be made only on motion for good cause and after notice is given to the person to be examined.

REQUESTS FOR ADMISSION

A party may serve on any other party a written request for admission of the truth of any matter that is relevant to the case. The request may relate to statements, opinions of fact or law, or the genuineness of documents.

The party to whom the request is directed must file a written answer within a prescribed number of days after service of the request. The answer must state, under the penalties of perjury, (1) a denial of the matter; (2) a reason why the answering party cannot truthfully admit or deny the matter; or (3) an objection, with reasons, to the request. If such an answer is not filed, the matter is considered by the court to be admitted.

REVIEWING WHAT YOU LEARNED

After studying the text, write the answers to each of the following questions.

1. How do methods of discovery used in the past compare with those of today? ____________

2. List the seven most common methods of discovery. ____________

3. To whom may interrogatories be asked? ____________

4. Who signs the answers to the interrogatories? ____________

5. Name the two principal types of depositions. ____________

6. Depositions are taken before whom? The testimony is taken down by whom? ____________

7. What occurs after the testimony of a deposition is transcribed by the stenographer? ________

____

____

____

8. Describe the back-and-forth questioning procedure that occurs when a deposition on written questions occurs. ________

____

____

____

9. When may depositions be used in court? ________

____

____

____

10. How must a party who is requested to produce documents respond? ________

____

____

____

11. For what purposes may a person request permission to enter on land of another? ________

____

____

____

____

____

12. When may the court order a party to submit to a physical or mental examination? ________

____

____

____

____

____

13. How must a party who is requested to admit a particular matter respond? ________

____

____

____

____

1

UNDERSTANDING LEGAL CONCEPTS

Indicate whether each statement is true or false. Then, change the italicized word or phrase of each *false* statement to make it true.

Answers

_______________ **1.** Attorneys *never* enter into agreements about different aspects of a case.

_______________ **2.** After an action has begun, any *party to a suit* may ask written questions of any other party to a suit.

_______________ **3.** Interrogatories must be answered in writing and signed by the *attorney* answering them under the penalties of perjury.

_______________ **4.** A deposition is the testimony of a witness given under oath *in* open court.

_______________ **5.** If a subpoena duces tecum is to be served on a person to be examined, the materials to be produced *must be* listed on the notice.

_______________ **6.** When depositions are taken, lawyers for each side *examine and cross-examine* the witnesses.

_______________ **7.** A deposition of a witness *may not be* used at a trial if the witness is dead.

_______________ **8.** Any party may serve on *any other party* a request to permit entry on the other's land.

_______________ **9.** The court may order a party to submit to a physical *but not* a mental examination.

_______________ **10.** If a party to whom a request for admission is directed fails to answer, the matter is considered by the court to be *admitted.*

CHECKING TERMINOLOGY

From the list of legal terms that follows, select the one that matches each definition.

- **a.** bill of particulars
- **b.** cross questions
- **c.** demand for bill of particulars
- **d.** deponent
- **e.** deposition
- **f.** deposition on oral examination
- **g.** deposition on written questions
- **h.** discovery
- **i.** impeach
- **j.** interrogatories
- **k.** motion for order compelling discovery

Answers

____ **1.** A person or organization participating or having a direct interest in a legal proceeding.

____ **2.** Methods that allow each party to obtain information from the other party and from witnesses about a case before going to court.

____ **3.** A form of discovery in a civil action in which parties are given a series of written questions to be answered under oath.

____ **4.** The testimony of a witness, given under oath but not in open court, and later reduced to writing.

____ **5.** An order commanding a person to appear and testify in a legal action (select two answers).

____ **6.** An order commanding a person to appear and bring certain papers or other materials that are pertinent to a legal action.

____ **7.** A person authorized to administer oaths, attest to and certify documents, take acknowledgments, and perform other official acts.

____ **8.** The giving of false testimony under oath.

____ **9.** One who gives testimony under oath.

l. notary public
m. party to a suit
n. perjury
o. recross questions
p. redirect questions
q. stipulate
r. stipulation
s. subpoena
t. subpoena ad testificandum
u. subpoena duces tecum
v. verbatim

____**10.** An agreement between the parties to an action regulating any matter relative to the proceedings.
____**11.** Call in to question.
____**12.** Questions asked by a deponent in response to questions asked at a deposition.
____**13.** Further questions asked by a deponent in response to redirect questions.
____**14.** A deposition in which lawyers examine and cross-examine a witness who has received in advance written questions to be answered.
____**15.** A written statement of the particulars of a complaint showing the details of the amount owed.
____**16.** Word for word.
____**17.** Agree.
____**18.** A motion asking the court to order the other party to produce certain writings, photographs, or other requested items.

UNRAVELING LEGALESE

Use simple, non-legal language, with the help of the glossary, to rewrite this case quote in the space below so that it is shorter and can be understood by a layperson without losing its meaning.

> If the court is satisfied that the perpetuation of the testimony may prevent a failure or delay of justice, it shall make an order designating or describing the persons whose depositions may be taken and specifying the subject matter of the examination and whether the depositions shall be taken upon oral examination or written interrogatories. [Rule 27(3) Federal Rules of Civil Procedure]

USING LEGAL LANGUAGE

Read the following story and fill in the blank lines with legal terms taken from the list of terms at the beginning of this chapter.

Before going to trial, attorney Mary Grey entered into an agreement, called a(n) ____________________, with the opposing attorney, admitting certain facts. She also used certain methods of ____________________ to obtain information from the other party and from witnesses about the case. She sent 30 questions, called ____________________, to be answered under oath by Conrad Allen, the defendant, who was a(n) ____________________ to the suit. She also sent a(n) ____________________, rather than a plain ____________________, to Leroy Henning, a witness, commanding him to bring with him certain payroll records of the defendant to a(n) ____________________, which is the testimony of a witness given under oath but not in open court. Because written questions were submitted to the ____________________, Leroy, in advance, this was known as a(n) ____________________. After receiving the questions, Leroy sent ____________________ to be answered by the plaintiff. The plaintiff, in turn, responded with further questions, called ____________________ to be answered by Leroy. The testimony was taken before a(n) ____________________, who was authorized to administer oaths, and written down ____________________—that is, word for word—by a stenographer. When the case goes to court, the questions and answers may be used to ____________________—that is, call in to question—Leroy's testimony. If Leroy gives false testimony, it is known as ____________________.

PUZZLING OVER WHAT YOU LEARNED

Caveat: Do **not** allow squares for spaces between words and punctuation (apostrophes, hyphens, etc.) when filling in crossword.

Across

1. An order commanding a person to appear and bring certain papers or other materials that are pertinent to a legal action.
3. An order commanding a person to appear and testify in a legal action.
8. The testimony of a witness, given under oath but not in open court, and later reduced to writing.
11. Call in to question.
12. Methods that allow each party to obtain information from the other party and from witnesses about a case before going to court.
14. Further questions asked by a deponent in response to redirect questions.
15. An agreement between the parties to an action regulating any matter relative to the proceedings.
16. Word for word.

Down

2. A written statement of the particulars of a complaint showing the details of the amount owed.
3. Agree.
4. A person authorized to administer oaths, attest to and certify documents, take acknowledgments, and perform other official acts.
5. Further questions asked by an examiner at a deposition in response to cross questions.
6. Questions asked by a deponent in response to questions asked at a deposition.
7. A form of discovery in a civil action in which parties are given a series of written questions to be answered under oath.
9. A person or organization participating or having a direct interest in a legal proceeding.
10. One who gives testimony under oath.
13. The giving of false testimony under oath.

1

CHAPTER 6

Pretrial Hearing and Jury Trial

ANTE INTERROGATORY

The examination of jurors by the court to see that they stand indifferent is referred to as the (A) venire, (B) voir dire, (C) array, and (D) venue.

CHAPTER OUTLINE

Pretrial Hearing
Right to Jury Trial
Selecting the Venire
Impaneling the Jury
Examination and Challenge of Jurors

KEY TERMS

alderpeople *(AL·der·pee·pel)*
alternate jurors *(AL·ter·net JOOR·ors)*
array *(a·RAY)*
bench trial *(tryl)*
capital criminal case *(KAP·i·tel KRIM·i·nel kase)*
challenge *(CHAL·enj)*
challenge for cause *(CHAL·enj for kaws)*
challenge to the array *(CHAL·enj to the a·RAY)*
foreperson *(FORE·per·son)*
impaneled *(im·PAN·eld)*
indifferent *(in·DIF·rent)*
jurors *(JOOR·ors)*
jury *(JOOR·ee)*
jury panel *(JOOR·ee PAN·el)*
jury pool *(JOOR·ee pool)*
jury waived trial *(JOOR·ee waved tryl)*
master *(MAS·ter)*
motion in limine *(MOH·shun in LIM·e·nee)*
motion to quash the array *(MOH·shun to kwash the a·RAY)*
one day–one trial jury system *(JOOR·ee SYS·tem)*
peremptory challenges *(per·EMP·ter·ee CHAL·en·jes)*
petit jury *(PET·ee JOOR·ee)*
pretrial hearing *(PRE·tryl HEER·ing)*
selectpeople *(sel·EKT·pee·pel)*
talesmen *(TAILZ·men)*
taleswomen *(tailz·WO·men)*
venire *(ven·EYE·ree)*
voir dire *(vwar deer)*
writ of venire facias *(ven·EYE·ree FAY·shes)*

PRETRIAL HEARING

Before a trial is held in the superior court, a **pretrial hearing** usually occurs. This hearing is for the purpose of speeding up the trial. Only the attorneys for each side are required to attend the hearing, but many attorneys like to bring their clients to be available for questions that may arise. The attorneys appear before the judge to consider the possibility of doing the following:

1. Simplifying the issues
2. Amending the pleadings
3. Obtaining admissions of fact
4. Limiting the number of expert witnesses
5. Referring the case to a master*
6. Settling the case
7. Agreeing on damages
8. Discussing other matters that may aid in the disposition of the action

Attorneys may make a variety of motions to the court during the pretrial hearing stage. A **motion in limine** is a pretrial motion asking the court to prohibit the introduction of prejudicial evidence by the other party. A report of the pretrial hearing becomes a part of the record of the case and may be read to the jury at the trial.

RIGHT TO JURY TRIAL

The right to a trial by jury in all criminal cases and in civil cases involving more than $20 is found in Article III and the Sixth and Seventh Amendments of the U.S. Constitution. Under the rules of civil procedure, any party may demand a jury trial on the other party no later than 10 days after the service of the last pleading. If a jury trial is not requested, a trial without a jury, called a **jury waived trial** or **bench trial,** will usually be held.

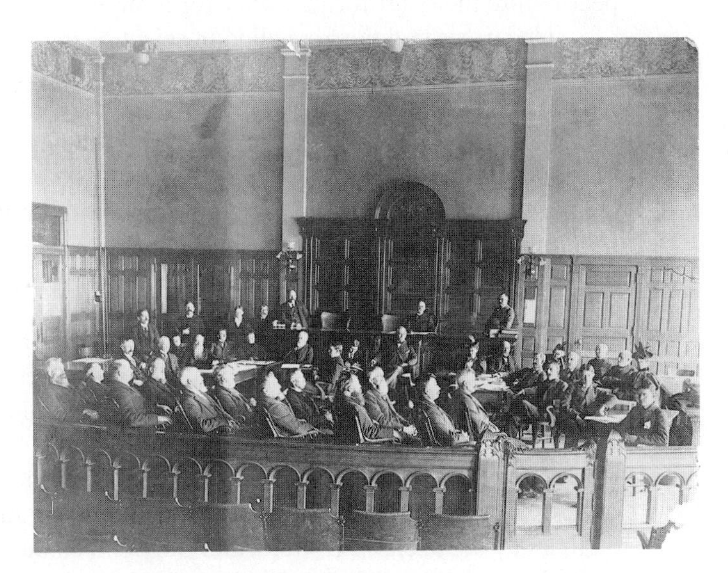

Figure 6-1 The 1895 Morrison Will case at Richmond, Indiana (illustrated here), lasted 128 days and was the longest jury trial in the United States up until that time. Almost a century later, the *Kemner v. Monsanto Co.* toxic waste trial lasted more than a year and a half and is in the *Guinness Book of World Records* as the longest jury trial in history. How many people serve on a petit jury? How many decide the case? (Courtesy of the Library of Congress, Prints and Photographs Division, reproduction number LC-USZ62-104009.)

*A **master** is a lawyer appointed by the court to hear testimony in the case and to report back to the court as to his or her findings or conclusions.

A **jury** (from the Latin *jurare,* meaning "to swear") is a group of people, called **jurors,** selected according to law and sworn to determine the facts in a case. The ordinary jury of 12 people used for the trial of a civil or criminal action is known as a **petit jury** to distinguish it from a grand jury, which issues indictments. The system of selecting the jury varies from state to state. One system is described here.

Selecting the Venire

The **jury pool** or large group of people from which juries are selected is called the **jury panel** or the **venire.** Sometimes it is referred to as the **array.** The selection of the venire has changed in recent years. Many jurisdictions have done away with the traditional method and replaced it with the "one day–one trial" system. Both methods are described here.

Traditional Method. Under the traditional method of selecting jurors, each city and town is required to prepare a list each year of everyone of good moral character, who is eligible to serve on a jury. Each name on the list is placed on a separate ballot and kept in a ballot box by the city or town clerk. Before each sitting of the court (a sitting lasts one month), the clerk of court sends a **writ of venire facias** to each city and town within the court's jurisdiction. This writ orders the city or town to provide a designated number of jurors for the next sitting of the court. Jurors' names are then drawn from the ballot box by the mayor and alderpeople of a city and by the selectpeople of a town. **Alderpeople** are men and women elected to serve as members of the legislative body of a city. **Selectpeople** are men and women elected to serve as the chief administrative authority of a town. Jurors whose names are drawn by the cities and towns are summoned to appear before the court for jury duty for a month.

Under this traditional method of selecting the venire, members of the clergy, lawyers, practicing physicians and surgeons, nurses, public school teachers, and certain other people are exempt from jury duty. Persons 70 years of age or older and parents who are responsible for the daily care of a child under the age of 15 may elect to be exempt from jury duty if they so choose. The judge may exempt others from jury duty if it is best for the public interest or if such duty will impose an undue hardship on the person selected. In addition, no person who would be embarrassed by hearing the testimony or by discussing the case in the jury room is required to serve as a juror on sexually related cases.

One Day–One Trial Method. Another method of jury selection is coming into wider use. Called the **one day–one trial jury system,** it is designed to provide the courts with juries consisting of fair cross sections of the community and to reduce the burden of jury duty on certain classes of citizens.

The system varies from state to state. Under the Massachusetts system, a new group of jurors appears in the jury pool (venire) each day. Jurors who are not selected for a trial on that day are excused from further duty and cannot be called again for three years. Jurors who are selected for a trial serve only for that trial and no longer.

Under this system, there are no exemptions from jury duty. Generally, every citizen 18 years old or older who can speak and understand the English language and is physically fit must serve. Citizens 70 years old or older may choose not to serve. To be eligible to serve, persons must have been a resident or inhabitant for six months or more in the county in which they are summoned. Jurors are selected randomly by computer from an annual census list provided by the cities and towns. Each juror, when summoned, is entitled to one postponement of up to one year from the date summoned. This postponement allows a juror to choose a more convenient date if the assigned date is not suitable.

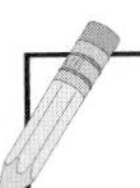

WORD WISE

"People" Rather than "Men"

The use of "man" or "men" as a generic term was found to be obsolete in 1971 by both the National Council for Teachers of English and the *Oxford English Dictionary.* Use of "people" in this chapter, such as *alderpeople* and *selectpeople,* reflects this shift.

Alternatives to the generic terms "man" and "men" include person, people, human being(s), civilization, society, individual(s), somebody, someone, anyone, all of us, everyone, humankind, humanity, the public, citizen(s), worker(s), member(s) and women and men.

Each juror, when summoned, may request a transfer of courthouse location if the juror encounters a hardship in reporting to the assigned location.

Under this particular state's system, jurors must be compensated by their employers for the first three days of jury duty at their normal rate of pay and by the county after that at a rate of $50 per day.

IMPANELING THE JURY

On the day the jurors are summoned to court, the clerk of court places each juror's name on a ballot and puts it in a ballot box. When a case is ready for trial, the members of the venire are brought into open court. Twelve of their names are picked out of the ballot box, and those chosen take seats in the jury box. In some states, if the case is expected to be lengthy, 14 or 16 jurors are **impaneled** (enrolled) to hear the case instead of 12, but before deliberating, the jury is reduced (by lot) to 12 members who decide the case. Those who are removed are retained as **alternate jurors** (additional jurors impaneled in case of sickness or removal of any of the 12 who are deliberating). In some states, including California, alternate jurors are chosen separately from regular jurors at the beginning of the trial and designated as such. The plaintiff and defendant may stipulate that the jury shall consist of any number less than 12 if they wish to do so.

Figure 6-2 Members of the jury must stand indifferent—they must have a neutral or unbiased opinion before the trial begins.

In some states, the judge chooses one of the members of the jury to be the **foreperson** (the presiding member of a jury who speaks for the group). In other states, the foreperson is elected by members of the jury.

If at least seven jurors have been chosen for a case, but not enough jurors are left on the venire to make up a complete jury, the judge has the power to send the sheriff out onto the street to obtain bystanders or people from the county at large to serve on the jury. Jurors who are chosen this way are called **talesmen** and **taleswomen.**

EXAMINATION AND CHALLENGE OF JURORS

Members of the jury must stand indifferent—that is, they must have a neutral or unbiased opinion before the trial begins. To establish such indifference, the jurors are examined under oath. This examination is called the **voir dire,** a French word meaning "to speak the truth." The court attempts to determine whether any of the jurors

1. Are related to either party or either attorney
2. Have any interest in the case
3. Have expressed or formed an opinion about it
4. Are aware of any bias or prejudice that they may have in the case
5. Know of any reason why they do not stand indifferent

Any juror who does not stand indifferent is replaced (by lot) by another juror from the venire.

Either attorney may **challenge** (call or put into question) members of the jury and ask the court to have them removed from the jury. A **challenge to the array,** sometimes called a **motion to quash the array,** is a challenge to the entire jury because of some irregularity in the selection of the jury. If allowed by the court, the entire jury must step down and a new jury is selected. **Challenges for cause** are challenges to individual jurors when it is believed that a juror does not stand **indifferent**—that is, impartial, unbiased, and disinterested. No limit exists to the number of challenges for cause that may be made. **Peremptory challenges** are challenges for which no reason need be given. State law varies as to the number of peremptory challenges allowed. In a **capital criminal case** (one in which the death penalty may be inflicted) in Massachusetts, each side is entitled to as many peremptory challenges as there are jurors. In a noncapital criminal case and in a civil case, each side is entitled to four peremptory challenges and an additional one if 14 jurors are selected, or two additional challenges if 16 jurors are selected.

In 1986, the U.S. Supreme Court held that peremptory challenges based on race are unconstitutional.

WEB WISE

Since *anyone* can publish *anything* on the Web, here are **5 W's** to ask whenever you consider the information you find there:

Who created the site?
Does the author have suitable credentials?
Is the "author" an organization or association?

What type of site is it?
.edu = educational
.com = commercial
.org = organization
.gov = government
.net = network/utilities
.mil = military

When was the site created or updated?
Is the site being maintained, or has it been abandoned?

Where can you find more information?
Are sources documented with footnotes or links?

Why was this site created?
To sell, entice?
To inform, give facts and data?
To persuade?
To advocate a point of view?

REVIEWING WHAT YOU LEARNED

After studying the text, write the answers to each of the following questions.

1. Who may demand a jury trial? ______________________________

2. What is the purpose of a pretrial hearing? ______________________________

3. Under the traditional method of selecting a jury, who is exempt from jury duty? How long do jurors serve? ______________________________

4. Under the one day—one trial system of jury selection, who is exempt from jury duty? How long do jurors serve? ______________________________

5. Describe the method that is used to impanel a jury in a particular trial. ____________

6. When may more than 12 jurors hear a case? How many jurors ultimately decide such a case? ____

7. In what two ways may jury forepersons be selected? ____________

8. When may the judge send the sheriff out into the street to obtain jurors? ____________

9. List two of the five points that would cause a juror not to stand indifferent. ____________

10. How many challenges for cause may be made?

11. In Massachusetts, how many peremptory challenges may be made in a capital criminal case? In a noncapital criminal case or a civil case?

UNDERSTANDING LEGAL CONCEPTS

Indicate whether each statement is true or false. Then, change the italicized word or phrase of each *false* statement to make it true.

Answers

______ **1.** The ordinary jury of 12 people used for the trial of a civil or criminal action is known as a *petit* jury.

______ **2.** A pretrial hearing is held for the purpose of *delaying* the trial as much as possible.

______ **3.** When a writ of venire facias is sent to a city, the mayor and alderpeople *personally choose* the names of people for jury duty.

______ **4.** Under the traditional method of selecting the venire, *members of the clergy and lawyers* are exempt from jury duty.

______ **5.** Under the one day–one trial system of jury selection, practicing physicians and surgeons, nurses, and public school teachers *are exempt* from jury duty.

______ **6.** Under the U.S. Constitution, peremptory challenges *may* be based on race.

______ **7.** When a case is ready for trial, the names of 12 members of the venire are *picked out of a ballot box* to serve on the jury.

______ **8.** If at least seven jurors have been chosen for a case, but not enough jurors are left on the venire to make up a complete jury, the judge *may* send the sheriff out onto the street and obtain bystanders to serve on the jury.

______ **9.** Members of the jury *must* stand indifferent.

______ **10.** When jurors are challenged, a limit exists to the number of *challenges for cause* that may be made.

CHECKING TERMINOLOGY

From the list of legal terms that follows, select the one that matches each definition:

a. alderpeople
b. alternate jurors
c. array
d. bench trial
e. capital criminal case
f. challenge
g. challenge for cause
h. challenge to the array
i. foreperson
j. impaneled

Answers

____ **1.** A case in which the death penalty may be inflicted.

____ **2.** The presiding member of a jury who speaks for the group.

____ **3.** Members of a jury.

____ **4.** A challenge of a juror for which no reason need be given.

____ **5.** A challenge to the entire jury because of some irregularity in the selection of the jury (select two answers).

____ **6.** Bystanders or people from the county at large chosen by the court to act as jurors when there are not enough people left on the venire.

____ **7.** The large group of people from which a jury is selected for a trial (select four answers).

____ **8.** A system designed to provide the courts with juries consisting of fair cross sections of the community and to reduce the burden of jury duty on certain classes of citizens.

k. indifferent
l. jurors
m. jury
n. jury panel
o. jury pool
p. jury waived trial
q. master
r. motion in limine
s. motion to quash the array
t. one day–one trial jury system
u. peremptory challenge
v. petit jury
w. pretrial hearing
x. selectpeople
y. talesmen and taleswomen
z. venire
aa. voir dire
bb. writ of venire facias

____ **9.** Listed as members of the jury.
____ **10.** People elected to serve as members of the legislative body of a city.
____ **11.** A written order to cities and towns to provide a designated number of jurors for the next sitting of the court.
____ **12.** A challenge of a juror made when it is believed that the juror does not stand indifferent.
____ **13.** Impartial, unbiased, and disinterested.
____ **14.** The ordinary jury of 6 or 12 people used for the trial of a civil or criminal action.
____ **15.** Additional jurors impaneled in case of sickness or removal of any of the regular jurors who are deliberating.
____ **16.** To speak the truth. The examination of jurors by the court to see that they stand indifferent.
____ **17.** A trial without a jury (select two answers).
____ **18.** A group of people selected according to law and sworn to determine the facts in a case.
____ **19.** A lawyer appointed by the court to hear testimony in a case and report back to the court as to his or her findings or conclusions.
____ **20.** A pretrial motion asking the court to prohibit the introduction of prejudicial evidence by the other party.

UNRAVELING LEGALESE

Use simple, non-legal language, with the help of the glossary, to rewrite this quote in the space below so that it is shorter and can be understood by a layperson without losing its meaning.

> In civil cases, each party shall be entitled to three peremptory challenges. Several defendants or several plaintiffs may be considered as a single party for the purposes of making challenges, or the court may allow additional peremptory challenges and permit them to be exercised separately or jointly. [28 U.S.C. 1870]

USING LEGAL LANGUAGE

Read the following story and fill in the blank lines with legal terms taken from the list of terms at the beginning of this chapter.

The plaintiff's attorney, Mary Grey, attended a(n) ______________________________ before the judge prior to the trial in an attempt to speed up the trial. Mary wanted a jury trial instead of referring the case to a(n) ______________________________—that is, a lawyer appointed by the court to hear testimony. In addition, she did not want a(n) ______________________ ______________________ or a(n) ______________________, which is a trial without a jury. The clerk of court sent a(n) ______________________ to each city and town within the court's jurisdiction to obtain jurors for the next sitting of the court. When the trial began, jurors were selected by lot from the ______________________ (the jury pool), and after the ______________________ was held to be sure that they stood ______________________, 14 jurors were ______________________ to hear the case. The number included two ______________________ who would be used in case of sickness or removal of any of the regular jurors. No ______________________ for cause existed, but several ______________________ did, which required no reason to be given. The lawyers did not wish to stipulate to a lesser number of jurors, and no need to obtain ______________________ existed—that is, bystanders or people from the county at large selected to serve on the jury. This trial was not a(n) ______________________, because it did not involve the death penalty. A woman was chosen to be the ______________________, who would speak for the group.

PUZZLING OVER WHAT YOU LEARNED

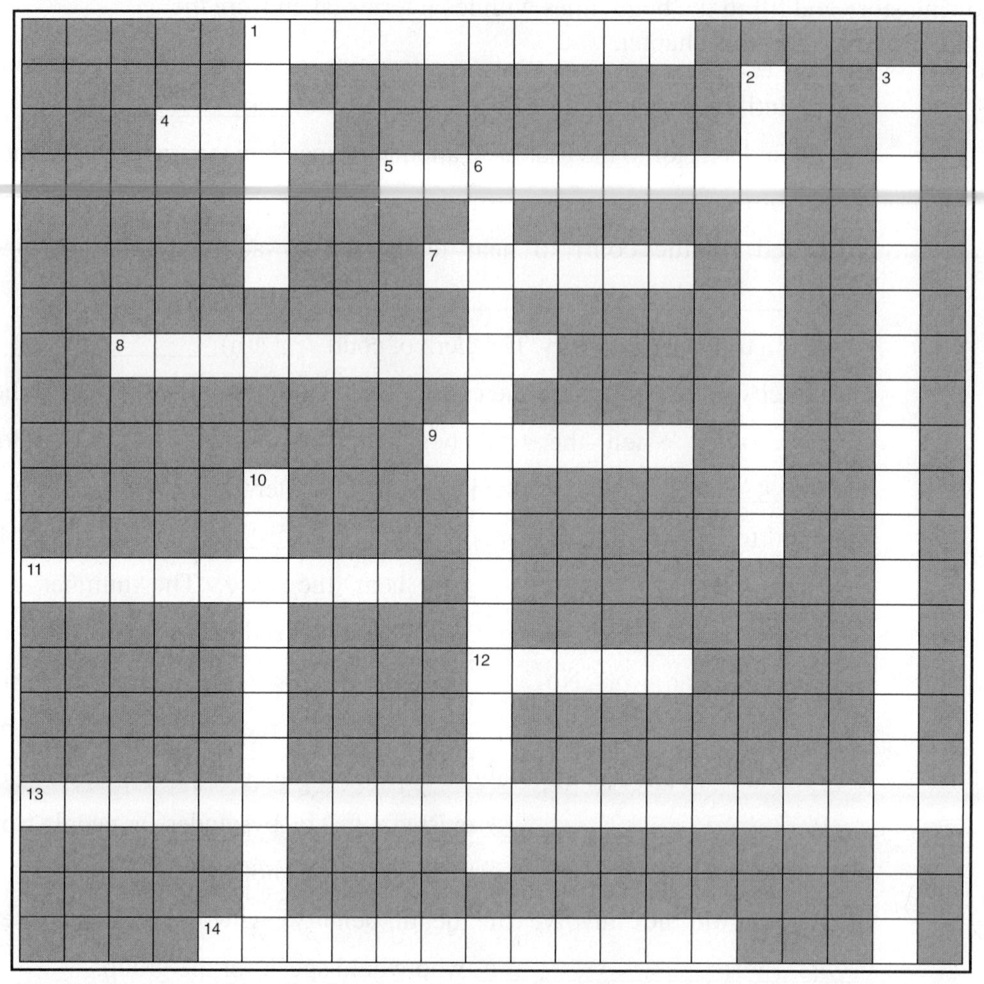

Caveat: Allow squares for spaces between words and punctuation (apostrophes, hyphens, etc.) when filling in crossword.

Across

1. Large group of people from which a jury is selected for a trial.
4. Group of people sworn to determine the facts in a case.
5. Listed as members of the jury.
7. Jury pool.
8. Ordinary jury of twelve people used for a trial.
9. Lawyer appointed by the court to hear testimony and report findings to the court.
11. Examination of jurors by the court to see that they stand indifferent.
12. Another name for venire.
13. Written order to cities and towns to provide jurors for the next court sitting.
14. People elected to serve as chief administrative authority of a town.

Down

1. Members of a jury.
2. Impartial, unbiased, and disinterested.
3. Challenges of jurors when it is believed they do not stand indifferent.
6. A hearing before the judge prior to a trial.
10. People elected to serve as members of the legislative body of a city.

CHAPTER 7
Steps in a Trial

ANTE INTERROGATORY

The decision of a jury is called a (A) judgment, (B) judgment n.o.v., (C) decree, (D) verdict.

CHAPTER OUTLINE

KEY TERMS

adjudicating *(a·JOO·di·kay·ting)*
adjudication *(a·joo·di·KAY·shun)*
admissible evidence *(ad·MISS·e·bel EV·i·dens)*
affirm *(a·FERM)*
appeal *(a·PEEL)*
appeal bond
appellant *(a·PEL·ent)*
appellee *(a·pel·EE)*
case in chief *(Cheef)*
circumstantial evidence *(ser·kum·STAN·shel EV·i·dens)*
closing argument *(AR·gyoo·ment)*
consent decree *(kon·SENT de·KREE)*
court of equity *(EK·wi·tee)*
cross-examination *(kross-eg·zam·in·AY·shun)*
decree *(de·KREE)*
defendant in error *(de·FEN·dent in ERR·er)*
deliberate *(dee·LIB·e·rate)*
direct evidence *(de·REKT EV·i·dens)*
direct examination *(de·REKT eg·zam·in·AY·shun)*
DNA
DNA sample
documentary evidence *(dok·u·MENT·ta·ree EV·i·dens)*
equity *(EK·wi·tee)*
exhibit *(eg·ZIB·it)*
hung jury *(JOOR·ee)*
injunction *(in·JUNK·shun)*
judgment *(JUJ·ment)*
judgment notwithstanding the verdict *(VER·dikt)*
judgment n.o.v.
judgment on the merits *(MER·its)*
judgment on the pleadings *(PLEED·ings)*
jury charge *(JOOR·ee charj)*
leading questions *(LEE·ding)*
mistrial *(MIS·tryl)*
motion for a directed verdict *(de·REK·ted VER·dikt)*
non obstante verdicto *(non ob·STAN·tee ver·DIK·toh)*
opening statement *(O·pen·ing STATE·ment)*
polling the jury *(POLE·ing)*

preliminary injunction *(pre·LIM·i·ner·ee in·JUNK·shun)*
prima facie case *(PRY·mah FAY·shee)*
questions of fact *(KWES·chens)*
questions of law
real evidence *(reel EV·i·dens)*
rebuttal *(re·BUT·el)*
relevant evidence *(REL·e·vent EV·i·dens)*
remand *(re·MAND)*
respondent *(re·SPON·dent)*
reverse *(re·VERSE)*
ripe for judgment *(JUJ·ment)*
sequester *(see·KWEST·er)*
set aside *(a·SIDE)*
summation *(sum·AY·shun)*
testimonial evidence *(tes·ti·MOH·nee·el EV·i·dens)*
vacate *(VA·kate)*
verdict *(VER·dikt)*
verdict contrary to law *(KON·trare·ee)*

Steps in a Jury Trial

1. Plaintiff's opening statement
2. Plaintiff's case in chief
3. Defendant's opening statement
4. Defendant's case in chief
5. Requests for instructions to the jury
6. Final arguments (summation)
7. Instructions to the jury (jury charge)
8. Jury's verdict
9. Court's judgment or decree
10. Appeal
11. Execution in civil cases
12. Sentencing in criminal cases

PLAINTIFF'S OPENING STATEMENT

After the jury is impaneled, the plaintiff's attorney makes an **opening statement.** The attorney outlines the case by telling the jury (the judge in a nonjury trial) what the evidence will prove. The opening statement must set forth a **prima facie case**—that is, be legally sufficient to win the case unless it is rebutted by contrary evidence.

PLAINTIFF'S CASE IN CHIEF

Next, the plaintiff's attorney puts in the **case in chief**—that is, he or she introduces evidence to prove the allegations that were made in the pleadings and in the opening statement. Evidence that is pertinent and proper to be considered in reaching a decision following specific rules is known as **admissible evidence.** Evidence tending to prove or disprove an alleged fact is termed **relevant evidence.** Evidence is classified as testimonial, documentary, or real. **Testimonial evidence** consists of oral testimony of witnesses made under oath in open court. **Documentary evidence** consists of such evidence as written contracts, business records, correspondence, wills, and deeds. **Real evidence** consists of actual objects that have a bearing on the case, such as an item of clothing, a weapon found at the scene of the crime, a photograph, a chart, a model, fingerprints, or **DNA** (deoxyribonucleic acid)—the double strand of molecules that carries a cell's unique genetic code. A **DNA sample** is biological evidence of any nature that is utilized to conduct DNA analysis. Tangible items that are introduced as evidence are referred to as **exhibits.**

When a witness testifies as to something he or she observed, such as "I saw that man shoot the gun," it is called **direct evidence** because the testimony directly relates to the fact in issue. (Did that man shoot the gun?) When the testimony relates to some fact other than the fact in issue, such as "I heard the sound of a gun being fired and then saw that man run past me," it is called **circumstantial evidence.**

To begin this phase of the trial, the plaintiff's attorney calls his or her first witness to the witness stand. The examination of one's own witness is called **direct examination.** The attorney must ask questions in such a way as to draw the information from the witness in the witness's own words without asking **leading questions** (questions that suggest to the witness the desired answer). When the plaintiff's attorney has no further questions, the witness may be questioned by the opposing attorney, which is called **cross-examination.** Leading questions are allowed on cross-examination. The plaintiff's attorney may conduct a redirect examination on issues brought up in the cross-examination, which may be followed by a re-cross-examination by the defendant's attorney.

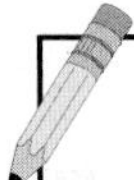

WORD WISE

Around

The Latin root "circum" used in the term "circumstantial evidence" means "around." The distance around a circle is its circumference. Besides the concrete image and implied action, "circum" can also indicate the *idea* of "around." *Circumstantial evidence* relies on proving facts indirectly; it "goes around" evidence from which other facts are to be inferred.

After all of the plaintiff's witnesses are examined in this way and all other evidence that the plaintiff has is introduced, the plaintiff's attorney rests the case. At this point, the defendant's attorney may make a **motion for a directed verdict**—that is, ask the court to find in favor of the defendant without giving the case to the jury. The motion will be allowed if the court finds that the evidence is insufficient as a matter of law to support a verdict in the plaintiff's favor.

DEFENDANT'S OPENING STATEMENT

After the plaintiff's attorney rests the case, the defendant's attorney makes an opening statement. He or she outlines the defendant's side of the case and tells the jury of the evidence that will be introduced to rebut or to contradict the plaintiff's evidence.

DEFENDANT'S CASE IN CHIEF

The defendant's attorney must introduce the evidence that is necessary to support the defensive claims that were made in the defendant's answer and in the opening statement. As before, one cannot ask leading questions of one's own witnesses.

After all of the defendant's witnesses have been examined and cross-examined, the defendant's attorney rests the case. At this point, the plaintiff's attorney may come in **rebuttal**—that is, introduce evidence that will destroy the effect of the evidence introduced by the other side. Either party may make a motion for a directed verdict at this time.

REQUESTS FOR INSTRUCTIONS TO JURY

At the close of the evidence, the attorneys may file written requests that the judge instruct the jury on the law as set forth in the requests. The judge must inform the attorneys of his or her decision on the requests before they give their final arguments to the jury.

FINAL ARGUMENTS

Each attorney is given 30 minutes (unless reduced or extended by the court beforehand) to argue his or her side of the case to the jury or to the judge in a nonjury trial. In this **closing argument,** or **summation,** the attorneys summarize the evidence that has been introduced in their favor.

INSTRUCTIONS TO JURY

Jurors are not expected to know the law. For this reason, the jury must be told what the law is in that particular case. After the closing arguments, the judge tells the jury the law that must be applied. This is called the **jury charge.** When it **deliberates**—considers the case slowly and carefully—the jury must apply that law to the facts in making its decision. In highly publicized cases, jurors are sometimes **sequestered**—that is, isolated or set apart from society in a hotel during the deliberation period to prevent them from being exposed to outside influences.

VERDICT

The decision of the jury is called the **verdict.** In a criminal case, the jury must agree unanimously to reach a verdict. If it cannot do so, a **mistrial** (an invalid trial of no consequence) is called, and a new trial may be held. In a civil case, five-sixths of the members of the jury must reach agreement to arrive at a verdict unless the plaintiff and the defendant agree that a different majority of the jurors will be taken as the verdict. It is

Figure 7-1 The term *non sequitor* means "it does not follow." When jurors are *sequestered,* they are set apart from society during the deliberation period to prevent them from being exposed to outside influences. (NON SEQUITOR © Wiley Miller. Dist. by UNIVERSAL PRESS SYNDICATE. Reprinted with permission. All rights reserved.)

called **polling the jury** when individual jurors are asked whether they agree with the verdict given by the jury foreperson. A deadlocked jury is often referred to as a **hung jury.**

WEB WISE

- For an overview of evidence, go to the Legal Information Institute (LII) at **www.law.cornell.edu.** When there, put your curser on "Law about . . ." and double click "All topics." On the list that follows, click "Evidence." In addition to the Federal Rules of Evidence, you will find federal and state cases on the subject.
- Look for practice and procedure information for your state by going to **www.findlaw.com.** When there, click "jurisdiction," then click the name of your state.

JUDGMENT OR DECREE

Following the jury's verdict, the court issues a **judgment,** also called an **adjudication,** which is the decision of a court of law. The judgment is the act of the trial court finally **adjudicating** (determining) the rights of the parties. This determination is the court's decision in the case. A case is said to be **ripe for judgment** when it reaches the stage when everything has been completed except the court's decision. A **judgment on the merits** is a court decision based on the evidence and facts introduced. In contrast, a **judgment on the pleadings** will be rendered without hearing evidence if the court determines that it is clear from the pleadings that one party is entitled to win the case as a matter of law. Similarly, if the judge believes that the jury's verdict is incorrect as a matter of law (a **verdict contrary to law**), he or she may issue a **judgment notwithstanding the verdict,** also called a **judgment n.o.v.** (from the Latin **non obstante verdicto**), which is a judgment in favor of one party notwithstanding a verdict in favor of the other party.

The decision of a court of equity is called a **decree. Equity** means that which is just and fair. A **court of equity** is a court that administers justice according to the system of equity. It is able to grant relief to people when no adequate remedy is otherwise available. To illustrate, a court of law can usually do nothing more than award money to an injured party. In contrast, a court of equity can issue an **injunction**—that is, order someone to do or refrain from doing a particular act. Sometimes a court of equity will issue a **preliminary injunction** before hearing the merits of a case to prevent injustice. A **consent decree** is a decree that is entered by consent of the parties, usually without admitting guilt or wrongdoing. This type of decree cannot be appealed because the parties have agreed to it.

APPEAL

A party bringing an appeal is called an **appellant.** A party against whom an appeal is brought is called an **appellee,** a **respondent,** or a **defendant in error.** Only questions of law may be raised on appeal. **Questions of law** are questions relating to the application or interpretation of law. Such questions are not decided by a jury. **Questions of fact**—that is, questions about the activities that took place between the parties that caused them to go to court—are for the jury to decide and cannot be appealed unless the jury is plainly wrong as a matter of law. To be heard by an appellate court, an appeal must be filed within a prescribed period of time, often 30 days from the entry of judgment.

When an appellate court takes a case and agrees with the lower court decision, it will **affirm**—that is, approve—the decision. In contrast, when an appellate court disagrees with a lower court decision, it will **reverse** or **set aside** (make void) the decision, or it will **vacate** (annul) the judgment and **remand** (send back) the case to the lower court for further proceedings. An **appeal bond** is often required as security to guarantee the cost of an appeal, especially in civil cases.

REVIEWING WHAT YOU LEARNED

After studying the text, write the answers to each of the following questions.

1. List the steps in the order that they occur in a jury trial. ______________________________

____

____

____

____

2. What is one requirement of an opening statement? ______________________________

____

____

____

____

3. Differentiate among testimonial evidence, documentary evidence, and real evidence. ________

____

____

____

____

4. Give an example of testimony that is (a) direct evidence and (b) circumstantial evidence. ____

____

____

____

____

5. When are leading questions allowed and not allowed? ______________________________

____

____

____

____

6. When may a motion for a directed verdict be allowed? ______________________________

____

____

____

____

7. When may the plaintiff's attorney introduce rebuttal evidence? ______________________

____

____

____

____

8. What is the difference between questions of law and questions of fact, and which may be raised on appeal? ______________________

____

____

____

9. To reach a verdict, how must the jury agree in a criminal case? ______________________

____

____

____

____

10. What is the difference between a judgment and a writ of execution? ______________________

____

____

____

____

UNDERSTANDING LEGAL CONCEPTS

Indicate whether each statement is true or false. Then, change the italicized word or phrase of each *false* statement to make it true.

Answers

______________ **1.** In the *opening statement,* the attorney outlines the case by telling the jury what the evidence will prove.

______________ **2.** When a witness testifies as to something he or she observed, such as "I saw that man shoot the gun," it is called *circumstantial* evidence.

______________ **3.** Leading questions are allowed on *direct* examination.

______________ **4.** After the plaintiff's attorney rests the case, the defendant's attorney *makes an opening statement.*

______________ **5.** When final arguments are made, the plaintiff's attorney argues *first.*

______________ **6.** A jury never decides questions of *fact.*

______________ **7.** In a criminal case, the jury must agree unanimously to reach a *verdict.*

______________ **8.** Following the jury's verdict, the court issues a *judgment.*

______________ **9.** The decision of a court of equity is called a *decree.*

______________ **10.** Only questions of *fact* may be raised on appeal.

1

CHECKING TERMINOLOGY (PART A)

From the list of legal terms that follows, select the one that matches each definition.

a. adjudicating
b. adjudication
c. admissible evidence
d. affirm
e. appeal
f. appeal bond
g. appellant
h. appellee
i. case in chief
j. circumstantial evidence
k. consent decree
l. court of equity
m. cross-examination
n. decree
o. defendant in error
p. deliberate
q. direct evidence
r. direct examination
s. DNA
t. DNA sample
u. documentary evidence
v. equity
w. exhibit
x. hung jury
y. injunction
z. judgment
aa. judgment notwithstanding the verdict
bb. judgment n.o.v.
cc. judgment on the merits
dd. judgment on the pleadings
ee. respondent

Answers

____ **1.** The examination of one's own witness.
____ **2.** A bond often required as security to guarantee the cost of an appeal, especially in civil cases.
____ **3.** Approve.
____ **4.** A deadlocked jury; one that cannot agree.
____ **5.** A tangible item that is introduced in evidence.
____ **6.** Determining finally by a court.
____ **7.** Evidence that directly relates to the fact in issue.
____ **8.** A party bringing an appeal.
____ **9.** A court decision based on the evidence and facts introduced.
____**10.** A party against whom an appeal is brought (select three answers).
____**11.** A judgment rendered in favor of one party notwithstanding a verdict in favor of the other party (select two answers).
____**12.** A court that administers justice according to the system of equity.
____**13.** A judgment rendered without hearing evidence if the court determines that it is clear from the pleadings that one party is entitled to win the case.
____**14.** That which is just and fair.
____**15.** Evidence that is pertinent and proper to be considered in reaching a decision following specific rules.
____**16.** The decision of a court of equity.
____**17.** Evidence that relates to some fact other than the fact in issue; indirect evidence.
____**18.** The decision of a court of law.
____**19.** Evidence consisting of such documents as written contracts, business records, correspondence, wills, and deeds.
____**20.** A court judgment.
____**21.** The examination of an opposing witness.
____**22.** A request to a higher court to review the decision of a lower court.
____**23.** The introduction of evidence to prove the allegations that were made in the pleadings and in the opening statement.
____**24.** An order of a court of equity to do or refrain from doing a particular act.
____**25.** The double strand of molecules that carries a cell's unique genetic code.
____**26.** Biological evidence of any nature that is utilized to conduct DNA analysis.
____**27.** A decree that is entered by consent of the parties.
____**28.** To consider slowly and carefully.

CHECKING TERMINOLOGY (PART B)

From the list of legal terms that follows, select the one that matches each definition.

a. closing argument
b. jury charge
c. leading questions
d. mistrial
e. motion for a directed verdict
f. non obstante verdicto
g. opening statement
h. polling the jury
i. preliminary injunction
j. prima facie case
k. questions of fact
l. questions of law
m. real evidence
n. rebuttal
o. relevant evidence
p. remand
q. reverse
r. ripe for judgment
s. sequester
t. set aside
u. summation
v. testimonial evidence
w. vacate
x. verdict
y. verdict contrary to law

Answers

____ **1.** Send back.
____ **2.** In a jury trial, a motion asking the court to find in favor of the moving party as a matter of law, without having the case go to the jury.
____ **3.** Questions about the activities that took place between the parties that caused them to go to court.
____ **4.** Final statements by the attorneys summarizing the evidence that has been introduced (select two answers).
____ **5.** The decision of a jury.
____ **6.** Actual objects that have a bearing on the case, such as an item of clothing, a weapon found at the scene of a crime, a photograph, a chart, or a model.
____ **7.** Notwithstanding a verdict.
____ **8.** Annul.
____ **9.** Instructions to a jury on matters of law.
____ **10.** Evidence tending to prove or disprove an alleged fact.
____ **11.** An attorney's outline to the jury of anticipated proof.
____ **12.** Legally sufficient for proof unless rebutted or contradicted by other evidence.
____ **13.** A procedure in which individual jurors are asked whether they agree with the verdict given by the jury foreperson.
____ **14.** Questions that suggest to the witness the desired answer.
____ **15.** Oral testimony of witnesses made under oath in open court.
____ **16.** Questions relating to the application or interpretation of law.
____ **17.** An invalid trial of no consequence.
____ **18.** Make void (select two answers).
____ **19.** The introduction of evidence that will destroy the effect of the evidence introduced by the other side.
____ **20.** An injunction issued by a court before hearing the merits of a case.
____ **21.** A verdict that is incorrect as a matter of law.
____ **22.** The stage of a trial when everything has been completed except the court's decision.
____ **23.** To isolate or set apart from society.

UNRAVELING LEGALESE

Use simple, non-legal language, with the help of the glossary, to rewrite this quote in the space below so that it is shorter and can be understood by a layperson without losing its meaning.

> If the jury has returned a guilty verdict, the court may set aside the verdict and enter an acquittal. If the jury has failed to return a verdict, the court may enter a judgment of acquittal. [Rule 31(c)(2) Federal Rules of Criminal Procedure]

SHARPENING YOUR LATIN SKILLS

In the space provided, write the definition of each of the following legal terms, referring to the glossary when necessary.

certiorari ______________________________

non obstante verdicto ______________________________

prima facie ______________________________

subpoena ______________________________

subpoena ad testificandum ______________________________

subpoena duces tecum ______________________________

venire ______________________________

venire facias ______________________________

USING LEGAL LANGUAGE

Read the following story and fill in the blank lines with legal terms taken from the list of terms at the beginning of this chapter.

The plaintiff's attorney, Mary Grey, was required to set forth a(n) __________________________ in her opening statement before the jury. Her evidence consisted of a photograph, which was __________________________; payroll records, which were __________________________; and oral statements of a witness, which were __________________________. On the stand, Mary's witness, Leroy Henning, said, "I am the payroll clerk, and these payroll records are true and correct." This was __________________________ evidence, not __________________________, and because she was examining her own witness, Mary's examination was called __________________________. Mary could not ask __________________________, which suggest to the witness the desired answer. The opposing attorney could do so, however, on __________________________. At the close of Mary's case, the opposing attorney made a(n) __________________________, asking the court to find in favor of his client. This request was denied, and the case went to the jury, whose decision is called a(n) __________________________. Following this decision, the court issued its __________________________, which is sometimes called a __________________________ in a court of equity. Mary's client won the case, and the opposing attorney decided not to __________________________ to a higher court because only __________________________ may be raised at that time. Had he done so, his client would have been called the __________________________ and would have had to put up a(n) __________________________ as security.

PUZZLING OVER WHAT YOU LEARNED

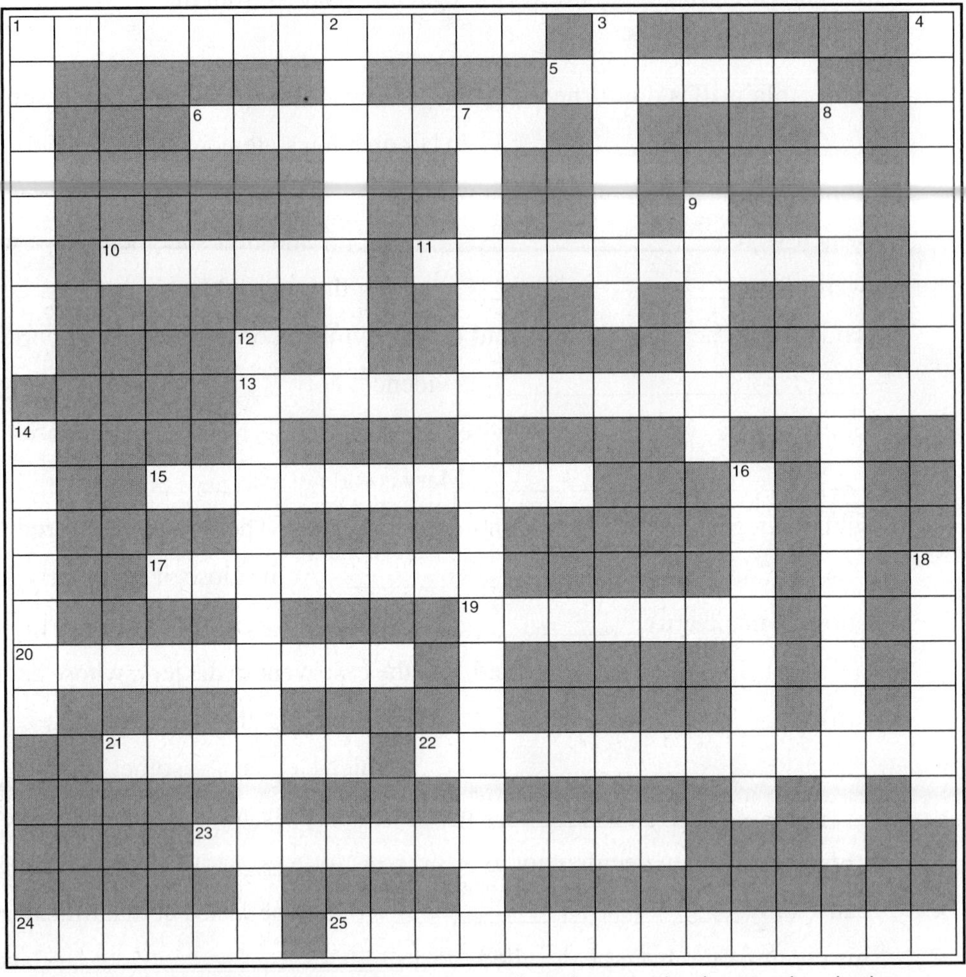

Caveat: Do not allow squares for spaces between words and punctuation (apostrophes, hyphens, etc.) when filling in crossword.

Across

1. Actual objects that have a bearing on the case, such as an item of clothing or a weapon found at the scene of the crime.
5. Decision of a court of equity.
6. Make void; reverse.
10. Approve.
11. Instructions to a jury on matters of law.
13. An attorney's outline to the jury of anticipated proof.
15. To consider slowly and carefully.
17. A deadlocked jury; one that cannot agree.
19. A tangible item that is introduced in evidence.
20. Closing argument.
21. A request to a higher court to review the decision of a lower court.
22. A court judgment.
23. A judgment rendered in favor of one party notwithstanding a verdict in favor of the other party.
24. That which is just and fair.
25. Evidence that directly relates to the fact in issue.

Down

1. The introduction of evidence that will destroy the effect of the evidence introduced by the other side.
2. Biological evidence of any nature that is utilized to conduct DNA analysis.
3. The decision of a jury.
4. A party bringing an appeal.
7. Evidence consisting of documents.
8. The examination of one's own witness.
9. Annul.
12. A procedure in which individual jurors are asked whether they agree with the verdict given by the jury foreperson.
14. Make void; set aside.
16. An invalid trial of no consequence.
18. Send back.

PART TWO

TERMS USED IN CRIMINAL LAW

2

In our society, criminal law not only dominates the news, it also penetrates deeply into our culture by way of TV thrillers, violent movies, and suspense-filled mystery stories. Part Two discusses of many of the crimes that we have heard about or have been exposed to since childhood. After defining a crime and explaining its components, Chapter 8 highlights the three broad classes of crimes and describes accomplices and criminal defenses. Chapter 9 explains the elements of crimes and discusses crimes against property, including larceny, embezzlement, bribery, extortion, coercion, receipt of stolen goods, and forgery. Chapter 10 explores crimes against the person such as robbery, mayhem, assault, battery, and rape, in addition to crimes against human habitation; that is, burglary and arson. The subject of homicide is explained in Chapter 11. Crimes against morality, including adultery, fornication, bigamy, polygamy, incest, sodomy, miscegenation, abortion, pornography, and drug abuse are examined in Chapter 12.

CHAPTER 8

Crimes, Accomplices, and Defenses

2

ANTE INTERROGATORY

Being tried twice for the same offense is (A) entrapment, (B) petit treason, (C) double jeopardy, (D) ex post facto.

CHAPTER OUTLINE

Crimes Mala in Se and Mala Prohibita
Principal Criminal Categories
Treason
Felonies and Misdemeanors
Accomplices
Principal in the First Degree
Principal in the Second Degree
Accessory before the Fact
Accessory after the Fact
Criminal Defenses
Cyberlaw

KEY TERMS

accessory after the fact *(ak-SESS·o·ree)*
accessory before the fact
accomplice *(a·COM·pliss)*
actus reus *(AHK·tus REE·us)*
aiding and abetting *(a·BET·ing)*
alibi *(AL·i·by)*
common law *(KOM·on)*
conspiracy *(kon·SPIR·a·see)*
constructively *(kon·STRUC·tiv·lee)*
cybercrime *(SY·ber·krym)*
cyberlaw *(SY·ber·law)*
defense *(de·FENSE)*
double jeopardy *(DUB·el JEP·er·dee)*
entrapment *(en·TRAP·ment)*
exclusionary rule *(eks·KLOO·shun·a·ree)*
ex post facto *(eks post FAK·to)*
felony *(FEL·en·ee)*
fruits of the poisonous tree doctrine *(DOK·trin)*
good faith exception to the exclusionary rule *(ex·SEP·shun)*
high treason *(hy TREE·zun)*
hot pursuit doctrine *(pur·SOOT DOK·trin)*
illegal profiling *(ill·EE·gul PRO·fyl·ing)*
incarceration *(in·kar·ser·AY·shun)*
insanity *(in·SAN·i·tee)*
mala in se *(MAL·ah in seh)*
mala prohibita *(MAL·ah pro·HIB·i·ta)*
mens rea *(menz RAY·ah)*
misdemeanor *(mis·de·MEEN·er)*
penal laws *(PE·nel)*
petit treason *(PET·ee TREE·zun)*
plain view doctrine *(DOK·trin)*
principal in the first degree *(PRIN·se·pel)*
principal in the second degree *(de·GREE)*
search warrant *(WAR·ent)*
self-defense *(de·FENSE)*
stop and frisk rule
treason *(TREE·zun)*

A crime consists of either the commission or the omission of a voluntary act (known as **actus reus**) punishable by a fine, imprisonment, or both. No act is criminal unless it is both prohibited and penalized by the law of the place where it is committed. In addition, to protect the innocent, the English common law required the act to be committed with a particular state of mind known as **mens rea,** which means criminal intent.

Laws that impose a penalty or punishment for a wrong against society are called **penal laws.** The U.S. Constitution prohibits Congress or any state from passing a law that is **ex post facto** (after the fact)—that is, one that holds a person criminally responsible for an act that was not a crime at the time of its commission. Similarly, the Fifth Amendment of the U.S. Constitution prevents people from being tried twice for the same offense, which is known as freedom from **double jeopardy.**

WEB WISE

- For an overview of criminal law and a link to your state criminal code, go to **www.law.cornell.edu/topics/criminal.html.**
- Read about computer crime by going to **www.cybercrime.gov.**
- The website of the U.S. Department of Justice is located at **www.usdoj.gov.**

CRIMES MALA IN SE AND MALA PROHIBITA

Crimes are divided into two classes: those that are wrong in and of themselves, such as murder, rape, and robbery; and those that are not in themselves wrong but are criminal simply because they are prohibited by statute. The former are called crimes **mala in se** (wrongs in themselves) and require a wrongful or unlawful intent on the part of the perpetrator. The latter are called crimes **mala prohibita** (prohibited wrongs) and require no wrongful intent on the part of the perpetrator. All that is necessary is the doing of the act regardless of the intent of the actor. Under the **common law**—that is, the law used in England and the American colonies before the American Revolution—all crimes were mala in se.

To illustrate a crime mala prohibita, a 1906 state statute made it a crime to transport intoxicating liquor within the state without a license. A truck driver in the employ of a common carrier (which was bound to accept all packages offered to it for transportation and which had no right to compel a shipper to disclose the package's contents) was convicted of violating the statute when he transported an unmarked sugar barrel filled with liquor. Nothing about the appearance of the barrel caused suspicion as to its contents, and the truck driver was ignorant of the fact that it contained intoxicating liquor. The appellate court upheld the conviction, saying that the only fact to be determined is whether the defendant did the act. The court held that knowledge of the wrongdoing or wrongful intent was immaterial in the case of a crime mala prohibita. The court said that the legislature has the power to prohibit certain acts regardless of moral purity or ignorance.

PRINCIPAL CRIMINAL CATEGORIES

Crimes are divided into three principal groups: treason, felonies, and misdemeanors.

Treason

Treason was divided into **high treason** (acts against the king) and **petit treason** (acts against one's master or lord) under the common law of England. Such a division was never followed in this country, however. Instead, **treason** is defined in the U.S. Constitution as levying war against the United States or giving aid and comfort to the nation's enemies. The charge of treason has only been brought a few dozen times in U.S. history. The first treason charge since the end of World War II was brought in 2006 against a California man who allegedly appeared in propaganda videos for Al Queda during the war on terrorism.

Felonies and Misdemeanors

A **felony** is a major crime, although its exact definition differs from state to state. It is defined in some states as "punishment by hard labor" and in others as "an infamous crime" or a crime subject to "infamous punishment." A **misdemeanor,** conversely, is a less serious crime than a felony. Many states distinguish between a felony and a misdemeanor by the length of **incarceration** (confinement) involved. For example, in Massachusetts, "A crime punishable by death or imprisonment in the state prison is a felony. All other crimes are misdemeanors." In that state, the minimum sentence in a state prison is two and one-half years. Many states have classified felonies and misdemeanors according to punishment using a lettering or numbering system. A "class A felony," for example, would have a different punishment from a "class B felony." Murder, rape, armed robbery, and assault with a deadly weapon are examples of felonies. Misdemeanors call for a lighter penalty, such as a fine or jail sentence in a place other than a state prison. Disturbing the peace, simple assault, and petty larceny are examples of misdemeanors.

ACCOMPLICES

The crime of conspiracy takes place when two or more people agree to commit an unlawful act. **Conspiracy** is the getting together of two or more people to accomplish some criminal or unlawful act. The crime of conspiracy exists even when the crime or unlawful act that was agreed upon is never carried out. In some states, proof of an agreement between the parties to commit a criminal or unlawful act is all that is necessary to convict the parties of conspiracy. In many states, however, it is necessary to prove, in addition, that the parties took some action toward the commission of the crime or unlawful act for a conviction to come about. Anyone who takes part with another in the commission of a crime is called an **accomplice.**

Principal in the First Degree

A **principal in the first degree** is a person who actually commits a felony either by his or her own hand or through an innocent agent. A principal in the first degree is the one who pulls the trigger or strikes the blow. One who intentionally places poison in a glass, for example, would be considered a principal in the first degree even though the glass containing the poison was delivered to the victim by an innocent third person.

Principal in the Second Degree

A **principal in the second degree** is one who did not commit the act, but who was actually or constructively present, aiding and abetting another in the commission of a felony. **Aiding and abetting** means participating in the crime by giving assistance or encouragement. One who is positioned outside as a lookout, for example, while his or her companions are inside committing burglary, would be considered **constructively** present—that is, made present by legal interpretation. In a Nevada case, a lookout stationed miles away sent a smoke signal to fellow robbers signaling that a stagecoach was coming. The court found the lookout guilty as a principal in the second degree, holding that the lookout was constructively present even though he was miles away from the scene of the crime.

At common law, and in most states today, a principal in the second degree is subject to the same punishment as that given to a principal in the first degree.

Accessory before the Fact

An **accessory before the fact** is one who procures, counsels, or commands another to commit a felony but who is not present when the felony is committed. Mere knowledge that a crime is going to be committed by another person is not enough to become an accessory before the fact to the crime that is subsequently committed by the other person,

Figure 8-1 A principal in the second degree is one who did not commit the act, but who was actually or constructively present, aiding and abetting another in the commission of a felony. A principal in the second degree can be subject to the same punishment as that given to a principal in the first degree.

however. It must be shown that the accessory before the fact was active in inducing or bringing about the felony.

An accessory before the fact will be responsible for the natural and probable consequences that ensue from the crime that he or she induced but not for a crime of a substantially different nature. Thus, if one person procures another to beat someone up, and the beating results in death, the one who procured the beating would be an accessory before the fact to the killing, because it is a natural and probable consequence of beating someone up.

Conversely, in the situation in which one person hires a man to beat up a woman and he rapes her instead, the procurer would not be an accessory before the fact to the rape, because it is a crime of a substantially different nature than that which was ordered by the procurer.

Some states still follow the common law rule that an accessory before the fact cannot be tried in court until a principal is first convicted. Many states, however, now hold that an accessory before the fact may be tried without regard to the principal and may be found guilty even though the principal is acquitted.

In general, an accessory before the fact is subject to the same punishment as that given to a principal.

WORD WISE

"Mal-" . . . "Mala"

"Mal(e)" is a prefix or word part used in many legal terms to mean bad, wrong, or fraudulent.

malconduct	malefaction	malefactor
malice	malicious	malfeasance

"Mala" is the plural form of the Latin word "malum," which also means bad, evil, or wrongful.

"Mala" appears in many legal phrases, including

mala fides	bad faith
mala in se	wrongs in themselves
mala praxis	malpractice
mala prohibita	prohibited wrongs or offenses

Accessory after the Fact

An **accessory after the fact** is one who receives, relieves, comforts, or assists another with knowledge that the other person has committed a felony. To be convicted of being an accessory after the fact, a felony must have been committed by another person, and the accessory after the fact must intend that that person avoid or escape detention, arrest, trial, or punishment.

At common law, a wife could not be held liable as an accessory after the fact under the theory that she was under her husband's coercion. Modern statutes have extended that exception, although for a different reason, to include close relatives as well. The reason is that it would be natural for spouses and close relatives to protect their loved ones who are in trouble with the law. Rhode Island and Massachusetts, for example, do not allow a criminal's spouse, parent, grandparent, child, grandchild, brother, or sister to be convicted of being an accessory after the fact to the criminal.

CRIMINAL DEFENSES

Evidence offered by a defendant to defeat a criminal charge or civil lawsuit is known as a **defense.** Some common criminal defenses are alibi, entrapment, insanity, and self-defense. **Alibi** is a defense that places the defendant in a different place than the crime scene, so that it would have been impossible to commit the crime. **Entrapment** may be used as a defense when a police officer induces a person to commit a crime that the person would not have committed otherwise. **Insanity** is a defense available to mentally ill defendants who can prove that they did not know the difference between right and wrong or did not appreciate the criminality of their conduct. **Self-defense** is an excuse for the use of force in resisting attack. Victims of attack may use no more force than is necessary to stop the attack and, except in their own home, must retreat if possible under many state laws.

The U.S. Constitution provides broad protection for criminal defendants. For example, under the Fourth Amendment, a **search warrant** (a written order of the court authorizing law enforcement officers to search and seize certain property) must generally be obtained before officers may enter private property without permission. A search warrant is not needed to seize items that are in plain view of a lawfully positioned police officer under the **plain view doctrine.** Likewise, a search warrant is not needed, under the **hot pursuit doctrine,** when police pursue a fleeing suspect into a private area. Similarly, under the **stop and frisk rule,** a police officer who believes a person is acting suspiciously and could be armed may stop and frisk the suspect for weapons without a search warrant. The same is true when police lawfully arrest someone. Police officers are also allowed to stop and search a motor vehicle, and to order all passengers out of the vehicle, but only when they have probable cause to do so.

CONSTITUTION WISE

Protection for Criminal Defendants

right to trial by jury	Gives criminal defendants the right to a speedy and public jury trial.	6th Amendment
right to confront witnesses	Gives criminal defendants the right to be confronted with witnesses against them.	6th Amendment
self-incrimination protection	Gives criminal defendants the right to refuse to testify against themselves.	5th Amendment
cruel and unusual punishment forbidden	Protects criminal defendants from being subject to excessive bail and cruel and unusual punishment.	8th Amendment
double jeopardy protection	Protects criminal defendants from being tried twice for the same offense.	5th Amendment

Illegal profiling may also be used as a defense. **Illegal profiling** is a law enforcement action, such as a detention or arrest, based solely on race, religion, national origin, ethnicity, gender, or sexual orientation rather than on a person's behavior or on information identifying a person as having engaged in criminal activity.

Under the **exclusionary rule,** evidence obtained by an unconstitutional search or seizure cannot be used at the trial of a defendant. Similarly, under the **fruit of the poisonous tree doctrine,** evidence derived from an illegal search is inadmissible. Thus, law enforcement officers could not use as evidence illegal weapons found in a building they had unlawfully searched while looking for illicit drugs. The **good faith exception to the exclusionary rule** makes admissible evidence discovered by officers acting in a good faith but mistaken belief that the search was valid.

CYBERLAW

Cyberlaw, the area of law that involves computers and their related problems, is a term that has recently come into common usage. **Cybercrimes**—criminal activity associated with a computer—include such crimes as identity theft, stalking, extortion, blackmail, vandalism, and terrorism.

Figure 8-2 Illegal profiling is a law enforcement action, such as a detention or arrest, based solely on race, religion, national origin, ethnicity, gender, or sexual orientation.

REVIEWING WHAT YOU LEARNED

After studying the text, write the answers to each of the following questions:

1. Who brings the action in a criminal case? ____
2. What is an ex post facto law? ____
3. How does a crime that is mala in se differ from a crime that is mala prohibita? ____
4. List the three classifications of crimes. ____
5. What is the difference between a felony and a misdemeanor? ____
6. What is the difference between a principal in the first degree and a principal in the second degree?
7. How does the punishment of a principal in the first degree compare with that of a principal in the second degree? ____
8. What is the difference between an accessory before the fact and an accessory after the fact?
9. Is the punishment for an accessory before the fact the same as that for a principal to a crime?
10. Under Rhode Island and Massachusetts law, who cannot be held liable as an accessory after the fact? ____

UNDERSTANDING LEGAL CONCEPTS

Indicate whether each statement is true or false. Then, change the italicized word or phrase of each *false* statement to make it true.

Answers

_______________ **1.** A crime is an offense against *the individual victim alone.* It *is not* a wrong against all of society.

_______________ **2.** A felony is a *less* serious crime than a misdemeanor.

_______________ **3.** A crime that is wrong in and of itself is called a crime *mala in se.*

_______________ **4.** *Petit treason* is a crime that is defined in the U.S. Constitution.

_______________ **5.** No act is criminal unless it is both *prohibited and penalized* by the law of the jurisdiction in which it is committed.

_______________ **6.** One who intentionally places poison in a glass is a *principal in the first degree* even though the glass containing the poison is delivered to the victim by an innocent third person.

_______________ **7.** A *principal in the second degree* is one who procures, counsels, or commands another to commit a felony but who is not present when the felony is committed.

_______________ **8.** Mere knowledge that a crime is going to be committed by another person *is enough* for someone to become an accessory before the fact.

_______________ **9.** At common law, a wife *could not* be held as an accessory after the fact to a crime committed by her husband under the theory that she was under the husband's coercion.

_______________ **10.** In general, an *accessory before the fact* is subject to the same punishment as that given to a principal.

CHECKING TERMINOLOGY

From the list of legal terms that follows, select the one that matches each definition.

a. accessory after the fact
b. accessory before the fact
c. accomplice
d. actus reus
e. aiding and abetting
f. alibi
g. common law
h. conspiracy
i. constructively
j. cybercrime
k. cyberlaw

Answers

____ **1.** Evidence discovered by officers acting in good faith but under the mistaken belief that a search that was valid, can be used at the trial of a defendant.

____ **2.** A voluntary act.

____ **3.** A minor crime; not a felony.

____ **4.** Wrong in and of itself.

____ **5.** Evidence offered by a defendant to defeat a criminal charge or civil lawsuit.

____ **6.** One who actually commits a felony.

____ **7.** A major crime, punishable by imprisonment in a state prison.

____ **8.** One who procures, counsels, or commands another to commit a felony but who is not present when the felony is committed.

____ **9.** Tried twice for the same offense.

____ **10.** After the fact.

l. defense
m. double jeopardy
n. entrapment
o. exclusionary rule
p. ex post facto
q. felony
r. fruit of the poisonous tree doctrine
s. good faith exception to the exclusionary rule
t. high treason
u. hot pursuit doctrine
v. illegal profiling
w. incarceration
x. insanity
y. mala in se
z. mala prohibita
aa. mens rea
bb. misdemeanor
cc. penal laws
dd. petit treason
ee. plain view doctrine
ff. principal in the first degree
gg. principal in the second degree
hh. search warrant
ii. self-defense
jj. stop and frisk rule
kk. treason

_____**11.** One who did not commit the act but who was present, aiding and abetting another in the commission of a felony.

_____**12.** A defense available to mentally ill defendants who can prove that they did not know the difference between right and wrong or did not appreciate the criminality of their conduct.

_____**13.** Prohibited wrong.

_____**14.** The statutory and case law used in England and in the American colonies before the American Revolution.

_____**15.** A written order of the court authorizing law enforcement officers to search and seize certain property.

_____**16.** One who receives, relieves, comforts, or assists another with knowledge that the other has committed a felony.

_____**17.** An excuse for the use of force in resisting attack.

_____**18.** Acts against the king (under the English common law).

_____**19.** A defense that may be used when a police officer induces a person to commit a crime that the person would not have otherwise committed.

_____**20.** Participating in a crime by giving assistance or encouragement.

_____**21.** A search warrant is not needed to seize items that are in plain view of a lawfully positioned police officer.

_____**22.** A defense that places the defendant in a different place than the crime scene, so that it would have been impossible to commit the crime.

_____**23.** Acts against one's master or lord (under the English common law).

_____**24.** The getting together of two or more people to accomplish some criminal or unlawful act.

_____**25.** Anyone who takes part with another in the commission of a crime.

_____**26.** Laws that impose a penalty or punishment for a wrong against society.

_____**27.** Criminal intent.

_____**28.** A search warrant that is not needed when police pursue a fleeing suspect into a private area.

_____**29.** A rule that allows police officers who believe a person is acting suspiciously and could be armed to stop and frisk the suspect without a search warrant.

_____**30.** Made so by legal interpretation.

_____**31.** Evidence generated or derived from an illegal search or seizure that cannot be used at the trial of a defendant.

_____**32.** Evidence obtained by an unconstitutional search or seizure that cannot be used at the trial of a defendant.

_____**33.** Levying war against the United States or giving aid and comfort to its enemies.

_____**34.** A law enforcement action, such as a detention or arrest, based solely on race, religion, national origin, ethnicity, gender, or sexual orientation.

UNRAVELING LEGALESE

With the help of the glossary, rewrite the following sentence in the space below, substituting each of the italicized terms with a word or phrase that has the same meaning.

> Both defendants were *acquitted* upon an *indictment* charging them, with others, with a conspiracy to commit the identical *felonies* for which each has now been convicted as an *accessory before the fact.*

USING LEGAL LANGUAGE

Read the following story and fill in the blank lines with legal terms taken from the list of terms at the beginning of this chapter.

> Abigail hired two ____________________, Bonnie and Clyde, to rob a bank. She waited at home while the others carried out the act, which was a(n) ____________________, because it was an offense against the public at large. Bonnie, with a state of mind known as ____________________, went into the bank and committed the robbery, while Clyde, who was ____________________ and ____________________, waited outside in the get-away car. Abigail would be classified as a(n) ____________________, Bonnie a(n) ____________________, and Clyde a(n) ____________________ to robbery, which is a(n) ____________________ rather than a(n) ____________________. It is also a crime that is mala ____________________ because it is wrong in and of itself. After the commission of the crime, Bonnie and Clyde drove to the home of their sister, Dinah, who took them in, knowing that they had robbed the bank. Dinah was found not guilty of being a(n) ____________________, because she is a close relative. She could not be tried—that is, ____________________—a second time for the same offense because it would put her in ____________________, which is against the U.S. Constitution. When Abigail, Bonnie, and Clyde agreed to commit the robbery and took action to carry it out, they committed the crime of ____________________. Once they were convicted, they were called ____________________. They had no ____________________—that is, evidence to defeat the criminal charges against them—and they had no ____________________ that placed them in a different place than the crime scene.

2

PUZZLING OVER WHAT YOU LEARNED

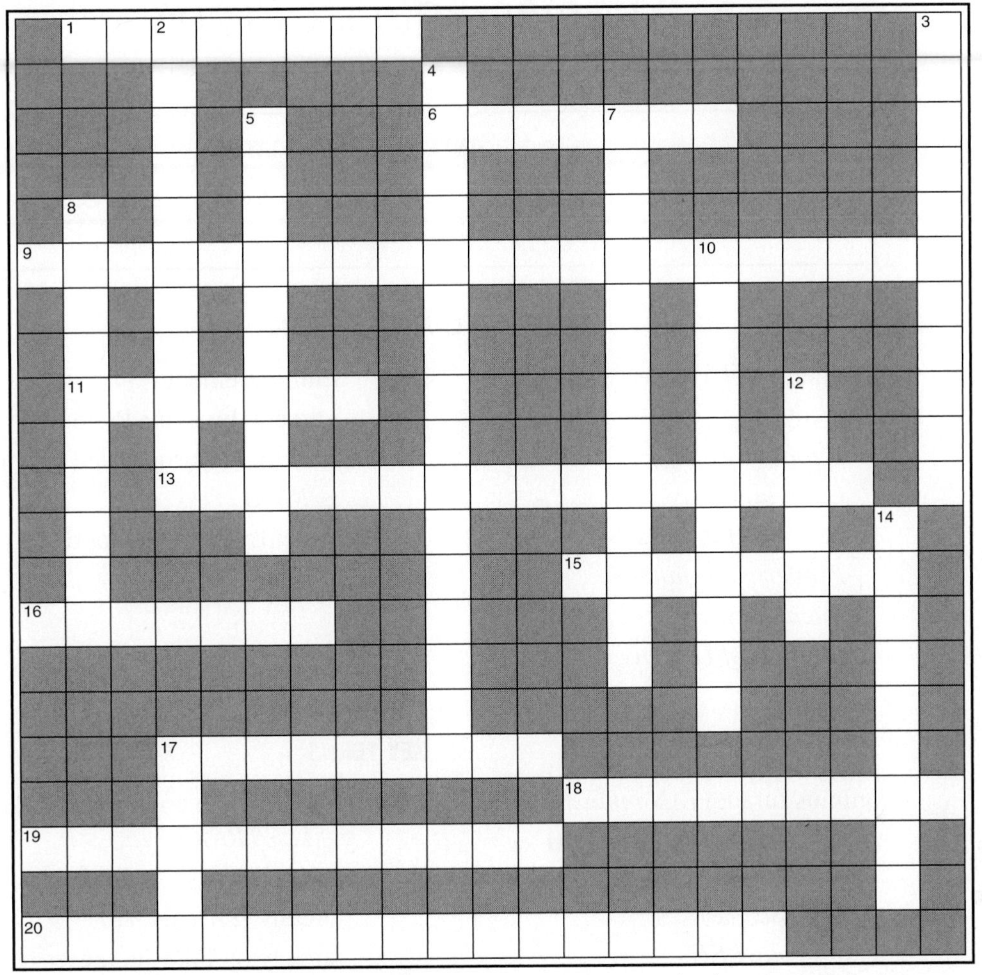

Caveat: Do not allow squares for spaces between words and punctuation (apostrophes, hyphens, etc.) when filling in crossword.

Across

1. A defense available to mentally ill defendants.
6. The levying of war against the United States or giving aid and comfort to its enemies.
9. One who receives, relieves, comforts, or assists another with knowledge that the other has committed a felony.
11. Criminal intent.
13. Evidence obtained by an unconstitutional search or seizure that cannot be used at the trial of a defendant.
15. Wrong in and of itself.
16. Evidence offered by a defendant to defeat a criminal charge or civil lawsuit.
17. A voluntary act.
18. The case law used in England and the American colonies before the American Revolution.
19. Acts against one's master or lord.
20. Participating in a crime by giving assistance or encouragement.

Down

2. An excuse of the use of force in resisting attack.
3. After the fact.
4. A rule that allows police officers who believe a person is acting suspiciously and could be armed to stop and frisk that person for weapons without a search warrant.
5. The getting together of two or more people to accomplish some criminal or unlawful act.
7. A written order of the court authorizing law enforcement officers to search and seize certain property.
8. Anyone who takes part with another in the commission of a crime.
10. Acts against the king (under the English common law).
12. A major crime, punishable by imprisonment in a state prison.
14. Laws that impose a penalty or punishment for a wrong against society.
17. A defense that places the defendant in a different place than the crime scene so that it would have been impossible to commit the crime.

CHAPTER 9

Crimes Against Property

ANTE INTERROGATORY

The giving or receiving of a reward to influence any official act is (A) coercion, (B) embezzlement, (C) bribery, (D) extortion.

2

CHAPTER OUTLINE

Elements of Crimes
Larceny
- *Wrongful Taking*
- *Carrying Away*
- *Personal Property*
- *Property of Another*
- *Intent to Steal*
- *Degrees of Larceny*

Embezzlement
Larceny by False Pretenses
Bribery, Extortion, and Coercion
- *RICO*

Receipt of Stolen Goods
Forgery

KEY TERMS

animus furandi *(AN·i·mus fer·AN·day)*
asportation *(as·por·TA·shun)*
attempted larceny *(a ·TEMPT· ed LAR ·sen·ee)*
bailee *(bay·LEE)*
bribery *(BRY·be·ree)*
chattels *(CHAT·els)*
chose in action *(shohz in AK·shun)*
circumstantial evidence *(ser·kum·STAN·shel EV·i·dens)*
coercion *(ko·ER·shen)*
computer fraud *(frawd)*
constructive possession *(kon·STRUK·tiv po·SESH·en)*
criminal fraud *(KRIM·i·nel frawd)*
custody *(KUS·te·dee)*
efficacy *(EF·i·ka·see)*
embezzlement *(em·BEZ·ul·ment)*
extortion *(eks·TOR·shun)*
forgery *(FOR·jer·ee)*
fraud in esse contractus *(ESS·ay kon·TRAKT·es)*
grand larceny *(LAR·sen·ee)*
larceny *(LAR·sen·ee)*
larceny by false pretenses *(PRE·ten·sez)*
mail fraud *(frawd)*
personal property *(PER·son·al PROP·er·tee)*
petit larceny *(PET·ee LAR·sen·ee)*
petty larceny *(PET·ee LAR·sen·ee)*
possession *(po·SESH·en)*
prosecution *(pros·e·KYOO·shun)*
racketeering *(rak·a·TEER·ing)*
real property *(PROP·er·tee)*
receiving stolen goods *(re·SEEV·ing STOH·len)*
RICO *(REE·coh)*
uttering *(UT·er·ing)*
wire fraud *(frawd)*

ELEMENTS OF CRIMES

To be criminal, in addition to having to be committed voluntarily with wrongful intent, acts must have exact definitions. This is so there can be no question about what is against the law. At common law, exact definitions came about by assigning specific elements to each crime. No person could be convicted of a crime unless each element of the crime was proved beyond a reasonable doubt. Most states still define crimes in this manner. This chapter discusses the elements of some of the most commonly committed crimes against property.

LARCENY

The common law definition of **larceny** is the wrongful taking and carrying away of personal property of another with the intent to steal. Broken down into its elements, the crime consists of the following:

1. A wrongful taking
2. A carrying away
3. Personal property
4. Of another
5. With intent to steal

Wrongful Taking

A wrongful taking means a trespass to someone else's possession of personal property. More precisely, it is the exercise of dominion and control over the personal property in the possession of another, without the right to do so.

Carrying Away

In addition to the wrongful taking, a carrying away must occur, which is called an **asportation** in legal terminology. This act involves a removal of the property from the place it formerly occupied.

To illustrate, in a case in which a thief attempted to steal a fur coat from a store dummy but was unable to do so because the coat was attached to the dummy by a chain, the court held that no larceny occurred, because the coat was not carried away. Instead, this would have been the crime of **attempted larceny** (an attempt to commit larceny, falling short of its commission), but this offense was not placed in the original charge. The defendant was protected by the right to freedom from double jeopardy. In another case, a thief opened a cash register and picked up some bills but dropped them back into the register drawer when he was discovered by the owner. In holding that a carrying away occurred, the court said: "If he had actually taken the money into his hand, and lifted it from the place where the owner had placed it, so as to entirely sever it from the spot where it was so placed, with the intention of stealing it, he would be guilty of larceny, though he may have dropped it into the place it was lying, upon being discovered, and had never had it out of the drawer."

Personal Property

The subject matter of larceny must be **personal property** (also called goods or **chattels**), which is defined as everything that is the subject of ownership not coming under the category of real estate. A negotiable instrument, such as a check, draft, or promissory note, was not the subject of larceny at common law as it was not personal property. Such an instrument is called a **chose in action,** which is evidence of a right to property but not the property itself. For example, a check is evidence of the right to the amount of money for which the check is written, but it is not the money itself. Statutes have been enacted by most states making it a crime to commit larceny of choses in action.

The item stolen must be capable of being owned to be the subject of larceny. Older cases held that it was not larceny to steal a dead body, as a dead body could have no owner; however, it was larceny to steal the casket containing the body as well as the clothing on the body, as these things were owned by the personal representatives of the decedent's estate. Wild animals having no owner could not be the subject of larceny for the same reason, even though they were taken from another's land.

Real property (land or anything permanently affixed thereto) is not the subject of larceny unless made so by statute. Thus, such things as growing trees, fences, doors or other fixtures, seaweed, and minerals or stone not yet mined or quarried are not the subject of common law larceny. The cutting down and carrying away of a standing tree would not be larceny; however, the carrying away of wood already cut would be larceny. Statutes have been passed by some states making it larceny to steal many things not included in common law larceny.

Property of Another

The general rule is that a person cannot commit larceny of his or her own property, with the exception of stealing his or her own property from a **bailee** (one to whom it has been rightfully entrusted). The property must be taken from the possession of another. The law, however, distinguishes between possession and custody. **Custody** is the care and keeping of anything; **possession** is the detention and control of anything. A person is said to have constructive possession of property when it is held in custody for that person by another. **Constructive possession** is possession not actual but assumed to exist. For example, a supermarket cashier has custody of the money in the cash register. The store itself (or the store owner) has possession of it. Anyone stealing it from the cashier commits larceny from the possession of the owner, which is true even if the cashier is the thief.

Intent to Steal

An essential element of larceny is called **animus furandi,** an intent to steal. This term means the intent to deprive the owner of the property permanently. Thus, at common law, the borrowing of a neighbor's horse without consent but with the intent to return it later in the day was not considered to be larceny. (It was, if anything, a trespass to personal property.) Some more recent cases, although still requiring intent to steal, define larceny as "appropriating the goods to a use inconsistent with the owner's rights," thus avoiding the problem mentioned earlier.

The intent to steal must exist at the time of the taking. A person who takes another's goods with permission or with the intent to return them, and later changes his or her mind and decides to steal them, is guilty of embezzlement rather than common law larceny. Embezzlement is discussed later.

Degrees of Larceny

By statute, larceny is divided into two degrees, **petit larceny** (usually referred to as **petty larceny**) and **grand larceny.** The former is usually a misdemeanor; the latter is a felony. Although the states differ in their distinction between the two, one common distinction makes it a misdemeanor to steal property with a value of $250 or less (petty larceny) and a felony to steal property with a value exceeding $250 (grand larceny).

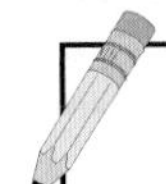

WORD WISE

"Animus" [Latin for mind; intention]

Examples	*Meaning*
animus cancellandi	intent to cancel or destroy (as applied to wills)
animus capiendi	intent to capture or take
animus defamandi	intent to defame
animus derelinquendi	intent to abandon or relinquish
animus lucrandi	intent to make a gain or profit (become lucrative)
animus recuperandi	intent to recover or recuperate
animus signandi	intent to sign an instrument (as a will)
animus testandi	intent to make a will (testament)

EMBEZZLEMENT

Embezzlement, which is essentially a breach of trust, consists of the same elements as larceny except that instead of "wrongful taking," a "rightful taking" occurs. The crime did not exist at common law but was created by statute to fill the gap in the law of larceny when someone, such as an employee or bailee, was entrusted with property of another and appropriated it to his or her own use, or when property was stolen before it came into the possession of the owner.

To illustrate, if a customer pays a supermarket cashier money for groceries and the cashier puts the money directly into his or her pocket rather than into the cash register, it is embezzlement because the money did not come to the possession of the supermarket before it was stolen. It would have been larceny, however, if the cashier had first placed the money into the cash register and stolen it later, as it would have come into the constructive possession of the store before it was stolen.

LARCENY BY FALSE PRETENSES

Larceny by false pretenses, also called **criminal fraud,** is another crime created by statute to fill a gap in common law larceny. In general, it is the act of knowingly and deliberately obtaining the property of another by false pretenses with intent to defraud. The elements of this crime are quite similar to the elements of the tort of deceit, which is discussed in a later chapter.

Some states have consolidated larceny, embezzlement, and larceny by false pretenses into one statute so that need no longer exists for the **prosecution** (the state bringing the action) to distinguish among them. The defendant is merely charged with violating that particular chapter and section of the statute, which includes all three common law crimes.

Figure 9-1 Bribery is the giving or receiving of a reward to influence any official act. (*Source: The Legal Lampoon*, Wiley Milles, p. 51 Andrew McMeel Publishing, 4520 Main St., Kansas City, MO 64111)

BRIBERY, EXTORTION, AND COERCION

It is illegal to give money or other items to public officials to sway their official activity. The giving or receiving of a reward to influence any official act is called **bribery** and is against the law. It is also illegal for public officials to demand payment from others for doing official acts. This type of action is known as **extortion** and is defined as the corrupt demanding or receiving by a person in office of a fee for services that should be performed gratuitously. **Coercion,** also a crime, means compelling someone to do something by threat or force.

RICO

A federal statute referred to as **RICO** (an acronym for the Racketeer Influenced and Corrupt Organizations Act) is designed to stop organized criminal activity from invading legitimate businesses. Under RICO, it is illegal to conduct a legitimate business with funds obtained from a pattern of racketeering activity. **Racketeering** (activities of organized criminals who extort money from legitimate businesses) includes many kinds of criminal activity, such as arson, robbery, bribery, and extortion. Also included in the definition of racketeering are the white-collar crimes of **mail fraud, wire fraud,** and **computer fraud** (the offense of using mail, wire, or computers to obtain money, property, or services by false pretenses).

RECEIPT OF STOLEN GOODS

It is a crime to buy, receive, or aid in the concealment of stolen or embezzled property, knowing it to have been stolen. This is the crime of **receiving stolen goods.** To constitute the crime, the goods must have been stolen at the time they are received, the receiver must have knowledge that the goods were stolen, and the receiver must have felonious intent.

One of the major issues in determining the guilt or innocence of people accused of the crime is whether or not they actually knew that the goods were stolen. If they either knew or believed that the property was stolen at the time it came into their possession or if at any time while it was in their possession they ascertained that it was stolen property and undertook to deprive the owner of the rightful use of it, they may be convicted of the crime. If they did not know that the goods were stolen, they cannot be found

WEB WISE

Need to find out what an acronym like RICO stands for?

Web Address	*Definition*
http://www.ucc.ie/acronym	The **Acronym Database** allows you to find out what an acronym means; you may also search for a word to see what acronyms it is used in.
http://www.acronymfinder.com	**Acronym Finder** lets you search more than 200,000 acronyms and abbreviations.
http://www.stands4.com	**Stands4** allows you to browse by category or do a specific search.

guilty. **Circumstantial evidence** (evidence of an indirect nature), such as paying an unreasonably low purchase price for goods, is often used to prove that the accused had knowledge that the goods were stolen.

FORGERY

Forgery is defined as the fraudulent making or altering of a writing whereby the rights of another might be prejudiced. The subject matter of forgery must be a writing or document that has some legal **efficacy** (effectiveness) such as a deed, mortgage, will, promissory note, check, receipt, or other writing. The forgery of a person's signature to a will that is invalid because of an improper number of witnesses would not be a forgery, because the will had no legal efficacy because of insufficient witnesses.

People can commit forgery by signing their own name if they fraudulently hold themselves out to be someone else of that same name, sign another's name with intent to defraud, or write something in above another's existing signature. It has also been held to be forgery to obtain someone's genuine signature by **fraud in esse contractus**—that is, fraud as to the essential nature of the contract—as when a person signs a promissory note thinking he or she is signing a receipt or other instrument.

Fraudulent intent is necessary to commit forgery. Thus, if someone is authorized to sign another's name, or reasonably believes that he or she has that authority, it would not be the crime of forgery to sign the other's name.

Uttering a forged negotiable instrument, such as a check or promissory note, is also a crime. **Uttering** means offering a forged negotiable instrument to another person, knowing it to be forged and intending to defraud.

REVIEWING WHAT YOU LEARNED

After studying the text, write the answers to each of the following questions:

1. List the five elements of common law larceny.

2. Describe a wrongful taking.

3. What is a carrying away?

4. Of what must the subject matter of larceny consist?

5. Describe and give an example of a chose in action.

6. Why did the court hold that it was not larceny to steal a dead body?

7. When is real property the subject of larceny?

8. When is it considered larceny to steal one's own property?

9. Describe the difference between possession and custody.

10. Define intent to steal.

11. At common law, is borrowing with intent to return considered to be larceny? Why or why not?

12. When must the intent to steal exist to constitute larceny?

13. Name the two degrees of larceny. ________

14. What is the amount that divides the two degrees of larceny by statute in some states? ________

15. In comparing the crimes of larceny and embezzlement, what is the one element that differs?

16. What have some states done by statute to larceny, embezzlement, and larceny by false pretenses so that no need exists to distinguish among them?

17. In what way does bribery differ from extortion?

UNDERSTANDING LEGAL CONCEPTS

Indicate whether each statement is true or false. Then, change the italicized word or phrase of each *false* statement to make it true.

Answers

________ **1.** In addition to a wrongful taking, a carrying away must occur to constitute *larceny.*

________ **2.** The subject matter of larceny must be *personal property.*

________ **3.** Older cases held that it *was* larceny to steal a dead body.

________ **4.** The cutting down and carrying away of a standing tree *was* larceny at common law.

________ **5.** One cannot commit larceny of *one's own* property except from a bailee.

________ **6.** To constitute larceny, the property must be taken from another's *custody.*

________ **7.** An essential element of *larceny* is an intent to steal.

________ **8.** Petty larceny is usually a *misdemeanor,* and grand larceny is a *felony.*

________ **9.** Embezzlement includes a *wrongful* taking.

________ **10.** The crime of bribery is *the same as* the crime of extortion.

CHECKING TERMINOLOGY

From the list of legal terms that follows, select the one that matches each definition:

- **a.** animus furandi
- **b.** asportation
- **c.** attempted larceny
- **d.** bailee
- **e.** bribery
- **f.** chattels
- **g.** chose in action
- **h.** circumstantial evidence
- **i.** coercion
- **j.** computer fraud
- **k.** constructive possession
- **l.** criminal fraud
- **m.** custody
- **n.** efficacy
- **o.** embezzlement
- **p.** extortion
- **q.** forgery
- **r.** fraud in esse contractus
- **s.** grand larceny
- **t.** larceny
- **u.** larceny by false pretenses
- **v.** mail fraud
- **w.** personal property
- **x.** petit larceny
- **y.** possession
- **z.** prosecution
- **aa.** racketerring
- **bb.** real property
- **cc.** receiving stolen goods
- **dd.** RICO
- **ee.** uttering
- **ff.** wire fraud

Answers

____ **1.** Using the computer to obtain money, property, or services by false pretenses.
____ **2.** Using mail to obtain money, property, or services by false pretenses.
____ **3.** The care and keeping of anything.
____ **4.** A federal statute designed to stop organized criminal activity from invading legitimate businesses.
____ **5.** One to whom personal property is given under a bailment contract.
____ **6.** Activities of organized criminals who extort money from legitimate businesses.
____ **7.** Everything that is the subject of ownership not coming under the category of real estate (select two answers).
____ **8.** The corrupt demanding or receiving by a person in office of a fee for services that should be performed gratuitously.
____ **9.** Possession not actual but assumed to exist.
____ **10.** The party by whom criminal proceedings are started or conducted; the state.
____ **11.** An intent to steal.
____ **12.** Effectiveness.
____ **13.** Compelling someone to do something by threat or force.
____ **14.** Using the wires to obtain money, property, or services by false pretenses.
____ **15.** At common law, the wrongful taking and carrying away of personal property of another with the intent to steal.
____ **16.** The giving or receiving of a reward to influence any official act.
____ **17.** The detention and control of anything.
____ **18.** Larceny that is a felony.
____ **19.** Knowingly and deliberately obtaining the property of another by false pretenses with intent to defraud (select two answers).
____ **20.** The carrying away of goods.
____ **21.** The fraudulent appropriation of property by a person to whom it has been entrusted.
____ **22.** The ground and anything permanently attached to it, including land, buildings, and growing trees, and the airspace above the ground.
____ **23.** Evidence of a right to property but not the property itself.
____ **24.** Larceny that is a misdemeanor rather than a felony.
____ **25.** An attempt to commit larceny, falling short of its commission.
____ **26.** Evidence of an indirect nature.
____ **27.** Offering a forged negotiable instrument to another person, knowing it to be forged and intending to defraud.
____ **28.** The fraudulent making or altering of a writing whereby the rights of another might be prejudiced.

UNRAVELING LEGALESE

With the help of the glossary, rewrite the following sentence in the space below, substituting each of the underlined terms with a word or phrase that has the same meaning.

> If a person honestly receives the possession of the goods, chattels, or money of another upon any trust, express or implied and, after receiving them, fraudulently converts them to his or her own use, he or she may be guilty of the crime of embezzlement, but cannot be guilty of that of larceny, except as embezzlement is by statute made larceny.

USING LEGAL LANGUAGE

Read the following story and fill in the blank lines with legal terms taken from the list of terms at the beginning of this chapter.

A blind woman named Alice bought some items of stolen furniture from a corrupt salesperson. She could not be convicted of ____________ because she did not know that the goods were stolen, and no ____________ was uncovered, such as the payment of a low price, to prove that she had such knowledge. The corrupt salesperson committed ____________ when he told Alice that she was signing a receipt when she was actually signing a check made out to the crook. Even though Alice signed her own name, it was a(n) ____________, and the check certainly had some legal ____________. The corrupt salesperson committed the crime of ____________ when he tried to cash the check at a local bank. Oddly, it was probably the crime of ____________ when the bank employee took the check, because she had been entrusted with it, and the judge said that the check that was taken was actually a(n) ____________ rather than an item of ____________. When an automobile was stolen from the bank's parking lot, however, the attorney for the ____________ claimed that it was the crime of ____________, which is divided into two degrees: ____________ and ____________. The attorney claimed that the thief had the intent to steal, known as ____________, and that a(n) ____________ existed—that is, a carrying away of goods, which are also called ____________. Because the owner of the car had control of it, he had ____________ rather than ____________ of the car, and he was not a(n) ____________. In addition, because the owner's possession was actual rather than assumed, this case did not involve ____________. No fraud occurred; therefore, the crime was not ____________, which is also called ____________. Because this crime had nothing to do with land, ____________ was not involved. The crime of ____________ occurred, however, when the thief paid the prosecuting attorney $1,000 to drop the case. It would have been ____________ if the thief had compelled someone to do something by threat or force.

PUZZLING OVER WHAT YOU LEARNED

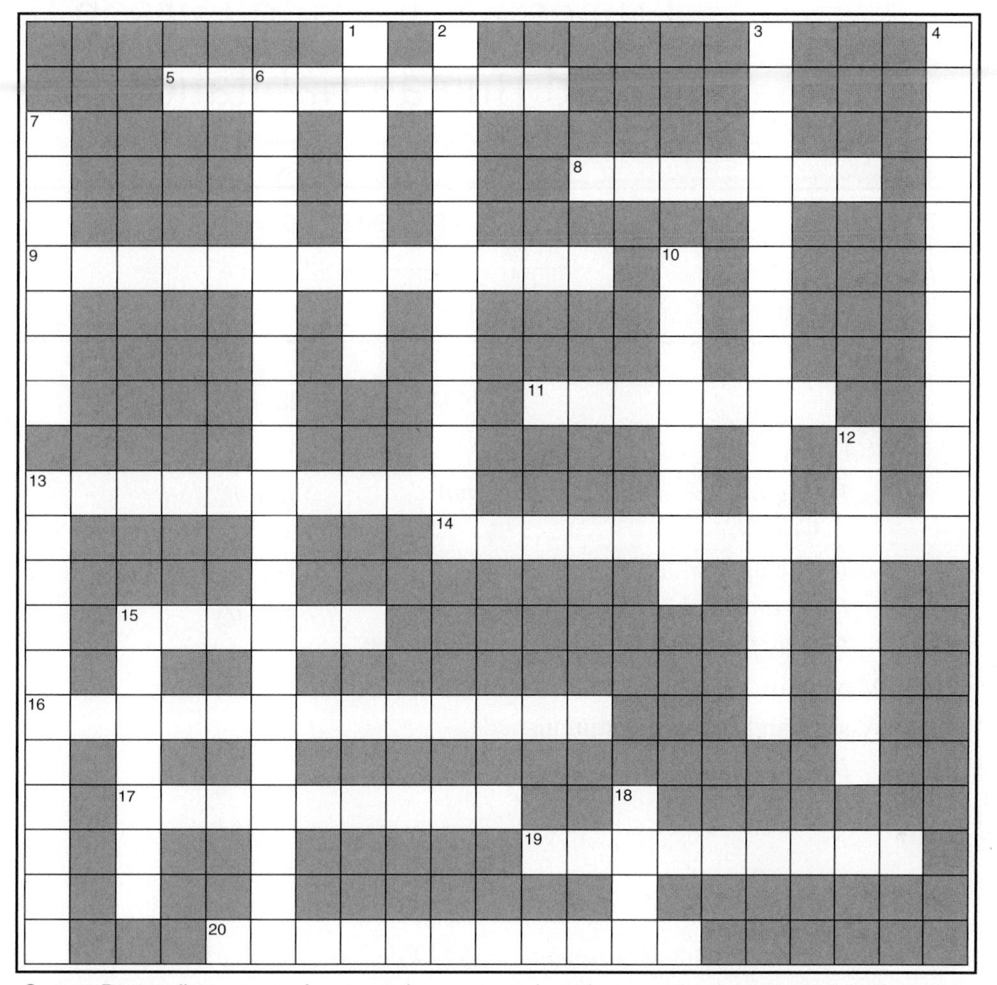

Caveat: Do not allow squares for spaces between words and punctuation (apostrophes, hyphens, etc.) when filling in crossword.

Across

5. Using the wires to obtain money, property, or services by false pretenses.
8. The fraudulent making or altering of a writing.
9. Evidence of a right to property but not the property itself.
11. The care and keeping of anything.
13. The detention and control of anything.
14. Larceny that is a felony.
15. One to whom personal property is given under a bailment contract.
16. Knowingly and deliberately obtaining the property of another by false pretenses with intent to defraud.
17. The corrupt demanding or receiving by a person in office of a fee for services that should be performed gratuitously.
19. Using mail to obtain money, property, or services by false pretenses.
20. The carrying away of goods.

Down

1. Effectiveness.
2. Activities of organized criminals who extort money from legitimate businesses.
3. An attempt to commit larceny, falling short of its commission.
4. Larceny that is a misdemeanor rather than a felony.
6. The buying, receiving, or aiding in the concealment of stolen or embezzled property, knowing it to have been stolen.
7. The wrongful taking and carrying away of personal property of another with the intent to steal.
10. Anything that is the subject of ownership other than real property.
12. Compelling someone to do something by threat or force.
13. A criminal action. The party by whom criminal proceedings are started or conducted; the state.
15. The giving or receiving of a reward to influence any official act.
18. Racketeer Influenced and Corrupt Organizations Act.

2

CHAPTER 10

Crimes against the Person and Human Habitation

ANTE INTERROGATORY

One of the elements of common law burglary is (A) in the nighttime, (B) a carrying away, (C) in the daytime, (D) personal property.

CHAPTER OUTLINE

Robbery
- *Taking from the Person or Personal Custody*
- *Taking against the Other's Will*
- *Force and Violence*
- *Penalty for Robbery*

Mayhem

Assault and Battery Distinguished
- *Battery*
- *Assault*

Rape
- *Statutory Rape*

Domestic Violence and Stalking

Crimes against Human Habitation
- *Burglary*
- *Arson*

KEY TERMS

aggravated assault *(AG·ra·va·ted a·SALT)*
arson *(AR·sen)*
assault *(a·SALT)*
attempted arson *(a·TEMT·ed)*
battery *(BAT·er·ee)*
breaking *(BRAKE·ing)*
burglary *(BUR·gler·ee)*
carnal knowledge *(KAR·nel NOL·ej)*
convicted *(kon·VICT·ed)*
curtilage *(KUR·til·ej)*
dangerous weapon *(DAYN·jer·ess WEP·en)*
deadly weapon *(DED·lee WEP·en)*
domestic violence *(do·MES·tik VY·o·lense)*
dwelling house *(DWEL·ing)*
lesser-included offense *(o·FENSE)*
maim *(maym)*
mayhem *(MAY·hem)*
nighttime
rape
rape shield laws *(sheeld)*
restraining order *(re·STRANE·ing)*
robbery *(ROB·e·ree)*
sexual assault *(SEKS·yoo·el a·SALT)*
stalking *(STAW·king)*
statutory arson *(STAT·shoo·tore·ee AR·sen)*
statutory burglary *(STAT·shoo·tore·ee BUR·gler·ee)*
statutory rape *(STAT·shoo·tore·ee)*
summarily *(sum·EHR·i·lee)*
unlawful sexual intercourse *(un·LAW·ful SEKS·yoo·el IN·ter·kors)*

Crimes against the person were considered to be more serious than crimes against property at common law and were subject to a harsher punishment.

ROBBERY

Robbery is defined as the wrongful taking and carrying away of the personal property of another from the other's person or personal custody, and against the other's will by force and violence. The essence of the crime is the exertion of force against another to steal personal property from that person. The elements of robbery consist of the following:

1. Wrongful taking
2. Carrying away
3. Personal property of another
4. From the person or personal custody
5. Against the other's will with force and violence

2

WEB WISE

- Log onto the Internet Law Library at **www.lawguru.com** for links to the text of the U.S. Constitution, state constitutions, and other legal subjects.
- Look up U.S. Supreme Court opinions from 1893 to the present by going to **www.findlaw.com.** At that site, you can look for cases by specific year, by citation, by the name of a party, or by specific words used in the opinion.

Because all of the elements of larceny are included in the crime of robbery, larceny is a lesser included offense of robbery. A **lesser included offense** is a crime that contains some but not all elements of a greater offense, making it impossible to commit the greater offense without also committing the lesser offense. One can be convicted of either the greater or the lesser offense but not both. The first three elements of robbery are discussed in Chapter 2 under the larceny heading. The last two elements, which are different, are discussed here.

Taking from the Person or Personal Custody

One of the principal differences between larceny and robbery is that in robbery a taking "from the person" occurs, whereas in larceny it does not. To constitute robbery, the taking must be from the person or in the presence of the one in possession of the goods at the time of the robbery.

In a case in which a man held a woman at gunpoint in his room and ordered her to telephone her maid to deliver the woman's jewels to his room, the court, in holding the crime to be robbery, said: "A thing is in the presence of a person, in respect to robbery, which is so within his reach, inspection, observation, or control, that he could, if not overcome by violence or prevented by fear, retain his possession of it."

When the owner is kept in one room of the house and is forced to tell where his or her property may be found in another room, and the assailant goes there and takes the property, it has been held that such a taking is a robbery.

Taking against the Other's Will

The taking must be against the will of the person in possession of the goods. If the person from whom the goods are stolen is unaware of the crime's occurrence, as when a pocket is picked, the crime is larceny rather than robbery.

Force and Violence

Some force or violence must be used against the possessor of the goods to constitute robbery. The degree of force is immaterial so long as it is sufficient to obtain the victim's property against his or her will. The court, for example, held that the dispensing of a drug to a person so as to make him unconscious in order to steal his property was enough force to constitute robbery.

An intimidation, or a putting in fear, will take the place of the force required in the crime. Thus, even though no actual force is used but victims are put in fear, as when threatened by a superior force or by the threat of harm to their persons or property, the element of force and violence will be satisfied.

Penalty for Robbery

In general, the penalty for robbery is greater than that for larceny. For example, in Massachusetts, the punishment for robbery (whether armed or unarmed) is "imprisonment in the state prison for life or for any term of years." In contrast, grand larceny is punished by "imprisonment in the state prison for not more than five years or by a fine of not more than $2,500 and imprisonment in jail for not more than two years."

MAYHEM

At common law, **mayhem** was violently depriving others of the use of such members as may render them less able in fighting, either to defend themselves or to annoy their adversary. Examples of mayhem were cutting off a person's hand, foot, or finger and putting out an eye. It was not mayhem to cut off another's nose or ear or to disfigure a person in a way that did not interfere with the ability to fight. Interestingly, it was mayhem to knock out a person's front tooth, but it was not mayhem to knock out a back tooth, because such a tooth was not needed to bite someone while fighting. Mayhem was a misdemeanor at common law, except for castration, which was a felony.

In modern times, mayhem has become a felony in most states and includes many types of disfiguration. It is commonly called **maim,** which means to cripple or mutilate in any way. To illustrate, a typical present-day statute reads in part:

Whoever, with malicious intent to maim or disfigure, cuts out or maims the tongue, puts out or destroys an eye, cuts or tears off an ear, cuts, slits or mutilates the nose or lip, or cuts off or disables a limb or member of another person . . . shall be punished by imprisonment in the state prison for not more than twenty years or by a fine of not more than one thousand dollars and imprisonment in jail for not more than two and one half years.

ASSAULT AND BATTERY DISTINGUISHED

An **assault** is an attempt to commit a battery; a **battery** is the actual contact or touching of another without permission or privilege. Thus, the shooting of a gun at another is the assault; the bullet striking the person is the battery. An assault can and often does occur without a battery, but battery necessarily includes an assault.

Battery

A battery is the unpermitted physical contact with another person in an angry, revengeful, rude, insolent, or reckless manner. It may also be defined as the unlawful application of force on another person. The intentional pushing or hitting of someone or grabbing someone's purse or wallet would be a battery. An accidental bumping of another in a crowded room, however, would not be a battery because the crime requires a general criminal intent or reckless behavior on the part of the perpetrator.

Assault

An assault is an attempt, real or apparent, to commit a battery. Some overt act, such as the movement of an arm or pointing of a gun toward the victim, is required to accomplish the crime. Mere threats or words alone are not enough to commit the offense. A criminal assault may occur even though a battery is impossible, as when an unloaded gun is aimed at another, or even though the victim is unaware of the offense and is not put in fear.

The Texas code has merged the separate crime of battery into the state's definition of assault and included threatening to assault someone as part of that crime.

Simple assault and battery is generally a misdemeanor. **Aggravated assault,** which is an assault committed with the intention of committing some additional crime, is a felony by statute in most states. Examples of aggravated assault are assault with intent to murder, assault with a **dangerous** or **deadly weapon** (an item that is, from the way it is used, capable of causing death or serious bodily injury), assault with intent to commit unarmed robbery, and assault with intent to commit a felony.

To illustrate, Boston Bruins hockey player Marty McSorley was found guilty by a Canadian court of *assault with a weapon* when he slashed Vancouver Canucks player Donald Brashear in the head with a hockey stick during a game.

RAPE

At common law, **rape** was defined as the unlawful, forcible carnal knowledge by a man of a woman, against her will, or without her consent. The essential elements of the crime follow:

1. Carnal knowledge
2. Force by the man
3. Nonconsent by the woman

Carnal knowledge meant the slightest penetration of the sexual organ of the woman by the sexual organ of the man. The force by the man had to be such as would overcome physical resistance by the woman, and the woman had to resist "to the uttermost" to prove that force occurred and that she did not consent to the act. The punishment for the crime was death.

It was impossible, under the common law, for a woman to commit the crime of rape, because the definition required carnal knowledge "by a man of a woman." A woman could be **convicted** (found guilty) of rape, however, as a principal in the second degree or as an accessory to the crime if she aided another in its commission. Similarly, a husband could not be convicted of raping his wife; however, he could be found guilty as a principal in the second degree by assisting another to do the act. The rape of a spouse is now a crime in many states.

Many states today have changed the definition of rape to include unnatural sexual acts on men as well as women and to include the threat of bodily harm as well as actual force on the victim. The following is an example of a modern rape statute:

> Whoever has sexual intercourse or unnatural sexual intercourse with a person, and who compels such person to submit by force and against his will or compels such person to submit by threat of bodily injury, shall be punished by imprisonment in the state prison for not more than twenty years; and whoever commits a second or subsequent such offense shall be punished by imprisonment in the state prison for life or for any term of years.

2

WORD WISE

Prefix "Carn-" (Latin for "flesh")

Term	*Meaning*
carnal	Fleshly; of or pertaining to the flesh or body (adjective)
carnage	Destruction of life; slaughter of many people as in battle (noun)
carnaged	Covered with carnage or slaughtered bodies (adjective)
carnalism	The practice of what is carnal; sensualism (noun)
carnalist	A person who pursues sensual, especially sexual, pleasure (noun)
carnality	State of being flesh; fleshiness (noun)
carnalize	To make carnal or rob of spirituality; to sensualize (verb)
carnally	Corporeally; bodily (adverb)
carnalness	Carnal quality or state; sensuality (noun)
carnivorous	Flesh-eating (adjective)

The same statute provides for a punishment of up to life imprisonment in cases in which the rape results in serious bodily injury or is committed by more than one person. **Rape shield laws** have been passed to help prevent rape victims from being victimized. In addition, some states require people charged with rape to be tested for AIDS.

Sexual assault is much broader than rape, sometimes defined as any unwanted sexual contact.

Statutory Rape

Statutory rape, referred to as **unlawful sexual intercourse** in California, is sexual intercourse with a child under the age set by the particular state statute regardless of whether the child consented or not. It is often referred to as *child abuse.* At common law, a child under the age of 10 was considered incapable of consenting, and sexual intercourse with a child of that age was rape even when the child consented. Present-day statutes, which vary from state to state, have increased the age to 12, 16, and even 18 years in some states. Thus, sexual intercourse with a person under that particular age is rape even if the child consented to or encouraged the act.

DOMESTIC VIOLENCE AND STALKING

In recent years, states have enacted laws attempting to decrease the amount of **domestic violence** (the abuse of a closely related person, such as a present or former spouse or cohabitant). Among other things, states have made it easier for victims to obtain restraining orders against their attackers. A **restraining order** is an order forbidding a person from doing a particular act. A temporary restraining order is often given **summarily** (quickly), followed by a hearing, which may or may not result in a permanent restraining order. In California, police officers must give domestic violence victims a "Victims of Domestic Violence" card, notifying them of their rights and of the availability of counseling centers and 24-hour counseling service telephone numbers.

Many states in recent years have made it a crime, called **stalking,** to follow someone around, threatening him or her with violence. **Stalking** is the willful, malicious, and repeated following, harassing, and threatening of another person, intending to place the person in fear of death or serious bodily injury.

CRIMES AGAINST HABITATION

The crimes of burglary and arson were considered to be crimes against habitation under the common law. For this reason, their definitions include, among other elements, a dwelling house.

Burglary

Burglary, under common law, is defined as the breaking and entering of a dwelling house of another, in the nighttime, with intent to commit a felony. All of the following elements of the crime must be proved by the state to convict someone of the crime of common law burglary:

1. A breaking
2. An entering
3. A dwelling house of another
4. In the nighttime
5. With the intent to commit a felony.

Breaking. A **breaking** is the putting aside of the dwelling house, which is relied on as security against intrusion. It can consist of such an activity as opening a door or window (whether locked or unlocked), opening a screen, opening a shutter or blind, digging under a sill, or even climbing down a chimney. At common law, it was held not to be a breaking when a window was left partly open and a burglar raised it further to enter. Modern decisions, however, have held such an act to be a breaking.

Entering. To constitute a burglary, an entry must occur of some part of the body or of some instrument by which the felony is sought to be accomplished. The entry may consist of an arm, leg, head, or the slightest part of the body such as a finger or foot. An interesting case arose when a person bored a hole with an auger up through the floor of a grain storage area that was part of a dwelling house, causing the grain to spill out of the hole into a sack placed below it. The court held that an entry occurred when the auger entered the storage area.

Dwelling House of Another. A **dwelling house** is a house in which the occupier and his or her family usually reside and includes all outbuildings within the curtilage, such as a garage or other outbuilding. **Curtilage** means the enclosed space of ground and buildings immediately surrounding a dwelling house, sometimes enclosed by a fence or wall. The requirement that the dwelling house be of another refers to occupancy rather than ownership. A landlord, for example, may be guilty of burglary for entering a house owned by him or her but rightfully occupied by tenants, if the other elements of burglary are present.

Nighttime. In ancient times, **nighttime** was defined as that period between sunset and sunrise during which the face of a person could not be discerned by the light of day (not including moonlight). In modern times, the word "nighttime" has been defined more precisely. For example, one state statute reads:

> If a crime is alleged to have been committed in the nighttime, nighttime shall be deemed the time between one hour after sunset on one day and one hour before sunrise on the next day; and the time of sunset and sunrise shall be ascertained according to mean time in the place where the crime was committed.

Intent to Commit a Felony. Under the common law definition of burglary, the breaking and entering must be done with the intent to commit a felony within the house. If the person breaking in intended merely to commit a misdemeanor, the crime would not be common law burglary. In an interesting case that occurred in the 1860s, a group of men, in the nighttime, broke into and entered a dwelling house of a person with the intent to cut off his ear. The men were found not guilty of burglary, because the cutting off of an ear was not a felony at the time. It was merely a misdemeanor because one did not need an ear to protect oneself. Today, in most states, the crime would be a felony.

Statutory Burglary. Many states have enacted statutes making it a criminal offense to do acts not included in the common law crime of burglary. Such crimes are sometimes referred to as **statutory burglary.** They include breaking and entering a building other than a dwelling house, and breaking and entering with the intent to commit a misdemeanor.

Arson

The common law definition of **arson,** which is still followed in many states, is the willful and malicious burning of the dwelling house of another. Broken down into its elements, the common law crime consists of the following elements:

1. A burning
2. Of a dwelling house
3. Of another
4. With malice

The mere scorching or blackening of the wood of a dwelling house is not enough to constitute arson. Some portion of the house must actually have been on fire so that the wood or other building material is charred to constitute the crime of arson. If someone attempts to commit the crime of arson but falls short of its commission, the crime of **attempted arson** is committed. This crime is also a punishable offense.

Because the common law crime of arson was directed toward the protection of people rather than property, the burning of a building other than a dwelling house was not considered to be arson.

The dwelling house must have been occupied by someone other than the perpetrator of the crime, and the fire must have been set intentionally and not through negligence or by accident.

Statutory Arson. Although most states have retained the common law definition of arson and still follow it, they have added, by statute, other forms of arson such as the burning of a building other than a dwelling house and the burning of one's own house to collect insurance. This act is referred to as **statutory arson** in contrast to common law arson.

REVIEWING WHAT YOU LEARNED

After studying the text, write the answers to each of the following questions:

1. List the five elements of robbery. ____________

2. The first three elements of robbery are the same as those for what other crime? ____________

3. What is one of the principal differences between larceny and robbery? ____________

4. Give an example of something that would be mayhem today but was not considered to be mayhem at common law. ____________

5. What is the difference between assault and battery? ____________

6. What is the difference between simple assault and battery and aggravated assault? ____________

7. List the three essential elements of rape at common law. ____________

8. Explain how a woman in earlier times or a husband could be guilty of rape. ____________

9. In what way have many states changed the common law definition of rape? ____________

10. How does statutory rape (unlawful sexual intercourse) differ from ordinary rape? ____________

11. List the elements of common law burglary. ______________________________

12. Describe the present law with respect to a breaking when a burglar enters a partially open window. ______________________________

13. Describe the intent necessary for a person to be convicted of common law burglary. ______________________________

14. What is statutory burglary, and why does a need for the term exist? ______________________________

15. List the four elements of common law arson. ______________________________

16. Describe the amount of burning that must occur to constitute arson. ______________________________

17. Describe statutory arson. ______________________________

UNDERSTANDING LEGAL CONCEPTS

Indicate whether each statement is true or false. Then, change the italicized word or phrase of each *false* statement to make it true.

Answers

______________ 1. At common law, crimes against the person were *not as serious as* crimes against property.

______________ 2. One of the principal differences between larceny and robbery is that in *robbery* a taking "from the person" occurs, whereas in *larceny* it does not.

______________ 3. A *battery* is an attempt to commit an *assault.*

______________ 4. The accidental bumping of another in a crowded room *is* a battery.

______________ 5. If the person from whom goods are stolen is unaware of the crime's occurrence, the crime is *larceny* rather than *robbery.*

______________ 6. Many states today have changed the definition of rape to include *unnatural sexual acts* on men as well as women.

______________ 7. Sexual intercourse with a child under the age set by state statute *is* rape even though the child consented to or encouraged the act.

______________ 8. Opening an *unlocked* door or window is considered a breaking.

______________ 9. A landlord *may be* guilty of burglary for entering a house owned by him or her but rightfully occupied by a tenant if the other elements of burglary are present.

______________ 10. Attempted arson *is not* a punishable offense.

CHECKING TERMINOLOGY

From the list of legal terms that follows, select the one that matches each definition.

a. aggravated assault
b. arson
c. assault
d. attempted arson
e. battery
f. breaking
g. burglary
h. carnal knowledge
i. convicted
j. curtilage
k. dangerous weapon
l. deadly weapon
m. domestic violence
n. dwelling house
o. lesser included offense
p. maim
q. mayhem
r. nighttime
s. rape
t. rape shield laws
u. restraining order
v. robbery
w. stalking
x. statutory arson
y. statutory burglary
z. statutory rape
aa. summarily
bb. unlawful sexual intercourse

Answers

____ **1.** Quickly.

____ **2.** The willful, malicious, and repeated following, harassing, and threatening of another person, intending to place the person in fear of death or serious bodily injury.

____ **3.** An item that is, from the way it is used, capable of causing death or serious bodily injury (select two answers).

____ **4.** Laws passed to help prevent rape victims from being victimized.

____ **5.** At common law, violently depriving others of the use of such members as may render them less able in fighting.

____ **6.** To cripple or mutilate in any way.

____ **7.** An attempt to commit a battery.

____ **8.** The unpermitted, unprivileged touching of another person; the unlawful application of force on another person.

____ **9.** An assault committed with the intention of committing some additional crime.

____ **10.** An order forbidding a person to perform a particular act.

____ **11.** The abuse of a closely related person such as a present or former spouse or cohabitant.

____ **12.** The wrongful taking and carrying away of the personal property of another from the other's person or personal custody, against his or her will by force and violence.

____ **13.** At common law, the unlawful, forcible carnal knowledge by a man of a woman, against her will, or without her consent.

____ **14.** Sexual intercourse; the slightest penetration of the sexual organ of the woman by the sexual organ of the man.

____ **15.** A crime that contains some but not all elements of a greater offense, making it impossible to commit the greater offense without also committing the lesser offense.

____ **16.** Sexual intercourse with a child under the age set by state statute regardless of whether the child consented or not (select two answers).

____ **17.** Found guilty of a crime.

____ **18.** The willful and malicious burning of the dwelling house of another.

____ **19.** An attempt to commit the crime of arson, falling short of its commission.

____ **20.** The burning of a building other than a dwelling house or the burning of one's own house to collect insurance.

____ **21.** At common law, the breaking and entering of a dwelling house of another, in the nighttime, with intent to commit a felony.

____ **22.** The putting aside of the dwelling house that is relied on as security against intrusion.

(continues on p. 116)

2

____**23.** A house in which the occupier and family usually reside, including all outbuildings within the curtilage.

____**24.** The enclosed space of ground and buildings immediately surrounding a dwelling house.

____**25.** Burglary that does not contain all of the elements of common law burglary.

2

UNRAVELING LEGALESE

Use simple, non-legal language, with the help of the glossary, to rewrite this quote in the space below so that it is shorter and can be understood by a layperson without losing its meaning.

> To ascertain the meaning of the word "maliciously" in the statute we must turn to the common law, for the statute was undoubtedly drawn against that background. At common law, the offense of arson consisted of the willful and malicious burning of the house of another. But the meaning given to the word "malicious" when used in defining the crime of arson is quite different from the literal meaning. The malice which is a necessary element in the crime of arson need not be express, but may be implied; it need not take the form of malevolence or ill will, but it is sufficient if one deliberately and without justification or excuse sets out to burn the dwelling house of another.

USING LEGAL LANGUAGE

Read the following story and fill in the blank lines with legal terms taken from the list of terms at the beginning of this chapter.

The suspect was charged with ______________________ when he sexually attacked a young woman late at night as she entered her house. Since the young woman was an adult, it was not the crime of ______________________, which is called ______________________ in California. The suspect was not ______________________ of the crime, because the state could not prove the element of ______________________. The state was able to prove, however, a(n) ______________________ and a(n) ______________________ because the suspect had lunged at the young woman with a knife, which struck her hand. A knife is considered to be a(n) ______________________ or a(n) ______________________. The suspect was found guilty of ______________________ and also ______________________, which was called ______________________ at common law, because the knife had cut off the tip of the young woman's finger. The entire incident was not considered to be ______________________ because it was not the exertion of force against another person in order to steal from that person. Also, it was not ______________________ because the suspect had not repeatedly followed and harassed the young woman. In addition, after ______________________ into the woman's garage, which was part of the ______________________ because it was within the ______________________, the suspect deliberately set fire to a pile of rubbish. The fire scorched some molding before it went out. Because the wood did not char, the suspect could be convicted of ______________________ but not ______________________ along with the crime of ______________________. Had this building been a factory, the crimes might have been ______________________ and ______________________.

PUZZLING OVER WHAT YOU LEARNED

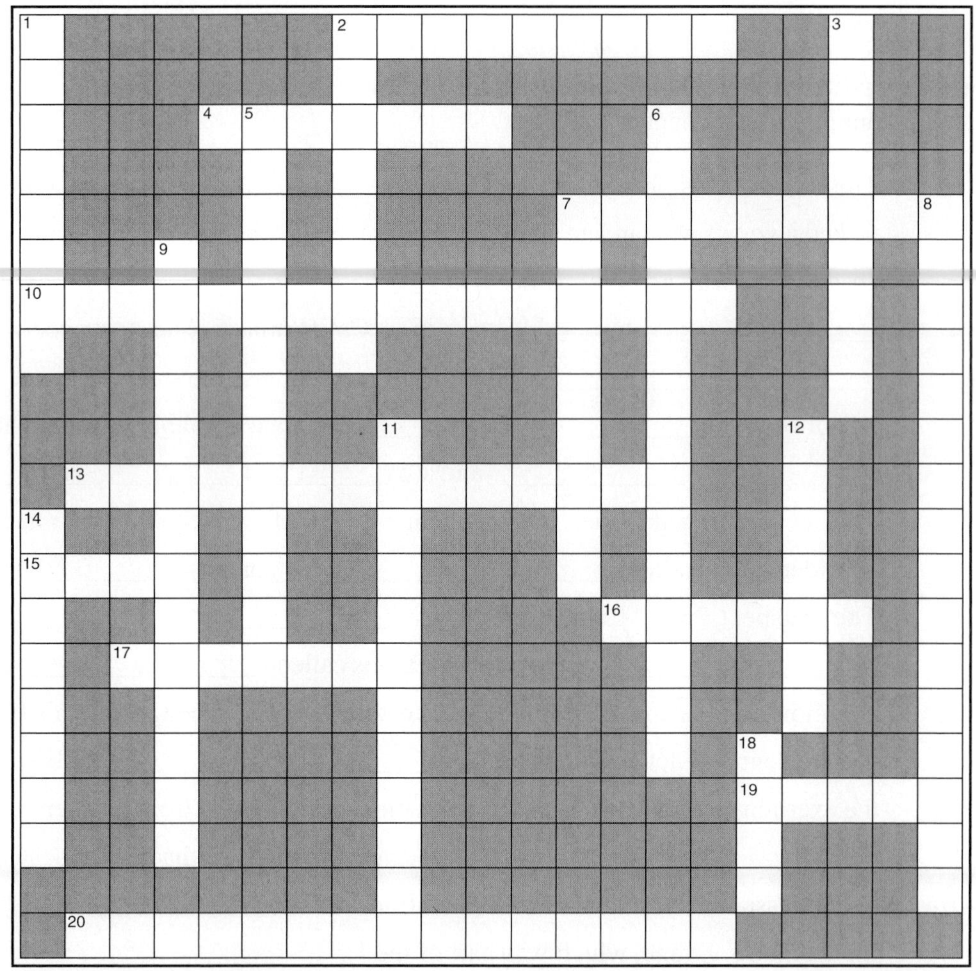

Caveat: Do not allow squares for spaces between words and punctuation (apostrophes, hyphens, etc.) when filling in crossword.

Across

2. Quickly.
4. The intentional creation of a reasonable apprehension of an imminent battery. An attempt to commit a battery.
7. Found guilty of a crime.
10. An order forbidding a person from doing a particular act.
13. Laws passed to help prevent rape victims from being victimized.
15. The unlawful, forcible carnal knowledge by a man of a woman, against her will, or without her consent.
16. Violently depriving others of the use of such members as may render them less able in fighting.
17. Intentional contact with another person without that person's permission and without justification.
19. The willful and malicious burning of a dwelling house of another.
20. Sexual intercourse.

Down

1. The breaking and entering of a dwelling house another, in the nighttime, with intent to commit felony.
2. The willful, malicious, and repeated following, harassing, and threatening of another person, intending to place the person in fear of death or serious bodily injury.
3. The time between one hour after sunset on on day and one hour before sunrise on the next c
5. Any unwanted sexual contact.
6. An item that is, from the way it is used, capabl causing death or serious bodily injury.
7. The enclosed space of ground and buildings immediately surrounding a dwelling house.
8. The abuse of a closely related person, such as a present or former spouse or cohabitant.
9. An attempt to commit the crime of arson, falling short of its commission.
11. An item that is, from the way it is used, capabl of causing death or serious bodily injury.
12. The wrongful taking and carrying away of personal property of another from the other person or personal custody against his or her will with force and violence.
14. The putting aside of the dwelling house that is relied on as security against intrusion.
18. To cripple or mutilate in any way.

CHAPTER 11
Homicide

ANTE INTERROGATORY

The killing of a human being by a human being is the definition of (A) euthanasia, (B) homicide, (C) manslaughter, (D) murder.

CHAPTER OUTLINE

Justifiable Homicide
- *Self Defense*
- *Exclusions under Common Law*

Proximate Cause

Felonious Homicide
- *Murder*
- *Suicide*
- *Degrees of Murder*
- *Manslaughter*

KEY TERMS

capital crime *(KAP·i·tel)*
castle doctrine *(KAS·el DOK·trin)*
corpus delicti *(KOR·pus de·LIK·tie)*
euthanasia *(yooth·e·NAY·zha)*
excusable homicide *(eks·KYOO·se·bel HOM·i·side)*
felon *(FEL·en)*
felonious homicide *(fe·LONE·ee·us HOM·i·side*
felony murder *(FEL·en·ee MER·der)*
feticide *(FET·e·side)*
first-degree murder *(de·GREE MER·der)*
fratricide *(FRAT·re·side)*
genocide *(JEN·o·side)*
homicide *(HOM·i·side)*
infanticide *(in·FANT·e·side)*
involuntary manslaughter *(in·VOL·en·ter·ee MAN·slaw·ter)*
justifiable homicide *(jus·ti·FY·a·bel HOM·i·side)*
malice *(MAL·iss)*
manslaughter *(MAN·slaw·ter)*
matricide *(MAT·ri·side)*
murder *(MER·der)*
patricide *(PAT·ri·side)*
premeditated malice aforethought *(pre·MED·i·tay·ted MAL·iss a·FORE·thawt)*
proximate cause *(PROK·si·met)*
right-to-die laws
second-degree murder *(SEK·end-de·GREE MER·der)*
self-defense *(de·FENSE)*
sororicide *(so·ROR·i·side)*
suicide *(SOO·i·side)*
uxoricide *(ux·OR·i·side)*
viable *(VI·a·bel)*
voluntary manslaughter *(VOL·en·ter·ee MAN·slaw·ter)*
year-and-a-day rule

Homicide is the killing of a human being by a human being. The term comes from the Latin *homo* (man) and *cidere* (to kill). Other terms with the same suffix include the following:

feticide: killing a fetus in the womb—abortion
fratricide: killing one's brother
genocide: killing a racial or political group
infanticide: killing an infant soon after birth
matricide: killing one's mother
patricide: killing one's father
sororicide: killing one's sister
suicide: killing oneself
uxoricide: killing one's wife

JUSTIFIABLE HOMICIDE

Justifiable homicide, which is also known as **excusable homicide,** is the taking of human life when an excuse exists. It includes the legal execution of murderers, the killing of others during battle, the killing of a fleeing suspect by a police officer to prevent escape after the commission of a felony, and the killing of another in self-defense.

Self Defense

Self defense is an excuse for the use of force in resisting attack, especially for killing an assailant. Before it can be used as a justification for homicide, the danger must appear so imminent that the only possible way to escape death or bodily injury is to kill the assailant. In addition, except when in one's own house (and in some southern and western states), one must retreat if possible before killing an assailant. When in one's own house, one need not retreat before using deadly force when being attacked. Frequently referred to as the **castle doctrine,** the rule is based on the common law principle that one's home is one's castle.

Exclusions under Common Law

At common law, the killing of an unborn child in its mother's womb was not homicide because to be such, the child must have had a circulation independent of its mother—that is, it must have breathed and thus have supplied oxygen to its own lungs. Such an act, however, could amount to criminal abortion. Modern decisions in many states have changed this rule, making it homicide to kill an unborn child in its mother's womb when the child is **viable**—that is, having the appearance of being able to live.

At common law, the death of the victim must have occurred within a year and a day after the blow occurred for the defendant to be convicted of a homicide. This rule, known as the **year-and-a-day rule,** is still followed in most states in the United States today. Some states, including Massachusetts, New Jersey, New York, Ohio, Oregon, and Pennsylvania have abolished the year-and-a-day rule because modern medical techniques allow injured people to be kept alive for long periods of time. California has increased the time under the rule to three years and one day.

NON SEQUITUR by Wiley

Figure 11-1 *Justifiable homicide*, also called *excusable homicide*, is the taking of human life when a valid legal excuse exists. (©1993, Universal Press Syndicate. Reprinted with permission.)

PROXIMATE CAUSE

To be convicted of homicide, it must be shown that the defendant's act was the **proximate cause**—that is, the dominant cause of death. It need not, however, be the sole cause of death. For example, a defendant who inflicted a gunshot wound on another was found guilty of the homicide even though the victim was negligently treated by a physician and died from lockjaw. In addition, the **corpus delicti** (the body on which a crime has been committed) must be accounted for to convict someone of homicide. Proof of death must exist. The term "corpus delicti" also refers to all the elements that must be proved in a particular crime. As discussed in Chapter 3, for example, the corpus delicti of robbery consists of five elements: (1) wrongful taking, (2) carrying away, (3) personal property of another, (4) from the person or personal custody, and (5) against the other's will with force and violence.

FELONIOUS HOMICIDE

Felonious homicide is homicide done with the intent to commit a felony. It is a **capital crime** in some states—that is, one that is punishable by death. It is divided into two kinds: murder and manslaughter. A person who commits a felony is called a **felon.**

Murder

Murder is defined as the unlawful killing of a human being by another with malice aforethought. **Malice** is evil intent. It is the state of mind that is reckless of law and of the legal rights of others that prompts one to take the life of another without just cause or provocation. When malice is present, the actor is motivated by cruelty, hostility, or revenge.

Suicide

Suicide was held to be murder at common law, and the punishment was the forfeiture of the deceased's goods to the state and burial under the highway leading into town so that henceforth every person, wagon, and animal going in and out of town would run over the body. Suicide is not punished in the United States and generally is not considered a crime because of the fact that the perpetrator cannot be punished. In some states, anyone who counsels another to commit suicide and who is present when the act is committed would be considered a principal in the second degree to the crime of murder. The U.S. Supreme Court decided in 1997 that states may ban doctor-assisted suicides, and most states have done so. The Florida law states, for example:

> Every person deliberately assisting another in the commission of self-murder shall be guilty of manslaughter, a felony of the second degree. . . .

Oregon is the only state that has enacted an assisted suicide law. That state's Death with Dignity Act allows doctors to prescribe lethal doses of medication to terminally ill people who have six months left to live. The federal government is attempting to have the Oregon law declared illegal.

Euthanasia, which is not the same as assisted suicide, is the act of painlessly putting to death someone suffering from an incurable disease as an act of mercy, and it is illegal in the United States. However, **right-to-die laws,** which are laws that allow dying people to refuse extraordinary treatment to prolong life, are very popular. Right-to-die laws are discussed in Chapter 22.

Degrees of Murder

No degrees of murder existed at common law; however, by statute in many states, the crime has been divided into two and sometimes three degrees. Under early statutes, the punishment for murder in the first degree was death, and the punishment for murder in the second degree was life imprisonment. Today, punishment for the crime varies from state to state.

First-Degree Murder. With some variations from state to state, **first-degree murder** is defined as murder committed in any of the following ways:

1. With deliberately premeditated malice aforethought, or
2. With extreme atrocity or cruelty, or
3. While in the commission or attempted commission of a felony, which is sometimes referred to as a **felony murder.**

Deliberately **premeditated malice aforethought** means thinking over, deliberating on, or weighing in the mind beforehand. Examples of murder committed with extreme atrocity or cruelty are those committed with repeated violent blows, sexual attacks, or repeated stabbing. Examples of felony murders are those committed in connection with rape, robbery, kidnapping, and sometimes arson and burglary.

Second-Degree Murder. In some states, murder that is not found to be in the first degree is **murder in the second degree.** Other states differentiate the two degrees depending on whether the malice was express or implied, the latter being second-degree murder. Still others base the difference on whether or not deliberation or premeditation occurred.

Manslaughter

Manslaughter is the unlawful killing of one human being by another without malice aforethought. The major difference between murder and manslaughter is that malice is essential in all degrees of murder, whereas it is not present in manslaughter. Manslaughter is either voluntary or involuntary.

Voluntary Manslaughter. **Voluntary manslaughter** occurs when an intention to kill exists but through the violence of sudden passion, occasioned by some great provocation. The provocation must be such that a reasonable person might naturally be induced to commit the act. For example, a husband comes home unexpectedly and finds his wife in the act of adultery. He becomes enraged and, in a fit of irresistible passion, kills the wife or the third person. When voluntary manslaughter occurs, an intent to kill exists, but it is done in the heat of passion without malice.

Involuntary Manslaughter. **Involuntary manslaughter** is the unintentional killing of another while in the commission of an unlawful act not amounting to a felony or in the commission of a wanton or reckless act. For example, the accidental killing of a pedestrian while driving at a high speed along a thickly settled, residential street could be involuntary manslaughter.

2

WORD WISE

"Manslaughter"—A Sexist Term

Should we continue to use the term "manslaughter" even though it is sexist? *The Dictionary of Bias-Free Usage: A Guide to Nondiscriminatory Language* (1991) recommends continuing to use the word until a nonsexist term is created to replace it. The language associated with English and American law, courts, and government is largely male oriented because men, in the past, dominated the field. Women, for example, were not allowed to vote until 1920 in this country and did not often hold policymaking positions. When the Founding Fathers wrote that "all men are created equal" in the Declaration of Independence, they meant men specifically, not generically—and even more precisely, white, male property owners. In government, terms like "city fathers," "favorite son candidate," and "gentlemen's agreement" remain in common usage. Can you suggest a nonsexist term that might realistically replace the word "manslaughter"?

REVIEWING WHAT YOU LEARNED

After studying the text, write the answers to each of the following questions.

1. What is the difference between justifiable homicide and felonious homicide? ______

2. What must appear before self-defense can be used as a justification for homicide? ______

3. What must be shown to be convicted of homicide? ______

4. At common law, what was the punishment for suicide? ______

5. In some states, what happens to one who counsels another to commit suicide and is present when the act is committed? ______

6. At common law, what were the degrees of murder? ______

7. Under early statutes, what was the punishment for murder in the first degree and murder in the second degree? ______

8. Generally, first-degree murder is murder committed in what three ways? ______

9. What is second-degree murder? ______

10. What is the difference between murder and manslaughter? ______

11. When does voluntary manslaughter occur? ______

12. When does involuntary manslaughter occur? ______

UNDERSTANDING LEGAL CONCEPTS

Indicate whether each statement is true or false. Then, change the italicized word or phrase of each *false* statement to make it true.

Answers

_______________ 1. Legal execution is an example of *felonious* homicide.

_______________ 2. Except when a person is in his or her own home, he or she *must* retreat if possible before killing an assailant in self-defense.

_______________ 3. At common law, the killing of an unborn child in its mother's womb *was not* homicide.

_______________ 4. The corpus delicti *must be* accounted for to convict someone of homicide.

_______________ 5. *Malice* is defined as the unlawful killing of a human being by another.

_______________ 6. *Three* degrees of murder existed at common law.

_______________ 7. Deliberately *premeditated malice aforethought* means thinking over, deliberating on, or weighing in the mind beforehand.

_______________ 8. The major difference between murder and manslaughter is that malice is essential in all degrees of *murder,* whereas it is not present in *manslaughter.*

_______________ 9. *Involuntary manslaughter* includes an intent to kill, but it is done in the heat of passion without malice.

_______________ 10. The accidental killing of a pedestrian while violating the speed limit is an example of *voluntary manslaughter.*

2

CHECKING TERMINOLOGY

From the list of legal terms that follows, select the one that matches each definition.

a. capital crime
b. castle doctrine
c. corpus delicti
d. euthanasia
e. excusable homicide
f. felon
g. felonious homicide
h. felony murder
i. feticide
j. first-degree murder
k. fratricide
l. genocide
m. homicide
n. infanticide
o. involuntary manslaughter
p. justifiable homicide
q. malice
r. matricide
s. manslaughter
t. murder
u. patricide
v. premediated malice aforethought
w. proximate cause
x. right-to-die laws
y. second-degree murder
z. self-defense
aa. sororicide
bb. suicide
cc. uxoricide
dd. viable
ee. voluntary manslaughter
ff. year-and-a-day rule

Answers

____ **1.** The killing of a human being by a human being.
____ **2.** The taking of a human life when an excuse exists (select two answers).
____ **3.** Homicide done with the intent to commit a felony.
____ **4.** A body on which a crime has been committed.
____ **5.** The unlawful killing of a human being by another with malice aforethought.
____ **6.** Evil intent; that state of mind that is reckless of law and of the legal rights of others.
____ **7.** A person who commits a felony.
____ **8.** Murder committed with deliberately premeditated malice aforethought, or with extreme atrocity or cruelty, or while in the commission of a crime punishable by life in prison.
____ **9.** Murder that is not found to be in the first degree.
____ **10.** The unlawful killing of one human being by another without malice aforethought.
____ **11.** The unlawful killing of another without malice when an intention to kill exists but through the violence of sudden passion.
____ **12.** The unintentional killing of another while in the commission of an unlawful act or while in the commission of a reckless act.
____ **13.** An excuse for the use of force in resisting attack, especially for killing an assailant.
____ **14.** The dominant cause that produces an injury or death.
____ **15.** The act of painlessly putting to death someone suffering from an incurable disease as an act of mercy.
____ **16.** Killing oneself.
____ **17.** Thinking over, deliberating on, or weighing in the mind beforehand.
____ **18.** Laws that allow dying people to refuse extraordinary treatment to prolong life.
____ **19.** Killing a fetus in a womb—abortion.
____ **20.** Killing one's brother.
____ **21.** Killing a racial or political group.
____ **22.** Killing an infant soon after birth.
____ **23.** Killing one's mother.
____ **24.** Killing one's father.
____ **25.** Killing one's sister.
____ **26.** Killing one's wife.
____ **27.** Death must have occurred within a year and a day after the blow occurred for a defendant to be convicted of homicide.

____**28.** Murder committed while in the commission or attempted commission of a felony.

____**29.** Having the appearance of being able to live.

____**30.** A crime that is punishable by death.

____**31.** When being attacked in one's house, a person need not retreat before using deadly force.

UNRAVELING LEGALESE

Use simple, non-legal language, with the help of the glossary, to rewrite this quote so that it is shorter and can be understood by a layperson without losing its meaning.

> It has long been settled that the word "deliberately" in the expression "deliberately premeditated malice aforethought" as used in our statute does not mean slowly. It has reference to the purposeful character of the premeditated malice rather than to the time spent in premeditation. In substance, while it must be shown that there must be a plan to murder formed after the matter had been made a subject of deliberation and reflection, yet, in view of the quickness with which the mind may act, the law cannot set any limit to the time. It may be a matter of days, hours, or even seconds. It is not so much a matter of time as of logical sequence. First the deliberation and premeditation, then the resolution to kill, and lastly the killing in pursuance of the resolution; and all this may occur in a few seconds.

USING LEGAL LANGUAGE

Read the following story and fill in the blank lines with legal terms taken from the list of terms at the beginning of this chapter.

A gruesome killing was discovered when the maid found the ______________________, on the floor, riddled with bullet holes. The victim was not an infant or a father or a mother; therefore, the crime could not have been ______________________, ______________________, or ______________________. It turned out that the butler shot his wife, making the crime ______________________. The shooting was held to be the ______________________, or dominant cause that produced the death. This case was not one in which the killer had an excuse for the use of force in resisting attack; therefore, he could not claim ______________________. When the killer was executed by the state, it was a type of ______________________ known as ______________________ or ______________________ rather than ______________________, of which the killer was guilty. The ______________________ had been convicted of ______________________, which is ______________________ committed with deliberately premeditated ______________________ aforethought. Although it found malice, the jury decided against ______________________, because premeditation had occurred. ______________________ is the unlawful killing of one human being by another without malice aforethought. Because of the malice in this case, the killing was neither ______________________ nor ______________________. It was, however, a(n) ______________________, because it is punishable by death in that state.

PUZZLING OVER WHAT YOU LEARNED

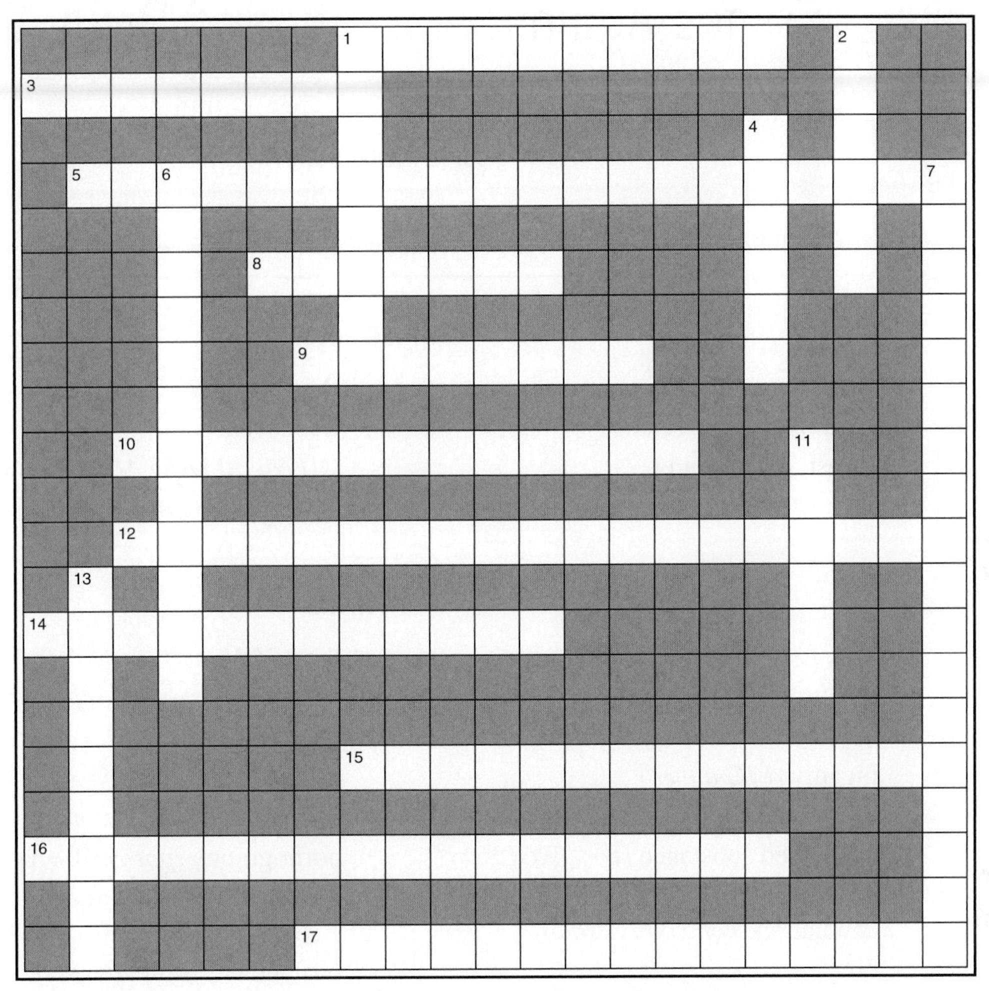

Caveat: Allow squares for spaces between words and punctuation (apostrophes, hyphens, etc.) when filling in crossword.

Across

1. Killing one's brother.
3. The killing of a human being by a human being.
5. The taking of a human life when an excuse exists.
8. Self-destruction.
9. Killing a racial or political group.
10. Murder committed while in the commission of a felony.
12. Death must occur within year and day for a person to be guilty of homicide.
14. Unlawful killing of human being by another without malice.
15. The body on which a crime has been committed.
16. Laws that allow dying people to refuse extraordinary treatment.
17. The dominant cause that produces an injury or death.

Down

1. Killing a fetus in the womb—abortion.
2. Evil intent.
4. Having the appearance of being able to live.
6. An excuse for the use of force in resisting attack.
7. The taking of a human life when an excuse exists.
11. Unlawful killing of a human being by another with malice aforethought.
13. Killing one's mother.

CHAPTER 12

Crimes Against Morality and Drug Abuse

ANTE INTERROGATORY

With some variations, most states prohibit marriage between people who are related by (A) fornication, (B) affinity, (C) consanguinity, (D) miscegenation.

2

CHAPTER OUTLINE

Adultery and Fornication
Bigamy and Polygamy
Incest and Sodomy
Miscegenation and Abortion Laws
Pornography
Drug Abuse
Federal Drug Abuse Laws
State Drug Abuse Laws

KEY TERMS

abortion *(a·BOR·shun)*
adultery *(a·DUL·ter·ee)*
affinity *(a·FIN·i·tee)*
bigamy *(BIG·a·mee)*
consanguinity *(kon·san·GWIN·i·tee)*
controlled substance *(kon·TROLED SUB·stanse)*
copulation *(kop·yoo·LA·shun)*
drugs
drug trafficking *(TRAF·ik·ing)*
fact finder *(fakt FINE·der)*
fornication *(for·ni·KA·shun)*
impediment *(im·PED·i·ment)*
incest *(IN·sest)*
miscegenation *(mis·sej·e·NA·shun)*
obscenity *(ob·SEN·i·tee)*
ordinance *(OR·di·nense)*
polygamy *(po·LIG·a·mee)*
pornography *(por·NAW·graf·ee)*
preponderance of evidence *(pre·PON·der·ense ov EV·i·dens)*
pro-choice *(pro-choys)*
pro-life *(pro-life)*
prurient interest *(PROO·ree·ent IN·trest)*
reasonable doubt *(REE·zen·e·bel dowt)*
sodomy *(SOD·e·mee)*

ADULTERY AND FORNICATION

Adultery is voluntary sexual intercourse by a married person with someone other than his or her spouse or by an unmarried person with a married person. In addition to being a ground for divorce, it is a crime in many states. The statute of one state reads:

> A married person who has sexual intercourse with a person not his spouse, or an unmarried person who has sexual intercourse with a married person shall be guilty of adultery and shall be punished by imprisonment in the state prison for not more than three years, or in jail for not more than two years, or by a fine of not more than $500.

To convict someone of the crime of adultery, the prosecution must prove beyond a reasonable doubt that the illegal act occurred. In contrast, to obtain a divorce on the ground of adultery, it is merely necessary to prove by a preponderance of evidence that the illegal act occurred. Preponderance of evidence is evidence of the greatest weight, indicating that it is more likely than not that the act occurred. The subject of adultery is discussed further in Chapter 38.

Fornication, which is sexual intercourse between two unmarried persons, is also a crime in some states. The Massachusetts statute reads:

> Whoever commits fornication shall be punished by imprisonment for not more than three months or by a fine of not more than thirty dollars.

As of 2007 Florida, Michigan, Mississippi, North Carolina, North Dakota, Virginia, and West Virginia have laws prohibiting an unmarried man and woman from living together as if they were married. The Florida statute reads:

> If any man and woman, not being married to each other, lewdly and lasciviously associate and cohabit together, or if any man or woman, married or unmarried, engages in open and gross lewdness and lascivious behavior, they shall be guilty of a misdemeanor of the second degree.

Many states have done away with laws that made adultery and fornication crimes. Many other states have kept the laws on their books, but seldom enforce them.

BIGAMY AND POLYGAMY

Bigamy is the state of a man who has two wives, or of a woman who has two husbands, living at the same time. **Polygamy** is the state of having several wives or husbands at the same time. All states in the United States consider bigamy and polygamy to be criminal offenses. In addition, a marriage contracted while either party thereto has a wife or husband is void and of no legal effect unless the previous marriage has been terminated by annulment, divorce, or death of that spouse. In some states, if one of the parties entered the marriage in good faith without knowledge of the **impediment**—that is, the hindrance to the making of a contract (the fact that the other spouse is married)—the second marriage will become valid upon the death or divorce of the former spouse if the parties continue to live together in good faith on the part of one of them.

WORD WISE

Numbers

Word Element	*Meaning*	*Examples*
uni-	one	unilateral, universe
bi-, di-, du-	two	bilateral, dichotomy, duet
tri-	three	trifurcate, tricycle
quadr-, quart-	four	quadrangle, quartet
quint-, penta-	five	quintuplets, pentagon
ses-, sext-, hexa-	six	sestet, sextet, hexagon
sept-	seven	septet
oct-	eight	octagon, octet
non-, nov-	nine	nonagon, novena
deca-	ten	decathlon, decade

Figure 12-1 In 1842, Brigham Young announced that polygamy was a basic tenant of the Church of Jesus Christ of Latter-Day Saints. At his death in 1877, he had more than 20 wives and 47 children. The church abandoned the practice of polygamy in 1890. What is the legal effect, under today's law, of a subsequent marriage when an earlier marriage has not ended by death, annulment, or divorce? (Courtesy of the Library of Congress, Prints and Photographs Division, reproduction numbers LC-USZ62-89570.)

INCEST AND SODOMY

Incest is sexual intercourse between people who are related by **consanguinity** (blood) or affinity in such a way that they cannot legally marry. **Affinity** is the relationship that one spouse has to blood relatives of the other.

At common law, people could not marry the following relatives:

Consanguinity	**Affinity**
Mother or father	Stepmother or stepfather
Grandmother or grandfather	Step-grandmother or step-grandfather
Daughter or son	Stepdaughter or stepson
Granddaughter or grandson	Step-granddaughter or step-grandson
Aunt or uncle	Mother-in-law or father-in-law
Sister or brother	Grandmother-in-law or grandfather-in-law
Niece or nephew	Daughter-in-law or son-in-law Grand-daughter-in-law or grandson-in-law

Today, many states no longer prohibit marriages between people who are related by affinity. With some variations, most states still prohibit marriages between people who are related by consanguinity.

Sodomy was formerly referred to in state statutes as the "abominable and detestable crime against nature." The crime has been interpreted by the courts as referring to oral intercourse, anal penetration, and bestiality, the later being carnal **copulation** (sexual intercourse) by a man or woman with a beast. In 2003, the U.S. Supreme Court case of *Lawrence* v. *Texas* held anti-sodomy laws to be unconstitutional. The Court said that the parties' right to liberty under the due process clause gives them the full right to engage in private conduct without government intervention.

MISCEGENATION AND ABORTION LAWS

At one time, many states prohibited marriage between people of different races, which was called **miscegenation.** Such marriages were often held to be illegal and void, and the parties thereto were punished. The U.S. Supreme Court has held miscegenation statutes to be against the law. They violate the equal protection clause and the due process clause of the Fourteenth Amendment of the U.S. Constitution.

The question of whether to legally allow a pregnant woman to have an **abortion** (the act of stopping a pregnancy) is an extremely emotional issue. Many people are **pro-life**—they believe that abortions should not be allowed except in the case of rape or incest and when necessary to save the life of the mother. They believe that an abortion takes the life of a human being and is no different from killing someone who is alive. Others are **pro-choice**—they believe that a pregnant woman should have the choice of having an abortion or not, without interference from the government.

In 1973 in *Roe* v. *Wade,* the U.S. Supreme Court held that laws prohibiting abortion were unconstitutional. The Court said that during the first three months of pregnancy, a woman can have an abortion; the decision is up to her without interference by the state. States are allowed to pass laws to protect the mother's health during the second three months of pregnancy by making rules as to who can perform abortions and where they can be performed. State laws may prohibit abortions during the last three months of pregnancy, the Court said, with exceptions to protect the life or health of the mother.

In 1989, the U.S. Supreme Court held, in *Webster* v. *Reproductive Health Services,* that states may ban public employees from performing abortions in public hospitals other than to save the life of the mother and that states may pass laws requiring doctors to determine through various tests whether a fetus at least 20 weeks old is viable. In the 1991 case of *Rust* v. *Sullivan,* the U.S. Supreme Court upheld laws that prohibit agencies that receive federal or state funding from giving information on or performing abortions. In 1992, in the case of *Planned Parenthood* v. *Casey,* the U.S. Supreme Court reaffirmed its essential holdings in the *Roe* v. *Wade* case. In addition, the Court upheld laws that require minors seeking an abortion to obtain a parent's or guardian's consent but struck down laws that require wives to notify husbands of an intended abortion.

In 2003, in *Scheidler* v. *NOW,* the U.S. Supreme Court held that federal racketeering laws, such as RICO, could not be used as the foundation for criminal charges against pro-life protesters who rally outside abortion clinics. Four years later, in 2007, the same court held that the Partial Birth Abortion Ban Act passed by Congress in 2003 is constitutional. It does not violate a woman's right to have an abortion even though it contains no exception if needed to preserve a woman's life. Partial birth abortion procedures, now illegal, involved partially removing the fetus intact from a woman's uterus and cutting or crushing its skull.

PORNOGRAPHY

Pornography, in general, refers to material or conduct that shows or describes some kind of sexual activity and is designed to make people become sexually aroused. The term that is more commonly used by courts and legislatures to describe pornography is **obscenity.**

The First and Fourteenth Amendments to the U.S. Constitution, which give to all Americans the right of free speech and free expression, do not protect obscenity. Each individual state may, under a U.S. Supreme Court decision, enact laws regulating obscenity. The Court has set forth a three-part test to determine whether material is obscene, and all three parts of the test must be present for material to be obscene. The three-part test follows:

1. An average person, applying modern community standards, would find that the work taken as a whole appeals to prurient interests. **Prurient interest** means a shameful or morbid interest in sex. Local, rather than national, standards may be used as a guide.
2. The matter must show or describe sexual conduct in a way that is openly offensive. The sexual conduct that is not allowed to be shown or described must also be clearly defined by state law. This guideline exists so that people will know exactly what is considered to be obscene by the state.
3. The work, taken as a whole, has no serious literary, artistic, political, or scientific value.

A drive-in theater showed a movie in which people were nude. The theater was located in such a position that the screen could be seen from two public streets and a nearby church parking lot. A local **ordinance** (law passed by a city council) made it unlawful for a drive-in theater to show films containing nudity when the screen was visible from a public street or public place. The theater was charged by the city with violating the ordinance. The U.S. Supreme Court held that the city ordinance was unconstitutional because it was too broad. It prevented drive-in theaters from showing movies containing any nudity at all, however innocent or educational. The court said, "clearly, all nudity cannot be deemed obscene even as to minors."

DRUG ABUSE

The abuse of **drugs** (chemical substances that have an effect on the body or mind) has been a major national concern since the 1960s. Both federal and state laws deal with drug abuse.

Federal Drug Abuse Laws

The Federal Controlled Substances Act places strict controls on drugs. Under the act, five schedules have been established. Drugs are placed on one of five schedules, depending on their medical use, potential for abuse, and potential for dependence. A drug that is included on any of the five schedules is called a **controlled substance.** Drugs that are placed on schedule I, such as heroin, are strictly controlled. They have little or no medical use, are usually addictive, and have a high potential for abuse. Drugs that are placed on schedule V, such as codeine cough medicine, are not as strictly controlled.

Penalties for violating federal drug abuse laws are found in the United States Sentencing Guidelines. They range from imprisonment for one year and a $1,000 fine to imprisonment for life. Penalties also include the forfeiture of personal property, such as motor vehicles, boats, and aircraft, and real property used to facilitate the possession of a controlled substance.

The law has a provision allowing minor punishment without giving the offender a criminal record if an offender is in possession of only a small amount of drugs. In such cases, the government has the option of imposing a civil fine of up to $10,000 rather than a criminal penalty. In determining the amount of the fine, the offender's income and assets are considered. For a first offense for which the offender has paid all fines, can pass a drug test, and has not been convicted of a crime after three years, the proceedings can be dismissed. When this occurs, the drug offender can lawfully say that he or she had never been prosecuted, either criminally or civilly, for a drug offense. This law may not be used if (1) the drug offender has been previously convicted of a federal or state drug offense; or (2) the offender has been fined twice under this special program.

The federal act imposes penalties on persons for illegal **drug trafficking.** This activity is the unauthorized manufacture or distribution of any controlled substance or the possession of such a substance with the intention of manufacturing or distributing it illegally. The penalty for being convicted of a first offense of drug trafficking of a schedule I or II drug is not less than 5 years or more than 40 years in prison. The penalty increases to not less than 10 years or more than life in prison for a second offense. The penalty increases even more for the trafficking of very great quantities of illegal drugs.

The Drug Enforcement Administration enforces the federal drug laws. It also strives to cut off the sources of supply of illegal drugs before they reach people who might use them.

State Drug Abuse Laws

Many states have adopted the Uniform Controlled Substances Act and have made it part of their state law. The uniform law is similar to the Federal Controlled Substances Act. It contains the same five schedules that are found in the federal act and provides a procedure for adding, removing, and transferring drugs from one schedule to another. It also contains controls that are similar to those found in the federal act. It does not, however, establish penalties for violation of the law. Instead, the act leaves it up to each state to set its own penalties.

REVIEWING WHAT YOU LEARNED

After studying the text, write the answers to each of the following questions:

1. What is the difference between fornication and adultery? ____________________
2. What is the status of a marriage contracted while either party has a spouse still living? ____________________
3. Under what circumstance will a bigamous marriage become valid in some states? ____________________
4. Name five relationships by consanguinity that one cannot legally marry. ____________________
5. Name three relationships by affinity that one could not legally marry at common law. ____________________
6. What is the difference between being related by consanguinity and being related by affinity? ____________________
7. Explain the present legal status of miscegenation statutes. ____________________
8. When is abortion legal? ____________________
9. Describe the three-part test that must be used to determine whether or not material is obscene. ____________________
10. The Federal Controlled Substances Act places drugs on different schedules depending on what three considerations? ____________________
11. Give an example of a drug that is placed on schedule I of the Federal Controlled Substances Act. ____________________
12. In what way does the Uniform Controlled Substances Act deal with penalties for drug abuse? ____________________

2

UNDERSTANDING LEGAL CONCEPTS

Indicate whether each statement is true or false. Then, change the italicized word or phrase of each *false* statement to make it true.

Answers

__________ **1.** In addition to being a ground for divorce, adultery is a *crime* in many states.

__________ **2.** Fornication *is not* a crime in *any* state.

__________ **3.** All states in the United States consider bigamy, *but not* polygamy, to be criminal.

__________ **4.** Incest and sodomy are *synonymous.*

__________ **5.** With some variations, most states *still prohibit* marriage between people who are related by consanguinity.

__________ **6.** The U.S. Supreme Court has held miscegenation statutes to be *valid and legal.*

__________ **7.** During the first *six* months of pregnancy, a woman can have an abortion without interference by the state under the 1973 Supreme Court decision.

__________ **8.** The First and Fourteenth Amendments to the U.S. Constitution *do not* protect obscenity.

__________ **9.** The penalties are *greater* for the illegal trafficking of drugs on schedule I than they are for drugs on schedule V under the Federal Controlled Substances Act.

__________ **10.** The Uniform Controlled Substances Act *establishes* penalties for violation of the law.

2

CHECKING TERMINOLOGY

From the list of legal terms that follows, select the one that matches each definition.

a. abortion
b. adultery
c. affinity
d. beyond a reasonable doubt
e. bigamy
f. consanguinity
g. controlled substance
h. copulation
i. drugs
j. drug trafficking
k. fact finder
l. fornication
m. impediment
n. incest
o. miscegenation
p. obscenity
q. ordinance
r. polygamy
s. pornography
t. preponderance of evidence
u. pro-choice
v. pro-life
w. prurient interest
x. reasonable doubt
y. sodomy

Answers

____ **1.** Voluntary sexual intercourse by a married person with someone other than his or her spouse or by an unmarried person with a married person.
____ **2.** The state of a man who has two wives, or of a woman who has two husbands, living at the same time.
____ **3.** Related by blood.
____ **4.** Disability or hindrance to the making of a contract.
____ **5.** The act that state statutes often describe as an "abominable and detestable crime against nature."
____ **6.** Doubt based on reason.
____ **7.** Evidence of the greatest weight.
____ **8.** The act of stopping a pregnancy.
____ **9.** Material or conduct that shows or describes some kind of sexual activity and is designed to make people become sexually aroused (select two answers).
____ **10.** A law passed by a city council.
____ **11.** The unauthorized manufacture or distribution of any controlled substance or the possession of such a substance with the intention of manufacturing or distributing it illegally.
____ **12.** The jury, or the judge in a nonjury trial.
____ **13.** Sexual intercourse between two unmarried persons.
____ **14.** The state of having several wives or husbands at the same time.
____ **15.** Sexual intercourse between people who are related by consanguinity or affinity in such a way that they cannot legally marry.
____ **16.** The relationship that one spouse has to blood relatives of the other.
____ **17.** Marriage between people of different races.
____ **18.** Chemical substances that have an effect on the body or mind.
____ **19.** A shameful or morbid interest in sex.
____ **20.** Favoring legislation that disallows abortion.
____ **21.** A drug that is included in any of the five schedules established by the Federal Controlled Substances Act.
____ **22.** Sexual intercourse.
____ **23.** The fact finder is fully persuaded that the accused has committed the crime.
____ **24.** Favoring legislation that allows abortion.

SHARPENING YOUR LATIN SKILLS

In the space provided, write the definition of each of the following legal terms, referring to the glossary when necessary.

actio criminalis ______________________________

actus reus ______________________________

animus furandi ______________________________

corpus delicti ______________________________

doli capaz ______________________________

ex post facto ______________________________

malum in se ______________________________

malum prohibita ______________________________

mens rea ______________________________

nolle prosequi ______________________________

UNRAVELING LEGALESE

Use the glossary to write the definitions of each of the italicized terms in the following syllabus from the U.S Supreme Court case of *Scheidler* v. *NOW.*

> *Respondents,* an organization that supports the legal availability of *abortion* and two facilities that perform abortions, filed a *class action alleging* that *petitioners,* individuals, and organizations that oppose legal abortion, violated *RICO* by engaging in a nationwide *conspiracy* to shut down abortion clinics through "a pattern of *racketeering* activity" that included acts of *extortion* in violation of the Hobbs Act.

USING LEGAL LANGUAGE

Read the following story and fill in the blank lines with legal terms taken from the list of terms at the beginning of this chapter.

Janice's husband, Rodney, who was white, became acquainted with some people who were taking ____________________, which is the name for illegal drugs. Because he did not manufacture or distribute the ____________________, he could not be convicted of ____________________ Rodney's friends often watched X-rated movies, which were allowed by a local ____________________—that is, a law passed by the city—but which were close to being ____________________, because, among other points, they appealed to ____________________, which means a shameful or morbid interest in sex. Without divorcing Janice, Rodney married another woman, thereby committing the crime of ____________________. Both of these marriages were later dissolved. Rodney then met Doris, an Asian woman, with whom he had sexual intercourse. This crime was one of ____________________ because they were not married to each other. Because neither of them was married to anyone else, it was not the crime of ____________________, and because they were not related by ____________________ or ____________________, it was not the crime of ____________________. When she became pregnant, Doris decided to carry the baby to term—that is, not have a(n) ____________________. The fact that the two were of different races did not prohibit them from getting married, because all ____________________ statutes are now illegal.

PUZZLING OVER WHAT YOU LEARNED

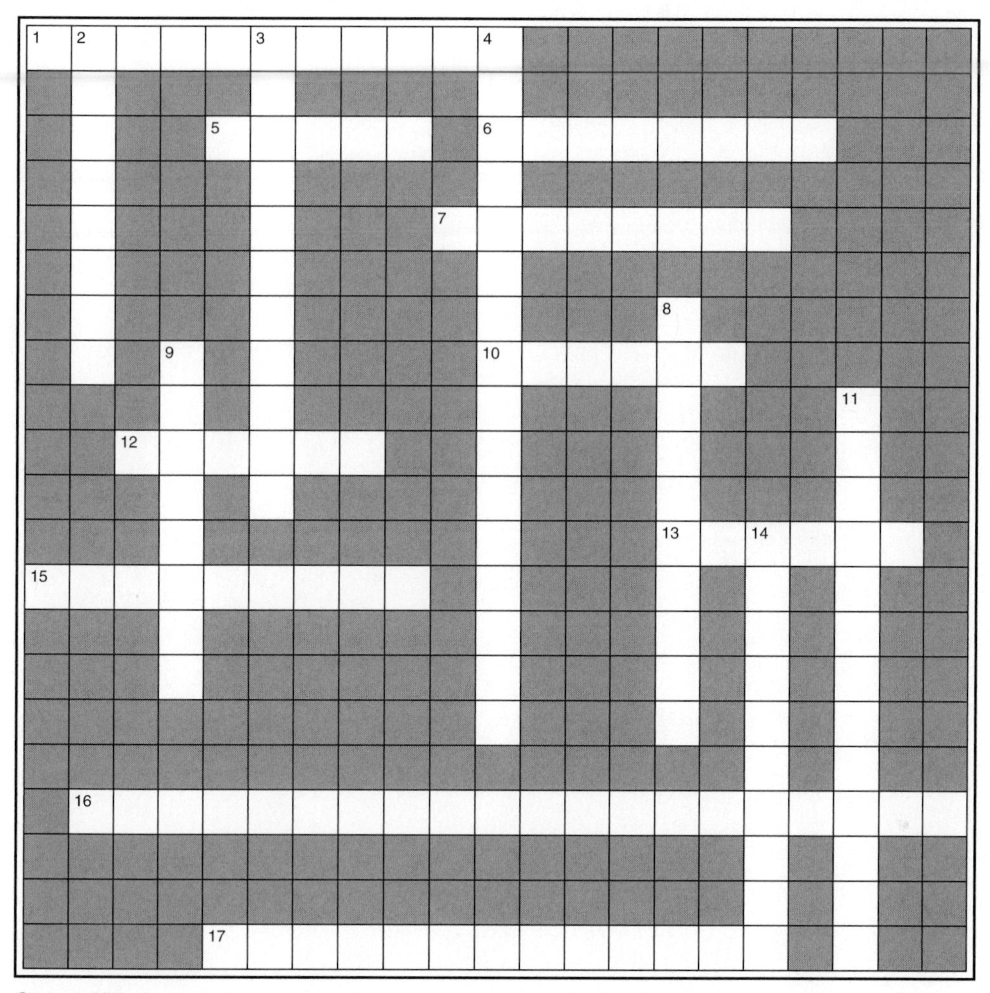

Caveat: Allow squares for spaces between words and punctuation (apostrophes, hyphens, etc.) when filling in crossword.

Across

1. The jury or the judge in a nonjury trial.
5. Chemical substances that have an effect on the body or mind.
6. Related by marriage.
7. The state of having several wives or husbands at the same time.
10. The state of a person with two spouses living at the same time.
12. Act often described as an "abominable and detestable crime against nature."
13. Sexual intercourse between people related by consanguinity.
15. Law passed by a city council.
16. A drug that is included in a schedule of the Federal Controlled Substances Act.
17. Marriage between people of different races.

Down

2. Sexual intercourse by a married person with someone other than a spouse.
3. Sexual intercourse between two unmarried persons.
4. Doubt based on reason.
8. Disability or hindrance to the making of a contract.
9. The act of stopping a pregnancy.
11. Related by blood.
14. Sexual intercourse.

PART THREE

TERMS USED IN LAW OF TORTS

3

Some wrongful acts, although not in themselves criminal, may cause injuries to other people. To provide monetary relief to people who suffer losses from the wrongs of others, the law of torts has developed over the years. Chapter 13 defines the elements of a tort action and then discusses imputed liability, liability of minors, immunity from tort liability, and joint tortfeasors. Chapter 14 explains the intentional torts of assault and battery, infliction of emotional distress, deceit, defamation, malicious prosecution, trespass, and conversion. The most common tort—negligence—is saved for last, where its elements, degrees, and defenses are examined in Chapter 15.

CHAPTER 13

Torts and Tortfeasors

ANTE INTERROGATORY

A tort is defined as (A) a breach of contract, (B) a wrong against the public at large, (C) a wrong against a town government, (D) a wrong against an individual.

CHAPTER OUTLINE

Elements of a Tort Action
Imputed Liability
Liability of Minors
Immunity from Tort Liability
Charitable Immunity
Sovereign Immunity
Joint Tortfeasors

3

KEY TERMS

agent *(AY·jent)*
cybertort *(SY·ber·tort)*
doctrine of charitable immunity *(DOK·trin ov CHAR·i·ta·bel im·YOO·ni·tee)*
doctrine of respondeat superior *(res·PON·dee·at soo·PEER·ee·or)*
doctrine of sovereign immunity *(SOV·er·in im·YOO·ni·tee)*
Good Samaritan statutes *(sem·EHR·i·ten STAT·shoot)*
immune *(im·YOON)*
imputed liability *(im·PEW·ted ly·a·BIL·i·tee)*
joint liability *(joynt ly·a·BIL·i·tee)*
joint tortfeasors *(tort·FEE·zors)*
master *(MAS·ter)*
principal *(PRIN·se·pel)*
right of contribution *(kon·tri·BYOO·shun)*
servant *(SER·vent)*
several liability *(SEV·er·el ly·a·BIL·i·tee)*
tort
tortfeasor *(tort·FEE·zor)*

A tort, which means "wrong" in French (from the Latin *tortus,* meaning "twisted"), is a wrong against an individual, as opposed to a crime, which is a wrong against the public at large. A tort action is a civil suit brought by the injured party to recover money damages to compensate him or her for losses caused by the tortious act of the **tortfeasor** (the one who commits the tort). It differs from a criminal action, which is brought by the state to punish the defendant for the wrongdoing. In some situations, such as in the case of assault and battery, the wrong is both a tort and a crime. In such a case, the state can bring a criminal action against the defendant, and the injured party can bring a separate tort action against the defendant for the same occurrence. The term **cybertort** means a tort associated with a computer.

In comparing a tort with a breach of contract, a tort is a breach of duty imposed by law, whereas a breach of contract is a breach of duty imposed by agreement of the parties.

ELEMENTS OF A TORT ACTION

Although each tort has its own particular elements that must be alleged and proved by the plaintiff to win a case, four basic elements are common to all torts. In general, the plaintiff must allege and prove all of the following:

1. The existence of a duty owed to the plaintiff by the defendant
2. A violation of that duty
3. A showing that the violation was the cause of the plaintiff's injuries
4. Damages

Several years ago, an intoxicated person tipped over while paddling a canoe on a lake. The proprietor of a boathouse watched on shore while the person yelled for help and finally drowned. The proprietor was sued by the decedent's estate for negligence (a tort to be discussed later) for not attempting to rescue the drowning person. The court held in favor of the boathouse proprietor, saying that he owed no duty to go to the rescue of the person who was drowning.

The rule that people are not legally bound to help others who are in trouble has been modified somewhat in recent years. For example, the janitor of a building was held to be negligent when he failed to turn off the electricity to an elevator when told that a child had climbed through the opening in the elevator car's roof. The child was killed when the elevator was set in motion by an unsuspecting person. In that case, the court held that the janitor owed a duty to go to the aid of the child by shutting off the electricity.

WORD WISE

Homonyms

Homonyms are words that have the same pronunciation but differ in meaning. Here are some examples:

Word	*Meaning*	*Examples*
principle	Rule; precept	It would be contrary to my *principles* to vote for that person.
		There were no guiding *principles* to follow when we landed on the moon.
principal	Chief; main	The *principal* of the school was the *principal* objector to the plan to invest the *principal* at 3 percent.
counsel	Advice; deliberation; one who gives advice	I asked my aunt's *counsel* before making my investments.
		The defendant consulted his *counsel* before answering the question.
council	An assembly	The city *council* discussed the matter at its last meeting.
		Council Bluffs, Iowa, commemorates the *council* that Lewis and Clark held with the Indians on the high bluffs.

Although in most cases people are not legally bound to help others, if they do so and are negligent, they will be liable for any injuries they cause. For this reason, people in the medical field would sometimes refuse to assist injured people at accident scenes or in other emergencies. States have passed laws, known as Good Samaritan statutes, to alleviate this problem. **Good Samaritan statutes** provide that physicians, nurses, and certain other medical personnel will not be liable for negligent acts that occur when they voluntarily, without a fee, render emergency care or treatment outside of the ordinary course of their practice.

IMPUTED LIABILITY

Although everyone is responsible for their own torts, in some situations one person may be held responsible for the torts that are committed by another person, which is known as **imputed liability.** It happens most frequently when an employee commits a tort while work for an employer. Under the **doctrine of respondeat superior, masters** (employers) can be held responsible for the torts of their **servants** (employees) that are committed within the scope of employment. Similarly, **principals** (people who authorize others to act for them) can be held responsible for the torts committed by their **agents** (people authorized to act) while acting within the scope of their authority. Similarly, a partner may be held liable for torts committed by another partner while acting in the ordinary course of the partnership.

LIABILITY OF MINORS

Minor children (those under the age of 18) are liable for their torts just the same as adults. It is usually impossible to collect court judgments from them, however, because in most cases they have no money. Under the common law, parents were not responsible for the torts of their minor child unless the act was committed in the parents' presence or while the minor was acting as the agent or servant of the parents. Some states have modified this rule by enacting statutes making parents liable up to a limited amount of money for the willful torts committed by their minor children.

IMMUNITY FROM TORT LIABILITY

In the past, charitable and governmental institutions could not be sued, with some exceptions, for their wrongdoings.

Charitable Immunity

Until recently, charitable institutions such as hospitals and churches were **immune**—that is, exempt—from tort liability. They could not be sued in tort for the wrongdoings of their agents or employees that occurred in the course of the charitable activity. This regulation was known as the **doctrine of charitable immunity.** By 1969, most U.S. states had abolished the doctrine of charitable immunity. To illustrate, in 1969, the Massachusetts Supreme Judicial Court (the highest court in that state) declared that it would abolish the doctrine in the next case involving that issue unless the legislature acted on the matter. This decision caused the Massachusetts legislature to pass a statute in 1971 abolishing the doctrine of charitable immunity in cases arising from a charity's commercial

Figure 13-1 In some states, parents are liable up to a limited amount of money for the intentional torts of their minor children.

activity and setting a limit of $20,000 on the amount that may be recovered from a charity for torts arising out of charitable activity.

Sovereign Immunity

The **doctrine of sovereign immunity,** which makes a governmental body immune from tort liability unless the government agrees to be held liable, stems from the old common law rule that "the king can do no wrong." For hundreds of years, under this doctrine, individuals could not sue the federal, state, or local government for its torts unless a statute allowed a suit for that particular wrong. This doctrine has also been modified by the U.S. Congress and by statute in many states.

For example, the U.S. government has waived its sovereign immunity to allow civil suits for actions arising out of negligent acts of its agents. To bring such an action, strict rules under the Federal Tort Claims Act must be followed precisely.

Under the Massachusetts Tort Claims Act, public employers (state and local governmental agencies) are liable for personal injury, property damage, or death caused by the negligent or wrongful act or omission of any public employee while acting within the scope of employment up to $100,000. In addition, the public employee whose negligent or wrongful act or omission caused the claim cannot be sued if the act occurred while he or she was acting within the scope of employment and if it was not an intentional tort. Before suit may be brought under the act, a claim must be presented in writing, within two years after the cause of action arose, to the executive officer of the public employer involved. The public employer has six months in which to pay the claim, deny it, refer it to arbitration, or reach a settlement. Only then may the suit be brought against the public employer, and it must be brought within three years after the cause of action arose.

JOINT TORTFEASORS

If more than one person participates in the commission of a tort, they are called **joint tortfeasors.** They may be held either jointly or severally liable for their wrongdoings. **Joint liability** means that all joint tortfeasors must be named as defendants in the lawsuit. **Several liability** means that the joint tortfeasors may be sued separately for the wrongdoing. By statute in some states, if one joint tortfeasor is required to pay more than his or her share to the injured party, he or she may sue the other joint tortfeasor for the excess. This regulation is known as the **right of contribution** between joint tortfeasors.

REVIEWING WHAT YOU LEARNED

After studying the text, write the answers to each of the following questions:

1. What is the difference between a tort and a crime? ______

2. Give an example of a wrong that is both a tort and a crime. ______

3. How does a tort differ from a breach of contract? ______

4. What four basic requirements must the plaintiff allege and prove to recover for a tort? ______

5. Describe a situation in which one person may be held responsible for the torts that are committed by another person. ______

6. What liability do minor children have for their torts? ______

7. In what way are parents liable today for torts committed by their children? ______

8. Describe the statute enacted in 1971 by the Massachusetts legislature dealing with the tort liability of a charitable organization. ______

9. Describe the main features of the Massachusetts Tort Claims Act. ______

10. What is the difference between joint liability and several liability? ______

UNDERSTANDING LEGAL CONCEPTS

Indicate whether each statement is true or false. Then, change the italicized word or phrase of each *false* statement to make it true.

Answers

_______________ **1.** A tort is a wrong against *society.*

_______________ **2.** Under the doctrine of *respondeat superior,* a governmental body is immune from tort liability.

_______________ **3.** In the past, charitable institutions and government bodies were immune from *tort* liability.

_______________ **4.** Master is the legal name that means *employer.*

_______________ **5.** *Several* liability means that all joint tortfeasors must be named as defendants in a lawsuit.

_______________ **6.** Minor children are liable for their *torts* just the same as adults.

_______________ **7.** In comparing a tort with a breach of contract, a tort is a breach of duty imposed by *the parties,* whereas a breach of contract is a breach of duty imposed by *law.*

_______________ **8.** A *tort* is a criminal action brought by the state to punish the defendant for the wrongdoing.

_______________ **9.** If one joint tortfeasor is required to pay more than his or her share to the injured party, he or she *may* sue the other joint tortfeasor for the excess.

_______________ **10.** An *agent* is a person who is authorized to act on behalf of another and subject to the other's control.

3

CHECKING TERMINOLOGY

From the list of legal terms that follows, select the one that matches each definition.

a. agent
b. doctrine of charitable immunity
c. doctrine of respondeat superior
d. doctrine of sovereign immunity
e. Good Samaritan statutes
f. immune
g. imputed liability

Answers

____ **1.** A wrong against an individual.

____ **2.** One who commits a tort.

____ **3.** Vicarious responsibility for the torts committed by another person.

____ **4.** A legal doctrine under which a master is responsible for the torts of his or her servants that are committed within the scope of employment.

____ **5.** An employer.

____ **6.** An employee.

____ **7.** A person who authorizes an agent to act on his or her behalf and subject to his or her control.

____ **8.** A person authorized to act on behalf of another and subject to the other's control.

____ **9.** Exempt.

h. joint liability
i. joint tortfeasors
j. master
k. principal
l. right of contribution
m. servant
n. several liability
o. tort
p. tortfeasor

____**10.** A legal doctrine under which charitable institutions are immune from tort liability.
____**11.** A legal doctrine under which governmental bodies are immune from tort liability.
____**12.** Two or more people who participate in the commission of a tort.
____**13.** Liability under which all joint tortfeasors must be named as defendants in a lawsuit.
____**14.** Liability under which joint tortfeasors may be sued separately in a lawsuit.
____**15.** The right to share a loss among joint tortfeasors or other codefendants.
____**16.** Laws providing that physicians, nurses, and certain other medical personnel will not be liable for negligent acts that occur when they voluntarily, without a fee, render emergency care or treatment outside of the ordinary course of their practice.

UNRAVELING LEGALESE

Use simple, non-legal language, with the help of the glossary, to rewrite this quote from the Federal Tort Claims Act so that it is shorter and can be understood by a layperson without losing its meaning.

> The United States shall be liable, respecting the provisions of this title relating to tort claims, in the same manner and to the same extent as a private individual under like circumstances, but shall not be liable for interest prior to judgment or for punitive damages. If, however, in any case wherein death was caused, the law of the place where the act or omission complained of occurred provides, or has been construed to provide, for damages only punitive in nature, the United States shall be liable for actual or compensatory damages, measured by the pecuniary injuries resulting from such death to the persons respectively, for whose benefit the action was brought, in lieu thereof.

USING LEGAL LANGUAGE

Read the following story and fill in the blank lines with legal terms taken from the list of terms at the beginning of this chapter.

Amy and Barry, while working for the Red Cross, committed a ____________ when they violated a duty imposed on them by law. Because they committed the wrongful act together, they were joint ____________, but because they could be sued separately, their liability was ____________ rather than ____________. Because the doctrine of ____________ no longer applies, the Red Cross, which is the ____________ of Amy and Barry, has ____________ liability for the torts of its ____________ under the doctrine of ____________. If it turns out that Amy is required to pay more than Barry for the damages they caused, Amy has the right of ____________ to recover the excess from Barry. This case is not one involving the doctrine of ____________, because it does not involve a governmental body being ____________ from tort liability, nor does it involve a(n) ____________ or ____________—that is, a person who authorizes another to act or one who is authorized to act.

3

PUZZLING OVER WHAT YOU LEARNED

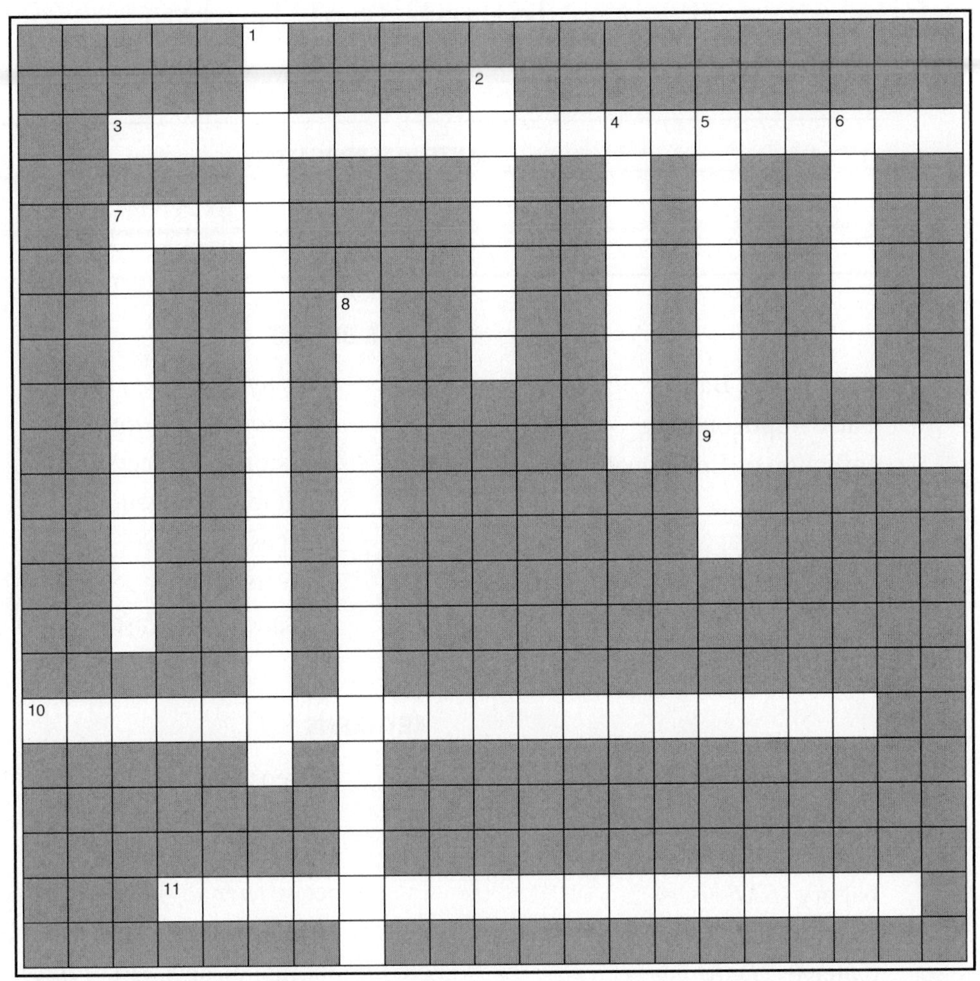

Caveat: Allow squares for spaces between words and punctuation (apostrophes, hyphens, etc.) when filling in crossword.

Across

3. Doctrine under which a master is responsible for the torts of his or her servants.
7. A wrong against an individual.
9. People authorized to act on behalf of others and subject to the others' control.
10. Doctrine under which charitable institutions are immune from tort liability.
11. Two or more people who participate in the commission of a tort.

Down

1. Vicarious responsibility for the torts committed by another person.
2. Employers.
4. Employees.
5. People who authorize agents to act on their behalf and subject to their control.
6. Exempt.
7. One who commits a tort.
8. Liability under which all joint tortfeasors must be named as defendants.

3

CHAPTER 14

Intentional Torts

ANTE INTERROGATORY

Defamation that is communicated by a writing is called (A) slander, (B) libel, (C) conversion, (D) deceit.

CHAPTER OUTLINE

KEY TERMS

acquitted *(a·KWIT·ed)*
actionable *(AK·shun·a·bel)*
assault *(a·SALT)*
battery *(BAT·er·ee)*
conversion *(kon·VER·shun)*
damages *(DAM·e·jez)*
deceit *(dee·SEET)*
defamation *(de·fa·MA·shun)*
emotional distress *(e·MO·shun·al dis·TRES)*
false arrest *(a·REST)*
false imprisonment *(im·PRIS·on·ment)*
fraud *(frawd)*
intentional torts *(in·TEN·shun·al)*
invasion of privacy *(in·VA·shun ov PRY·va·see)*
libel *(LY·bel)*
malicious prosecution *(ma·LISH·us pros·e·KYOO·shun)*
misrepresentation *(mis·rep·rez·en·TA·shun)*
nuisance *(NOO·sens)*
per se *(per say)*
private nuisance *(PRI·vet NOO·sens)*
public nuisance *(PUB·lik NOO·sens)*
right of privacy *(PRI·va·see)*
scienter *(si·EN·ter)*
slander *(SLAN·der)*
tortious *(TOR·shus)*
trespass *(TRES·pass)*
trespass de bonis asportatis *(de BO·nis as·por·TAH·tis)*
unintentional torts *(un·in·TEN·shun·al)*
waste
willful torts

Tortious (wrongful) acts may be committed either intentionally or unintentionally. Those that are committed intentionally—that is, deliberately rather than by accident or mistake—are known as **intentional** or **willful torts.** Conversely, those that are committed accidentally, such as negligence, are referred to as **unintentional torts.**

ASSAULT AND BATTERY

Assault and battery are examples of intentional torts that are also crimes. In such cases, the state can bring a criminal action, and, in addition, victims can bring a tort suit against the wrongdoer. **Battery** is defined as the intentional contact with another person without that person's permission and without justification. **Assault** is the intentional creation of a reasonable apprehension of an imminent battery. Pointing a gun at someone is an assault; the bullet striking the person is a battery.

Verbal threats alone, in most states, are not enough to be an assault. To convert a threat into an assault requires some act to indicate that the battery will ensue immediately. Although every battery includes an assault, an assault does not necessarily require a battery.

FALSE IMPRISONMENT

False imprisonment (also called **false arrest**) is the intentional confinement of a person without legal justification. It is a restraint on a person's liberty. The person who is confined need not be held within an enclosure of any kind or even touched by the other person. It is considered to be a confinement if a person apprehends that physical force will be used if he or she attempts to leave.

Many cases of false imprisonment arise out of situations in which suspected shoplifters are detained by store proprietors without reasonable grounds for doing so. The person who is detained sues the store for damages arising from the false imprisonment.

Store owners, in some states, have the protection of statutes that allow the detention, for a reasonable length of time and in a reasonable manner, of a person suspected of shoplifting if reasonable grounds for such suspicion exist. Generally, it is reasonable to detain a person if goods that were not purchased are concealed in the clothing or among the belongings of a shopper.

INFLICTION OF EMOTIONAL DISTRESS

Under earlier law, except in the case of false imprisonment, one could not recover damages from another for the infliction of emotional distress unless the emotional suffering was accompanied by some outer physical injury such as a break in the skin or a broken bone.

This earlier law was changed by court decisions and state statutes. For example, in a 1976 case, the manager of a restaurant called a meeting of all waitresses and told them that some stealing was occurring and that the identity of the person responsible was unknown. He said that until the person responsible was discovered, he would begin firing all the present waitresses in alphabetic order. He then fired a waitress whose name began with the letter "A," having no evidence that she had been involved in the thefts. She became greatly upset and began to cry, sustaining emotional distress and mental anguish. The court allowed her to recover damages for her emotional suffering.

The intentional tort of **emotional distress** is defined as emotional suffering caused by the infliction of extreme and outrageous intentional conduct by another.

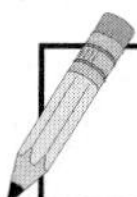

WORD WISE

Suffixes

Many words in this chapter are a combination of the basic part of a word, called a root, and a suffix, which is a word element that follows the root. Some of the words use suffixes to form nouns; others form adjectives. Some suffixes form both nouns and adjectives.

Suffixes that Form Nouns

Suffix	*Meaning*	*Examples*
-ment	State, quality, act of	imprisonment statement
-sion, -tion	Act or state of	defamation recognition

Suffixes that Form Adjectives

Suffix	*Meaning*	*Examples*
-able, -ible	Capable of	actionable visible
-al	Like, relating to	emotional intentional

Suffixes that Form Nouns or Adjectives

Suffix	*Meaning*	*Examples*
-ery, -ary, -ory, -ry	Relating to; connected with	robbery (noun) customary (adjective)
-ful	Full of	spoonful (noun) plentiful (adjective)

DECEIT

The tort of **deceit,** which is also known as **fraud** or *fraudulent misrepresentation,* comes about when one person, by false representation of material facts, induces another to act and thereby suffer a financial loss. To recover for this tort, the plaintiff must allege and prove all of the following five elements:

1. A misrepresentation of a material, existing fact
2. Made with knowledge of its falsity
3. Made with the intent that it be relied on
4. That it was reasonably relied on
5. Damages

To be actionable, the **misrepresentation** (false or deceptive statement or act) must be of a material, existing fact. It is not actionable if it is an opinion or a promise of something to happen in the future.

The misrepresentation must be made with knowledge of its falsity. This act is known as the **scienter** requirement, which is from the Latin word meaning "knowingly." This element of deceit may be satisfied if the person who made the misrepresentation had actual knowledge of its falsity or made it recklessly without regard to its truth or falsity. In some states, it may also be satisfied if the person who made the misrepresentation actually had no knowledge of its falsity but was susceptible of knowledge—that is, was in a position in which he or she was expected to know.

To illustrate the latter, in some states if a buyer asks a homeowner who is selling a house, "Does the house have termites?" and the homeowner does not know whether it does or not but replies, "No, it does not have termites," the court will hold that the homeowner was susceptible of knowledge and therefore satisfied the knowledge requirement.

The person who makes the misrepresentation must intend that the other person rely on it. Suppose, for example, that A made false representations when he sold goods to B. B then sold the goods to C. C would have no right of action against A for the misrepresentations because A did not intend that C rely on them.

In addition, the person to whom the misrepresentation was made must reasonably rely on it. Suppose, for example, that a prospective buyer of a house says to the owner, "Does the house have termites?" and the owner replies, "No, it does not have termites." If the buyer, before buying, has the house inspected by a termite inspector who negligently fails to discover termites that are in the house, the buyer could not sue the seller for deceit, because the buyer did not rely on the seller's misrepresentation.

To recover for deceit, the injured party must prove that he or she suffered some **damage** (financial loss) as a result of the misrepresentation.

DEFAMATION

Defamation is the wrongful act of damaging another's character or reputation by the use of false statements. It is divided into two classes, libel and slander. **Libel** is defamation that is communicated by a writing, drawing, photograph, television program, or other means that is directed toward the sense of sight. **Slander** is defamation that is communicated by the spoken word. It is a communication that is directed toward the sense of hearing.

To be **actionable**—that is, to furnish legal ground for a lawsuit—both libel and slander must be communicated to a third person. Unless a third person hears or sees the defamatory material, no one can sue.

Libel

Because of its more permanent, longer-lasting form and its ability to reach more people, libel is considered to be more serious than slander. It is actionable **per se**—that is, in and of itself. Suit can be brought in all instances of libel.

Slander

Slander, conversely, is not actionable per se. It is actionable only in the following situations:

1. When someone is falsely accused of committing a crime of moral turpitude
2. When someone is falsely accused of having a contagious disease, such as leprosy, AIDS, or venereal disease
3. When someone makes a false statement that injures a person in his or her business, profession, or trade
4. When the injured person can prove that he or she suffered special damages from the slanderous statements

Slander that does not fall within the preceding four categories cannot be a reason to sue.

WEB WISE

- To read current information about defamation, go to **www.findlaw.com.** At that site, click "Legal Subjects." From the list that follows, select "Injury and Tort Law." Then click "Findlaw Library," followed by "Defamation/Libel/Slander."
- For a summary of your state law on wiretapping and eavesdropping, log on to **www.google.com.** Type in the words "wiretapping and eavesdropping laws" and click "State-by-state summaries."

Privileges and Defenses to Defamation

The law gives privileges to certain people, making them immune from suit for slander and libel. Judges, lawyers, and witnesses, while they are participating in trials, and members of the legislature, during its sessions, have an absolute privilege against defamation suits. They cannot be sued for libel or slander.

Newspapers have a qualified privilege when they report about public events and matters of public concern. Actual malice on the part of the newspaper must be proved for someone to recover damages from the newspaper in such cases. Public figures such as actors, actresses, and politicians must prove that the defamatory material was spoken or written with actual malice before they can recover damages against others for defamation.

Truth is an absolute defense against libel or slander.

INVASION OF PRIVACY

The **right of privacy** encompasses the right to be left alone, the right to be free from uncalled-for publicity, and the right to live without unreasonable interference by the public in private matters. A violation of the right of privacy is known as **invasion of privacy.** Using someone's photograph without permission for advertising purposes, wiretapping someone's house, and publishing someone's medical or financial condition are examples of invasion of privacy. In 2002, a special federal appeals court gave the U.S. government permission to use secret wiretaps as a weapon against terrorism.

Figure 14-1 An acquittal is a discharge from civil or criminal liability. (NON SEQUITOR © Wiley Miller. Dist. By UNIVERSAL PRESS SYNDICATE. Reprinted with permission. All rights reserved.)

MALICIOUS PROSECUTION

The right of action for the tort of **malicious prosecution** arises when one person has unsuccessfully brought criminal or civil charges against another with malice and without probable cause. The one against whom the charges were brought may bring a tort suit against the person who brought the charges for malicious prosecution. To bring such a suit, all of the following must be proved:

1. Criminal or civil charges were brought against the plaintiff.
2. The plaintiff was **acquitted**—that is, discharged from accusation.
3. The defendant brought the charges maliciously and without probable cause.

TRESPASS

The intentional and unauthorized entry on the land of another is called **trespass.** Suit may be brought against a trespasser by the one who is in possession of the land whether or not he or she has suffered any damages from the trespass. It has been held to be a trespass to do any of the following: step on another's land without permission, hit a golf ball into another's airspace, and string a wire into another's airspace.

Trespass to personal property is a tort called **trespass de bonis asportatis** (trespass for goods carried away). To recover for this tort, it is necessary to prove that actual damages occurred as a result of the trespass.

CONVERSION

Conversion is the wrongful exercise of dominion and control over the personal property in the possession of another. It is different from trespass in that it is using another's property as though it belonged to the wrongdoer rather than interfering with the owner's possession as in trespass. Some examples of conversion are misdelivery of goods by a carrier, theft of goods, failure to return borrowed goods, and sale of goods belonging to another without authority.

NUISANCE AND WASTE

The tort of **nuisance** involves the use of one's property in a way that causes annoyance, inconvenience, or discomfort to another. The emission of smoke, offensive odors, and loud noises often generate nuisance lawsuits. Airlines are sometimes sued, for example, by people who live near airports because of the loud noise, smoke, and odors of the planes taking off. The tort is called a **public nuisance** when the disturbance affects the community at large and a **private nuisance** when it disturbs one neighbor only.

Another tort, called **waste,** is the abuse or destructive use of property that is in one's rightful possession. A tenant who damages the landlord's property, for example, commits the tort of waste.

REVIEWING WHAT YOU LEARNED

After studying the text, write the answers to each of the following questions.

1. What must occur to convert a verbal threat into an assault? ____________________

2. Out of what situations do many false imprisonment cases arise? ____________________

3. What five elements must the plaintiff allege and prove to recover for fraud or deceit? ____________________

4. Give an example of a person not relying on a misrepresentation and thus not being able to recover for fraud or deceit. ____________________

5. What is the difference between libel and slander? ____________________

6. To whom must libel and slander be communicated to be actionable? ____________________

7. When is libel actionable? ____________________

8. When is slander actionable? ____________________

9. What people enjoy an absolute privilege against defamation suits? ____________________

10. What must be proved for someone to recover for libel from a newspaper when it reports about public events and matters of public concern? ____________________

11. What three elements must be proved for one to recover for malicious prosecution? ____________________

12. Give three examples of trespass to real property. ____________________

13. Give three examples of conversion. ____________________

3

UNDERSTANDING LEGAL CONCEPTS

Indicate whether each statement is true or false. Then, change the italicized word or phrase of each *false* statement to make it true.

Answers

1. In the case of false imprisonment, the person confined *must be* held within an enclosure of some kind.
2. Although every battery includes an assault, an *assault* does not necessarily require a battery.
3. Verbal threats alone *are* enough to be an assault.
4. To be actionable fraud, the misrepresentation *must be* an opinion or a promise of something to happen in the future.
5. To recover for emotional suffering, the plaintiff must prove that the emotional suffering was caused by the *extreme and outrageous* intentional conduct of the defendant.
6. To be actionable, *both* libel and slander must be communicated to a third person.
7. *Libel* is defamation that is directed toward the sense of hearing.
8. *Slander* is actionable per se.
9. Hitting a golf ball into another's airspace is *not* a trespass.
10. Failing to return borrowed goods is an example of *conversion*.

CHECKING TERMINOLOGY

From the list of legal terms that follows, select the one that matches each definition.

a. acquitted
b. actionable
c. assault
d. battery
e. conversion
f. damages
g. deceit
h. defamation
i. emotional distress
j. false arrest
k. false imprisonment
l. fraud
m. intentional torts
n. invasion of privacy
o. libel
p. malicious prosecution
q. misrepresentation
r. nuisance
s. per se
t. private nuisance
u. public nuisance
v. right of privacy
w. scienter
x. slander
y. tortious
z. trespass
aa. trespass de bonis asportatis
bb. unintentional torts
cc. waste
dd. willful torts

Answers

____ **1.** The wrongful act of damaging another's character or reputation by the use of false statements.

____ **2.** Defamation that is communicated by a writing or by other means that is directed toward the sense of sight.

____ **3.** Defamation that is communicated by the spoken word.

____ **4.** In and of itself; taken alone.

____ **5.** Prosecution begun in malice without probable cause.

____ **6.** The intentional and unauthorized entry on the land of another.

____ **7.** The wrongful exercise of dominion and control over the personal property in another's possession.

____ **8.** Wrongful; implying or involving tort.

____ **9.** Torts that are committed intentionally (select two answers).

____ **10.** The intentional contact with another person without that person's permission and without justification.

____ **11.** The intentional creation of a reasonable apprehension of an imminent battery.

____ **12.** The intentional confinement of a person without legal justification (select two answers).

____ **13.** A misrepresentation of a material, existing fact, knowingly made, that causes someone reasonably relying on it to suffer damages (select two answers).

____ **14.** A false or deceptive statement or act.

____ **15.** The monetary loss suffered by a party as a result of a wrong.

____ **16.** Discharged from accusation.

____ **17.** Furnishing legal ground for a lawsuit.

____ **18.** Trespass for goods carried away.

____ **19.** Emotional suffering caused by the infliction of extreme and outrageous intentional conduct by another.

____ **20.** Knowingly.

____ **21.** Torts that are committed accidentally.

____ **22.** A violation of the right of privacy.

____ **23.** The use of one's property in a way that causes annoyance, inconvenience, or discomfort to another.

____ **24.** A nuisance that affects the community at large.

____ **25.** The right to be left alone, the right to be free from uncalled-for publicity, and the right to live without unreasonable interference by the public in private matters.

____ **26.** The abuse or destructive use of property that is in one's rightful possession.

____ **27.** A nuisance that disturbs one neighbor only.

UNRAVELING LEGALESE

Use simple, non-legal language, with the help of the glossary, to rewrite this case quote so that it is shorter and can be understood by a layperson without losing its meaning.

> Under New York law, trespass is the intentional invasion of another's property. To be liable, the trespasser need not intend or expect the damaging consequences of his intrusion; rather, he need only intend the act which amounts to or produces the unlawful invasion. The intrusion itself must at least be the immediate or inevitable consequence of what the trespasser willfully does, or which he does so negligently as to amount to willfulness.

USING LEGAL LANGUAGE

Read the following story and fill in the blank lines with legal terms taken from the list of terms at the beginning of this chapter.

While looking at cars in a used car lot, Henry recognized a car that had once belonged to his friend Sam. He knew that the car had been abused by Sam and was in poor condition. A salesperson, noticing Henry looking at the car, went up to Henry and said: "This car's a beauty! It belonged to a little old lady who took it out only on Sunday morning to drive to church." Angered by this ______________________ and knowing that the salesperson was committing ______________________, which is also known as ______________________, Henry picked up a hubcap that was on the ground, threw it at the salesperson, but missed. Legally, this action was ______________________ but not ______________________. In any case, it was a(n) ______________________ act. The salesperson, now enraged, grabbed an innocent passerby, thinking she was with Henry. He detained the passerby in his office for 10 minutes, thereby committing the tort of ______________________, which is also called ______________________. Later that day, Henry accidentally sold his next-door neighbor's lawn mower to a stranger at his yard sale. When his next-door neighbor, Martha, learned of the ______________________, she called up her friend Mildred and told her that Henry was a no-good dirty rat. Although this statement was a form of ______________________, it was not actionable ______________________, because it was not one of the four situations for which suit may be brought. Later, Martha wrote a letter to the editor of the local newspaper, saying that Henry was a no-good dirty rat. The newspaper refused to print the letter because it did not want to be sued for ______________________, which is actionable ______________________. When Henry heard that Martha had written the letter to the newspaper, he went outside, picked up a huge pile of trash from his yard, and dumped it all over Martha's front lawn, thereby committing the tort of ______________________. He then swore out a criminal complaint against Martha for disturbing the peace. Martha was tried for the crime and found not guilty. She then sued Henry in tort for ______________________ ______________________.

PUZZLING OVER WHAT YOU LEARNED

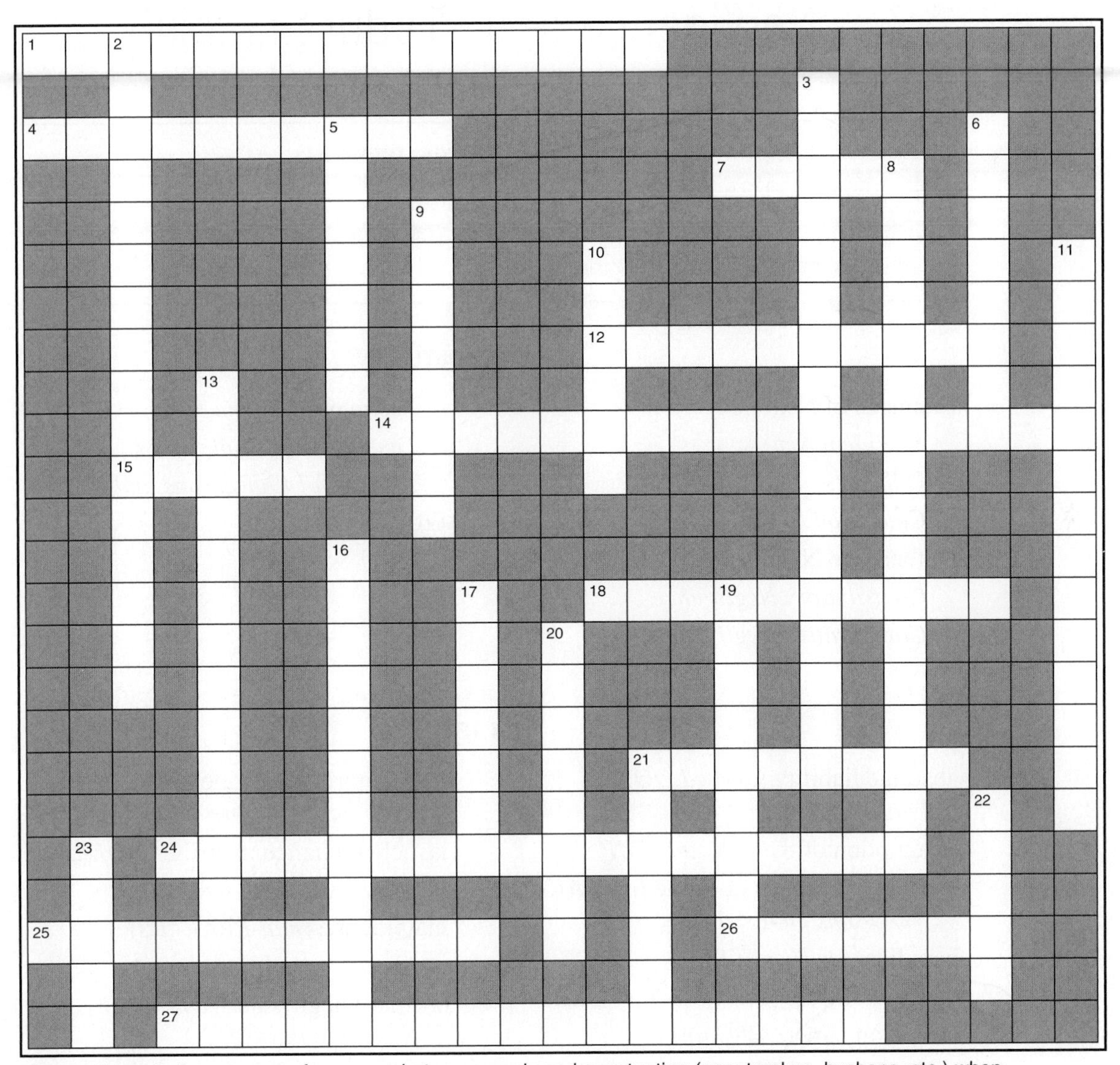

Caveat: Do **not** allow squares for spaces between words and punctuation (apostrophes, hyphens, etc.) when filling in crossword.

Across

1. A nuisance that disturbs one neighbor only.
4. Furnishing legal ground for a lawsuit.
7. The abuse or destructive use of property that is in one's rightful possession.
12. The wrongful exercise of dominion and control over the personal property of another.
14. The intentional confinement of a person without legal justification.
15. Defamation that is communicated by a writing.
18. The wrongful act of damaging another's character or reputation by the use of false statements.
21. Knowingly.
24. Torts that are committed accidentally.
25. Another name for false imprisonment.
26. The monetary loss suffered by a party as a result of a wrong.
27. A violation of the right of privacy.

Down

2. Torts that are committed intentionally.
3. A false or deceptive statement or act.
5. The intentional contact with another person without that person's permission and without justification.
6. The use of one's property in a way that causes annoyance to another.
8. Emotional suffering caused by the infliction of extreme and outrageous intentional conduct by another.
9. The intentional and unauthorized entry on the land of another.
10. Another name for fraud.
11. The right to be left alone.
13. A nuisance that affects the community at large.
16. Another name for intentional torts.
17. The intentional creation of a reasonable apprehension of an imminent battery.
19. Discharged from accusation.
20. Wrongful; implying or involving tort.
21. Defamation that is communicated by the spoken word.
22. In and of itself; taken alone.
23. A misrepresentation of a material, existing fact, knowingly made, that causes someone reasonably relying on it to suffer damages.

CHAPTER 15

Negligence and Product Liability

ANTE INTERROGATORY

The doctrine that protects children who trespass is called the (A) attractive nuisance doctrine, (B) contributory negligence doctrine, (C) comparative negligence doctrine, (D) assumption of the risk doctrine.

CHAPTER OUTLINE

Elements of Negligence
- *Negligent Act*
- *Damages*
- *Causation*

Defenses to Negligence
- *Contributory Negligence*
- *Comparative Negligence*
- *Assumption of the Risk*
- *Discharge in Bankruptcy*
- *Statutes of Limitations and Repose*

Product Liability

KEY TERMS

absolute liability *(ab·so·LOOT ly·a·BIL·i·tee)*
assumption of the risk *(a·SUMP·shun)*
attractive nuisance doctrine *(a·TRAK·tiv NOO·sens DOK·trin)*
bare licensee *(ly·sen·SEE)*
business invitee *(BIZ·ness in·vy·TEE)*
causation *(kaw·ZAY·shun)*
comparative negligence *(kom·PAR·e·tiv NEG·li·jens)*
contributory negligence *(kon·TRIB·u·tor·ee NEG·li·jens)*
culpable negligence *(KUL·pa·bel NEG·li·jens)*
damages *(DAM·e·jez)*
dangerous instrumentalities *(DAYN·jer·ess in·stroo·men·TAL·i·tees)*
fact finder *(fakt FINE·der)*
foreseeable *(fore·SEE·a·bel)*
gratuitous guest *(gra·TOO·i·tes)*
gross negligence *(NEG·li·jens)*
humanitarian doctrine *(hew·man·i·TAR·ee·en DOK·trin)*
last clear chance doctrine *(DOK·trin)*
liability *(ly·a·BIL·i·tee)*
malpractice *(mal·PRAK·tiss)*
negligence *(NEG·li·jens)*
ordinary negligence *(OR·di·ner·ee NEG·li·jens)*
pain and suffering *(SUF·er·ing)*
privity of contract *(PRIV·i·tee ov KON·trakt)*
product liability *(PROD·ukt ly·a·BIL·i·tee)*
proximate cause *(PROK·si·met kaws)*
prudent *(PROO·dent)*
reasonable care *(REE·zen·e·bel)*
res ipsa loquitur *(reyz IP·sa LO·kwe·ter)*
statute of limitations *(STAT·shoot ov lim·i·TA·shuns)*
statute of repose *(STAT·shoot ov re·POSE)*
strict liability *(strikt ly·a·BIL·i·tee)*

3

supervening cause *(su·per·VEEN·ing)*
willful, wanton, and reckless conduct *(WIL·ful WON·ten and REK·les KON·dukt)*
wrongful death action *(RONG·ful deth AK·shun)*
wrongful death statutes *(RONG·ful deth STAT·shoots)*

Negligence occurs when one person suffers a loss because of the carelessness of another person. It is an unintentional tort and is the subject matter of more lawsuits than any other tort. **Negligence** is defined as the failure to use the amount of care and skill that a reasonably prudent person would have used under the same circumstances and conditions.

ELEMENTS OF NEGLIGENCE

To recover for negligence, the injured party must prove all of the following:

1. A negligent act
2. Damages
3. Causation

3

Negligent Act

Whether or not an act is negligent is normally a question of fact (rather than a question of law) to be decided by the fact finder. The **fact finder** is the jury in a jury trial or the judge in a nonjury trial. The fact finder must ask the question: "Did the defendant do (or fail to do) that which a reasonably **prudent** (cautious) person would have done under the same circumstances and conditions?" If the defendant is a child, the fact finder must ask: "Did the defendant exercise the degree of care that a reasonably prudent child of the same age, intelligence, and experience would have exercised under the same circumstances and conditions?" If the defendant is a physician, the fact finder must ask: "Did the defendant exercise the degree of care and skill of the average qualified physician, considering the advances in the medical profession?" Negligence of a physician, attorney, or other professional is commonly referred to as **malpractice.**

For a negligent act to occur, a duty must be owed by the defendant to the plaintiff, and a breach of that duty must occur. Until recently, the law recognized different *degrees of care* owed to different people. The duty of care owed to a **business invitee** (one invited on the premises for a business or commercial purpose) was to refrain from **ordinary negligence** (the want of ordinary care). The duty of care owed to a **gratuitous guest** (one invited on the premises for nonbusiness purposes) was to refrain from gross negligence. **Gross negligence** is extreme negligence. Under this older law, a gratuitous guest could not recover for damages caused by a host's ordinary negligence. The duty of care owed to a trespasser and a **bare licensee** (a person allowed on another's premises by operation of law such as a firefighter or police officer) was to refrain from **willful, wanton, and reckless conduct.** This conduct, also called **culpable negligence,** is the intentional commission of an act that a reasonable person knows would cause injury to another. It is more serious than gross negligence.

Many states have eliminated the different degrees of negligence. Instead, they hold that property owners owe a duty to use **reasonable care** toward everyone who is rightfully on their premises. This degree of care is one that a reasonable person would have used under the circumstances then known. Because a trespasser is not rightfully on the premises, the duty of care owed to such a person is to refrain from willful, wanton, and reckless conduct.

One exception to the latter rule is the **attractive nuisance doctrine,** which protects children who are enticed to trespass on another's property because of an attraction that exists there such as a swimming pool in a backyard. In states that follow the doctrine, property owners owe a duty to refrain from ordinary negligence, rather than willful, wanton, and reckless conduct, toward children who are attracted to the premises by a condition that normally attracts children, even though they are trespassers.

Doctrine of Res Ipsa Loquitur. To recover for negligence, evidence must be introduced by the plaintiff to prove the negligent act of the defendant. Sometimes the plaintiff has no evidence to prove that a negligent act was committed by the defendant; however, the plaintiff can prove that he or she was injured by an act that normally does not occur unless someone is negligent such as in a rear-end automobile collision. The doctrine of **res ipsa loquitur,** which means "the thing speaks for itself," can sometimes be used by the plaintiff when he or she cannot prove an actual negligent act of the defendant. Under this doctrine, the mere fact that an act occurred can be used by the jury (or by the judge in a nonjury trial) to infer that the defendant was negligent. When the doctrine is used, the case can go to the jury if it is probable (not just possible) that a negligent act of the defendant caused the plaintiff's injury.

Absolute Liability. People who handle **dangerous instrumentalities** such as explosives or wild animals are liable, regardless of fault, for injuries to others caused by the dangerous item. Such liability regardless of fault is known as **absolute** or **strict liability.**

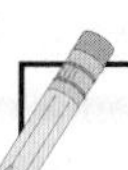

WORD WISE

Res Ipsa Loquitur ("the thing speaks for itself")

The "ipsa" in *res ipsa loquitur* is a form of the Latin term *ipse* meaning "myself, himself, herself, or itself." Here are some other uses of the term:

ipse dixit = he himself said it (something asserted but not proved).

ipso facto = by the fact (or act) itself (by the mere effect or nature of an act or fact).

ipso jure = by the law itself (by the mere operation of the law).

Damages

To recover for negligence, the plaintiff must prove **damages**—that is, some actual loss. Even though a negligent act may be committed by the defendant, no recovery by the plaintiff can occur unless he or she suffers damages. Various kinds of damages are discussed in Chapter 18.

The amount of damages that the plaintiff can recover is the amount of money that will place the plaintiff in the same position that he or she was in immediately before the negligent act occurred. Damages include the cost of hospital and medical treatment, any loss of wages, and an amount of money to compensate for **pain and suffering** (physical discomfort and emotional trauma) endured by the plaintiff.

When someone dies as a result of another's negligence, the suit that is brought is called a **wrongful death action,** which is a suit brought by the decedent's personal representative against the negligent party for the benefit of the decedent's heirs. Such suits are governed by **wrongful death statutes** found in each state.

Causation

To recover for negligence, the plaintiff must prove **causation**—that is, that the negligent act of the defendant was the direct and **proximate cause** (the dominant, or moving, cause) of the plaintiff's injuries. In determining proximate cause, the court asks whether the harm that resulted from the conduct was **foreseeable** (known in advance; anticipated) when it took place. In a case in which an intoxicated person was served liquor in a bar and on leaving the bar drove negligently into another car, killing someone, the court held that the bartender's act of serving a drink to the intoxicated person was the proximate cause of death. The court said that the bartender could have foreseen that the intoxicated person would be driving home and might cause death or injury to another.

No recovery can occur, conversely, if a break in the chain of causation exists. For example, when a car owner leaves the key in a car (which is a statutory violation in some states) and a thief steals the car and injures someone while driving negligently, the act of leaving the key in the car is not the direct and proximate cause of the injury. Rather, the negligent act of the thief was a **supervening cause**—that is, a new occurrence that became the proximate cause of the injury. The injured party cannot recover from the car owner.

3

DEFENSES TO NEGLIGENCE

The principal defenses to negligence actions are (1) contributory negligence, (2) comparative negligence, (3) assumption of the risk, (4) discharge in bankruptcy, and (5) running of the statute of limitations.

Contributory Negligence

Contributory negligence is negligence on the part of the plaintiff that contributed toward the injuries and was a proximate cause of them. Under the doctrine of contributory negligence, when the plaintiff sues the defendant for negligence, if the defendant can prove that the plaintiff was also negligent, no matter how slight, the plaintiff can recover nothing. An exception exists under a rule known as the **last clear chance doctrine** in some states and as the **humanitarian doctrine** in others. Under this doctrine, a defendant who had the last clear chance to have avoided injuring the plaintiff is liable even though the plaintiff had also been contributorily negligent.

Many states no longer follow the doctrine of contributory negligence, because of its unfairness to plaintiffs who were only slightly negligent. These states have adopted the doctrine of comparative negligence in its place.

Comparative Negligence

Under the doctrine of **comparative negligence,** each party's negligence is compared, and the plaintiff's damages are reduced in proportion to his or her negligence. In determining by what amount the plaintiff's damages are to be diminished, the negligence of the plaintiff is compared to the total of all persons against whom recovery is sought. The combined total of the plaintiff's negligence and all the negligence of all defendants must equal 100 percent. For example, in a case in which the total damages are $100,000, if the jury finds that the plaintiff was 40 percent negligent and the defendant was 60 percent negligent, the plaintiff will recover $60,000. In the same case, if the jury finds that each party was 50 percent negligent, the plaintiff will recover $50,000. If the jury finds that the plaintiff was 51 percent negligent and the defendant was 49 percent negligent, the plaintiff will recover nothing.

Assumption of the Risk

In a suit for negligence, if the defendant can show that the plaintiff knew of the risk involved and took the chance of being injured, he or she may claim **assumption of the risk** as a defense. This defense has sometimes been used by baseball clubs when they are sued by spectators who are injured by baseballs hit into the stands.

Discharge in Bankruptcy

A cause of action for negligence against a defendant cannot be sued on if the defendant is discharged in bankruptcy and the plaintiff's claim is included among the defendant's debts.

Statutes of Limitations and Repose

Every cause of action has a time limit for bringing suit. A **statute of limitations** is a time limit, set by statute, within which a suit must be commenced after the cause of action accrues. A cause of action accrues when a suit may be brought for damages. In negligence cases, the statute of limitations begins to run either on the date of the injury or on the date that the injury is or should have been discovered. A **statute of repose,** on the other hand, places an absolute time limit for bringing a cause of action regardless of when the cause of action accrues. The following is an example of a statute that contains both a statute of limitations and a statute of repose.

> An action of tort for damages arising out of any deficiency or neglect on the design, planning, construction, or general administration of an improvement to real property shall be commenced only within three years next after the cause of action accrues; provided, however, that in no event shall such actions be commenced more than six years after the substantial completion of the improvement and the taking of possession for occupancy by the owner.

The first part of the statute (a statute of limitations) contains a time limit of three years from the date of injury for bringing suit, which could be any number of years after the completion of the improvement. The second part (a statute of repose), however, places an absolute time limit for bringing a suit of six years following the completion and taking of possession by the owner.

PRODUCT LIABILITY

Liability (legal responsibility) of manufacturers and sellers to compensate people for injuries suffered because of defects in their products is a tort known as **product liability.** Under modern legal theory, people who are injured by defective products can bring suit against the manufacturers or sellers of the products whether or not they purchased them. There is no requirement of **privity of contract** (relationship between contracting parties) to recover for injuries from defective goods. In addition, it is not necessary to prove a negligent act on the part of the manufacturer or seller. Under a theory of **strict liability,** manufacturers and sellers are liable without regard to fault. They can be held liable if it can be shown that the product was sold in a defective condition, that it was unreasonably dangerous to the user or consumer, and that the defective condition was the proximate cause of the injury or damage.

REVIEWING WHAT YOU LEARNED

After studying the text, write the answers to each of the following questions:

1. Name the tort that is the subject matter of more lawsuits than any other tort. ______________

2. List three elements that an injured party must prove to recover for negligence. ______________

3. Who is the fact finder in a jury trial? In a nonjury trial? ______________

4. What degree of care must be exercised by a child to avoid negligence? ______________

5. What degree of care must be exercised by a physician to avoid negligence? ______________

6. Until recently, what degree of care was owed to a business invitee? To a gratuitous guest? To a bare licensee? ______________

7. What degree of care is owed to the preceding people (question 6) under modern law in many states? ______________

8. What degree of care is owed to a trespasser? ______________

9. When may the doctrine of res ipsa loquitur be used to prove negligence? ______________

10. What is the amount of money that the plaintiff can recover in a negligence action? ______________

11. Damages include what three elements? ______________

12. What must the plaintiff prove relative to causation to recover for negligence? ______________

13. List five defenses to negligence. ____________

14. What is the difference between contributory negligence and comparative negligence? ____________

15. What defense is sometimes used by a baseball club when it is sued by a spectator who is injured by a ball that is hit into the stands? ____________

16. What is the difference between a statute of limitations and a statute of repose? ____________

UNDERSTANDING LEGAL CONCEPTS

Indicate whether each statement is true or false. Then, change the italicized word or phrase of each *false* statement to make it true.

Answers

______ 1. Whether or not an act is negligent is normally a question of *law*.

______ 2. For a *negligent* act to occur, a duty must be owed by the defendant to the plaintiff, and a breach of that duty must occur.

______ 3. In states that follow the attractive nuisance doctrine, property owners owe a duty to refrain from *gross negligence* toward children who are attracted to the premises by a condition that normally attracts children.

______ 4. When the doctrine of res ipsa loquitur is used, the case can go to the jury if it is *probable* that a negligent act of the defendant caused the plaintiff's injury.

______ 5. Even though a negligent act may be committed by the defendant, no recovery by the plaintiff can occur unless he or she *suffers damages.*

______ 6. When a thief steals a car with keys left in it and injures a pedestrian, the pedestrian *can* recover from the car owner for damages.

______ 7. Many states *no longer* follow the doctrine of contributory negligence, because of its unfairness to plaintiffs who were only slightly negligent.

______ 8. Contributory negligence is negligence on the part of the *defendant,* which contributed toward the injuries and was a proximate cause of them.

______ 9. In a case involving comparative negligence, if the jury finds that the plaintiff was 51 percent negligent and the defendant was 49 percent negligent, the plaintiff will recover *nothing.*

______ 10. *No* time limit exists for bringing suit for the tort of negligence.

3

CHECKING TERMINOLOGY

From the list of legal terms that follows, select the one that matches each definition.

a. absolute liability
b. assumption of the risk
c. attractive nuisance doctrine
d. bare licensee
e. business invitee
f. causation
g. comparative negligence
h. contributory negligence
i. culpable negligence
j. damages
k. dangerous instrumentalities
l. fact finder
m. foreseeable
n. gratuitous guest
o. gross negligence
p. humanitarian doctrine
q. last clear chance doctrine
r. liability
s. malpractice
t. negligence
u. ordinary negligence
v. pain and suffering
w. privity of contract
x. product liability
y. proximate cause
z. prudent
aa. reasonable care
bb. res ipsa loquitur

Answers

____ **1.** Extreme negligence.
____ **2.** One invited on the premises for a business or commercial purpose.
____ **3.** The thing speaks for itself.
____ **4.** A time limit, set by statute, within which a suit must be commenced after the cause of action accrues.
____ **5.** The intentional commission of an act that a reasonable person knows would cause injury to another (select two answers).
____ **6.** A relationship between contracting parties.
____ **7.** The failure to use that amount of care and skill that a reasonably prudent person would have used under the same circumstances and conditions.
____ **8.** A person allowed on another's premises by operation of law, such as a fire fighter or police officer.
____ **9.** A doctrine under which a defendant who had the last clear chance to have avoided injuring the plaintiff is liable even though the plaintiff had also been contributorily negligent (select two answers).
____ **10.** A monetary loss suffered by a party as a result of a wrong.
____ **11.** Plaintiff assumes consequences of injury; employee agrees that dangers of injury shall be at his or her own risk.
____ **12.** Professional misconduct; negligence of a professional.
____ **13.** The degree of care that a reasonable person would have used under the circumstances then known.
____ **14.** Liability of manufacturers and sellers to compensate people for injuries suffered because of defects in their products.
____ **15.** The proportionate sharing between the plaintiff and the defendant of compensation for injuries, based on the relative negligence of the two.
____ **16.** A new occurrence that became the proximate cause of the injury.
____ **17.** One invited on the premises for nonbusiness purposes.
____ **18.** The jury in a jury trial or the judge in a nonjury trial.
____ **19.** Physical discomfort and emotional trauma.
____ **20.** Liability for an act that causes harm without regard to fault or negligence (select two answers).
____ **21.** A suit brought by a decedent's personal representative for the benefit of the decedent's heirs, claiming that death was caused by the defendant's negligent act.
____ **22.** Cautious.
____ **23.** Hazardous items such as explosives and wild animals.
____ **24.** Legislative enactments that govern wrongful death actions.
____ **25.** The want of ordinary care.

cc. statute of limitations

dd. statute of repose

ee. strict liability

ff. supervening cause

gg. willful, wanton, and reckless conduct

hh. wrongful death action

ii. wrongful death statutes

____**26.** A doctrine establishing property owners' duty to use ordinary care toward trespassing children who might reasonably be attracted to their property.

____**27.** Negligence on the part of the plaintiff, which contributed toward the injuries and was a proximate cause of them.

____**28.** An absolute time limit for bringing a cause of action regardless of when the cause of action accrues.

____**29.** Known in advance; anticipated.

____**30.** The dominant, or moving, cause.

____**31.** The direct and proximate cause of someone's injuries.

____**32.** Legal responsibility.

SHARPENING YOUR LATIN SKILLS

In the space provided, write the definition of each of the following legal terms, referring to the glossary when necessary.

nul tort ____________________

per se ____________________

res ____________________

res ipsa loquitur ____________________

respondeat superior ____________________

scienter ____________________

3

UNRAVELING LEGALESE

Use simple, non-legal language, with the help of the glossary, to rewrite this case quote so that it is shorter and can be understood by a layperson without losing its meaning.

> The correctness of the judge's initial instruction to the jury that the status of the plaintiff Joseph Pridgen as he went through the escape hatch and got on the roof of the elevator car was that of a trespasser is too obvious to require any discussion in support thereof. The judge's later instruction on the nature and extent of the authority's duty toward Joseph after he slipped off the car roof and became trapped was in accord with the rule of many other jurisdictions that although an owner or occupier of land owes a trespasser only the duty to refrain from willful, wanton, or reckless conduct, where a trespasser is in a position of peril or in a helpless situation and his presence becomes known, the owner then has a duty to use reasonable care to avoid injuring him.

USING LEGAL LANGUAGE

Read the following story and fill in the blank lines with legal terms taken from the list of terms at the beginning of this chapter.

While shopping in a grocery store, Alison slipped on some fat that had accumulated in front of the meat counter. Alison was a(n) _________________________ (customer), and the _________________________ (carelessness) of the store employees, who were not _________________________ (cautious), caused the accident. Because the wrongful act was not extreme, the degree of wrong would probably be considered _________________________ rather than _________________________. The physician who treated Alison for her injuries was capable and not responsible for _________________________ _________________________, although the amount of the physician's bill became part of Alison's _________________________. When Alison arrived home, she noticed a police car in front of her house and saw a police officer inside. The officer, who was a(n) _________________________, told her that a neighborhood child had wandered without permission into Alison's pool area and had almost drowned. A friend of Alison, who was visiting at the time, rescued the child from drowning. The legal status of the friend was that of a(n) _________________________. Because the child was a trespasser, Alison's obligation to her would normally have been to refrain from _________________________ unless the _________________________ doctrine required her to use ordinary care.

Should the case go to court, the jury, which is the _________________________, will have to determine whether the child was negligent if the state follows the doctrine of _________________________ or the percentage of negligence of each party if the state follows the doctrine of _________________________. Because it is not probable but merely possible that Alison was negligent, the plaintiff would not be able to use the doctrine of _________________________ to prove the case. Similarly, it is doubtful that Alison can use the defense of _________________________ or _________________________ if suit is brought promptly.

3

PUZZLING OVER WHAT YOU LEARNED

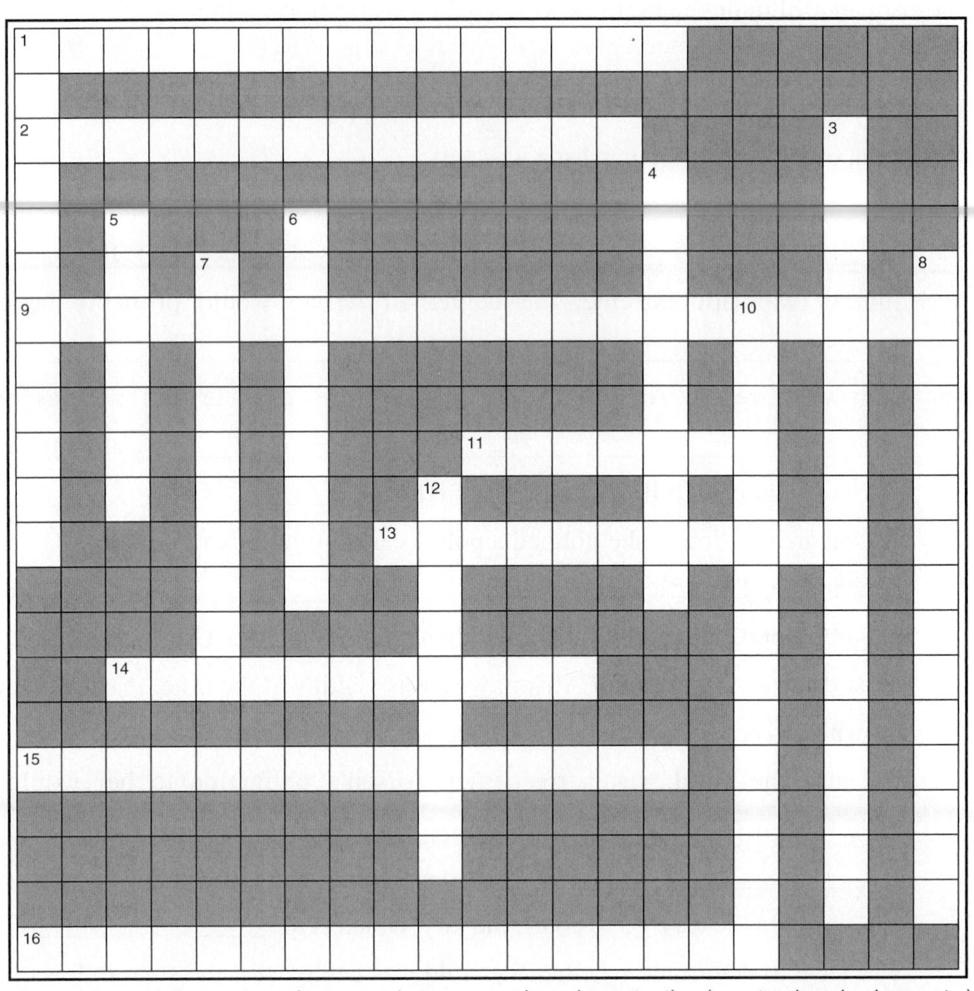

Caveat: Do **not** allow squares for spaces between words and punctuation (apostrophes, hyphens, etc.) when filling in crossword.

Across

1. One invited on the premises for a business or commercial purpose.
2. The degree of care that a reasonable person would have used under the circumstances then known.
9. The proportionate sharing between the plaintiff and the defendant of compensation for injuries, based on the relative negligence of the two.
11. Cautious
13. Professional misconduct; negligence of a professional.
14. Known in advance; anticipated.
15. Extreme negligence.
16. A relationship between contracting parties.

Down

1. A person allowed on another's premises by operation of law, such as a fire fighter or police officer.
3. The want of ordinary care.
4. The failure to use that amount of care and skill that a reasonably prudent person would have used under the same circumstances and conditions.
5. A monetary loss suffered by a party as a result of a wrong.
6. Legal responsibility.
7. The jury in a jury trial or the judge in a nonjury trial.
8. The thing speaks for itself.
10. One invited on the premises for nonbusiness purposes.
12. The direct and proximate cause of someone's injuries.

PART FOUR

TERMS USED IN LAW OF CONTRACTS

The law of contracts lies at the core of most personal and business transactions that we become involved with during our lifetime. A contract occurs whenever we buy or sell something, give or receive services for a fee, employ someone or become employed, rent an apartment, or attend college, and at many other times during our lives. Chapter 16 breaks down the subject of contracts into various classifications. Contract requirements, including consideration, writing essentials, defective agreements, and illegality, are examined in Chapter 17. After discussing the subjects of assignment and delegation of contracts, Chapter 18 surveys the various methods of ending contractual obligations.

CHAPTER 16

Formation of Contracts

ANTE INTERROGATORY

In most cases, contracts made by minors are (A) misdemeanors, (B) void, (C) voidable, (D) illegal.

CHAPTER OUTLINE

Contract Formation
Contract Classifications
Express and Implied Contracts
Bilateral and Unilateral Contracts
Valid, Void, Voidable, and Unenforceable Contracts
Executed and Executory Contracts

KEY TERMS

acceptance *(ak·SEP·tense)*
avoid *(a·VOID)*
bargain *(BAR·gen)*
bilateral contract *(by·LAT·er·el KON·trakt)*
capacity *(ka·PAS·e·tee)*
commerce clause *(KOM·ers)*
condition precedent *(kon·DISH·en pree·SEE·dent)*
contract *(KON·trakt)*
contract implied in fact *(KON·trakt im·PLIDE)*
contract implied in law
counteroffer *(KOWN·ter·off·er)*
disaffirm *(dis·a·FERM)*
executed *(EK·se·kew·ted)*
executory *(eg·ZEK·yoo·tor·ee)*
express contract *(eks·PRESS KON·trakt)*
full, faith, and credit clause *(CRED·it)*
implied contract *(im·PLIDE KON·trakt)*
infant *(IN·fent)*
invitation to deal *(in·vi·TA·shun)*
invitation to negotiate *(ne·GO·shee·ate)*
majority *(ma·JAW·ri·tee)*
necessaries *(NE·se·ser·ees)*
nullity *(NUL·i·tee)*
offer *(OFF·er)*
offeree *(off·er·EE)*
offeror *(off·er·OR)*
quasi *(KWAY·zi)*
quasi contract *(KWAY·zi KON·trakt)*
ratify *(RAT·i·fy)*
rejection *(re·JEK·shun)*
restitution *(res·ti·TEW·shun)*
revocation *(rev·o·KA·shun)*
supremacy clause *(soo·PREM·i·see)*
unenforceable contract *(un·en·FORS·e·bel KON·trakt)*
unilateral contract *(yoon·i·LAT·er·el KON·trakt)*
unjust enrichment *(un·JUST en·RICH·ment)*
valid *(VAL·id)*
void
voidable *(VOID·e·bel)*

CONTRACT FORMATION

In its simplest terms, a **contract** is any agreement that is enforceable in a court of law.

To reach an agreement, one party (called the **offeror**) makes an **offer** (a proposal) to another party (called the **offeree**) to enter into a legal agreement. If the offeree assents to the terms of the offer, an **acceptance** occurs and an agreement, sometimes called a **bargain,** comes into existence. To illustrate, if one person says to another, "I'll sell you my car for $495" (the offer) and the other person replies, "I'll buy it" (the acceptance), a contract comes into existence the moment the words of acceptance are spoken. If instead, the other person replies, "I don't want it," it is a **rejection**—the refusal by the offeree of an offer. A rejection brings an offer to an end. When the other person responds with a different offer instead of accepting the one that was made, it is called a **counteroffer.** Like a rejection, a counteroffer ends an offer. A **revocation** occurs when the offeror has a change of mind and calls back the offer before it is accepted by the offeree.

When an offer (or contract) contains a condition precedent, the parties are not obligated until the prerequisite is carried out. For example, if I agree to buy your car if you have the brakes fixed, I would have no obligation to buy it unless you have the repair made. A **condition precedent** is an event that must first occur before an agreement (or deed or will) becomes effective.

Some things, such as advertisements, price tags, prices on merchandise, signs, and prices in catalogs are not usually treated as offers. Instead, they are called **invitations to negotiate** or **invitations to deal.** For this reason, a contract does not usually arise when a customer offers to buy a mismarked product unless the store accepts the customer's offer and agrees to sell the product at the mismarked price.

CONSTITUTION WISE

Meaningful Clauses

commerce clause	Gives Congress the power to regulate commerce with foreign nations and among the different states.	Art. IV, s. 1
supremacy clause	Makes the U.S. Constitution and federal laws the supreme law of the land.	Art. VI, s.1
full, faith, and credit clause	Requires each state to recognize the laws and court decisions of every other state.	Art. IV, s. 1

4

CONTRACT CLASSIFICATIONS

Contracts may be classified in the following ways:

1. Express and implied
2. Bilateral and unilateral
3. Valid, void, voidable, and unenforceable
4. Executed and executory

Express and Implied Contracts

An **express contract** is one in which the terms of the contract are stated by the parties, either orally or in writing. An **implied contract** is one in which the terms of the contract are not stated by the parties.

Two types of implied contracts are a contract implied in fact and a contract implied in law. A **contract implied in fact** is a contract that arises from the conduct of the parties rather than from their express statements. For example, when you board a bus and pay the fare without saying anything to the driver and the driver says nothing to you, no express contract exists because the terms were not stated; however, a contract implied in fact exists that the bus driver will take you to a destination along that bus's particular route.

Unjust enrichment occurs when one person retains money, property, or other benefit that in equity and justice belongs to another. Sometimes, to prevent unjust enrichment, the court will impose a contract on the parties when one actually does not exist or when an express contract cannot be enforced. This court-imposed obligation is called a **contract implied in law** or **quasi contract.** The term **quasi** means "as if" or "almost as it were." A person who has been unjustly enriched at the expense of another is required to make **restitution**—that is, restore the other person to his or her original position prior to the loss.

Bilateral and Unilateral Contracts

Contracts are classified according to the number of promises made by the parties. A **bilateral contract** is a contract containing two promises, one made by each party to the contract. One party makes a promise in exchange for the other party's promise. For example, if someone says, "I'll sell you my car for $495," and the other party replies, "I'll buy it," a bilateral contract comes into existence, because both parties made promises.

A **unilateral contract** is a contract containing only one promise in exchange for an act. Suppose, for example, that a person offers a $100 reward for the return of a lost dog. The only way the offer can be accepted is by the actual return of the lost dog to the offeror. When that happens, the offer is accepted.

In a bilateral contract, consideration is found in the promises of each party. In a unilateral contract, consideration is found in the promise of the offeror and the act of the offeree.

Valid, Void, Voidable, and Unenforceable Contracts

A **valid** contract is one that is good; it meets the requirements of law. A **void** contract, conversely, is not good; it is a **nullity** and has no legal effect. An illegal contract, such as one charging a greater amount of interest than is allowed by law, is void.

A **voidable** contract is one that may be **disaffirmed** or **avoided** (repudiated; gotten out of) by one of the parties, if he or she wishes, because of some rule of law that excuses that party's performance. It is sometimes said that a voidable contract is one that is valid unless voided. For example, a contract entered into between an **infant** (the legal name for a minor) and an adult is voidable, except for necessaries, by the infant but not by the adult. **Necessaries** are food, clothing, shelter, and medical care that are needed by the infant but not being supplied by the parent or guardian.

Although infants are responsible for paying for the fair value of their necessaries, at their option they may disaffirm most other contracts on the ground that they lack **capacity** (legal competency) to contract. When infants reach **majority** (adulthood), they may **ratify**—that is, approve or confirm—earlier contracts made during their minority and thus be bound by them. Infants reach majority on the day before their eighteenth birthday.

An **unenforceable contract** is one that is valid but cannot be enforced for some legal reason. An oral contract for the sale of real property is an example of an unenforceable contract. Such a contract is required to be in writing to be enforceable.

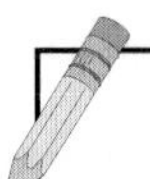

WORD WISE

Necessaries v. Necessities

The definition of "necessities" in standard dictionaries lists food, clothing, and shelter as specific items necessary to sustain life. In legal dictionaries, however, the term is given a broader meaning as well as a different spelling. For example, a "see necessaries" reference is listed under the term "necessities" in *Black's Law Dictionary*. This is because, in the legal use of the term, "necessaries" include not only what maintains life but also what is required to preserve the standard of living to which an individual is accustomed. Thus, "necessaries" often relate to the standard established by the rank, position, and earning power of a buyer or his or her parent or spouse.

$25,000.00
REWARD

FOR INFORMATION LEADING TO THE ARREST AND CONVICTION OF THE PERSON OR PERSONS WHO PARTICIPATED IN THE HOLDUP OF A BRINK'S, INCORPORATED MESSENGER ON JANUARY 28, 1980 AT OR ABOUT 9:50 A.M. AT THE DEDHAM INSTITUTION FOR SAVINGS, 741 PROVIDENCE HIGHWAY, DEDHAM, MASSACHUSETTS.

ANY PERSONS HAVING SUCH INFORMATION ARE REQUESTED TO CALL THE DEDHAM POLICE DEPARTMENT: 326-1212 OR THE F.B.I.: 742-5533 IN BOSTON. ALL CONVERSATIONS WILL BE HELD CONFIDENTIAL AND SECRET.

IN CASE OF DUPLICATION OF INFORMATION OR DISPUTE, THE BOARD OF DIRECTORS OF BRINK'S, INCORPORATED SHALL BE THE SOLE JUDGE AS TO WHOM THE REWARD OR A SHARE THEREOF SHOULD BE PAID. THIS REWARD SHALL BE CANCELLED ON AND AFTER MAY 1, 1980.

BRINK'S, INCORPORATED
500 NEPONSET AVENUE
BOSTON, MASSACHUSETTS 02107
(617) 288-0800

Figure 16-1 A reward offer is an example of a unilateral contract, which comes into existence when the offer is accepted by the performance of an act.

Executed and Executory Contracts

Contracts that are completely carried out are said to be **executed.** Those that have come into existence but are not yet carried out are **executory.** For example, when one person says to another, "I'll sell you my car for $495," and the other replies, "I'll buy it," the contract has come into existence but is in its executory stage. When the car is delivered and the money paid, the contract is executed.

REVIEWING WHAT YOU LEARNED

After studying the text, write the answers to each of the following questions.

1. Explain how a contractual agreement is reached.

____

____

____

2. Why does a contract not usually arise when a customer offers to buy a mismarked product?

____

____

____

3. Give an example of a contract implied in fact.

____

____

____

4. For what reason does the court impose a contract on the parties when a quasi contract arises?

____

____

____

5. What is the difference between a bilateral contract and a unilateral contract? ______________

____

____

____

____

6. Give an example of a void contract, a voidable contract, and an unenforceable contract. _____

____

____

____

____

7. How does an executory contract differ from an executed contract? ______________

____

____

____

____

UNDERSTANDING LEGAL CONCEPTS

Indicate whether each statement is true or false. Then, change the italicized word or phrase of each *false* statement to make it true.

Answers

_______________ 1. A *rejection* occurs when an offeror has a change of mind and calls back an offer before it is accepted.

_______________ 2. Prices on merchandise and in catalogs are usually treated as *offers*.

_______________ 3. Boarding a bus and putting money in the coin slot without saying anything to the driver is a *quasi contract*.

_______________ 4. A *bilateral contract* results when someone says, "I'll sell you my stereo for $100," and the other party replies, "I'll buy it."

_______________ 5. A *voidable* contract is one that is valid unless voided.

_______________ 6. An oral contract for the sale of real property is an example of a contract that is *void*.

_______________ 7. Infants *may* ratify contracts at any time during their minority.

_______________ 8. When someone says, "I'll sell you my stereo for $100," and the other party replies, "I'll buy it," a contract comes into existence, and it is in its *executory* stage.

_______________ 9. It is known as a *rejection* when the offeree declines an offer.

_______________ 10. A *void* contract is said to be a nullity.

4

CHECKING TERMINOLOGY

From the list of legal terms that follows, select the one that matches each definition.

a. acceptance
b. avoid
c. bargain
d. bilateral contract
e. capacity
f. commerce clause
g. condition precedent
h. contract
i. contract implied in fact
j. contract implied in law
k. counteroffer
l. disaffirm
m. executed
n. executory
o. express contract
p. full, faith, and credit clause
q. implied contract
r. infant
s. invitation to deal
t. invitation to negotiate
u. majority
v. necessaries
w. nullity
x. offer
y. offeree
z. offeror
aa. quasi
bb. quasi contract
cc. ratify
dd. rejection
ee. restitution
ff. revocation

Answers

____ **1.** Any agreement that is enforceable in a court of law.
____ **2.** A contract in which the terms are stated or expressed by the parties.
____ **3.** The refusal by an offeree of an offer.
____ **4.** A proposal made by an offeror.
____ **5.** A contract containing two promises, one made by each party.
____ **6.** Good; having legal effect.
____ **7.** A clause in the U.S. Constitution making the U.S. Constitution and federal laws the supreme law of the land.
____ **8.** Approve; confirm.
____ **9.** The assent to the terms of an offer.
____ **10.** Occurs when one person retains money, property, or other benefit that in equity and justice belongs to another.
____ **11.** A clause in the U.S. Constitution requiring each state to recognize the laws and court decisions of every other state.
____ **12.** Carried out or performed.
____ **13.** The legal name for a minor.
____ **14.** A contract that cannot be enforced for some legal reason.
____ **15.** To get out of a voidable contract; repudiate (select two answers).
____ **16.** Not good; having no legal effect.
____ **17.** The taking back of an offer by an offeror before it has been accepted by an offeree.
____ **18.** One who makes an offer.
____ **19.** A clause in the U.S. Constitution giving Congress the power to regulate commerce with foreign nations and among the different states.
____ **20.** Capable of being disaffirmed or voided.
____ **21.** A contract in which the terms are not stated or expressed by the parties.
____ **22.** A response to an offer in which the terms of the original offer are changed.
____ **23.** A contract that is imposed by the court to prevent unjust enrichment (select two answers).
____ **24.** As if; almost as it were.
____ **25.** Full age; adulthood.
____ **26.** Legal competency.
____ **27.** A contract containing one promise in exchange for an act.
____ **28.** That which is yet to be executed or performed.
____ **29.** One to whom an offer is made.
____ **30.** Agreement.
____ **31.** Restore an injured person to his or her original position prior to a loss.

gg. supremacy clause
hh. unenforceable contract
ii. unilateral contract
jj. unjust enrichment
kk. valid
ll. void
mm. voidable

____**32.** A request to an individual or the public to make an offer (select two answers).

____**33.** A contract that arises from the conduct of the parties rather than from their express statements.

____**34.** Food, clothing, shelter, and medical care that are needed by an infant but not supplied by a parent or guardian.

____**35.** Nothing; as though it had not occurred.

UNRAVELING LEGALESE

Use simple, non-legal language, with the help of the glossary, to rewrite this case quote so that it is shorter and can be understood by a layperson without losing its meaning.

> If a proposal is nothing more than an invitation to the person to whom it is made to make an offer to the proposer, it is not such an offer as can be turned into an agreement by acceptance. Proposals of this kind, although made to definite persons and not to the public generally, are merely invitations to trade; they go no further than what occurs when one asks another what he [or she] will give or take for certain goods. Such inquiries may lead to bargains, but do not make them. They ask for offers which the proposer has a right to accept or reject as he [or she] pleases.

USING LEGAL LANGUAGE

Read the following story and fill in the blank lines with legal terms taken from the list of terms at the beginning of this chapter.

> Monica placed a sign on her car that read, "FOR SALE: $1,000." Seeing the sign, Alex approached Monica and said, "I'll give you $800 for it." Monica replied, "I'll take $900 for it." The sign was a(n) ____________________, or ____________________. Alex's statement was a(n) ____________________, and Monica's response was a(n) ____________________, which required a(n) ____________________ on the part of Alex to create a(n) ____________________. Alex did not answer immediately, causing Monica to change her mind about the $900 offer and to take it back, but before she voiced her

_________________, Alex answered with a(n) _________________ by saying "I don't want it at that price." Alex left Monica and took a bus to visit his nephew. This action resulted in a(n) _________________ between Alex and the bus company, because the terms of the contract were not stated. Because the contract arose from the conduct of the parties, it was a contract _________________. When Alex got off the bus, he noticed that he was being followed by a small poodle that looked just like one that was advertised as being lost in the newspaper he had just read. The advertisement offered a reward of $150 to anyone who returned the lost poodle to its owner. Alex went to the address given in the newspaper and returned the dog to its owner, thus creating a(n) _________________. While there, he noticed a car for sale in front of the house and said to the dog owner, "I'll take that car instead of the $150 reward." Alex was the _________________; the dog owner was the _________________. The dog owner replied, "It's a deal." At this point, the contract was in its _________________ stage, because it had not been carried out completely. When the dog owner turns the car over to Alex, the contract will be _________________. In addition, because the terms of the contract were stated, this agreement was a(n) _________________. It was not a contract _________________ (which is also known as a(n) _________________), because no unjust enrichment occurred. Because both parties made promises, it was a(n) _________________. The contract met the requirements of law; therefore, it was _________________. Alex said to his 14-year-old nephew, Otto: "I'll sell you my baseball glove for $15." Otto replied: "I'll buy it." This contract was _________________ because of Otto's age. He was still a(n) _________________ and could disaffirm all contracts except for _________________ unless he _________________ them after reaching _________________. Otto then said to Alex: "I'll bet you $2,000 that the White Sox will win the pennant this year." Alex asked: "Where will you get the money if you lose?" "From a loan shark at 50 percent per annum interest," Otto answered. This loan would involve charging a greater amount of interest than is allowed by law. Such a contract is a(n) _________________ and is absolutely _________________. This type of agreement is *not* an example of a(n) _________________ contract, which is a contract that is valid but that cannot be enforced for some legal reason.

4

PUZZLING OVER WHAT YOU LEARNED

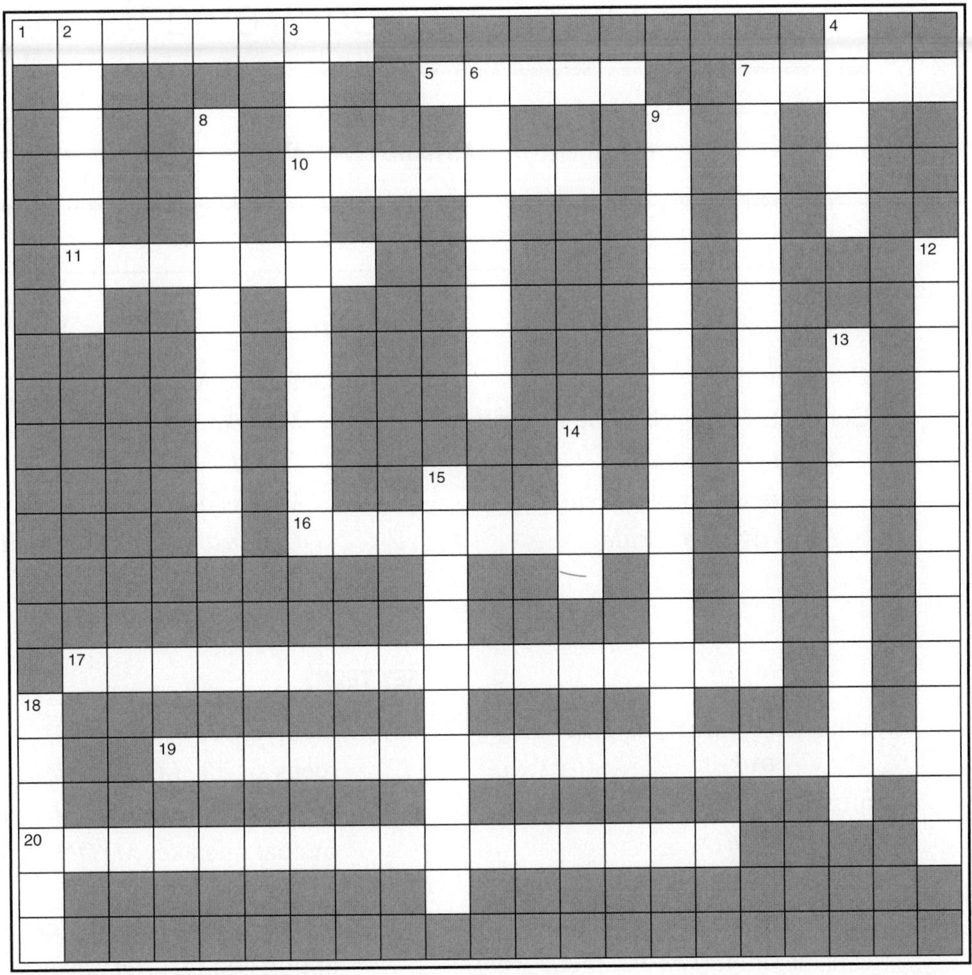

Caveat: Allow squares for spaces between words and punctuation (apostrophes, hyphens, etc.) when filling in crossword.

Across

1. Any agreement that is enforceable in a court of law.
5. To get out of a voidable contract.
7. As if; almost as it were.
10. Nothing; as though it had not occurred.
11. One to whom an offer is made.
16. The refusal by an offeree of an offer made by an offerer.
17. A contract in which the terms are stated or expressed by the parties.
19. A request to an individual or the public to make an offer.
20. A contract in which the terms are not stated or expressed by the parties.

Down

2. One who makes an offer.
3. A response to an offer in which the terms of the original offer are changed.
4. Good; having legal effect.
6. Capable of being disaffirmed or voided.
7. A contract imposed by law to prevent unjust enrichment.
8 The assent to the terms of an offer.
9. A contract that arises from the conduct of the parties.
12. Another name for a quasi contract.
13. Food, clothing, shelter, and medical care that are needed.
14. Not good; having no legal effect.
15. The taking back of an offer by an offeror before it has been accepted.
18. Approve; confirm.

4

CHAPTER 17
Contract Requirements

ANTE INTERROGATORY

The letters "L.S." next to a party's signature on a written contract mean (A) place of the seal, (B) legal signature, (C) locus supra, (D) legal standing.

CHAPTER OUTLINE

Consideration
Contracts Required to Be in Writing
Statute of Frauds
Requirements of a Writing
Parol Evidence Rule
Defective Agreements
Mistake
Fraud
Duress and Undue Influence
Unconscionable Contracts
Legality

KEY TERMS

adhesion contract *(ad·HEE·shen KON·trakt)*
affirm *(a·FIRM)*
avoid *(a·VOID)*
bilateral mistake *(by·LAT·er·el mis·TAKE)*
boilerplate *(BOY·ler·plate)*
consideration *(kon·sid·er·AH·shun)*
deceit *(dee·SEET)*
detriment *(DET·ri·ment)*
duress *(der·ESS)*
e-signature *(ee-SIG·na·choor)*
exculpatory clause *(eks·KUL·pa·toh·ree)*
failure of consideration *(FAYL·yer ov kon·sid·er·AH·shun)*
firm offer *(OFF·er)*
forbearance *(for·BARE·ense)*
fraud *(frawd)*
fraud in esse contractus *(ESS·ay kon·TRAKT·es)*
fraud in the inducement *(in·DEWSS·ment)*
in pari delicto *(in PAH·ree de·LIK·toh)*
lack of consideration *(kon·sid·er·AH·shun)*
locus *(LOH·kus)*
locus sigilli *(LOH·kus se·JIL·i)*
memorandum *(mem·o·RAN·dum)*
mutual mistake *(MYOO·choo·el mis·TAKE)*
nudum pactum *(NOO·dum PAK·tum)*
option contract *(OP·shen KON·trakt)*
parol evidence rule *(pa·ROLE EV·i·dens)*
promisee *(prom·i·SEE)*
promisor *(prom·i·SOHR)*
promissory estoppel *(PROM·i·sore·ee es·TOP·el)*
rescind *(ree·SIND)*
rescission *(ree·SISH·en)*
seal
statute of frauds *(STAT·shoot ov frawds)*
unconscionable *(un·KON·shun·a·bel)*
undue influence *(UN·dew IN·flew·ens)*
unilateral mistake *(yoon·i·LAT·er·el mis·TAKE)*
usury *(YOO·zer·ee)*

CONSIDERATION

To be binding on the parties, an agreement must have **consideration,** which is an exchange of benefits and detriments by the parties to the agreement. It is the cement that binds the parties to the contract. The Latin phrase describing this concept is *quid pro quo,* meaning "what for what" or "one thing for another." To illustrate, when one person says to another, "I'll sell you my car for $495" and the other replies, "I'll buy it," the promise to give up the car was a **detriment** (the giving up of a legal right) to the offeror and a benefit to the offeree. The promise to pay $495 was a detriment to the offeree and a benefit to the offeror. Because each party suffered a detriment and received a benefit, the agreement contained consideration and was a binding contract on the parties.

Suppose a man says to a woman, "I'm going to give you my car as a gift," and the woman replies, "Fine, I'll accept it." No binding contract comes into existence in this situation because no detriment was promised by the offeree in exchange for the benefit promised by the offeror, who said he would give the car as a gift. The one who made the promise (the **promisor**) is under no legal obligation to give the car to the one to whom the promise was made (the **promisee**), because the agreement is a **nudum pactum**—that is, a barren promise with no consideration.

In a bilateral contract, consideration is found in the promises made by each party. In a unilateral contract, it is found in the promise of one and in the act of the other, and, therefore, it does not come about until the act is completed.

In the past and still today in some states, a **seal** on a contract furnished consideration when none existed. This mark, impression, the word "seal," or the letters "L.S." are placed on a written contract next to the party's signature. "L.S." stands for **locus sigilli,** which means the place of the seal.

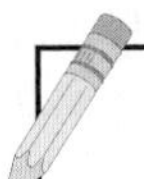

WORD WISE

One "Locus"; Several "Loci"

Most nouns in the English language form plurals by adding "s" to the singular. However, some nouns adapted from Latin, Greek, French, or Italian rely on the original language for the plural. Here are some examples:

Singular	*Plural*
locus	loci
medium	media
datum	data
beau	beaux
memorandum	memoranda
criterion	criteria
phenomenon	phenomena
stimulus	stimuli
radius	radii
larva	larvae
crisis	crises
matrix	matrices

4

Figure 17-1 The Latin phrase *quid pro quo*, means "what for what" or "one thing for another." It is sometimes used in law to describe consideration.

An **option contract** is a binding promise by an offeror to hold an offer open and requires consideration from the offeree to make it binding. An exception occurs when a merchant promises in writing to hold an offer open for the sale of goods. This promise by a merchant is known as a **firm offer** and requires no consideration to be binding.

In a lawsuit, the defense of **lack of consideration** refers to a barren promise containing no consideration in the agreement. In contrast, the defense of **failure of consideration** refers to a contract containing consideration that is not in fact given to the party being sued.

Under a doctrine known as **promissory estoppel,** no consideration is necessary when someone makes a promise that induces another's action or **forbearance** (refraining from taking action) and injustice can be avoided only by enforcing the promise. For example, Peter Giron, in Pennsylvania, e-mailed Jack Kenealy in Massachusetts, offering him a job. Without answering the e-mail, Kenealy quit his job, gave up his apartment, and moved to Pennsylvania. Giron refused to give Kenealy the job. Because Kenealy relied on Giron's promise and changed his position significantly, a court of equity would "estop" Giron from using the defense of no consideration if sued by Kenealy. The issue would have been avoided if Kenealy had e-mailed Giron back, accepting the offer and creating a bilateral contract.

CONTRACTS REQUIRED TO BE IN WRITING

The law requires only certain contracts to be in writing; others are fully enforceable even though they are oral.

Statute of Frauds

Under a rule of law known as the **statute of frauds,** certain contracts must be in writing to be enforceable. With some variations from state to state, the following contracts must be in writing to be enforceable:

1. Contracts that are not to be completed within a year
2. Promises to answer for the debt or default of another
3. Contracts for the sale of an interest in real property

4. Contracts in which marriage is the consideration
5. Promises by personal representatives of estates to pay debts of the estate personally
6. Promises to leave something to someone in a will
7. With four exceptions, contracts for the sale of goods of $500 or more

Requirements of a Writing

The writing that is necessary to satisfy the statute of frauds is called a **memorandum.** It may consist of any writing (such as words on a piece of scrap paper, receipt, or check) so long as it meets the following requirements:

1. Identifies the parties to the contract
2. States the terms of the contract
3. Identifies the **locus** if land—that is, the exact parcel of land under contract
4. States the price
5. Is signed by the person against whom enforcement is sought

If the parties agree, the federal law and many state laws allow contracts to be signed with an **e-signature** (electronic signature)—a method of signing an electronic message that identifies the sender and signifies his or her approval of the message's content.

Parol Evidence Rule

The law assumes that when a contract is reduced to writing, all of its terms are contained in the writing. Consequently, under a special rule of evidence known as the **parol evidence rule,** oral evidence of prior or contemporaneous negotiations between the parties is not admissible in court to alter, vary, or contradict the terms of a written agreement. Because of this rule, it is important to include all terms that are orally agreed upon whenever a contract is reduced to writing.

DEFECTIVE AGREEMENTS

Certain agreements are defective and are therefore not recognized as valid, binding contracts. The most common of these are agreements involving mutual mistake, fraud, duress, and undue influence. Unconscionable contracts may also be declared unenforceable by the courts.

Mistake

When both parties are mistaken about an important aspect of an agreement that they entered into, so that no meeting of the minds occurs, it is known as a **bilateral** or **mutual mistake,** and the contract is voidable at the option of either party. In contrast, when only one of the parties makes a mistake, it is known as a **unilateral** (one-sided) **mistake,** and the contract cannot be **avoided** (made void) by the parties.

Fraud

Fraud, called **deceit** in tort law, occurs when one party to the contract makes a misrepresentation of a material, existing fact that the other party to the contract relies on and thereby suffers damages. If the defrauded party was induced by fraud to enter into the contract, it is called **fraud in the inducement,** and the contract is voidable at the option of the injured party. If, conversely, fraud as to the essential nature of the transaction occurred, such as telling a blind man that he is signing a receipt when it is really a check, it is called **fraud in esse contractus,** and the contract is void. A defrauded party always has the right to **rescind** (cancel) the contract and to return any consideration received. Thus, **rescission** (cancellation) restores the parties to their original positions. A defrauded party may choose, instead, to keep the consideration and **affirm** (approve) the contract and bring suit for damages.

The five elements that must be proved by the party claiming fraud are discussed in more detail in Chapter 14 in the section on deceit.

Duress and Undue Influence

Contracts that are entered into because of duress or undue influence may also be avoided by the injured party. **Duress** is the overcoming of a person's free will by the use of threat or physical harm. **Undue influence** is the overcoming of a person's free will by misusing a position of trust and taking advantage of the other person who is relying on the trust relationship.

Unconscionable Contracts

Some contracts (or parts of them) are so harshly one-sided and unfair that they shock the conscience of the court. These are called **unconscionable** by the courts and will not be enforced. Sometimes **adhesion contracts** fall into this category. These are contracts that are drawn by one party to that party's benefit and must be accepted as is on a take-it-or-leave-it basis if a contract is to result. Adhesion contracts often contain **boilerplate,** which is standard language used commonly in documents of the same type. Boilerplate is found in legal form books or stored on law-office computers for use when drafting legal documents. **Exculpatory clauses** (clauses that are used to escape legal responsibility) are looked on with disfavor by the court. However, such clauses will usually be enforced if they do not offend public policy and the bargaining power between the parties is equal.

LEGALITY

To be valid and enforceable, contracts must be within the framework of the law. Illegal contracts are utterly void; they have no legal effect. **Usury,** for example, which is the charging of a greater amount of interest than is allowed by law, is illegal in every state. Gambling is illegal in many states with exceptions such as state lotteries, horse and dog racing, and bingo. Sunday contracts are illegal in some states, with certain specific exceptions. Contracts in restraint of trade, such as agreements not to compete, are also illegal, along with other types of contracts that are opposed to public policy.

Except when the parties are not **in pari delicto** (in equal fault), the court will not aid either party to an illegal contract. It will leave the parties where they placed themselves.

REVIEWING WHAT YOU LEARNED

After studying the text, write the answers to each of the following questions.

1. Give an example of a contract containing consideration. ______

2. Give an example of an agreement that does not contain consideration. ______

3. Where is consideration found in a bilateral contract? In a unilateral contract? ______

4. List seven kinds of contracts that must be in writing to be enforceable. ______

5. What are the requirements of a memorandum that will satisfy the statute of frauds? ______

6. Explain the meaning and significance of the parol evidence rule. ______

7. Describe the kind of contract that is voidable because of a mistake, and compare it with the kind of contract that is not voidable because of a mistake. ______

8. List the five elements of fraud. ______

9. Describe an unconscionable contract. ______

10. Describe three kinds of contracts that are illegal and void in many states. ______

UNDERSTANDING LEGAL CONCEPTS

Indicate whether each statement is true or false. Then, change the italicized word or phrase of each *false* statement to make it true.

Answers

__________________ **1.** A binding contract *comes* into existence when one person says to another, "I'm going to give you my stereo as a gift," and the other replies, "Fine, I'll accept it."

__________________ **2.** In the past, and still today in some states, a seal on a contract *furnishes* consideration when none exists.

__________________ **3.** Under a rule of law known as the *statute of limitations,* certain contracts must be in writing to be enforceable.

__________________ **4.** Contracts for the sale of an interest in *real property* must be in writing to be enforceable.

__________________ **5.** With four exceptions, contracts for the sale of goods of *$600* or more must be in writing to be enforceable.

__________________ **6.** A memorandum *may* consist of words on a piece of scrap paper, receipt, or check.

__________________ **7.** The law assumes that when a contract is reduced to writing, *all* of its terms are contained in the writing.

__________________ **8.** When a mutual mistake occurs, a contract *cannot* be avoided by the parties.

__________________ **9.** When a person is induced by fraud to enter into a contract, it is called fraud in the inducement, and the contract is *void.*

__________________ **10.** Illegal contracts are *void;* they have no legal effect.

4

CHECKING TERMINOLOGY

From the list of legal terms that follows, select the one that matches each definition.

a. adhesion contract
b. affirm
c. avoid
d. bilateral mistake
e. boilerplate
f. consideration
g. deceit
h. detriment
i. duress
j. e-signature
k. exculpatory clause
l. failure of consideration

Answers

____ **1.** The giving up of a legal right.

____ **2.** Place; locality.

____ **3.** Cancellation.

____ **4.** In equal fault.

____ **5.** Standard language commonly used in documents of the same type.

____ **6.** The overcoming of a person's free will by misusing a position of trust and taking advantage of the other person who is relying on the trust relationship.

____ **7.** One who makes a promise.

____ **8.** Oral evidence of prior or contemporaneous negotiations between the parties is not admissible in court to alter, vary, or contradict the terms of a written agreement.

____ **9.** Refraining from taking action.

____ **10.** The overcoming of a person's free will by the use of threat or physical harm.

m. firm offer
n. forbearance
o. fraud
p. fraud in esse contractus
q. fraud in the inducement
r. in pari delicto
s. lack of consideration
t. locus
u. locus sigilli
v. memorandum
w. mutual mistake
x. nudum pactum
y. option contract
z. parol evidence rule
aa. promisee
bb. promisor
cc. promissory estoppel
dd. rescind
ee. rescission
ff. seal
gg. statute of frauds
hh. unconscionable
ii. undue influence
jj. unilateral mistake
kk. usury

____**11.** A clause that is used in a contract to escape legal responsibility.

____**12.** A contract that is drawn by one party to that party's benefit and must be accepted, as is, on a take-it-or-leave-it basis if a contract is to result.

____**13.** A misrepresentation of a material, existing fact, knowingly made, that causes someone reasonably relying on it to suffer damages (select two answers).

____**14.** The writing that is necessary to satisfy the statute of frauds.

____**15.** A mark, impression, the word "seal," or the letters "L.S." placed on a written contract next to the party's signature.

____**16.** Approve.

____**17.** So harshly one-sided and unfair that the court's conscience is shocked.

____**18.** Fraud as to the essential nature of the transaction.

____**19.** A defense available when the consideration provided for in an agreement is not in fact given to the party being sued.

____**20.** A mistake made by only one party to a contract.

____**21.** To annul, cancel, or make void.

____**22.** One to whom a promise is made.

____**23.** A defense available to a party being sued when no consideration is contained in the agreement that is sued on.

____**24.** Cancel.

____**25.** A binding promise to hold an offer open.

____**26.** A doctrine under which no consideration is necessary when someone makes a promise that induces another's action or forbearance and injustice can be avoided only by enforcing the promise.

____**27.** A merchant's written promise to hold an offer open for the sale of goods.

____**28.** Place of the seal.

____**29.** When both parties are mistaken about an important aspect of an agreement (select two answers).

____**30.** Certain contracts must be in writing to be enforceable.

____**31.** Barren promise with no consideration.

____**32.** An exchange of benefits and detriments by the parties to an agreement.

____**33.** Fraud that induces another to enter into a contract.

____**34.** The charging of a greater amount of interest than is allowed by law.

____**35.** A method of signing an electronic message.

UNRAVELING LEGALESE

Use simple, non-legal language, with the help of the glossary, to rewrite this case quote so that it is shorter and can be understood by a layperson without losing its meaning.

> The use of "benefit" and "detriment" in this connection needs explanation. While correct if properly understood, it is liable to misconstruction. "Benefit" does not refer to any pecuniary gain arising out of the transaction, nor "detriment" in any pecuniary loss. It is not possible to wait until the transaction is concluded and the books balanced to see whether the consideration existed originally. "Benefit" as used in this rule means that the promisor has, in return for a promise, acquired some legal right to which he [or she] would not otherwise have been entitled; "detriment" means that the promisee has, in return for the promise, forgone some legal right which he [or she] would otherwise have been entitled to exercise.

USING LEGAL LANGUAGE

Read the following story and fill in the blank lines with legal terms taken from the list of terms at the beginning of this chapter.

> The smooth-talking salesperson promised a free cataract operation to an elderly woman who was almost blind. The salesperson was the ____________________ and the elderly woman was the ____________________; however, because the elderly woman promised nothing in exchange for the cataract operation, she suffered no ____________________. For this reason, no ____________________ occurred, and the agreement was a ____________________. Had the promise been in writing and put under ____________________ by the use of the letters "L.S." (which stand for ____________________), it would have been binding in some states. The salesperson also committed ____________________ or ____________________ when he lied to the elderly woman. He talked her into buying some worthless land with a shack on it by telling her that the ____________________ was beautiful high ground when it was actually swampland. The type of fraud was ____________________, because the salesperson's lie induced the woman to enter into the contract. Because the salesperson was not in a position of trust, the wrongful act was not ____________________ and it was not

_________________________, because the woman's free will was not overcome by threats or physical harm. It was _________________________, however, when the salesperson told the woman that she was signing a second copy of the contract when she was actually signing a check for $10,000. The writing that the woman signed met the requirements of a(n) _________________________ and, for that reason, was sufficient to satisfy the _________________________. Because it was drawn up by the seller to the seller's advantage and offered to the woman on a take-it-or-leave-it basis, the court might consider the contract to be a(n) _________________________ _________________________. In addition, the court might consider the contract to be _________________________, because the woman agreed to buy a shack on an acre of worthless swampland for $250,000. Under the terms of the contract, she was to pay $100,000 in cash and sign a note for the balance at 50 percent per annum interest, which is _________________________. Although the _________________________ does not allow prior oral statements by the parties into evidence in court to alter the terms of a written agreement, an exception exists when fraud is committed. In addition, because both parties were mistaken as to the existence of the subject matter when they signed the contract (the shack on the property had burned down two days before the contract was signed), the contract was voidable. The mistake was a(n) _________________________, which is also known as a(n) _________________________, not a(n) _________________________.

PUZZLING OVER WHAT YOU LEARNED

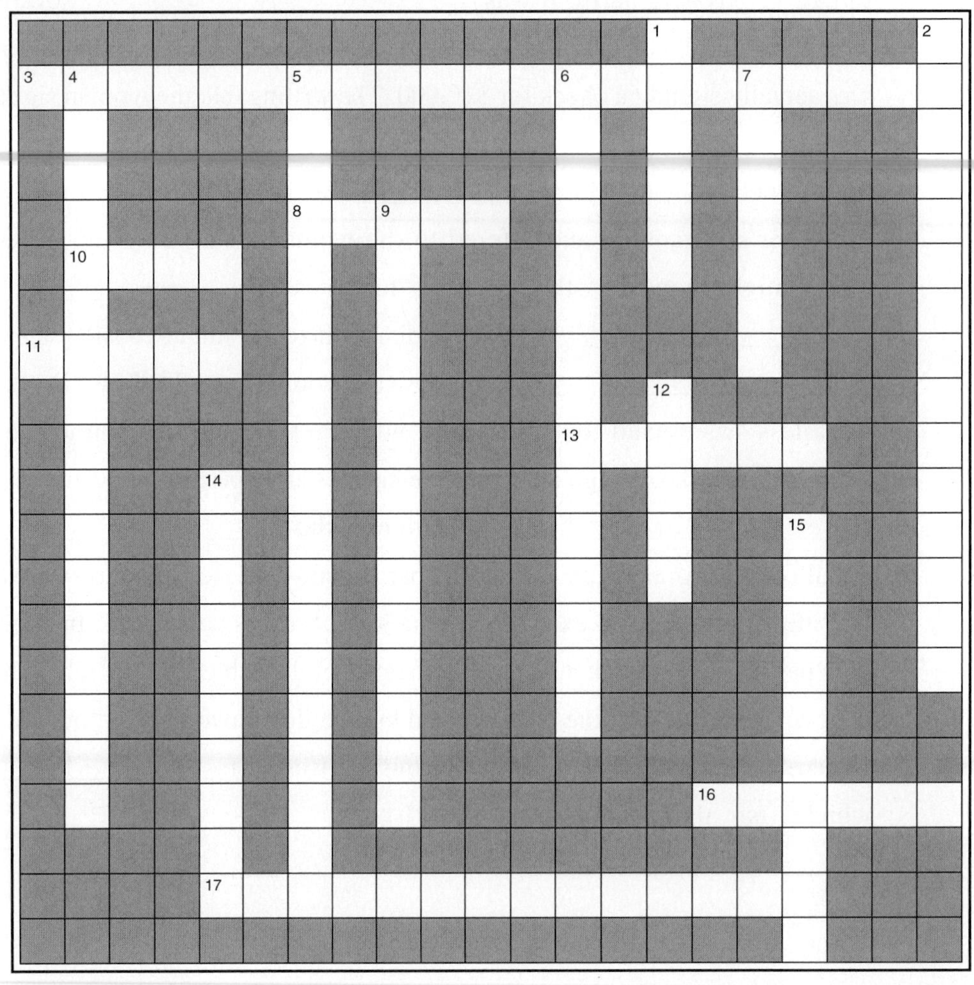

Caveat: Allow squares for spaces between words and punctuation (apostrophes, hyphens, etc.) when filling in crossword.

Across

3. A defense available when no consideration is contained in an agreement.
8. The charging of a greater amount of interest than is allowed by law.
10. A mark, impression, the word "seal," or the letters "L.S."
11. Place; locality.
13. The overcoming of a person's free will by the use of threat or physical harm.
16. Approve.
17. Another name for a bilateral mistake.

Down

1. Misrepresentation of a material, existing fact knowingly made.
2. Overcoming a person's free will by misusing a position of trust.
4. One-sided contract that must be accepted as is.
5. Fraud that induces another to enter into a contract.
6. In equal fault.
7. Annulled, canceled, or made void.
9. So harshly one-sided and unfair as to shock the court's conscience.
12. Another name for deceit.
14. The writing that is necessary to satisfy the statute of frauds.
15. A merchant's written promise to hold an offer open for the sale of goods.

CHAPTER 18

Third Parties and Discharge of Contracts

ANTE INTERROGATORY

Damages that are agreed upon by the parties at the time of the execution of the contract in the event of a subsequent breach are called (A) consequential damages, (B) exemplary damages, (C) incidental damages, (D) liquidated damages.

CHAPTER OUTLINE

Third-Party Beneficiaries
Assignment and Delegation
Ending Contractual Obligations
   Performance
   Agreement
   Impossibility
   Operation of Law
   Breach of Contract

KEY TERMS

accord and satisfaction *(a·KORD and sat·is·FAK·shun)*
anticipatory breach *(an·TISS·i·pa·tore·ee)*
assignee *(ass·en·EE)*
assignment *(a·SINE·ment)*
assignor *(ass·en·OR)*
bankruptcy *(BANK·rupt·see)*
breach of contract *(KON·trakt)*
compensatory damages *(kom·PEN·se·tor·ee DAM·e·jez)*
consequential damages *(kon·se·KWEN·shel DAM·e·jez)*
damages *(DAM·e·jez)*
delegation *(del·e·GA·shun)*
exemplary damages *(egs·ZEMP·le·ree DAM·e·jez)*
impossibility *(im·pos·i·BIL·i·tee)*
incidental damages *(in·si·DEN·tel DAM·e·jez)*
legal tender *(LEE·gul TEN·der)*
liquidated damages *(lik·wi·DAY·ted DAM·e·jez)*
mitigate *(MIT·i·gate)*
nominal damages *(NOM·i·nel DAM·e·jez)*
novation *(no·VAY·shun)*
performance *(per·FORM·ens)*
privity of contract *(PRIV·i·tee ov KON·trakt)*
punitive damages *(PYOON·i·tiv)*
reasonable time *(REE·zen·e·bel)*
specific performance *(spe·SIF·ic per·FORM·ens)*
statute of limitations *(STAT·shoot ov lim·i·TA·shuns)*
substantial performance *(sub·STAN·shel per·FORM·ens)*
tender of payment *(TEN·der)*
tender of performance *(per·FORM·ens)*
third-party beneficiary *(ben·e·FISH·ee·air·ee)*
time is of the essence *(ESS·ens)*
toll *(tohl)*

4

THIRD-PARTY BENEFICIARIES

A **third-party beneficiary** is someone for whose benefit a promise is made but who is not a party to the contract. For example, A enters into a contract with B to provide services for C. Because the contract is between A and B, C is not in **privity of contract**—the legal name for the relationship that exists between contracting parties. C, instead, is a third-party beneficiary. When contracting parties intend to benefit a third person, the third person can enforce the contract between the contracting parties without being in privity of contract.

ASSIGNMENT AND DELEGATION

Parties who enter into contracts receive rights and incur duties. For example, if I agree to sell you my car for $2,000 and you agree to buy it from me for that price, I receive the right to the money and incur the duty to give you the car. Your rights and duties are the opposite. With some exceptions and unless otherwise agreed, rights and duties can be transferred to other people.

The transfer of a right is called an **assignment.** The person who transfers the right is called the **assignor,** and the person to whom the right is transferred is called the **assignee.** In the preceding example, if before receiving the $2,000 from you I assign it to a third person, you would have to pay the money to the third person upon learning of the assignment.

The transfer of a duty is known as a **delegation.** Duties to perform personal services cannot be delegated without the consent of the person for whom the duty is to be performed.

When two contracting parties agree that one of them will transfer both rights and duties to a third person, and the remaining party and the third person agree to deal solely with each other, privity of contract changes, and a novation occurs. A **novation** is an agreement whereby an original party to a contract is replaced by a new party, creating a completely new contract and ending the original one.

WEB WISE

- Look for a discussion of contract law at **www.findlaw.com.** At that site, select the tab "For Legal Professionals," then click "Practice Areas," followed by "Contracts."
- Read more about the assignment of contracts by going to **www.google.com** and typing in the words "Contract Assignment."

ENDING CONTRACTUAL OBLIGATIONS

The principal ways that contractual obligations end are as follows:

1. Performance
2. Agreement
3. Impossibility
4. Operation of law
5. Breach of contract

Performance

Most contracts come to an end by **performance**—that is, the parties do as they agreed to do under the terms of the contract. At common law, the parties were required to do absolutely everything they agreed to do, without exception, to be in a position to bring suit against the other party for breach of contract. Under today's law, the doctrine of **substantial performance** allows a contracting party to sue the other party for breach even though slight omissions or deviations were made in his or her own performance of the contract.

The time for performance of a contract is sometimes important to the parties. If a time for performance is stated in a written contract, the court may allow additional time for its performance without recognizing a breach. If a time for performance is stated in the writing and the words **time is of the essence** (meaning time is critical) are added, however, a breach of contract will occur at the end of the stated time if the contract has not been performed. If no time for performance is put in the contract, it must be performed within a **reasonable time.** This time, left to the discretion of the judge, or jury may be fairly allowed depending on the circumstances.

To be in a position to bring a suit against another for breach of contract, it is necessary to make tender. **Tender of performance** means to offer to do that which one has agreed to do under the terms of the contract. **Tender of payment** means to offer to the other party the money owed under the contract. For the sale of goods under the Uniform Commercial Code, tender of payment may be made by any means or in any manner that is commonly used in the ordinary course of business. The seller may demand legal tender but must give the buyer a reasonable time to obtain it. **Legal tender** is coin, paper, or other currency that is sufficient under law for the payment of debts.

Agreement

Sometimes when there is a dispute, instead of completing the terms of a contract, the parties will agree to end the contract altogether. Other times they will agree to perform in a different manner from that agreed upon originally. This latter arrangement is called an accord. When the agreed-upon performance is completed, it is known as a satisfaction. Together, this arrangement is known as an **accord and satisfaction.**

Impossibility

Contracts that are impossible to perform, not merely difficult or costly to do so, may be discharged by **impossibility.** Legal reasons for this kind of discharge of performance include the following:

1. Death of a person who was to perform personal services
2. Destruction of the exact subject matter of the contract
3. Subsequent illegality of that particular performance

Operation of Law

Sometimes contracts will be discharged by operation of law. The filing of bankruptcy, for example, discharges the contractual obligations of the debtor. **Bankruptcy** (discussed in Chapter 42) is a legal process under the Federal Bankruptcy Act that aims to give debtors who are overwhelmed with debt a fresh start and to provide a fair way of distributing a debtor's assets among all creditors.

Contract rights are also discharged by the operation of **statutes of limitations.** These are laws that set forth time limits for bringing legal actions. For example, in the case of a breach of contract for the sale of goods, suit must be brought within four years from the date of the breach to be actionable. Other time limits vary from state to state for different causes of actions.

WORD WISE

Prefixes That Mean "Not"

Prefix	*Examples*
dis-	disbelief, disaffirm, dishonor
in-	indirect, intestate
im- (before *p, b, m*)	immature, impeach, impossibility
il- (before *l*)	illegal, illegitimate child
ir- (before *r*)	irregular, irreconcilable differences, irrevocable trust
non-	nonliving, nonsuit
un-	unscrupulous, unconscionable, undisclosed principal, unenforceable

Statutes of limitations are tolled—that is, they do not run—while a plaintiff is under a disability such as infancy or mental illness. Similarly, they do not run while a defendant is out of the state and not under the jurisdiction of the court. In the case of a lawsuit for money owed, part payment of the debt has the effect of starting the full statutory period of time running all over again from the beginning. The word **toll** means to bar, defeat, or take away. Thus, to toll the statute of limitations means to show facts that remove its bar of the action.

4

Breach of Contract

A **breach of contract** occurs when one of the parties fails to carry out the terms of the contract. When the breaching party announces before the time for performance that he or she is not going to perform, it is known as an **anticipatory breach.** Some states allow suit to be brought at that moment; other states require the injured party to wait until the time for performance before bringing suit to test the breaching party's ability to perform.

When a breach of contract occurs, the injured party may bring suit for **damages,** which is the money lost as a result of the breach. **Nominal damages**—that is, damages in name only—are sometimes recovered in the amount of $0.01 or $1 by a party who wins a lawsuit but suffers no actual monetary loss. **Compensatory damages** are damages that compensate the plaintiff for actual losses resulting from the breach. **Punitive** or **exemplary damages,** such as those that are double or triple the amount of actual damages, are occasionally awarded to the plaintiff as a measure of punishment for the defendant's wrongful acts. **Liquidated damages** are damages that are agreed upon by the parties at the time of the execution of the contract in the event of a subsequent breach. **Incidental**

damages may be awarded to the injured party to cover reasonable expenses that indirectly result from a breach of contract. **Consequential damages** are losses (such as lost profits) that flow not directly from the breach but from the consequences of it.

Whenever a contract is breached, the injured party owes a duty to the breaching party to **mitigate** the damages—that is, keep them as low as possible.

Sometimes the court will order the breaching party to do that which he or she agreed to do under the terms of the contract. This order is known as **specific performance** and is used only when the subject matter of the contract is either unique or rare, so that money damages are not an adequate remedy for the injured party. Because the court considers real property to be unique, it will often order a contract for the purchase or sale of real property to be specifically performed.

REVIEWING WHAT YOU LEARNED

After studying the text, write the answers to each of the following questions:

1. Explain the difference between an assignment and a delegation. ______

2. List the five ways that contractual obligations come to an end. ______

3. If the time for performance is not mentioned in a contract, when must the contract be performed? ______

4. What is necessary to be in a position to bring suit against another for breach of contract? ______

5. Explain the difference between accord and satisfaction. ______

6. List three legal reasons for discharging a contract for impossibility. ______

7. Describe two situations that toll the statute of limitations. ______

8. How do nominal damages, punitive damages, liquidated damages, incidental damages, and consequential damages differ from one another? ______

9. When may the court order specific performance of a contract? ______

UNDERSTANDING LEGAL CONCEPTS

Indicate whether each statement is true or false. Then, change the italicized word or phrase of each *false* statement to make it true.

Answers

______ **1.** The transfer of a *duty* is known as an assignment.

______ **2.** With some exceptions and unless otherwise agreed, rights and duties *cannot* be transferred to other people.

______ **3.** Most contracts come to an end by *agreement.*

______ **4.** If a time for performance is stated in a written contract, the court *may* allow additional time for its performance.

______ **5.** If no time for performance is put in a contract, it must be performed within a *reasonable* time.

______ **6.** When parties agree to perform in a different manner than originally agreed upon and the new performance is completed, it is called an accord and *completion.*

______ **7.** The law of *bankruptcy* aims to give debtors who are overwhelmed with debt a fresh start.

______ **8.** In the case of a breach of contract for the sale of goods, suit must be brought within *six* years from the date of the breach to be actionable.

______ **9.** Whenever a contract is breached, the *breaching* party owes a duty to keep the damages as low as possible.

______ **10.** *Specific performance* is used only when the subject matter of a contract is either unique or rare, so that money damages are not an adequate remedy for the injured party.

CHECKING TERMINOLOGY

From the list of legal terms that follows, select the one that matches each definition.

a. accord and satisfaction
b. anticipatory breach
c. assignee
d. assignment
e. assignor
f. bankruptcy
g. breach of contract
h. compensatory damages
i. consequential damages
j. damages
k. delegation
l. exemplary damages
m. impossibility
n. incidental damages
o. legal tender
p. liquidated damages
q. mitigate
r. nominal damages
s. novation
t. performance
u. privity of contract
v. punitive damages
w. reasonable time
x. specific performance
y. statute of limitations
z. substantial performance
aa. tender of payment
bb. tender of performance
cc. third-party beneficiary
dd. time is of the essence
ee. toll

Answers

____ **1.** The transfer of a right from one person to another.
____ **2.** One who transfers a right by assignment.
____ **3.** One to whom a right is transferred by assignment.
____ **4.** The transfer of a duty by one person to another.
____ **5.** Coin, paper, or other currency that is sufficient under law for the payment of debts.
____ **6.** An agreement to perform in a different manner than originally called for and the completion of that agreed-upon performance.
____ **7.** A method of discharging a contract that is impossible to perform, not merely difficult or costly.
____ **8.** A legal process that aims to give debtors who are overwhelmed with debt a fresh start and to provide a fair way of distributing a debtor's assets among all creditors.
____ **9.** The failure of a party to a contract to carry out the terms of the agreement.
____ **10.** The announcement, before the time for performance, by a party to a contract that he or she is not going to perform.
____ **11.** Compensation in money for loss or injury.
____ **12.** Damages as a measure of punishment for the defendant's wrongful acts (also called punitive damages).
____ **13.** Damages that are agreed upon by the parties at the time of the execution of a contract in the event of a subsequent breach.
____ **14.** Reasonable expenses that indirectly result from a breach of contract.
____ **15.** Losses that flow not directly from a breach of contract but from the consequences of it.
____ **16.** The relationship that exists between two or more contracting parties.
____ **17.** An agreement whereby an original party to a contract is replaced by a new party.
____ **18.** Discharging a contract by doing that which one agreed to do under the terms of the contract.
____ **19.** A doctrine allowing a contracting party to sue the other party for breach even though slight omissions or deviations were made in his or her own performance of the contract.
____ **20.** Time is critical.
____ **21.** A period of time, left to the discretion of the judge or jury, that may be fairly allowed depending on the circumstances.
____ **22.** To offer to do that which one has agreed to do under the terms of a contract.
____ **23.** To offer to the other party the money owed under a contract.
____ **24.** Law that sets forth time limits for bringing legal actions.
____ **25.** To bar, defeat, or take away.
____ **26.** Damages in name only.

____**27.** Damages as a measure of punishment for the defendant's wrongful acts (also called *exemplary* damages).

____**28.** Lessen; keep as low as possible.

____**29.** An order by the court ordering a breaching party to do that which he or she agreed to do under the terms of the contract.

____**30.** Damages that compensate the plaintiff for actual losses resulting from the breach.

____**31.** Someone for whose benefit a promise is made but who is not a party to the contract.

UNRAVELING LEGALESE

Use simple, non-legal language, with the help of the glossary, to rewrite this case quote, so that it is shorter and can be understood by a layperson without losing its meaning.

> However, the analysis of the facts on this appeal leaves no room for doubt that the case at bar falls into the category of those assignments where an attempt is made to transfer the rights and to delegate the duties of the assignor under an executory bilateral contract whose terms and the circumstances make plain that the personal qualification and action of the assignor, with respect to both his [or her] benefits and burdens under the contract, were essential inducements in the formation of the contract.

SHARPENING YOUR LATIN SKILLS

In the space provided, write the definition of each of the following legal terms, referring to the glossary when necessary.

assumpsit ____________________

ex contractu ____________________

gratis ____________________

in pari delicto ____________________

locus sigilli ____________________

non assumpsit ____________________

nudum pactum ____________________

quasi ____________________

USING LEGAL LANGUAGE

Read the following story and fill in the blank lines with legal terms taken from the list of terms at the beginning of this chapter:

Needing a car for a trip she was planning, Holly entered into a contract to buy a late-model Toyota from Enrique for $7,000. Time was of the __________ with regard to this contract, because Holly planned to leave on the trip the next day. Before carrying out the contract, however, Holly's trip was canceled. She decided to transfer her right to the car to her friend Maxine. The transfer of a right is called a(n) __________ rather than a(n) __________, which is a transfer of a duty. Holly was the __________, and Maxine was the __________. Enrique agreed to deal solely with Maxine and to release Holly from all obligations under the contract, thus creating a(n) __________. Enrique and Maxine were in __________, which is the legal name for the relationship that existed between them. When the time for __________—that is, the carrying out of the contract—arrived, Enrique made __________ by offering to turn the car over to Maxine. She offered to pay him with Mexican pesos, which is not __________ in the United States. Enrique refused the __________ but then reached an agreement with Maxine to change the price for the car to $6,000 and to postpone the time for performance for a week. This agreement to change the performance is called a(n) __________. When the agreed-upon performance is completed, it will be known as a(n) __________. The next day Maxine told Enrique that she had changed her mind and was not going to buy the car. Because this occurred before the time for performance had arrived, it is known as a(n) __________. Enrique would not be able to ask the court to order __________, because the subject matter of the contract was not unique. Similarly, because the parties had not agreed on damages at the time of the execution of the contract, no __________ existed. If Enrique suffered no actual monetary loss because of the __________ by Maxine, he would be able to recover only __________ from her in court plus __________ to take care of any reasonable expenses resulting from the breach. Enrique owed a duty to Maxine to __________ the damages—that is, keep them as low as possible. This case was not one involving __________ or __________ such as double or triple the amount of actual damages. The __________ __________—that is, the time limit for bringing suit—had not run out.

PUZZLING OVER WHAT YOU LEARNED

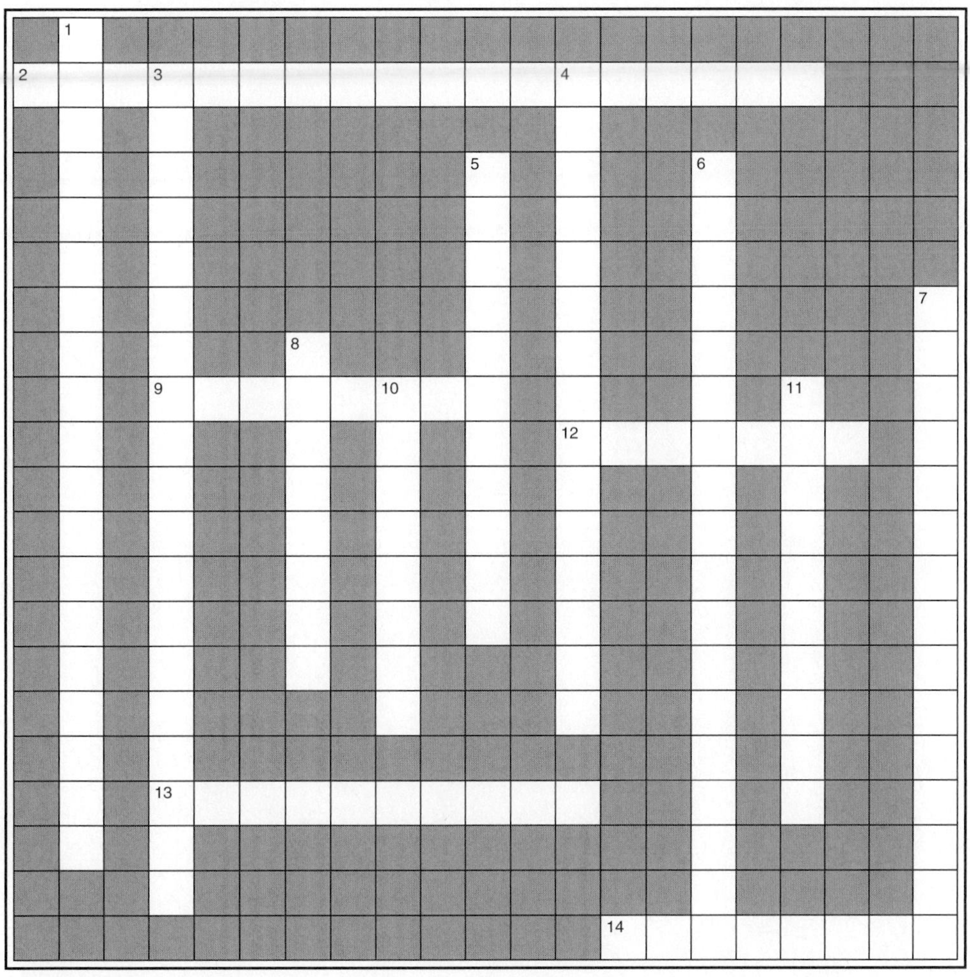

Caveat: Allow squares for spaces between words and punctuation (apostrophes, hyphens, etc.) when filling in crossword.

Across

2. The failure of a party to a contract to carry out its terms.
9. One who transfers a right by assignment.
12. Compensation in money for loss or injury.
13. The transfer of a right from one person to another.
14. One to whom a right is transferred by assignment.

Down

1. The relationship that exists between two or more contracting parties.
3. Announcement before time for performance of a breach of contract.
4. Damages in name only.
5. Discharging a contract by doing that which one agreed to do.
6. Damages agreed to at the time of the execution of a contract.
7. A time that may be fairly allowed depending on the circumstances.
8. Lessen; keep as low as possible.
10. An agreement whereby an original party to a contract is replaced.
11. The transfer of a duty by one person to another.

PART FIVE

TERMS USED IN LAW OF PERSONAL PROPERTY AND AGENCY

We are surrounded by personal property from the moment we are born to the moment we die. In fact, whether good or bad, much of our lives is spent in the pursuit of more personal property of one kind or another. In addition, we are touched by the law of agency in many aspects of our lives, either by dealing with people who are principals, agents, employers, and employees or by being involved in those roles ourselves. Chapter 19 discusses contracts for the sale of goods (a common type of personal property) followed by an explanation of bailments. Chapter 20 covers the subject of intellectual property, including patents, copyrights, trademarks, and trade secrets. Chapter 21 begins by distinguishing among the different kinds of agency relationships and continues with an examination of the various kinds of agents, the authority of agents, and the subject of vicarious liability.

5

CHAPTER 19

Personal Property and Bailments

ANTE INTERROGATORY

When you borrow a cup of sugar from a neighbor with the intention of returning the sugar, it is known as a (A) bailment for the sole benefit of the bailor, (B) mutuum, (C) mutual benefit bailment, (D) bailment for the sole benefit of the bailee.

CHAPTER OUTLINE

Sale of Goods
- *Electronic Commerce*
- *Warranties*
- *Auction Sales*

Bailments

KEY TERMS

auction sale *(AWK·shen)*
auction with reserve *(ree·ZERV)*
auction without reserve
bailee *(bay·LEE)*
bailment *(BALE·ment)*
bailment for the sole benefit of the bailee *(bay·LEE)*
bailment for the sole benefit of the bailor *(bay·LOR)*
bailor *(bay·LOR)*
bidder *(BID·er)*
bill of sale
bulk transfer *(TRANS·fer)*
chattels *(CHAT·els)*
chose in action *(shohz in AK·shun)*
conforming goods *(kon·FORM·ing)*
contract to sell *(KON·trakt)*
cover *(KUV·er)*
cure *(kyoor)*
destination contract *(des·te·NAY·shun KON·trakt)*
donee *(doh·NEE)*
donor *(doh·NOR)*
e-commerce *(ee-KOM·ers)*
express warranty *(eks·PRESS WAR·en·tee)*
fixture *(FIKS·cher)*
f.o.b. the place of destination *(des·te·NAY·shun)*
f.o.b. the place of shipment *(SHIP·ment)*
full warranty *(WAR·en·tee)*
fungible goods *(FUN·ji·bel)*
future goods *(FEW·cher)*
goods
gratuitous bailment *(gra·TOO·i·tes BAYL·ment)*
identified goods *(eye·DENT·i·fyd)*
implied warranty *(im·PLIDE WAR·en·tee)*
intangible personal property *(in·TAN·je·bel PER·son·al PROP·er·tee)*
limited warranty *(LIM·i·ted WAR·en·tee)*
merchant *(MER·chent)*
mutual benefit bailment *(MYOO·choo·el BEN·e·fit BAYL·ment)*
mutuum *(MYOO·choo·um)*
nonconforming goods *(non·kon·FORM·ing)*

output contract *(OWT·put KON·trakt)*
personal property *(PER·son·al PROP·er·tee)*
personalty *(PER·sen·el·tee)*
requirements contract *(re·KWIRE·ments KON·trakt)*
risk of loss
sale
sale on approval *(a·PROOV·el)*
sale or return *(re·TURN)*
shipment contract *(SHIP·ment KON·trakt)*
tangible personal property *(TAN·je·bel PER·son·al PROP·er·tee)*
title *(TY·tel)*
tortious bailee *(TOR·shus bay·LEE)*
trade fixture *(FIKS·cher)*
Uniform Commercial Code *(YOON·i·form ke·MERSH·el kode)*
warranty of fitness for a particular purpose *(WAR·en·tee ov FIT·ness)*
warranty of merchantability *(WAR·en·tee ov mer·chent·a·BIL·e·tee)*
warranty of title *(WAR·en·tee ov TY·tel)*

Broadly speaking, **personal property,** also called **personalty** or **chattels,** is anything that is the subject of ownership other than real property. **Tangible personal property** is property that has substance and that can be touched, such as a pencil, an item of clothing, or an automobile. **Intangible personal property,** conversely, is property that is not perceptible to the senses and cannot be touched, such as ownership interests in partnerships or corporations; patents, copyrights, and trademarks (discussed in Chapter 14); and claims against others, both in tort and in contract. These interests and claims, including checks and promissory notes, are also called **choses in action,** which means evidence of the right to property but not the property itself.

When personal property is physically attached to real property, it is known as a **fixture** and becomes part of the real property. A built-in dishwasher and a permanently installed lighting unit are examples of fixtures. In contrast, when a business tenant physically attaches personal property, such as machinery, that is necessary to carry on the trade or business to real property, it is called a **trade fixture.** It does not become part of the real property and may be removed by the business tenant upon termination of the tenancy.

SALE OF GOODS

The **Uniform Commercial Code (UCC),** which is a law in every state, governs different types of commercial transactions. A familiar transaction that is governed by the UCC, except in Louisiana, is a contract for the sale of goods, whether you deal with a business or another private party. **Goods** may be defined as anything that is movable. Your books, clothing, motor vehicles, computers, furniture, food, animals, and growing crops are all examples of goods—another name for tangible personal property. If the goods are not yet in existence (such as goods not yet manufactured) or under anyone's control (such as fish not yet caught), they are known as **future goods.** If they are the type of goods that are usually sold by weight or measure and are stored in bulk quantities, such as grain or oil, they are called **fungible goods.** These are defined as goods of which any unit is the same as any like unit.

If the goods are in accordance with the obligations under the contract, they are called **conforming goods.** In contrast, if the goods are not the same as those called for under the contract or are defective, they are called **nonconforming goods.** Sellers who deliver nonconforming goods are allowed to **cure** (correct) the defect if they do so within the contract period. If the defect is not cured, buyers have the right to **cover** the sale—that is, buy similar goods from someone else and bring suit for the difference between the agreed price and the cost of the purchase. **Identified goods** is the name given to specific goods that have been selected as the subject matter of a contract. Goods must be identified as goods to which a contract refers before title to them can pass from a seller to a buyer.

A contract for *services* is not governed by the UCC because it is not a sale of goods. Such a contract is governed by the common law of contracts, discussed in Chapters 16–18.

A **sale** is defined by the Uniform Commercial Code as the passing of **title** (ownership) from the seller to the buyer for a price. Sometimes a **bill of sale,** which is a signed writing evidencing the transfer of personal property from one person to another, is given by the seller to the buyer. If title is to pass at a future time, the transaction is called a **contract to sell** rather than a sale. A **sale on approval** occurs when the goods are for the buyer's use rather than for resale, and they may be returned even though they conform to the contract. Such goods remain the property of the seller until the buyer's approval is expressed or a reasonable time elapses. In contrast, a **sale or return** occurs when the goods are primarily for resale and may be returned even though they conform to the contract. In this latter instance, title passes to the buyer at the time of sale but reverts to the seller if the goods are returned. A gift is not a sale, because the person receiving the gift (the **donee**) pays no price to the person making the gift (the **donor**).

Sometimes businesses will dispose of their entire stock of merchandise and supplies in one transaction. This disposal is called a **bulk transfer** which is defined as a transfer not in the ordinary course of business but in bulk of a major part of the materials, supplies, merchandise, or other inventory of an enterprise. When a bulk transfer is made, all creditors of the transferor must be notified of the forthcoming transfer at least 10 days before the transfer occurs. This notice gives creditors time, if they wish, to attach the goods before they are transferred. In this way, creditors can have the goods sold under the supervision of the court and obtain the money owed them.

Unique terms are used to describe certain contracts for goods. A contract to sell "all the goods a company manufactures" or "all the crops a farmer grows" is called an **output contract.** In contrast, a contract to buy "all the fuel needed for one year" is called a **requirements contract.** A contract under which the seller turns the goods over to a carrier for delivery to a buyer is termed a **shipment contract** and is often designated **f.o.b. the place of shipment** (such as Boston), meaning free onboard (no delivery charges) to the place of shipment. In a shipment contract, title to the goods and **risk of loss** (responsibility in case of damage or destruction) pass to the buyer when the goods are turned over to a carrier. On the other hand, a contract that requires the seller to deliver goods to a destination is called a **destination contract** and is designated **f.o.b. the place of destination** (such as Chicago). In a destination contract, title and risk of loss pass to the buyer when the goods are tendered at their destination.

Electronic Commerce

Shopping online, paying bills, and doing business on the Internet have become a way of life for many people. The general term that describes this practice is **e-commerce** (electronic commerce)—the buying and selling of goods and services or the transfer of money over the Internet.

WEB WISE

Learn more about e-commerce at the following sites:

- **http://www.google.com** and key in "e-commerce"
- **http://www.ilr.cornell.edu** and click "search."
- **http://e-comm.webopedia.com/**

Warranties

Sellers of goods often guarantee their products by making promises or statements of fact about them. This guarantee is known as an **express warranty** and comes about when sellers, as part of a transaction, make statements of fact or promises about the goods, describe them, or show samples of them. Under federal law, when a **full warranty** is given for consumer goods, the seller must repair or replace without cost to the buyer defective goods or refund the purchase price. Any express warranty that does less must be labeled a **limited warranty.**

An **implied warranty** is one that is imposed by law rather than given voluntarily by the seller. Two kinds are (1) the warranty of merchantability and (2) the warranty of fitness for a particular purpose.

The **warranty of merchantability** is made whenever merchants sell goods. It is not given by private parties. Merchants warrant, among other guarantees, that their goods are fit for the ordinary purpose for which they are to be used. A **merchant** is a person who sells goods of the kind sold in the ordinary course of business or who has knowledge or skills peculiar to those goods.

The **warranty of fitness for a particular purpose** is made when any buyer relies on a seller's skill and judgment in selecting the goods. When this happens, the seller impliedly warrants that the goods are fit for the purpose for which they are to be used.

Implied warranties may be excluded by the seller by indicating in a conspicuous fashion that they are excluded or by writing "as is" or "with all faults" on the sales slip. Exclusion of these warranties is not effective when express warranties are made for consumer goods.

Another warranty that is made by all sellers of goods, whether merchants or not, is called the **warranty of title.** This warrants that the title being conveyed is good, that the transfer is rightful, and that no unknown liens on the goods exist. Unlike implied warranties, the warranty of title cannot be excluded by the seller.

Auction Sales

An **auction sale** is a sale of property to the highest **bidder** (offeror). In an **auction with reserve,** the auctioneer may withdraw the goods without accepting the highest bid. In contrast, in an **auction without reserve,** the auctioneer must sell the goods to the highest bidder. An auction is *with reserve* unless otherwise stated by the auctioneer.

BAILMENTS

A **bailment** occurs whenever one person places personal property in the possession of another person without intending to transfer title to that person. For example, a bailment occurs when someone leaves a car with an auto repair shop to be fixed, or loans a lawnmower

Figure 19-1 A guarantee is another name for an express warranty. The Uniform Commercial Code would not apply in this transaction, however, because it is a contract for services rather than for goods. NON SEQUITUR © Wiley Miller. Dist. By UNIVERSAL PRESS SYNDICATE. Reprinted with permission. All rights reserved.

to a neighbor, or takes care of a friend's goldfish for a week. The one who owns the goods and places them in the possession of another person is the **bailor.** The one who takes possession of the goods is the **bailee.** It is not a bailment when someone borrows something, such as a cup of sugar, and intends to return a similar amount of the same goods, because the exact item that was borrowed will not be returned. Instead of a bailment, that type of borrowing is known as a **mutuum.**

It is called a **mutual benefit bailment** when both the bailor and the bailee benefit from the transactions. For example, when someone leaves a watch with a jeweler to be repaired, the watch owner receives the benefit of having the watch repaired, and the jeweler receives the benefit of being paid for the service rendered. In this type of bailment, the bailee owes a duty to use ordinary care toward the property and would be responsible for ordinary negligence if the goods are lost or damaged.

A **gratuitous bailment** is one in which no consideration is given by one of the parties in exchange for the benefits bestowed by the other. It may be for the sole benefit of either the bailor or the bailee. For example, if someone stores his or her car in a friend's garage for safekeeping while away on a trip, it would be a **bailment for the sole benefit of the bailor.** In this type of bailment, the bailee owes a duty to use only slight care over the property and would be responsible only for gross negligence, because he or she is receiving no benefit. When someone loans a camera or other item to a friend, conversely, it is a **bailment for the sole benefit of the bailee.** Here, the bailee owes a duty to use great care with the property and would be responsible for slight negligence in the event of loss or damage to the bailed property.

A **tortious bailee** is one who has wrongful possession of another's goods. For example, a person who takes another's goods without authority, or keeps another's goods after they should be returned, or uses another's goods for a purpose other than agreed upon is a tortious bailee.

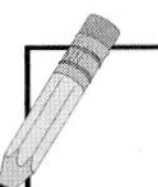

WORD WISE

More Words Ending in "or" and "ee"

assignor (ass·en·OR)	A person who transfers contract rights or property to another
assignee (ass·en·EE)	One to whom contract rights or property is transferred
bailor (bay·LOR)	One who transfers goods to another temporarily
bailee (bay·LEE)	One to whom goods are transferred temporarily
consignor (kon·sine·OR)	A party shipping goods under a bill of lading
consignee (kon·sine·EE)	A party to whom goods are shipped under a bill of lading
donor (doh·NOR)	One who makes a gift
donee (doh·NEE)	One to whom a gift is made

REVIEWING WHAT YOU LEARNED

After studying the text, write the answers to each of the following questions:

1. Name and give an example of each of the two kinds of personal property. ______________

____

____

____

2. What is the difference between a fixture and a trade fixture? ______________

____

____

____

3. What do goods include? ______________

____

____

____

4. What is the name given to the type of goods that are usually sold by weight or measure and are stored in bulk quantities? ______________

____

____

____

5. Why is a gift not a sale? ______________

____

____

____

6. When do express warranties come about? ______________

____

____

____

7. What is the difference between a full warranty and a limited warranty? ______________

____

____

____

8. When is the warranty of merchantability made, and what does it include? ______________

____

____

____

9. When is the warranty of fitness for a particular purpose made? ______________________________

10. How may implied warranties be excluded?

11. What is the warranty of title, and who makes it?

12. When does a bailment occur? ______________

13. Why is it not a bailment when someone borrows a cup of sugar from a neighbor? ____________

14. Give an example of a mutual benefit bailment.

15. Give an example of a bailment for the sole benefit of the bailor. ______________

16. Why does the bailee in a bailment for the sole benefit of the bailorowe a duty to use only slight care over the property? ______________

17. Give an example of a tortious bailee. ________

UNDERSTANDING LEGAL CONCEPTS

Indicate whether each statement is true or false. Then, change the italicized word or phrase of each *false* statement to make it true.

Answers

______ **1.** *Tangible* personal property is property that is not perceptible to the senses and cannot be touched.

______ **2.** Goods that are not yet in existence or under anyone's control are called *fungible* goods.

______ **3.** Under federal law, when a *limited* warranty is given for consumer goods, the seller must repair or replace without cost to the buyer defective goods or refund the purchase price.

______ **4.** The warranty of *merchantability* is made whenever merchants sell goods.

______ **5.** Implied warranties *may be* excluded by writing "as is" on the sales slip.

______ **6.** The warranty of *title* cannot be excluded by the seller.

______ **7.** It is a *bailment* when someone borrows a cup of sugar from a neighbor.

______ **8.** In a mutual benefit bailment, the bailee owes a duty to use *slight* care toward the property.

______ **9.** In a bailment for the sole benefit of the bailee, the bailee owes a duty to use *great* care with the property.

______ **10.** A person who uses another's goods for a purpose other than agreed upon is a *tortious bailee.*

CHECKING TERMINOLOGY (PART A)

From the list of legal terms that follows, select the one that matches each definition.

a. auction sale
b. auction with reserve
c. auction without reserve
d. bailee
e. bailment
f. bailment for the sole benefit of the bailee
g. bailment for the sole benefit of the bailor
h. bailor
i. bidder
j. bill of sale
k. bulk transfer
l. chose in action
m. conforming goods
n. contract to sell
o. cover
p. cure
q. destination contract
r. donee
s. donor
t. e-commerce
u. express warranty
v. fixture
w. f.o.b. the place of destination
x. f.o.b. the place of shipment
y. full warranty
z. fungible goods
aa. future goods
bb. goods

Answers

____ **1.** Offeror.
____ **2.** Correct.
____ **3.** A contract under which title to goods is to pass at a future time.
____ **4.** Personal property that is physically attached to real property and becomes part of the real property.
____ **5.** An auction in which the auctioneer may withdraw the goods without accepting the highest bid.
____ **6.** Goods that are not yet in existence or under anyone's control.
____ **7.** Goods that are in accordance with the obligations under the contract.
____ **8.** Anything that is movable.
____ **9.** A gratuitous bailment benefiting only the bailor.
____ **10.** An auction in which the auctioneer must sell the goods to the highest bidder.
____ **11.** Free on-board (no delivery charges) to the place of shipment.
____ **12.** A contract that requires the seller to deliver goods to a destination.
____ **13.** A signed writing evidencing the transfer of personal property from one person to another.
____ **14.** The relationship that exists when possession (but not ownership) of personal property is transferred to another for a specific purpose.
____ **15.** A sale of property to the highest bidder.
____ **16.** Free on-board (no delivery charges) to the place of destination.
____ **17.** A person who receives a gift.
____ **18.** The owner of personal property that has been temporarily transferred to a bailee under a contract of bailment.
____ **19.** An express warranty given for consumer goods under which the seller must repair or replace without cost to the buyer defective goods or refund the purchase price.
____ **20.** Evidence of the right to property but not the property itself.
____ **21.** A statement of fact or promise that goods have certain qualities.
____ **22.** The person to whom personal property is delivered under a contract of bailment.
____ **23.** A person who gives a gift.
____ **24.** Goods such as grain or oil, of which any unit is the same as any like unit.
____ **25.** A transfer not in the ordinary course of business but in bulk of a major part of the materials, supplies, merchandise, or other inventory of an enterprise.
____ **26.** The right of a buyer, after breach by a seller, to purchase similar goods from someone else.
____ **27.** A gratuitous bailment benefiting only the bailee.
____ **28.** The buying and selling of goods and services or the transfer of money over the Internet.

5

CHECKING TERMINOLOGY (PART B)

From the list of legal terms that follows, select the one that matches each definition.

- **a.** chattels
- **b.** gratuitous bailment
- **c.** identified goods
- **d.** implied warranty
- **e.** intangible personal property
- **f.** limited warranty
- **g.** merchant
- **h.** mutual benefit bailment
- **i.** mutuum
- **j.** nonconforming goods
- **k.** output contract
- **l.** personal property
- **m.** personalty
- **n.** requirements contract
- **o.** risk of loss
- **p.** sale
- **q.** sale on approval
- **r.** sale or return
- **s.** shipment contract
- **t.** tangible personal property
- **u.** title
- **v.** tortious bailee
- **w.** trade fixture
- **x.** Uniform Commercial Code
- **y.** warranty of fitness for a particular purpose
- **z.** warranty of merchantability
- **aa.** warranty of title

Answers

____ **1.** Ownership.

____ **2.** A loan of goods, on the agreement that the borrower may consume them, returning to the lender an equivalent in kind and quantity.

____ **3.** A law in every state that governs different types of commercial transactions.

____ **4.** A bailment for the sole benefit of either the bailor or the bailee, in which no consideration is given by one of the parties in exchange for the benefits bestowed by the other.

____ **5.** Property that has substance and that can be touched.

____ **6.** A contract to sell "all the goods a company manufactures" or "all the crops a farmer grows."

____ **7.** An implied warranty, given by merchants in all sales unless excluded, that goods are fit for the ordinary purpose for which such goods are used.

____ **8.** An express warranty given for consumer goods that is less than a full warranty.

____ **9.** A sale of goods that are primarily for resale and may be returned even though they conform to the contract.

____ **10.** Anything that is the subject of ownership other than real property (select three answers).

____ **11.** A guarantee that title is good, that the transfer is rightful, and that no unknown liens on the goods exist.

____ **12.** The passing of title from the seller to the buyer for a price.

____ **13.** A warranty that is imposed by law rather than given voluntarily.

____ **14.** An implied warranty, given when a buyer relies on any seller's skill and judgment in selecting goods, that they will be fit for a particular purpose.

____ **15.** Goods that are not the same as those called for under the contract.

____ **16.** A contract under which the seller turns the goods over to a carrier for delivery to a buyer.

____ **17.** Goods that have been selected as the subject matter of a contract.

____ **18.** A sale of goods that are for the buyer's use rather than for resale and that may be returned even though they conform to the contract.

____ **19.** A bailment in which both the bailor and the bailee receive some benefit.

____ **20.** Responsibility in case of damage or destruction.

____ **21.** Personal property, necessary to carry on a trade or business, that is physically attached to real property but does not become part of the real property.

____ **22.** Property that is not perceptible to the senses and that cannot be touched.

____ **23.** A contract to buy "all the fuel (or other goods) needed for one year."

____ **24.** A person who sells goods of the kind sold in the ordinary course of business or who has knowledge or skills peculiar to those goods.

____ **25.** A person who is wrongfully in possession of another's personal property.

UNRAVELING LEGALESE

Use simple, non-legal language, with the help of the glossary, to rewrite this case quote so that it is shorter and can be understood by a layperson without losing its meaning.

> The doctrine is now well settled that a sale of timber or other product of the soil, which is to be severed from the freehold by the vendee under a special license to enter on the land for that purpose is, in contemplation of the parties, a sale of chattels only, and cannot be regarded as passing an interest in the land, and is not for that reason required to be in writing as being within the statute of frauds.

USING LEGAL LANGUAGE

Read the following story and fill in the blank lines with legal terms taken from the list of terms at the beginning of this chapter.

Roland went shopping for an outdoor gas grill to give to his friend Rita for her birthday. Broadly speaking, the grill would be called ____________________, ____________________, or ____________________, because it is the subject of ownership other than real property. Because it has substance and can be touched, it is ____________________. It is also called ____________________, because it is movable. The grill that Roland looked at had a 90-day guarantee, which is known as a(n) ____________________ in legal terminology. It was not a(n) ____________________, however, because any defective part had to be shipped at the buyer's expense to the factory for repair or replacement. For that reason, the guarantee is known as a (n) ____________________. In addition, a(n) ____________________ would exist—that is, a type of guarantee that is imposed by law. Called the ____________________, it guarantees that the goods are fit for the ordinary purpose for which they are to be used and is made when goods are sold by a(n) ____________________—that is, one who sells goods of the kind sold in the ordinary course of business. This guarantee was not a(n) ____________________, because Roland did not rely on the seller's skill and judgment in selecting the grill. When Roland bought the grill, it was a(n) ____________________ because ____________________ (ownership) passed from the seller to the buyer for a

5

price. Had title passed at a future time, it would have been called a(n) ______________________________. Under its ______________________________, the store guaranteed that title to the grill was good and that its transfer was rightful. When Roland gave the grill to Rita, he was the ______________________________, and she was the ______________________________. The next morning, Rita left the gas tank in the possession of a bottled-gas company to be filled and picked up later, creating a(n) ______________________________. Rita was the ______________________________; the bottled-gas company was the ______________________________. Because both parties benefited from the transaction, it was a(n) ______________________________. The gas that was put into the tank is known as ______________________________, because any unit is the same as any like unit. Rita paid for the gas by check, which is a(n) ______________________________, or a type of ______________________________. Rita's neighbor Ruth borrowed not only her grill but also some hot dogs that Rita had in the freezer. The loan of the grill was a(n) ______________________________, because no consideration was given, and the loan of the hot dogs was a(n) ______________________________, because the identical ones would not be returned. Ruth moved away without returning Rita's grill, becoming a(n) ______________________________.

PUZZLING OVER WHAT YOU LEARNED

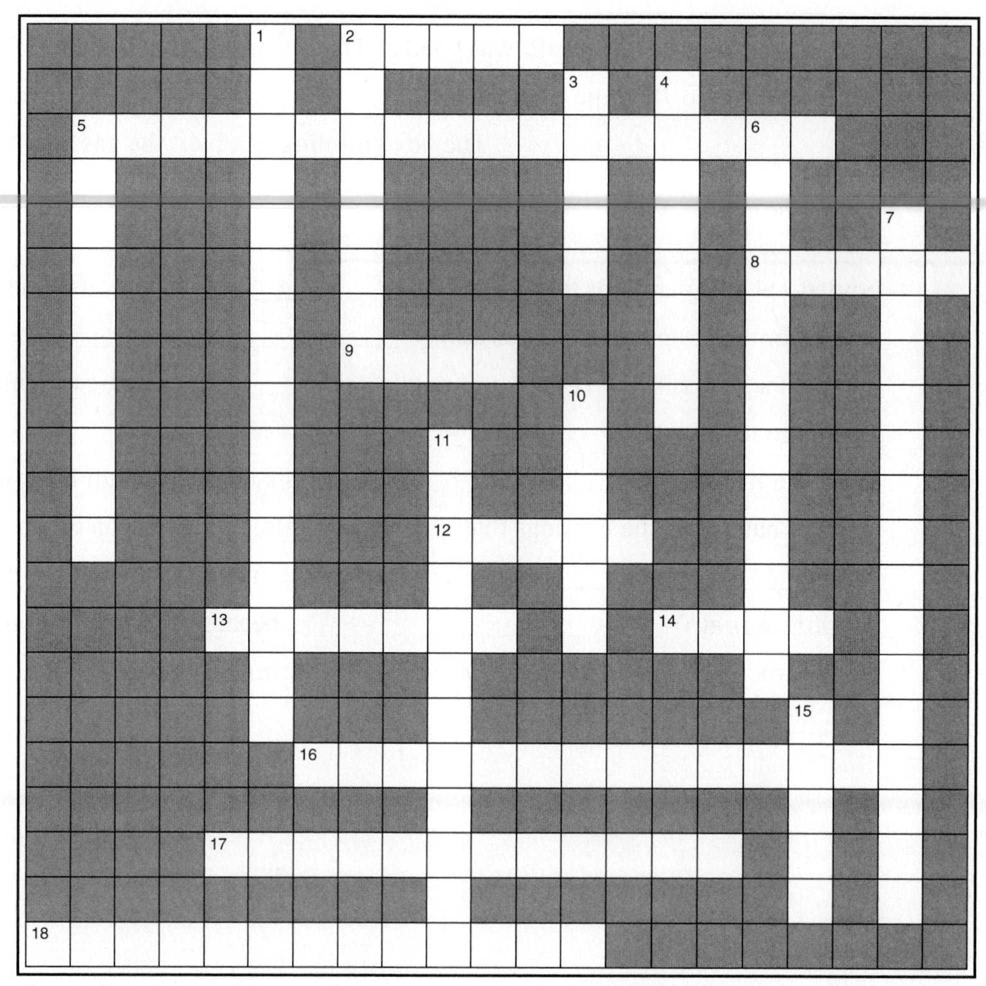

Caveat: Allow squares for spaces between words and punctuation (apostrophes, hyphens, etc.) when filling in crossword.

Across

2. The right of a buyer, after breach by a seller, to purchase similar goods from someone else.
5. Anything that is the subject of ownership other than real property.
8. A person who gives a gift.
9. The passing of title from the seller to the buyer for a price.
12. Ownership.
13. Personal property attached to real property.
14. Correct.
16. Goods such as grain or oil, of which any unit is the same as any like unit.
17. Written evidence of the transfer of personalty from one person to another.
18. A transfer in bulk of the majority of a merchant's inventory.

Down

1. Evidence of the right to property but not the property itself.
2. Anything that is the subject of ownership other than real property.
3. Anything that is movable.
4. Person who sells goods of the kind sold in the ordinary course of business.
5. Another name for personal property.
6. Personal property attached to real property necessary for business.
7. Contract under which title to goods is passed at a future time.
10. Owner of personal property that has been temporarily transferred to a bailee.
11. Goods that are not yet in existence or under anyone's control.
15. A person who receives a gift.

5

CHAPTER 20
Intellectual Property

ANTE INTERROGATORY

A patent is a grant by the U.S. government of the exclusive right to make, use, and sell an invention for (A) 50 years, (B) 25 years, (C) 17 years, (D) 10 years.

CHAPTER OUTLINE

Patents
Copyrights
Trademarks
Trade Secrets

KEY TERMS

confidentiality agreement *(kon·fe·den·shee·AL·i·tee a·GREE·ment)*
copyright *(KOP·ee·rite)*
copyright infringement *(KOP·ee·rite in·FRINJ·ment)*
due process clause *(dew PRO·sess)*
enjoin *(en·JOYN)*
equal protection clause *(EE·kwell pro·TEK·shen)*
fair-use doctrine *(DOK·trin)*
generic term *(jen·ER·ik)*
injunction *(in·JUNK·shun)*
intellectual property *(in·te·LEK·choo·el PROP·er·tee)*
nondisclosure agreement *(non·dis·KLOH·zher a·GREE·ment)*
patent *(PAT·ent)*
patent infringement *(PAT·ent in·FRINJ·ment)*
privileges and immunities clause *(PRIV·i·leg·es and im·YOON·i·teez)*
public domain *(PUB·lik doh·MAYN)*
service mark *(SER·viss·mark)*
trademark *(TRADE·mark)*
trade secret *(SEE·kret)*

5

Intellectual property is an original work fixed in a tangible medium of expression. The term is a broad, encompassing term used to describe the fields of patents, copyrights, trademarks, and trade secrets. Examples of intellectual property are literary and artistic works, inventions, audio and video recordings, computer programs, and trade secrets. Owners of such property are given protection by the government to prevent their creative works from being taken and used without authority by others.

PATENTS

For protection, inventors may have their inventions patented by the U.S. Patent and Trademark Office in Arlington, Virginia. A **patent** is a grant by the U.S. government of the exclusive right to make, use, and sell an invention for 20 years. A *utility patent* is granted for inventing a new process or item of manufacture. In contrast, a *design patent* is given (for a 14-year period) on the way an item is fashioned; that is, the way it looks. Utility and design patents can be obtained for the same invention. A *plant patent* is issued for asexually producing a new plant; that is, by other than the use of seeds, for example, by grafting. To be patented, an item must be novel and not be obvious to a person with ordinary skill in that particular field. When the 20-year period expires, the invention loses its protection and becomes part of the **public domain**—that is, becomes owned by the public. At that time, the invention may be made, used, or sold by anyone.

A **patent infringement** is the unauthorized making, using, or selling of a patented invention during the term of the patent. Federal courts have the power to enjoin anyone from infringing on another's patent. **Enjoin** means to require a person to perform or to abstain from some act, and it is usually done by the court's issuance of an **injunction,** which is an order to do or refrain from doing a particular act.

COPYRIGHTS

A **copyright** is the exclusive right given to an author, composer, artist, or photographer to publish and sell exclusively a work for the life of the author plus 70 years. Such things as literary works; pantomime and choreographic works; pictorial, graphic, and sculptural works; motion pictures and other audiovisual works; and sound recordings may be copyrighted. Computer programs fall under the category of literary works and may also be copyrighted.

In 1998, Congress enacted the Sonny Bono Act, which extended the life of a copyright from 50 to 70 years after the author's death. The act was held to be constitutional by the U.S. Supreme Court in 2003.

To register a copyright, it is necessary to fill out a government form and send it with the proper fee and two copies of the work to the U.S. Copyright Office in Washington, D.C. Although formerly required, it is now optional to put © or the word "copyright" followed by the date and the name of the owner on the work.

Copyrighted work may not be reproduced without permission of the owner of the copyright. The unauthorized use of copyrighted material is known as **copyright infringement.** Under the **fair-use doctrine,** however, the fair use of a copyrighted work for purposes such as criticism, comment, news reporting, teaching (including multiple copies for classroom use), scholarship, or research is not a copyright infringement.

TRADEMARKS

A **trademark** is any word, name, symbol, or device used by a business to identify goods and distinguish them from those manufactured or sold by others. **Servicemark** is the term used to describe trademark protection for services.

In addition to being established by usage under the common law, trademarks may be obtained from state governments by following state trademark laws. The most common type of trademark, however, is one obtained by registering with the U.S. Patent and Trademark Office. A federal trademark provides protection for 10 years and may be renewed for additional 10-year periods. Under the federal law, an application to register a trademark may be filed six months before the mark is used in commerce. The mark then becomes reserved and cannot be used by anyone else for six months. An additional six-month reservation period is allowed, and other extensions may be obtained by showing good cause. The trademark registration becomes effective when the mark is actually used in the ordinary course of trade.

Although not required by law, notice that a trademark is registered with the federal government may be given by using the symbol ® or by using the phrase "Registered in U.S. Patent & Trademark Office" or "Reg. U.S. Pat. & Tm. Off." If the mark is not federally registered, the symbol ® may not be used. The symbol ™ or ℠ may be used, however, to give notice of the trademark or servicemark established by usage under the common law. No symbol has been established to designate state-registered trademarks.

Trademark protection can be lost by nonuse or by the mark becoming a generic term used by a large segment of the public for a long period of time. A **generic term** is a term that relates to, or is characteristic of, a whole group. "Corn flakes," "nylon," "escalator," and "yo-yo" are examples of trademarks that were lost by becoming generic terms. To prevent products from losing their trademarks, businesses use the word "brand" after their product name. They also place advertisements in journals reminding people that their products are trademarked. For example, the Xerox Corporation advertised: "You can't Xerox a Xerox on a Xerox, but we don't mind if you copy a copy on a Xerox copier."

TRADE SECRETS

A **trade secret** is a plan, process, or device that is used in business and is known only to employees who need to know the secret to accomplish their work. Examples of trade secrets are customer lists, chemical formulas, food recipes, manufacturing processes, marketing techniques, and pricing methods.

Figure 20-1 This trademark for Ivory Soap was registered by Procter & Gamble in 1879. Under current law, how long does a federal trademark last? (Courtesy of the Library of Congress, Prints and Photographs Division, reproduction number LC-USZ62-77907.)

5

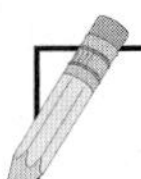

WORD WISE

The "Gen" in GENERIC

The root "gen-" may mean "birth, origin, or race" as in:

gene
generation
genesis

Or it may mean "type" as in:

gender
generic
genus

How the word is used in the context of a sentence will generally show whether "gen-" indicates "birth" or "type" in a particular word. Consider the use of "gen-" in the following terms found in the text:

miscegenation
general agent
primogeniture
genocide
generic term

CONSTITUTION WISE

Meaningful Clauses

privileges and immunities clause	Requires states to give out-of-state citizens the same rights as they give their own citizens.	Art. IV, s. 2; 14th Amend.
equal protection clause	Requires that similarly situated persons receive similar treatment under the law.	14th Amend.
due process clause	No person shall be deprived of life, liberty, or property without fairness and justice (due process of law).	5th Amend; 14th Amend.

5

Businesses often protect trade secrets by having employees sign **nondisclosure** or **confidentiality agreements,** agreeing to refrain from disclosing trade secrets to others. Even without such an agreement, however, courts prohibit employees from disclosing their employer's trade secrets both while they are employed and after they leave the employment. When this employee duty is violated, courts will often enjoin the use of the trade secret by others to whom the secret has been given.

Figure 20-2 The equal protection clause of the U.S. Constitution requires that similarly situated persons receive similar treatment under the law.

REVIEWING WHAT YOU LEARNED

After studying the text, write the answers to each of the following questions.

1. Name the fields that "intellectual property" describes. ____________________

2. What are the requirements for an invention to be patented? ____________________

3. Describe what happens to an invention when the protection period covered by a patent expires. ____________________

4. What may a court do when a patent infringement occurs? ____________________

5. Explain the procedure to copyright a work. ____________________

6. When is the copying of a copyrighted work not an infringement? ____________________

7. In what three ways may a trademark be obtained? ____________________

8. How may a trademark be reserved? ____________________

9. When does a trademark registration become effective? ____________________

10. For how long may the federal trademark protection period be renewed? ____________________

11. How may trademark protection be lost? ____________________

12. Give three examples of trade secrets. ____________________

13. How do businesses often protect their trade secrets? ____________________

14. In what other way are trade secrets protected? ____________________

UNDERSTANDING LEGAL CONCEPTS

Indicate whether each statement is true or false. Then, change the italicized word or phrase of each *false* statement to make it true.

Answers

______ 1. A patent owner has the exclusive right to make, use, and sell an invention for *50 years.*

______ 2. *State* courts have the power to enjoin anyone from infringing on another's patent.

______ 3. Copyright protection lasts for *the life of the author.*

______ 4. It is now *optional* to put © or the word "copyright" followed by the date and the name of the owner on a copyrighted work.

______ 5. The fair use of copyrighted work for purposes of teaching, *including multiple copies for classroom use,* is allowed.

______ 6. *Trademark* is the term used to describe protection for services.

______ 7. Trademark protection may be obtained from *state governments.*

______ 8. The most common type of trademark is obtained by *usage under the common law.*

______ 9. A registered trademark provides protection for *15 years.*

______ 10. Trademark protection *can* be lost by the mark becoming a generic term.

CHECKING TERMINOLOGY

From the list of legal terms that follows, select the one that matches each definition.

a. confidentiality agreement
b. copyright
c. copyright infringement
d. due process clause
e. enjoin
f. equal protection clause
g. fair-use doctrine
h. generic term
i. injunction
j. intellectual property
k. nondisclosure agreement
l. patent
m. patent infringement
n. privileges and immunities clause
o. public domain
p. servicemark
q. trademark
r. trade secret

Answers

____ **1.** To require a person to perform or to abstain from some act.
____ **2.** An order to do or refrain from doing a particular act.
____ **3.** A term used to describe trademark protection for services.
____ **4.** A clause in the U.S. Constitution requiring states to give out-of-state citizens the same rights as they give their own citizens.
____ **5.** The unauthorized use of copyrighted material.
____ **6.** A grant by the U.S. government of the exclusive right to make, use, and sell an invention for 20 years.
____ **7.** A rule stating that the use of a copyrighted work for purposes such as criticism, comment, news reporting, teaching, scholarship, or research is not a copyright infringement.
____ **8.** Any word, name, symbol, or device used by a business to identify goods and distinguish them from those manufactured or sold by others.
____ **9.** An agreement to refrain from disclosing trade secrets to others (select two answers).
____ **10.** An original work fixed in a tangible medium of expression.
____ **11.** Owned by the public.
____ **12.** A clause in the U.S. Constitution requiring that no person shall be deprived of life, liberty, or property without fairness and justice.
____ **13.** A term that means relating to, or characteristic of, a whole group.
____ **14.** A plan, process, or device that is used in business and is known only to employees who need to know the secret to accomplish their work.
____ **15.** The unauthorized making, using, or selling of a patented invention during the term of the patent.
____ **16.** The exclusive right given to an author, composer, artist, or photographer to publish and sell exclusively a work for the life of the author plus 70 years.
____ **17.** A clause in the U.S. Constitution requiring similarly situated persons to receive similar treatment under the law.

UNRAVELING LEGALESE

Use simple, non-legal language, with the help of the glossary, to rewrite this case quote so that it is shorter and can be understood by a layperson without losing its meaning.

> Copyright law protects original expressions of ideas but it does not safeguard either the ideas themselves or banal expressions of them. Thus, in assessing whether substantial similarity exists, an overall impression of similarity may not be enough. If such an impression flows from similarities as to elements that are not themselves copyrightable, it will not satisfy the predicate requirement of originality necessary to ground a finding of actionable copying.

USING LEGAL LANGUAGE

Read the following story and fill in the blank lines with legal terms taken from the list of terms at the beginning of this chapter.

Millin, an inventor, obtained ____________ on two products she had invented, giving her the exclusive right to make, use, and sell them for 20 years. Since she had obtained one of them more than 20 years ago, it was now in the ____________. The other type of ____________ (original work fixed in a tangible medium of expression) was much newer and was copied by a competitor, causing Millin to bring a(n) ____________ suit for the unauthorized making of the product. Millin won the case, and the court ____________ the competitor by issuing a(n) ____________ ordering it to refrain from making Millin's product. When Millin began to sell the product, she obtained a(n) ____________ for it to identify it and to distinguish it from products made by others. She did not obtain a(n) ____________, because the product was a good rather than a service. To prevent the product from becoming a(n) ____________, Millin used the word "brand" in all product advertisements. For further protection, Millin required all of her employees to sign ____________, also called ____________, agreeing to refrain from disclosing ____________ to others. The product turned out to be so successful that she wrote a book about her success. A(n) ____________ gave her the exclusive right to publish the book except for a limited amount of copying that could be done by others under a rule known as the ____________.

5

PUZZLING OVER WHAT YOU LEARNED

Caveat: Do **not** allow squares for spaces between words and punctuation (apostrophes, hyphens, etc.) when filling in crossword.

Across

2. The unauthorized making, using, or selling of a patented invention during the term of the patent.
6. An order to do or refrain from doing a particular act.
9. A term used to describe trademark protection for services.
10. Any word, name, symbol, or device used by a business to identify goods and distinguish them from those manufactured or sold by others.
11. The exclusive right given to an author, composer, artist, or photographer, to publish and sell exclusively a work for the life of the author plus 70 years.
12. A clause in the U.S. Constitution requiring that no person shall be deprived of life, liberty, or property without fairness and justice.
13. A clause in the U.S. Constitution requiring similarly situated persons to receive similar treatment under the law.

Down

1. To require a person to perform or to abstain from some act.
2. Owned by the public.
3. An original work fixed in a tangible medium of expression.
4. A rule stating that the use of a copyrighted work for purposes such as criticism, comment, news reporting, teaching, scholarship, or research is not a copyright infringement.
5. A term that means relating to or characteristic of a whole group.
7. A grant by the U.S. government of the exclusive right to make, use, and sell an invention for 20 years.
8. A plan, process, or device that is used in business and is known only to employees who need to know the secret to accomplish their work.

CHAPTER 21
Law of Agency

ANTE INTERROGATORY

One who performs services under the direction and control of another is known as a(n) (A) agent, (B) servant, (C) independent contractor, (D) consignee.

CHAPTER OUTLINE

KEY TERMS

agency *(AY·jen·see)*
agency by estoppel *(AY·jen·see by es·TOP·el)*
agency by ratification *(AY·jen·see by rat·i·fi·KAY·shun)*
agent *(AY·jent)*
apparent authority *(a·PAR·ent aw·THAW·ri·tee)*
attorney in fact *(a·TERN·ee)*
consignee *(kon·sine·EE)*
consignment *(kon·SINE·ment)*
consignor *(kon·sine·OR)*
del credere agent *(del KREH·de·reh AY·jent)*
employee *(em·PLOY·ee)*
employer *(em·PLOY·er)*
express authority *(eks·PRESS aw·THAW·ri·tee)*
factor *(FAK·ter)*
general agent *(JEN·e·rel AY·jent)*
implied authority *(im·PLIDE aw·THAW·ri·tee)*
impute *(im·PEWT)*
independent contractor *(in·de·PEN·dent KON·trak·ter)*
malfeasance *(mal·FEE·zense)*
master *(MAS·ter)*
misfeasance *(mis·FEE·zense)*
nonfeasance *(non·FEE·zense)*
power of attorney *(POW·er ov a·TERN·ee)*
principal *(PRIN·se·pel)*
respondeat superior *(res·PON·dee·at soo·PEER·ee·or)*
servant *(SER·vent)*
special agent *(SPESH·el AY·jent)*
third party *(PAR·tee)*
undisclosed principal *(un·dis·KLOZED PRIN·se·pel)*
vicarious liability *(vy·KEHR·ee·us)*

5

It is common in our society to have one person act on behalf of another in dealing with third parties. For example, when salespeople sell goods and collect money, they are acting on behalf of the owner of the establishment; when corporate executives sign contracts, they are acting on behalf of the stockholders who own the business.

RELATIONSHIPS DISTINGUISHED

When discussing this subject matter, three types of relationships need to be distinguished: (1) principal-agent, (2) employer-employee, and (3) employer-independent contractor.

An **agency** relationship exists when one person, called an **agent,** is authorized to act on behalf of, and under the control of, another person, called a **principal.** The person with whom the agent deals is known as the **third party.** When a principal authorizes an agent to enter into a contract on the principal's behalf, the resulting contract is between the principal and the third party. The authorized agent is not a party to the contract and cannot be sued for its breach. Only when an agent acts without authority or fails to disclose the existence of the agency relationship can the agent be held liable on the contract by the third party.

When the third party deals with an agent and is not aware of the agency relationship, the principal is called an **undisclosed principal.** In such a case, privity of contract exists between the third party and the agent, and the agent can be held liable on the resulting contract. In the event of a suit for breach of contract, the third party may elect to hold either the principal or the agent liable.

An employment relationship exists when one person, called an **employee** (formerly known as a **servant**), performs services under the direction and control of another, called an **employer** (formerly known as a **master**). Employees may also be agents if they have been authorized to enter into contracts with third parties on behalf of their employers.

Independent contractors differ from employees in that they perform services for others but are not under the others' control. People who have independent contractors perform work for them do not withhold taxes from their pay and are not responsible for their wrongdoings.

KINDS OF AGENTS

A **general agent** is one who is authorized to conduct all of a principal's activity in connection with a particular business. A person hired to manage a business would be an example of a general agent. A **special agent,** conversely, is one who is authorized to carry out a single transaction or to perform a specified act. For example, a person authorized to sell a house for someone who is away on a trip would be a special agent.

Sometimes goods are sold on **consignment**—that is, they are left by a bailor (**consignor**) with a bailee (**consignee**) who tries to sell them. Title to the goods does not pass between these parties, and the goods may be returned if not sold. The bailee to whom the goods are consigned for sale is a type of agent called a **factor.** If the factor sells consigned goods on credit and guarantees to the consignor that the buyer will pay for them, the factor is known as a **del credere agent.**

AUTHORITY OF AGENTS

Agents are often given their authority expressly, which may be done either orally or in writing. **Express authority** is authority that is given explicitly. Sometimes agents are appointed formally by a written instrument known as a **power of attorney,** which is a formal writing that authorizes an agent to act for a principal. When a power of attorney is used, the agent is referred to as an **attorney in fact.**

In addition to the express authority given them, agents have a certain amount of **implied authority.** This authority is to perform incidental functions that are reasonably and customarily necessary to enable them to accomplish the overall purpose of the agency.

Apparent authority comes about when a principal, through some act, makes it appear that an agent has authority when none exists. This type of authority is also known as **agency by estoppel** because the principal will be stopped from denying that an agency relationship existed if he or she attempts to do so.

WORD WISE

Negative Prefixes—A Further Clarification

Prefix	*Meaning*	*Examples*
mis-	incorrect; improper	misspell
		misfeasance
		misdemeanor
		mistrial
		misrepresentation
mal-	bad; evil	malice
		malfeasance
		malpractice
non-	not	nonentity
		nonfeasance
		nonmarital child
		nonconforming use

When an agent acts on behalf of a principal without authority to do so, but the principal later approves of the act, it is known as an **agency by ratification.**

Sometimes agents fail to act when they are supposed to, or they act improperly. Three terms are used to describe such situations. **Misfeasance** is the improper doing of an act, **malfeasance** is the doing of an act that ought not to be done at all, and **nonfeasance** is the failure to do an act that ought to be done.

VICARIOUS LIABILITY

Principals and employers are responsible under a rule known as the doctrine of **respondeat superior** (let the superior respond) for the torts of their agents and employees that are committed within the scope of authority (in the case of agents) and within the scope of employment (in the case of employees). Principals and employers are said to have **vicarious liability,** which means that the wrongdoings of their agents and employees are **imputed** (charged) to them. Injured parties may recover damages from either the principal (or employer) or the agent (or employee). Usually, they recover from the former, because that person is in a better position to pay the damages.

REVIEWING WHAT YOU LEARNED

After studying the text, write the answers to each of the following questions.

1. Name the three relationships that need to be distinguished when discussing agency law. ______
2. When a principal authorizes an agent to enter into a contract, between whom is the contract?
3. When can an agent be held liable on a contract by a third party? ______
4. When an undisclosed principal is involved, whom may a third party hold liable in the event of a suit for breach of contract? ______
5. When may employees also be agents? ______
6. Describe two advantages of hiring independent contractors. ______
7. Give an example of a general agent and a special agent. ______
8. Describe the method of selling goods on consignment. ______
9. Why is apparent authority also called *agency by estoppel?* ______
10. From whom may injured parties recover damages when employees commit torts within the scope of their employment? ______

5

UNDERSTANDING LEGAL CONCEPTS

Indicate whether each statement is true or false. Then, change the italicized word or phrase of each *false* statement to make it true.

Answers

____________ **1.** When a principal authorizes an agent to enter into a contract on the principal's behalf, the resulting contract is between the *agent* and third party.

____________ **2.** An agent who contracts on behalf of an undisclosed principal *can* be held liable on the contract.

____________ **3.** Employees *may also be* agents if they have been authorized to enter into contracts with third parties on behalf of their employers.

____________ **4.** People who have independent contractors perform work for them *must* withhold taxes from their pay.

____________ **5.** A person hired to manage a business is an example of a *special* agent.

____________ **6.** When goods are sold on consignment, title to the goods *does not pass* between the consignor and the consignee.

____________ **7.** Agents may be appointed expressly, *either orally or in writing.*

____________ **8.** When agents are given express authority to perform certain acts, they have *no* implied authority.

____________ **9.** Apparent authority comes about when *an agent* makes it appear that the agent has authority when none exists.

____________ **10.** Someone who is injured by an employee's wrongful act may recover damages from *either* the employer or the employee.

CHECKING TERMINOLOGY

From the list of legal terms that follows, select the one that matches each definition.

- **a.** agency
- **b.** agency by estoppel
- **c.** agency by ratification
- **d.** agent
- **e.** apparent authority
- **f.** attorney in fact
- **g.** consignee
- **h.** consignment
- **i.** consignor
- **j.** del credere agent
- **k.** employee
- **l.** employer
- **m.** express authority
- **n.** factor
- **o.** general agent
- **p.** implied authority
- **q.** impute
- **r.** independent contractor
- **s.** malfeasance
- **t.** master
- **u.** misfeasance
- **v.** nonfeasance
- **w.** power of attorney
- **x.** principal
- **y.** respondeat superior
- **z.** servant
- **aa.** special agent
- **bb.** third party
- **cc.** undisclosed principal
- **dd.** vicarious liability

Answers

____ **1.** A rule of law that makes principals and employers responsible for the torts of their agents and servants committed within the scope of their authority or employment.

____ **2.** To charge; to lay the responsibility or blame.

____ **3.** Liability that is imputed to principals and employers because of the wrongdoings of their agents and employees.

____ **4.** A relationship that exists when one person is authorized to act under the control of another person.

____ **5.** A factor who sells consigned goods on credit and who guarantees to the consignor that the buyer will pay for the goods.

____ **6.** A bailee to whom goods are consigned for sale.

____ **7.** One who is authorized to act for another.

____ **8.** One who authorizes another to act on his or her behalf.

____ **9.** One who performs services under the direction and control of another (select two answers).

____ **10.** One who performs services for another but who is not under the other's control.

____ **11.** An agent who is authorized to conduct all of a principal's activity in connection with a particular business.

____ **12.** An agent who is authorized to carry out a single transaction or to perform a specified act.

____ **13.** Authority that is given explicitly.

____ **14.** A formal writing that authorizes an agent to act for a principal.

____ **15.** Authority to perform incidental functions that are reasonably and customarily necessary to enable an agent to accomplish the overall purpose of the agency.

____ **16.** Authority that comes about when a principal, through some act, makes it appear that an agent has authority when none actually exists (select two answers).

____ **17.** The failure to do an act that ought to be done.

____ **18.** A relationship that occurs when someone performs an act on behalf of another without authority to do so, but the other person later approves of the act.

____ **19.** The process of delivering goods to a bailee, called a factor, who attempts to sell them and who may return those that are unsold.

____ **20.** One who is not known by a third party to be a principal for an agent.

____ **21.** The doing of an act that ought not to be done at all.

____ **22.** In agency law, one who deals with an agent in making a contract with the agent's principal.

____**23.** An agent who is authorized to act under a power of attorney.

____**24.** One who makes a consignment.

____**25.** One to whom a consignment is made.

____**26.** One who employs the services of others in exchange for wages or salaries (select two answers).

____**27.** The improper doing of an act.

SHARPENING YOUR LATIN SKILLS

In the space provided, write the definition of the following legal terms, referring to the glossary when necessary.

caveat ____________________

caveat emptor ____________________

caveat venditor ____________________

nulla bona ____________________

respondeat superior ____________________

UNRAVELING LEGALESE

Use simple, non-legal language, with the help of the glossary, to rewrite this case quote so that it is shorter and can be understood by a layperson without losing its meaning.

> A servant is defined as a person employed to perform personal service for another in his [or her] affairs, and who, in respect to his [or her] physical movements in the performance of the service is subject to the other's control or right to control, while an agent is defined as a person who represents another in contractual negotiations or transactions akin thereto. The reason assigned for the importance of making the distinction is that an agent who is not at the same time acting as a servant cannot ordinarily make his [or her] principal liable for incidental negligence in connection with the means incidentally employed to accomplish the work entrusted to his [or her] care.

USING LEGAL LANGUAGE

Read the following story and fill in the blank lines with legal terms taken from the list of terms at the beginning of this chapter.

Darlene, who was the general manager and thus a(n) ____________________ for Johnson Service Co., hired Amos to work as a(n) ____________________ or ____________________ under the company's direction and control. The company was the ____________________ or ____________________ of Amos. One year later, Amos took a three-week vacation trip to Europe. Because his house was for sale at the time, he appointed Betsy to be his ____________________ solely for the purpose of selling the house in the event a buyer came along while he was away. Because he used a formal written instrument called a(n) ____________________ to make the appointment, Betsy became known as a(n) ____________________. Claude learned that the house was for sale and went to look at it. Betsy, meanwhile, was at the house and had just removed the well cover to see how much water was in it when Claude arrived. She introduced herself to him and showed him around, not telling him that she was not the owner. Claude decided to buy the house and signed a contract agreeing to do so. Betsy signed as the seller, not telling Claude that this was a(n) ____________________ relationship and that she was a(n) ____________________ acting on behalf of Amos, the ____________________, and that Claude was a(n) ____________________. Amos would be described as a(n) ____________________, because Claude was not aware of the particular relationship. As he walked from the house, Claude fell into the uncovered well and was injured. Under a doctrine known as ____________________, Amos would be ____________________ liable—that is, Betsy's negligent act of leaving the well uncovered would be ____________________ to him. After recuperating from his injuries, Claude converted part of his new house into a small gift shop where he sold other people's goods on ____________________, which is an arrangement under which title to the goods did not pass to Claude and he could return those that did not sell. People who left goods in his store for sale were called ____________________. Claude, who was known as a(n) ____________________, was also a type of agent called a(n) ____________________. Whenever he sold goods on credit and guaranteed payment, he was a(n) ____________________. Claude hired Eva to paint the shop for him. She was a(n) ____________________, because she was not under Claude's control in doing the work. One day, Claude left the gift shop to go fishing and told Eva to look after business while she painted. Eva had ____________________ to take care of incidental functions that were reasonably and customarily necessary to accomplish her purpose. Before Claude returned, Eva sold an expensive antique for one-tenth of its value to a knowledgeable customer. Claude attempted to rescind the sale on the ground that Eva had no authority, but he failed in his attempt because Eva had __________________________; this was a(n) __________________________, because Claude made it appear that Eva had authority by leaving the store in her care.

5

PUZZLING OVER WHAT YOU LEARNED

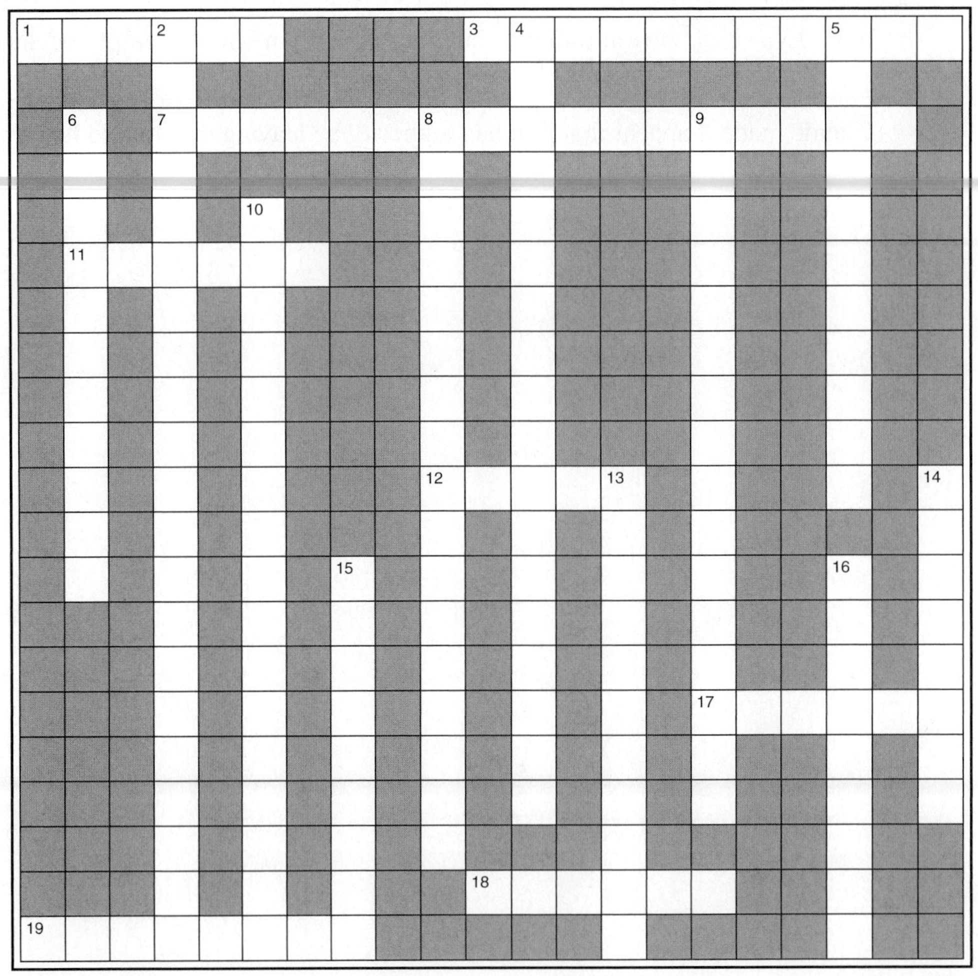

Caveat: Allow squares for spaces between words and punctuation (apostrophes, hyphens, etc.) when filling in crossword.

Across

1. To charge; to lay the responsibility or blame.
3. The doing of an act that ought not to be done at all.
7. A factor who sells consigned goods on credit with a guarantee of payment.
11. A bailee to whom goods are consigned for sale.
12. One who is authorized to act for another.
17. Relationship that exists when one person is authorized to act for another.
18. One who employs the services of others in exchange for wages.
19. One who performs services under the direction and control of another.

Down

2. One who is not known by a third party to be a principal for an agent.
4. Authority caused by a principal making it appear that a non-agent has authority.
5. The failure to do an act that ought to be done.
6. The improper doing of an act.
8. Authority that is given explicitly.
9. An agent who is authorized to act under a power of attorney.
10. A formal writing that authorizes an agent to act for a principal.
13. One who deals with an agent in making a contract with the agent's principal.
14. One who employs the services of others in exchange for wages.
15. One to whom a consignment is made.
16. One who authorizes another to act on his or her behalf.

6

PART SIX

TERMS USED IN LAW OF WILLS AND ESTATES

The drafting of wills is a customary part of the practice of most law offices because many people realize that a will is an important document and should be drafted professionally. Even law offices that specialize in other areas of law often draft wills as part of their practice. Litigation relating to the settling of estates is also very common in the United States. Chapter 22 explains who may make a will, describes the requirements of drafting and executing a proper will, and examines advance directives. Chapter 23 discusses the methods of revoking a will and explains the failure of legacies and devises, including lapse and ademption. The principal clauses in a will are outlined in Chapter 24, and spousal protection, dower and curtesy, pretermitted children, distinctive relationships, and the law of intestacy comprise Chapter 25. The types of personal representatives are discussed in Chapter 26, and the procedure for settling an estate is outlined in Chapter 27. The parties to a trust and the various kinds of trusts are explored in Chapter 28.

6

CHAPTER 22

Wills, Testaments, and Advance Directives

ANTE INTERROGATORY

A person who makes or has made a will is a(n) (A) executor, (B) testatrix, (C) devisor, (D) testator.

CHAPTER OUTLINE

Parties to a Will
Statutory Requirements
  Eighteen Years of Age
  Sound Mind
  Writing
  Signature
  Attestation and Subscription
  Testator's Presence
  Two or More Competent Witnesses
Advance Directives

KEY TERMS

advance directive *(ad·VANS de·REK·tiv)*
agent *(AY·jent)*
attest *(a·TEST)*
attesting witness *(a·TEST·ing WIT·nes)*
beneficiary *(ben·e·FISH·ee·air·ee)*
bequeath *(be·KWEETH)*
bequest *(be·KWEST)*
decedent *(de·SEE·dent)*
devise *(de·VIZE)*
devisee *(dev·i·ZEE)*
devisor *(dev·i·ZOR)*
directive to physicians *(der·EK·tiv to fi·ZI·shens)*
durable power of attorney *(DER·ebel POW·er ov a·TERN·ee*
estate planning *(es·TATE PLAN·ing)*
exordium clause *(eks·ORD·ee·um)*
health care declaration *(dek·la·RAY·shun)*
health care proxy *(PROK·see)*
holographic will *(hol·o·GRAF·ik)*
intestate share *(in·TESS·tate)*
legacy *(LEG·a·see)*
legatee *(leg·a·TEE)*
legator *(leg·a·TOR)*
living will
medical directive *(MED·i·kel der·EK·tiv)*
medical power of attorney *(MED·i·kel POW·er ov a·TERN·ee)*
nuncupative will *(NUN·kyoo·pay·tiv)*
personal property *(PER·son·al PROP·er·tee)*
proponent *(pro·PO·nent)*
real property *(reel PROP·er·tee)*
right-to-die laws
soundness of mind
springing power *(SPRING·ing POW·er)*
subscribe *(sub·SKRIBE)*
surrogate *(SER·o·get)*
testament *(TES·te·ment)*
testamentary capacity *(test·e·MEN·ter·ee ka·PAS·e·tee)*
testamentary disposition *(test·e·MEN·ter·ee dis·po·ZI·shun)*
testate *(TES·tate)*
testator *(tes·tay·TOR)*
testatrix *(tes·tay·TRIX)*
Uniform Probate Code (UPC) *(YOON·i·form PRO·bate kode)*
will
will and testament *(TES·te·ment)*

The branch of the law known as **estate planning** involves arranging a person's assets in a way that maintains and protects the family most effectively both during and after the person's life. The fields of taxation, insurance, property ownership, trusts, and wills are important facets of estate planning.

The term **will** is an Anglo-Saxon word that originally referred to an instrument that disposed of **real property** (land and anything that is permanently attached to it). Even today, a gift of real property in a will has a special name. It is called a **devise.** The person who makes the gift of real property is called the **devisor,** and the person to whom the gift is made is called the **devisee.**

The term **testament,** which is Latin, referred to an instrument that disposed of **personal property** (things other than real property) under early English law. A gift of personal property in a will today is known as a **bequest** or a **legacy.** The person who makes a gift of personal property in a will is called a **legator,** and the person to whom the gift is made is called a **legatee.**

Under early English law, **will and testament** disposed of both real and personal property. In practice today, the distinction between the two terms is not made. Thus, the terms "will" and "will and testament" are used interchangeably. It is common, however, to see the phrase "I give, devise, and bequeath. . . ." in a will referring to both real and personal property, the verb **bequeath** meaning "to give personal property in a will."

PARTIES TO A WILL

The person who makes a will is called a **testator,** if a man, and a **testatrix,** if a woman. A **beneficiary** is someone who actually receives a gift under a will. The word **testate** refers to the state of a person who has made a will, and the phrase **testamentary disposition** means a gift of property that is not to take effect until the one who makes the gift dies.

STATUTORY REQUIREMENTS

Today, in the United States, each state has enacted its own statutes governing the formalities of executing wills. Sixteen states (see Figure 22-1) have adopted the **Uniform Probate Code (UPC),** which is a uniform law attempting to standardize and modernize laws relating to the affairs of **decedents** (deceased persons), minors, and certain other people who need protection. The UPC has changed the definitions of some commonly used legal terms. For example, the term **devise** refers to a gift of either real or personal property in states that have adopted the UPC. Correspondingly, the term **devisee** refers to a person who receives a gift of either real or personal property under a will.

A typical state statute (non-UPC) reads, in part, as follows:

> Every person eighteen years of age or older and of sound mind may by his last will in writing, signed by him or by a person in his presence and by his express direction, and attested and subscribed in his presence by two or more competent witnesses, dispose of his property, real and personal.

An analysis of the preceding statute reveals the following requirements for executing a will in that particular state:

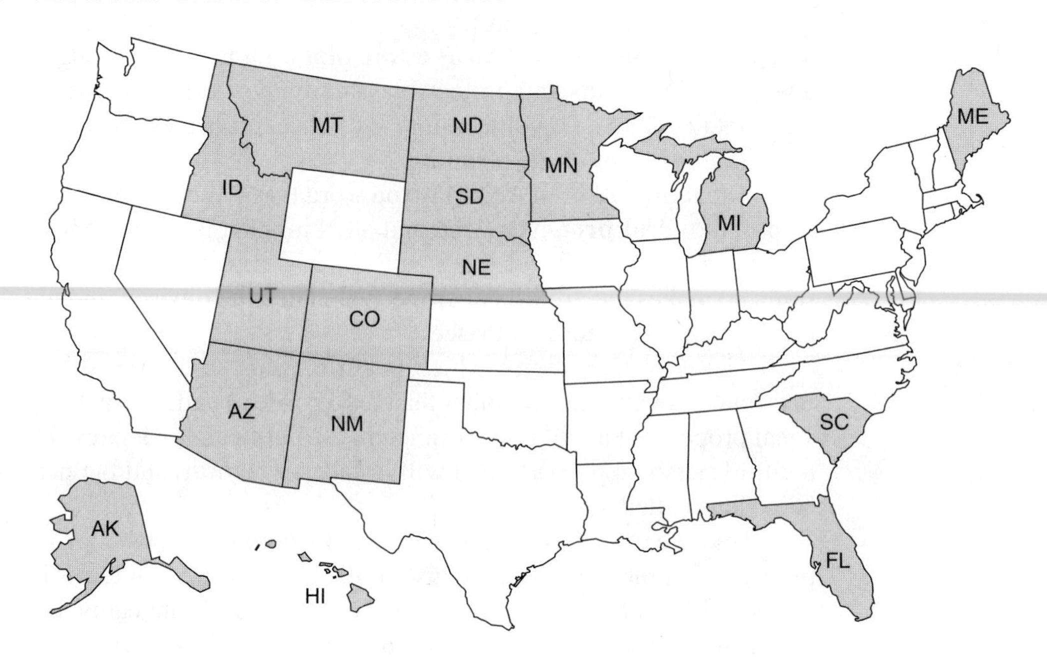

Figure 22-1 States that have adopted the Uniform Probate Code.

1. 18 years of age
2. Sound mind
3. Writing
4. Signed
5. Attested
6. Subscribed in the testator's presence
7. Two or more competent witnesses

WORD WISE

To Write

Both the root "graph" used in "holographic" and the root "scrib" used in "subscribe" mean "to write." Other words with these roots are:

Word	*Meaning*
circumscribe [*circum* (around) + *scribe*]	To draw a line around
manuscript [*manu* (by hand) + *script*]	A document written by hand
telegraph [*tele* (far) + *graph*]	Message sent over a distance
autograph [*auto* (self) + *graph*]	Written with one's own hand

Eighteen Years of Age

Although most state laws set the minimum age for making a will at 18, a few states allow wills to be made at an earlier age for military personnel and married persons. People become 18 years of age on the day before their eighteenth birthday, because the law considers persons as having lived an entire day if they live any part of that day. Since the day of birth is counted, a child will have lived 365 days on the day before the child's first birthday.

Sound Mind

Soundness of mind, which is often referred to as **testamentary capacity,** may be proved by showing that at the time of the execution of the will, the testator met all of the following requirements:

1. The testator had the ability to understand and carry in mind, in a general way, the nature and extent of property owned, and his or her relationship to those persons who would naturally have some claim to the estate.
2. The testator was free from delusions that might influence the disposition of his or her property.
3. The testator had the ability to comprehend the nature of the act—that is, knew that he or she was making a will.

Generally, if the question of soundness of mind is raised in a contested will case, only the following people are allowed to testify as to the testator's mental condition: the witnesses to the will, the testator's family physician, and experts of skill and experience in the knowledge and treatment of mental diseases. The **proponent** of the will—that is, the one who presents the will to the court for allowance—has the burden of proving the soundness of mind of the testator.

Writing

The writing required by the statute may be printed, typewritten, or written entirely in the hand of the testator. The last is called a **holographic will.** A will need not be under seal. With exceptions, only a soldier in the military service or a mariner at sea may make a **nuncupative will** (oral), which is limited to the disposition of personal property.

Signature

Under the preceding statute, the signature of the testator may be anywhere on the instrument. Thus, in a case in which a testator wrote his name in the **exordium clause** (the first paragraph) of his handwritten will but failed to sign it at the end, the court allowed the will. Some states require that the testator sign at the end of the will.

The signature need not be in any particular form. It may be made by an X or any other mark of the testator so long as it is intended to be the testator's signature. Under this particular statute, another person may sign for the testator if it is done in the testator's presence and by his or her express direction. Also, under this statute, the testator is not required to sign in the presence of the witnesses.

Attestation and Subscription

To **attest** means to bear witness to the testator's signature. To **subscribe** means to write below or underneath. An early English case held that "to attest" and "to subscribe" are different actions. Attestation is the act of the senses; subscription is the act of the hand. The one is mental; the other mechanical. To attest to a will is to know that it was published

Figure 22-2 A person becomes 18 on the day before his or her eighteenth birthday.

as a will; to subscribe is only to write on the same paper the names of the witnesses for the sole purpose of identification.

A will was held to be properly executed when the testator acknowledged his or her signature, which he or she had previously placed thereon, by showing the paper to the witness, stating that it was his will, and requesting the person to sign it as a witness. In another case, a will was disallowed by the court because the testator intentionally covered up his signature so that the witnesses could not see it. In that case, the court said that a person does not acknowledge a signature to be his when no signature can be seen by the witness. In a contrasting case, however, a will was allowed by the court when the signature of the testator was unintentionally covered up by a fold in the paper.

Attesting witnesses (people who witness the signing of a document) should sign below the testator's signature and after the testator signs the instrument. They may subscribe by making a mark as well as by writing their names in full if they do so with the intent to subscribe to the will. In a case in which a witness unintentionally wrote his correct first name but the middle initial and last name of the person who signed above his name, the court, in allowing the will, said that any form of writing adopted by the witness is sufficient to satisfy the statute.

Testator's Presence

The witnesses must subscribe in the presence of the testator. It has been said that witnesses are not in the presence of the testator unless they are within the testator's sight; however, a person may take note of the presence of another by the other senses, as hearing or touch.

If two blind people, for example, are in the same room talking together, no question exists that they are in each other's presence.

A will was disallowed in a case in which the witnesses watched the testator (who was ill in bed) sign the will and then withdrew to another room to subscribe as witnesses. The court held that the witnesses did not subscribe in the presence of the testator.

Two or More Competent Witnesses

Under the statute set forth earlier, a will must have two witnesses. That particular state statute continues on to read:

> Any person of sufficient understanding shall be deemed to be a competent witness to a will, . . . but a beneficial devise or legacy to a subscribing witness or to the husband or wife of such witness shall be void unless there are two other subscribing witnesses to the will who are not similarly benefited thereunder.

This statement means that if a beneficiary or a beneficiary's spouse witnesses a will, he or she cannot take the gift that was given under the will unless extra witnesses receive nothing under the will. Note that no age requirement of a witness exists under the preceding statute. The only requirement is that the witness be "of sufficient understanding." Some states have age requirements for witnesses.

All states but three in the United States require two witnesses to a will. Pennsylvania has no witness requirement unless the testator signs by mark, Louisiana calls for two witnesses plus a notary public, and Vermont clings to the three-witness requirement of earlier times. Notwithstanding this requirement, holographic wills need not be witnessed in over half the states. Some states allow witnesses who are named as beneficiaries to inherit under the will. Still others, including California and Texas, allow witnesses who are named as beneficiaries in a will to inherit only an amount that does not exceed their **intestate share** (the amount they would have inherited had the decedent died without a will). In Florida, the entire will is void when any of the witnesses are named as beneficiaries.

ADVANCE DIRECTIVES

Right-to-die laws have become prevalent in recent years. These are laws that allow dying people to refuse extraordinary treatment to prolong life. In *Cruzan* v. *Director, Missouri Department of Health* (1990), the U.S. Supreme Court held that the right to refuse medical treatment is protected by the Fourteenth Amendment of the U.S. Constitution. In the *Cruzan* case, the court encouraged people to make **advance directives**—that is, written statements specifying whether they want life-sustaining medical treatment if they become desperately ill.

WEB WISE

- Find out about the U.S. Living Will Registry at **www.uslivingwillregistry.com.**
- Print out your own state's advance directive by going to **www.partnershipforcaring.org.**

Individual state laws regulate advance directives. Some states authorize the use of the **living will,** which is a written expression of a person's wishes to be allowed to die a natural death and not be kept alive by heroic or artificial methods. Other states use a health care proxy for the same purpose. **A health care proxy,** also called a **medical power of attorney,** is a written statement authorizing an **agent** or **surrogate** (person authorized to act for another) to make medical treatment decisions for another in the event of the other's inability to do so. Still other states use a durable power of attorney for this purpose. A **durable power of attorney** is a document authorizing another person to act on one's behalf with language indicating that it either is to survive one's incapacity or is to become effective when one becomes incapacitated. In the latter instance, the power is called a **springing power,** because it does not become effective until the person making it actually becomes incapacitated. A durable power of attorney is not limited to health care issues in most states. A living will is sometimes called a **directive to physicians,** a **medical directive,** or a **health care declaration.**

Many states have *surrogate decision-making laws* that permit a close relative or friend to make health care decisions for patients who have no advance directives.

REVIEWING WHAT YOU LEARNED

After studying the text, write the answers to each of the following questions:

1. What was the difference between a will and a testament under early law? ______________

____

____

____

____

2. List the seven requirements of executing a will under a typical state statute. ______________

____

____

____

____

3. When do people become 18 years old? ______

____

____

____

4. What three facts prove soundness of mind of a testator? ______________

____

____

____

____

5. Generally, who is considered competent to give an opinion of the testator's mental condition?

____

____

____

6. Generally, who may make an oral will? To what is it limited? ______________

____

____

____

7. What is the difference between attest and subscribe? ______________

____

____

____

8. Read the two state statutes that are provided in this chapter, and answer the following questions relating to them:

   a. Where on the will may the signature of the testator be located? ______________

   ____

   ____

   ____

b. In what form must the signature be? ______

c. Must the testator sign in the presence of the witnesses? ______

d. Where must the witnesses sign their names?

e. In whose presence must witnesses attest and subscribe? ______

f. How many witnesses must a will have? ______

g. Who may be a witness to a will? ______

h. What will result if a beneficiary or beneficiary's spouse witnesses a will? ______

9. Name three advance directives that are in common use. ______

UNDERSTANDING LEGAL CONCEPTS

Indicate whether each statement is true or false. Then, change the italicized word or phrase of each *false* statement to make it true.

Answers

______ **1.** Originally, the term *will* referred to an instrument that disposed of personal property, and the term *testament* referred to an instrument that disposed of real property.

______ **2.** A devise is a gift of *personal* property in a will.

______ **3.** The word "testate" refers to the state of a person who dies *without* a will.

______ **4.** A person becomes 18 years of age on the *day before* his or her eighteenth birthday.

______ **5.** If the question of soundness of mind is raised in a contested will case, the witnesses to the will *may not* testify.

______ **6.** A nuncupative will is limited to the disposition of *real* property.

______ **7.** A will *may never be* signed by an "X."

______ **8.** Attestation is the act of the *senses;* subscription is the act of the hand.

______ **9.** In all states, a witness to a will *must be* 18 years of age.

______ **10.** Witnesses *must* subscribe in the presence of the testator.

CHECKING TERMINOLOGY

From the list of legal terms that follows, select the one that matches each definition.

- **a.** advance directive
- **b.** agent
- **c.** attest
- **d.** attesting witnesses
- **e.** beneficiary
- **f.** bequeath
- **g.** bequest
- **h.** decedents
- **i.** devise
- **j.** devisee
- **k.** devisor
- **l.** directive to physicians
- **m.** durable power of attorney
- **n.** estate planning
- **o.** exordium clause
- **p.** health care declaration
- **q.** health care proxy
- **r.** holographic will
- **s.** intestate share
- **t.** legacy
- **u.** legatee
- **v.** legator
- **w.** living will
- **x.** medical directive
- **y.** medical power of attorney
- **z.** nuncupative will
- **aa.** personal property
- **bb.** proponent
- **cc.** real property
- **dd.** right-to-die laws
- **ee.** soundness of mind
- **ff.** springing power
- **gg.** subscribe

Answers

____ **1.** Originally, a legal instrument stating a person's wishes as to the disposition of real property at death, but now referring to both real and personal property.

____ **2.** A legal instrument stating a person's wishes as to the disposition of personal property at death.

____ **3.** Someone who actually receives a gift under a will; also, one for whose benefit a trust is created.

____ **4.** A gift of real property in a will.

____ **5.** A woman who makes or has made a testament or will.

____ **6.** An oral will.

____ **7.** A gift of property that is not to take effect until the one who makes the gift dies.

____ **8.** A male who makes or has made a testament or will.

____ **9.** A person to whom real property is given by will.

____ **10.** Land and anything that is permanently attached to it.

____ **11.** Things other than real property.

____ **12.** A gift of personal property in a will (select two answers).

____ **13.** A person who gives real property by will.

____ **14.** The state of a person who has made a will.

____ **15.** Under early English law, a legal instrument that disposed of both real and personal property at death.

____ **16.** A person who receives a gift of personal property under a will.

____ **17.** Deceased persons.

____ **18.** An amount that is inherited when a decedent dies without a will.

____ **19.** A law attempting to standardize and modernize laws relating to the affairs of decedents, minors, and certain other people who need protection.

____ **20.** Sufficient mental ability to make a will (select two answers).

____ **21.** A will written entirely in the hand of the testator.

____ **22.** To bear witness to.

____ **23.** A person who makes a gift of personal property by will.

____ **24.** To sign below or at the end; to write underneath.

____ **25.** The introductory paragraph of a will.

____ **26.** To give personal property in a will.

____ **27.** Laws allowing dying people to refuse extraordinary treatment to prolong life.

____ **28.** A written expression of a person's wishes to be allowed to die a natural death and not be kept alive by heroic or artificial methods (select four answers).

hh. surrogate
ii. testament
jj. testamentary capacity
kk. testamentary disposition
ll. testate
mm. testator
nn. testatrix
oo. Uniform Probate Code (UPC)
pp. will
qq. will and testament

____**29.** A written statement specifying whether a person wants life-sustaining medical treatment if he or she becomes desperately ill.

____**30.** A power in a durable power of attorney that does not become effective until the person making it actually becomes incapacitated.

____**31.** A document authorizing another person to act on one's behalf with language indicating that it either is to survive one's incapacity or is to become effective when one becomes incapacitated.

____**32.** A written statement authorizing an agent or surrogate to make medical treatment decisions for another in the event of the other's inability to do so (select two answers).

____**33.** A person authorized to act for another (select two answers).

____**34.** People who witness the signing of a document.

____**35.** Arranging a person's assets in a way that maintains and protects the family most effectively both during and after a person's life.

____**36.** One who proposes or argues in support of something.

UNRAVELING LEGALESE

Use simple, non-legal language, with the help of the glossary, to rewrite this case quote so that it is shorter and can be understood by a layperson without losing its meaning.

> A subscribing witness cannot sign before the testator has signed. The statute not only requires them (the witnesses) to attest, but to subscribe. It is not sufficient for the witnesses to be called upon to witness the testator's signature, or to stand by while he makes or acknowledges it, and be prepared to testify afterwards to his sanity and due execution of the instrument, but they must subscribe. This subscription is the evidence of their previous attestation, and to preserve the proof of that attestation in case of their death or absence when after the testator's death, the will shall be presented for probate.

6

USING LEGAL LANGUAGE

Read the following story and fill in the blank lines with legal terms taken from the list of terms at the beginning of this chapter.

When Jason signed his last ______________________ and ______________________, he was not aware that the term "will" originally referred to an instrument that disposed of ______________________ and that the term "testament" originally referred to an instrument that disposed of ______________________. He was glad to be ______________________, however, which refers to the state of a person who has made a will. Jason is called a(n) ______________________, because he is a man. When his wife, Julia, signed her will, she was referred to as a(n) ______________________. These wills were not oral; therefore, they were not ______________________. They were not entirely in their own handwriting; therefore, they were not ______________________. The wills were witnessed by two ______________________. Jason and Julia both ______________________ (willed) their real estate to their children, which made them ______________________ and their children ______________________. They made a special ______________________ of their automobile to Julia's brother, James. This made them ______________________, and James was a(n) ______________________ as to this ______________________. Because they were both of sound mind, they had ______________________, and the ______________________ was valid. They were pleased to have accomplished some ______________________, which is the arranging of their assets in a way that would maintain and protect their family most effectively both while alive and after death.

PUZZLING OVER WHAT YOU LEARNED

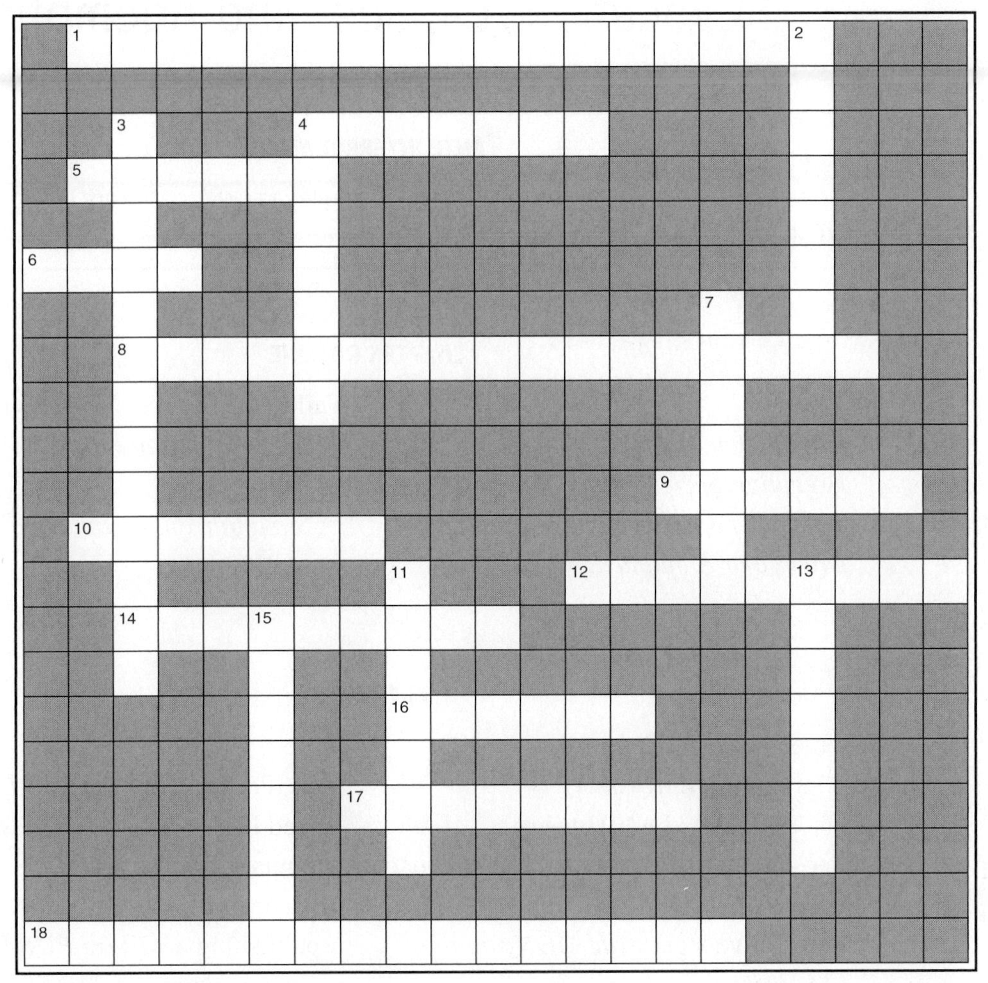

Caveat: Allow squares for spaces between words and punctuation (apostrophes, hyphens, etc.) when filling in crossword.

Across

1. Sufficient mental ability to make a will.
4. A person to whom real property is given by will.
5. A gift of real property in a will.
6. Instrument stating person's wishes as to real property at death.
8. Things other than real property.
9. A gift of personal property in a will.
10. A person who makes a gift of personal property by will.
12. A woman who makes or has made a testament or will.
14. Instrument stating person's wishes as to personal property at death.
16. To bear witness to.
17. To give personal property in a will.
18. A will written entirely in the hand of the testator.

Down

2. Deceased person.
3. Land and anything that is permanently attached to it.
4. A person who gives real property by will.
7. A gift of personal property in a will.
11. A person who receives a gift of personal property under a will.
13. The state of a person who has made a will.
15. A male who makes or has made a testament or will.

6

CHAPTER 23

Revocation, Lapses, and Ademption

ANTE INTERROGATORY

A legacy of money is called a (A) demonstrative legacy, (B) pecuniary legacy, (C) specific legacy, (D) lapsed legacy.

CHAPTER OUTLINE

Revocation
- *Destruction of Will*
- *Execution of New Will*
- *Subsequent Marriage*
- *Divorce or Annulment*

Failure of Legacies and Devises
- *Lapsed Legacies and Devises*
- *Ademption*
- *Simultaneous Deaths and Slayer Statutes*

KEY TERMS

adeemed *(a·DEEMD)*
ademption *(a·DEMP·shun)*
advancement *(ad·VANSE·ment)*
antilapse statute *(an·tee·LAPS STAT·shoot)*
codicil *(KOD·i·sil)*
demonstrative legacy *(de·MON·stre·tiv LEG·a·see)*
execute *(EK·se·kyoot)*
extinction *(eks·TINK·shun)*
general legacy *(JEN·e·rel LEG·a·see)*
general pecuniary legacy *(JEN·e·rel pee·KYOO·nee·er·ee LEG·a·see)*
intestate *(in·TESS·tate)*
intestate succession *(in·TESS·tate suk·SESH·en)*
issue *(ISH·oo)*
lapsed devise *(lapsd de·VIZE)*
lapsed legacy *(lapsd LEG·a·see)*
pecuniary gift *(pe·KYOO·nee·er·ee)*
predeceased *(pre·de·SEESD)*
republishing a will *(re·PUB·lish·ing)*
residuary clause *(re·ZID·joo·er·ee)*
revocable *(REV·e·ke·bel)*
revocation *(rev·o·KA·shun)*
revoke *(re·VOKE)*
satisfaction *(sat·is·FAK·shun)*
simultaneous deaths *(sy·mul·TAY·nee·us)*
slayer statute *(SLAY·er STAT·shoot)*
specific legacy *(spe·SIF·ic LEG·a·see)*

REVOCATION

The term **revoke** means to cancel or rescind. **Revocable** means capable of being revoked, and **revocation** means the act of revoking. With variations from state to state, a will may be revoked in the following ways:

1. Destruction of will (burning, tearing, cancelling, or obliterating)
2. Execution of new will (**execute** means to complete, to make, to perform, or to do, such as signing a will)
3. Subsequent marriage
4. Divorce or annulment of marriage (but only as to gifts made in a will to a former spouse)

Destruction of Will

When a will is revoked by burning, tearing, canceling, or obliterating, the act must be done with the intent to revoke the will. Thus, a will destroyed when the testator's house is accidentally burned would not, without the testator's intent, be revoked. In such a case, a copy of the signed *will, if* available, might be used in court as evidence of the unrevoked will.

The court in one case decided that when an elderly testatrix made marks on her previously executed will, she had no intention of revoking it, and the will was allowed. Other cases, however, have held that lines drawn through a line, paragraph, or portion of a will were effective to revoke those particular parts of the will that were marked out.

In another case, a testatrix left a sizable **pecuniary gift** (gift of money) in her will to a friend. Later, she decided to leave her friend a larger sum of money in the will. Without consulting a lawyer, she drew a line through the first amount and wrote above it the larger amount. When the testatrix died, her friend received nothing. The line drawn through the smaller amount effectively canceled that gift and the larger amount written above had no effect because the will had not been reexecuted by the testator or reattested and resubscribed by the proper number of witnesses after the change was made.

Execution of New Will

Frequently, testators wish to revoke or make changes in their wills. In fact, it is a good idea to review a will every five years or so to be sure that it still meets one's needs and desires. One way to revoke or change a will is to make a new will. Another way is to make a **codicil,** which is an alteration or addition to an existing will. A codicil must be executed with the same formalities as a will (signed by the testator and attested, and subscribed in the testator's presence by two or more competent witnesses) and must refer specifically to the existing will so as to identify it.

A will and codicil are read together as one instrument. A properly executed codicil has the effect of **republishing a will,** which means it will reestablish a will that has been formerly revoked or improperly executed.

Subsequent Marriage

In most states, the marriage of a person after executing a will has no effect on the will. However, subsequent marriage (after making a will) revokes the will in the following states: Connecticut, Georgia, Kansas, Kentucky, Massachusetts, Nevada, Oregon, Rhode Island, South Dakota, West Virginia, and Wisconsin. In those states, if it appears within the body of the will that it was made in contemplation of marriage, the will is not revoked. In Maryland and Tennessee, subsequent marriage revokes a will only when a child is born of the marriage, and in the state of Washington, it revokes only those gifts in the will to the surviving spouse.

Divorce or Annulment

In most states, a divorce or annulment revokes a gift in a will made to the former spouse. It does not revoke the entire will. Similarly, a divorce or annulment revokes any nomination of the former spouse as executor, trustee, conservator, or guardian, unless the will expressly provides otherwise.

FAILURE OF LEGACIES AND DEVISES

A gift made in a will may fail in two ways. The first occurs when the person who is to receive the gift (the devisee or legatee) dies before the testator. The second occurs when the gift itself is not owned by the testator at the time of death. These two situations are discussed subsequently.

Lapsed Legacies and Devises

When a legatee or devisee dies before the testator, the bequest or devise in the will to that person is called a **lapsed legacy** or **lapsed devise** and takes no effect. Instead, it falls into the residuary fund of the estate, which is established by the residuary clause of the will. The **residuary clause** is the clause of a will that leaves "all the rest, residue and remainder" of the estate to named beneficiaries after specific gifts, if any, are provided for. If no residuary clause is in a will and the legatees and devisees have **predeceased** (died before) the testator, the lapsed gift passes to the heirs according to the law of **intestate succession.** This law governs the distribution of property of one who dies without a will—that is, **intestate.**

Antilapse Statutes. Some states have enacted **antilapse statutes** designed to minimize the effect of lapse. Here is a typical one:

> If a devise or legacy is made to a child or other relation of the testator, who dies before the testator, but leaves issue surviving the testator, such issue shall, unless a different disposition is made or required by the will, take the same estate which the person whose issue they are would have taken if he had survived the testator. The words "child," "issue," and "other relation," as used in this section, shall include adopted children.

Under this statute, a gift that is made in a will to a child or other relative who predeceases the testator does not lapse. Instead, it passes to the issue of the child or other relative of the testator. **Issue** are all people who have descended from a common ancestor such as the decedent's children, grandchildren, great-grandchildren, and so forth.

If the testator does not want the issue of a deceased legatee or devisee to receive a gift under the antilapse statute, a statement to that effect must be made in the will. For example, a clause in a will leaving a gift "To my daughter, Shirley, if she shall survive me," would prevent the antilapse statute from taking effect.

Ademption

If the exact thing that is bequeathed or devised is not in existence or has been disposed of at the time of the testator's death, the legacy or devise is **adeemed** (taken away), and the legatee's or devisee's rights are gone. This is known as **ademption** or **advancement,** and occurs in either of two ways: satisfaction or extinction.

Satisfaction. A **satisfaction** is defined as the discharge of a legal obligation by paying a party what is due. Thus, a satisfaction takes place when all or part of the amount of a

WORD WISE

Prefixes that Mean "Against"

Prefix	*Examples*	*Meaning*
ant-	antonym	A word of opposite meaning
anti-	antilapse	To minimize lapse
contra-	contradict	To say the opposite
contro-	controversy	A dispute
ob-	obstruct	To block
oc- (before *c*)	occupy	To seize
of- (before *f*)	offend	To insult
op- (before *p*)	oppose	To set against
o- (before *m*)	omit	To neglect

general pecuniary legacy (a gift of money out of the general assets of the estate) is paid to the legatee during the testator's life with the intent that such payment is in lieu of the legacy. In such a case, the legatee will not receive the legacy when the testator dies because the gift is said to have been adeemed. It was given to the legatee while the testator was alive.

Legacies and devises are classified into three types—specific, general, and demonstrative. A **specific legacy** is a gift by will of a particular piece of personal property. For example, if a clause in a will reads, "I leave my 2003 Cadillac to my son, Timothy," the gift is a specific legacy. A **general legacy** is a gift (usually of money) that comes out of the estate generally. For example, if a clause in a will reads, "I leave $10,000 to my daughter, Jennifer," the gift is a general legacy. A **demonstrative legacy** is a combination of the two. When it is used, the testator intends to make a general gift but wishes to have it satisfied out of specific property. An example of a demonstrative legacy is a clause in a will that reads, "I bequeath $10,000 to my son, Matthew, and I direct that my shares of Symantic stock be sold and the proceeds applied to the payment of this gift."

Extinction. An **extinction** occurs by a destruction or disposal of a specific legacy by the testator during his or her lifetime. Thus, in the first example given earlier, if the testator does not own the 2003 Cadillac on death, the legacy will adeem by extinction. Timothy will not receive the car because it is not part of the decedent's estate.

A general legacy does not adeem by extinction unless the general assets of the estate are not enough to pay it. Similarly, a demonstrative legacy does not adeem. In the third example given earlier, if the testator does not own any shares of Symantic stock at the time of death, Matthew will still receive the $10,000 gift. It will come out of the general assets of the estate.

Simultaneous Deaths and Slayer Statutes

Simultaneous deaths are the deaths of two or more people in such a way that it is impossible to determine who died before whom. All states have adopted some version of the Uniform Simultaneous Death Act. This law comes into effect when the disposition of the

Figure 23-1 If the exact item that is bequested is not in existence at the time of the testator's death, the legacy is adeemed and the legatee's rights are gone.

decedents' property depends on who died first and this cannot be determined—often when two or more people die in a common disaster. The act allows the property of each decedent to be distributed as if he or she had survived, unless a will or trust provides otherwise.

People are not allowed to inherit from someone they murder. Instead, state laws, called **slayer statutes,** regard the murderer as having died before the victim, thus preventing any inheritance from going to the wrongdoer.

REVIEWING WHAT YOU LEARNED

After studying the text, write the answers to each of the following questions.

1. What four ways may a will be revoked, depending on state statute? ______________________

____

____

____

2. To revoke a will by burning, tearing, canceling, or obliterating, what must accompany the act?

____

____

____

3. How must a codicil be executed? ____________

4. A properly executed codicil republishes a will that is defective in what two ways? ____________

5. In the state of Washington, what effect does a subsequent marriage have on a will made before the marriage? In the state of Massachusetts?

6. What effect does a divorce or annulment have on a will made before the divorce or annulment?

7. What effect does a divorce have on the appointment of the former spouse as executor, trustee, conservator, or guardian unless the will shall expressly provide otherwise? ____________

8. In what two ways may a gift in a will fail?

9. Who will receive a gift that is made in a will to a legatee who dies before the testator if a residuary clause is in the will? If no residuary clause is in the will? ____________

10. Under the antilapse statute, what will happen to a gift made in a will to a child or other relative who predeceases the testator? What language can be used in a will to keep this from happening?

11. In what two ways may an ademption occur?

12. When may a gift adeem by satisfaction? ____________

13. Give an example of a specific legacy, a general legacy, and a demonstrative legacy. ____________

14. How may a gift adeem by extinction? ____________

UNDERSTANDING LEGAL CONCEPTS

Indicate whether each statement is true or false. Then, change the italicized word or phrase of each *false* statement to make it true.

Answers

______ **1.** A *codicil* must be signed by the testator and attested and subscribed in the testator's presence by two or more competent witnesses.

______ **2.** A properly executed codicil *will reestablish* a will that has been formerly revoked or improperly executed.

______ **3.** In *every state,* it is important for a person to make a new will after becoming married if he or she had a will before the marriage.

______ **4.** In most states, a divorce revokes a *will* that was made before the divorce.

______ **5.** When a legatee or devisee dies before the testator, the bequest or devise in the will to that person *falls into the residuary fund* of the estate.

______ **6.** Under an antilapse statute, a gift that is made in a will to a *friend* who predeceases the testator does not lapse.

______ **7.** A clause in a will leaving a gift "to my daughter, Linda, if she shall survive me," would *cause* the antilapse statute *to take* effect.

______ **8.** A *satisfaction* occurs when all or part of the amount of a general pecuniary legacy is paid to a legatee during the testator's life with the intent that such payment is in lieu of the legacy.

______ **9.** If a clause in a will reads: "I leave $10,000 to my daughter, Deborah," the gift is a *specific* legacy.

______ **10.** An *extinction* occurs by a destruction or disposal of a specific legacy by the testator during his lifetime.

CHECKING TERMINOLOGY

From the list of legal terms that follows, select the one that matches each definition:

a. adeemed
b. ademption
c. advancement
d. antilapse statute
e. codicil
f. demonstrative legacy
g. execute
h. extinction
i. general legacy
j. general pecuniary legacy
k. intestate
l. intestate succession
m. issue
n. lapsed devise
o. lapsed legacy
p. pecuniary gift
q. predeceased
r. republishing a will
s. residuary clause
t. revocable
u. revocation
v. revoke
w. satisfaction
x. simultaneous deaths
y. slayer statutes
z. specific legacy

Answers

____ **1.** The act of revoking.
____ **2.** Cancel or rescind.
____ **3.** Capable of being revoked.
____ **4.** To complete, to make, to perform, or to do, such as sign a will.
____ **5.** Gift of money.
____ **6.** An amendment to a will that must be executed with the same formalities as the will itself.
____ **7.** Reestablishing a will that has been formerly revoked or improperly executed.
____ **8.** The clause in a will that disposes of all of the testator's property not otherwise distributed.
____ **9.** A gift of personal property in a will that fails because the legatee predeceased the testator.
____ **10.** The act or process of an heir becoming beneficially entitled to the property of one who dies without a will.
____ **11.** Die before.
____ **12.** Having made no valid will.
____ **13.** All people who have descended from a common ancestor.
____ **14.** A bequest of a certain sum of money with a direction that it be paid out of a particular fund.
____ **15.** Taken away.
____ **16.** The testator's disposing of or giving to a beneficiary, while alive, that which was provided in a will, so as to make it impossible to carry out the will (select two answers).
____ **17.** Laws designed to minimize the effect of lapse.
____ **18.** The discharge of a legal obligation by paying a party what is due.
____ **19.** A gift of money out of the general assets of the estate (select two answers).
____ **20.** A gift by will of a particular article of personal property.
____ **21.** The act of extinguishing or putting to an end.
____ **22.** A gift of real property in a will that fails because the devisee predeceased the testator.
____ **23.** Laws enacted by legislatures stating that murderers cannot inherit from their victims.
____ **24.** The deaths of two or more people in a way that it is impossible to determine who died before whom.

UNRAVELING LEGALESE

Use simple, non-legal language, with the help of the glossary, to rewrite this case quote so that it is shorter and can be understood by a layperson without losing its meaning.

> It is well settled that if a legatee not a relation of the testator predeceases a testator, the legacy lapses unless the will provides otherwise. However, if the legacy is given to a group of people as a class, it will not cause the legacy to lapse; rather, it will pass to the survivors.

USING LEGAL LANGUAGE

Read the following story and fill in the blank lines with legal terms taken from the list of terms at the beginning of this chapter:

Because Jason sold the automobile that he had bequeathed to James before he died, a(n) ______________________ occurred. The automobile, which was a(n) ______________________ (kind of gift), ______________________ by extinction. The gift of money—that is, the ______________________, which is also known as a(n) ______________________ or ______________________—went to his children, who were his ______________________. Because they did not ______________________ (die before) him, it was not a(n) ______________________, and the house they inherited was not a(n) ______________________. The gift of $1,000 to Julie's brother, James, to be taken from the sale of stock, was a(n) ______________________. Because Jason died with a will, he did not die ______________________, and the laws of ______________________ did not apply to him. He had not made a(n) ______________________—that is, an addition to his will. Because he did not ______________________ (cancel or rescind) the instrument after he had ______________________ (signed) it, no ______________________ of the instrument had occurred. The ______________________ of the will gave all the rest, residue, and remainder of Jason's estate to his wife, Julie.

PUZZLING OVER WHAT YOU LEARNED

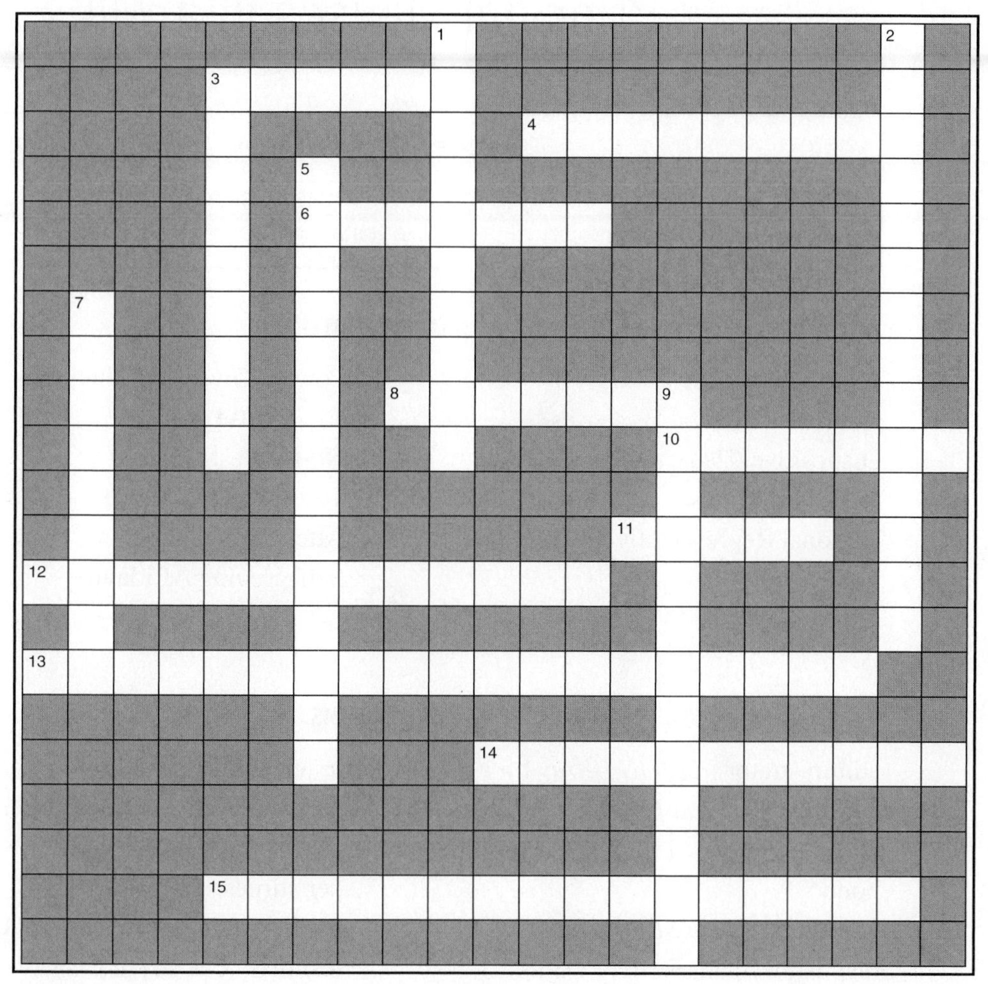

Caveat: Allow squares for spaces between words and punctuation (apostrophes, hyphens, etc.) when filling in crossword.

Across

3. Cancel or rescind.
4. The extinction or satisfaction of a legacy or devise before death.
6. To complete, to make, to perform, or to do, such as sign a will.
8. An amendment to a will that must be executed with the same formalities as a will.
10. Taken away.
11. All people who have descended from a common ancestor.
12. Gift of real property in a will that fails due to prior death of the devisee.
13. Reestablishing a will that has been formerly revoked.
14. Died before.
15. Clause in a will that disposes of all the testator's property not given out.

Down

1. The act of revoking.
2. A gift of money out of the general assets of the estate.
3. Capable of being revoked.
5. Gift of money.
7. Having made no valid will.
9. Gift of personal property in will that fails due to prior death of legatee.

6

CHAPTER 24
Principal Clauses in a Will

ANTE INTERROGATORY

The clause in a will that directly precedes the testator's signature is called the (A) residuary clause, (B) testimonium clause, (C) attestation clause, (D) exordium clause.

CHAPTER OUTLINE

Exordium Clause
Debts and Funeral Expenses
Dispositive Clauses
Residuary Clause
Personal Representative, Guardian, and Trustee
No Surety on Bond
Powers Given to Fiduciaries
Tax Clause
No-Contest Clause
Testimonium Clause
Attestation Clause
Self-proving Affidavit

KEY TERMS

administrator *(ad·MIN·is·tray·tor)*
administratrix *(ad·MIN·is·tray·triks)*
attestation clause *(a·tes·TAY·shun)*
bond
conservator *(kon·SER·ve·tor)*
dispositive clauses *(dis·POS·a·tiv)*
domicile *(DOM·i·sile)*
executor *(eg·ZEK·yoo·tor)*
executrix *(eg·ZEK·yoo·triks)*
exordium clause *(eks·ORD·ee·um)*
fiduciary *(fi·DOO·she·air·ee)*
guardian *(GAR·dee·en)*
guardian ad litem *(GAR·dee·en ad LY·tem)*
incorporation by reference *(in·kore·per·AY·shen by REF·e·renss)*
in terrorem clause *(in ter·RAW·rem)*
no-contest clause *(no-KON·test)*
per capita *(per KAP·i·ta)*
per stirpes *(per STIR·peez)*
publication clause *(pub·li·KAY·shun)*
residuary clause *(re·ZID·joo·er·ee)*
residuary estate *(re·ZID·joo·er·ee es·TATE)*
self-proving affidavit *(a·fi·DAY·vit)*
signature clause *(SIG·na·cher)*
surety *(SHOOR·e·tee)*
testimonium clause *(tes·ti·MOH·nee·um)*
trustee *(trus·TEE)*

A will need not follow any particular form. In fact, a properly drawn will is a highly individualized instrument tailored to the particular needs of the testator and the testator's family. A will drafted by a lawyer, however, will contain many of the following clauses.

EXORDIUM CLAUSE

The **exordium clause,** also called the **publication clause,** is the introductory paragraph setting out the full name and **domicile** (principal residence) of the testator and stating that he or she revokes all previous wills and codicils made at an earlier time.

DEBTS AND FUNERAL EXPENSES

A will commonly contains a clause directing that the just debts and funeral expenses be paid out of the residuary estate. The **residuary estate** is the estate remaining after individual items have been given out by the will.

DISPOSITIVE CLAUSES

The **dispositive clauses** make up the main part of the will. In these clauses, the testator names his or her beneficiaries and states exactly what each is to receive. Often, when the testator leaves the entire estate to one person or in equal shares to several people, the only dispositive clause is the residuary clause discussed later.

A gift made in a will to one's issue then living **per stirpes** (by right of representation) means that the children of any deceased heirs inherit their deceased parent's share. In contrast, a gift made to one's issue then living **per capita** (per head) means that heads are counted and all living issue share the amount of the gift equally.

A will's reference to another document, such as a list of items to be given to someone, makes it a part of the will and is known as **incorporation by reference.** To be valid, the document that is referred to must be in existence at the time the will is executed.

RESIDUARY CLAUSE

The **residuary clause** disposes of all of the testator's property not otherwise given out. If the residuary clause is omitted from the will or all of the residuary legatees and devisees predecease the testator, the residue usually passes to the heirs according to the law of intestate succession.

PERSONAL REPRESENTATIVE, GUARDIAN, AND TRUSTEE

Separate clauses are used to appoint the personal representative, guardian, and trustee in a will.

Except in states that have adopted the Uniform Probate Code, the **executor** (if a man) or **executrix** (if a woman) is the personal representative of the estate. He or she gathers the assets of the estate, pays the debts (including taxes and cost of administration), and distributes the remainder according to the testamentary provisions of the will. This distribution is done under the supervision of the probate court. If a testator fails to appoint an executor or if the executor predeceases the testator or otherwise fails to carry out the responsibility, a court will appoint someone else to perform the task. The person the court appoints to be the personal representative of the estate is called an **administrator** or **administratrix.**

It is common for people to name someone in their will to serve as guardian of their minor children. Adults sometimes need the services of a guardian as well. A **guardian** is one who legally has the care and management of the person, or person and property of a minor or incompetent. A **guardian ad litem** (for the suit) is a guardian appointed by a court to protect a minor who brings or defends a lawsuit. A **conservator,** conversely, is one who legally has the care and management of the property, but not the person, of someone who is incompetent.

A **trustee** is someone who is appointed in a will to hold property for the benefit of another when one or more of the gifts are left in trust. Trusts will be discussed in more detail in a later chapter.

NO SURETY ON BOND

A will usually contains a clause stating that the executor (often the guardian and trustee) is to serve without giving surety on his or her bond. In some states, without this clause in the will, the executor will have to have a **surety** on the bond—that is, either two persons or a surety company that will stand behind the executor's obligation. A **bond** is a promise by the personal representative and the sureties (if any) to pay the amount of the bond to the probate judge if the representative's duties are not faithfully performed.

POWERS GIVEN TO FIDUCIARIES

A clause is often included in the will to give the **fiduciaries** (people in positions of trust, such as the executor, guardian, and trustee) specific power and authority to conserve and manage the property under all foreseeable conditions. Without such a clause, the executor would be required to obtain permission (sometimes a license) from the court each time he or she wished to carry out an extraordinary administrative function such as selling real property belonging to the estate.

TAX CLAUSE

The purpose of the tax clause is to establish the source for the payment of death taxes. Often the clause directs that taxes be paid out of the residuary estate.

NO-CONTEST CLAUSE

A **no-contest clause,** also known as an **in terrorem** (in terror or warning) **clause,** attempts to disinherit any legatee, devisee, or beneficiary who contests the provisions of the will. In states that have adopted the Uniform Probate Code, such a clause is unenforceable if there is probable cause to contest the will.

TESTIMONIUM CLAUSE

The clause immediately preceding the testator's signature is called the **testimonium clause** or the **signature clause.** It is a declaration that the testator's signature is attached in testimony of the preceding part of the instrument and begins with the words "IN WIT-

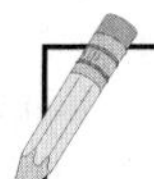

WORD WISE

Per

The Latin word *per* means "by," "through," "by way of," or "by means of."

per annum = by the year; annually (*annum* means "year")

per autre vie (also spelled pur autre vie) = for or during another's life; for the period that another person is alive (*autre* means "other"; *vie* means "life")

per capita = by heads; for each person; as individuals (*capita* means "heads")

per centum = (usually shortened to percent) by the hundred (*centum* means "hundred")

per curiam = by the court; an opinion of the whole court rather than an opinion of any one judge (*curiam* means "court")

per diem = by the day; an allowance or amount of so much per day (*diem* means "day")

per formam doni = by the form of a gift; by designation of the giver rather than by the operation of the law (*formam* means "form"; *doni* means "gift")

per fraudem = by fraud (*fraudem* means "fraud")

per infortunium = by misadventure or misfortune (*infortunium* means "misfortune")

per se = by itself, by herself, by himself, in isolation; unconnected to other matters (*se* means "itself," "herself," or "himself")

per stirpes = by (family) roots; by representation (*stirpes* means "stems" or "roots")

NESS WHEREOF" or "IN TESTIMONY WHEREOF." Often it contains a statement that the testator has initialed each of the previous pages.

ATTESTATION CLAUSE

The **attestation clause** precedes the witnesses' signatures and recites that the will was witnessed at the request of the testator and that it was signed by the witnesses in the presence of the testator and in the presence of each other.

The most desirable arrangement of the signature page of a will is to have at least three lines of the text of the will on the same page with the testimonium clause, the testator's signature, the attestation clause, and the witnesses' signatures.

SELF-PROVING AFFIDAVIT

In some states, a will will be allowed by the court without the testimony of witnesses if it contains a **self-proving affidavit** and no one objects to its allowance. This clause contains an affidavit by the testator that the testator declared the instrument to be his last will and that he signed it willingly as his free and voluntary act. It also contains affidavits by the witnesses that they signed the will as witnesses and that to the best of their knowledge the testator was 18 years of age or older, of sound mind, and under no constraint or undue influence.

Here is a self-proof clause that is authorized by statute in Massachusetts:

We, the undersigned witnesses, each do hereby declare in the presence of the aforesaid testator that the testator signed and executed this instrument as his last will in the presence of each of us, that he signed it willingly, that each of us hereby signs this will as witness in the presence of the testator, and that to the best of our knowledge the testator is eighteen (18) years of age or over, of sound mind, and under no constraint or undue influence.

________________ ________________

(witness) (address)

________________ ________________

(witness) (address)

COMMONWEALTH OF MASSACHUSETTS COUNTY OF ESSEX

Subscribed, sworn to and acknowledged before me by the said testator and witnesses this ________ day of ____________, 20___.

____

Notary Public

My commission expires:

REVIEWING WHAT YOU LEARNED

After studying the text, write the answers to each of the following questions:

1. What particular form must a will follow?

2. What is the name given to the first clause of a will in which the testator sets forth his name and domicile and states that he revokes all previous wills and codicils made by him? ____________

3. Why is the clause directing that the just debts and funeral expenses be paid out of the residuary estate often omitted from the will? ____________

4. On what occasion is the residuary clause the only dispositive clause in a will? ____________

5. What will happen to the residue of an estate if the residuary clause is omitted from a will?

6. What are the principal duties of the executor or executrix? ____________

7. On what occasions, when a person dies testate, will the court appoint an administrator or administratrix? ______________________

8. In some states, what will be required if a will does not state that the executor is to serve without giving surety on his or her bond? ________

9. If no "powers" clause is in a will, what will the executor be required to do each time he or she wishes to carry out an extraordinary administrative function? ______________________

10. What is the purpose of the tax clause in a will?

11. Where, on a will, is the testimonium clause located? What are the first few words of the testimonium clause? ______________________

12. Where, on a will, is the attestation clause located? ______________________

13. What is the most desirable arrangement of the signature page of a will? ______________________

14. Explain the reason for using a self-proving affidavit in a will. ______________________

UNDERSTANDING LEGAL CONCEPTS

Indicate whether each statement is true or false. Then, change the italicized word or phrase of each *false* statement to make it true.

Answers

________________ **1.** A will *must* follow a particular form.

________________ **2.** The exordium clause is the *last* clause in a will.

________________ **3.** The *residuary* estate is the estate remaining after individual items have been given out by the will.

________________ **4.** Often, when the testator leaves the entire estate to one person or in equal shares to several people, the only dispositive clause is the *residuary* clause.

________________ **5.** If the residuary clause is omitted from a will, the residue will usually pass to the heirs according to the law of *intestate succession.*

________________ **6.** In some states, a will will be allowed by the court *without* the testimony of witnesses if it contains a self-proving affidavit and no one objects to its allowance.

________________ **7.** The clause that precedes the witnesses' signatures is called the *testimonium* clause.

________________ **8.** If a testator fails to appoint an executor in a will, the court will appoint a *trustee* to perform the task.

________________ **9.** Unless a will contains a clause stating that the executor is to serve without giving surety on his or her bond, the *executor* will have to have a surety on the bond.

________________ **10.** The clause preceding the testator's signature is called the *attestation* clause.

CHECKING TERMINOLOGY

From the list of legal terms that follows, select the one that matches each definition.

a. administrator
b. administratrix
c. attestation clause
d. bond
e. conservator
f. dispositive clauses
g. domicile
h. executor
i. executrix
j. exordium clause
k. fiduciary
l. guardian
m. guardian ad litem
n. incorporation by reference
o. in terrorem clause
p. no-contest clause

Answers

____ **1.** The estate remaining after individual items have been given out by a will.

____ **2.** A person's principal place of abode; the place to which, whenever a person is absent, he or she has the present intent of returning.

____ **3.** The introductory paragraph of a will (select two answers).

____ **4.** A man nominated in a will of a decedent to carry out the terms of the will; a personal representative of an estate.

____ **5.** A person in a position of trust, such as an executor, administrator, guardian, or trustee.

____ **6.** A woman nominated in a will of a decedent to carry out the terms of the will; a personal representative of an estate.

____ **7.** The clauses in a will that disposes of all of the testator's property not otherwise given out.

____ **8.** The clause in a will that states exactly what each beneficiary is to receive.

____ **9.** A clause in a will containing an affidavit that allows the will to be allowed by the court without the testimony of witnesses.

____ **10.** A man appointed by the court to administer the estate of an intestate decedent.

q. per capita
r. per stirpes
s. publication clause
t. residuary clause
u. residuary estate
v. self-proving affidavit
w. signature clause
x. surety
y. testimonium clause
z. trustee

____**11.** A woman appointed by the court to administer the estate of an intestate decedent.

____**12.** One who legally has the care and management of the person, property, or both of a minor or incompetent.

____**13.** A person who holds property in trust for another.

____**14.** A clause in a will that attempts to disinherit any legatee, devisee, or beneficiary who contests the provisions of the will (select two answers).

____**15.** One who undertakes to stand behind another—that is, pay money or do any other act in the event that his or her principal fails to meet an obligation.

____**16.** The clause in a will that precedes the witnesses' signatures.

____**17.** A written instrument promising the payment of a sum of money if certain duties are not performed.

____**18.** The clause in a will that precedes the testator's signature (select two answers).

____**19.** By right of representation.

____**20.** One who legally has the care and management of the property, but not the person, of someone who is incompetent.

____**21.** Per head.

____**22.** A guardian appointed by a court to protect a minor who brings or defends a lawsuit.

____**23.** Making a document part of another document by referring to it in the second document and stating the intention of including it.

UNRAVELING LEGALESE

John Lennon was domiciled in New York when he executed his will. He was shot to death outside his New York apartment on December 8, 1980. Give the legal names of the following clause in Mr. Lennon's will and explain its legal implications.

> If any legatee or beneficiary under this will or the trust agreement between myself as Grantor and YOKO ONO LENNON and ELI GARBER as trustees, dated November 12, 1979 shall interpose objections to the probate of this Will, or institute or prosecute or be in any way interested or instrumental in the institution or prosecution of any action or proceeding for the purpose of setting aside or invalidating this Will, then and in each such case, I direct that such legatee or beneficiary shall receive nothing whatsoever under this Will or the aforementioned Trust.

USING LEGAL LANGUAGE

Read the following story and fill in the blank lines with legal terms taken from the list of terms at the beginning of this chapter.

In his will, Jason named his wife, Julie, to be the __________________________—that is, the personal representative of his estate—and said that she was to serve without giving __________________________ (naming someone to stand behind) on her official __________________________. Had he died without a will, Julie probably would have been appointed __________________________. The __________________________ in Jason's will set forth his name and __________________________—that is, his principal residence—and stated that he revoked all previous wills and codicils made by him. The __________________________ in his will listed the items that each beneficiary was to receive. The __________________________ gave all the rest, residue, and remainder of Jason's estate, called the __________________________, to his wife, Julie, who was named __________________________ to care for their minor daughter, Jennie, and __________________________ to hold property for Jennie's benefit. These latter positions made her a(n) __________________________, because she was in a position of trust. A(n) __________________________, also called a(n) __________________________, was not needed because Jason expected no beneficiary to contest the will. The will contained a(n) __________________________ preceding the testator's signature and a(n) __________________________ preceding the witnesses' signatures. The will ended with a(n) __________________________ that contained an affidavit by Jason that he declared the instrument to be his last will and that he signed it willingly as a free and voluntary act.

PUZZLING OVER WHAT YOU LEARNED

Caveat: Allow squares for spaces between words and punctuation (apostrophes, hyphens, etc.) when filling in crossword.

Across

1. One who undertakes to stand behind another.
3. A person who holds property in trust for another.
10. The introductory paragraph of a will.
12. Per head.
15. An instrument promising the payment of money if duties are not performed.
16. People in positions of trust.
17. One who has the care of the person and property of a minor.
18. Clauses in a will that state exactly what each beneficiary is to receive.

Down

2. Clause in a will that disposes of all property not otherwise given out.
4. A woman nominated in a will to carry out the terms of the will.
5. Estate remaining after individual items have been given out by a will.
6. One who legally has management of the property but not the person of an incompetent.
7. The introductory paragraph of a will.
8. By right of representation.
9. A woman appointed by the court to administer the estate of an intestate.
11. A person's principal place of abode.
13. A man nominated in a will to carry out the terms of the will.
14. A man appointed by the court to administer the estate of an intestate.

6

CHAPTER 25

Disinheritance and Intestacy

ANTE INTERROGATORY

When property reverts to the state, it is said to (A) escheat, (B) lapse, (C) adeem, (D) vest.

CHAPTER OUTLINE

Spousal Protection
Dower and Curtesy
Pretermitted Children
Homestead Protection
Distinctive Relationships
Intestacy
Rights of Surviving Spouse
Rights of Other Heirs

KEY TERMS

adoption *(a·DOP·shun)*
adoptive parents *(a·DOP·tiv)*
affiliation proceedings *(a·fil·ee·AY·shun pro·SEED·ings)*
bastards *(BAS·terds)*
collateral relatives *(ko·LAT·er·el REL·e·tivs)*
coparceners *(koh·PAR·se·ners)*
coverture *(KUV·er·cher)*
curtesy *(KUR·te·see)*
decedent *(de·SEE·dent)*
degree of kindred *(de·GREE ov KIN·dred)*
descendants *(de·SEN·dents)*
descent *(de·SENT)*
distribution *(dis·tre·BYOO·shun)*
dower *(DOW·er)*
elective share *(e·LEK·tiv)*
escheat *(es·CHEET)*
forced heir *(forssd air)*
forced share
full age *(ayj)*
half-blood
homestead *(HOME·sted)*
illegitimate children *(il·e·JIT·i·met CHIL·dren)*
intestacy *(in·TESS·te·see)*
intestate *(in·TESS·tate)*
intestate succession *(in·TESS·tate suk·SESH·en)*
kindred *(KIN·dred)*
legal fiction *(LEE·gul FIK·shun)*
life estate *(es·TATE)*
lineal ascendants *(LIN·ee·el a·SEN·dents)*
lineal descendants *(LIN·ee·el de·SEN·dents)*
majority *(ma·JAW·ri·tee)*
next friend
next of kin
nonmarital children *(non·MAR·i·tel)*
paternity proceeding *(pa·TERN·i·tee pro·SEED·ing)*
pretermitted child *(pre·ter·MIT·ed)*
primogeniture *(pry·mo·JEN·e·cher)*
probated *(PRO·bate·ed)*
vested *(VES·ted)*
waive a spouse's will *(SPOW·sez)*

SPOUSAL PROTECTION

Surviving spouses are protected against being disinherited by their husbands and wives. State laws allow surviving spouses to disclaim the provisions made for them in their deceased spouse's will and take a statutory sum, called an **elective share** or a **forced share,** instead. A surviving spouse who elects to disclaim the provisions of a deceased spouse's will is sometimes referred to as a **forced heir.**

Some states allow a disinherited spouse to take the amount he or she would have inherited had the spouse died without a will. Other states use a different formula to determine the amount of a spouse's inheritance. For example, in Massachusetts, the surviving husband or wife who wishes to **waive a spouse's will**—that is, renounce or disclaim it—must file a petition to do so with the court within six months after the spouse's will is **probated** (proved and allowed by the court). On waiving the will, the surviving spouse will be entitled to receive the following from the estate of the deceased spouse:

1. If the deceased spouse was survived by issue, one-third of all the real property and one-third of all the personal property, but of that share, no more than $25,000 outright and a life estate in the remainder. A **life estate** is an ownership interest whose duration is limited to the life of some person.

Figure 25-1 State laws allow surviving spouses to disclaim the provisions made for them in their deceased spouse's will and take a statutory sum called an elective or forced share instead.

2. If the deceased spouse was survived by no issue but **kindred** (blood relatives), $25,000 outright plus a life estate in one-half of the remaining real and one-half of the remaining personal property.
3. If the deceased spouse was survived by no issue or kindred, $25,000 outright plus one-half of the remaining real and personal property absolutely.

Under this particular state statute, a will cannot be waived by the surviving spouse if the deceased testator or testatrix had obtained a legal separation from the spouse before death.

DOWER AND CURTESY

Years ago in England, the rights of dower and curtesy developed as a way to protect the interest of a surviving spouse of one who owned real property. These rights were especially important in those days, when land was the chief form of income from either rents or profits from the land. **Dower** was a right that a widow had to a life estate in one-third of all real property owned by her husband during **coverture** (marriage). **Curtesy** was a right that a widower (a man) had, only if issue of the marriage were born alive, to a life estate in all real property owned by his wife at any time during coverture. Both dower and curtesy were exempt from the claims of the decedent's creditors—an important consideration today.

Many states today have either abolished common law dower and curtesy or amended it to treat men and women equally. They also apply it only to real property that was owned by a spouse on death rather than during coverture. This change eliminates the need to obtain a release of dower or curtesy of a spouse on a married person's deed.

Usually, a person cannot accept dower and at the same time waive the will of a deceased spouse. In states that follow this law, a surviving spouse of a person who dies testate has a choice of (1) accepting the provisions of the will, (2) waiving the will and taking the amount provided for by statute, or (3) taking the right of dower or curtesy. Usually, the last would not be elected unless the decedent's estate was insolvent, because the second choice would normally provide a greater inheritance.

PRETERMITTED CHILDREN

Sometimes a testator or testatrix will leave a child out of a will. When this occurs, the omitted child, called a **pretermitted child,** will receive nothing from the parent's estate unless the child can prove that the omission was unintentional—that is, done by mistake. Here is a typical statute:

> If a testator omits to provide in his will for any of his children, whether born before or after the testator's death, or for the issue of a deceased child, whether born before or after the testator's death, they shall take the same share of his estate which they would have taken if he had died intestate, unless they have been provided for by the testator in his lifetime or unless it appears that the omission was intentional and not occasioned by accident or mistake.

Under the statute, the burden is on the omitted child to prove that his or her omission from the will was unintentional. This must be done through another person (called a **next friend**) if the child is still a minor, because a person cannot bring a lawsuit until reaching **majority,** which means becoming of **full age**—that is, an adult. To avoid a will contest when a child is purposely omitted from a will, it is best to mention in the will that the child was omitted intentionally and that it was not done by accident or mistake.

HOMESTEAD PROTECTION

To allow families to remain in their homes when tragedy strikes, states have **homestead exemption laws,** which allow a head of household to designate a house and land as a homestead. A **homestead** is property that is beyond the reach of creditors and claims of others so long as the family uses it as a home. In many states, a homestead allowance up to a certain amount of money continues after the death of the head of household to provide a residence for the surviving spouse and minor children.

DISTINCTIVE RELATIONSHIPS

Half-blood relatives have one parent in common, but not both. For example, a half-sister might have the same mother but not have the same father as her half-brother. Under the laws of many states, half-blood relatives inherit the same as whole-blood relatives. In a few states, half-blood relatives inherit only when there are no whole-blood relatives. In Florida, half-blood kindred receive only half as much as whole-blood kindred unless there is no one of the whole blood.

Adoption is the legal process by which a child's legal rights and duties toward his or her natural parents are replaced by similar rights and duties toward his or her adopting parents. Under most state laws today, adopted children inherit from and through their **adoptive** (adopting) **parents** and not from their natural parents. The term **descendants** means those who are of the bloodstream (including adopted children) of a common ancestor. This paradox is known as a **legal fiction**—an assumption, for purposes of justice, of a fact that does not exist.

Children born out of wedlock, formerly called **bastards** but now referred to as **illegitimate children** or **nonmarital children,** inherit from their mother and any maternal ancestors. They inherit from and through their fathers who have acknowledged paternity, have been adjudicated to be their fathers in paternity proceedings, or have married their mothers. A **paternity proceeding,** also called an **affiliation proceeding,** is a court action to determine whether a person is the father of a child born out of wedlock.

INTESTACY

When people die without a will—that is, **intestate**—their personal property passes to others according to the law of the state where they were domiciled when they died. In contrast, their real property passes according to the law of the state in which the property is located. These laws were called the **laws of descent and distribution** under early English law, which distinguished real property from personal property. Real property descended to the eldest son of the **decedent** (deceased person) under a doctrine known as **primogeniture.** If parents had no sons, all daughters took the property together as a single heir (as **coparceners,** or joint heirs). Personal property of the decedent, in those early days, was distributed by church officials "for the good of the soul of the deceased." Thus, the word **descent** technically refers only to real property, and the word **distribution** refers to personal property.

Today, the law of **intestacy** (the state of dying without having made a valid will) is called the law of **intestate succession.** The early distinction between real and personal property is still followed. Ownership of real property becomes **vested** (fixed or absolute) in the decedent's heirs at the moment of death; ownership of personal property, however, passes to the administrator or administratrix to be distributed by him or her.

Present American statutes of intestate succession are based on the English Statute of 1670 and apply to both real and personal property. Under most state laws, after an amount is allotted to a surviving spouse, if any, the balance passes to the decedent's lineal descendants. **Lineal descendants** are people who are in a direct line of descent (downward) from the decedent—children, grandchildren, and great-grandchildren. When there are no living lineal descendants, the balance passes to the decedent's lineal ascendants. **Lineal ascendants** are people who are in a direct line of ascent (upward) from the decedent—parents, grandparents, and great-grandparents. When there are no living descendants or ascendants, the balance passes to the decedent's **collateral relatives**—those not in a direct line, such as brothers, sisters, nieces, nephews, uncles, aunts, and cousins. Although the statutes differ from state to state, a fairly typical one is discussed here.

WORD WISE

The Prefix "Co-"

This Latin prefix meaning "together" appears in hundreds of English words. Its four spelling variations (col-, com-, con-, and cor-) make pronunciation easier before various roots. Some examples are:

Word	*Meaning*
collaborate [*col* + *laborare* (to work)]	To work together
companion [*com* + *panis* (bread)]	Someone who accompanies another; originally, someone who shared bread
contact [*con* + *tact* (to touch)]	Touch by meeting
coparceners	Joint heirs
corroborate [*cor* + *roborare* (strength)]	To make certain; confirm

Rights of Surviving Spouse

Under the Massachusetts statute, if a person dies intestate, a surviving spouse is entitled to the following:

1. If the deceased is survived by issue, one-half of the estate
2. If the deceased is survived by kindred but no issue, $200,000 and one-half of the remainder of the estate
3. If the deceased is survived by no issue and no kindred, the whole estate

Rights of Other Heirs

Under this state statute, if a person dies intestate, his or her property will pass, subject to the rights of the surviving spouse (stated earlier), as follows:

1. If the deceased is survived by issue, the property will pass in equal shares to the surviving children. The issue of any deceased children take their parent's share by right of representation.
2. If the deceased is survived by no issue but a father or mother, the property will pass in equal shares to the father and mother or the survivor of them.

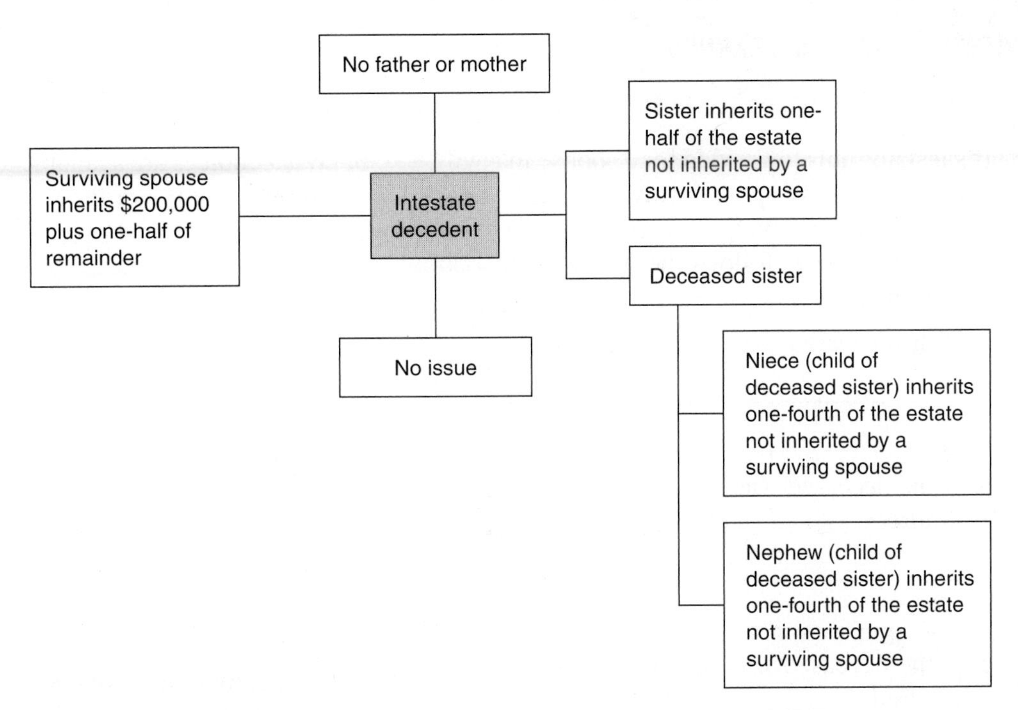

Figure 25-2 This chart illustrates the way in which property passes by intestate succession in Massachusetts to a decedent's siblings under the state statute. The decedent, who was survived by no issue, mother, or father, was survived by a spouse, one sister, and two children of a deceased sister.

3. If the deceased is survived by no issue and no mother or father, the property will pass in equal shares to brothers and sisters. The issue of any deceased brothers or sisters take their parent's share by right of representation (see Figure 25-2).
4. If the deceased is survived by no issue, and no mother or father, and no brothers or sisters or their issue (nieces or nephews), the property will pass in equal shares to the **next of kin** (those most nearly related by blood). To determine the closest relatives, each relationship is assigned a number called a **degree of kindred.** The relationship with the lowest number usually inherits to the exclusion of all others. For example, first cousins (fourth-degree kindred) would inherit before second cousins (sixth-degree kindred).
5. If the deceased is survived by no kindred and no surviving spouse, the property will **escheat**—that is, pass to the state.

REVIEWING WHAT YOU LEARNED

After studying the text, write the answers to each of the following questions:

1. If a testator fails to provide for a spouse in a will and the surviving spouse waives the will, how much will the surviving spouse be entitled to receive in a state that follows the statute mentioned in this chapter? ______
   a. If the deceased was survived by issue? ______
   b. If the deceased was survived by no issue but kindred? ______
   c. If the deceased was survived by no issue or kindred? ______
2. On what occasion may a will *not* be waived by the surviving spouse under that particular statute? ______
3. For what reason did the rights of dower and curtesy develop in early England? ______
4. What was the difference between dower and curtesy years ago in England? ______
5. What choices are available to a surviving spouse who does not like the provisions of the will of his or her spouse? ______
6. What must a pretermitted child prove to inherit from a parent's estate? ______
7. What should testators do to avoid a will contest when a child is purposely omitted from a will? ______
8. Differentiate between the words "descent" and "distribution." ______
9. Explain the difference between the vesting of real property and the passing of personal property under today's law. ______
10. How do half-blood relatives inherit under the laws of many states? ______

11. Under most state laws today, from whom do adopted children inherit? ____________________

____

____

____

12. When do nonmarital children inherit from and through their fathers? ____________________

____

____

____

13. Who will inherit and in what amount, under the law of intestate succession explained in this chapter, from the estate of a person who dies intestate survived by:

a. A spouse and two children ($120,000 estate)?

____

____

____

b. A spouse and a father and mother ($260,000 estate)? ____________________

____

____

c. A spouse and no issue or kindred ($120,000 estate)? ____________________

____

____

d. Three children ($120,000 estate)? ____________________

____

____

e. No issue or kindred and no surviving spouse ($120,000 estate)? ____________________

____

____

f. A spouse and a 96-year-old uncle ($400,000 estate)? ____________________

____

UNDERSTANDING LEGAL CONCEPTS

Indicate whether each statement is true or false. Then, change the italicized word or phrase of each *false* statement to make it true.

Answers

____________________ **1.** Under today's laws, if a surviving spouse is unhappy with the provisions of his or her spouse's will, he or she can *do nothing about* it.

____________________ **2.** Under the state statute referred to earlier, a will *cannot be* waived by the surviving spouse if the deceased testator or testatrix had obtained a legal separation from his or her spouse before death.

____________________ **3.** Years ago in England, *dower* was a right that a widower had if issue of the marriage were born alive, but not otherwise, to a life estate in all real property owned by his wife at any time during coverture.

____________________ **4.** Both dower and curtesy were exempt from the claims of the decedent's *creditors,* which is an important consideration today.

____________________ **5.** A child who is omitted from a parent's will can receive nothing from the parent's estate unless the child can prove that the omission was *unintentional.*

____________________ **6.** A person can bring a lawsuit by himself or herself at *any age.*

____________________ **7.** If a person dies without a will and is survived by heirs, the property will pass *to the state.*

_______________ **8.** Today, real property vests in the decedent's heirs at the moment of death of the owner, whereas *personal property* passes to the administrator or administratrix to be distributed by him or her.

9. Under the state statute referred to in this chapter, if a person dies intestate and is

_______________ **a.** Survived by *kindred but no issue,* a surviving spouse is entitled to one-half of the estate.

_______________ **b.** Survived by *no issue and no kindred,* a surviving spouse is entitled to the whole estate.

_______________ **c.** Survived by issue, his or her property will pass, subject to the rights of the surviving spouse, in equal shares, to the surviving *grandchildren.*

_______________ **d.** Survived by no issue but a father or mother, his or her property will pass, subject to the rights of the surviving spouse, to the surviving *father and mother.*

_______________ **e.** Survived by no issue and no mother or father, the decedent's property will pass, subject to the rights of the surviving spouse, to his or her *next of kin.*

_______________ **10.** Under some state statutes, illegitimate children inherit from their *father* and any *paternal* ancestor.

CHECKING TERMINOLOGY

From the list of legal terms that follows, select the one that matches each definition:

a. adoption
b. adoptive parents
c. affiliation proceeding
d. bastards
e. collateral relatives
f. coparceners
g. coverture
h. curtesy
i. decedent
j. degree of kindred
k. descendants
l. descent
m. distribution
n. dower
o. elective share
p. escheat
q. forced heir
r. forced share
s. full age
t. half-blood
u. homestead

Answers

____ **1.** Relatives who have one parent in common, but not both.

____ **2.** To die without a will.

____ **3.** A statutory sum given to a surviving spouse who disclaims the provisions made for him or her in a deceased spouse's will (select two answers).

____ **4.** At common law, the right of a widow to a life estate in one-third of all real property owned by her husband during coverture.

____ **5.** At common law, the right of a widower, if issue of the marriage were born alive, to a life estate in all real property owned by his wife during coverture.

____ **6.** Renounce or disclaim a spouse's will.

____ **7.** Blood relatives.

____ **8.** An ownership interest whose duration is limited to the life of some person.

____ **9.** A court action to determine whether a person is the father of a child born out of wedlock (select two answers).

____ **10.** Children born out of wedlock (select three answers).

____ **11.** The legal process in which a child's legal rights and duties toward his or her natural parents are replaced by similar rights and duties toward his or her adopting parents.

____ **12.** One acting for the benefit of an infant in bringing a legal action.

____ **13.** A child who is omitted by a testator from a will.

____ **14.** Marriage.

____ **15.** Adulthood (select two answers).

v. illegitimate children
w. intestacy
x. intestate
y. intestate succession
z. kindred
aa. legal fiction
bb. life estate
cc. lineal ascendants
dd. lineal descendants
ee. majority
ff. next friend
gg. next of kin
hh. nonmarital children
ii. paternity proceeding
jj. pretermitted child
kk. primogeniture
ll. probated
mm. vested
nn. waive a spouse's will

____**16.** The act or process of an heir becoming beneficially entitled to the property of one who dies without a will.

____**17.** Succession to the ownership of real property by inheritance (early English law).

____**18.** The apportionment and division of the personal property of an intestate among his or her heirs (early English law).

____**19.** The state of being the first born among several children of the same parents (early English law).

____**20.** Persons to whom an estate of inheritance descends jointly; joint heirs (early English law).

____**21.** The state of dying without having made a valid will.

____**22.** A surviving spouse who elects to disclaim the provisions of a deceased spouse's will.

____**23.** Parents who adopt a child.

____**24.** Those most nearly related by blood.

____**25.** The reversion of property to the state if the property owner dies without heirs.

____**26.** Fixed or absolute; not contingent.

____**27.** A deceased person.

____**28.** Proved and allowed by the court.

____**29.** Property that is beyond the reach of creditors' and others' claims as long as the family uses the property as a home.

____**30.** The relationship between a decedent and his or her relatives to determine who are most nearly related by blood.

____**31.** Relatives not in a direct line, such as brothers, sisters, nieces, nephews, uncles, aunts, and cousins.

____**32.** Those who are of the bloodstream (including adopted children) of a common ancestor.

____**33.** An assumption, for purposes of justice, of a fact that does not exist.

____**34.** People who are in a direct line of ascent (upward) from the decedent—parents, grandparents, and great-grandparents.

____**35.** People who are in a direct line of descent (downward) from the decedent—children, grandchildren, and great-grandchildren.

UNRAVELING LEGALESE

Use simple, non-legal language, with the help of the glossary, to rewrite this case quote so that it is shorter and can be understood by a layperson without losing its meaning.

> Turning to "issue" who are the nonmarital children of an intestate, the intestacy statute treats different classes of nonmarital children differently based on the presumed ease of establishing their consanguinity with the deceased parent. A nonmarital child is presumptively the child of his or her mother and is entitled by virtue of the presumption to enjoy inheritance rights as her issue. However, to enjoy inheritance rights as the issue of a deceased father, a nonmarital child, in the absence of the father's acknowledgment of paternity or marriage to the mother, must obtain a judicial determination that he or she is the father's child.

USING LEGAL LANGUAGE

Read the following story and fill in the blank lines with legal terms taken from the list of terms at the beginning of this chapter.

When Jason, the ____________________, died testate, his wife, Julie, who was of ____________________—that is, an adult—could choose to accept the provisions of the will, ____________________ (renounce or disclaim) the will, or take her right of ____________________, which at common law was the right to a(n) ____________________ in one-third of all real property owned by Jason during ____________________. Had she been a man, this right would be called ____________________. Jason's real property passed under the will by ____________________ to his devisee, and ____________________ at the moment of death. His personal property passed by ____________________ through his personal representative to his legatees. The will had to be ____________________—that is, proved and allowed by the court. Jason did not fail to provide for any of his children; therefore, no ____________________ would, if he or she had not reached ____________________, have to bring suit by a ____________________. He had no ____________________—that is, children born out of wedlock—and none of his children were of the ____________________—that is, had one parent in common, but not both. Had Jason died without a will, on death, his personal property would have passed to his heirs according to the law of ____________________ in the state where he died domiciled. His ____________________—that is, those most nearly related by blood and sometimes referred to as ____________________—would have inherited from his estate along with his surviving spouse.

6

PUZZLING OVER WHAT YOU LEARNED

Caveat: Allow squares for spaces between words and punctuation (apostrophes, hyphens, etc.) when filling in crossword.

Across

7. Another name for a forced share.
10. Right of a widow to a life estate in one-third of real property owned by a husband.
12. Surviving spouse who elects to disclaim the provisions of a spouse's will.
14. To die without a will.
16. The state of dying without having made a valid will.
17. Fixed or absolute.
18. Blood relatives.
19. Adulthood.

Down

1. Renounce or disclaim a spouse's will.
2. Succession to the ownership of real property by inheritance.
3. A statutory sum given to a surviving spouse who disclaims will's provisions.
4. A child who is omitted by a testator from a will.
5. One acting for the benefit of an infant in bringing a legal action.
6. Right of a widower to a life estate in real property owned by his wife.
8. An ownership interest whose duration is limited to someone's life.
9. Marriage.
11. Proved and allowed by the court.
13. A deceased person.
15. The reversion of property to the state if the owner dies without heirs.

6

CHAPTER 26

Personal Representative of the Estate

ANTE INTERROGATORY

A personal representative who is appointed by the court to handle the affairs of a decedent in a foreign state is called a(n) (A) public administrator, (B) special administrator, (C) ancillary administrator, (D) voluntary administrator.

CHAPTER OUTLINE

Estate Settlement
Titles of Personal Representatives
Successor Personal Representatives
Particular-Purpose Administrators

KEY TERMS

administrator *(ad·MIN·is·tray·tor)*
administrator ad litem *(ad LY·tem)*
administrator c.t.a.
administrator cum testamento annexo *(kum tes·ta·MENT·o an·EKS·o)*
administrator d.b.n.
administrator d.b.n.c.t.a.
administrator de bonis non *(de BO·nis non)*
administrator de bonis non cum testamento annexo
administrator pendente lite *(pen·DEN·tay LIE·tay)*
administrator with the will annexed *(an·EKSD)*
administrator w.w.a.
administratrix *(ad·MIN·is·tray·triks)*
ancillary administrator *(AN·sil·a·ree ad·MIN·is·tray·tor)*
Court of Ordinary *(OR·di·ner·ee)*
executor *(eg·ZEK·yoo·tor)*
executor de son tort *(eg·ZEK·yoo·tor day sown tort)*
executrix *(eg·ZEK·yoo·triks)*
fiduciary capacity *(fi·DOO·she·air·ee ka·PASS·e·tee)*
Orphan's Court
personal representative *(PER·son·al rep·re·ZEN·ta·tiv)*
Prerogative Court *(pre·ROG·a·tiv)*
Probate and Family Court *(PRO·bate)*
public administrator *(PUB·lik ad·MIN·is·tray·tor)*
special administrator *(SPESH·el ad·MIN·is·tray·tor)*
successor personal representatives *(suk·SESS·or PER·son·al rep·re·ZEN·ta·tiv)*
summary administration *(SUM·e·ree ad·min·is·TRAY·shun)*
Surrogate's Court *(SER·o·gets)*
voluntary administrator *(VOL·en·ter·ee ad·MIN·is·tray·tor)*
will contest

ESTATE SETTLEMENT

When a person dies owning property of any kind solely, the estate must be settled. This task is undertaken by the court, which acts through an executor or administrator (called the **personal representative**), who is appointed for that purpose and who acts in a **fiduciary capacity**—that is, a position of trust. The court that exercises this function is called by different names in different states. For example, in New York, it is called the **Surrogate's Court;** in Pennsylvania, the **Orphan's Court;** in New Jersey, the **Prerogative Court;** in Massachusetts, the **Probate and Family Court;** and in Georgia, the **Court of Ordinary.** In California, the Superior Court has jurisdiction over probate proceedings.

TITLES OF PERSONAL REPRESENTATIVES

In states that have adopted the Uniform Probate Code (see page 249), a personal representative is referred to as a **personal representative.** In other states, personal representatives are given different titles depending on the method by which they gained their position or the particular task they are to perform. An **executor** (if a man) or **executrix** (if a woman) is a person nominated in the will of a decedent to carry out the terms of the will. An **administrator** (if a man) or **administratrix** (if a woman) is a person appointed by the court to administer the estate of an intestate decedent.

Successor Personal Representatives

An **administrator de bonis non** (administrator of goods not administered), also known as **administrator d.b.n.,** is appointed by the court to complete the settlement of an estate in which a previously appointed administrator has died, resigned, or been removed. An **administrator cum testamento annexo** (**administrator with the will annexed**), also known as **administrator c.t.a.** or **administrator w.w.a.,** is appointed by the court to administer a testate estate in which no executor is nominated or in which the person named to be executor has, before being appointed, either died or been adjudged incompetent or refuses or neglects to perform the task. An **administrator de bonis non cum testamento annexo** (administrator of goods not administered with the will annexed), also known as **administrator d.b.n.c.t.a.,** is appointed by the court to take the place of a previously appointed executor or administrator cum testamento annexo who has died, resigned, or been removed. In Uniform Probate Code states, all of these people are referred to as **successor personal representatives.** They are appointed to succeed previously appointed personal representatives.

Particular-Purpose Administrators

A **special administrator** is one who is appointed by the court to handle the affairs of an estate for a limited time only, such as when a delay in the allowance of a will or dispute over the appointment of an executor occurs. The special administrator takes care of affairs that are urgent and in need of immediate attention.

A **public administrator** is an official who administers the estate of a person who dies intestate and no relative, heir, or other person appears who is entitled to act as administrator.

A **voluntary administrator** is a person who undertakes the informal administration of a small estate. Some states provide this as an easy method of settling small estates. For example, in Massachusetts, if an estate consists entirely of personal property the total value of which does not exceed an automobile and $15,000, a surviving spouse, child, parent, brother, or sister of the decedent may, after the expiration of 30 days from the date

WORD WISE

The Prefix "Ad-"

The Latin prefix "ad" means "to" or "toward." Its spelling variations facilitate pronunciation before different roots.

Prefix	*Example*
ad-	administrator
a- (before *sc, sp, st*)	ascend, aspect, astride
ac- (before *c* or *q*)	accept, acquit
af- (before *f*)	affect
ag- (before *g*)	aggravated
an- (before *n*)	annulment
ap- (before *p*)	approve
ar- (before *r*)	arraignment
as- (before *s*)	assault
at- (before *t*)	attempt

of death, file certain information and become a voluntary administrator. The powers of a voluntary administrator cease if a regular administrator or executor is appointed to settle the estate. In California, a similar procedure, known as **summary administration,** is used to settle estates that do not exceed $30,000.

An **ancillary administrator** is one who is appointed by the court to handle the affairs of a decedent in a foreign state. For example, if a decedent dies domiciled in New York owning real property in Connecticut, ancillary administration will have to be taken out in Connecticut in addition to there being a New York executor or administrator to settle the Connecticut real property. It is also necessary to take out ancillary administration if one is to bring suit or collect debts of a nonresident decedent.

An **administrator pendente lite** (pending suit) is a temporary administrator appointed by the court to protect estate assets when there is a **will contest** (a suit over the allowance or disallowance of a will). In contrast, an **administrator ad litem** (for the suit) is appointed by the court to supply a necessary party to a suit in which the estate has an interest, as when the estate is a party to a lawsuit.

An **executor de son tort** is the name given to a person who performs the duties of an executor without authority to do so. Such a person is said to be an intermeddler and is held responsible for his or her acts.

REVIEWING WHAT YOU LEARNED

After studying the text, write the answers to each of the following questions:

1. Name the personal representative who is nominated in a will. ______

2. Name the personal representative of an intestate estate. ______

3. If the original personal representative of an intestate estate dies before completing the task, what is the title given to the person who is appointed to take his or her place? ______

4. If the personal representative who is nominated in the will dies before the testator and then the testator dies, what is the title given to the person who is appointed to settle the estate? ______

5. If the personal representative who is nominated in the will begins but does not complete the task, what is the title given to the person who is appointed to settle the estate? ______

6. What kind of affairs does the special administrator usually handle? ______

7. When does a public administrator administer an estate? ______

8. When would an ancillary administrator be appointed in one state for a person who dies while domiciled in another state? ______

9. What is the difference between an administrator pendente lite and an administrator ad litem?

10. Why do you think an executor de son tort is said to be an intermeddler? ______

6

UNDERSTANDING LEGAL CONCEPTS

Indicate whether each statement is true or false. Then, change the italicized word or phrase of each *false* statement to make it true.

Answers

_______________ **1.** Another name for an executor or administrator is *personal representative.*

_______________ **2.** In California, the court that undertakes the settlement of estates is called the *Surrogate's Court.*

_______________ **3.** An *executor* is a male appointed by the court to administer the estate of an intestate decedent.

_______________ **4.** An *administratrix* is a woman nominated in a will to carry out the terms of the will.

_______________ **5.** An *administrator de bonis non* is appointed by the court to complete the settlement of an estate in which a previously appointed administrator has died, resigned, or been removed.

_______________ **6.** An administrator cum testamento annexo is also called an *administrator with the will annexed.*

_______________ **7.** An administrator de bonis non cum testamento annexo is appointed by the court to take the place of a previously appointed *executor* who has died, resigned, or been removed.

_______________ **8.** A *public* administrator is a person who undertakes the informal administration of a small estate.

_______________ **9.** The powers of a voluntary administrator *cease* if a regular administrator or executor is appointed to settle the estate.

_______________ **10.** A *voluntary* administrator is one who is appointed by the court to handle the affairs of a decedent in a foreign state.

CHECKING TERMINOLOGY

From the list of legal terms that follows, select the one that matches each definition.

a. administrator
b. administrator ad litem
c. administrator cum testamento annexo (c.t.a.)
d. administrator d.b.n.
e. administrator d.b.n.c.t.a.
f. administrator de bonis non

Answers

____ **1.** A man nominated in a will of a decedent to carry out the terms of the will; a personal representative of an estate.

____ **2.** A woman appointed by the court to administer the estate of an intestate decedent.

____ **3.** A person appointed by the court to complete the settlement of an estate in which a previously appointed administrator has died, resigned, or been removed (select two answers).

____ **4.** A person who undertakes the informal administration of a small estate.

____ **5.** A woman nominated in a will of a decedent to carry out the terms of the will; a personal representative of an estate.

6

g. administrator de bonis non cum testamento annexo
h. administrator pendente lite
i. administrator with the will annexed (w.w.a.)
j. administratrix
k. ancillary administrator
l. Court of Ordinary
m. executor
n. executor de son tort
o. executrix
p. fiduciary capacity
q. Orphan's Court
r. personal representative
s. Prerogative Court
t. Probate and Family Court
u. public administrator
v. special administrator
w. successor personal representatives
x. summary administration
y. Surrogate's Court
z. voluntary administrator
aa. will contest

____ **6.** A person appointed by the court to administer a testate estate in which no executor is nominated or in which the executor has died or for some reason does not settle the estate (select two answers).

____ **7.** A person who performs the duties of an executor without authority to do so.

____ **8.** A temporary administrator appointed by the court to protect estate assets when there is a will contest.

____ **9.** A position of trust.

____ **10.** People appointed to succeed previously appointed personal representatives.

____ **11.** An administrator appointed by the court to supply a necessary party to a suit in which the estate has an interest.

____ **12.** A suit over the allowance or disallowance of a will.

____ **13.** A male appointed by the court to administer the estate of an intestate decedent.

____ **14.** A person appointed by the court to replace a previously appointed executor who has died, resigned, or been removed (select two answers).

____ **15.** A person appointed by the court to handle the affairs of an estate for a limited time only to take care of urgent affairs.

____ **16.** An official who administers the estate of a person who dies intestate when no relative, heir, or other person appears who is entitled to act as administrator.

____ **17.** A person appointed by the court to handle the affairs of a decedent in a foreign state.

____ **18.** The executor or administrator of a deceased person.

____ **19.** The name given to the court that exercises the function of settling decedent's estates (select five answers).

____ **20.** An informal procedure used in California to settle estates that do not exceed $30,000.

UNRAVELING LEGALESE

Use simple, non-legal language, with the help of the glossary, to rewrite this case quote so that it is shorter and can be understood by a layperson without losing its meaning.

> Upon finding a fiduciary's violation of [a statute], the Surrogate is vested with discretion to select among a number of courses of relief, the most serious of which is revocation of letters and removal of the fiduciary. Removal of a fiduciary constitutes a judicial nullification of the testator's choice and may only be decreed when the grounds set forth in the relevant statutes have been clearly established. Accordingly the rule has long prevailed that "courts are required to exercise the power of removal sparingly and to nullify the testator's choice [of executor] only upon a clear showing of serious misconduct that endangers the safety of the estate; it is not every breach of fiduciary duty that will warrant removal [of an executor]."

USING LEGAL LANGUAGE

Read the following story and fill in the blank lines with legal terms taken from the list of terms at the beginning of this chapter:

In his will, Kevin named Katherine to be the person who would settle his estate when he died. She was called a(n) ________________________, which is the name given to a female ________________________ of an estate. In her will, Katherine named Kevin to be the ________________________. Kevin was killed in an automobile accident. His huge vegetable garden, from which he made a living, was just about to be harvested when Kevin died and needed immediate attention; thus, the court appointed a(n) ________________________ to take care of the garden at once. Because he was domiciled in Georgia when he died, Katherine was given her fiduciary appointment by the Court of ________________________, which is called the ________________________ in New York, the ____________________ in Pennsylvania, the ____________________ in New Jersey, and the ________________________ in Massachusetts. Six months later, while giving birth to a child, Katherine died. Because she had not completed the settlement of Kevin's estate, her brother-in-law, Keith, was appointed ____________________ to finish the job. Keith was also appointed the fiduciary to settle Katherine's estate. In that position, he was known as a(n) ________________________ because the person Katherine had named to complete the task had predeceased her. Katherine's newborn child, Kelley, who had inherited a sizable estate from her mother, lived only for six days and then died. Because she died without a will, Katherine's sister, Karen, was appointed ________________________ by the court to settle Kelley's estate. Had Karen been a man instead of a woman, she would have been called a(n) ________________________. Before completing her task, Karen became mentally ill and could not complete the job. Her friend, Kaleb, was appointed a(n) ________________________ by the court to finish the task. No need existed to appoint a(n) ________________________, because relatives could settle all of the estates involved here. A(n) ________________________ was not needed, because no out-of-state property was involved. None of these estates were small; therefore, none met the requirements for the appointment of a(n) ________________________.

PUZZLING OVER WHAT YOU LEARNED

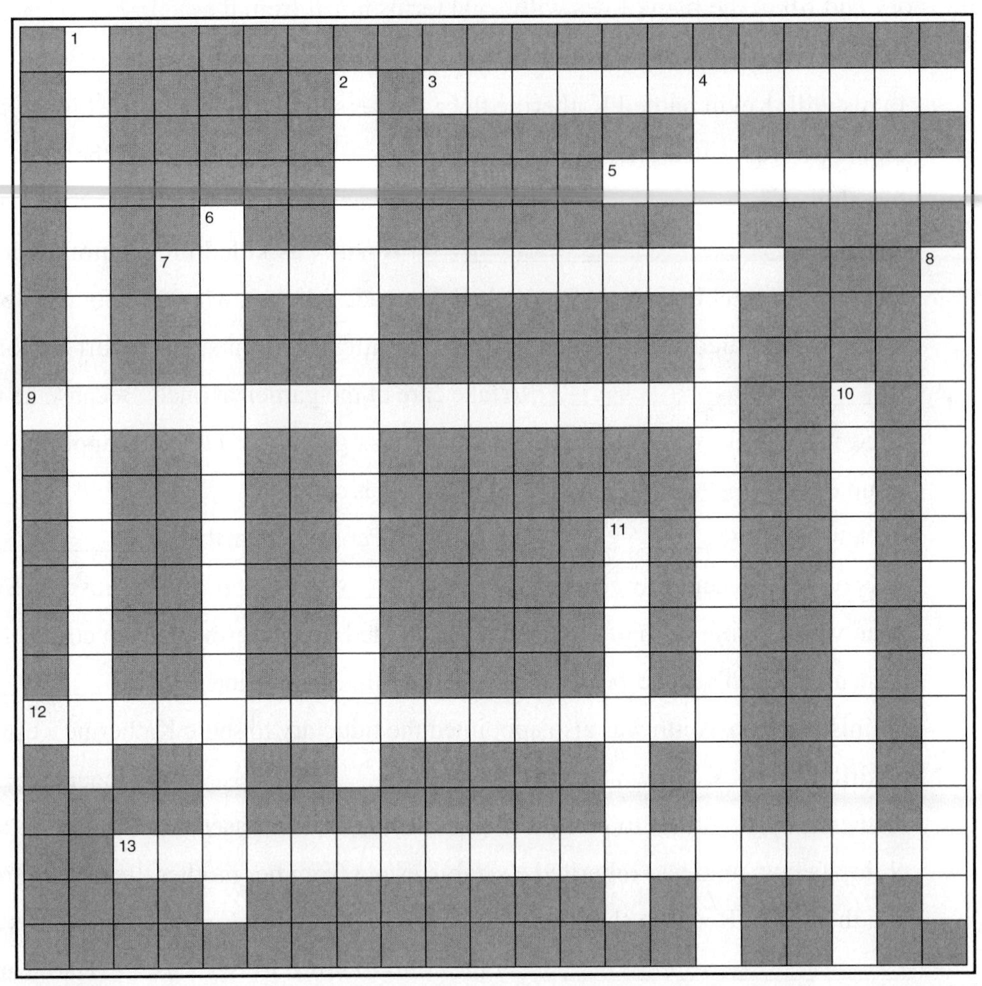

Caveat: Do **not** allow squares for spaces between words and punctuation (apostrophes, hyphens, etc.) when filling in crossword.

Across

3. The name given to the court that exercises the function of settling decedent's estates.
5. A man nominated in a will to carry out the terms of the will.
7. A woman appointed by the court to administer the estate of an intestate decedent.
9. A person appointed by the court to administer a testate estate in which no executor is nominated or in which the executor has died or for some reason does not settle the estate.
12. The name given to the court that exercises the function of settling decedent's estates.
13. An official who administers the estate of a person who dies intestate when no relative, heir, or other person appears who is entitled to act as administrator.

Down

1. A person who performs the duties of an executor without authority to do so.
2. A person appointed by the court to administer a testate estate in which no executor is nominated or in which the executor has died or for some reason does not settle the estate.
4. A person appointed by the court to handle the affairs of an estate for a limited time only to take care of urgent affairs.
6. A person appointed by the court to complete the settlement of an estate in which a previously appointed administrator has died.
8. The name given to the court that exercises the function of settling decedent's estates.
10. A male appointed by the court to administer the estate of an intestate decedent.
11. A woman nominated in a will to carry out the terms of the will.

6

CHAPTER 27
Settling an Estate

ANTE INTERROGATORY

A promise by the personal representative to pay an amount of money to the probate judge if the representative's duties are not faithfully performed is called a (A) covenant, (B) surety, (C) decree, (D) bond.

CHAPTER OUTLINE

Steps in Estate Settlement
- *Petitioning the Court*
- *Fiduciary's Bond*
- *Letters*
- *Inventory*
- *Federal Estate Tax*
- *Federal Gift Tax*
- *State Death Taxes*
- *Distribution and Accounting*

Contesting a Will

KEY TERMS

bond
burden of proof *(BER·den)*
decree *(de·KREE)*
estate tax *(es·TATE)*
fiduciary *(fi·DOO·she·air·ee)*
first and final account *(a·KOWNT)*
gifts causa mortis *(KAWS·ah MORE·tes)*
gifts made in contemplation of death *(kon·tem·PLAY·shun)*
gift tax
gross estate *(es·TATE)*
heir *(air)*
heirs at law *(airs)*
inheritance tax *(in·HER·i·tense)*
inter vivos *(IN·ter VY·vose)*
inventory *(IN·ven·tor·ee)*
judgment *(JUJ·ment)*
letters of administration *(ad·min·is·TRAY·shun)*
letters testamentary *(test·e·MEN·ter·ee)*
marital deduction *(MAR·i·tal de·DUK·shun)*
proponent *(pro·PO·nent)*
sponge tax *(spunj taks)*
sureties *(SHOOR·e·tees)*

STEPS IN ESTATE SETTLEMENT

Several steps are involved in the settling of an estate. These include petitioning the court for appointment, filing a bond, filing an inventory, making out tax returns, paying debts and expenses of administration, making distribution of the assets of the estate, and filing an account with the court.

6

Petitioning the Court

If the decedent died testate, the executor named in the will or some other interested person petitions the court for the allowance of the will and appointment as executor or administrator cum testamento annexo of the will. If the decedent died intestate, one or more of the heirs, next of kin, or creditors petition the court for appointment as administrator of the estate. An **heir,** in the broadest usage of the term, is a person who inherits property from a decedent's estate.

Notice of a hearing on the petition is given to all interested parties, including heirs at law, by service of process, mail, or newspaper publication, depending on the particular state statute. **Heirs at law** are people who would have inherited had the decedent died intestate. After a waiting period (usually three weeks), a hearing is held to decide on the petition, and the court issues a **decree** (decision of a court of equity) or **judgment** (decision of a court of law) that either allows or disallows the will, if one exists, and appoints the executor of the will or the administrator of the estate.

WORD WISE

Variations of "Heir": Related Terms and Spellings

heir [the *h* is silent; pronounced "air"]

heirdom *(AIR·dum)*

heirloom *(AIR·loom)*

The *i* disappears and the *h* is pronounced in these words:

heredity *(her·ED·i·tee)*

hereditament *(herr·e·DIT·a·ment)*

hereditary *(her·ED·i·terr·ee)*

A prefix is added in these words:

inherit *(in·HER·it)*

inheritance *(in·HER·i·tense)*

inheritor *(in·HER·i·tor)*

Fiduciary's Bond

Before being appointed, the executor or administrator (called a **fiduciary,** meaning a person who holds a position of trust) must file a bond with the court. A **bond** is a promise by the personal representative and the sureties (if any) to pay the amount of the bond to the probate judge if the representative's duties are not faithfully performed. **Sureties** are people who stand behind the personal representative in the event he or she fails to do the job. The amount of the bond is usually twice the value of the personal property of the estate. Sureties on the bond are often required unless the will otherwise provides or unless all interested parties consent to a bond without sureties.

Letters

When a satisfactory bond with sufficient sureties has been filed, the court issues a certificate of appointment to the personal representative. The certificate is known as **letters testamentary** in a testate estate and **letters of administration** in an intestate estate. In California, the judge signs an "order for probate" and the personal representative is given a form explaining the duties and liabilities of the position.

Inventory

After being appointed, one of the first duties of the personal representative is to file an inventory with the court. The **inventory** is a document that lists the assets of the estate together with their appraised value.

A waiting period (from nine months to a year) then elapses to give time for creditors to present their claims. After the time period runs out, creditors are barred from bringing claims, and the debts of the estate may be paid.

Federal Estate Tax

An **estate tax** is a tax imposed on the estate of a deceased person. A federal estate tax return (form 706) must be filed within nine months after the date of death when the gross estate exceeds an amount that is exempt from the tax. Two million dollars is exempt in 2007 and 2008. This increases to $3.5 million in 2009. The federal estate tax disappears altogether in 2010 but resurfaces in 2011, unless Congress decides otherwise, and taxes estates in which the gross estate exceeds $1 million. The **gross estate** for tax purposes includes all property that the decedent owned at death, including individually owned real or personal property, jointly owned real or personal property, life insurance, **inter vivos** (between the living) trusts, and **gifts made in contemplation of death.** Gifts made within three years of the date of death are presumed to be made in contemplation of death unless shown to the contrary. They are sometimes referred to as **gifts causa mortis.**

The following are deductible from the gross estate: debts of the decedent, funeral expenses, administration expenses, amounts given by will to charity, amounts inherited by a surviving spouse (called the **marital deduction**), and other miscellaneous items.

Federal Gift Tax

With exceptions, a federal **gift tax** is imposed on gifts totaling more than $1 million made during one's lifetime. However, anyone can make gifts of up to $12,000 per donee per year without being taxed. Any gift tax due is collected from the donor's estate, if the estate is large enough to be taxable, when the donor dies.

State Death Taxes

In addition to the federal estate tax, many states impose death taxes. They are called either **estate** or **inheritance taxes,** depending on whether the tax is imposed on the estate or on the people receiving the inheritance. An inheritance tax is a tax imposed on a person who inherits from a decedent's estate. California and many other states impose an estate tax equal to the credit allowed for state death taxes on the federal estate tax return if it is required to be filed. It is called a **sponge tax** because it soaks up money for the state that the estate is being given credit for in any event.

Distribution and Accounting

After the taxes and debts have been paid and the time has expired for creditors to submit claims, the remaining assets for the estate are distributed according to the terms of the will or the laws of intestate succession. Finally, an accounting, called the **first and final account,** if it is the only one, is prepared. This report details the amounts received and distributed by the personal representative of the estate. When the final account is allowed by the court, the estate is settled.

CONTESTING A WILL

A will may be contested only on one of the following grounds: (a) the will was improperly executed; (b) the testator was of unsound mind; or (c) the will's execution was obtained through the use of undue influence or fraud. If a will is contested on either of the first two grounds, the **proponent** of the will—that is, the person offering it for probate—has the **burden of proof** (the duty of proving a fact) either that the will was properly executed or that the testator was of sound mind. In contrast, if a will is contested on the ground of undue influence or fraud, the person claiming those acts must prove that they took place. A will may be contested only by someone who has an interest in opposing it, such as an heir at law or a devisee or legatee of an earlier-made will.

REVIEWING WHAT YOU LEARNED

After studying the text, write the answers to each of the following questions:

1. What is the first step in administering an estate if the decedent dies testate? ____________

____

____

____

____

2. How is notice of a hearing given to all interested parties? ____________

____

____

____

____

3. What is the significance of the decree or judgment that is issued after the court hearing?

____

____

____

____

4. When are sureties required on a personal representative's bond? ____________

____

____

____

____

5. What is the usual amount of the bond? ______

____

____

____

____

6. On what grounds may a will be contested?

____

____

____

____

7. If a will is contested on the ground that the testator was not of sound mind, who has the burden of proof? ______________________________

____

____

____

____

8. After being appointed, what is one of the first duties of the personal representative of an estate?

____

____

____

____

9. What is the length of time that creditors have to make claims against a decedent's estate? _____

____

____

____

____

10. In general, when must a federal estate tax return be filed? ______________________________

____

____

____

____

11. What does the gross estate include? _________

____

____

____

____

12. What is the final report that is prepared to close an estate? ______________________________

____

____

____

____

6

UNDERSTANDING LEGAL CONCEPTS

Indicate whether each statement is true or false. Then, change the italicized word or phrase of each *false* statement to make it true.

Answers

_______________ **1.** If the decedent died *intestate,* the executor named in the will or some other interested person petitions the court for the allowance of the will and appointment as executor.

_______________ **2.** Notice of a hearing on the petition is given to *all interested parties* by service of process, mail, or newspaper publication.

_______________ **3.** Before being appointed, the executor or administrator must file a *bond* with the court.

_______________ **4.** The amount of the bond is usually *three times* the value of the personal property of the estate.

_______________ **5.** Sureties on the fiduciary's bond are *never* required.

_______________ **6.** A certificate of appointment of the personal representative in a *testate* estate is known as letters of administration.

_______________ **7.** After being appointed, one of the first duties of the personal representative is to file an *inventory* with the court.

_______________ **8.** A waiting period from nine months to *a year* elapses to give creditors time to present their claims.

_______________ **9.** The gross estate, for tax purposes, *does not* include jointly owned property.

_______________ **10.** When the *final account* is allowed by the court, the estate is settled.

CHECKING TERMINOLOGY

From the list of legal terms that follows, select the one that matches each definition.

a. bond
b. burden of proof
c. decree
d. estate tax
e. fiduciary
f. first and final account
g. gifts causa mortis
h. gifts made in contemplation of death
i. gift tax
j. gross estate
k. heir
l. heirs at law

Answers

____ **1.** A person who inherits property.

____ **2.** The decision of a court of law.

____ **3.** People who undertake to pay money or to do any other act in the event that their principal fails to meet an obligation.

____ **4.** A certificate of appointment as executor of a will.

____ **5.** A detailed list of articles of property in an estate, made by the executor or administrator thereof.

____ **6.** A promise by the personal representative to pay an amount of money to the probate judge if the representative's duties are not faithfully performed.

____ **7.** A person in a position of trust, such as an executor, administrator, guardian, or trustee.

____ **8.** People who would have inherited had a decedent died intestate.

____ **9.** A person offering a will for probate.

____ **10.** The decision of a court of equity.

m. inheritance tax
n. inter vivos
o. inventory
p. judgment
q. letters of administration
r. letters testamentary
s. marital deduction
t. proponent
u. sponge tax
v. sureties

____**11.** A certificate of appointment as administrator of an estate.
____**12.** Gifts made within three years of the date of death. They are subject to the federal estate tax (select two answers).
____**13.** Amounts inherited from the estate of one's spouse. They are not subject to the federal estate tax.
____**14.** All property that the decedent owned at death, including individually and jointly owned property, life insurance, living trusts, and gifts made in contemplation of death.
____**15.** Between the living.
____**16.** A tax imposed on the estate of a deceased person.
____**17.** An accounting, if it is the only one, presented to the court in final settlement of a decedent's estate.
____**18.** A tax imposed on a person who inherits from a decedent's estate.
____**19.** A tax that soaks up money for the state that the estate is being given credit for in any event.
____**20.** The duty of proving a fact.
____**21.** A federal tax that is imposed (with exceptions) on gifts totaling more than $1 million made during one's lifetime.

UNRAVELING LEGALESE

Use simple, non-legal language, with the help of the glossary, to rewrite this statute quote so that it is shorter and can be understood by a layperson without losing its meaning.

> A person having custody of a will, other than a register of probate, shall, within thirty days after notice of the death of the testator, deliver such will into the probate court having jurisdiction of the probate thereof, or to the executors named in the will, who shall themselves deliver it into such court within said time; and if a person neglects without reasonable cause so to deliver a will, after being duly cited for that purpose by such court, he [or she] may be committed to jail by warrant of the court until he [or she] delivers it as above provided, and shall be liable to a person who is aggrieved for the damage sustained by him [or her] by reason of such neglect.

USING LEGAL LANGUAGE

Read the following story and fill in the blank lines with legal terms taken from the list of terms at the beginning of this chapter.

Soon after Kevin died, Karen filed a petition for the probate of the will and for the allowance of her ______________________, which was her promise to pay an amount of money to the probate judge if her duties are not faithfully performed. She was not required to have ______________________—that is, people who would stand behind her in the event she failed to do her job. She then notified his next of kin and all of his ______________________—that is, the people who inherited from his estate. After a waiting period, a hearing was held, and the court issued its decision, called a(n) ______________________ or ______________________, allowing the will. The court then issued Karen a certificate of her appointment called ______________________, because this was a testate case, rather than ______________________, which would have been issued had Kevin died intestate. She could now be called a(n) ______________________—that is, a person who holds a position of trust. Karen's first job was to file a(n) ______________________ listing the assets of the estate. Her next task was to file a federal estate tax return listing the ______________________, which includes the value of all property Kevin owned at his death, both in his own name and jointly with others, as well as life insurance, ______________________ (between the living) trusts, and gifts made within three years of death, called ______________________, or ______________________. Anything left to Kevin's surviving spouse, which is known as the ______________________, was not taxable. Many states now have a(n) ______________________, which is a tax equal to the credit allowed for state death taxes on the federal estate tax return.

PUZZLING OVER WHAT YOU LEARNED

Caveat: Do **not** allow squares for spaces between words and punctuation (apostrophes, hyphens, etc.) when filling in crossword.

Across

6. Amounts inherited from the estate of one's spouse.
8. All property that the decedent owned at death, including individually and jointly owned property, life insurance, living trusts, and gifts made in contemplation of death.
11. Between the living.
12. A detailed list of articles of property in an estate.
13. A tax imposed on the estate of a deceased person.
14. A person who inherits property.
15. The decision of a court of equity.
17. A person in a position of trust.
18. The decision of a court of law.

Down

1. A tax that soaks up money for the state that the estate is being given credit for in any event.
2. People who would have inherited had a decedent died intestate.
3. An accounting, if it is the only one, presented to the court in final settlement of a decedent's estate.
4. The duty of proving a fact.
5. A tax imposed on a person who inherits from a decedent's estate.
7. A certificate of appointment as executor of a will.
9. A person offering a will for probate.
10. A federal tax imposed on gifts totaling more than $1 million made during one's lifetime.
16. A promise by the personal representative to pay an amount of money to the probate judge if the representative's duties are not faithfully performed.

6

CHAPTER 28
Trusts

ANTE INTERROGATORY

The one who creates a trust is the (A) beneficiary, (B) settlor, (C) trustee, (D) cestui que trust.

CHAPTER OUTLINE

Parties to a Trust
Kinds of Trusts
Testamentary Trust
Living Trust
Spendthrift Trust
Charitable Trust
Sprinkling Trust
Implied Trust
Precatory Trust
Pour-Over Trust
Marital Deduction Trust

KEY TERMS

A–B trust
beneficial title *(ben·e·FISH·el TY·tel)*
beneficiary *(ben·e·FISH·ee·air·ee)*
bypass trust *(BY·pass)*
cestui que trust *(SES·twee kay)*
charitable remainder annuity trust (CRAT) *(CHAR·i·ta·bel re·MANE·der a·NYOO·i·tee)*
charitable remainder trust *(CHAR·i·ta·bel re·MANE·der)*
charitable remainder unitrust (CRUT) *(CHAR·i·ta·bel re·MANE·der YOO·nee·trust)*
charitable trust *(CHAR·i·ta·bel)*
constructive trust *(kon·STRUK·tiv)*
conveyance in trust *(kon·VAY·enss)*
corpus *(KOR·pus)*
credit-shelter trust *(Kred·et-SHEL·ter)*
Crummey powers *(KRUM·ee)*
cy pres doctrine *(sy pray DOK·trin)*
declaration of trust *(dek·la·RAY·shun)*
discretionary trust *(dis·KRE·shun·air·ee)*
donor *(doh·NOR)*
equitable title *(EK·wit·a·bel TY·tel)*
exemption equivalent trust *(eg·ZEMP·shun)*
grantor *(gran·TOR)*
implied trust *(im·PLIDE)*
inter vivos trust *(IN·ter VY·vose)*
irrevocable living trust *(ir·REV·e·ke·bel)*
legal title *(LEE·gul TY·tel)*
living trust
marital deduction *(MAR·i·tal de·DUK·shun)*
marital deduction trust
pour-over trust *(pore-O·ver)*
precatory trust *(PREK·a·tore·ee)*
public trust *(PUB·lik)*
qualified terminable interest property (QTIP) trust *(KWAH·li·fide TERM·in·a·bel IN·trest PROP·er·tee)*
resulting trust *(re·ZULT·ing)*
revocable living trust *(REV·e·ke·bel)*
rule against perpetuities *(per·pe·TYOO·i·teez)*
settlor *(set·LOR)*

spendthrift *(SPEND·thrift)*
spendthrift trust
spray trust
sprinkling trust *(SPRINK·ling)*
testamentary trust *(test·e·MEN·ter·ee)*
Totten trust *(TOT·en)*
trust
trust deed
trustee *(trus·TEE)*
trust fund
trust indenture *(in·DEN·cher)*
trustor *(trus·TOR)*
trust principal *(PRIN·se·pel)*
trust property *(PROP·er·tee)*
trust res *(reyz)*

PARTIES TO A TRUST

A **trust** is a right of ownership to property held by one person for the benefit of another. When a trust is established, the **legal title** (full, absolute ownership) in a particular item of property is separated from the **equitable** or **beneficial title** (the right to beneficial enjoyment) in the same property. The person who establishes the trust is called the **settlor,** the **trustor,** the **grantor,** or the **donor.** The person who holds the legal title to the property for the other's benefit is called the **trustee.** The person who holds the equitable or beneficial title is known as the **beneficiary.** The beneficiary, also known as the **cestui que trust,** is the one for whom the trust is created and who receives the benefits from it. The property that is held in trust is called the **corpus,** the **trust res,** the **trust fund,** the **trust property,** or the **trust principal.**

A typical trust is one in which a husband gives property to a trustee either during his lifetime or by will when he dies, to be held in trust with instructions to pay the income from the property to his wife as long as she lives and on her death to divide what remains among his children.

KINDS OF TRUSTS

Many different kinds of trusts exist. The most common ones are described briefly in this chapter.

Testamentary Trust

A **testamentary trust** is a trust that is created by will. It comes into existence only on the death of the testator. The terms of the trust together with the names of the trustee and the beneficiaries are set out in the body of the will itself. Here is the beginning of a typical trust clause in a will:

> I direct that each share of my residuary estate payable to an individual under the age of 25 shall be held in trust for that individual under Article III. (Article III of the will contains the provisions of the trust.)

Living Trust

A **living trust,** also called an **inter vivos trust,** is created by the settlor while he or she is alive and is established by either a conveyance in trust or a declaration of trust. The instrument creating the trust is called a **trust deed** or a **trust indenture.** In a **conveyance**

in trust, the settlor conveys away the legal title to a trustee to hold for the benefit of either the settlor or another as beneficiary. In a **declaration of trust,** the settlor declares in writing that he or she is holding the legal title to the property as trustee for the benefit of some other person (beneficiary) to whom he or she now conveys the equitable (beneficial) title.

WORD WISE

Cestui Que Trust (Ses·twee kay trust) ("trust beneficiary")

Cestui is a French term meaning "to him" or "to her." Here are some other "cestui" phrases:

cestui que use = someone for whose use and benefit land, tenements, etc., are held by another. The *cestui que use* may receive profits and benefits of the estate, but the legal title and possession rest with the other.

cestui que vie = the person whose life determines the duration of the trust, gift, estate, or insurance contract. The *cestui que vie* is the person on whose life the insurance is written.

A living trust may be either irrevocable or revocable. If it is an **irrevocable living trust,** the settlor loses complete control over the trust corpus during his or her lifetime and cannot change the trust. The advantage of an irrevocable trust is that the income from the trust is not taxable to the settlor. The trust itself or the beneficiaries pay the taxes on the trust's income. Such a trust has a disadvantage, however, in that it may never be changed. The settlor can never get back that which he or she put in trust regardless of the circumstances.

A **revocable living trust** may be rescinded or changed by the settlor at any time during his or her lifetime. It has neither estate tax nor income tax benefits. Such a trust, however, can serve the purpose of relieving the cares of management of money or property as well as other purposes.

Spendthrift Trust

A **spendthrift** is one who spends money profusely and improvidently. A **spendthrift trust** is designed to provide a fund for the maintenance of a beneficiary and, simultaneously, to secure it against the beneficiary's improvidence or incapacity. In some states, all trusts are considered such. In other states, such as Massachusetts, to create a spendthrift trust, a clause must be placed in the trust instrument to the effect that the beneficiary cannot assign either the income or the principal of the trust and that neither the income nor the principal of the trust can be reached by the beneficiary's creditors. Still other states do not permit spendthrift trusts to be established.

Charitable Trust

A **charitable** or **public trust** is one established for charitable purposes such as the advancement of education; relief to the aged, ill, and poor; and promotion of religion. To be valid, the person to be benefited must be uncertain. A **charitable remainder trust** is a trust in which the donor, or a beneficiary, retains the income from the trust for life or other period, after which the trust corpus is given to a charity. Under a **charitable remainder annuity trust,** a fixed *amount* of income is given annually to a beneficiary, and the remainder is given to a charity. Under a **charitable remainder unitrust,** a fixed *percentage* of income (at least 5 percent of the trust corpus) is given annually to a beneficiary with the remainder going to a charity.

A charitable trust can be written to last indefinitely; it is not affected by the rule against perpetuities. The **rule against perpetuities** provides that every interest in property is void unless it must vest, if at all, not later than 21 years after some life in being, plus the period of gestation, at the time of the creation of the interest. For example, a trust established for "my grandchildren who shall reach the age of 21" would be void because other children may be born to the settlor and they would not be "lives in being" when the trust was created. Some states have rewritten the rule to provide that property interests must vest either no later than 21 years after some life in being at the time of the creation of the interest or within 90 years of such creation.

When the original purpose of a charitable trust can no longer be fulfilled, instead of causing the trust to end, the court may apply the **cy pres doctrine,** a doctrine meaning "as near as possible." Under this doctrine, the court allows the trust fund to be held for another purpose that meets as nearly as possible the intent of the settlor.

WEB WISE

These sites are good starting points for looking up information about trusts and other legal subjects:

- **http://www.yahoo.com/law**
- **http://www.catalaw.com**
- **http://www.law.cornell.edu**
- **http://www.lawcrawler.com**

Sprinkling Trust

A **sprinkling** or **spray trust** allows the trustee to decide how much will be given to each beneficiary at the trustee's discretion rather than allowing the settlor to make the decision. Such a trust is also called a **discretionary trust.** The advantage of this type of trust is that the trustee can determine the tax brackets of the beneficiaries and pay less tax by giving more money to those beneficiaries in the lowest tax brackets. It also has built-in spendthrift provisions. The chief objection is that it gives the trustee too much control over the distribution of the trust property.

Implied Trust

A trust that arises by implication of law from the conduct of the parties is known as an **implied trust.** Two examples of implied trusts are resulting trusts and constructive trusts.

A **resulting trust** arises when a transfer of property is made to one person but the purchase price for the property is paid by another person. In such a case, a trust results in favor of the person who furnished the consideration. This allows the person who actually paid for the property to obtain title to it (under the theory of a resulting trust) if he or she wishes to do so.

A **constructive trust** is imposed by law to avoid the unjust enrichment of one party at the expense of the other when the legal title to the property was obtained by fraud.

Totten Trusts and Crummey Powers

Two legal terms used in the law of trusts are derived from the names of cases. A **Totten trust** is a bank account in the name of the depositor as trustee for another person. While alive, the depositor can deposit and withdraw from the account. Upon the depositor's death, the account belongs to the named beneficiary. The name of the trust comes from a 1906 New York case, *In re Totten,* 71 N.E. 748.

Crummey powers give trust beneficiaries the right to withdraw each year the money that is contributed to the trust that year. This term comes from the case of *Crummey* v. *Commissioner,* 397 F.2d 82 (1968).

Precatory Trust

A **precatory trust** is an express trust that sometimes arises from the use of polite language by a testator in a will. For example, a testatrix wrote in her will: "I give and bequeath unto my husband . . . the use, income, and improvement of all the estate . . . for and during the term of his natural life, in the full confidence that upon my decease he will, as he has heretofore done, continue to give and afford my children [enumerating them] such protection, comfort and support as they or either of them may stand in need of." The court held this to be a trust for the benefit of the children.

Pour-Over Trust

A **pour-over trust** is a misnomer. It is actually a provision in a will leaving a bequest or devise to the trustee of an existing living trust. When the testator dies, the will pours the particular gift into the trust—thus the name "pour-over trust."

Marital Deduction Trust

A **marital deduction trust** is a trust that is arranged to make maximum use of the marital deduction that is found in the federal estate tax law. The **marital deduction** is the amount that passes from a decedent to a surviving spouse and is not taxable under the federal estate tax law.

One type of marital deduction trust, called a **credit-shelter trust,** an **A–B trust,** a **bypass trust,** or an **exemption equivalent trust,** reduces the taxation of the second spouse to die by limiting the amount in that person's estate to a sum that is not taxable. With this type of trust, the property of the first spouse to die passes to a two-part trust rather than to the surviving spouse. Trust A is an irrevocable trust that provides only income to the surviving spouse for life, with the principal passing to someone else (such as children) upon the surviving spouse's death, tax free. Trust B, for an amount that is tax exempt (see Chapter 27), is for the benefit of the surviving spouse. When the surviving spouse dies, that estate is not large enough to be taxable.

Another marital deduction trust, called a **qualified terminable interest property (QTIP) trust,** gives all trust income to a surviving spouse for life, payable at least annually, with the principal passing to someone else upon the spouse's death. This trust provides for the surviving spouse for life, yet leaves the principal untouched for someone else when the surviving spouse dies.

REVIEWING WHAT YOU LEARNED

After studying the text, write the answers to each of the following questions:

1. When a trust is created, how is title to the property separated? ______________________________

2. List four names that are used to describe a person who establishes a trust. ______________________________

3. List five names that are used to describe the property that is held in trust. ______________________________

4. How is a testamentary trust created? When does it come into existence? ______________________________

5. What is another name for a living trust? ______________________________

6. Describe what occurs when a conveyance of trust is created. ______________________________

7. Describe what occurs when a declaration of trust arises. ______________________________

8. What are the advantages and disadvantages of an irrevocable living trust? ______________________________

6

9. What is necessary for a charitable or public trust to be valid? ______

10. What is the advantage of a sprinkling or spray trust? ______

11. What is the difference between a resulting trust and a constructive trust? ______

12. Why is the term **pour-over trust** a misnomer?

UNDERSTANDING LEGAL CONCEPTS

Indicate whether each statement is true or false. Then, change the italicized word or phrase of each *false* statement to make it true.

Answers

______ 1. When a trust is established, the *legal title* in a particular item of property is separated from the equitable or beneficial title in the same property.

______ 2. A *testamentary* trust comes into existence only on the death of the testator.

______ 3. An *inter vivos* trust is a trust that is created by will.

______ 4. In a *declaration of* trust, the settlor conveys away the legal title to a trustee to hold for the benefit of either the settlor or the beneficiary.

______ 5. The advantage of a *revocable* living trust is that the income from the trust is not taxable to the settlor.

______ 6. A *spendthrift* trust is designed to provide a fund for the maintenance of a beneficiary and, simultaneously, to secure it against his or her improvidence or incapacity.

______ 7. For a *charitable* trust to be valid, the person to be benefited must be uncertain.

______ 8. The chief objection to a sprinkling or spray trust is that it gives the *trustee* too much control over the distribution of the trust property.

______ 9. A *resulting* trust is imposed by law to avoid the unjust enrichment of one party at the expense of the other when the legal title to the property was obtained by fraud.

______ 10. A precatory trust is an *implied* trust that sometimes arises from the use of polite language by a testator in a will.

CHECKING TERMINOLOGY (PART A)

From the list of legal terms that follows, select the one that matches each definition.

a. A–B trust
b. beneficial title
c. beneficiary
d. bypass trust
e. cestui que trust
f. charitable remainder annuity trust (CRAT)
g. charitable remainder trust
h. charitable remainder unitrust (CRUT)
i. charitable trust
j. constructive trust
k. conveyance in trust
l. credit-shelter trust
m. Crummey powers
n. cy pres doctrine
o. declaration of trust
p. equitable title
q. exemption equivalent trust
r. implied trust
s. inter vivos trust
t. irrevocable living trust
u. legal title
v. living trust
w. marital deduction
x. marital deduction trust
y. pour-over trust
z. precatory trust
aa. public trust

Answers

____ **1.** A trust that is created by the settlor when he or she is alive (select two answers).

____ **2.** A trust established for charitable purposes (select two answers).

____ **3.** Full, absolute ownership.

____ **4.** An express trust that arises from the use of polite, noncommanding language by a testator in a will.

____ **5.** The amount that passes from a decedent to a surviving spouse and is not taxable under the federal estate tax law.

____ **6.** A trust in which a fixed amount of income is given annually to a beneficiary and the remainder is given to a charity.

____ **7.** A written declaration by a settlor that he or she is holding legal title to property as trustee for the benefit of another person.

____ **8.** The right to beneficial enjoyment (select two answers).

____ **9.** Authority that gives trust beneficiaries the right to withdraw each year the money that is contributed to the trust that year.

____ **10.** An implied trust that arises in favor of one who is defrauded when title to property is obtained by fraud.

____ **11.** As nearly as possible.

____ **12.** A type of marital deduction trust that reduces the taxation of the second spouse to die by limiting the amount in that person's estate to a sum that is not taxable (select four answers).

____ **13.** A trust that is arranged to make maximum use of the marital deduction that is found in the federal estate tax law.

____ **14.** A trust in which a fixed percentage of income (at least 5 percent of the trust corpus) is given annually to a beneficiary and the remainder is given to a charity.

____ **15.** A provision in a will leaving a bequest or devise to the trustee of an existing living trust.

____ **16.** A trust that may not be rescinded or changed by the settlor at any time during his or her lifetime.

____ **17.** A trust that arises by implication of law from the conduct of the parties.

____ **18.** A trust in which the donor, or a beneficiary, retains the income from the trust for life or other period, after which the trust corpus is given to a charity.

____ **19.** A transfer of legal title to property by the settlor to a trustee to hold for the benefit of a beneficiary.

____ **20.** One for whose benefit a trust is created (select two answers).

CHECKING TERMINOLOGY (PART B)

From the list of legal terms that follows, select the one that matches each definition.

- **a.** corpus
- **b.** discretionary trust
- **c.** donor
- **d.** grantor
- **e.** qualified terminable interest property (QTIP) trust
- **f.** resulting trust
- **g.** revocable living trust
- **h.** rule against perpetuities
- **i.** settlor
- **j.** spendthrift
- **k.** spendthrift trust
- **l.** spray trust
- **m.** sprinkling trust
- **n.** testamentary trust
- **o.** Totten trust
- **p.** trust
- **q.** trust deed
- **r.** trustee
- **s.** trust fund
- **t.** trust indenture
- **u.** trustor
- **v.** trust principal
- **w.** trust property
- **x.** trust res

Answers

____ **1.** A trust that may be rescinded or changed by the settlor at any time during his or her lifetime.

____ **2.** A person who establishes a trust (select four answers).

____ **3.** A person who holds legal title to property in trust for another.

____ **4.** A trust designed to provide a fund for the maintenance of a beneficiary and, at the same time, to secure it against the beneficiary's improvidence or incapacity.

____ **5.** The principle that no interest in property is good unless it must vest, if at all, not later than 21 years after some life in being, plus the period of gestation, at the creation of the interest.

____ **6.** A bank account in the name of the depositor as trustee for another person.

____ **7.** A marital deduction trust that gives all trust income to a surviving spouse for life, payable at least annually, with the principal passing to someone else upon the spouse's death.

____ **8.** The body, principal sum, or capital of a trust (select five answers).

____ **9.** A trust that is created by will and that comes into existence only on the death of the testator.

____ **10.** An instrument that creates a living trust (select two answers).

____ **11.** An implied trust that arises in favor of the payor when property is transferred to one person after being paid for by another person.

____ **12.** A right of ownership to property held by one person for the benefit of another.

____ **13.** A trust that allows the trustee to decide how much will be given to each beneficiary at the trustee's discretion (select three answers).

____ **14.** One who spends money profusely and improvidently.

SHARPENING YOUR LATIN SKILLS

In the space provided, write the definition of each of the following legal terms, referring to the glossary when necessary.

ad litem ______________________________

corpus ______________________________

cum testamento annexo ______________________________

de bonis non ______________________________

pendent elite ______________________________

per capita ______________________________

per stirpes ______________________________

UNRAVELING LEGALESE

Give the legal names of the following trust clause and explain its advantages and disadvantages.

> Trustee shall pay to or apply for the benefit of my children, herein referred to as income beneficiaries, at least annually, and in such proportions as trustee in its absolute discretion may from time to time determine, all of the net income of the trust estate.

USING LEGAL LANGUAGE

Read the following story and fill in the blank lines with legal terms taken from the list of terms at the beginning of this chapter.

Leon decided to put $10,000 in ______________ for the benefit of his daughter, Lois. He created a(n) ______________, which is also known as a(n) ______________, while he was alive by the use of an instrument called either a(n) ______________ or a(n) ______________. It was not called a(n) ______________, because it was not created by will. Because Leon transferred legal title to the money to another, the transaction was known as a(n) ______________ rather than a(n) ______________, which it would have been called had he retained legal title to the money. Leon could rescind this trust whenever he wished; therefore, it was known as a(n) ______________ rather than a(n) ______________. Because he established it, Leon could be referred to as the ______________, the ______________, the ______________, or the ______________. Lois was known as the ______________. Leon's wife, Laura, was given legal title to the money; therefore, she was called the ______________. The money itself could be termed the ______________, the ______________, the ______________, the ______________, or the ______________. Called a(n) ______________, the instrument was designed to provide a fund for Lois and, at the same time, to protect against her improvidence because she was a(n) ______________—that is, one who spends money profusely. It was not a(n) ______________ or ______________, because it was not for charitable purposes; thus, the rule known as the ______________ was applicable. Leon did not give Laura discretion in the trust to decide how much would be given to different beneficiaries. For that reason, this was not a(n) ______________ or a(n) ______________. Because the trust did not arise by implication of law from the conduct of the parties, it was not either one of the ______________—that is, a(n) ______________ or a(n) ______________. In addition, because it did not arise from the use of polite language in a will, it was not a(n) ______________.

PUZZLING OVER WHAT YOU LEARNED

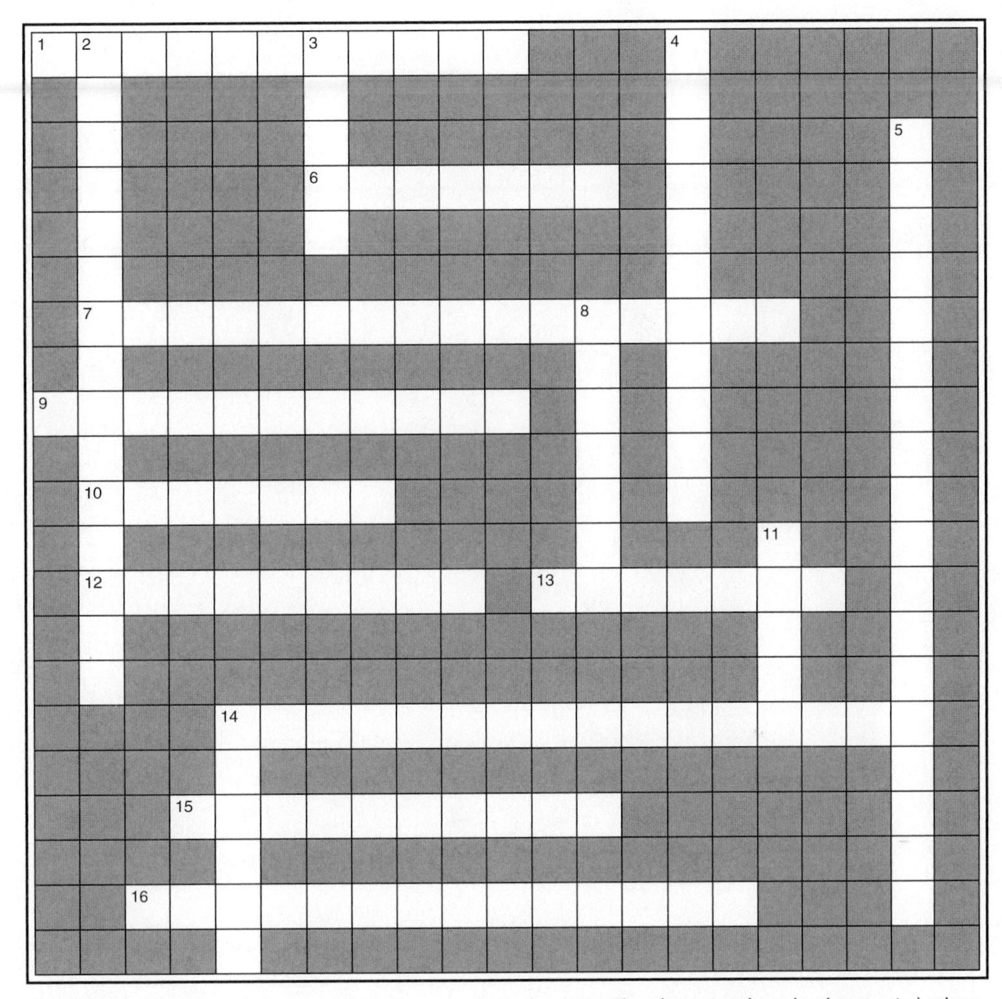

Caveat: Allow squares for spaces between words and punctuation (apostrophes, hyphens, etc.) when filling in crossword.

Across

1. Full, absolute ownership.
6. Person who establishes a trust.
7. The right to beneficial enjoyment.
9. One for whose benefit a trust is created.
10. Person who holds legal title to property in trust for another.
12. The body, principal sum, or capital of a trust.
13. A person who establishes a trust.
14. One for whose benefit a trust is created.
15. The body, principal sum, or capital of a trust.
16. The body, principal sum, or capital of a trust.

Down

2. The right to beneficial enjoyment.
3. Right of ownership to property held by one person for another.
4. A trust that allows the trustee to decide how much to give each beneficiary.
5. A trust that is created by will.
8. A person who establishes a trust.
11. A person who establishes a trust.
14. The body, principal sum, or capital of a trust.

PART SEVEN

TERMS USED IN LAW OF REAL PROPERTY

7

Some law firms specialize in the field of real property law, other firms work in the field as part of a general practice, and still others work in the field only occasionally or not at all. Knowledge of real property law, in any event, is important to all of us because we all must reside somewhere, whether we own the property, rent it, or live there with someone else who does. Chapter 29 explains the various estates in real property that are available to property owners. Co-ownership of real property is discussed in Chapter 30, and the methods of acquiring title to real property are outlined in Chapter 31. The requirements of a valid deed and the different types of deeds are examined in Chapter 32, followed by a discussion of mortgages in Chapter 33. Title search procedures are explained in Chapter 34. The law relating to airspace and water rights is covered in Chapter 35, and easements, restrictions, and zoning regulations are discussed in Chapter 36. Landlord and tenant law is the focal point of Chapter 37.

7

CHAPTER 29

Estates in Real Property

ANTE INTERROGATORY

The largest estate that one can own in land is a (A) determinable fee, (B) fee tail, (C) fee simple, (D) life estate.

CHAPTER OUTLINE

Freehold Estates
- *Fee Simple Estate*
- *Fee Tail Estate*
- *Determinable Fee Estate*
- *Life Estate*

Leasehold Estates

KEY TERMS

apt words
condition subsequent *(kon·DISH·en SUB·se·kwent)*
defeasible estate *(de·FEEZ·i·bel es·TATE)*
determinable fee *(de·TER·min·e·bel)*
determine *(de·TER·min)*
esquire *(ES·kwyr)*
estate *(es·TATE)*
estate pur autre vie *(per OH·tra vee)*
estate tail male
estate tail special *(SPESH·el)*
fee
fee simple absolute *(SIM·pel ab·so·LOOT)*
fee simple determinable *(de·TER·min·e·bel)*
fee simple estate *(es·TATE)*
fee tail estate *(es·TATE)*
freehold estate *(FREE·hold es·TATE)*
leasehold estate *(LEESS·hold es·TATE)*
life estate *(es·TATE)*
life tenant *(TEN·ent)*
possibility of reverter *(pos·i·BIL·i·tee ov re·VERT·er)*
real property *(PROP·er·tee)*
remainder interest *(re·MANE·der IN·trest)*
reversionary interest *(re·VER·zhen·e·ree IN·trest)*
revert *(re·VERT)*
waste

Ownership of interests in **real property**—that is, the ground and anything permanently attached to it—in the United States follows the estate concept that developed under the English feudal system. **Estates** (ownership interests) in real property are divided into two groups: freehold estates and leasehold estates.

FREEHOLD ESTATES

A **freehold estate** is an estate in which the holder owns the land for life or forever. At common law, only freehold estates were considered to be real property. There are four types of freehold estates:

1. Fee simple
2. Fee tail
3. Determinable fee
4. Life

Fee Simple Estate

The **fee simple estate** (sometimes called **fee** or **fee simple absolute**) is the largest estate that one can own in land, giving the holder absolute ownership that descends to the owner's heirs on his or her death. In addition, it can be sold or granted out by the owner at will during the owner's lifetime. In early conveyances, a fee simple estate was created by a deed containing the words "To (a person) and his heirs." If the words "and his heirs," called the **apt words** (the suitable words), were omitted from the deed, the grantee received only a life estate. Today, by statute, the words "and his heirs" are no longer required to be in a deed to create a fee simple estate.

Fee Tail Estate

A **fee tail estate** restricts ownership of real property to a particular family bloodline. It was created by statute in England in 1285 (when land was the basis for the family fortune) as a way to keep real property in the family forever. Under the statute, the property

Origin of Real Property Law

The Feudal System

Under the feudal system in England, which began in the year 1066 when William the Conqueror took over England after the Battle of Hastings, the king was the personal owner of all land in the kingdom. In exchange for services, the king granted land in large tracts to his tenants-in-chief (barons) who, in turn, granted land to lesser lords. These lesser lords granted land to still lesser noblemen. In exchange for use of the land, continuous services were required. Thus was created a pyramid with the king at the top and the people who worked the land at the bottom. Rights in the land moved down the pyramid (each step down being a lesser right) while a constant flow of services moved up.

In its early stage, feudalism was a military system designed to protect the king. Since the king was short of money, he used land to purchase military services. Thus, the highest type of ownership of land was a military tenure called knight's service. The vassal swore allegiance to the king and also agreed to give him the services of a number of knights and squires (depending on the amount of land received) for 40 days in the year. The services were perpetual. The land reverted to the king if the knights were not productive.

Today in the United States, the term **esquire** is used as a title (abbreviated Esq.) following the name of an attorney, in place of the prefixes Mr., Mrs., Miss, or Ms. In English nobility, esquire (abbreviated squire) was a social rank higher than a gentleman but lower than a knight.

Oath of Fealty

In return for land, each tenant down the line swore *fealty* (allegiance) and agreed to do *homage* (a particular service) to his landlord in a ceremony called *feoffment.* The landlord was called the *feoffor* and the tenant was called the *feoffee.* The feoffee made the following oath of fealty:

> I become your man from this day forward of life and limb and of earthly worship, and unto you shall be true and faithful, and bear to you faith for the tenements that I claim to hold of you, saving the faith that I owe unto our sovereign lord the king.

Tenant's Service

The tenant's service to his lord varied greatly. *Cornage* required the tenant to blow a horn to warn the country on the approach of the king's enemies. *Villeinage* required the tenant to plow the lord's land and make his hedges. A *tenant in sergeanty* was a servant such as a chamberlain, an armoror, a cook, or an esquire. Churches held land in *frank-almoign* (free alms) in exchange for services such as the saying of masses for the donor. *Socage* tenure required the oath of faithfulness but only nominal services for the land such as the giving of one red rose at midsummer, or the delivery of one peppercorn annually. This was often done when a father parceled out land to his children. The word *nominal* means "in name only; not real or substantial."

Life Estate

In the early feudal period, the greatest estate that one could own was a life estate, and that could not be transferred by a tenant without his lord's assent. When the tenant died, the lord was under no obligation to accept the tenant's heir as successor; however, he customarily did so in exchange for a payment called *relief.* This was the forerunner of our present estate tax. When a tenant died leaving an infant heir, the child became the ward of the lord, who kept the child's income and profit from the land, during minority, in exchange for support, education, and protection. The lord also had the power to choose the minor's spouse. Wardships and marriages were bought and sold by the lord, and upon his death, they passed by will or intestate succession to the lord's heirs.

Fee Simple Estate

As time went on, a lord could accept, if he wished, the tenant's heir in advance by granting land "to him and his heir." The heir at that time would usually be the tenant's eldest son. If the grant was "to him and his heirs," it was a grant to the tenant, then the tenant's heir, then the heir's heir, and on down the line. These words eventually became the words which created a *fee simple estate* (absolute ownership of property). When a tenant died without heirs, his property *escheated,* that is, reverted to the lord. None of this law applied to women who, in those days, had few legal rights.

Gradually, statutes were passed in England allowing tenants to transfer their property rights to others without permission of the lord and also to pass their interest in the land to their heirs. The feudal system was finally abolished in England in 1660 by King Charles II.

could not be alienated. If the bloodline became extinct, the property reverted to the original owner's line.

At common law, an estate tail was created by the apt words in a deed "To (the grantee) and the heirs of his body" and was often given by a parent to a child as part of a marriage settlement. The word "tail" comes from the French word *tailler,* meaning "to carve." The idea was that the grantor was carving an estate to his liking. Variations included the **estate tail special,** in which land was given to both the husband and wife and the heirs of their two bodies, and the **estate tail male,** which restricted ownership to men in the family line.

As time went on in England, methods were devised that allowed property in an estate tail to be alienated from the family line. Today, the estate tail has been either abolished or made ineffective by state statutes.

Determinable Fee Estate

A **determinable fee,** also called a **fee simple determinable,** is an estate in real property that is capable of coming to an end automatically because of the happening of some event. If the event occurs, the estate **determines**—that is, comes to an end. If the event never occurs, the estate is absolute. To illustrate, if a person conveys real property to a particular church "so long as the premises shall be used for church purposes," the church has a fee simple determinable. The property will **revert** (go back) to the grantor or his or her heirs if it is not used for church purposes. The grantor has a **possibility of reverter** interest in the property because it is always possible that the event will occur.

A similar type of **defeasible estate**—that is, one that can be lost or defeated—is called a *fee simple subject to a* **condition subsequent** (a qualification that comes later). This exists when a condition is placed in a deed, making it possible to have the ownership terminated at a future time. For example, if a deed contains the language "subject to the condition that the premises never be used for the sale of alcohol" and the property is later used for the sale of alcohol, the former owner (or his or her heirs) could bring legal action to take back the property. The estate does not automatically come to an end, as in the case of a determinable fee; rather, legal action must be taken to end it.

WORD WISE

The "Vert" in Revert

The Latin root "vert" and its variation "vers" mean "turn." For example, the term "revert" [*re* (back) + *vert* (turn)] means "to go back" or "to return."

"Vert" may mean "turn" in the physical or literal sense, as in the word "invert" [*in* + *vert* = to turn in], which could include turning inside out or upside down or reversing the order.

"Vert" may also be used in a nonphysical sense, as in the word "advertise," where consumer attention is hopefully "turned" toward a product or service.

Consider how the root functions in these words: adversary, vertigo, perverse, diversion.

7

Life Estate

A **life estate** is an estate limited in duration to either the life of the owner or the life of another person. It may be created by deed, will, or operation of law.

If A either deeds or wills real property "to B for life and on B's death to C," B will own an estate for life, and C will own **a remainder interest** (an interest that takes effect after another estate is ended) in fee simple. Life tenants may convey their interest to others; however, they can only convey that which they own, nothing greater. Thus, if B conveys his or her interest (a life estate) to D, D will own a life estate for the duration of B's life, after which the property will belong to C, the holder of the fee. It is known as an **estate pur autre vie** when one holds property for the duration of the life of another person.

When a person grants a life estate, either by will or by deed, to another and retains the fee, he or she is said to have a **reversionary interest** (a right to the future enjoyment of property that one originally owned). On the death of the life tenant, the estate reverts to the owner or the owner's heirs.

Legal life estates are created by the operation of some law. For example, the rights of dower and curtesy and the right of a surviving spouse to waive the will of a deceased spouse sometimes create life estates, depending on state statutes.

Owners of life estates, known as **life tenants,** own legal title to the property during their lifetime. They must pay the taxes but are entitled to possession of the property and to any income that comes from it. Life tenants are responsible to the owners of the fee for the commission of **waste.** This is the destruction, alteration, or deterioration of the premises, other than from natural causes or from normal usage.

Figure 29-1 Life tenants are responsible to the owners of the fee for the commission of waste.

LEASEHOLD ESTATES

A **leasehold estate** is an estate that is less than a freehold estate. At common law, and in most states today, leasehold estates are treated as personal property rather than real property. There are four types of leasehold estates:

1. *Tenancy for years*—an estate for a definite or fixed period of time.
2. *Periodic tenancy*—an estate that continues for successive periods until one of the parties terminates it by giving notice to the other party.
3. *Tenancy at will*—an estate for an indefinite period of time.
4. *Tenancy at sufferance*—an estate held wrongfully, held over after termination of a rightful tenancy, consisting of illegal possession only.

Leasehold estates are discussed in detail in Chapter 37.

REVIEWING WHAT YOU LEARNED

After studying the text, write the answers to each of the following questions:

1. Estates in real property are divided into what two groups?
2. List four freehold estates.
3. What will happen to an estate owned solely by an individual in fee simple when the owner dies? When may the owner sell or grant out the property?
4. What was the original purpose of the estate in fee tail? What was an estate tail male?
5. Give an example of a conveyance that is a determinable fee.
6. In what three ways may a life estate be created?
7. What is the difference between a remainder interest and a reversionary interest?
8. If A conveys her interest in real property to B for B's life, and upon B's death to C, and B thereafter conveys her interest to D, who will own the property when B dies?
9. Give an example of a law that will create a life estate.
10. What is the difference between a freehold estate and a leasehold estate?
11. List four leasehold estates.

UNDERSTANDING LEGAL CONCEPTS

Indicate whether each statement is true or false. Then, change the italicized word or phrase of each *false* statement to make it true.

Answers

_______________ **1.** Ownership of interests in land in the United States follows the estate concept that developed under the *English feudal system.*

_______________ **2.** A freehold estate is an estate in which the holder owns the land *only for life.*

_______________ **3.** A fee simple estate *cannot* be sold during the owner's lifetime.

_______________ **4.** Today, by statute, the words "and his heirs" are *no longer required* to be in a deed to create a fee simple estate.

_______________ **5.** Today, the *estate tail* has been either abolished or made ineffective by state statutes.

_______________ **6.** A determinable fee is an estate in real property that *never comes to an end.*

_______________ **7.** Legal action *must be* taken to end an estate in fee simple subject to a condition subsequent if the condition occurs.

_______________ **8.** A life estate may *not be* created by will.

_______________ **9.** When a person grants a life estate to another and retains the fee, he or she is said to have a *remainder* interest.

_______________ **10.** Life tenants are responsible to the owners of the fee for the commission of *waste.*

7

CHECKING TERMINOLOGY

From the list of legal terms that follows, select the one that matches each definition.

a. apt words
b. condition subsequent
c. defeasible estate
d. determinable fee
e. determine
f. esquite
g. estate
h. estate pur autre vie
i. estate tail male
j. estate tail special
k. fee
l. fee simple absolute
m. fee simple determinable
n. fee simple estate

Answers

____ **1.** Ownership interest.

____ **2.** The largest estate that one can own in land, giving the holder the absolute ownership and power of disposition during life and descending to the owner's heirs at death (select three answers).

____ **3.** A freehold estate that restricts ownership of real property to a particular family blood line.

____ **4.** A freehold estate restricting ownership to men in the family line.

____ **5.** Come to an end.

____ **6.** An estate that can be lost or defeated.

____ **7.** An estate limited in duration to either the life of the owner or the life of another person.

____ **8.** A right to the future enjoyment of property that one originally owned.

____ **9.** Destruction, alteration, or deterioration of a premises other than from natural causes or from normal use.

____ **10.** An estate in which the holder owns the land for life or forever.

____ **11.** Suitable words.

o. fee tail estate
p. freehold estate
q. leasehold estate
r. life estate
s. life tenant
t. possibility of reverter
u. real property
v. remainder interest
w. reversionary interest
x. revert
y. waste

____**12.** A freehold estate restricting ownership to a husband and wife and the heirs of their two bodies.

____**13.** An estate in real property that is capable of coming to an end automatically because of the happening of some event (select two answers).

____**14.** Go back.

____**15.** A qualification that comes later.

____**16.** An interest that takes effect after another estate is ended.

____**17.** The owner of a life estate.

____**18.** An estate that is less than a freehold estate.

____**19.** An interest in property due to the possibility that an event will occur that causes the property to revert to the grantor.

____**20.** The ground and anything permanently attached to it.

____**21.** An estate that a person holds for the duration of the life of another person.

____**22.** A title following the name of an attorney in place of the prefixes Mr., Mrs., Miss, or Ms.

UNRAVELING LEGALESE

Use simple, non-legal language, with the help of the glossary, to rewrite this case quote so that it is shorter and can be understood by a layperson without losing its meaning.

> The thirteenth paragraph of the will reads as follows: "All the rest and residue of my estate of whatever nature and wherever situated I give, devise and bequeath to my brother, Luman O. Pendell, with the right to use the property during his lifetime, and at his death to be divided equally among my nieces and nephews." The Probate Court instructed the executor that Luman is entitled "to use the principal and income of said property. We hold that the right to "use" the property in the will before us is not a right to consume it. We think that the "use" of the property given to Luman was the right to the income of the property during his life, and not a right to alienate or consume it and thus to deprive the nieces and nephews of their expected interest in it.

USING LEGAL LANGUAGE

Read the following story and fill in the blank lines with legal terms taken from the list of terms at the beginning of this chapter.

Harvey owned a(n) __________________________ in real property, which was limited to the duration of his life. It is not a(n) __________________________—that is, an estate that a person holds for the duration of the life of another. He was known as a(n) __________________________ and was responsible to others for the commission of __________________________, which is the destruction or deterioration of the premises. On Harvey's death, the __________________________—that is, the ownership interest—went to Harriet, a new owner who had a(n) __________________________, which took effect after Harvey's estate ended. It was not a(n) __________________________, because title did not __________________________—that is, go back—to an earlier owner. Similarly, it was not a(n) __________________________ designed to restrict ownership of real property to a particular family blood line, with its variations of __________________________ and __________________________. The deed conveying title to Harriet contained the __________________________—that is, the suitable words—to give her the largest estate that one can own in land. This estate has various names, including __________________________, __________________________ and just plain __________________________. The estate was not a(n) __________________________—that is, an estate in real property that is capable of coming to an end—nor was it __________________________, meaning one that can be lost or defeated. It was not a fee simple subject to a(n) __________________________, because no conditions were in the deed. In addition, it was not a(n) __________________________, because it was not less than a(n) __________________________, which is an estate in which the holder owns the land for life or forever.

7

PUZZLING OVER WHAT YOU LEARNED

Caveat: Allow squares for spaces between words and punctuation (apostrophes, hyphens, etc.) when filling in crossword.

Across

4. The ground and anything permanently attached to it.
6. The largest estate that one can own in land.
7. Destruction, alteration, or deterioration of a premises.
8. Estate limited in duration to the life of the owner or another person.
10. Comes to an end.
11. Go back.
12. Suitable words.
13. The largest estate that one can own in land.
14. A freehold estate restricting ownership to a husband, wife, and bodily heirs.

Down

1. An estate in which the holder owns land for life or forever.
2. The largest estate that one can own in land.
3. Owners of a life estate.
5. A freehold estate restricting ownership to men in the family line.
9. A freehold estate that restricts ownership of real property to a family bloodline.

CHAPTER 30

Multiple Ownership of Real Property

7

ANTE INTERROGATORY

The form of co-ownership of real property in which a deceased co-owner's share passes to his or her heirs is (A) tenancy in common, (B) joint tenancy, (C) tenancy by the entirety, (D) tenancy in partnership.

CHAPTER OUTLINE

Co-Ownership of Real Property
- *Tenants in Common*
- *Joint Tenants*
- *Community Property*
- *Tenants by the Entirety*
- *Tenants in Partnership*

Multi-Ownership of Real Property
- *Condominiums*
- *Cooperatives*
- *Timesharing*

KEY TERMS

common areas *(KOM·on AIR·ee·uz)*
community property *(kom·YOON·i·tee PROP·er·tee)*
concurrent ownership *(kon·KER·ent OH·ner·ship)*
condominium *(kon·de·MIN·ee·um)*
condominium association *(kon·de·MIN·ee·um a·so·see·AY·shun)*
cooperative apartment *(koh·OP·er·a·tive a·PART·ment)*
co-ownership *(koh-OH·ner·ship)*
co-tenants *(koh-TEN·entz)*
creditors *(KRED·et·ers)*
interval ownership *(IN·ter·vel OH·ner·ship)*
joint tenancy *(TEN·en·see)*
joint tenancy with the right of survivorship *(ser·VIVE·or·ship)*
joint tenants *(TEN·entz)*
levy on execution *(LEV·ee on ek·se·KYOO·shen)*
master deed *(MAS·ter deed)*
moiety *(MOY·e·tee)*
partition *(par·TI·shun)*
proprietary lease *(pro·PRY·e·ter·ee)*
several *(SEV·er·el)*
tenancy by the entirety *(TEN·en·see by the en·TY·re·tee)*
tenancy in partnership *(TEN·en·see in PART·ner·ship)*
tenants in common *(TEN·entz in KOM·on)*
timesharing
unit deed *(YOON·it)*
units *(YOON·its)*
unity of interest *(YOON·i·tee ov IN·trest)*
unity of possession *(YOON·i·tee ov po·SESH·en)*
unity of time *(YOON·i·tee)*
unity of title *(YOON·i·tee ov TY·tel)*

CO-OWNERSHIP OF REAL PROPERTY

When real property is owned separately by one person, it is referred to as being owned **severally.** In contract, when real property is owned by more than one person, it is called **concurrent ownership** or **co-ownership,** and the owners are known as **co-tenants.** It is said that co-owners of property own by moieties. **Moiety** means a part, portion, or fraction. The most common co-tenant relationships are tenants in common, joint tenants, tenants by the entirety, and tenants in partnership.

Tenants in Common

When two or more persons own real property as **tenants in common,** each person owns an undivided share, and on one owner's death, that person's share passes to his or her heirs or devisees. Tenants in common have **unity of possession,** which means that each owner is entitled to possession of the entire premises. This tenancy may be created by deed or by will, but more commonly it comes about by operation of law, such as when a person dies intestate, leaving real property to two or more heirs. Such heirs will take the property as tenants in common.

Any of the tenants in common may sell or grant out their interests to others without permission of the other co-tenants, and any new owners become tenants in common with the remaining owners. One tenant's interest is not necessarily the same as another tenant's interest. For example, one person might own a one-half interest with two others who each own a one-quarter interest, all as tenants in common.

Tenants in common may separate their interests in the property by petitioning the court for a partition of the premises. When a **partition** occurs, the court either divides the property into separate parcels, so that each co-tenant will own a particular part outright, or orders the property sold and divides the proceeds of the sale among the co-tenants. **Creditors** (people who are owed money) may reach the interest of a tenant in common and have the interest sold or hold it with the remaining tenants in common.

Joint Tenants

When two or more persons own real property as joint tenants, the estate created is a single estate with multiple ownership. It is known as **joint tenancy** or **joint tenancy with the right of survivorship. Joint tenants** are two or more persons holding one and the same interest, accruing by one and the same conveyance, commencing at one and the same time, and held by one and the same undivided possession. Each tenant owns the entire estate, subject to the equal rights of the other joint tenants. All joint tenants' interests are equal (**unity of interest**), and all have the right to possession of the entire estate (**unity of possession**). All owners must take title at the same time (**unity of time**), and each must receive title from the same instrument or conveyance, such as a will or a deed (**unity of title**). On the death of one joint tenant, the entire ownership remains in the other joint tenants and does not pass to the heirs or devisees of the decedent.

A joint tenant may grant out his or her interest to a new owner without permission of the other joint tenants, but the new owner becomes a tenant in common with the remaining joint tenants. Similarly, a joint tenant may petition the court for a partition of the estate, which would end the joint tenancy. Creditors may levy on the interests of a joint tenant on execution and take over the joint tenant's interest as a tenant in common with the remaining joint tenants. To **levy on execution** means to collect a sum of money by putting into effect the judgment of a court.

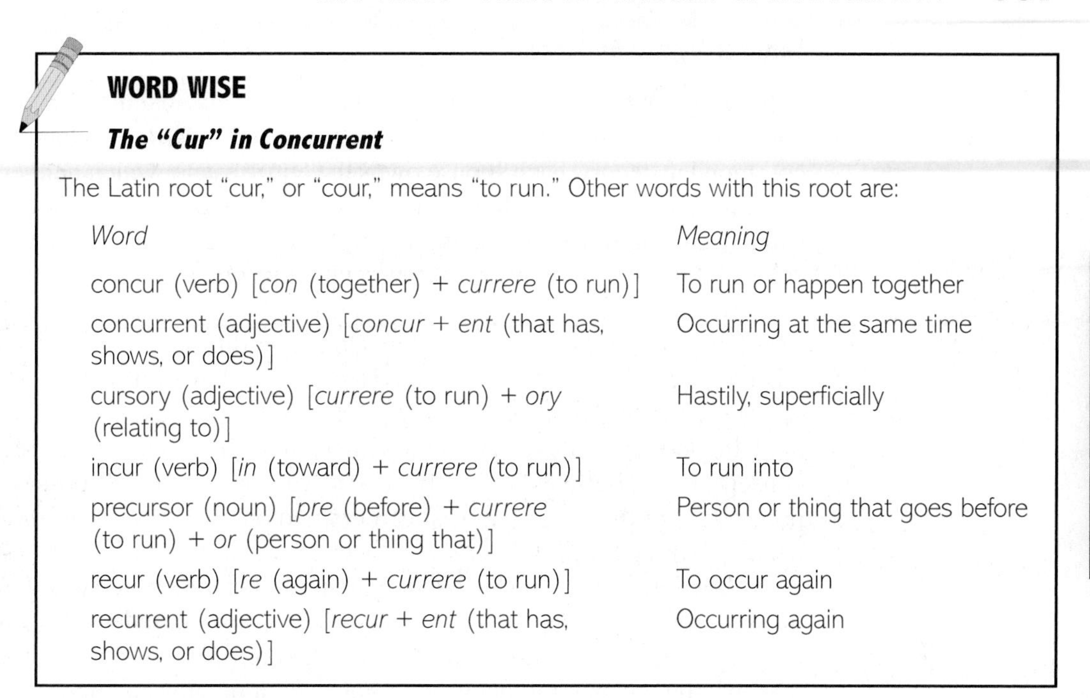

WORD WISE

The "Cur" in Concurrent

The Latin root "cur," or "cour," means "to run." Other words with this root are:

Word	*Meaning*
concur (verb) [*con* (together) + *currere* (to run)]	To run or happen together
concurrent (adjective) [*concur* + *ent* (that has, shows, or does)]	Occurring at the same time
cursory (adjective) [*currere* (to run) + *ory* (relating to)]	Hastily, superficially
incur (verb) [*in* (toward) + *currere* (to run)]	To run into
precursor (noun) [*pre* (before) + *currere* (to run) + *or* (person or thing that)]	Person or thing that goes before
recur (verb) [*re* (again) + *currere* (to run)]	To occur again
recurrent (adjective) [*recur* + *ent* (that has, shows, or does)]	Occurring again

Community Property

A system of ownership of property by husbands and wives that originated in Spain, called community property, is followed in the states indicated on the map in Figure 30-1. **Community property** is property (other than a gift or inheritance) acquired by a husband or wife during marriage that belongs to both spouses equally. Under this system, property acquired by the efforts of either spouse during marriage belongs to both spouses equally—that is, each spouse owns an undivided one-half interest in the whole premises.

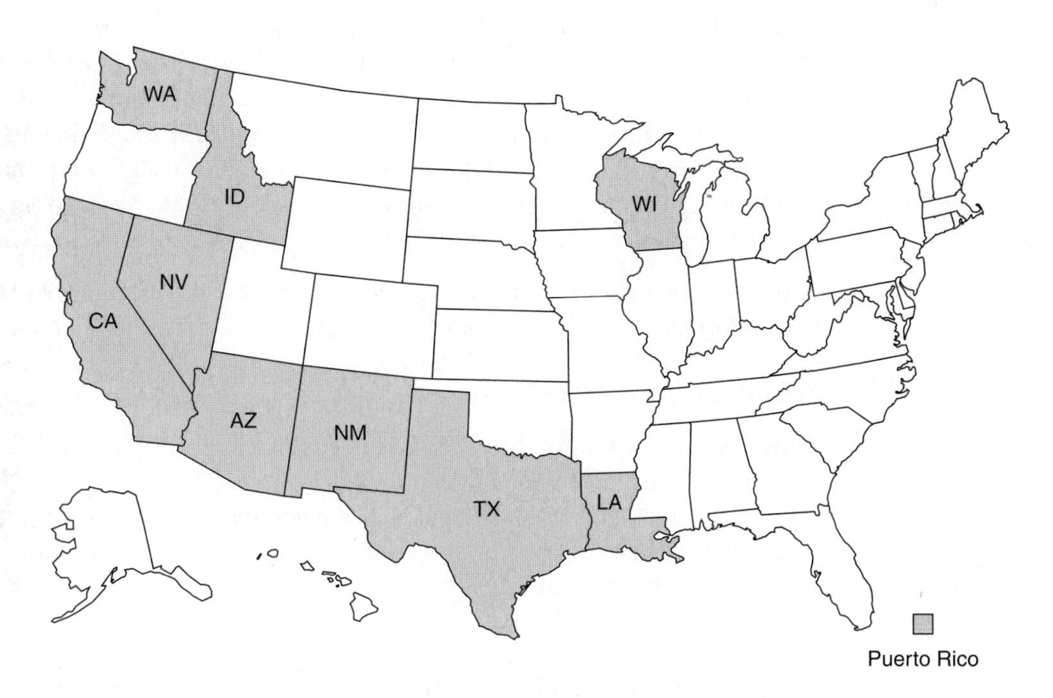

Figure 30-1 Community property jurisdictions

Tenants by the Entirety

A **tenancy by the entirety** may be held only by a husband and wife and is based on the common law doctrine that a husband and wife are regarded, in law, as one person. Under common law theory, each spouse owns the entire estate, which neither can destroy by any separate act. The husband, however, has the entire control over the estate, including the exclusive right to possession and the right to all rents and profits. On the death of either spouse, the survivor owns the entire estate outright.

Under the common law rule, the husband may transfer his interest in the tenancy to someone else without his wife's consent. In addition, his interest may be attached and taken on execution by his creditors. His interest, however, is limited to merely the right to possession of the property and profits from it, plus exclusive title only if he survives his wife. He cannot defeat his wife's interest in the estate while she is alive without her consent. If she outlives her husband, the wife will gain full possession and title to the property, regardless of what has been granted out by the husband or attached by the husband's creditors.

The wife, unlike the husband, may not transfer her interest in the tenancy by the entirety to someone else without the husband's consent, under common law theory. Similarly, her interest may not be attached or taken on execution by her creditors. For these reasons, the tenancy by the entirety has been a popular method of ownership by a husband and wife for protection against attaching creditors. Neither spouse can defeat the other spouse's interest in the estate without the other's consent, and a court has no power to partition a tenancy by the entirety.

In recent years, because of the unequal rights of spouses in the tenancy by the entirety, some states no longer use it as a form of co-ownership of real property. Other states have modified the common law version to give equal rights to the spouses, while at the same time retaining the feature of protection against attachment by creditors. Here is an example of a modern state statute:

> A husband and wife shall be equally entitled to the rents, products, income or profits and to the control, management and possession of property held by them as tenants by the entirety. The interest of a debtor spouse in property held as tenants by the entirety shall not be subject to seizure or execution by a creditor of such debtor spouse so long as such property is the principal residence of the nondebtor spouse; provided, however, both spouses shall be liable jointly or severally for debts incurred on account of necessaries furnished by either spouse or to a member of their family.

A divorce, by operation of law, automatically converts a tenancy by the entirety owned by the former spouses into a tenancy in common.

Tenants in Partnership

Tenancy in partnership is a form of ownership of real property that is available to business partners if they choose to use it. It is governed by the Uniform Partnership Act in those states that have adopted it. Under the act, individual partners cannot transfer their interests in the property to others unless all of them do so, and individual partners' interests in the property are not subject to attachment or execution except on a claim against the partnership.

On the death of a partner, the decedent's rights in specific partnership property become vested in the surviving partners, who may possess such property only for partnership purposes. Death causes a dissolution of a partnership, however, and the surviving partners must account to the estate of the decedent and pay over to the estate the value of the deceased partner's equity in the partnership.

MULTI-OWNERSHIP OF REAL PROPERTY

Separate ownership of property by different people is accomplished by way of condominiums, cooperatives, and time-sharing arrangements.

Condominiums

A **condominium** is a parcel of real property, portions of which, called **units,** are owned separately in fee simple by individual owners, and the remainder of which, called the **common areas,** is owned as tenants in common by all the unit owners. Common areas include entrances, hallways, sidewalks, swimming pools, yards, roofs, and outside walls and are maintained and managed by a **condominium association,** consisting of unit members. Unit owners pay monthly maintenance fees in addition to real property taxes. An ownership interest in a condominium is considered to be real property. A **master deed,** describing the entire property that is owned by the condominium association, is recorded at the registry of deeds, together with restrictions that are placed on the use of the property. The transfer of ownership of each unit is accomplished by the use of a **unit deed,** which is a deed to the individual unit being transferred.

Cooperatives

A **cooperative apartment** is a dwelling unit in which the occupants lease individual units and, at the same time, own shares of stock in the corporation that owns the building. The corporation owns the complex, which is occupied by the tenants who are the stockholders of the nonprofit corporation. The lease is known as a **proprietary lease** because it is a lease to an owner of the property. Tenants pay rent to the corporation, and the corporation maintains the property and pays the real property taxes. An ownership interest in a cooperative is personal property rather than real property, and a transfer of ownership is accomplished by selling the stock in the controlling corporation.

Timesharing

Timesharing, also called **interval ownership,** is a fee simple ownership of a unit of real property in which the owner can exercise the right of possession for only an interval, such as a week or two, each year. Other people possess the property at other intervals of the year. Like condominium owners, interval owners have the right to use the common areas of the property. An ownership interest in a time-share is considered to be real property, unless it is established by a lease, and the transfer of ownership is accomplished with the use of a deed to the individual unit being transferred. Timesharing is popular in vacation and resort areas of the country.

REVIEWING WHAT YOU LEARNED

After studying the text, write the answers to each of the following questions:

1. List the four most common co-tenant relationships.
2. Each tenant in common is entitled to possession of what part of the premises?
3. What happens to the interest in real property of a tenant in common at death?
4. May tenants in common grant out their interests in real property without permission to do so from the other co-tenants? May joint tenants do so? May tenants by the entirety do so?
5. How may tenants in common separate their interests in the property from other tenants in common?
6. Name the four unities in a joint tenancy.
7. What happens to a joint tenant's interest in real property at death?
8. Who may own real property as tenants by the entirety?
9. Describe ownership rights of a husband and a wife under the community property system.
10. What jurisdictions follow the community property system?
11. What rights does the husband have that the wife does not have under the common law theory of tenants by the entirety?

12. Why is a tenancy by the entirety a popular method of ownership by a husband and wife?

13. In what way have some states modified the common law version of the tenancy by the entirety?

14. Under a tenancy in partnership, when is a partner's interest subject to attachment?

15. When a partner dies, who owns the property under tenancy in partnership?

UNDERSTANDING LEGAL CONCEPTS

Indicate whether each statement is true or false. Then, change the italicized word or phrase of each *false* statement to make it true.

Answers

1. Real property may be owned severally—that is, by *two or more persons.*

2. When two or more people own real property as tenants in common, each owner is entitled to the possession of *his or her part of the premises only.*

3. Any of the tenants in common *may* grant out their interests to others without permission of the other co-tenants.

4. All joint tenants' interests *are* equal.

5. If a joint tenant grants out his or her interest to a new owner, the new owner becomes a *joint tenant* with the remaining joint tenants.

6. Under common law, the husband, in a tenancy by the entirety, had the *exclusive* right to possession of the premises.

7. Under common law, a wife *can* transfer her interest in a tenancy by the entirety to someone else without her husband's consent.

8. The court *has no power* to partition a tenancy by the entirety.

9. A divorce, by operation of law, automatically converts a tenancy by the entirety into a *joint tenancy.*

10. In a *tenancy in partnership,* individual partners cannot transfer their interests in the property to others unless all of them do so.

7

CHECKING TERMINOLOGY

From the list of legal terms that follows, select the one that matches each definition:

a. common areas
b. community property
c. concurrent ownership
d. condominium
e. condominium association
f. cooperative apartment
g. co-ownership
h. co-tenants
i. creditors
j. interval ownership
k. joint tenancy
l. joint tenancy with the right of survivorship
m. joint tenants
n. levy on execution
o. master deed
p. moiety
q. partition
r. proprietary lease
s. several
t. tenancy by the entirety
u. tenancy in partnership
v. tenants in common
w. timesharing
x. unit deed
y. units
z. unity of interest
aa. unity of possession
bb. unity of time
cc. unity of title

Answers

____ **1.** Property (other than a gift or inheritance) acquired by a husband or wife during marriage that belongs to both spouses equally.
____ **2.** Two or more owners of real property.
____ **3.** The individual portions of a condominium that are owned separately in fee simple by individual owners.
____ **4.** Equal interest in property by all owners.
____ **5.** A dwelling unit in which the occupants lease individual units and, at the same time, own shares of stock in the corporation that owns the building.
____ **6.** Separate, individual, and independent.
____ **7.** The division of land held by joint tenants or tenants in common into distinct portions so that they may hold them separately.
____ **8.** The part of a condominium or cooperative apartment building that is owned as tenants in common by all the unit owners.
____ **9.** Two or more persons holding one and the same interest, accruing by one and the same conveyance, commencing at one and the same time, and held by one and the same undivided possession.
____ **10.** Ownership in which each person has an interest in partnership property and is a co-owner of such property.
____ **11.** A lease to an owner of the property.
____ **12.** Owned by more than one person (select two answers).
____ **13.** All owners of property taking title at the same time.
____ **14.** The estate owned by joint tenants (select two answers).
____ **15.** People who are owed money.
____ **16.** A type of joint tenancy held by a husband and wife that offers protection against attachment and that cannot be terminated by one spouse alone.
____ **17.** A group of condominium unit owners that manages and maintains a condominium.
____ **18.** Equal rights to possession of the entire property by all owners.
____ **19.** Two or more persons holding an undivided interest in property, with each owner's interests going to his or her heirs on death rather than to the surviving co-owners.
____ **20.** A fee simple ownership of a unit of real property in which the owner can exercise the right of possession for only an interval, such as a week or two, each year (select two answers).
____ **21.** A deed to the individual unit being transferred.
____ **22.** A parcel of real property, portions of which are owned separately in fee simple by individual owners, and the remainder of which is owned as tenants in common by all the unit owners.
____ **23.** All owners of property receiving title from the same instrument.

____**24.** To collect a sum of money by putting into effect the judgment of a court.

____**25.** A part, portion, or fraction.

____**26.** A deed to a condominium that describes the entire property that is owned by the condominium association.

UNRAVELING LEGALESE

Use simple, non-legal language, with the help of the glossary, to rewrite this case quote so that it is shorter and can be understood by a layperson without losing its meaning.

> The nature of a tenancy by the entirety is thoroughly established by our decisions. It is founded on the common law doctrine of the unity of husband and wife as constituting in law but one person. A conveyance to a husband and wife as tenants by the entirety creates one indivisible estate in them both and in the survivor, which neither can destroy by any separate act. Both husband and wife are seised of such an estate as one person, and not as joint tenants or tenants in common. Alienation by either the husband or wife will not defeat the right of the survivor to the entire estate on the death of the other.

USING LEGAL LANGUAGE

Read the following story and fill in the blank lines with legal terms taken from the list of terms at the beginning of this chapter.

James and Kathleen, who were business partners, took title to a parcel of real property as ________________________ to protect their interests from being attached except on a claim against the partnership. When the partnership was dissolved, Kathleen bought out James's interest and owned the property ________________________—that is, separately. She sold the property to Larry, Mary, and Nancy, who took title as ________________________, which means that on the death of one of them, the entire ownership would remain in the surviving owners. They were called ________________________, because of the ________________________ ownership, and they had the following unities: ____________________, ____________________, ____________________, and ________________________. Mary decided to sell her interest in the property but couldn't find a buyer. To avoid having the court ________________________ the property—that is, divide it into separate parcels—Larry and Nancy bought Mary's share. They decided to take title as ________________________ so that if one of them died, his or her share would go to his or her heirs. Later, however, when Larry and Nancy got married, they had their attorney change the way in which they owned the property to ________________________ so that they would have protection against attaching ________________________ (people who are owed money), who could ________________________ to collect money owed them by putting into effect a court judgment. They did not live in a(n) ________________________ jurisdiction in which all property (other than a gift or inheritance) acquired by either of them during marriage would belong to both equally. Eventually, Larry and Nancy sold the property and bought a ________________________, which is a parcel of real property, portions of which, called ________________________, are owned separately in fee simple by individual owners, and the remainder of which, called the ________________________, is owned as tenants in common by all the owners.

PUZZLING OVER WHAT YOU LEARNED

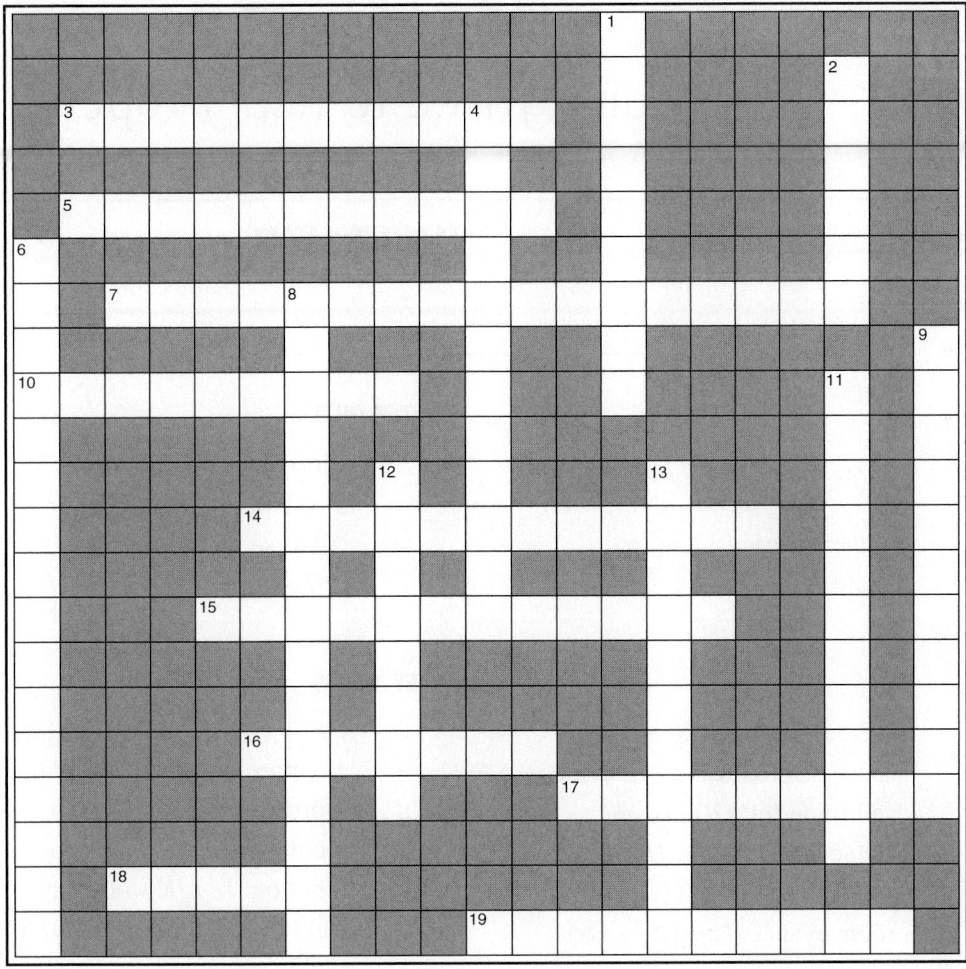

Caveat: Do not allow squares for spaces between words and punctuation (apostrophes, hyphens, etc.) when filling in crossword.

Across

3. A parcel of real property, portions of which are owned separately in fee simple by individual owners, and the remainder of which is owned as tenants in common by all the unit owners.
5. Owned by more than one person.
7. Property (other than a gift or inheritance) acquired by a husband or wife during marriage that belongs to both spouses equally.
10. The division of land held by tenants in common into distinct portions so that they may hold them separately.
14. The estate owned by joint tenants.
15. Two or more persons holding one and the same interest, accruing by one and the same conveyance, commencing at one and the same time, and held by one and the same undivided possession.
16. Separate, individual, and independent.
17. Two or more owners of real property.
18. The individual portions of a condominium that are owned separately in fee simple by individual owners.
19. A deed to a condominium that describes the entire property owned by the condominium association.

Down

1. People to whom money is owed.
2. A part, portion, or fraction.
4. All owners of a property receiving title from the same instrument.
6. A lease to an owner of the property.
8. Equal interest in a property by all owners.
9. The part of a condominium or apartment that is owned as tenants in common by all unit owners.
11. A fee simple owner of a unit of real property in which the owner can exercise the right of possession for only an interval each year.
12. A deed to an individual condominium unit.
13. All owners of a property taking title at the same time.

7

CHAPTER 31
Acquiring Title to Real Property

ANTE INTERROGATORY

An increase of land caused by the slow action of water upon its borders is known as (A) tacking, (B) seisin, (C) dereliction, (D) accretion.

CHAPTER OUTLINE

Original Grant
Deed
Inheritance
Sale on Execution
Mortgagee's Foreclosure Sale
Tax Title
Adverse Possession
Slow Action of Water

KEY TERMS

accretion *(a·KREE·shun)*
adverse possession *(AD·verse po·SESH·en)*
alluvion *(a·LOO·vee·en)*
attachment *(a·TACH·ment)*
convey *(kon·VAY)*
conveyance *(kon·VAY·enss)*
deed
disseised *(di·SEEZD)*
divested *(dy·VEST·ed)*
erosion *(e·RO·shen)*
foreclose *(for·KLOZE)*
infancy *(IN·fen·see)*
mortgagee *(more·gej·EE)*
mortgagee's foreclosure sale *(more·gej·EES for·KLOH·zher)*
mortgagor *(more·gej·OR)*
record owner *(REK·erd)*
reliction *(re·LIK·shun)*
right of redemption *(re·DEMP·shun)*
seal
seisin *(SEE·zin)*
sheriff's sale *(SHERR·ifs)*
tacking
vendee *(ven·DEE)*
vendor *(ven·DOR)*

Title to real property may be acquired in the following ways:

1. Original grant
2. Deed
3. Inheritance
4. Sale on execution
5. Mortgagee's foreclosure sale
6. Tax title
7. Adverse possession
8. Slow action of water

ORIGINAL GRANT

Originally, land in America was owned by the various foreign governments that had settled here, such as England, France, Spain, and Mexico. Individuals obtained title to the land by grants from the crowns of those countries. After the American Revolution, any land that was not owned by individuals became the property of either the state or the federal government, which **conveyed** (transferred) much of it out by public grant to homesteaders or settlers under laws enacted by Congress.

DEED

The most common method of acquiring title to real property is by the use of a deed signed by the grantor and delivered to the grantee. A **deed** is a formal written instrument used to transfer title from one person to another. It is also known as a **conveyance.** The transfer can be as a result of a sale or a gift. A person who transfers property or goods by sale is a **vendor.** A purchaser or buyer of property or goods is a **vendee.** Traditionally, a deed was required to be under seal to be effective; however, many states have done away with that requirement by statute. A **seal** is a mark or impression (originally made with wax) placed next to the party's signature. Some states require that a deed be witnessed; others have no such requirement. The deed is discussed in detail in Chapter 32.

INHERITANCE

When people die owning real property either separately or with others as tenants in common, title to the property vests in their heirs or devisees at the moment of death. No deed is necessary for them to receive title because title passes to them by operation of law. Such vesting of title, however, is subject to being **divested** (taken away) by the executor or administrator of the estate if it is necessary to obtain money from the sale of the property to pay estate taxes, administrative expenses, and other claims against the estate.

When someone dies owning real property with others as joint tenants, the surviving joint tenants own the entire property outright at the moment of death of the decedent. In this case, it is not necessary to probate the estate to obtain title because title passes automatically to the surviving joint tenants. It is usually necessary to obtain estate tax releases for the surviving joint tenants to have clear title to the property, however.

SALE ON EXECUTION

At the beginning of a lawsuit, the plaintiff will often attach the defendant's real property. An **attachment** has the effect of bringing the property under the jurisdiction of the court as security for the debt. If the defendant loses the case and does not pay the amount of the judgment to the plaintiff, the sheriff may levy and sell on execution the real property that was attached. This is often referred to as a **sheriff's sale** and is done by public auction after a prescribed amount of time and notice, set by state statute, is given to the property owner.

MORTGAGEE'S FORECLOSURE SALE

A **mortgagee's foreclosure sale** occurs when the holder of a mortgage on real property (the **mortgagee**) is not paid and decides to sell the property to obtain the amount owed by the homeowner (the **mortgagor**). The sale is by auction and occurs under the jurisdiction of the court. The proceeds of the sale are applied to the payment of the mortgage

Figure 31-1 No deed is necessary to pass title to real property to heirs or devisees when the owner dies. Title examiners check the probate records to ascertain title in lieu of a deed.

debt, with any surplus going to the mortgagor. Some states have a statutory power of sale provision for mortgages that regulates the foreclosure sale and must be strictly followed when a foreclosure sale occurs. Foreclosure sales under a deed of trust (see Chapter 33) typically are not subject to court supervision.

TAX TITLE

Municipalities have the power to take real property for unpaid taxes. Usually, a city or town must first make a demand for payment on the record owner of the property. The **record owner** is the person who appears to be the owner of the property according to the records at the registry of deeds. If the tax is not paid within a certain number of days after demand, the tax collector may take the property for the city or town, or sell it at a public auction. In some states, this is done by a foreclosure suit brought by the taxing authority.

A purchaser of real property at a tax sale, however, takes the property subject to the former owner's **right of redemption** (right to take the property back). The latter can get the property back on the payment to the city or town of the back taxes, interest, and expenses incurred in the tax title sale. The purchaser of tax title property, to obtain clear title, must petition the court to **foreclose** (terminate) the right of redemption. Only when the court does this does title become absolute in the owner who purchased it at the tax sale.

ADVERSE POSSESSION

Title to real property may be obtained by taking actual possession of the property openly, notoriously, exclusively, under a claim of right, and continuously for the statutory pe-

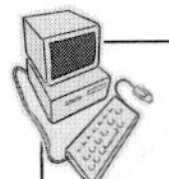

WEB WISE

Finding information on the Web is made easier with Subject Directories and Search Engines. Subject Directories are listings of web sites arranged by subject, chosen by human beings, and are helpful when you need general information on popular or scholarly subjects. In contrast, Search Engines rely on computer programs to search the Web for sites containing the word or words you type in a search box. If you are looking for something specific, use a Search Engine. The chart below describes the main differences between the two search tools:

Subject Directory	*Search Engine*
■ Built by **human** selection	■ Built by **computer** program
■ Organized into **subject** categories	■ **Ranked** by a computer algorithm
■ **Never** contains every word of the web page	■ Contains the **full text** of web pages
■ Often **small and specialized** result list	■ **Huge** result list
■ Often **evaluated** and annotated	■ User needs to evaluate
A Legal Subject Directory is FindLaw **http://www.findlaw.com**	*A Legal Search Engine is FindLaw's "Law Crawler"*

riod, which is 20 years in many states. This method of obtaining title to real property, called **adverse possession,** developed at common law under the theory that two persons (unless they are co-owners) could not have **seisin** (possession of a freehold) of the same land at the same time. If one person took possession of land under a claim of right, the real owner was said to be **disseised** (dispossessed) and would have to bring an action to regain possession within 20 years or be forever barred from doing so.

In calculating the 20-year or other statutory period, any uninterrupted continuous use by previous nonowner occupiers may be added to the time period. Such an accumulation of possession by different occupiers who are not record owners is called **tacking.**

Certain disabilities on the part of the true owner (including **infancy**—that is, under the age of majority—insanity, imprisonment, and absence from the United States), if they occur at the beginning of the adverse possession, will give the true owner a longer time to regain possession of the premises.

In some states, clear record title by adverse possession may be had by simply filing an affidavit with the proper office. Other states require a court proceeding to obtain clear title.

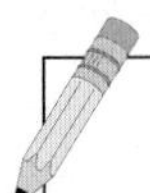

WORD WISE

Seise or Seize?

The legal term "seisin" means "possession"; the term "disseised" means "dispossessed." "Seise" is the legal variation of the word "seize," which has the broader meaning of grasping something suddenly and forcibly. Both words have the same pronunciation.

SLOW ACTION OF WATER

Any addition to the soil made by nature, such as the gradual accumulation of soil on land next to a stream caused by the action of water, is called **accretion.** Another term used to describe this addition to the soil is **alluvion.** Such addition to the soil belongs to the owner of the soil to which it is added. In contrast, when one side of a stream gains soil by the slow action of water, the opposite side of the stream often loses soil. This process is known as **erosion,** which is defined as the gradual eating away of the soil by the operation of currents or tides.

Real property owners sometimes gain additional land when adjoining water permanently recedes. This gradual recession of water, leaving land permanently uncovered, is referred to as **reliction.**

REVIEWING WHAT YOU LEARNED

After studying the text, write the answers to each of the following questions:

1. List the ways that title may be acquired to real property. ______
2. From whom did individuals originally obtain title to land in America? ______
3. What happened, after the American Revolution, to land that was not owned by individuals? ______
4. What is the most common method of acquiring title to real property, and what are the requirements of this method? ______
5. When an individual owner of real property dies, who becomes the immediate owner of the property? To what is this ownership subject? ______
6. Briefly describe a sale on execution. ______
7. When does a mortgagee's foreclosure sale occur? ______
8. Why does the purchaser of real property at a tax sale take a risk? ______

9. How long must one possess real property to own it by adverse possession? ______________________

____

____

____

____

____

10. Who becomes the owner of soil that is gradually added to land adjoining a stream as a result of the action of water? ______________________

____

____

____

____

UNDERSTANDING LEGAL CONCEPTS

Indicate whether each statement is true or false. Then, change the italicized word or phrase of each *false* statement to make it true.

Answers

______________ **1.** Originally, land in America was owned by the various *foreign governments* that had settled here.

______________ **2.** Traditionally, a deed was required to be under seal to be effective; however, many states *have* done away with that requirement.

______________ **3.** *Some* states have no requirement that a deed be witnessed.

______________ **4.** When people die owning real estate separately, *a deed* is necessary to pass title to their heirs.

______________ **5.** For title to pass to a surviving joint tenant, it *is necessary* to probate the estate of a deceased joint tenant.

______________ **6.** An attachment has the effect of bringing property under the jurisdiction of *the court* as security for a debt.

______________ **7.** A mortgagee's foreclosure sale is a *private sale* that occurs under the jurisdiction of the court.

______________ **8.** A purchaser of real property at a tax sale takes the property subject to the former owner's right to *take the property back.*

______________ **9.** In calculating the time period to obtain title by adverse possession, any uninterrupted use by previous nonowner occupiers *may not be* added to the time period.

______________ **10.** Any addition to the soil made by nature, such as the *very rapid* accumulation of soil on land next to a stream, is called accretion.

CHECKING TERMINOLOGY

From the list of legal terms that follows, select the one that matches each definition.

- **a.** accretion
- **b.** adverse possession
- **c.** alluvion
- **d.** attachment
- **e.** convey
- **f.** conveyance
- **g.** deed
- **h.** disseised
- **i.** divested
- **j.** erosion
- **k.** foreclose
- **l.** infancy
- **m.** mortgagee
- **n.** mortgagee's foreclosure sale
- **o.** mortgagor
- **p.** record owner
- **q.** reliction
- **r.** right of redemption
- **s.** seal
- **t.** seisin
- **u.** sheriff's sale
- **v.** tacking
- **w.** vendee
- **x.** vendor

Answers

____ **1.** A formal written instrument used to transfer title to real property, from one person to another (select two answers).

____ **2.** A mark or impression, originally made with wax placed next to a party's signature.

____ **3.** The act of taking or seizing property by the use of a writ, summons, or other judicial order and bringing it into the custody of the court.

____ **4.** One who borrows money and gives a mortgage—that is, pledges property—to the lender as security for the loan.

____ **5.** A sale of property at public auction conducted by a sheriff.

____ **6.** Right to take property back.

____ **7.** Title to real property obtained by taking actual possession of it openly, notoriously, exclusively, under a claim of right, and continuously for a period of time set by statute.

____ **8.** Dispossessed.

____ **9.** Any gradual addition to the soil made by nature, such as the gradual accumulation of soil on land next to a stream caused by the action of water (select two answers).

____ **10.** To transfer.

____ **11.** Taken away.

____ **12.** One who lends money and takes back a mortgage as security for the loan.

____ **13.** One who appears to be the owner of real property according to the records at the registry of deeds.

____ **14.** A sale of real property that terminates all rights of the mortgagor in the property covered by the mortgage.

____ **15.** Terminate.

____ **16.** Possession of a freehold.

____ **17.** The addition of previous occupants' possession to one's own possession to meet the statutory period for adverse possession.

____ **18.** The gradual eating away of the soil by the operation of currents or tides.

____ **19.** The gradual recession of water leaving land permanently uncovered.

____ **20.** Under the age of majority.

____ **21.** A purchaser or buyer of property or goods.

UNRAVELING LEGALESE

Use simple, non-legal language, with the help of the glossary, to rewrite this case quote so that it is shorter and can be understood by a layperson without losing its meaning.

> It is settled that where accretions are made to land along the seashore, the line of ownership follows the changing waterline. The circumstances that the building of the breakwaters by public authority may have aided the operation of natural causes in the deposit of the accretions, as inferred by the trial judge, does not modify the general rule that the littoral proprietor is entitled to his [or her] proportionate share of such accretions.

USING LEGAL LANGUAGE

Read the following story and fill in the blank lines with legal terms taken from the list of terms at the beginning of this chapter.

Arlene inherited some real property that adjoined a river. Title to the property vested in Arlene at the moment of death of the decedent but was subject to being ______________________ to pay claims against the estate. Arlene was the ______________________, because she was the person who appeared to be the owner according to the records at the Registry of Deeds. She received a notice in the mail from her bank saying that a(n) ______________________ was about to occur, because she was behind in her mortgage payments. She was the ______________________; the bank was the ______________________. Arlene took the money that she had saved to pay property taxes and other creditors and used it to pay the money owed on the mortgage. One of her creditors brought suit against her and placed a(n) ______________________ on her property, which had the effect of bringing it under the jurisdiction of the court as security for the debt. To prevent a(n) ______________________ —that is, a sale on execution of the property—Arlene paid the amount that was owed to the creditor. She then had the property lines surveyed and discovered that the garage belonging to her next-door neighbor, Ben, extended four feet onto her land. Although Ben had owned the property for 10 years, the garage had been placed there by Carl, the previous owner, 22 years earlier. Ben can add his 10 years of ownership to that of Carl's under a method called ______________________. Ben obtained title to the land under the garage by ______________________, a method that developed at common law under the theory that two persons could not have ______________________ of the same land at the same time. If one person took possession of land under a claim of right, the real owner was said to be ______________________—that is, dispossessed—of the property. Because Arlene had failed to pay the property tax, the local tax collector took the property and sold it at a public auction to Darlene. The ______________________—that is, the transfer to Darlene—was made by the use of a(n) ______________________, which is a formal written instrument used to transfer title from one person to another. The instrument was under ______________________, which is a mark or impression next to the party's signature. Darlene bought the property subject to Arlene's ______________________—that is, the right to take the property back—unless Darlene is successful in petitioning the court to ______________________ (terminate) that right. By then, a considerable amount of land had been added to the property by ______________________, which is also called ______________________, caused by the slow action of the adjoining river.

PUZZLING OVER WHAT YOU LEARNED

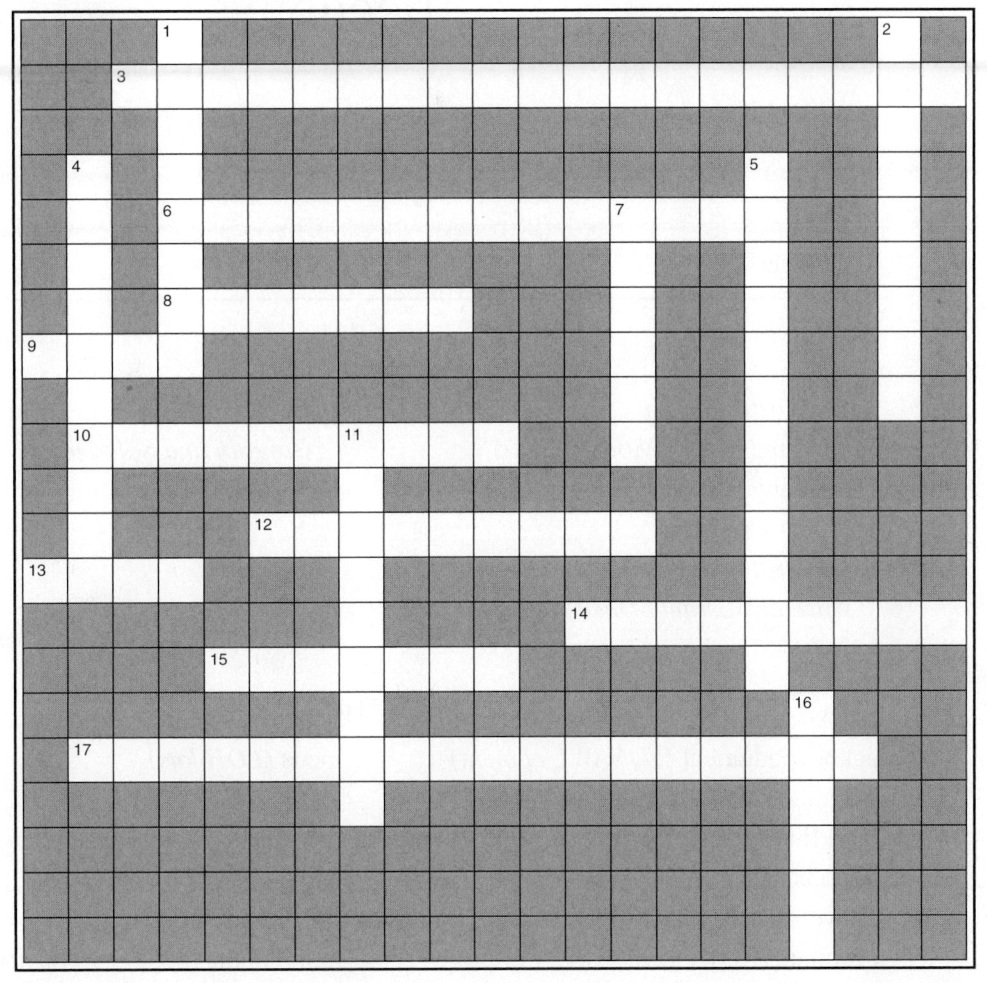

Caveat: Allow squares for spaces between words and punctuation (apostrophes, hyphens, etc.) when filling in crossword.

Across

3. Right to take property back.
6. A sale of property at public auction conducted by a sheriff.
8. Gradual eating away of the soil by the operation of currents or tides.
9. A written instrument used to transfer title of real property.
10. Act of taking property and bringing it into the custody of the court.
12. One who borrows money and gives a mortgage to the lender as security.
13. A mark or impression.
14. Dispossessed.
15. Under the age of majority.
17. Title to real property obtained by taking actual possession of it.

Down

1. Taken away.
2. Terminate.
4. A written instrument used to transfer title of real property.
5. One who appears to be the owner of real property according to the records.
7. Possession of a freehold.
11. One who lends money and takes back a mortgage as security for a loan.
16. To transfer.

7

CHAPTER 32

Deeds

ANTE INTERROGATORY

The most desirable form of a deed, which gives assurances that title is good, is a (A) bargain and sale deed, (B) quitclaim deed, (C) special warranty deed, (D) general warranty deed.

CHAPTER OUTLINE

Sealed Instrument
Requirements of a Modern Deed
Describing Real Property
Types of Deeds
  General Warranty Deed
  Special Warranty Deed
  Quitclaim Deed
  Bargain and Sale Deed

KEY TERMS

acknowledgment *(ak·NAWL·ej·ment)*
bargain and sale deed *(BAR·gen)*
base lines
bounds
conveyancing *(kon·VAY·ens·ing)*
covenant *(KOV·e·nent)*
deed
deed without covenants *(KOV·e·nents)*
encumbrance *(en·KUM·brens)*
fiduciary deed *(fi·DOO·she·air·ee)*
full covenant and warranty deed *(KOV·e·nent and WAR·en·tee)*
general warranty deed *(JEN·e·rel WAR·en·tee)*
government survey system *(GUV·ern·ment SUR·vey SYS·tem)*
grantee *(gran·TEE)*
grantor *(gran·TOR)*
habendum clause *(ha·BEN·dum)*
heirlooms *(AIR·looms)*
hereditaments *(herr·e·DIT·a·ments)*
limited warranty deed *(LIM·i·ted WAR·en·tee)*
locus *(LOH·kus)*
locus sigilli *(LOH·kus se·JIL·i)*
meridians *(mer·ID·ee·ens)*
metes *(meets)*
metes and bounds
monuments *(MON·yoo·ments)*
plat
plat book
plat map
plot
quitclaim deed *(KWIT·klame)*
range *(rainj)*
rectangular survey system *(rek·TANG·yoo·ler SUR·vey SYS·tem)*
section *(SEK·shun)*
special warranty deed *(SPESH·el WAR·en·tee)*
tenements *(TEN·e·mentz)*
township *(TOUN·ship)*
tract of land *(trakt)*
warrant *(WAR·ent)*

Centuries ago in England, before the use of the deed, real property was transferred from one person to another in a public ceremony known as *livery of seisin.* The one transferring the property would hand the other a clod of dirt or a twig from a tree, symbolizing the transfer. The ceremony was called *livery in deed* when it took place on the property itself, and *livery in law* when it was done in sight of the property but not actually on it.

SEALED INSTRUMENT

As time went on and more people learned to read and write, the written deed replaced the formal ceremony of transferring real property. In those days, a person's seal was of foremost importance. One reason was that the seal was more difficult to forge than a handwritten signature. Any contract that was under seal and contained **covenants** (promises) was called a **deed.**

Later, but still under the common law, a deed became defined as "a writing under seal by which lands, tenements, or hereditaments are conveyed for an estate not less than freehold." **Tenements** were defined as "everything of a permanent nature which may be holden, and in a more restrictive sense, houses or dwellings." **Hereditaments** were "things capable of being inherited, including not only lands and everything thereon, but also **heirlooms**" (valued possessions with sentimental value passed down through generations within a family).

Originally, a seal was an impression on wax, paper, wafer, or some other firm substance upon which an impression could be made. As time went on, the impression was replaced by a round, red paper seal pasted on the instrument, or the word "seal," or a phrase such as "Witness my hand and seal," or the letters "L.S." (the abbreviation for **locus sigilli**—the place of the seal) written beside a party's signature. Whatever method is used to put a deed under seal is not the same as a notary public's seal used by a notary to acknowledge an instrument. Each of the seals are separate and distinct, one having nothing to do with the other.

Today, a **deed** may be defined as a formal written instrument by which title to real property is transferred from one person to another. The deed is the most common method of **conveyancing** (transferring title to real property from one person to another). By statute, in many states, a deed is no longer required to be under seal.

The person who transfers title is known as the **grantor,** and the person to whom title is transferred is known as the **grantee.**

REQUIREMENTS OF A MODERN DEED

A deed must convey a present ownership interest to the grantee, even though the grantee's right to possess the premises may be delayed until a later time. For a conveyance to be valid, a deed must meet the following requirements:

1. Be in writing
2. Identify the grantor
3. Be signed by the grantor
4. Identify the grantee
5. Contain words of conveyance, such as "grant," "convey," or "transfer"
6. Describe the **locus** (exact parcel) being conveyed

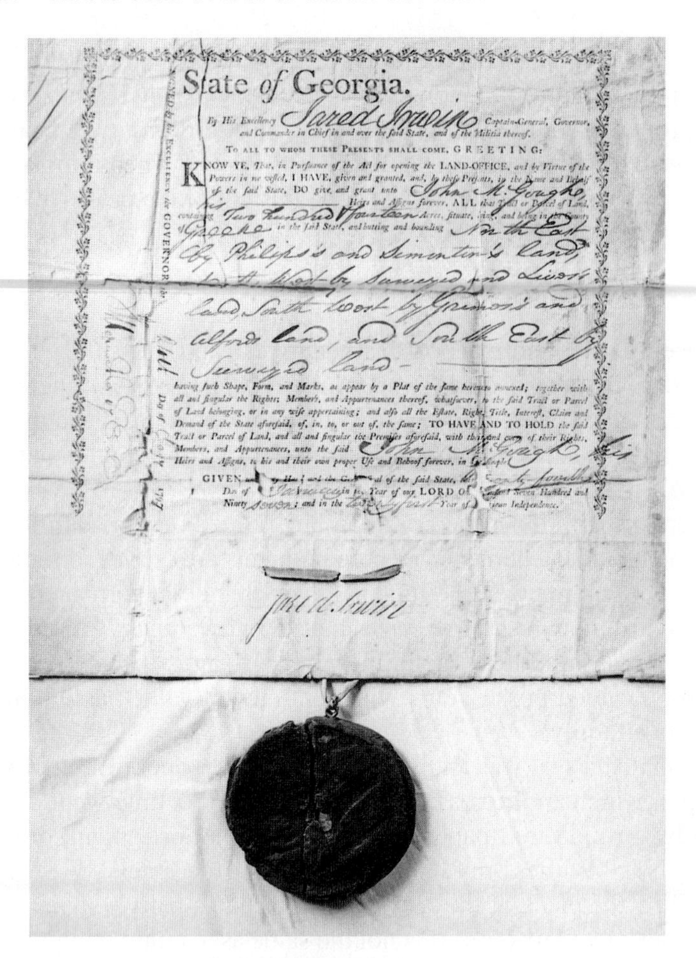
State of Georgia.

By His Excellency Jared Irwin Captain-General, Governor, and Commander in Chief in and over the said State, and of the Militia thereof.

To all to whom these Presents shall come, GREETING:

KNOW YE, That, in Pursuance of the Act for opening the LAND-OFFICE, and by Virtue of the Powers in me vested, I HAVE, given and granted, and, by these Presents, in the Name and Behalf of the said State, DO give, and grant unto John M. Gougho, his Heirs and Assigns forever, ALL that Tract or Parcel of Land, containing Two hundred & fourteen Acres, situate, lying, and being in the County of Greene in the said State, and butting and bounding North East by Philips's and Simonton's land, North West by Surveyed and [illegible] land, South West by [illegible] and Alfords land, and South East by Surveyed land –

having such Shape, Form, and Marks, as appear by a Plat of the same hereunto annexed; together with all and singular the Rights, Members, and Appurtenances thereof, whatsoever, to the said Tract or Parcel of Land belonging, or in any wise appertaining; and also all the Estate, Right, Title, Interest, Claim and Demand of the State aforesaid, of, in, to, or out of, the same; TO HAVE AND TO HOLD the said Tract or Parcel of Land, and all and singular the Premises aforesaid, with their and every of their Rights, Members, and Appurtenances, unto the said John M. Gough, his Heirs and Assigns, to his and their own proper Use and Behoof forever, in Fee Simple.

GIVEN [illegible] Seal of the said State, [illegible] Day of [illegible] in the Year of our LORD One Thousand Seven Hundred and Ninety [illegible]; and in the [illegible] Year of American Independence.

Jared Irwin

Figure 32-1 This early deed conveying land in Greene County, Georgia, illustrates a wax seal that was required to be on deeds to pass title at that time. What type of seal is required to be on a deed in your state today? (Courtesy of the Library of Congress, Prints and Photographs Division, reproduction number LC-USF34-044309-D.)

7. Be delivered to the grantee
8. Be accepted by the grantee

To be effective as to third parties, a deed must also be recorded. To be recorded (explained in Chapter 34), a deed must be acknowledged. An **acknowledgment** is a formal declaration before an authorized official, by a person who executes an instrument, that it is his or her free act and deed. A certificate of acknowledgment, signed and sealed by the official (usually a notary public), is placed at the bottom of the deed following the signature of the grantor.

DESCRIBING REAL PROPERTY

There are three principal systems in use today to describe real property in a deed: (1) by the metes and bounds system, (2) by the rectangular survey system, and (3) by reference to a plat or survey.

Metes and bounds is a system of describing real property by its outer boundaries, with reference to courses, distances, and **monuments** (visible marks indicating boundaries). **Metes** are the distances between points and **bounds** are the directions of the boundaries that enclose a parcel of land. This system came from England and is used in the eastern part of the country. Here is an example:

> Beginning at the Southwesterly corner of the wall, by Haverhill Road, (Main Street) and land now owned by Raymond Pearl (formerly owned by B. Ford Parsons) and thence running
>
> Easterly — by said wall and fence and by land of said Pearl about four hundred thirty-four (434) feet to a corner of the fence by land now of Charles M. Moulton; thence running
>
> Northerly — by the wall, and by land of said Moulton, one hundred sixty-seven feet (167) to land now or formerly of Charles F. Austin; thence running
>
> Westerly — by said land about four hundred and forty-four (444) to said Haverhill Road (Main Street); thence running
>
> Southerly — by said Haverhill Road (Main Street) one hundred eighty-eight feet (188) to the point begun at.

Following the Revolutionary War, the United States Congress ordered a survey of the vast area of land west of the original 13 colonies. The **rectangular survey system,** also known as the **government survey system,** was established at that time. It is a method of describing real property based on the property's relationship to intersecting lines called **base lines** (running east and west) and *principal* or *prime* **meridians** (lines running north and south). The intersections of the lines create 24-mile squares, which are further divided into 6-mile squares called **townships.** Each township is divided into 26 equal squares called sections. A **section** is a square mile of land, containing 640 acres. A row of townships running north and south is called a **range.**

A third method of describing real property is by reference to a recorded survey that is made when a **tract of land** (a large piece of land) is subdivided. A map of the subdivision, called a **plat, plat map,** or **plot,** is drawn. The size and shape of each lot is designated, and the plat is given a name or number so that it can be identified. When it is recorded, the plat is entered into a **plat book** at the registry of deeds.

TYPES OF DEEDS

There are four types of deeds in general use today:

1. General warranty deed
2. Special warranty deed
3. Quitclaim deed
4. Bargain and sale deed.

The first two deeds contain warranties. The latter two do not.

General Warranty Deed

A **general warranty deed,** sometimes known as a **full covenant and warranty deed,** is the most desirable form of deed from the viewpoint of the grantee because it **warrants** (gives assurances) that the title is good. The typical general warranty deed contains the following four covenants made by the grantor to the grantee:

1. The grantor has good title.
2. No **encumbrances** (liens or claims by others) exist.
3. The grantor has good right to sell and convey the property.
4. The grantor will warrant and defend the title against the claims of all persons.

Because of its lengthy covenants, the warranty deed is extremely long and wordy. To illustrate, the clause called the **habendum clause,** which defines the extent of ownership, reads as follows in a long-form warranty deed:

> TO HAVE AND TO HOLD THE GRANTED PREMISES, with all the privileges and appurtenances thereto belonging, to the said (grantee), and his [or her] heirs and assigns, to their own use and behoof forever.

Similarly, the clause containing the covenants in a long-form general warranty deed reads:

> And I hereby, for myself and my heirs, executors, and administrators, COVENANT with the grantee and his [or her] heirs and assigns that I am lawfully seized in fee simple of the granted premises; that they are free from all encumbrances; that I have good right to sell and convey the same as aforesaid; and that I will, and my heirs, executors, and administrators shall, WARRANT AND DEFEND the same to the grantee and his [or her] heirs and assigns forever against the lawful claims and demands of all persons.

To avoid the use of such lengthy and complicated language, many states have created short forms of deeds, which give the same warranties as the long forms but use fewer words. For example, the words "convey and warrant" create a general warranty deed in Alaska, Illinois, Kansas, Michigan, Minnesota, and Wisconsin. The words "warrant generally" mean the same in Pennsylvania, Vermont, Virginia, and West Virginia deeds. The

WORD WISE

More Words Ending in "or" and "ee"

grantor (*gran·TOR*)	One who transfers real property to another.
grantee (*gran·TEE*)	One to whom real property is transferred.
mortgagor (*more·gej·OR*)	One who borrows money and gives a mortgage as security.
mortgagee (*more·gej·EE*)	One who lends money and takes a mortgage as security.
obligor (*ob·li·GOR*)	One bound by contract to perform an obligation.
obligee (*ob·li·GEE*)	One to whom an obligation is owed under a contract.
pledgor (*plej·OR*)	One who gives property to another as security for a loan.
pledgee (*plej·EE*)	One to whom property is given as security for a loan.
promisor (*prom·i·SOHR*)	One who makes a promise.
promisee (*prom·i·SEE*)	One to whom a promise is made.

words "grant, bargain, and sell" create a general warranty deed in Arkansas, Florida, Idaho, Missouri, and Nevada. Finally, the words "with warranty covenants" mean the same in Massachusetts deeds.

Special Warranty Deed

A **special warranty deed,** sometimes called a **limited warranty deed,** warrants that no defects arose in the title during the time that the grantor owned the property, but no warranty is made as to defects that arose before the grantor owned the property. In a special warranty deed, the grantor warrants the following:

1. The premises are free from all encumbrances made by the grantor.
2. The grantor will warrant and defend the title only against claims through him or her.

As in the case of the general warranty deed, many states have created short forms of special warranty deeds. For example, the words "warrant specially" create a special warranty deed in Mississippi, Pennsylvania, Vermont, Virginia, and West Virginia. The word "grant" means the same in California, Idaho, and North Dakota deeds. The words "with quitclaim covenants" are used to create a special warranty deed in Massachusetts.

Quitclaim Deed

A **quitclaim deed** (called a **deed without covenants** or a **fiduciary deed** in some states) conveys only the grantor's interest, if any, in the real property and contains no warranties. It is commonly used when a deed is necessary to cure a defect in the chain of title or when the grantor is not sure whether his or her title is good or bad. Executors, administrators, and other fiduciaries often use this form of deed when conveying real property.

Bargain and Sale Deed

A **bargain and sale deed** conveys the land itself rather than merely the interest that the grantor has in the property, as is done in a quitclaim deed. The form is the same as a warranty deed except that the covenants (warranties) are omitted. Consideration is required in a bargain and sale deed.

REVIEWING WHAT YOU LEARNED

After studying the text, write the answers to each of the following questions:

1. What was considered to be a deed under the early days of common law? ______

2. List the requirements of a valid deed. ______

3. What are the four types of deeds that are in general use today? ______

4. Why is a general warranty deed the most desirable form of deed from the viewpoint of the grantee? How many covenants are made in a general warranty deed? ______

5. What have many states done to avoid the use of long and complicated language in a deed? ______

6. Describe the two warranties made in a special warranty deed. ______

7. When is a quitclaim deed commonly used? ______

8. Describe the form of a bargain and sale deed. ______

UNDERSTANDING LEGAL CONCEPTS

Indicate whether each statement is true or false. Then, change the italicized word or phrase of each *false* statement to make it true.

Answers

______________ **1.** In the early days of common law, a deed and a sealed instrument were *practically synonymous.*

______________ **2.** For a conveyance to be valid, a deed must be *delivered* to the grantee.

______________ **3.** A general warranty deed *is not* the most desirable form of deed from the viewpoint of the grantee.

______________ **4.** A general warranty deed *does not* contain a warranty that the grantor has good title.

______________ **5.** To avoid use of lengthy and complicated language, many states have created *short forms* of deeds.

______________ **6.** The *habendum clause* begins with the words "TO HAVE AND TO HOLD."

______________ **7.** A special warranty deed protects against defects that arose *before* the grantor owned the property.

______________ **8.** A quitclaim deed contains *a warranty that title is good.*

______________ **9.** A *quitclaim* deed is commonly used when a deed is necessary to cure a defect in the chain of title.

______________ **10.** Consideration *is not* required in a bargain and sale deed.

7

CHECKING TERMINOLOGY

From the list of legal terms that follows, select the one that matches each definition.

a. acknowledgment
b. bargain and sale deed
c. base lines
d. bounds
e. conveyancing
f. covenant
g. deed
h. deed without covenants
i. encumbrance
j. fiduciary deed
k. full covenant and warranty deed
l. general warranty deed
m. government survey system
n. grantee
o. grantor
p. habendum clause
q. heirlooms
r. hereditaments
s. limited warranty deed
t. locus
u. locus sigilli
v. meridians
w. metes
x. metes and bounds
y. monuments
z. plat
aa. plat book
bb. plat map
cc. plot
dd. quitclaim deed
ee. range

Answers

____ **1.** Valued possessions with sentimental value passed down through generations within a family.

____ **2.** A place.

____ **3.** A map designating the size and shape of a specific land area (select three answers).

____ **4.** To give assurance.

____ **5.** A claim, lien, charge, or liability attached to and binding real property.

____ **6.** A square mile of land, containing 640 acres, in the United States government survey.

____ **7.** A system of describing real property by its outer boundaries, with reference to courses, distances, and monuments.

____ **8.** A deed that conveys land itself, rather than people's interests therein, and requires consideration.

____ **9.** The portion of a deed beginning with the words *To have and to hold,* which defines the extent of the ownership of the property granted.

____ **10.** A person to whom real property is transferred.

____ **11.** Visible marks indicating boundaries.

____ **12.** A row of townships running north and south in the United States government survey.

____ **13.** A promise or assurance.

____ **14.** A six-square-mile portion of land in the United States government survey.

____ **15.** Horizontal lines running east and west in the United States government survey.

____ **16.** Vertical lines running north and south in the United States government survey.

____ **17.** A deed containing warranties under which the grantor guarantees the property to be free from all encumbrances made during the time that he or she owned the property and to defend the title only against claims through him or her (select two answers).

____ **18.** A method of describing real property based on the property's relationship to intersecting lines running east and west and lines running north and south (select two answers).

____ **19.** Transferring title to real property.

____ **20.** A formal written instrument by which title to real property is transferred from one person to another.

____ **21.** A person who transfers real property to another.

____ **22.** A large piece of land.

____ **23.** A deed containing warranties under which the grantor guarantees the property to be free from all encumbrances and to defend the title against the claims of all persons (select two answers).

ff. rectangular survey system

gg. section

hh. special warranty deed

ii. tenements

jj. township

kk. tract of land

ll. warrant

____**24.** Everything of a permanent nature that may be possessed and, in a more restrictive sense, houses or dwellings.

____**25.** Directions of the boundaries that enclose a parcel of land.

____**26.** A book that is recorded at the registry of deeds containing plat maps.

____**27.** Things capable of being inherited, including not only lands and everything thereon but also heirlooms.

____**28.** A deed to real property in which the grantor transfers only his or her interest, if any, in the property and gives no warranties of title (select three answers).

____**29.** Distances between points.

____**30.** Place of the seal.

____**31.** A formal declaration before an authorized official, by a person who executes an instrument, that it is his or her free act and deed.

UNRAVELING LEGALESE

Use simple, non-legal language, with the help of the glossary, to rewrite this case quote so that it is shorter and can be understood by a layperson without losing its meaning.

> The certificate of acknowledgment furnishes formal proof of the authenticity of the execution of the instrument when presented for recording. The certificate of acknowledgment is of evidentiary character, and the taking of the acknowledgment has always been regarded in this Commonwealth as a ministerial and not as a judicial act, and the recitals contained in the certificate may be contradicted, and so may the certificate of a judge before whom is proved the execution of the deed where the grantor dies without acknowledging the instrument and where the certificate from the judge is obtained in order to have the instrument recorded.

USING LEGAL LANGUAGE

Read the following story and fill in the blank lines with legal terms taken from the list of terms at the beginning of this chapter.

Clifford purchased a parcel of real property from Diane, who was the executrix of an estate. In the ____________, which was the formal written instrument by which title was transferred, Diane was the ____________, and Clifford was the ____________. The instrument, which conveyed only the grantor's interest and contained no warranties, is called a(n) ____________ in some states, a(n) ____________ in others, and a(n) ____________ in still others. The ____________ system is used to describe the property by its outer boundaries, with reference to courses, distances, and ____________ (visible marks indicating boundaries). ____________ are the distances between points, and ____________ are the directions of the boundaries that enclose a parcel of land. Later, Clifford sold the property to Emily, who was schooled in the subject of ____________—that is, transferring title to real property—and wanted the kind of deed that ____________ (gives assurances) that title is good. Emily insisted that Clifford give her a deed containing four promises or guarantees called ____________. This type of deed is known as a(n) ____________ in some states and a(n) ____________ in others. The ____________ in this deed begins with the words "To have and to hold." The day after receiving title, Emily transferred the exact parcel—that is, the ____________—to Frank by giving him a(n) ____________, which is called a(n) ____________ in some states and warrants that the premises are free from all ____________ made by the grantor. In her state, the ____________, which conveys the land itself and requires consideration, is not used.

PUZZLING OVER WHAT YOU LEARNED

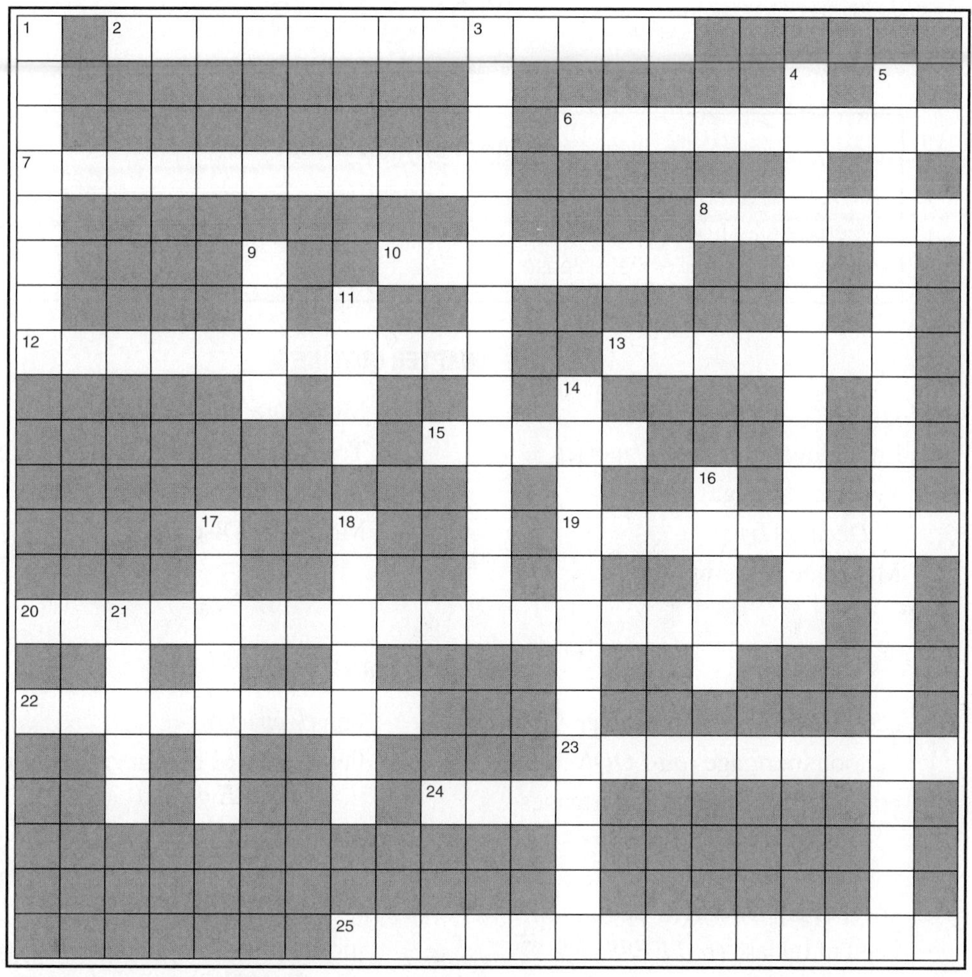

Caveat: Do **not** allow squares for spaces between words and punctuation (apostrophes, hyphens, etc.) when filling in crossword.

Across

2. Things capable of being inherited, including not only lands and everything thereon but also heirlooms.
6. Horizontal lines running east and west in the United States government survey.
7. A claim, lien, charge, or liability attached to and binding real property.
8. Directions of the boundaries that enclose a parcel of land.
10. A person who transfers real property to another.
12. A large piece of land.
13. To give assurance.
15. A place.
19. Everything of a permanent nature that may be possessed and, in a more restrictive sense, houses or dwellings.
20. A deed that conveys land itself, rather than people's interest therein, and requires consideration.
22. Visible marks indicating boundaries.
23. Lines running north and south in the United States government survey.
24. A formal written instrument by which title to real property is transferred from one person to another.
25. The portion of a deed beginning with the words *to have and to hold,* which defines the extent of the ownership of the property granted.

Down

1. A promise or assurance.
3. A system of describing real property by its outer boundaries, with reference to courses, distances, and monuments.
4. Another name for *quitclaim deed.*
5. Another name for *quitclaim deed.*
9. A map designating the size and shape of a specific land area.
11. Another name for *plot.*
14. A deed to real property in which the grantor transfers only his or her interests, if any, in the property and gives no warranties of title.
16. Distances between points.
17. Another name for *plot.*
18. A person to whom real property is transferred.
21. A row of townships running north and south in the United States government survey.

CHAPTER 33
Mortgages

7

ANTE INTERROGATORY

A clause in a mortgage or note that causes the entire balance of the loan to become due when a default occurs is a(n) (A) acceleration clause, (B) default clause, (C) redemption clause, (D) power of sale clause.

CHAPTER OUTLINE

Historical Background
Prevailing Mortgage Theories
Types of Mortgages
Deed of Trust
Mortgage Redemption
Mortgage Foreclosure
Transfer of Mortgaged Premises
Junior Mortgages
Mortgage Discharge

KEY TERMS

acceleration clause *(ak·sel·er·AH·shun)*
balloon mortgage *(ba·LOON MORE·gej)*
common law theory of mortgages *(KOM·on law THEE·ree ov MORE·ge·jes)*
court of equity *(EK·wi·tee)*
deed of release *(re·LEESS)*
deed of trust
default *(de·FAWLT)*
defeasance clause *(de·FEE·senz)*
deficiency judgment *(de·FISH·en·see JUJ·ment)*
equitable theory of mortgages *(EK·wit·a·bel THEE·ree ov MORE·ge·jes)*
equity of redemption *(EK·wi·tee ov re·DEMP·shun)*
fixed-rate mortgage *(fiksd-rate MORE·gej)*
flexible-rate mortgage *(FLEKS·i·bel-rate MORE·gej)*
foreclose *(for·KLOZE)*
graduated-payment mortgage *(GRAD·yoo·ay·ted MORE·gej)*
junior mortgage *(JOO·nyer MORE·gej)*
lien *(leen)*
lien theory of mortgages *(leen THEE·ree ov MORE·ge·jes)*
mortgage *(MORE·gej)*
mortgage assignment *(MORE·gej a·SINE·ment)*
mortgage assumption *(MORE·gej a·SUMP·shun)*
mortgage deed *(MORE·gej)*
mortgage discharge *(MORE·gej DIS·charj)*
mortgagee *(more·gej·EE)*
mortgage take-over *(MORE·gej)*
mortgagor *(more·gej·OR)*
partial release *(PAR·shell re·LEESS)*
power of sale clause *(POW·er)*
promissory note *(PROM·i·sore·ee)*
redeem *(re·DEEM)*
right of redemption *(rite ov re·DEMP·shun)*
second mortgage *(SEK·end MORE·gej)*
security *(se·KYOOR·i·tee)*
title theory of mortgages *(TY·tel THEE·ree ov MORE·ge·jes)*
variable-rate mortgage *(VAR·ee·a·bel-rate MORE·gej)*

People who buy real property usually do not have enough money to pay for the property outright. They must borrow it. Lenders, however, wish to have some **security** for their loan—that is, something they can sell to get their money back in case of default. A **mortgage,** sometimes called a **mortgage deed,** meets this need. It is a conveyance of real property for the purpose of securing a debt. The one who borrows money and gives a mortgage to the lender as security for the loan is the **mortgagor.** The one who lends money and takes back a mortgage as security for the loan is the **mortgagee.** In addition to signing a mortgage deed when the loan is made, the mortgagor signs a **promissory note,** which is a written promise by the borrower to pay a sum of money to the lender.

HISTORICAL BACKGROUND

Mort means "dead" and *gage* means "pledge." In early times, a mortgage was a "dead pledge." The mortgagor pledged the property to the mortgagee and gave up possession of the property as well as all income from it until the debt was paid. In addition, the mortgagor lost all title to the property if the debt was not paid precisely when it was due. As time went on, the **court of equity,** which is a court designed to do that which is just and fair, allowed the mortgagor additional time after a default to **redeem** (buy back) the property. Current legal theories governing mortgages follow.

PREVAILING MORTGAGE THEORIES

Two principal legal theories relating to mortgages are followed in the United States. They are the common law theory and the lien theory.

Under the **common law theory** (called the **title theory** in some states), a mortgage is a conveyance of title by the mortgagor to the mortgagee. A clause in the mortgage, known as the **defeasance clause,** provides that the mortgage deed shall be void on payment of the obligation. The mortgagor has the right to possession of the premises and the right to all rents and profits from the property. The mortgagee has no right to enter the premises unless a **default** (the failure to perform a legal duty) by the mortgagor occurs, but he or she does have the right to prevent waste through court action.

Under the **lien theory** (called the **equitable theory** in some states), a mortgage is not regarded as a conveyance of title to the mortgagee but merely a lien against the property. A **lien** is a claim or charge on the property for the payment of a debt. Under this mortgage theory, the mortgagor retains legal title to the premises.

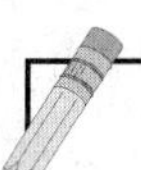

WORD WISE

The Prefix "Equi-" in Equity

The Latin prefix *equi* means "equal" and is used in many English words. Here are some examples:

Words	*Meaning*
equiangular	equal angles
equidistant	equally distant
equilateral	equal sides
equinox	equal nights
equity	equal treatment

Some states follow a modified form of the title theory of mortgages. For example, in Missouri, the mortgagee has a lien before a default of the mortgage but obtains legal title to the property after a default.

TYPES OF MORTGAGES

There are a variety of mortgages in use today. A **fixed-rate mortgage** is a mortgage with an interest rate that does not change during the life of the mortgage. A **variable-rate mortgage,** also called a **flexible-rate mortgage,** is a mortgage with an interest rate that fluctuates according to changes in an index to which it is connected. A **graduated-payment mortgage** is a mortgage under which payments increase gradually over the life of the loan. A **balloon mortgage** is a mortgage with low fixed payments during the life of the loan, ending with one large final payment.

Deed of Trust

In some states, a **deed of trust** is used instead of a mortgage. This instrument conveys title to a third party (often a title insurance company), called a **trustee,** who holds it as security for the debt. When the debt is paid, title is returned to the borrower. If the borrower defaults, however, the trustee sells the property without going to court to pay the amount of the debt to the lender.

MORTGAGE REDEMPTION

Under modern laws, the mortgagor has the **equity of redemption,** which is the right to redeem the property any time before the completion of a foreclosure proceeding by paying the amount of the debt, interest, and costs. In addition, in some states, the mortgagor has the **right of redemption,** which is a statutory right to redeem the property even after a foreclosure sale. In states that recognize this latter right, a buyer at a mortgage foreclosure sale does not receive good title to the premises until the time for the mortgagor's right

Figure 33-1 A variable-rate mortgage is a mortgage with an interest rate that fluctuates according to an index to which it is connected.

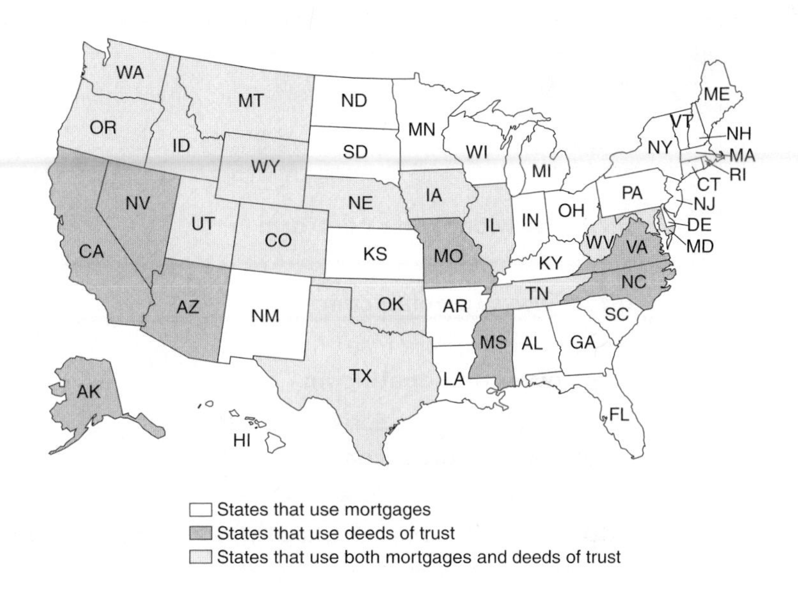

Figure 33-2 States that use mortgages, deeds of trust, and those that use both mortgages and deeds of trust.

of redemption elapses, which ranges from six months to two years after the foreclosure sale, depending on the state.

MORTGAGE FORECLOSURE

Foreclose means to "shut out," "bar," or "terminate." Thus, a foreclosure proceeding terminates the mortgagor's equity of redemption in the property. The mortgagee has a right to foreclose when the mortgagor defaults in the payment of the debt or fails to follow a condition (requirement) of the mortgage. An **acceleration clause** in the mortgage or note causes the entire balance of the loan to become due when a default occurs.

The most common method of foreclosure is by judicial sale, which is a sale at public auction under the jurisdiction of the court. Another method of foreclosure is by "power of sale" under the terms of a **power of sale clause** found in the mortgage instrument. This clause allows the mortgagee to hold the foreclosure sale alone, without involving the court. Still another method of foreclosure found in some states allows the mortgagee to enter and possess the premises for a specific period of time. This method may be used only when the entry and possession can be made peaceably.

Sometimes a foreclosure sale does not bring enough money to pay off the amount owed to the mortgagee. When this occurs, the court may issue a deficiency judgment against the mortgagor. A **deficiency judgment** is a judgment for the amount remaining due on the mortgage after a foreclosure sale.

TRANSFER OF MORTGAGED PREMISES

Usually when mortgagors sell real property, they convey it free and clear of the mortgage by paying it off out of the proceeds of the sale. Sometimes, however, a buyer will agree to buy property with the mortgage still on it—that is, "subject to the mortgage." This

WEB WISE

Mortgage information abounds on the Web. Here are a few reliable choices:

Bank Rate Monitor
http://www.bankrate.com/brm

Homefair.com
http://www.homefair.com

Homepath (from Fannie Mae)
http://www.homepath.com

Mortgage Market Information Services, Inc.
http://www.interest.com

Mortgage Payment Calculator
http://www.ffb.com/calculators/mortgage_calc.cfm

agreement means that the new buyer takes the property subject to the mortgagee's rights. Only the equity of redemption is sold. The original mortgagor must still pay the mortgagee, and the mortgagee can foreclose against the new buyer if a default of the mortgage payments by the mortgagor occurs.

Sometimes a mortgagor will sell the premises "subject to the mortgage that the grantee assumes and agrees to pay." This is commonly referred to as a **mortgage takeover** or a **mortgage assumption.** In this situation, the new buyer not only takes the property subject to the mortgagee's rights but also agrees to pay the balance of the mortgage payments to the mortgagee as they fall due. The original mortgagor is still liable on the debt, however, and becomes a surety on the loan. He or she must pay the mortgage if the new buyer, who took it over, fails to do so.

It is common for banks who are mortgagees to put "due on sale" clauses in their mortgages to the effect that if title to the property vests in someone other than the mortgagor, the mortgage is immediately due and payable. This language prevents the assumption of a mortgage by another person without the bank's permission.

Mortgagees often transfer their interests in mortgages to other parties. This transfer is done by the use of an instrument known as a **mortgage assignment.** When this occurs, the original mortgagor makes the mortgage payments to the new mortgagee to whom the mortgage has been assigned.

JUNIOR MORTGAGES

A **junior mortgage,** also called a **second** (or third) **mortgage,** is a mortgage on the equity of redemption, or a mortgage subject to a prior mortgage. Junior mortgagees may foreclose only on their mortgagors' equity of redemption, and their foreclosure is subject to the rights of the first mortgagee. If a first mortgagee forecloses, the second mortgagee's recourse is to pay the mortgagor's debt and then foreclose also. As a practical matter, however, both mortgages are foreclosed in the same proceeding; the proceeds of the sale are paid to the first mortgagee, and any balance remaining is paid to junior mortgagees.

MORTGAGE DISCHARGE

When a mortgage debt is paid, the mortgagor signs a **mortgage discharge,** which is a document stating that the mortgage debt is satisfied. The mortgage discharge is recorded at the registry of deeds. A **deed of release** (a deed releasing property from an encumbrance) is sometimes used for this purpose, especially by a trustee of a deed of trust to divest the trustee of legal title and revest title in the original owner. A **partial release** is used to show that specified parcels are released from the encumbrance.

REVIEWING WHAT YOU LEARNED

After studying the text, write the answers to each of the following questions.

1. What need does the mortgage meet? ________

2. In addition to signing a mortgage deed when a loan is made, what else does a mortgagor sign?

3. What was a mortgage in early times? ________

4. Describe the difference between the mortgagor and the mortgagee. ________

5. Who holds the legal title to the property under the common law mortgage theory? Under the lien theory? ________

6. Who has the right to possession under the common law mortgage theory? ________

7. Name four types of mortgages. ________

8. What is the difference between the equity of redemption and the right of redemption? ________

9. Name three methods of foreclosure. ________

10. If a new buyer takes the property subject to a mortgage, what can the mortgagee do if a default of the mortgage payments by the mortgagor occurs? ________

11. If a first mortgagee forecloses on the mortgage, what is the second mortgagee's recourse?

____

____

____

12. Describe the way that a deed of trust is used to provide security for a debt. _______________

____

____

____

UNDERSTANDING LEGAL CONCEPTS

Indicate whether each statement is true or false. Then, change the italicized word or phrase of each *false* statement to make it true.

Answers

_______________ 1. The mortgagor is the *lender.*

_______________ 2. In early times, a mortgage was a *dead pledge* because the property owner gave up possession of the property until the debt was paid.

_______________ 3. As time went on, the court of equity allowed the *mortgagor* additional time after a default to redeem the property.

_______________ 4. Under the *lien* theory of mortgages, a mortgage is a conveyance of title by the mortgagor to the mortgagee.

_______________ 5. Under the common law theory, the *mortgagee* has the right to possession of the premises.

_______________ 6. The right of redemption is the right to redeem the property *any time before* the completion of a foreclosure proceeding.

_______________ 7. The most common method of foreclosure is by *entry and possession* of the premises.

_______________ 8. When property is sold "subject to the mortgage," the *original mortgagor* must still pay the mortgagee.

_______________ 9. When a *mortgagee* transfers an interest in a mortgage to another, it is known as a mortgage assignment.

_______________ 10. A junior mortgagee's foreclosure is subject to the rights of the *first mortgagee.*

CHECKING TERMINOLOGY

From the list of legal terms that follows, select the one that matches each definition.

- **a.** acceleration clause
- **b.** balloon mortgage
- **c.** common law theory of mortgages
- **d.** court of equity
- **e.** deed of release
- **f.** deed of trust
- **g.** default
- **h.** defeasance clause
- **i.** deficiency judgment
- **j.** equitable theory of mortgages
- **k.** equity of redemption
- **l.** fixed-rate mortgage
- **m.** flexible-rate mortgage
- **n.** foreclose
- **o.** graduated-payment mortgage
- **p.** junior mortgage
- **q.** lien
- **r.** lien theory of mortgages
- **s.** mortgage
- **t.** mortgage assignment
- **u.** mortgage assumption
- **v.** mortgage deed
- **w.** mortgage discharge
- **x.** mortgagee
- **y.** mortgage take-over
- **z.** mortgagor
- **aa.** partial release
- **bb.** power of sale clause

Answers

____ **1.** Assurance (usually in the form of a pledge or deposit) given by a debtor to a creditor to make sure a debt is paid.

____ **2.** One who lends money and takes back a mortgage as security for the loan.

____ **3.** Buy back.

____ **4.** The right of a mortgagor to redeem the property any time before the completion of a foreclosure proceeding by paying the amount of the debt, interest, and costs.

____ **5.** A clause in a mortgage providing that the mortgage deed shall be void on payment of the obligation.

____ **6.** A claim or charge on the property for the payment of a debt.

____ **7.** A statutory right to redeem the property even after a foreclosure sale.

____ **8.** An agreement by a new owner of real property to pay the former owner's mortgage (select two answers).

____ **9.** A mortgage with an interest rate that fluctuates according to changes in an index to which it is connected (select two answers).

____ **10.** A clause in a mortgage or note that causes the entire balance of the loan to become due when a default occurs.

____ **11.** A mortgage with an interest rate that does not change during the life of the mortgage.

____ **12.** A mortgage subject to a prior mortgage (select two answers).

____ **13.** A conveyance of real property for the purpose of securing a debt (select two answers).

____ **14.** One who borrows money and gives a mortgage to the lender as security for the loan.

____ **15.** A court designed to do that which is just and fair.

____ **16.** A failure to perform a legal duty.

____ **17.** To shut out, bar, or terminate.

____ **18.** The transfer of a mortgagee's interest in a mortgage to another person.

____ **19.** A mortgage with low fixed payments during the life of the loan, ending with one large final payment.

____ **20.** A written promise by a borrower to pay a sum of money to a lender.

____ **21.** A mortgage under which payments increase gradually over the life of the loan.

____ **22.** An instrument used in some states that replaces a mortgage, by which the legal title to real property is placed in a trustee to secure the repayment of a debt.

____ **23.** A judgment for the amount remaining due on the mortgage after a foreclosure sale.

____ **24.** A deed releasing property from an encumbrance.

cc. promissory note
dd. redeem
ee. right of redemption
ff. second mortgage
gg. security
hh. title theory of mortgages
ii. variable-rate mortgage

____**25.** A document stating that a mortgage debt is satisfied.

____**26.** The legal theory that a mortgage is a conveyance of title, which becomes void on payment of the obligation (select two answers).

____**27.** The legal theory that a mortgage is not a conveyance of title but merely a lien against the property (select two answers).

____**28.** A clause in a mortgage allowing the mortgagee to hold a foreclosure sale without involving the court when a default in payment of the mortgage occurs.

____**29.** A document stating that specified parcels of property are released from an encumbrance.

UNRAVELING LEGALESE

Use simple, non-legal language, with the help of the glossary, to rewrite this case quote so that it is shorter and can be understood by a layperson without losing its meaning.

> A mortgage of real estate is, as between the parties a conveyance in fee, defeasible upon the performance of the conditions therein stated. The payment of the mortgage notes at or before maturity, or the due performance of any other condition that is expressed in the mortgage, terminates the interests of the mortgagee without any formal release or discharge and revests the legal title to the mortgagor. Upon the fulfillment of the conditions of the mortgage, the mortgagor is entitled to the note and a discharge of the mortgage in order to remove a cloud upon the record title to his [or her] premises.

USING LEGAL LANGUAGE

Read the following story and fill in the blank lines with legal terms taken from the list of terms at the beginning of this chapter.

When Steve and Linda bought their house, they gave a(n) ______________________ —that is, a conveyance of real property for the purpose of securing a debt—to the bank as ______________________ for the loan. They were called the ______________________; the bank was the ______________________. The instrument contained a(n) ______________________ providing that the mortgage deed would be void on payment of the obligation. It also contained a(n) ______________________, which allows the mortgagee to hold a foreclosure sale without involving the court when a default in payment of the mortgage occurs. Steve and Linda hold the ______________________, which is the right to ______________________ (buy back) the property any time before the completion of a foreclosure proceeding. The state where they live does not recognize the ______________________, which is the right to redeem the property even after a foreclosure sale. Similarly, their state does not use the ______________________ in place of a mortgage, which involves conveying title to a third party to hold as security for the debt. Steve and Linda gave a(n) ______________________, also known as a(n) ______________________, which is a mortgage subject to a prior mortgage, to Elliott, who sold them their house. Soon thereafter, Elliott made a(n) ______________________—that is, a transfer of his mortgage interest—to an out-of-town lending institution. The instrument represented a(n) ______________________, which is a claim or charge on the property for the payment of a debt. Possibly, when Steve and Linda sell their house, a(n) ______________________ or a(n) ______________________ will occur, wherein the new owner agrees to pay their existing mortgage. They were very careful not to ______________________—that is, fail to perform their legal duty—on either of their obligations, because they did not want anyone to ______________________ (shut out, bar, or terminate) their equity of redemption.

7

PUZZLING OVER WHAT YOU LEARNED

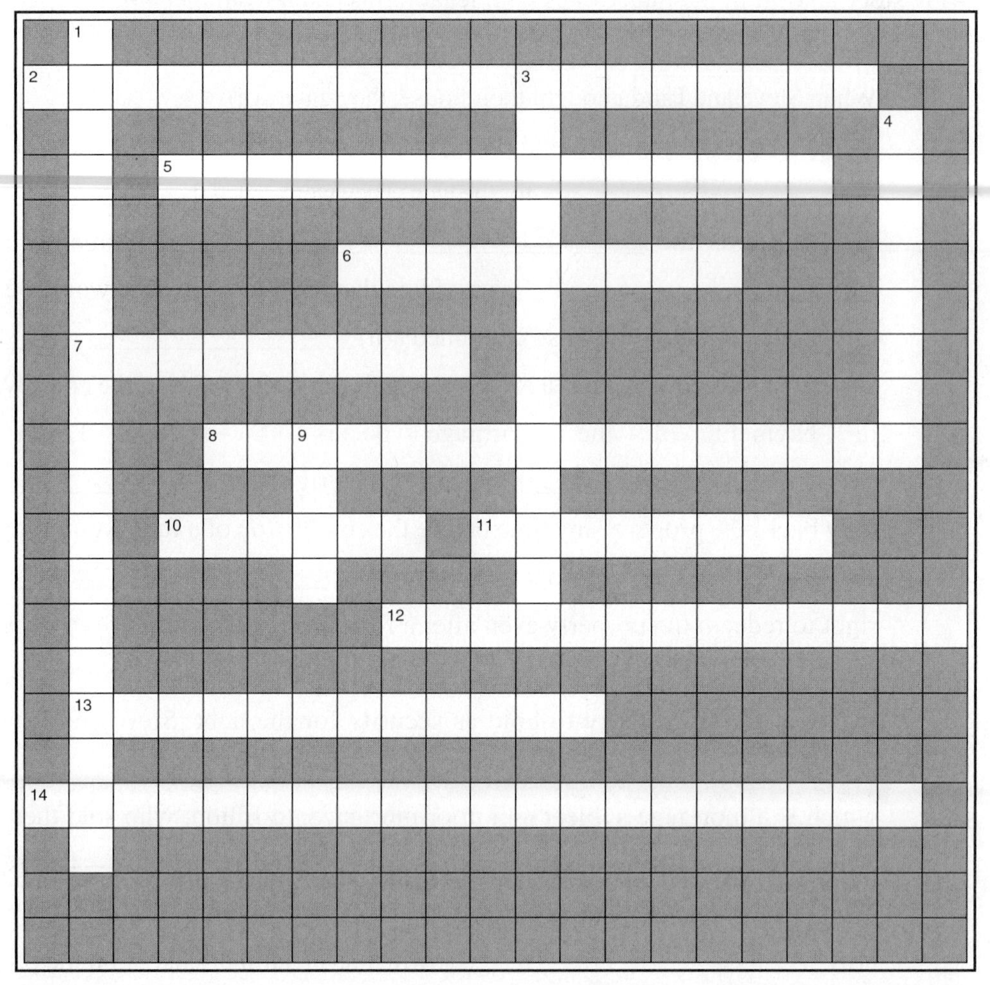

Caveat: Allow squares for spaces between words and punctuation (apostrophes, hyphens, etc.) when filling in crossword.

Across

2. A mortgage with an interest rate that does not change.
5. A written promise by a borrower to pay a sum of money to a lender.
6. One who lends money and takes back a mortgage as security for the loan.
7. To shut out, bar, or terminate.
8. Mortgage with low fixed payments during its life, ending with one large payment.
10. Buy back.
11. Assurance, usually in pledge form, given to make sure a debt is paid.
12. Instrument by which legal title to real property is placed in trust as security.
13. Legal theory that a mortgage is a conveyance of title.
14. Clause in a mortgage allowing the mortgagee to hold a foreclosure sale.

Down

1. Statutory right to redeem property even after a foreclosure sale.
3. A conveyance of real property for the purpose of securing a debt.
4. Another name for a mortgage deed.
9. A claim or charge on the property for the payment of a debt.

CHAPTER 34
Recording System

ANTE INTERROGATORY

When an owner inherits real property, (A) a deed to that owner will be on record, (B) a notation to that effect will be found in the grantor index, (C) a notation to that effect will be found in the grantee index, (D) no deed to the owner will be on record.

7

CHAPTER OUTLINE

Purpose of Title Search
Records that Are Examined
   Record Books
   Grantor and Grantee Indexes
Title Search Procedure
   Starting Point
   Outlining Chain of Title
   Rundown
   Abstract or Copy of Each Instrument
   Report
Torrens System
Real Estate Closing

KEY TERMS

abstract *(AB·strakt)*
abstract of title *(AB·strakt ov TY·tel)*
actual notice *(AK·shoo·el NO·tiss)*
chain of title *(TY·tel)*
clear title *(TY·tel)*
condemnation *(kon·dem·NAY·shun)*
constructive notice *(kon·STRUK·tiv NO·tiss)*
eminent domain *(EM·i·nent doh·MAYN)*
escrow *(ES·krow)*
et al. *(et ahl)*
et ux. *(et uks)*
folio *(FO·lee·oh)*
grantee index *(gran·TEE IN·deks)*
grantor index *(gran·TOR IN·deks)*
homestead rights *(HOME·sted rites)*
lis pendens *(lis PEN·denz)*
real estate closing *(reel es·TATE KLOS·ing)*
real estate settlement *(reel es·TATE SET·el·ment)*
record owner *(REK·erd)*
registered land *(REJ·is·terd)*
report *(re·PORT)*
rundown
title reference *(TY·tel REF·e·renss)*
title search *(TY·tel)*
Torrens system *(TOR·enz SYS·tem)*
volume *(VOL·yoom)*

From early colonial times, a system has been used in this country to record in a public place instruments (such as deeds, mortgages, and attachments) that affect title to real property. The records are kept in the registry of deeds in the county where the land is located. Anyone may go to the registry of deeds and examine the documents that are recorded there.

Whenever an instrument is recorded at a registry of deeds, it is considered to be notice to the public of the existence of that instrument. Anyone searching the title and finding the instrument will have **actual notice**—that is, notice actually received—of the existence of the instrument. Everyone else in the world is said to have **constructive notice** of its existence, which is notice imputed by law. Constructive notice has the same legal effect as actual notice.

When an instrument is recorded, it is delivered to the office of the registry of deeds, where it is indexed and copied. The date and time of its reception are written down to establish its priority over later-recorded instruments. With exceptions in some states, an earlier-recorded instrument takes priority over a later-recorded instrument unless the person recording first has actual notice of an earlier instrument that was not recorded. For example, if A conveys land to B (and B does not record the deed) and sometime later A conveys the same land to C (and C records the deed), C will take title to the land unless he or she had actual notice of the conveyance to B.

PURPOSE OF A TITLE SEARCH

A **title search** is an examination of all recorded instruments that affect the title to a particular parcel of property (the locus) for the past 50 or more years. The purpose of a title search is twofold:

1. To determine who is the **record owner** of the property—that is, the owner according to the records filed at the registry of deeds
2. To determine if **clear title** exists—that is, title free from any outstanding mortgages, liens, or other encumbrances of record

RECORDS THAT ARE EXAMINED

The following records are examined in the course of a title search:

- Record books
- Grantor index
- Grantee index
- Attachment index
- Bankruptcy index
- Federal and state tax lien index
- Plan books
- Atlases
- Probate records when property owners have died

Record Books

Whenever an instrument is recorded at the registry of deeds, it is photocopied, assigned volume and page numbers, and placed in a permanent volume called a **record book.** Record books contain all instruments and documents, in chronological order, that are recorded at the registry of deeds. People can find a particular instrument or document quickly if they know the book (or **volume**) number and the page (or **folio**) number where the instrument is recorded.

Grantor and Grantee Indexes

The grantor and grantee indexes are used to find the instruments that are recorded in the record books. The **grantor index** lists by year, in alphabetic order, the name of anyone who is named in an instrument as conveying away an interest in real property, either voluntarily or involuntarily. It lists, for example, the names of grantors, mortgagors, people whose property has been attached or on whose property liens have been placed, and people who sign agreements that are recorded. It also lists people whose land has been taken through **condemnation,** which is the process of taking private property for public use through the power of eminent domain. **Eminent domain** is the power of the government to take property for a public use. The index lists the date the instrument was recorded, the name of the grantee, the book and page numbers where the instrument may be found, and a short description of the instrument.

The **grantee index** lists by year, in alphabetic order, the name of anyone to whom an interest in real property is granted, such as the grantee of a deed and the mortgagee of a mortgage. When a mortgage is discharged, it is listed in the grantee index under the mortgagee's name. This index also lists the date that the instrument was recorded, the name of the grantor, the book and page numbers where the instrument may be found, and a short description of the instrument.

TITLE SEARCH PROCEDURE

The following steps are taken in the course of completing a title search:

1. Finding a starting point
2. Outlining a chain of title
3. Running down the grantor index
4. Copying or abstracting each instrument found in the grantor index
5. Completing a report

Starting Point

The customary starting point for a title search is 50 years back to a point when a deed was recorded. This guideline is general, however, and cannot be followed in all cases. In many instances, it is necessary to begin at a point further back in time.

The first step in tracing back to the starting point is to look at the deed held by the current owner of the property. This deed should contain a title reference just below the property description. A **title reference** is a sentence indicating from whom the grantor in that deed received the property. A typical title reference reads as follows: "Being the same premises conveyed to me by deed of John Doe, et ux., dated August 7, 1977, and recorded with Essex South District Registry of Deeds in book 6543, page 219." The term **et ux.** means "and wife." The term **et al.** means "and another" or "and others."

The next step is to look up the deed that was given in the title reference, copy it, and see if that deed also has a title reference. If it has, you can look at that deed for another title reference. If every deed in the chain of title has a title reference you will soon find your way back 50 years to a starting point by referring to the title reference in each deed.

If you do not have the current owner's deed or if any of the deeds in the chain of title do not contain a title reference, you must look in the grantee index under the last owner's name during every year that the owner might possibly have obtained the property. If he or she received the property by deed, it will be listed in the grantee index.

WORD WISE

Abbreviations

Abbreviation	*Abbreviation for*
aff'd	affirmed
a.k.a.	also known as
arg.	arguendo (in the course of the argument)
ct.	court
d.b.a.	doing business as
e.g.	exempli gratia (for the purpose of example; for instance)
et al.	et alius (and another)
et als.	et alii (and others)
etc.	et cetera (and others; and the rest)
et.seq.	et sequentes and et sequentia (and the following)
et ux.	et uxor (and wife)
ev., evid.	evidence
i.e.	id est (that is)
ltd.	limited
n.k.a.	now known as
non pros.	non prosequitur (plaintiff does not follow up or proceed)
rem'g	remanding
viz.	videlicet (to wit; that is to say)

If an owner inherited the property, no deed will be on record. Individually owned real property passes automatically, without a deed, to the heirs or devisees of a deceased person, but the decedent's estate must be probated. A typically worded title reference in such a situation reads as follows: "For title see Estate of John Doe, Essex Probate No. 123456."

If no title reference is found in a deed and nothing can be found under the last owner's name in the grantee index, it is a clue that the property was inherited. It is then necessary to find the name of the decedent. The probate court indexes may be used for that purpose. Once a decedent's name is located, the inventory of his or her estate must be checked to verify that that particular property is included in the assets of the estate. The petition for administration of the estate or for probate of the will (and the will itself) must also be checked to determine who inherited the property.

Outlining Chain of Title

An outline of the chain of title is invaluable when doing a title search because it helps to clear up confusion that often occurs when working with many different deeds and recorded instruments. An outline is prepared as follows:

As you work your way back 50 years, make a copy of each deed that you find in the chain of title. Arrange the copies in chronological order with the oldest deed on top and the most recent deed on the bottom. Next, set up a sheet of paper with the following column heads: Date, Grantor, and Grantee. Using the column heads, list by number each deed on a separate line chronologically (from old to new), writing its date, name of grantor, and name of grantee. The result will be an outline of the **chain of title** (series of successive conveyances), excluding probates, of the property you are searching.

If every owner's title was received by deed, every grantee on the list will be the next grantor on the list, such as A to B, B to C, C to D, etc. A break in the chain usually indicates that an owner died and that the property passed by way of probate rather than by deed. A notation to this effect, listing the date of death, probate docket number, and names of heirs should be listed chronologically on the outline.

Refer to the outline when you get confused or lose track of things as you complete the title search.

Rundown

The most important part of the title search is the rundown of the grantor index. The **rundown** is accomplished by examining the grantor index under the name of each owner in the **chain of title** during the years that he or she owned the property. Title examiners use a specially lined rundown sheet (one for each owner in the chain of title) to assist them in doing the rundown. The lines on the rundown sheet correspond with those in the grantor index. Every item found in the grantor index pertaining to that locus is listed on the rundown sheet for that owner.

This part of the title examination requires extreme care and accuracy. If it is done correctly, every item that was ever granted out by every owner and every attachment or lien that was ever recorded from 50 years ago to the day you are at the registry of deeds will be discovered.

Abstract of Each Instrument

The next step, after the rundown is completed, is to abstract or copy most of the instruments that were found in the rundown. To **abstract** means to copy in abbreviated form the meaningful parts of an instrument. Title examiners use special forms for this purpose. In recent years, to save time, entire instruments are copied on copying machines instead of being abstracted. The complete set of abstracts and copies (one for each instrument found in the rundown) is sometimes referred to as an **abstract of title,** which is a condensed history of the title to that particular locus.

Report

Finally, a report is prepared that summarizes the status of the title. The **report** identifies the locus, names the present owner, gives the dates between which the title was searched, and states whether or not the title is subject to any of the following encumbrances:

attachments and executions
bankruptcy
debts
dower or curtesy
easements (either subject to or with the benefit of)
estate taxes
homestead rights (personal rights to the use of the home property free from claims of creditors)
legacies
liens
lis pendens (a pending suit)
miscellaneous defects
municipal liens
outstanding mortgages
restrictions
tax sales

TORRENS SYSTEM

The **Torrens system** is a method of land registration that establishes clear title to land. Property that is registered in this way is called **registered land.** It was first adopted in Australia and is used in England and many states in this country.

To register land under the Torrens system, a petition for registration is filed with the land court together with a deed and a plan of the land. The court will have the title searched, and notice of the petition will be published in the newspaper. In addition, notice of the petition will be posted on the land, and notice will be sent to all interested parties. If anyone raises an objection to the land being registered, a hearing will be held to settle the issues that are raised. If the court finds that the petitioner has proper title for registration, a decree will be issued registering the land and confirming that title is absolutely clear except for anything noted on the certificate. From that point on, each owner of the property will receive a certificate of title rather than a deed to the property. Any encumbrances are noted on the certificate.

REAL ESTATE CLOSING

When title to real property is transferred from a seller to a buyer, it is known as a **real estate closing** or **settlement.** The seller delivers the deed to the buyer and receives payment for the property. If a mortgage is involved, the mortgagee's attorney usually supervises the transaction to be sure that the title is clear when the deed and mortgage are recorded. In some states, instead of attending a formal closing, the parties go into **escrow.** This arrangement is for completing a real estate transaction by placing the papers and money on a conditional basis with an escrow agent until title is clear and all instruments are recorded.

REVIEWING WHAT YOU LEARNED

After studying the text, write the answers to each of the following questions:

1. Where are records that affect title to real property kept? ______________________________

____

____

____

2. Who may examine documents that are recorded at the registry of deeds? ______________________________

____

____

____

____

____

3. In general, when will an earlier-recorded instrument not take priority over a later-recorded instrument? ______________________________

____

____

____

4. Describe the twofold purpose of a title search.

____

____

____

____

____

5. List eight records that may be examined in the course of a title search. ______

6. What do record books contain? ______

7. What is the difference between the grantor index and the grantee index? ______

8. What is the customary starting point for a title search? ______

9. Describe briefly how a title examiner works his or her way back to the starting point. ______

10. What index is used to work back to a starting point if a deed does not contain a title reference?

11. Describe how title passes when someone inherits real property. ______

12. When someone inherits property and the decedent's name is known, what must be checked at the probate court to verify title? ______

13. What is the most important part of the title search, and how is it accomplished? ______

14. Describe the special rundown sheet that is used by title examiners and explain what is listed on it.

15. What will be discovered if a rundown is done correctly? ______

16. What is meant by abstracting each instrument?

17. Explain briefly the title examiner's report.

18. Explain the purpose of the Torrens systems.

UNDERSTANDING LEGAL CONCEPTS

Indicate whether each statement is true or false. Then, change the italicized word or phrase of each *false* statement to make it true.

Answers

_______________ **1.** *Only county employees* may examine the papers that are recorded at the registry of deeds.

_______________ **2.** Whenever an instrument is recorded at a registry of deeds, it is considered to be notice to *the public* of the existence of that instrument.

_______________ **3.** Constructive notice has the same legal effect as *actual notice.*

_______________ **4.** With exceptions in some states, an earlier-recorded instrument takes priority over a later-recorded instrument unless the person recording it has *constructive* notice of an earlier instrument that was not recorded.

_______________ **5.** The purpose of a title search is to determine who is the *record owner* of the property and to determine if the title is clear.

_______________ **6.** The *grantor* index lists by year, in alphabetic order, the name of anyone to whom an interest in real property is granted.

_______________ **7.** The customary starting point for a title search is *100 years* back to a point when a warranty deed was recorded.

_______________ **8.** If an owner inherited the property, a deed to the person who inherited it *will not be* on record.

_______________ **9.** The *least* important part of the title search is the rundown of the grantor index.

_______________ **10.** The Torrens system is a system of land registration that establishes *clear title* to land.

CHECKING TERMINOLOGY

From the list of legal terms that follows, select the one that matches each definition.

a. abstract
b. abstract of title
c. actual notice
d. chain of title
e. clear title
f. condemnation
g. constructive notice
h. eminent domain
i. escrow
j. et al.
k. et ux.
l. folio
m. grantee index
n. grantor index

Answers

____ **1.** Notice actually received.

____ **2.** Notice imputed by law.

____ **3.** An examination of all recorded instruments that affect the title to a particular parcel of property for the past 50 or more years.

____ **4.** The owner of real property according to the records filed at the registry of deeds.

____ **5.** Title that is free from any outstanding mortgages, liens, or other encumbrances of record.

____ **6.** An index that lists by year, in alphabetic order, the name of anyone who is named in an instrument as conveying away an interest in real property.

____ **7.** The power of the government to take property for a public purpose.

____ **8.** An index that lists by year, in alphabetic order, the name of anyone to whom an interest in real property is granted.

____ **9.** A sentence in a deed indicating from whom the grantor in that deed received the property.

o. homestead rights
p. lis pendens
q. real estate closing
r. real estate settlement
s. record owner
t. registered land
u. report
v. rundown
w. title reference
x. title search
y. Torrens system
z. volume

____**10.** And wife.

____**11.** An examination of the grantor index under the name of each owner in the chain of title during the years that he or she owned the property.

____**12.** "And another" or "and others".

____**13.** To copy in abbreviated form the meaningful parts of an instrument.

____**14.** Book.

____**15.** A condensed history of the title to a particular locus.

____**16.** A statement that identifies the locus, names the present owner, gives the dates between which the title was searched, and lists all liens or encumbrances to which the property is subject.

____**17.** A method of land registration that establishes clear title to land.

____**18.** Page.

____**19.** The procedure in which title to real property is transferred from a seller to a buyer (select two answers).

____**20.** An arrangement for completing a real estate transaction by placing the papers and money on a conditional basis with an agent until title is clear and all instruments are recorded.

____**21.** A pending suit.

____**22.** Personal rights to the use of the home property free from claims of creditors.

____**23.** The process of taking private property for public use through the power of eminent domain.

____**24.** A series of successive conveyances of real property.

____**25.** Land that is recorded under the Torrens system of land registration.

UNRAVELING LEGALESE

Use simple, non-legal language, with the help of the glossary, to rewrite this case quote so that it is shorter and can be understood by a layperson without losing its meaning.

> A deed duly signed, sealed, and delivered is sufficient as between the original parties to it, to transfer the whole title of the grantor to the grantee, though the instrument of conveyance may not have been acknowledged or recorded. The title passes by the deed, and not by the registration. No seisin remains in the grantor, and he [or she] has literally nothing in the premises which he [or she] can claim for himself, transmit to his [or her] heirs at law, or convey to any other person. But when the effect of the deed upon the rights of third persons, such as creditors or bona fide purchasers, is to be considered, the law requires something more, namely, either actual notice, or the further formality of registration, which is constructive notice. It may not be very logical to any that, after a man [or woman] has literally parted with all his [or her] right and estate in a lot of land, there still remains in his [or her] hands an attachable and transferable interest in it, of exactly the same extent and value as if he [or she] had made no conveyance whatever. But, for the protection of bona fide creditors and purchasers, the rule has been established that although an unrecorded deed is binding upon the grantor, his [or] heirs and devisees, and also upon all persons having actual notice of it, it is not valid and effectual as against any other persons. As to all such other persons, the unrecorded deed is a mere nullity. So far as they are concerned, it is no conveyance or transfer which the statute recognizes, or binding on them, or as having any capacity adversely to affect their rights as purchasers or attaching creditors. As to them, the person who appears of record to be the owner is to be taken as the true and actual owner, and his [or] apparent seisin is not divested or affected by any unknown and unrecorded deed that he [or she] may have made.

USING LEGAL LANGUAGE

Read the following story and fill in the blank lines with legal terms taken from the list of terms at the beginning of this chapter:

Before buying a parcel of real property, Monica decided to complete a(n) ______________________, which is an examination of all recorded instruments that affect the title to the property. She wanted to determine if the person she was buying the property from was the ______________________—that is; the owner according to the records filed at the Registry of Deeds—and if the title was ______________________, meaning free from all encumbrances. The property was not registered under the ______________________, which is a system establishing clear title to land. To find the present owner's deed, she looked under that person's name in the ______________________, which lists the name of anyone to whom an interest in real property is granted. After locating that deed, Monica looked at the ______________________, which is a sentence indicating from whom the present owner received the property. This information allowed her to work her way back to a starting point. She then completed the ______________________ by examining the ______________________ under the name of each owner in the chain of title during the years that that person owned the property. Next, she ______________________ —that is, copied in abbreviated form—each instrument, including the ______________________ (book) and ______________________ (page) of the instrument. She knew that the words ______________________ mean "and another" and that ______________________ means "and wife." Monica had ______________________ of all the instruments she looked at, whereas everyone else in the world who did not actually see them had ______________________ of their existence. None of the property involved was taken by ______________________ for public purposes by the government through the process of ______________________. After completing the ______________________, which is a condensed history of the title, Monica made out a(n) ______________________, which listed, among other items, all encumbrances that she found to be on the property.

7

PUZZLING OVER WHAT YOU LEARNED

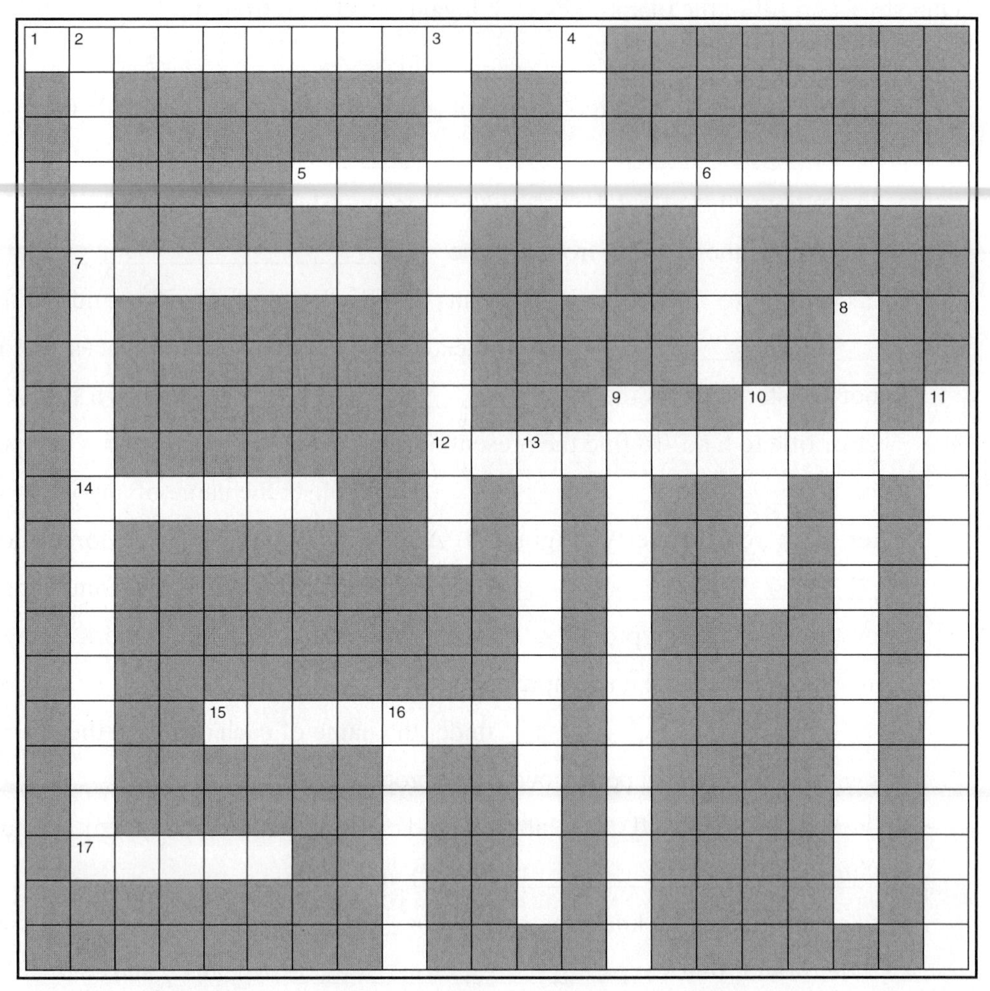

Caveat: Allow squares for spaces between words and punctuation (apostrophes, hyphens, etc.) when filling in crossword.

Across

1. Notice actually received.
5. Sentence in a deed indicating from whom the grantor received the property.
7. Examination of the grantor index under the name of each owner during years owned.
12. Owner of real property according to the records filed at the registry.
14. Book.
15. To copy in abbreviated form the meaningful parts of an instrument.
17. And another.

Down

2. Notice imputed by law.
3. Examination of all recorded instruments affecting title to a parcel.
4. Placing papers and money on a conditional basis with an agent.
6. And wife.
8. The taking of land by the government for a public purpose.
9. Index listing by year, in alphabetic order, of anyone conveying away property.
10. Page.
11. Index listing by year, in alphabetic order, of anyone to whom real property is granted.
13. Title that is free from outstanding liens or other encumbrances.
16. Statement that lists all liens or encumbrances to which property is subject.

CHAPTER 35

Airspace and Water Rights

ANTE INTERROGATORY

A landowner's right to have land supported by the soil beneath is known as the right of (A) lateral support, (B) littoral support, (C) subjacent support, (D) subterranean support.

CHAPTER OUTLINE

7

KEY TERMS

abutters *(a·BUT·ers)*
air rights
emblements *(EM·ble·ments)*
fructus industriales *(FRUK·tes in·dus·tree·AL·es)*
fructus naturales *(FRUK·tes nach·er·AL·es)*
great pond
lateral support *(LAT·e·rel su·PORT)*
littoral owners *(LIT·o·rel OH·ners)*
navigable airspace *(NAV·i·ga·bel AIR·spays)*
navigable stream *(NAV·i·ga·bel)*
percolating waters *(PER·ko·late·ing)*
prior appropriation doctrine *(PRY·er a·pro·pree·AY·shun DOK·trin)*
riparian owners *(ry·PARE·ee·en OH·ners)*
riparian rights doctrine *(ry·PARE·ee·en rites DOK·trin)*
small pond
subjacent support *(sub·JAY·sent)*
subterranean waters *(sub·ter·AYN·ee·en)*

At common law, ownership of real property extended from the center of the earth to the "periphery of the universe." A landowner owned not only a portion of the earth's crust but also the ground under it and the airspace over it. This law still exists today, with limitations, however.

AIRSPACE

People who own real property today also own the airspace above the surface of their property. The rights to the area above the earth's surface are called **air rights.** However, people no longer own to the "periphery of the universe" or to "the heavens," as some common law cases held. The U.S. Congress has enacted legislation that gives the public the right of freedom of transit through the navigable airspace of the United States. The **navigable airspace** is generally above 1,000 feet over populated areas and above 500 feet over water and unpopulated areas. In airport cases, the courts have tried to strike a balance between the landowner's right to exclusive possession, free from intrusion, and the public's interest in air travel. Some courts have held that landowners own the airspace to the height of their effective possession—that is, as high as they can effectively use the airspace over their property.

Projecting eaves of a building, leaning walls, wire strung over another's land 20 or 30 feet above the surface, an arm thrust into the space over a neighbor's land, a horse kicking into another's airspace, the projection of a board or other structure over another's ground, and shots fired over another's land have all been held by the court to be acts of trespass.

Trees

Trees and other perennial growth that returns each year without replanting, called **fructus naturales,** are considered to be part of the real property. *Fructus* is Latin for "fruit." A tree belongs to the person on whose land the trunk is located. **Abutters** (people who own adjoining land) have the right to cut off trespassing branches in their airspace and trespassing roots at the boundary line of their property. In the latter situation, however, they must support their neighbors' land if they excavate at the boundary line. A landowner's right to have land supported by the adjoining land is known as the right of **lateral support.** The right to have land supported by the soil beneath is known as the right of **subjacent support.** A tree that is exactly on the boundary line belongs to the abutters jointly, and neither can remove or injure it without consent of the other.

WORD WISE

Below and Above

Prefix	*Meaning*	*Examples*
sub-	under, below	subjacent
		subterranean
suc- (before *c*)	" "	succumb
suf- (before *f*)	" "	suffocate
sup- (before *p*)	" "	support
sus- (before *c, p, t*)	" "	suspect
super-	above, beyond	supervise
sur-	" "	surface

Crops produced annually by labor and industry rather than by nature are called **fructus industriales** or **emblements** and are treated as personal property rather than real property. Tenants who rent property may take their own emblements with them at the termination of their lease. Similarly, when real property is sold, emblements may be retained by the seller unless the parties agree otherwise. Emblements pass as personal property to the executor or administrator of a decedent's estate rather than vesting in the heirs as in the case of real property.

Figure 35-1 A tree belongs to the person on whose land the trunk is located. Abutters have the right to cut off trespassing branches in their airspace.

WATER RIGHTS

People who own land have certain rights and duties with respect to the water that flows over, under, and beside their land.

Rivers and Streams

The **riparian rights doctrine,** which is followed in many states, gives all riparian owners equal rights to the reasonable use of the water that flows past their borders. **Riparian owners** are people who own land along the banks of a river or stream. The **prior appropriation doctrine,** followed in some western states where water is scarce, allows the first person who puts water to beneficial use the right to do so even though the flow of water is cut off to other riparian owners.

Early mill acts in some eastern states allowed water to be dammed up even though it flooded upper riparian owners and disturbed the supply of water to lower riparians.

Modern statutes regulate the construction of dams, however, and both federal and state laws regulate water pollution.

When a stream is the boundary line between two parcels of land, each abutter owns to the center of the stream if it is nonnavigable. If the stream is navigable, however, each abutter owns only to the bank of the stream, the stream and bed being owned by the state. A **navigable stream** in some states is defined as one that ebbs and flows with the tide; in others, it is defined as a stream that is capable of being navigated by commercial vessels.

Surface Water

Rainwater on the surface of the earth may not be artificially channeled by a property owner in such a way that it damages the property of an abutter. Unless drainage easements are obtained to drain the water onto another's land, such water must be left to its natural watercourse, which is allowed even if it damages an abutter's property.

Subterranean and Percolating Waters

Waters that lie wholly beneath the surface of the ground are called **subterranean waters.** Waters that pass through the ground beneath the surface of the earth without any definite channel are known as **percolating waters.** These latter may be either rainwater that is slowly infiltrating through the soil or water seeping through the banks or the bed of a stream.

At common law, property owners had an absolute right to all the water that was under their land. Modern laws, however, designed to protect a larger segment of society, give property owners the right to use only that amount of water under their land that is reasonably necessary to satisfy their needs. Nearby property owners who are injured by the unreasonable and excessive use of underground waters by other property owners are given legal protection.

Ponds

In New England states, a **small pond** (under 10 acres) is owned by the person who owns the ground underneath. A **great pond** (10 acres or more) is owned by the state, with private ownership extending to the lower water mark.

Land Abutting the Ocean

People whose property abuts the ocean or a large lake are called **littoral owners.** The law varies from state to state concerning the ownership of land that abuts the ocean. In Maine and Massachusetts, ownership of real property abutting the ocean extends to the low water mark but not more than 100 rods from the high water mark. Such ownership in the land between high and low tide, however, is subject to the right of the public to navigate and fish. This law was enacted by the early colonial government to encourage colonists to build their homes near the ocean.

The United Nations Convention on the Law of the Seas, adopted in 1982, governs the ownership of international waters. Under this law, countries abutting international waters own, with exceptions, as far out as 12 nautical miles at low tide.

Figure 35-2 John Bull, the British equivalent of Uncle Sam, is shown in this July 1916 cartoon. How far out into the ocean do individual countries own before reaching international waters? (Courtesy of the Library of Congress, Prints and Photographs Division, reproduction number LC-USZ62-85731.)

REVIEWING WHAT YOU LEARNED

After studying the text, write the answers to each of the following questions:

1. What was the extent of ownership of real property at common law? ______________________

2. Who has the right to use the navigable airspace in the United States? ______________________

3. In airport cases, what rights do the courts try to balance? ______________________

4. Give two examples of a trespass into another's airspace. ______________________

5. Who owns a tree that is on the edge of a lot? What right does the adjoining lot owner have as to that tree? ______________________

6. What is the difference between fructus naturales and fructus industriales? ______________________

7. Describe the prior appropriation doctrine. Where is this doctrine followed? ______________________

8. When a stream is the boundary line between two parcels of land, where is the dividing line if the stream is nonnavigable? If the stream is navigable? ______________________

9. Under modern laws, what are the rights of property owners to the use of water that lies under their land? ______________________

10. What is the difference between a small pond and a great pond? ______________________

UNDERSTANDING LEGAL CONCEPTS

Indicate whether each statement is true or false. Then, change the italicized word or phrase of each *false* statement to make it true.

Answers

______ 1. People who own real property today *do not own* the airspace above their property.

______ 2. A tree that is exactly on the boundary line belongs to the abutters jointly, and *neither* can remove or injure it without consent of the other.

______ 3. Abutters who excavate at their boundary line have *no duty* to provide support to their neighbor's land to prevent it from caving in.

______ 4. Crops that are produced annually by labor and industry are considered to be *real property.*

______ 5. The *riparian rights* doctrine allows the first person who puts water to beneficial use the right to do so even though the flow of water is cut off to other riparian owners.

______ 6. When a stream is the boundary line between two parcels of land, each abutter owns to the *center of the stream* if it is non-navigable.

______ 7. Rainwater on the surface of the earth *may not be* artificially channeled by a property owner in such a way that it damages the property of an abutter.

______ 8. *Percolating waters* may be either rainwater or water seeping through the banks of a stream.

______ 9. Modern laws give property owners the right to use only that amount of water under their land that is *reasonably necessary* to satisfy their needs.

______ 10. A *small pond* is owned by the state, with private ownership extending to the lower water mark.

CHECKING TERMINOLOGY

From the list of legal terms that follows, select the one that matches each definition:

- **a.** abutter
- **b.** air rights
- **c.** emblements
- **d.** fructus industriales
- **e.** fructus naturales
- **f.** great pond
- **g.** lateral support
- **h.** littoral owners
- **i.** navigable airspace
- **j.** navigable stream
- **k.** percolating waters
- **l.** prior appropriation doctrine
- **m.** riparian owners
- **n.** riparian rights doctrine
- **o.** small pond
- **p.** subjacent support
- **q.** subterranean waters

Answers

____ **1.** Trees and other natural growth.

____ **2.** A person who owns adjoining land.

____ **3.** Crops produced annually by labor and industry (select two answers).

____ **4.** The space above 1,000 feet over populated areas and above 500 feet over water and unpopulated areas.

____ **5.** To hold up at the side.

____ **6.** Waters that pass through the ground beneath the surface of the earth without any definite channel.

____ **7.** A principle of law giving all riparian owners equal rights to the reasonable use of the water that flows past their borders.

____ **8.** People who own land along the banks of a river or stream.

____ **9.** A principle of law allowing the first person who puts water to beneficial use the right to do so even though the flow of water is cut off to other riparian owners.

____ **10.** A pond that is under 10 acres in size.

____ **11.** A pond that is 10 acres or more in size.

____ **12.** A stream that ebbs and flows with the tide or is capable of being navigated by commercial vessels.

____ **13.** Rights to the area above the earth's surface.

____ **14.** To hold up from below.

____ **15.** Waters that lie wholly beneath the surface of the earth.

____ **16.** People whose property abuts the ocean or a large lake.

UNRAVELING LEGALESE

Use simple, non-legal language, with the help of the glossary, to rewrite this case quote so that it is shorter and can be understood by a layperson without losing its meaning.

> In the first place, it seems very clearly settled that, upon all rivers not navigable, (and all rivers are to be deemed not navigable above where the sea ebbs and flows), the owner of land adjoining the river, is prima facie owner of the soil to the central line, or thread of the river, subject to an easement for the public to pass along and over it with boats, rafts, and river craft. This presumption will prevail, in all cases, in favor of the riparian proprietor, unless controlled by some express words of description which exclude the bed of the river, and bound the grantee on the bank or margin of the river.

7

USING LEGAL LANGUAGE

Read the following story and fill in the blank lines with legal terms taken from the list of terms at the beginning of this chapter.

Nathan and Martha's property adjoined a river on one side and a 12-acre pond, called a(n) ______________________ rather than a(n) ______________________, on the other. ______________________ slowly infiltrated through the soil from the bottom of the pond and settled below the surface, becoming known as ______________________. Because the river was a(n) ______________________, Nathan and Martha owned the land only to its bank. All the ______________________—that is, people along the riverbank—were governed by a principle of law known as the ______________________, which gives all owners equal rights to the reasonable use of the water that flows past their borders. Their state did not follow the ______________________, which allows the first person who puts water to beneficial use the right to do so at the expense of other property owners. Trees and other natural growth, known as ______________________, were on the property. Nathan and Martha had planted a large crop of vegetables, which may be referred to as ______________________ or ______________________. Although their ______________________ was excavating a gravel pit on the adjoining lot, Nathan and Martha had the right to have their land supported by the land next to it, called ______________________, and by the land under it, called ______________________. Nathan and Martha's ownership of the airspace above their property, known as ______________________, did not extend as high as the ______________________—that is, the space above 1,000 feet over populated areas.

PUZZLING OVER WHAT YOU LEARNED

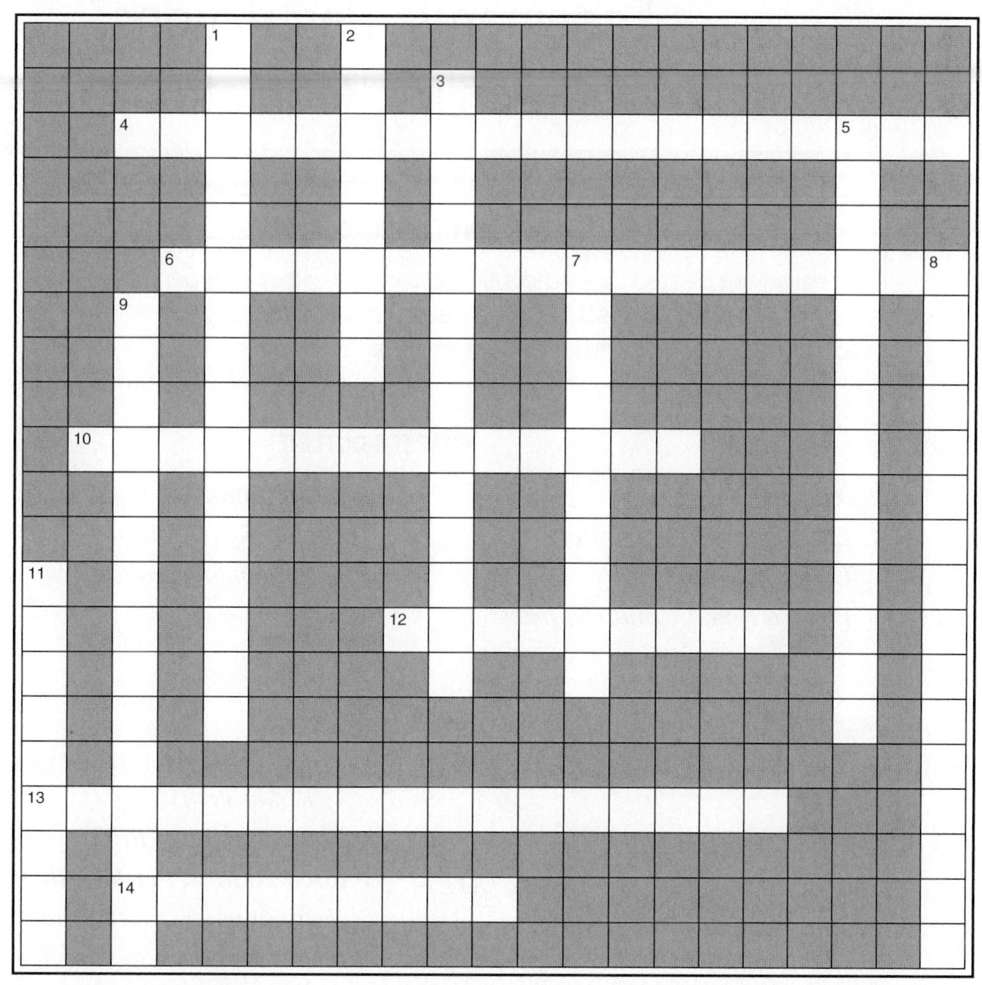

Caveat: Do **not** allow squares for spaces between words and punctuation (apostrophes, hyphens, etc.) when filling in crossword.

Across

4. Crops produced annually by labor and industry.
6. Waters that lie wholly beneath the surface of the earth.
10. People whose property abuts the ocean or large lake.
12. A pond that is 10 acres or more in size.
13. Waters that pass through the ground beneath the surface of the earth without any definite channel.
14. Rights to the area above the earth's surface.

Down

1. Trees and other natural growth.
2. People who own adjoining land.
3. People who own land along the banks of a river or stream.
5. To hold up at the side.
7. Crops produced annually by labor and industry.
8. To hold up from below.
9. A stream that ebbs and flows with the tide or is capable of being navigated by commercial vessels.
11. A pond that is under 10 acres in size.

7

7

CHAPTER 36

Easements, Restrictions, and Zoning Regulations

ANTE INTERROGATORY

An easement created by long-continued use of another's property openly, notoriously, continuously, and adversely is an (A) easement by necessity, (B) easement by prescription, (C) easement in gross, (D) easement appurtenant.

CHAPTER OUTLINE

KEY TERMS

appurtenant *(a·PER·ten·ent)*
bylaw
derogate *(DEH·ro·gate)*
dominant estate *(DOM·i·nent es·TATE)*
dominant tenement *(DOM·i·nent TEN·e·ment)*
easement *(EEZ·ment)*
easement appurtenant *(EEZ·ment a·PER·ten·ent)*
easement by prescription *(EEZ·ment by pre·SKRIP·shun)*
easement in gross *(EEZ·ment in gross)*
easement of necessity *(EEZ·ment ov ne·SESS·e·tee)*
grant
nonconforming use *(non·kon·FORM·ing)*
ordinance *(OR·di·nense)*
personal covenant *(PER·son·al KOV·e·nent)*
profit à prendre *(PROF·et a PRAWN·dra)*
reservation *(rez·er·VAY·shun)*
restrictions *(re·STRIK·shuns)*
restrictive covenants *(re·STRIK·tiv KOV·e·nents)*
right of way
servient estate *(SER·vee·ent es·TATE)*
servient tenement *(SER·vee·ent TEN·e·ment)*
tract *(trakt)*
usufruct *(YOO·se·frukt)*
usufructuary *(yoo·se·FRUK·shoo·a·ree)*
variance *(VAR·ee·enss)*
zoning

EASEMENTS

An **easement** (also called a **right of way**) is the right to use the land of another for a particular purpose. For example, suppose that A owns two acres of land between a highway and a lake. She divides the land into two parcels, sells the parcel adjoining the highway to B, and keeps the parcel adjoining the lake for herself. In her deed to B, A will include an easement giving B the right to pass and repass over A's land to reach the lake. She will also include a reservation in the deed, reserving to herself an easement to pass and repass over B's land to reach the highway. Thus, an easement may be created by **grant** (conveyance) by using the same formalities required of a deed, and it may be created by **reservation** (the act of keeping back) by reserving in a deed an easement for the person who is conveying the property away. It is known as an **easement appurtenant** when the easement benefits a particular **tract** (parcel) of land, such as the easement described here.

The one who enjoys the easement and to whom it attaches is called the **dominant tenement.** The one on whom the easement is imposed is called the **servient tenement.** Easements are said to run with the land—that is, they pass to all future transferees unless terminated by merger or abandonment.

In addition to being given to pass and repass over another's property, easements, called easements in gross, are often given for the right to use the airspace over another's land for electric and telephone wires and for the right to put gas and drainage pipes under someone else's ground. An **easement in gross** is an easement that is not attached to any parcel of land but is merely a personal right to use the land of another.

Easement by Prescription

An **easement by prescription** is an easement that is obtained by long-continued use. It is obtained in the same manner in which title to real property is obtained by adverse possession. To obtain an easement by prescription, someone must use the property of another openly, notoriously, continuously, and adversely for the statutory period, which is 20 years in many states.

Owners of real property may prevent others from obtaining easements by prescription over their land by interrupting the continuous use of the premises by the one attempting to gain the easement. For example, by statute in one state, the property owner may post a notice of his or her intent to prevent the acquisition of an easement in a conspicuous place on the property for six successive days, or have the notice served by a sheriff on persons who use the property and record the notice with the registry of deeds.

Easements of Necessity

The law does not allow land to be inaccessible. Therefore, if people convey part of their land in such a way that they deprive themselves of access to the remainder of it, they have, by implication, an **easement of necessity** over the granted portion. This easement is indispensable to the enjoyment of the dominant estate.

Profit à Prendre and Usufruct

A special type of easement, called a **profit à prendre,** allows the dominant tenement to remove something, such as sand, gravel, or timber, from the servient property. A similar term that is used in states with a civil law background is **usufruct**—the right to use the *profits* of property that belongs to another. For example, the right to use the timber from someone else's land, the wool from someone else's sheep, the grain from someone else's field, or the rent from someone else's building would be a *usufruct* in Texas and Louisiana. A **usufructuary** is a person who has a usufruct.

RESTRICTIONS

Limitations on the use of property, called **restrictions,** are sometimes placed in a deed or written out in a separate instrument and recorded with the deed by the grantor. Such restrictions, also called **restrictive covenants,** arise in either of the following ways:

1. Large parcels of land are divided into lots under a general building scheme, and restrictions are placed on the use of the land.
2. Landowners convey away part of their land and impose restrictions on either the land conveyed out or the land retained.

The following excerpt from a deed is an example of a restriction:

> No structure of a temporary character, trailer, basement, tent, shack, garage, barn, or other outbuilding shall be used on any lot at any time as a residence either temporarily or permanently.

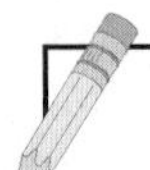

WORD WISE

The "Rog" in Derogate

The Latin root "rog" or "rogat" means "to ask." Some words with this root are:

Word	*Meaning*
derogate [*de* (away from) + *rogare* (to ask)]	To take away
interrogate [*inter* (between) + *rogare* (to ask)]	To question formally
prerogative [*pre* (before) + *rogare* (to ask)]	Prior right or privilege

A restrictive covenant in a deed will be binding on all future transferees—that is, it will run with the land—if it is **appurtenant** to—that is, belongs to or touches and concerns—the grantor's remaining land and provides some benefit to that remaining land. It must also be recorded at the registry of deeds. Restrictions on heights of buildings, setbacks, and types of use are commonly held to be appurtenant restrictions. The land that is benefited by the restrictions is called the **dominant estate.** The land that bears the burden of restrictions is known as the **servient estate.**

If a restrictive covenant in a deed is not appurtenant or provides no benefit to a dominant estate or is not recorded, it is said to be a **personal covenant** only—that is, binding only on the grantee and not on future transferees. Restrictions based on race, religion, or national origin are void. In some states, they result in criminal penalty.

Restrictions on real property will not be enforced by the courts when they become obsolete, such as when a material change has occurred in the neighborhood or when the continuation of the restriction would impede the use of the land for which it is best suited. In some states, a restriction will run out at the end of a statutory period, such as 30 years from the date of the deed or instrument creating it.

ZONING REGULATIONS

Zoning is the process of regulating the use of land by designating specific areas for certain uses. Most cities and towns today have enacted zoning laws that place restrictions on the use of the land to protect the health, safety, and general welfare of their inhabitants. A law enacted by a city is called an **ordinance;** a law enacted by a town is known as a **bylaw.**

Nonconforming Uses and Variances

When a zoning ordinance or bylaw is enacted, it does not apply to existing buildings or structures or to presently existing uses of land. A **nonconforming use** (a use not allowed by the new law but permitted if already being done) cannot be enlarged or changed and will be terminated by nonuse for a particular period of time.

A **variance** (exception to the zoning regulation) may be granted, after a public hearing, by a board of appeals if it can be shown that strict enforcement of the zoning law would cause substantial hardship and that the granting of a variance would not cause a substantial detriment to the public good or would not substantially **derogate** (take away from) the intent and purpose of the ordinance or bylaw.

REVIEWING WHAT YOU LEARNED

After studying the text, write the answers to each of the following questions:

1. What is the difference between an easement created by grant and an easement created by reservation? ______________________________

2. If A grants an easement to B to pass and repass over A's land, who is the dominant tenement and who is the servient tenement? ______________

3. How is an easement by prescription obtained? How may it be prevented? ______________

4. In what two ways do restrictions result? _____

5. When will a restrictive covenant in a deed be binding on all future transferees? ____________

6. What is the difference between a dominant estate and a servient estate as these terms apply to restrictions? ______________________________

7. How are restrictions based on race, religion, or national origin treated by the law? __________

8. When will restrictions on real property not be enforced by the courts? ________________

9. What limitations are placed on a nonconforming use? ______________________________

10. What must be shown to obtain a variance?

UNDERSTANDING LEGAL CONCEPTS

Indicate whether each statement is true or false. Then, change the italicized word or phrase of each *false* statement to make it true.

Answers

______ **1.** The person on whom an easement is imposed is called the *dominant* tenement.

______ **2.** Easements *cannot be* given for the right to use the airspace over another's land for electric wires.

______ **3.** To obtain an easement by prescription, someone must use the property of another *secretly* for the statutory period.

______ **4.** The law *does not* allow land to be inaccessible.

______ **5.** A restrictive covenant in a deed *will be* binding on all future transferees if it is appurtenant to the grantor's remaining land and provides some benefit to that remaining land.

______ **6.** Restrictions based on race, religion, or national origin are *void.*

______ **7.** Most cities and towns today have enacted zoning laws that *place restrictions* on the use of the land.

______ **8.** A law enacted by a city is called a *bylaw.*

______ **9.** A nonconforming use *cannot be* enlarged or changed.

______ **10.** A variance may be granted by the board of *selectpeople* if it can be shown that strict enforcement of the zoning law would cause a substantial hardship.

7

CHECKING TERMINOLOGY

From the list of legal terms that follows, select the one that matches each definition:

a. appurtenant
b. bylaw
c. derogate
d. dominant estate
e. dominant tenement
f. easement
g. easement appurtenant
h. easement by prescription
i. easement in gross
j. easement of necessity
k. grant
l. nonconforming use

Answers

____ **1.** Take away from.
____ **2.** An exception to the zoning regulation.
____ **3.** A law enacted by a town.
____ **4.** A law enacted by a city.
____ **5.** A use not allowed by the new law but permitted if already being done.
____ **6.** A promise that is binding on one person only and does not run with the land.
____ **7.** Land that bears the burden of a restriction or easement.
____ **8.** Belonging to; touching and concerning; annexed.
____ **9.** Limitations on the use of real property (select two answers).
____ **10.** Land that is benefited by a restriction or easement.
____ **11.** An easement created by long-continued use of another's property openly, notoriously, continuously, and adversely.
____ **12.** One on whom an easement is imposed.
____ **13.** One who enjoys an easement and to whom it attaches.

m. ordinance
n. personal covenant
o. profit à prendre
p. reservation
q. restrictions
r. restrictive covenants
s. right of way
t. servient estate
u. servient tenement
v. tract
w. usufruct
x. usufructuary
y. variance
z. zoning

____**14.** The right to use the land of another for a particular purpose (select two answers).

____**15.** The act of keeping back.

____**16.** A person who has a usufruct.

____**17.** Conveyance.

____**18.** The process of regulating the use of land by designating specific areas for certain uses.

____**19.** An easement that is indispensable to the enjoyment of the dominant estate.

____**20.** A special type of easement that allows the dominant tenement to remove something, such as sand, gravel, or timber, from the servient property.

____**21.** An easement that benefits a particular tract of land.

____**22.** The right to use the profits of property that belongs to another.

____**23.** Parcel.

____**24.** An easement that is not attached to any parcel of land but is merely a personal right to use the land of another.

UNRAVELING LEGALESE

Use simple, non-legal language, with the help of the glossary, to rewrite this case quote so that it is shorter and can be understood by a layperson without losing its meaning.

> In the absence of express statement, an intention that a restriction upon one lot shall be appurtenant to a neighboring lot is sometime[s] inferred from the relation of the lots to each other. But in many cases, there has been a scheme or plan for restricting the lots in a tract undergoing development to obtain substantial uniformity in building and use. The existence of such a building scheme has often been relied on to show an intention that the restrictions imposed upon the several lots shall be appurtenant to every other lot in the tract included in the scheme. In some cases the absence of such a scheme has made it impossible to show that the burden of the restriction was intended to be appurtenant to neighboring land.

USING LEGAL LANGUAGE

Read the following story and fill in the blank lines with legal terms taken from the list of terms at the beginning of this chapter:

When Opal sold a portion of her real property to Oliver to build a house on, she ____________________—that is, conveyed—to him a(n) ____________________, which is also called a(n) ____________________, to allow him to drive across one side of her remaining land. In addition, she included a(n) ____________________ in the deed, allowing her to drive across his land. In this latter instance, Opal was the ____________________ tenement, and Oliver was the ____________________ tenement. Because a neighbor had been driving across the other side of her land openly, notoriously, and continuously for more than 20 years, the neighbor had obtained a(n) ____________________. This was not a(n) ____________________, because it was not indispensable to the enjoyment of the dominant estate. Opal placed ____________________, which are also called ____________________, in the deed stating that no pigs could be raised on the lot. Because the lot was ____________________ to—that is, touching and concerning her remaining lot—it was not merely a(n) ____________________, which would have bound Oliver only and would not have run with the land. Opal's remaining land was the ____________________, because it was benefited, and Oliver's land was the ____________________, because it bore the burden of the restriction. A zoning law, called a(n) ____________________ in a town or a(n) ____________________ in a city, was in effect that required house lots to be larger than the one involved here. Oliver could not claim a(n) ____________________—that is, a use already in existence—but he was able to prove a hardship and obtain a(n) ____________________, which allowed him to build on the smaller lot, because it did not substantially ____________________—that is, take away from—the intent and purpose of the law.

PUZZLING OVER WHAT YOU LEARNED

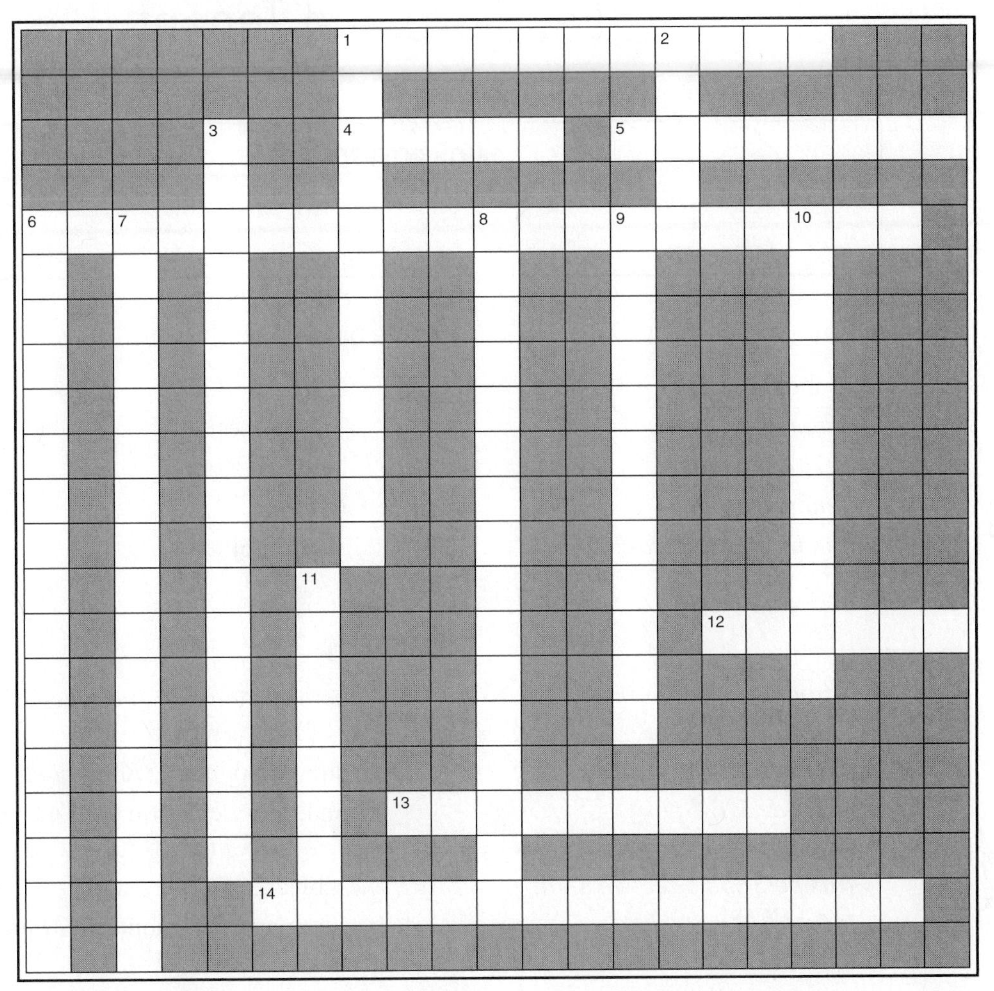

Caveat: Allow squares for spaces between words and punctuation (apostrophes, hyphens, etc.) when filling in crossword.

Across

1. The act of keeping back.
4. Conveyance.
5. An exception to the zoning regulation.
6. An easement that benefits a particular tract of land.
12. The process of regulating the use of land.
13. A law enacted by a city.
14. Land that bears the burden of a restriction or easement.

Down

1. Right to use the land of another for a particular purpose.
2. Parcel.
3. One who enjoys an easement and to whom it attaches.
6. Easement that is not attached to any parcel of land but is a personal right.
7. One on whom an easement is imposed.
8. Easement that allows the dominant tenement to remove something from the property.
9. Limitations on the use of real property.
10. Belonging to; touching and concerning; annexed.
11. Take away from.

7

7

CHAPTER 37
Landlord and Tenant

ANTE INTERROGATORY

A tenancy for an indefinite period of time is a tenancy (A) at will, (B) at sufferance, (C) for years, (D) from year to year.

CHAPTER OUTLINE

Leasehold Estates
- *Tenancy for Years*
- *Periodic Tenancy*
- *Tenancy at Will*
- *Tenancy at Sufferance*

License
The Lease
Tenants' Rights
Eviction
Tort Liability

KEY TERMS

constructive eviction *(kon·STRUK·tiv e·VIK·shun)*
deed-poll *(deed-pole)*
demise *(de·MIZE)*
dispossessory warrant proceedings *(dis·po·SESS·o·ree WAR·ent pro·SEED·ings)*
ejectment *(e·JEKT·ment)*
eviction *(e·VIK·shun)*
forcible entry and detainer *(FORSS·i·bel EN·tree and de·TAYN·er)*
holdover tenant *(HOLD·o·ver TEN·ent)*
indenture *(in·DEN·cher)*
landlord
lease *(leess)*
leasehold estate *(LEESS·hold es·TATE)*
lessee *(less·EE)*
lessor *(less·OR)*
license *(Ly·sense)*
licensee *(ly·sen·SEE)*
periodic tenancy *(peer·ee·ODD·ik TEN·en·see)*
quiet enjoyment *(KWY·et en·JOY·ment)*
retaliatory eviction *(re·TAL·ee·a·tore·ee e·VIK·shun)*
sublease *(SUB·leess)*
summary ejectment *(SUM·eree e·JEKT·ment)*
summary process *(SUM·e·ree PROSS·ess)*
tenancy at will *(TEN·en·see)*
tenancy for years *(TEN·en·see)*
tenancy from year to year *(TEN·en·see)*
tenant *(TEN·ent)*
tenant at sufferance *(TEN·ent at SUF·er·ense)*
underlease *(UN·der·leess)*
unlawful detainer *(de·TAYN·er)*
warranty of habitability *(WAR·en·tee ov hab·i·ta·BIL·i·tee)*

A lease is a contract granting the use of certain real property by its owner (called the **lessor** or **landlord**) to another (called the **lessee** or **tenant**) for a specified period in return for the payment of rent. In their strictest meaning, the terms *lessor* and *lessee* refer only to the parties to a lease. In contrast, the terms *landlord* and *tenant* are broad terms that refer to the parties under a tenancy at will as well as the parties under a lease.

LEASEHOLD ESTATES

The interest that is conveyed by a lease is called a **leasehold estate** and was treated as personal property at common law. The following are leasehold estates:

1. Tenancy for years
2. Periodic tenancy
3. Tenancy at will
4. Tenancy at sufferance

Tenancy for Years

A **tenancy for years** is an estate for a definite or fixed period of time no matter how long or how short. Such a tenancy can be for 1 month, 6 months, 1 year, 5 years, 99 years, or any period of time so long as it is ascertained. By statute in some states, a tenancy for 100 years or more creates a fee simple estate. This rule of law prompted the use of 99-year leases.

WORD WISE

Compound Words

Compound words are made by joining two or more words already in usage to create a new word with a new meaning. Some compound words found in this chapter are:

Word	*Meaning*
holdover	To hold over from a previous time period
landlord	A lord (person with authority or power) over land
leasehold	To hold by lease
sublease	A lease that is sub (less than) the full time period
underlease	A lease that is under (less than) the full time period

Some states require that a tenancy for years be in writing to be enforceable; others require a writing only if the time period exceeds one-year. In some states, leases for long periods of time must be recorded to be effective as to third parties. For example, a lease for seven years or more (or a notice thereof) must be recorded at the registry of deeds, under Massachusetts law, to be valid as to persons other than the lessor. Under this statute, if the owner of a building rents the building to a lessee for 10 years and the lease is not recorded, the owner can sell the building to someone else, and the new owner will not be bound by the lease.

Periodic Tenancy

A **periodic tenancy,** which is also called a **tenancy from year to year** (or from month to month, or from week to week) is a tenancy that continues for successive periods until one of the parties terminates it by giving notice to the other party. The notice requirement differs from state to state but is often the period between rent days. This tenancy may be created by implication if the landlord accepts rent from a tenant whose lease has run out or who is wrongfully in possession of the premises. Some states that do not recognize periodic tenancies treat the latter situation as a tenancy at sufferance.

Tenancy at Will

A **tenancy at will** is an estate in real property for an indefinite period of time. No writing is required to create this tenancy, and it may be terminated at the will of either party by giving the proper statutory notice.

Tenancy at Sufferance

A tenant who wrongfully remains in possession of the premises after the tenancy has expired is called a **holdover tenant** or a **tenant at sufferance.** Such a tenant has no estate or title but holds possession wrongfully. He or she is not entitled to notice to vacate and is liable to pay rent for the period of occupancy.

LICENSE

A lease differs from a license in that a lease conveys an interest in land and transfers possession, whereas a **license** conveys no property right or interest to the land but merely allows the licensee to do certain acts that would otherwise be a trespass. Lodgers who occupy rooms and advertisers who place signs on buildings are examples of **licensees** (people who have permission to do certain acts).

THE LEASE

A lease is an express contract between the parties in which real property is **demised** (leased) by the lessor to the lessee. The lease is usually executed in duplicate and signed by both parties (called an **indenture**), although a lease signed by the lessor only (a **deed-poll**) will be binding if accepted by the lessee. No particular form is necessary so long as the instrument identifies the parties, describes the demised premises, sets out the terms of the lease, provides for possession by the lessee, and contains consideration.

An *assignment* of a lease occurs when the lessee conveys the interest in the demised premises to another person for the balance of the term of the lease. It is called a **sublease** (or **underlease**) if the transfer is for a part of the term but not for the remainder of it.

TENANTS' RIGHTS

Tenants have the right to **quiet enjoyment** of the demised premises, which means that they have the right to possess the property and to be undisturbed in that possession. Thus, if the landlord locks out the tenant or interferes with the tenant's possession in any way, it is a breach of the tenant's right to quiet enjoyment.

When real property is rented for residential purposes, an implied warranty exists by the landlord that the premises are fit for human habitation, which is known as the implied **warranty of habitability.** In general, to be habitable, the property must meet the sanitary code of the local community. Legislation in some states allows the tenant to pay the rent to the court, instead of to the landlord, when the property is not fit for human habitation and violates the sanitary code. This action places the court in a position to prevent tenants from being evicted for complaining about the property they rent being uninhabitable. In other states, the tenant, after giving notice to the landlord, can correct a sanitary code defect at the tenant's own expense and withhold rent up to the cost of having the defect corrected.

EVICTION

An **eviction** is the act of depriving a person of the possession of real property either by reentry or by legal process. A landlord may not use force to evict a tenant. Instead, the landlord must give the tenant whatever notice is required by state law and use legal process (described later) to evict a tenant.

Retaliatory eviction is the eviction of a tenant for reporting sanitary code or building code violations to the authorities. This type of eviction is illegal in most states today.

A **constructive eviction** occurs when the landlord does some act that deprives the tenant of the beneficial enjoyment of the premises. Examples are depriving the tenant of heat, light, power, or some other service that was called for under the lease. When a constructive or other illegal eviction occurs, the tenant has the right to leave the premises without being in breach of the lease. The tenant may also withhold rent for the length of the eviction.

Figure 37-1 An eviction in New York City, circa 1910–1920. When may a landlord use self-help or force to evict a tenant? (Courtesy of the Library of Congress, Prints and Photographs Division, reproduction number LC-USZ62-30768.)

The legal action used by landlords to evict tenants was called **ejectment** at common law. Today, the name given to the action varies from state to state, including **summary process, summary ejectment, forcible entry and detainer, dispossessory warrant proceedings,** and **unlawful detainer.**

The landlord is required to give the proper statutory notice to the tenant before commencing such action, and the court, in its discretion, may allow time for the tenant to find another place to live.

TORT LIABILITY

When a person is injured on rented or leased property, the one who is in control of that part of the premises where the injury occurs is generally responsible if the injury was caused by negligence. For example, the landlord may be responsible for injury to others caused by a defect in the common areas over which he or she has control, such as hallways, stairways, and so forth. Likewise, the tenant may be responsible for injury to persons caused by defects in the portion of the premises over which he or she has control.

Legislation in some states has changed this common law rule of liability by allowing the tenant to give notice to the landlord of any unsafe conditions in that part of the premises under the tenant's control and making the landlord responsible thereafter for injury caused by the unsafe condition if the landlord fails to correct the condition.

REVIEWING WHAT YOU LEARNED

After studying the text, write the answers to each of the following questions:

1. What is the difference between the terms *landlord* and *tenant* and the terms *lessor* and *lessee?*

2. A leasehold estate was what kind of property at common law? ______

3. List the four leasehold estates. ______

4. For what length of time may a tenancy for years last? ______

5. What does a tenancy for 100 years create in some states? ______

6. How may a periodic tenancy be created by implication? ______

7. Describe a tenancy at will, including the method for its termination. ______________________

____

____

____

____

8. What is another name for a tenant at sufferance? How much notice must be given to evict such a tenant? ______________________

____

____

____

____

9. Compare a lease with a license. ______________

____

____

____

____

10. Who usually signs a lease? ______________

____

____

____

____

11. Differentiate between an assignment of a lease and a sublease. ______________________

____

____

____

____

12. Recent legislation in some states provides for what remedy to a tenant if the premises are not fit for human habitation? ______________

____

____

____

13. What is the difference between a retaliatory eviction and a constructive eviction? __________

____

____

____

____

14. List five names given by different states to the eviction action. ______________________

____

____

____

____

15. Who is responsible for a negligently caused injury that takes place ______________________

a. In the common areas of an apartment building? ______________________

____

____

____

b. In an area of the building that is controlled by a tenant? ______________________

____

____

____

7

UNDERSTANDING LEGAL CONCEPTS

Indicate whether each statement is true or false. Then, change the italicized word or phrase of each *false* statement to make it true.

Answers

______ 1. The terms *lessor* and *lessee* are broad terms that refer to the parties under a tenancy at will as well as the parties under a lease.

______ 2. A *tenancy for years* can be for any period so long as it is ascertained.

______ 3. A periodic tenancy continues for *successive periods* until one of the parties terminates it by giving notice to the other party.

______ 4. A writing *is necessary* to create a tenancy at will.

______ 5. A tenant at sufferance *is not* entitled to notice to vacate.

______ 6. A lease differs from a license in that a *license* conveys an interest in land and transfers possession.

______ 7. An *assignment* occurs when the lessee conveys part of the term of a lease but not the remainder of it to another person.

______ 8. *Quiet enjoyment* means that a tenant has the right to possess the property and to be undisturbed in that possession.

______ 9. A *retaliatory* eviction occurs when the landlord deprives the tenant of heat, light, power, or some other service called for under the lease.

______ 10. When a person is injured on leased property, the one in control of that part of the premises where the injury occurs *is generally responsible* if the injury was caused by negligence.

CHECKING TERMINOLOGY

From the list of legal terms that follows, select the one that matches each definition.

a. constructive eviction
b. deed-poll
c. demise
d. dispossessory warrant proceedings
e. ejectment
f. eviction
g. forcible entry and detainer
h. holdover tenant
i. indenture
j. landlord

Answers

______ 1. A contract granting the use of certain real property by its owner to another for a specified period in return for the payment of rent.

______ 2. A person who owns real property and who rents it to another under a lease (select two answers).

______ 3. A person who has temporary possession of, and an interest in, real property of another under a lease (select two answers).

______ 4. The interest that is conveyed by a lease.

______ 5. An estate in real property for a definite or fixed period of time no matter how long or how short.

______ 6. An estate in real property that continues for successive periods until one of the parties terminates it by giving notice to the other party (select two answers).

______ 7. A lease given by a lessee to a third person conveying the same interest for a shorter term than the period for which the lessee holds it (select two answers).

k. lease
l. leasehold estate
m. lessee
n. lessor
o. license
p. licensee
q. periodic tenancy
r. quiet enjoyment
s. retaliatory eviction
t. sublease
u. summary ejectment
v. summary process
w. tenancy at will
x. tenancy for years
y. tenancy from year to year
z. tenant
aa. tenant at sufferance
bb. underlease
cc. unlawful detainer
dd. warranty of habitability

____ 8. The right of a tenant to possess the rented property and to be undisturbed in that possession.
____ 9. The legal action used by landlords to evict tenants (select six answers).
____ 10. An estate in real property for an indefinite period of time.
____ 11. A tenant who wrongfully remains in possession of the premises after a tenancy has expired (select two answers).
____ 12. A person who has permission to do certain acts.
____ 13. A grant or permission to do a particular thing.
____ 14. To lease.
____ 15. A deed or lease to which two or more persons are parties.
____ 16. A deed or lease in which only the party making the instrument executes it.
____ 17. Dispossession caused by the landlord doing some act that deprives the tenant of the beneficial enjoyment of the demised premises.
____ 18. The act of depriving a person of the possession of real property either by reentry or by legal process.
____ 19. The eviction of a tenant for reporting sanitary code or building code violations to the authorities.
____ 20. An implied warranty by a landlord that the premises are fit for human habitation.

7

SHARPENING YOUR LATIN SKILLS

In the space provided, write the definition of each of the following legal terms, referring to the glossary when necessary.

et al. ____________________

et seq ____________________

et ux ____________________

fructus industriales ____________________

fructus naturalis ____________________

habendum ____________________

lis pendens ____________________

locus ____________________

locus sigilli ____________________

pendente lite ____________________

UNRAVELING LEGALESE

Using simple, non-legal language, with the help of the glossary, rewrite this case quote so that it is shorter and can be understood by a layperson without losing its meaning:

> At common law, a tenant at sufferance is entitled to no notice of the termination of that status before the landlord moves against him [or her] to obtain possession. Neither is he entitled by statute to any such notice of termination. However, under Massachusetts general laws chapter 186, section 13, if the tenancy at will of premises occupied for dwelling purposes is terminated by operation of law as it was in this case (the property being sold), the landlord may not dispossess the tenant or bring an action to recover possession of the premises until after the expiration of a period equal to the interval between the days on which the rent reserved is payable, from the time when the tenant receives notice in writing of such termination. This means notice of the termination of the preceding tenancy at will and not of the existing tenancy at sufferance.

USING LEGAL LANGUAGE

Read the following story and fill in the blank lines with legal terms taken from the list of terms at the beginning of this chapter.

Priscilla rented an apartment to Peter under a one-year ______________________ (contract). Priscilla was the ______________________ or ______________________, and Peter was the ______________________ or ______________________ of the ______________________—that is, the interest that was conveyed by the lease. Both parties signed the contract; therefore, it was a(n) ______________________ rather than a(n) ______________________, which is signed only by one party. Because the arrangement was for a definite period of time, it was called a(n) ______________________ rather than a(n) ______________________ (or ______________________), which continues for successive periods until one party terminates it by giving notice to the other party. A month later, Peter transferred his interest in the tenancy to Paul for a three-month period by the use of a(n) ______________________, which is also called a(n) ______________________. It was not a(n) ______________________, because Peter was to return to finish the remainder of the lease. Priscilla did not deprive Paul of heat, light, power, or other services called for under the lease; therefore, no ______________________ occurred. Paul did not pay the rent, however, which caused Priscilla to seek a(n) ______________________, which is the act of depriving him of the possession of the property. Paul continued to stay on even after being evicted, thus becoming a(n) ______________________, which is also called a(n) ______________________. After Paul left, Priscilla ______________________ (leased) the premises to Prudence for an indefinite period of time, creating a(n) ______________________. Prudence allowed Pauline to live with her as a lodger, the latter being a(n) ______________________, because she had no property right or interest in the premises.

7

PUZZLING OVER WHAT YOU LEARNED

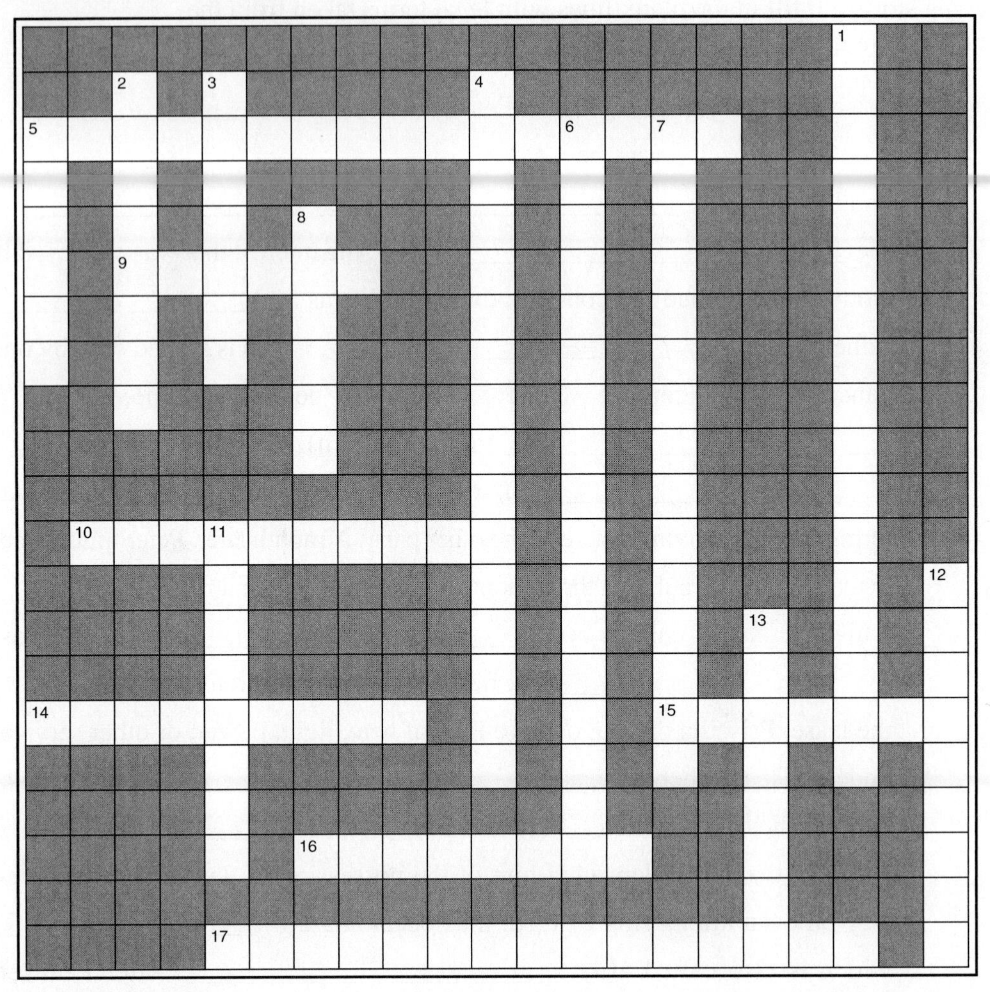

Caveat: Allow squares for spaces between words and punctuation (apostrophes, hyphens, etc.) when filling in crossword.

Across

5. The interest that is conveyed by a lease.
9. Person who has temporary possession of real property under a lease.
10. Lease given by a lessee to a third person for a shorter term.
14. Legal action used by landlords to evict tenants at common law.
15. A grant or permission to do a particular thing.
16. Lease given by a lessee to a third person for a shorter term.
17. Right of a tenant to the undisturbed possession of the rented property.

Down

1. Legal action used by landlords to evict tenants.
2. Person who owns real property and who rents it to another.
3. Leased
4. Estate that continues for successive periods until notice is given.
5. Person who owns real property and who rents it to another under a lease.
6. Estate in real property for a definite or fixed period of time.
7. Estate in real property for an indefinite period of time.
8. Person who has temporary possession of real property under a lease.
11. Act of depriving a person of the possession of real property.
12. A deed or lease to which two or more persons are parties.
13. Person who has permission to do certain acts.

PART EIGHT

TERMS USED IN FAMILY LAW

8

Although many couples today live together outside of wedlock, the institution of marriage remains firmly embedded in our culture. Divorce and dissolution of marriage also continue to occur at towering rates, and divorce courts and lawyers specializing in family law are heavily occupied. After a discussion of prenuptial contracts and marriage formalities, Chapter 38 compares annulment with marriage dissolution. It then examines the principal grounds for divorce. Chapter 39 discusses domicile and residence, foreign divorce, defenses to divorce actions, alimony, and support and custody of children.

CHAPTER 38
Marriage, Divorce, and Dissolution of Marriage

ANTE INTERROGATORY

Voluntary sexual intercourse by a married person with someone other than a spouse or by any unmarried person with a married person is (A) copulation, (B) adultery, (C) fornication, (D) impotency.

CHAPTER OUTLINE

Prenuptial Contracts
Marriage Formalities
Annulment of Marriage
Separation of Spouses
Divorce or Dissolution of Marriage
- *No-fault Divorce*
- *Fraud or Duress*
- *Adultery*
- *Cruelty*
- *Desertion*
- *Alcohol or Drug Addiction*
- *Impotency*
- *Nonsupport*
- *Conviction of a Felony*

KEY TERMS

adultery *(a·DUL·ter·ee)*
age of consent *(aje ov kon·SENT)*
alienation of affections *(ale·ee·a·NA·shun ov a·FEK·shuns)*
alleged *(a·LEJD)*
annulment *(a·NUL·ment)*
antenuptial contract *(an·tee·NUP·shel KON·trakt)*
banns of matrimony *(MAT·ri·mone·ee)*
breach of promise to marry *(PROM·iss)*
civil union *(SIV·el YOON·yun)*
cohabit *(koh·HAB·it)*
common law marriage *(KOM·on law MAHR·ej)*
community property *(kom·YOON·i·tee PROP·er·tee)*
conjugal *(KON·je·gel)*
consortium *(kon·SORE·shum)*
copulate *(KOP·yoo·late)*
co-respondent *(KOH-re·spond·ent)*
covenant marriage *(KOV·e·nent MAHR·ej)*
crime of moral turpitude *(MOR·el TER·pi·tood)*
criminal conversation *(KRIM·i·nel kon·ver·SAY·shun)*
cruelty *(KROO·el·tee)*
desertion *(des·ER·shun)*
discretion *(dis·KRE·shun)*
dissolution of marriage *(dis·o·LU·shun ov MAHR·ej)*
divorce *(de·VORSE)*
divorce from bed and board
heart balm statutes *(hart bahm STAT·shoots)*
impotency *(IM·pe·ten·see)*
incompatibility *(in·kom·pat·e·BIL·i·tee)*
irreconcilable differences *(ir·rek·en·SY·le·bel DIF·ren·sez)*

irretrievable breakdown *(ir·ree·TREE·ve·bel BRAKE·down)*
limited divorce *(LIM·i·ted de·VORSE)*
loss of consortium *(kon·SORE·shum)*
marriage *(MAHR·ej)*
marriage banns *(MAHR·ej)*
no-fault divorce *(de·VORSE)*
premarital contract *(pre·MAR·i·tel KON·trakt)*
prenuptial contract *(pre·NUP·shel KON·trakt)*
proxy marriage *(PROK·see MAHR·ej)*
reconciliation *(rek·on·sil·ee·AY·shun)*
separation of spouses *(sep·a·RAY·shun ov SPOW·sez)*
solemnized *(SAW·lem·nized)*

PRENUPTIAL CONTRACTS

A **prenuptial contract,** also called a **premarital** or **antenuptial contract,** is a written contract made in contemplation of marriage between prospective spouses setting forth, among other points, the rights each spouse will have to property brought into the marriage. A prenuptial contract takes effect on marriage. To be upheld by the court, the contract must be fair and reasonable, and the parties must fully disclose their assets to each other. In many states, when an attorney drafts a prenuptial contract, each party must be represented by a separate attorney—one attorney cannot represent both parties.

8

MARRIAGE FORMALITIES

The term **marriage** is defined by the federal government and most states as the union of one man and one woman. Massachusetts' highest court, however, held that its marriage law violated the Massachusetts constitution, leading to valid same-sex marriages in that state. The countries of Belgium, Canada, the Netherlands, South Africa, and Spain have also legalized same-sex marriages. Going in the opposite direction, at the beginning of 2007, 27 states had enacted laws banning same-sex marriages. The states of Vermont, Connecticut, and New Jersey have passed laws making civil unions legal. A **civil union** is a relationship in which same-sex couples have the same rights and duties as married couples. California's domestic partners law is a variation of the civil union.

Although the law continues to evolve, men and women who live together without being married have few, if any, **conjugal** rights beyond those given to single persons. In contrast, people who are married have legal rights that are deeply embedded in the law. These rights include protection of property, provisions for maintenance and support, and the right of inheritance.

Most states require marriages to be **solemnized**—that is, performed in a ceremonial fashion with witnesses present. Although no particular form of ceremony is required, state laws determine who is authorized to perform a marriage ceremony. In a unique ceremony in 2007, an American soldier in Iraq married his fiancée in Minnesota by the use of video teleconferencing.

A **common law marriage** is a marriage without a formal ceremony. It is allowed in only 14 jurisdictions in the United States* but has the same legal effect as a ceremonial marriage. To enter into a common law marriage, the couple must (1) agree by words

*Alabama, Colorado, the District of Columbia, Georgia, Idaho, Iowa, Kansas, Montana, Ohio, Oklahoma, Pennsylvania, Rhode Island, South Carolina, and Texas.

WORD WISE

Prefix Review

Key Term	*Prefix*	*Prefix Meaning*
prenuptial (*pre· NUP· shel*)	pre-	before
antenuptial (*an· tee· NUP· shel*)	ante-	before
cohabit (*koh· HAB· it*)	co-	together
incompatibility (*in· kom· pat· e· BIL· i· tee*)	in-	not
irretrievable (*ir· ree· TREE· ve· bel*)	ir-	not
impotency (*IM· pe· ten· see*)	im-	not
reconciliation (*rek· on· sil· ee· AY· shun*)	re-	again

8

to each other in the present tense that they are married, (2) **cohabit** (live together), and (3) hold themselves out to the community as husband and wife.

The Uniform Marriage and Divorce Act, which has been adopted in some states, allows a marriage by proxy when a party to the marriage cannot be present. A **proxy marriage** is a ceremonial marriage in which one of the parties is absent but represented by an agent who stands in his or her place.

The **covenant marriage** has been adopted in Arizona, Arkansas, and Louisiana in an attempt to decrease the divorce rate and to safeguard children from traumatic experiences. The parties agree to go through counseling before the marriage and also during the marriage to resolve conflicts. With exceptions, they can divorce only after a two-year separation.

Some religions require public notice of a marriage contract, called **banns of matrimony,** or **marriage banns,** for a certain number of weeks before the wedding date. This is to give anyone the opportunity to object to the marriage if there is just cause to do so. In addition, many state laws require a waiting period ranging from one to five days after the license is issued before the wedding can occur. Also, many states require the couple to have blood tests to determine the presence of rubella (German measles), venereal disease, sickle cell anemia, and AIDS.

ANNULMENT OF MARRIAGE

Marriages may be dissolved either by divorce or by annulment. An **annulment** is a judicial declaration that no valid marriage ever existed.

The principal grounds for annulment, which vary from state to state, are underage marriage, lack of marital intent, duress, fraud, pregnancy by someone other than the husband, incurable venereal disease, mental illness at the time of marriage, and physical incapacity.

At common law, the marriage of a girl under 12 or a boy under 14 was voidable. The marriage could be annulled by the court. Today, a marriage of a person below the age allowed by state law (called the **age of consent**) can be annulled at the court's **discretion.** This power is one that judges have to make decisions based on their own judgment and conscience.

Figure 38-1 A *proxy marriage,* allowed in some states, is a ceremonial marriage in which one of the parties is absent but represented by an agent. (NON SEQUITOR © Wiley Miller. Dist. By UNIVERSAL PRESS SYNDICATE. Reprinted with permission. All rights reserved.)

With some exceptions, the courts have held that a marriage entered into as a joke without any intent that the marriage be binding may be annulled as long as the parties to the marriage do not cohabit. For example, the Connecticut court annulled the marriage of a boy and girl who were married as a result of a "dare" by a group of teenagers out on a joy ride one evening. Neither party intended at the time to enter into the marital status, and they returned to their respective homes without cohabiting.

The courts have annulled marriages in cases in which the wife, at the time of the marriage, is pregnant by someone other than the husband. A woman who is incapable of bearing a child by her husband at the time of the marriage is unable to perform an important part of the marriage contract, according to these court decisions.

Most courts allow an annulment of a marriage when an undissolved prior marriage of one of the parties exists.

SEPARATION OF SPOUSES

Instead of issuing a divorce decree, the court may order a **separation of spouses,** also called a **limited divorce** or a **divorce from bed and board,** which is the discontinuance of cohabitation by the spouses. A separation for a statutory period of time, whether by agreement or judicial decree, is required in many states before a no-fault divorce action can be initiated.

DIVORCE OR DISSOLUTION OF MARRIAGE

A **divorce** (called **dissolution of marriage** in California) is the act of terminating a valid marriage by a court. A divorce requires a valid marriage to begin with, whereas an annulment does not. The principal grounds for divorce follow:

No-fault
Fraud or duress
Adultery
Cruelty

Desertion
Alcohol or drug addiction
Impotency
Nonsupport
Conviction of a felony

No-Fault Divorce

Almost all states have now enacted statutes, popularly known as **no-fault divorce** laws, that provide for the dissolution of marriage without regard to fault. Nevada has allowed a divorce on the ground of **incompatibility** for many years. In that state, instead of requiring a showing of fault, it is necessary to show only that the couple has a personality conflict so deep that no chance for a **reconciliation** (the renewal of amicable relations) exists. Common grounds for a no-fault divorce are **irretrievable breakdown** of the marriage and **irreconcilable differences.**

In some states, a choice exists between two procedures that may be followed to obtain a no-fault divorce. One procedure is used if both parties agree to the divorce; the other procedure is followed if the parties do not agree to it. The procedures differ from state to state.

In California, couples who, among other requirements, have no children, have been married less than five years, and own less than $25,000 worth of community property may divorce without going to court under a *summary dissolution* procedure. **Community property** is property other than a gift or inheritance, acquired by a husband or wife during marriage, that belongs to both spouses equally.

Fraud or Duress

Although most states allow an annulment rather than a divorce on the grounds of fraud and duress, a few states allow a divorce on both of these grounds.

Adultery

Adultery is voluntary sexual intercourse by a married person with someone other than a spouse or by an unmarried person with a married person. In addition to being a ground for divorce, it is a crime in many states.

Because of its private nature, adultery is most commonly proved by circumstantial evidence. In a divorce action, it is ordinarily enough to show that the **alleged** (claimed) adulterer had the opportunity together with the inclination or disposition to commit the act. For example, in a case in which a husband alleged adultery between his wife and a roomer who lived in the same house, the Illinois court held that adultery could be inferred because the marriage relationship between the husband and wife had not existed for years and the wife often visited bars and went on dates with other men. The court said that both the opportunity and the inclination existed.

To protect the character and reputation of innocent third persons, the name of the **co-respondent** (the person charged with committing adultery with the defendant) may not be used in the pleadings until a judge finds probable cause in a closed hearing.

In years past, a tort action, called **criminal conversation,** could be brought by a husband or wife against a third party who committed adultery with the husband's or wife's spouse. Damages for loss of **consortium** (the fellowship between a husband and wife) were often sought in such cases. So-called **heart balm statutes,** however, have been passed in most states abolishing this cause of action along with actions for **breach of promise to marry** (breaking off the engagement) and **alienation of affections** (willful and malicious interference with the marriage relation by a third party without justification or excuse).

WEB WISE

- Refer to a divorce law dictionary at **www.divorcenet.com/dictionary.html.**
- A divorce helpline is available at **inbox@divorcehelp.com.**
- Look for divorce forms at **www.divorce-forms.com.**
- For ongoing information about same-sex marriage laws in different states, log on to **www.marriagewatch.org.**

8

Cruelty

Cruelty is a common ground for divorce. It is called by different names, including the following, in different states:

Cruel and abusive treatment
Cruel and barbarous treatment
Cruel and inhuman treatment
Cruelty of treatment
Extreme and repeated cruelty
Extreme cruelty
Intolerable cruelty

Regardless of the name given to it, the requirements for proving cruelty are quite similar throughout the country. In general, plaintiffs must prove actual personal violence that endangers their life, limb, or health or that creates a reasonable apprehension of such danger and renders cohabitation unsafe or unbearable.

Usually more than a single act of violence must occur to obtain a divorce on this ground. For example, the court held that a single act by a husband of slapping a wife on the back—which was not severe, left no mark, and was the only act of violence in 25 years of marriage—was not a ground for divorce. In a contrasting case, however, the court said that one single incident of violence was enough to obtain a divorce when a husband, while drunk, struck, knocked down, and beat his wife in an argument, resulting in bruises on the wife's back, throat, arms, and legs.

Arguments alone, nagging, or the denial of sexual intercourse is not enough by itself to obtain a divorce on the grounds of cruelty. Mental suffering can be held to be cruelty if it impairs the health of the spouse. For example, a husband was allowed a divorce on the ground of cruelty when his wife persisted in seeing another man over his objections, because such conduct resulted in the deterioration of the husband's health.

Desertion

Desertion is defined as the voluntary separation of one spouse from the other, for the statutory period, without justification and with the intent of not returning. The abandoned spouse must not consent to the spouse's absence and must not have committed acts that justified the other's leaving. The time period for desertion varies from state to state.

Alcohol or Drug Addiction

Habitual drunkenness, by either alcohol or drugs, is a ground for divorce in most states. The habit must be confirmed (well established), persistent, voluntary, and excessive.

Impotency

Impotency is the incapacity of either party to consummate the marriage by sexual intercourse because of some physical infirmity or disarrangement. The test is the ability to **copulate,** which means to engage in sexual intercourse. It is not related to sterility, which is the inability to beget or bear a child.

Nonsupport

In many states, nonsupport is available only to the wife and not to the husband as a ground for divorce. In those states that have made the equal rights of men and women part of their state law, however, it is available to both spouses if the state recognizes it as a ground for divorce. The spouse against whom the divorce is sought must have sufficient ability to provide support and must willfully fail to do so.

Conviction of a Felony

Most states allow a divorce if either party is convicted of a felony or infamous crime or a **crime of moral turpitude** (a crime that is base, vile, and depraved). In some jurisdictions, life imprisonment automatically dissolves the marriage without further legal process; most states, however, require a divorce proceeding.

REVIEWING WHAT YOU LEARNED

After studying the text, write the answers to each of the following questions:

1. What is required for a prenuptial contract to be upheld by the court? ______

2. The legal rights given to people who are married include what? ______

3. What are the requirements for entering into a common law marriage? ______

4. List the principal grounds for an annulment. ______

5. At common law, the marriage of people under what age was voidable? ______

6. Today, a marriage of a person below what age can be annulled? ______

7. List the principal grounds for a divorce. ______

8. On what ground has Nevada allowed a divorce for many years? What must be shown to obtain such a divorce? ______

9. What are two common grounds for a no-fault divorce? ______

10. In a divorce action for adultery, it is ordinarily enough to show what two elements on the part of the alleged adulterer? ______

11. What is done to protect the character and reputation of innocent third persons in divorce actions for adultery? ______

12. What is generally required to obtain a divorce for cruelty? ______

13. Name three activities that, by themselves, are not enough to establish cruelty. ____________

14. To establish desertion, the abandoned spouse must not consent to what? ____________

15. What four words describe the habit necessary to establish habitual drunkenness? ____________

16. Explain the difference between impotency and sterility. ____________

17. What is required of the spouse against whom a divorce is sought on the ground of nonsupport? ____________

8

UNDERSTANDING LEGAL CONCEPTS

Indicate whether each statement is true or false. Then, change the italicized word or phrase of each *false* statement to make it true.

Answers

____________ **1.** To be upheld by the court, a prenuptial contract must be fair and reasonable, and the parties *must* fully disclose their assets to each other.

____________ **2.** Men and women who live together without being married have *many* rights beyond those given to single persons.

____________ **3.** Common law marriages are allowed in *all* jurisdictions in the United States.

____________ **4.** At common law, the marriage of a girl under *12* or a boy under 14 was voidable.

____________ **5.** An *annulment* requires a valid marriage to begin with.

____________ **6.** To prove adultery in a divorce action, it is ordinarily enough to show that the alleged adulterer had the *opportunity* together with the inclination to commit the act.

____________ **7.** The name of the co-respondent in a divorce action involving adultery may *not be* used in the pleadings until a judge finds probable cause in a closed hearing.

____________ **8.** Arguments or nagging is usually *enough* to obtain a divorce on the grounds of cruelty.

____________ **9.** To obtain a divorce for desertion, the abandoned spouse *must not* consent to the spouse's absence.

____________ **10.** The test to determine impotency is the ability to *beget or bear a child.*

CHECKING TERMINOLOGY

From the list of legal terms that follows, select the one that matches each definition.

a. adultery
b. age of consent
c. alienation of affections
d. alleged
e. annulment
f. antenuptial contract
g. banns of matrimony
h. breach of promise to marry
i. civil union
j. cohabit
k. common law marriage
l. community property
m. conjugal
n. consortium
o. copulate
p. co-respondent
q. covenant marriage
r. crime of moral turpitude
s. criminal conversation
t. cruelty
u. desertion
v. discretion
w. dissolution of marriage
x. divorce
y. divorce from bed and board
z. heart balm statutes
aa. impotency
bb. incompatibility

Answers

____ **1.** The act of terminating a valid marriage by a court (select two answers).
____ **2.** A judicial declaration that no valid marriage ever existed.
____ **3.** The power that a judge has to make a decision based on his or her own judgment and conscience.
____ **4.** A dissolution of marriage without regard to fault.
____ **5.** The renewal of amicable relations.
____ **6.** Voluntary sexual intercourse by a married person with someone other than a spouse or by any unmarried person with a married person.
____ **7.** The age at which one may be married under state law.
____ **8.** Conflicts in personalities and dispositions that are so deep as to be irreconcilable and irremediable and that render it impossible for the parties to continue to live together in a normal marital relationship (select three answers).
____ **9.** The person charged with committing adultery with the defendant in a divorce action.
____ **10.** In a divorce action, personal violence by one spouse that endangers the life, limb, or health of the other spouse.
____ **11.** The voluntary separation of one spouse from the other, for the statutory period, without justification and with the intent of not returning.
____ **12.** The incapacity of either party to consummate a marriage by sexual intercourse because of some physical infirmity or disarrangement.
____ **13.** Live together.
____ **14.** Claimed, asserted, or charged.
____ **15.** Public notice of a marriage contract for a certain number of weeks before the wedding date (select two answers).
____ **16.** A ceremonial marriage in which one of the parties is absent but represented by an agent who stands in his or her place.
____ **17.** Engage in sexual intercourse.
____ **18.** A contract made in contemplation of marriage between prospective spouses setting forth, among other points, the rights each spouse will have to property brought into the marriage (select three answers).
____ **19.** Performed in a ceremonial fashion with witnesses present.
____ **20.** A marriage without a formal ceremony.
____ **21.** Property (other than a gift or inheritance) acquired by a husband or wife during marriage that belongs to both spouses equally.
____ **22.** A crime that is base, vile, and depraved.
____ **23.** The willful and malicious interference with the marriage relation by a third party without justification or excuse.
____ **24.** The fellowship between a husband and wife.

8

cc. irreconcilable differences
dd. irretrievable breakdown
ee. limited divorce
ff. loss of consortium
gg. marriage
hh. marriage banns
ii. no-fault divorce
jj. premarital contract
kk. prenuptial contract
ll. proxy marriage
mm. reconciliation
nn. separation of spouses
oo. solemnized

____**25.** A tort action brought by a husband or wife against a third party who committed adultery with the husband's or wife's spouse.

____**26.** The discontinuance of cohabitation by the spouses (select three answers).

____**27.** Laws passed in most states abolishing actions for loss of consortium, breach of promise to marry, and alienation of affections.

____**28.** The destruction of fellowship between a husband and wife.

____**29.** Breaking off an engagement to marry.

____**30.** A marriage in which the parties agree to go through counseling before the marriage and also during the marriage to resolve conflicts.

____**31.** Pertaining to the marriage relationship.

8

UNRAVELING LEGALESE

Use the glossary to write the definitions of each of the italicized terms in the following case quote.

> It is to be observed that this is not a case of marriage prohibited by law such as a *bigamous* marriage or one prohibited by reason of *consanguinity* or *affinity* between the parties. Such a marriage is no marriage at all and is *void* without a *decree* of *divorce* or other legal process. While it doubtless is true that a decree of *nullity* ordinarily has the effect of making a marriage, even one which is *voidable,* void *ab initio,* this is a *legal fiction* which ought not to be pressed too far.

USING LEGAL LANGUAGE

Read the following story and fill in the blank lines with legal terms taken from the list of terms at the beginning of this chapter.

Although she looked older, Sonia was only 14 when she married Seth. This was below the ______________________, which is the age at which persons were allowed by the law of her state to marry; however, the couple did ______________________—that is, live together. Whether or not she could obtain a(n) ______________________, which is a judicial declaration that no valid marriage ever existed, was in the court's ______________________. She decided to seek a(n) ______________________, which is the act of terminating a marriage. Evidence existed that Seth had the opportunity together with the inclination to commit ______________________, which is a crime in many states in addition to being a ground for divorce. It was ______________________ (claimed) that he had gone to Sarah's apartment on several occasions. If Sarah was charged as being a(n) ______________________, her name could not be used in the pleadings without probable cause being found by a judge in a closed hearing. Seth had not committed ______________________, which is personal violence endangering a spouse's life, limb, or health. He had the ability to ______________________—that is, engage in sexual intercourse—ruling out Sonia's obtaining a divorce on the ground of ______________________. A divorce could not be obtained on the ground of ______________________, because no voluntary separation of one spouse from the other occurred. After thinking it over, Sonia decided to seek a(n) ______________________, which provides for the ______________________ without regard to fault. She considered getting a divorce in Nevada on the ground of ______________________, which required a showing that the couple had a personality conflict so deep that no chance for a(n) ______________________ existed. In some states, this ground for divorce is called ______________________, and in others, it is known as ______________________.

8

PUZZLING OVER WHAT YOU LEARNED

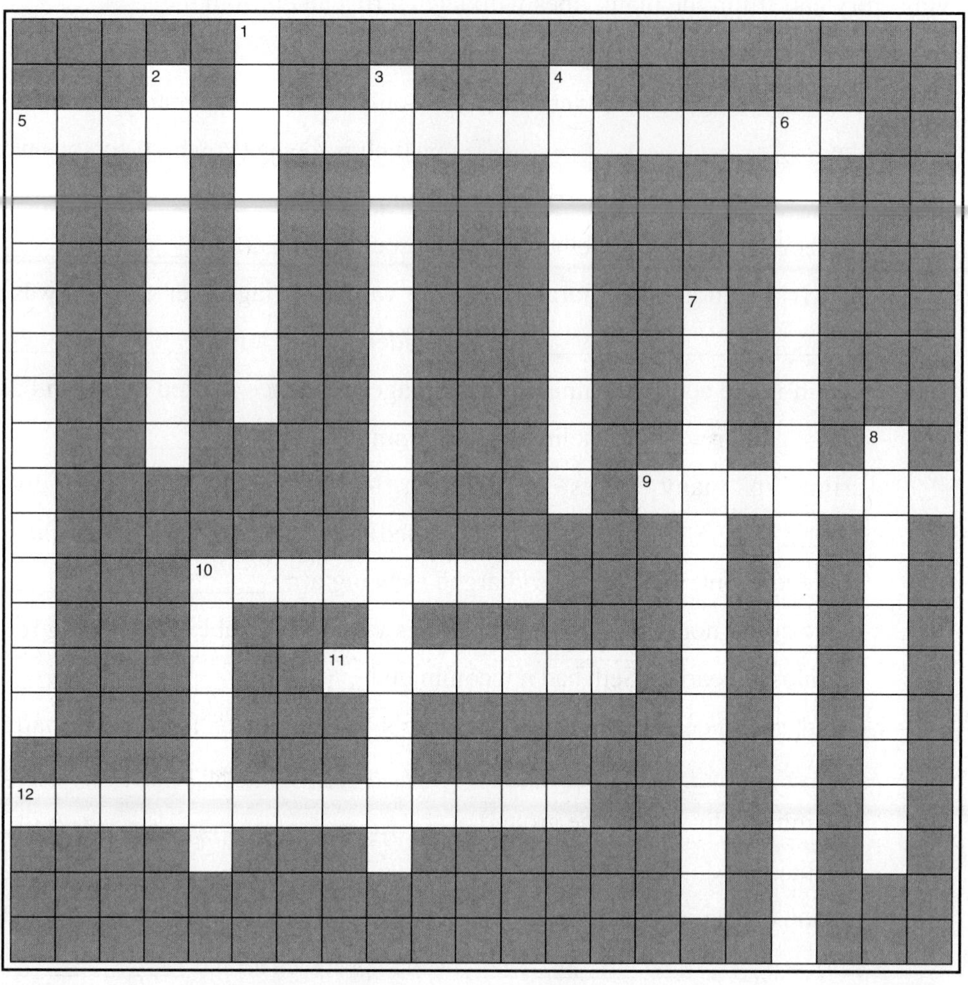

Caveat: Allow squares for spaces between words and punctuation (apostrophes, hyphens, etc.) when filling in crossword.

Across

5. A contract made in contemplation of marriage.
9. Live together.
10. Sexual intercourse by a married person with someone other than the spouse.
11. Act of terminating a valid marriage by a court.
12. Person charged with committing adultery with the defendant in a divorce action.

Down

1. Inability to have sexual intercourse.
2. Judicial declaration that no valid marriage ever existed.
3. Public notice of a marriage contract before the marriage.
4. Performed in a ceremonial fashion with witnesses present.
5. Ceremonial marriage in which one party is represented by an agent.
6. A marriage without a formal ceremony.
7. The age at which one may be married under state law.
8. Power that a judge has to make a decision based on his or her own conscience.
10. Claimed, asserted, or charged.

CHAPTER 39

Divorce Procedure

ANTE INTERROGATORY

Voluntary submission to the court's jurisdiction, either in person or by an agent, is (A) appearance, (B) collusion, (C) connivance, (D) comity.

CHAPTER OUTLINE

Domicile and Residence
Foreign Divorce
Defenses to Divorce Actions
Condonation
Connivance
Collusion
Recrimination
Alimony and Property Distribution
Support and Custody of Children

8

KEY TERMS

alimony *(AL·i·mohn·ee)*
appearance *(a·PEER·ens)*
bilateral foreign divorce *(by·LAT·er·el FOR·en de·VORSE)*
child support *(su·PORT)*
collusion *(ke·LOO·shen)*
comity *(KOM·i·tee)*
condonation *(kon·do·NAY·shun)*
connivance *(ke·NY·vens)*
custody of children *(KUS·te·dee)*
decree *(de·KREE)*
divided custody *(de·VIE·ded KUS·te·dee)*
domicile *(DOM·i·sile)*
emancipated *(e·MAN·si·pay·ted)*
equitable distribution laws *(EK·wit·a·bel dis·tre·BYOO·shun)*
ex parte foreign divorce *(eks PAR·tay FOR·en de·VORSE)*
foreign divorce *(FOR·en de·VORSE)*
foreign jurisdiction *(FOR·en joo·res·DIK·shen)*
forum *(FOR·em)*
full faith and credit clause *(KRED·et)*
interlocutory decree *(in·ter·LOK·ye·tore·ee de·KREE)*
joint custody *(joynt KUS·te·dee)*
judgment nisi *(JUJ·ment NIE·sie)*
libel *(LIE·bel)*
libelant *(lie·bel·AHNT)*
libelee *(lie·bel·EE)*
maintenance *(MAIN·ten·ens)*
pendente lite *(pen·DEN·tay LIE·tay)*
petition *(pe·TI·shun)*
petitioner *(pe·TI·shun·er)*
proceeding *(pro·SEED·ing)*
recrimination *(re·krim·i·NAY·shun)*
residence *(RES·e·dens)*
respondent *(re·SPON·dent)*
response *(re·SPONS)*
spousal support *(SPOWS·el su·PORT)*
temporary custody *(TEM·po·rare·ee KUS·te·dee)*

Changes have occurred over the years in the terminology that is used in divorce actions. Formerly, the person bringing a divorce action was called the **libelant** and the person against whom the action was brought was called the **libelee.** The pleading beginning the action was called a **libel.** Although some states still use these terms, many states, including Massachusetts, now use the terms *plaintiff* and *defendant* to describe the parties to a divorce action, and the initial pleading is called a *complaint.* The divorce court's decision, formerly called a **decree** (a decision of a court of equity), is now called a judgment in states that changed their terminology.

In California, the procedure for obtaining a dissolution of marriage is called a **proceeding,** and the process is begun by the filing of a **petition** (a written application for a court order) with the court. The parties to the proceeding are the **petitioner** (one who presents a petition to a court) and the **respondent** (one who is called on to answer a petition). The written answer filed by a respondent is known as a **response.**

Instead of issuing a final decision immediately, the courts of some states issue a provisional or temporary decision, called a **judgment nisi** in some states and an **interlocutory decree** in others. The provisional decision becomes final at the end of a statutory period of time unless a valid reason is shown for not issuing it.

DOMICILE AND RESIDENCE

In a divorce action or dissolution petition, jurisdiction is based on **domicile,** which is a person's principal place of abode. It is the place to which, whenever a person is absent, he or she has the present intent of returning. It cannot be abandoned or surrendered until another is acquired. It differs from a **residence** in that the latter is a place where a person actually lives, which may or may not be a domicile. People may have several residences, but they can have only one domicile at a particular time. For example, students may reside in a college dormitory in one state, spend their summer at a resort in another state, yet be domiciled at their home in a third state.

The plaintiff or petitioner in a divorce action must be domiciled within the jurisdiction of the court. Whether or not a legal domicile has been established is determined by the law of the **forum,** which is the place of litigation. The states are free to determine that a specific duration of residency is the equivalent of domicile.

All states except Alaska, South Dakota, and Washington require the plaintiff in a divorce action to reside in their state a minimum time before filing for divorce. The time period ranges from six weeks in a few states to one year in others.

FOREIGN DIVORCE

Before so many states allowed no-fault divorces, people would sometimes go to a **foreign jurisdiction** (another state or country) to obtain a **foreign divorce.** They did this because they did not have grounds for a divorce in their own state or because they wanted an immediate divorce without a waiting period. Nevada was attractive, because domicile could be established in six weeks and a divorce could be obtained on the ground of incompatibility. Mexico allowed quick, easy divorces (including those by mail order) at one time, but its laws have been amended, ending such practice.

Haiti and the Dominican Republic were once popular places to obtain overnight divorces. Jurisdiction was established by the fact that both parties submitted themselves to

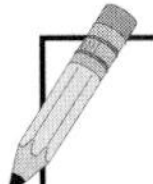

WORD WISE

Opposite Parties

appellant *(a·PEL·ent)*	A party bringing an appeal
appellee *(a·pel·EE)*	A party against whom an appeal is brought
defendant *(de·FEN·dent)*	A person against whom a legal action is brought
libelant *(lie·bel·AHNT)*	The plaintiff in a divorce action
libelee *(lie·bel·EE)*	The defendant in a divorce action
petitioner *(pe·TI·shun·er)*	One who presents a petition to a court
plaintiff *(PLAIN·tif)*	A person who brings a legal action against another
respondent *(re·SPON·dent)*	One who is called on to answer a petition

the jurisdiction of the court—the plaintiff in person and the defendant, in most cases, by filing an **appearance.** This voluntary submission to the court's jurisdiction, either in person or by an agent, was often accomplished by filing a power of attorney with the court without being personally present.

A **bilateral foreign divorce** occurs when both parties file an appearance, as mentioned earlier, in the foreign state or country. Such a divorce is recognized as valid by all states in this country under the **full faith and credit clause** of the U.S. Constitution. This clause requires that full faith and credit be given by each state to the judicial proceedings of every other state. The doctrine of **comity** applies a similar rule to judicial proceedings of foreign countries. This doctrine states that the courts of one jurisdiction will give effect to the laws and judicial decisions of another jurisdiction, not as a matter of obligation but out of deference and respect.

An **ex parte foreign divorce** occurs when one spouse appears in the foreign jurisdiction and the other spouse does not appear and fails to respond to the notice of divorce or service of process. This type of divorce may be attacked by the spouse who did not appear and declared void on the ground of lack of jurisdiction of the court granting the divorce. Such an attack may come when a spouse brings suit for separate support or when a spouse dies and the other spouse claims an inheritance.

DEFENSES TO DIVORCE ACTIONS

With the adoption of no-fault divorce laws, some states have eliminated the traditional defenses to divorce actions that had been available. These defenses were based on the theory that a divorce is granted because one party was at fault and the other was not.

Condonation

Condonation is the forgiveness of a matrimonial offense. It is a defense to a divorce action as long as the offense is not repeated and the wrongdoer remains faithful thereafter. The voluntary continuance of cohabitation or the resumption of sexual intercourse with knowledge of a marital offense usually amounts to condonation.

Connivance

The plaintiff's secret cooperation in the commission of a marital wrong committed by the defendant, called **connivance,** is a defense to a divorce action. A spouse who procures the commission of adultery, for example, or facilitates such an act is guilty of connivance. One cannot legally "smooth the path to the adulterous bed."

Collusion

An agreement between a husband and wife that one of them will commit a marital offense so that the other may obtain a divorce, an agreement not to defend a divorce action, and an agreement to withhold evidence in such an action are examples of **collusion,** which is a defense to a divorce action, other than no-fault.

Recrimination

The common law doctrine of **recrimination** held that neither party could obtain a divorce when both were guilty of a marital wrong. Before no-fault divorce laws, this defense was widely used in the United States. Conduct on the part of the plaintiff that constituted a ground for divorce was a defense to a divorce action. The offense by the plaintiff did not have to be the same offense alleged in the complaint for divorce; however, it did have to be a ground for divorce in that particular state.

ALIMONY AND PROPERTY DISTRIBUTION

Alimony (called **spousal support** in California) is an allowance made to a divorced spouse by a former spouse for support and maintenance. Its concept stems from the common law right of a wife to be supported by a husband during marriage. Today, however, many states award alimony or spousal support payments to either the ex-husband or the ex-wife. The power of the court to award alimony and spousal support is strictly statutory and comes solely from the statutes of the particular state making the award. In general, the court having jurisdiction to award a divorce also has the power to award alimony.

Alimony **pendente lite,** meaning litigation pending, is temporary alimony that may be granted to a spouse during the pendency of a divorce or separate support action. Temporary alimony rests largely in the discretion of the court and need not be awarded when the parties have entered into an agreement in that regard or when one spouse is voluntarily providing for the other spouse's support.

No set formula exists for determining the amount of alimony or spousal support that may be awarded. The determination rests in the sound discretion of the court. Such items as income and earning capacity, financial resources, future prospects, current obligations, dependents, and number of former and subsequent spouses are considered. Also considered are the spouse's situation in life, earning capacity, separate property, contribution to a spouse's property, age, health, obligations, and number of dependents.

Some jurisdictions will not award alimony or spousal support to a spouse who has a sufficient estate to provide for himself or herself. Similarly, a spouse who was at fault during the marriage will not be awarded alimony when the divorce was obtained for that reason.

The remarriage of a person who is receiving alimony or spousal support does not necessarily end a former spouse's obligation to pay it; however, that fact is usually a persuasive reason for a court to modify its judgment. The death of either party usually terminates the obligation to pay alimony or spousal support, although some state statutes authorize the continuance of alimony payments from the estate of the deceased spouse.

Courts, in most instances, will reserve the right to modify an alimony or spousal support award. Under some state laws, if the court does not reserve the right to do so in its judgment, the judgment cannot be changed after the expiration of the appeal period. Some states allow an alimony or spousal support award to be modified by agreement of the parties.

Many states have **equitable distribution laws** that give courts the power to distribute property equitably between the parties upon divorce. Both parties are usually required to disclose their financial situation and provide paycheck stubs and income tax returns. State statutes often provide criteria to be followed by the court in making the distribution.

SUPPORT AND CUSTODY OF CHILDREN

The legal obligations of parents to contribute to the economic maintenance and education of their children is known as **child support** or **maintenace.** Parents are required to support their minor children who are not **emancipated**—that is, freed from parental control. In a divorce proceeding, the parties may set the amount of child support by agreement, subject to approval of the court, or the court may determine the amount. Under the Uniform Reciprocal Enforcement of Support Act, which has been adopted by every state in the United States, a support order of one state can be enforced in every state.

The welfare or best interest of the child is the most important factor in determining the **custody of children,** that is, their care, control, and maintenance. In deciding who shall have custody of a child, the court considers such points as the stability of the person seeking custody; the physical safety of the child; and the emotional, social, spiritual, and economic needs of the child. The child's wishes are also considered in determining who shall have custody.

Temporary custody of children is often awarded to a parent, pending the outcome of a divorce or separation action. When the court orders **divided custody** of a child, it means that the child will live with each parent part of the year, the other parent usually having visitation rights. The parent with whom the child is living has complete control over the child during that period. In contrast, when the court orders **joint custody** of a child, both parents share the responsibility and authority of child rearing.

REVIEWING WHAT YOU LEARNED

After studying the text, write the answers to each of the following questions:

1. In former years, what terms described the plaintiff, the defendant, and the initial pleading in a divorce action? ______

2. What is jurisdiction based on in a divorce action or dissolution petition? ______

3. What is the difference between a residence and a domicile? ______

4. How many domiciles can a person have at any given time? ______

5. What law determines whether or not a legal domicile has been established? ______

6. What doctrine applies the full faith and credit rule to judicial proceedings of foreign countries? ______

7. In an ex parte foreign divorce, do one, both, or neither of the parties appear in the foreign jurisdiction? ______

8. On what ground may an ex parte foreign divorce be attacked, and when may it occur? ______

9. On what theory were the traditional defenses to divorce actions based? ______

10. What is the difference between connivance and collusion? ______

11. From what common law right does the concept of alimony and spousal support stem? _______

12. What points are considered in determining the amount of alimony and spousal support that may be awarded? _______

13. What is the most important factor in determining the custody of children? _______

UNDERSTANDING LEGAL CONCEPTS

Indicate whether each statement is true or false. Then, change the italicized word or phrase of each *false* statement to make it true.

Answers

_______ **1.** In many states, the person bringing a divorce action used to be called the *libelee*.

_______ **2.** In a divorce action, jurisdiction is based on the *residence* of the plaintiff.

_______ **3.** All states except *Alaska, South Dakota, and Washington* require the plaintiff in a divorce action to reside in their state a minimum time before filing for a divorce.

_______ **4.** The doctrine of *comity* applies to the acceptance of judicial proceedings of foreign countries.

_______ **5.** A bilateral foreign divorce may be attacked by the spouse who did not appear and declared void on the ground of *lack of jurisdiction* of the court granting the divorce.

_______ **6.** The *traditional defenses* to divorce actions were based on the theory that a divorce is granted because one party was at fault and the other was not.

_______ **7.** The common law doctrine of *connivance* held that neither party could obtain a divorce when both were guilty of a marital wrong.

_______ **8.** Today, *many* states award alimony or spousal support payments to either the ex-husband or the ex-wife.

_______ **9.** A set formula *exists* for determining the amount of alimony that may be awarded.

_______ **10.** A child's wishes *are not* considered in determining who shall have custody of the child.

CHECKING TERMINOLOGY

From the list of legal terms that follows, select the one that matches each definition:

- **a.** alimony
- **b.** appearance
- **c.** bilateral foreign divorce
- **d.** child support
- **e.** collusion
- **f.** comity
- **g.** condonation
- **h.** connivance
- **i.** custody of children
- **j.** decree
- **k.** divided custody
- **l.** domicile
- **m.** emancipated
- **n.** equitable distribution laws
- **o.** ex parte foreign divorce
- **p.** foreign divorce
- **q.** foreign jurisdiction
- **r.** forum
- **s.** full faith and credit clause
- **t.** interlocutory decree
- **u.** joint custody
- **v.** judgment nisi
- **w.** libel
- **x.** libelant
- **y.** libelee
- **z.** maintenance
- **aa.** pendente lite
- **bb.** petition
- **cc.** petitioner
- **dd.** proceeding
- **ee.** recrimination
- **ff.** residence

Answers

____ **1.** The plaintiff in a divorce action (no longer used by some states).

____ **2.** A person's principal place of abode; the place to which, whenever one is absent, he or she has the present intent of returning.

____ **3.** The place of litigation.

____ **4.** The voluntary submission to the court's jurisdiction, either in person or by an agent.

____ **5.** The initial pleading in a divorce action (no longer used by some states).

____ **6.** A rule of law requiring that full faith and credit be given by each state to the judicial proceedings of every other state.

____ **7.** A divorce that occurs when both parties make an appearance in a foreign state or country.

____ **8.** A divorce that occurs when one spouse appears in a foreign jurisdiction and the other spouse does not appear and fails to respond to the notice of divorce or service of process.

____ **9.** The forgiveness of a matrimonial offense.

____ **10.** An agreement between a husband and wife that one of them will commit a marital offense so that the other may obtain a divorce.

____ **11.** An allowance made to a divorced spouse by a former spouse for support and maintenance (select two answers).

____ **12.** The defendant in a divorce action (no longer used by some states).

____ **13.** A decision of a court of equity.

____ **14.** A provisional or temporary decision of a court (select two answers).

____ **15.** A place where a person actually lives.

____ **16.** Another state or country.

____ **17.** A doctrine stating that the courts of one jurisdiction will give effect to the laws and judicial decisions of another jurisdiction, not as a matter of obligation but out of deference and respect.

____ **18.** The plaintiff's secret cooperation in the commission of a marital wrong by the defendant, which is a common law defense to an action for divorce.

____ **19.** Conduct on the part of the plaintiff that constitutes a ground for divorce, which is a common law defense to an action for divorce.

____ **20.** Litigation pending.

____ **21.** The procedure in California for obtaining a dissolution of marriage.

____ **22.** A written application for a court order.

____ **23.** One who presents a petition to a court.

____ **24.** One who is called on to answer a petition.

____ **25.** The written answer to a petition filed by a respondent.

____ **26.** Freed from parental control.

8

gg. respondent
hh. response
ii. spousal support
jj. temporary custody

____**27.** The legal obligations of parents to contribute to the economic maintenance and education of their children (select two answers).

____**28.** The care, control, and maintenance of children.

____**29.** Custody in which the child will live with each parent part of the year, the other parent usually having visitation rights but not control of the child during that period.

____**30.** A divorce in a state or country other than where the party lives.

____**31.** Custody in which both parents share the responsibility and authority of child rearing.

____**32.** Custody of a child awarded to a parent on a temporary basis, pending the outcome of a divorce or separation action.

UNRAVELING LEGALESE

Use simple, non-legal language, with the help of the glossary, to rewrite this paragraph, substituting each of the italicized words with a word or phrase that has the same meaning.

> The evidence is undisputed that the *libellant* continued to live with the *libellee* in a complete marital relationship until a week before she signed her *libel* for divorce. While it is settled that *condonation* in such case is upon the *condition* that the spouse complained of will thereafter treat the other with *conjugal* kindness, and that breach of the condition may be shown by evidence which would not be sufficient to establish the principal charge. The evidence before us reveals no conduct on the part of the libellee which could be said to constitute a breach of the condition of condonation. The act alleged by the libellant to be a breach of that condition occurred when their nineteen-year-old son struck his father with a hammer. Such an event could hardly be classified as a breach of the condition of condonation on the part of the libellee. The *decree nisi* is reversed and a new decree is to be entered dismissing the libel.

USING LEGAL LANGUAGE

Read the following story and fill in the blank lines with legal terms taken from the list of terms at the beginning of this chapter.

Some years ago, before no-fault divorce was readily available, Rodney brought a divorce action against Heather on the ground of adultery. He was the ________________________, she was the ________________________, and the initial pleading was called a(n) ________________________. The ________________________—that is, the place of litigation—where Rodney brought the action was located in his principal place of abode, known as his ________________________. Because it was the place where he actually lived, it was also his ________________________. Before the action, Heather had agreed with Rodney to commit adultery so that he could divorce her, setting up the defense of ________________________ if Heather wanted to use it. In addition, Rodney secretly arranged to have his friend Rudolph spend the weekend with Heather while he was out of town, making available to her the defense of ________________________. In addition, Rodney deserted Heather, leaving her without means for support. Because this conduct was on the part of the plaintiff, which constituted a ground for divorce, it was also a defense called ________________________. Before the case went to trial, the parties forgave each other for their indiscretions, and the two resumed cohabitation, which created the defense of ________________________. Their reunion did not work out, however, and Heather decided to go to Haiti, a ________________________, to obtain an overnight divorce. Rodney refused to voluntarily submit to that court's jurisdiction by filing a(n) ________________________, which meant that this was a(n) ________________________ action rather than a(n) ________________________ action. As a result, the doctrine of ________________________, stating that the courts of one jurisdiction will give effect to the laws and judicial decisions of another jurisdiction, did not apply. Heather did not ask for ________________________—that is, an allowance for support and maintenance—as part of the court's ________________________ (decision).

PUZZLING OVER WHAT YOU LEARNED

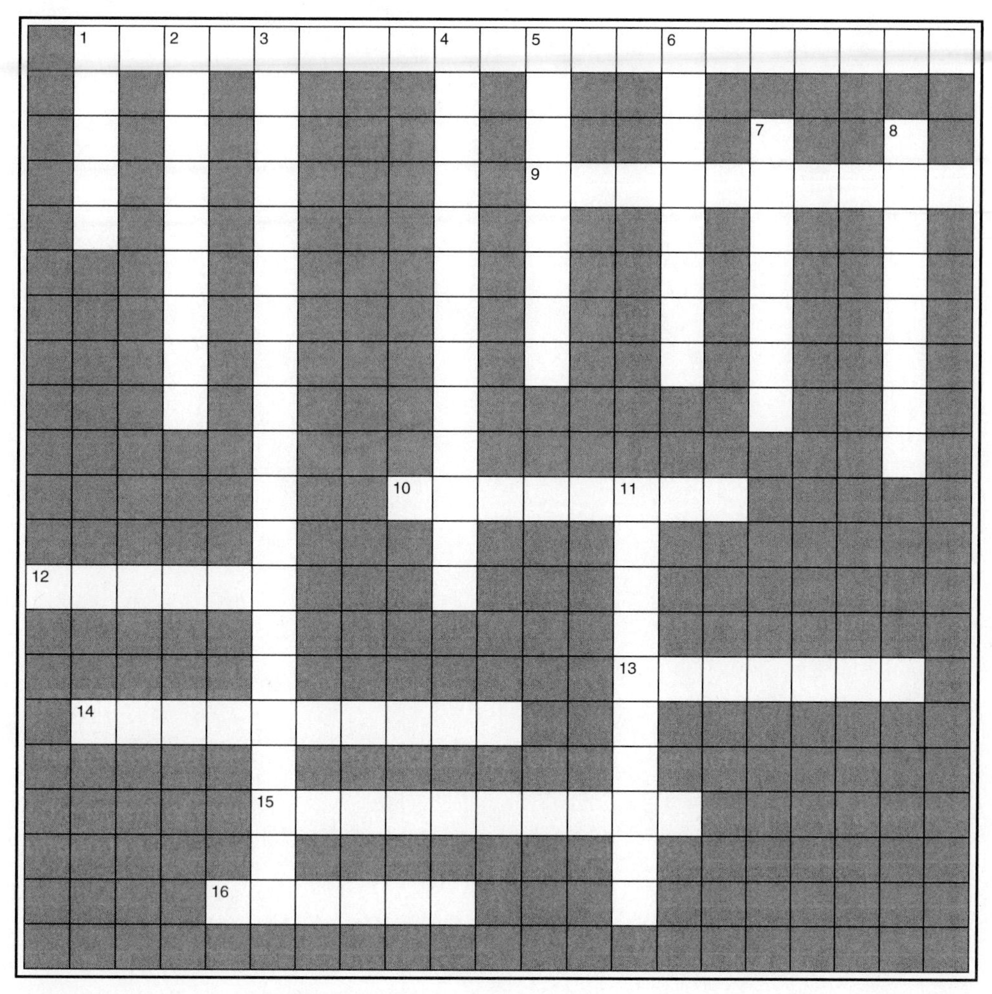

Caveat: Allow squares for spaces between words and punctuation (apostrophes, hyphens, etc.) when filling in crossword.

Across

1. Another state or country.
9. One who presents a petition to a court.
10. The plaintiff in a divorce action.
12. Courts of one jurisdiction will give effect to the laws of another.
13. Allowance made to a divorced spouse by a former spouse for support.
14. The procedure in California for obtaining a dissolution of marriage.
15. One who is called on to answer a petition.
16. A decision of a court of equity.

Down

1. The place of litigation.
2. Place where a person actually lives.
3. Provisional or temporary decision of a court.
4. A provisional judgment.
5. Written answer to a petition filed by a respondent.
6. Principal place of abode.
7. The defendant in a divorce action.
8. A written application for a court order.
11. Voluntary submission to the court's jurisdiction.

PART NINE

TERMS USED IN LAW OF NEGOTIABLE INSTRUMENTS

The law of negotiable instruments touches our lives daily. We are affected by this law every time we indorse our paycheck; pay for something by check; purchase a certificate of deposit; or borrow money to buy a house, automobile, or other expensive item. The built-in provisions of the law of negotiable instruments make checks, drafts, notes, and certificates of deposit highly useful in the business environment. The various kinds of negotiable instruments are discussed in Chapter 40, followed by an explanation of the law regarding the transfer of negotiable instruments.

9

CHAPTER 40
Negotiable Instruments

ANTE INTERROGATORY

The person making the promise to pay money on a note is called the (A) payee, (B) drawer, (C) drawee, (D) maker.

CHAPTER OUTLINE

Kinds of Negotiable Instruments
- *Drafts*
- *Notes*
- *Certificates of Deposit*

Transfer of Negotiable Instruments
- *Order and Bearer Paper*
- *Check 21 Act*

KEY TERMS

absolute defense *(ab·so·LOOT de·FENSE)*
acceptance *(ak·SEP·tense)*
acceptor *(ak·SEP·tor)*
allonge *(a·LONJ)*
bearer *(BARE·er)*
bearer paper *(BARE·er PAY·per)*
bill of exchange *(eks·CHANJ)*
bill of lading *(LAYD·ing)*
blank indorsement *(in·DORSE·ment)*
certificate of deposit *(ser·TIF·i·ket ov de·POS·et)*
certified check *(SER·ti·fide)*
check
Check 21 Act
co-maker *(KOH-may·ker)*
demand note *(de·MAND)*
dishonor *(dis·ON·er)*
domestic bill of exchange *(do·MES·tek bill ov eks·CHANJ)*
draft
drawee *(draw·EE)*
drawer *(draw·ER)*
fraud in esse contractus *(ESS·ay kon·TRAKT·es)*
full indorsement *(in·DORSE·ment)*
holder *(HOLD·er)*
holder in due course
indorsee *(in·dorse·EE)*
indorsement *(in·DORSE·ment)*
installment note *(in·STALL·ment)*
international bill of exchange *(in·ter·NASH·en·el bill ov eks·CHANJ)*
limited defense *(LIM·i·ted de·FENSE)*
maker *(MAY·ker)*
negotiation *(ne·go·shee·AY·shun)*
note
order paper
payee *(pay·EE)*
personal defense *(PER·son·al de·FENSE)*
promissory note *(PROM·i·sore·ee)*
qualified indorsement *(KWAH·li·fide in·DORSE·ment)*
real defense *(de·FENSE)*
restrictive indorsement *(re·STRIK·tiv in·DORSE·ment)*
sight draft
special indorsement *(SPESH·el in·DORSE·ment)*
substitute check *(SUB·te·toot)*
time draft
time note
trade acceptance *(ak·SEP·tense)*
universal defense *(yoon·i·VER·sel de·FENSE)*

9

The law of negotiable instruments is governed by the Uniform Commercial Code, which has been adopted in every state to govern various commercial transactions.

KINDS OF NEGOTIABLE INSTRUMENTS

Three kinds of negotiable instruments are drafts, notes, and certificates of deposit.

Drafts

A **draft** is a written instrument by which one person orders another person to pay money to a third person. The person who is ordered to pay the money need not do so unless he or she agrees to pay it. An agreement to pay the money, known as an **acceptance,** is indicated by writing "accepted" across the face of the instrument and signing it. If he or she refuses to accept the instrument when asked, it is called a **dishonor.** A person who draws a draft is known as a **drawer,** a person named in a draft who is ordered to pay money to a third person is called a **drawee,** a person named in a draft or note to whom payment is to be made is called a **payee,** and a drawee of a draft who signs it on the face agreeing to pay it is called an **acceptor.**

A **check** is the most common kind of draft. It is a draft that is drawn on a bank and payable on demand. A **certified check** is the same as an accepted draft because the bank guarantees it by marking "certified" on its face.

A **sight draft** is a draft that is payable when it is presented for payment to the drawee. A **time draft** is a draft that is payable at a particular time stated in the instrument. A draft that is payable "90 days after sight" is an example of a time draft.

WEB WISE

Besides text, the web includes a wide range of media. Here are some common types of file formats that are listed in the last part of the URL or web address:

.txt	Text file
.html and .htm	Hyper Text Markup Language document
.pdf	Adobe Acrobat format
.gif	Most common format for graphics
.jpg and .jpeg	Other graphics file formats
.wav	Sound file format
.au	Sound file format
.ra	Real Audio sound file
.mov and .qt	Quick Time Movie file
.zip	Compressed file
.avi	Movie file
.exe	Program file

A **trade acceptance** is a special kind of draft that is used, together with a bill of lading, by a seller of goods to extend credit or to be sure that payment for goods is received. A **bill of lading** is a document issued by a transportation company evidencing the receipt of goods for shipment. A seller in one city, for example, will ship goods to a buyer in a distant city and send a trade acceptance attached to a bill of lading to a bank in the distant city. The trade acceptance orders the buyer to pay the bank a certain amount of money. When the buyer pays the bank, the bank will release the bill of lading, which allows the buyer to pick up the goods from the freight company.

Under earlier law, before the Uniform Commercial Code, a draft was known as a **bill of exchange.** A **domestic bill of exchange** was drawn and payable in the United States. An **international bill of exchange** was drawn in one country and payable in another country.

Notes

A **note,** sometimes called a **promissory note,** is a written promise by one party, called the **maker,** to pay a sum of money to the order of another party, called the payee. If more than one maker is involved, they are referred to as **co-makers.**

A **demand note** is a note that must be paid whenever the holder demands it. A **time note** is payable at a particular time that is stated in the instrument. If a note is to be paid in multiple payments during a period, it is called an **installment note.**

Certificate of Deposit

A **certificate of deposit** is an instrument that is given by a bank to acknowledge the receipt of money by a depositor. The certificate contains promises by the bank to pay the money back to the depositor on a certain date with a stated amount of interest.

TRANSFER OF NEGOTIABLE INSTRUMENTS

9

The most important feature of a negotiable instrument is the ability to be transferred to other people who are given greater rights than their transferors had. This special type of transfer is known as **negotiation,** which is the transfer of an instrument in such form that the transferee becomes a holder. A **holder** is a person who is in possession of a negotiable instrument that has been issued or indorsed to that person's order or to bearer.

WORD WISE

Indorsement or Endorsement

When you look up the term "indorse" or its variations in a standard dictionary, you will be referred to "endorse," meaning either "to approve and support" or "to sign one's name on a commercial document or other instrument." The reverse is true when you use *West's Law Dictionary,* where "endorse" refers you to "indorse." Legal sources such as the Uniform Commercial Code, legal textbooks, and law dictionaries spell the term "indorse" rather than "endorse."

If the holder has taken the instrument for value, in good faith, and without any knowledge that it is overdue or that anyone has any claims or defenses to it, he or she is also called a **holder in due course.** It is this latter type of holder who is given special rights that other people do not have.

Holders in due course take instruments subject only to other people's **real defenses,** which are also known as **universal** or **absolute defenses.** These are the defenses of infancy, mental illness, illegality, duress, **fraud in esse contractus** (fraud as to the essential nature of the contract), bankruptcy, unauthorized signature, and material alteration. They are not subject to the **personal** or **limited defenses** of others, such as breach of contract, lack or failure of consideration, fraud in the inducement, lack of delivery of the instrument, and payment.

Instruments are negotiated either by delivery alone or by delivery and indorsement. An **indorsement** is the signature of an indorser, usually on the back of an instrument, for the purpose of transferring an instrument to someone else. A **blank indorsement** specifies no particular **indorsee** (person to whom a negotiable instrument is transferred by indorsement) and may consist of a mere signature. A **special indorsement,** sometimes called a **full indorsement,** specifies the person to whom or to whose order it makes the instrument payable. A **restrictive indorsement** purports to prohibit further transfer of the instrument by the use of such words as "for deposit only" or "pay any bank." A **qualified indorsement** limits the liability of the indorser by such words as "without recourse."

An indorsement must be written on the instrument or on a paper (called an **allonge**) so firmly affixed as to become a part of it.

Order and Bearer Paper

Negotiable instruments may be described as order paper or bearer paper. **Order paper** consists of instruments that are either originally drawn or indorsed "to the order of" particular payees or indorsees. Such paper requires the indorsement of the payee along with delivery to be negotiated. In contrast, **bearer paper**—that is, instruments made payable to "bearer" or to "cash," or indorsed in blank—needs no indorsement of the payee to be negotiated. Anyone in possession of such an instrument is called a **bearer.**

Check 21 Act

To facilitate check clearing and electronic check exchange, the **Check 21 Act** (named for the twenty-first century) authorizes a new negotiable instrument called a substitute check. A **substitute check** is a paper reproduction of the original check that contains an image of the front and back of the original check and can be processed just like the original check. A properly prepared substitute check is the legal equivalent of the original check for all purposes. Banks are not required to create substitute checks or to accept checks electronically. When they do, however, they warrant that (1) the substitute check contains an accurate image of the front and back of the original check, (2) it is the legal equivalent of the original check, and (3) no drawer, drawee, indorser, or depository bank will be asked to pay a check that it has already paid.

REVIEWING WHAT YOU LEARNED

After studying the text, write the answers to each of the following questions.

1. Describe the method used by drawees to indicate their agreement to pay drafts.

2. Name and define the parties to a draft.

3. Give an example of the way in which a seller of goods to a buyer in a distant city might use a trade acceptance.

4. Name and define the parties to a note.

5. Describe the most important feature of a negotiable instrument.

6. Name three real defenses.

7. Name three personal defenses.

8. Describe the difference between real and personal defenses as they relate to holders in due course.

9. Name and briefly describe four kinds of indorsements.

10. What is the difference between order paper and bearer paper?

UNDERSTANDING LEGAL CONCEPTS

Indicate whether each statement is true or false. Then, change the italicized word or phrase of each *false* statement to make it true.

Answers

__________ **1.** The person who is ordered to pay the money under an unaccepted draft *must* do so.

__________ **2.** A person who *draws* a draft is known as a *maker.*

__________ **3.** An acceptance of a draft is accomplished by writing *accepted* across the face of the instrument and signing it.

__________ **4.** A *check* is the most common kind of draft.

__________ **5.** A bill of exchange is another name for a *promissory note.*

__________ **6.** A negotiation is the transfer of an instrument in such form that the transferee becomes a *bearer.*

__________ **7.** Holders in due course are not subject to the *personal defenses* of others, such as breach of contract.

__________ **8.** A *restrictive* indorsement limits the liability of the indorser by such words as "without recourse."

__________ **9.** Bearer paper *may be* negotiated by delivery alone.

__________ **10.** *Order paper* requires the indorsement of the payee to be negotiated.

9

CHECKING TERMINOLOGY

From the list of legal terms that follows, select the one that matches each definition.

a. absolute defense
b. acceptance
c. acceptor
d. allonge
e. bearer
f. bearer paper
g. bill of exchange
h. bill of lading
i. blank indorsement
j. certificate of deposit
k. certified check
l. check
m. check 21 act
n. co-maker
o. demand note
p. dishonor
q. domestic bill of exchange
r. draft
s. drawee
t. drawer
u. fraud in esse contractus
v. full indorsement
w. holder
x. holder in due course
y. indorsee
z. indorsement
aa. installment note
bb. international bill of exchange
cc. limited defense
dd. maker
ee. negotiation
ff. note

Answers

____ **1.** A person who draws a draft.
____ **2.** A person named in a draft who is ordered to pay money to the payee.
____ **3.** A person named in a note or a draft to whom payment is to be made.
____ **4.** A person who promises to pay money to another on a note.
____ **5.** A person who, together with someone else, promises to pay money to another on a note.
____ **6.** A person who is in possession of a negotiable instrument that is payable to bearer, or to cash, or that has been indorsed in blank.
____ **7.** A person who is in possession of a negotiable instrument that has been issued or indorsed to that person's order or to bearer.
____ **8.** A holder who has taken a negotiable instrument for value, in good faith, and without any knowledge that it is overdue or that anyone has any claims or defenses to it.
____ **9.** A person to whom a negotiable instrument is transferred by indorsement.
____ **10.** A drawee of a draft who signs it on the face, agreeing to pay it.
____ **11.** A written instrument by which one person orders another person to pay money to a third person (select two answers).
____ **12.** The act by a drawee of writing "accepted" across the face of a draft and signing it, indicating that he or she agrees to pay it when due.
____ **13.** To refuse to accept or pay a negotiable instrument when it is presented.
____ **14.** A draft that is drawn on a bank and payable on demand.
____ **15.** A check that has been accepted, and thus guaranteed, by the bank on which it was drawn and has been marked to indicate such acceptance.
____ **16.** A draft that is payable when it is presented for payment to the drawee.
____ **17.** A draft that is payable at a particular time stated in the instrument.
____ **18.** A draft used with a bill of lading by a seller of goods to extend credit or to be sure that payment for goods is received.
____ **19.** A bill of exchange that is drawn and payable in the United States.
____ **20.** A document issued by a transportation company evidencing the receipt of goods for shipment.
____ **21.** A bill of exchange that is drawn in one country and payable in another country.
____ **22.** A written promise by one party to pay a sum of money to another party (select two answers).
____ **23.** A note that must be paid whenever the holder demands it.
____ **24.** An instrument that is given by a bank to acknowledge the receipt of money by a depositor.
____ **25.** The transfer of an instrument in such form that the transferee becomes a holder.

9

gg. order paper
hh. payee
ii. personal defense
jj. promissory note
kk. qualified indorsement
ll. real defense
mm. restrictive indorsement
nn. sight draft
oo. special indorsement
pp. subtitute check
qq. time draft
rr. time note
ss. trade acceptance
tt. universal defense

____**26.** A note that is payable at a particular time stated in the instrument.

____**27.** A defense that is good against everyone, including a holder in due course of a negotiable instrument (select three answers).

____**28.** A note that is to be paid in multiple payments during a period.

____**29.** An indorsement that specifies the person to whom or to whose order it makes the instrument payable (select two answers).

____**30.** An instrument that requires the indorsement of the payee and delivery to be negotiated.

____**31.** An indorsement that purports to prohibit further transfer of the instrument.

____**32.** Fraud as to the essential nature of the contract.

____**33.** A defense that can be used against a holder but not a holder in due course of a negotiable instrument (select two answers).

____**34.** An indorsement that specifies no particular indorsee and may consist of a mere signature.

____**35.** An indorsement that limits the liability of the indorser.

____**36.** A paper firmly affixed to a negotiable instrument for the writing of indorsements.

____**37.** An instrument that requires no indorsement of the payee to be negotiated.

____**38.** The signature of an indorser, usually on the back of an instrument, for the purpose of transferring an instrument to another.

____**39.** A federal law that authorizes a new negotiable instrument called a substitute check.

UNRAVELING LEGALESE

Use simple, non-legal language, to give an example of a real-life situation that illustrates the application of the Uniform Commercial Code [UCC] section set forth in the first paragraph. (The second paragraph is given to help you with the meaning of the terms in the first paragraph.)

> The person to whom an instrument is initially payable is determined by the intent of the person, whether or not authorized, signing as, or in the name or behalf of, the issuer of the instrument. The instrument is payable to the person intended by the signer even if that person is identified in that instrument by a name or other identification that is not that of the intended person. [UCC 310 (a)]
>
> "Issue" means the first delivery of an instrument by the maker or drawer, whether to a holder or nonholder, for the purpose of giving rights on the instrument to any person. [UCC 3–105 (a)] "Issuer" applies to issued and unissued instruments and means a maker or drawer of an instrument. [UCC 3–105 (c)]

9

USING LEGAL LANGUAGE

Read the following story and fill in the blank lines with legal terms taken from the list of terms at the beginning of this chapter:

> Nathan, who owned a salad-dressing business, owed $3,000 to Olive, from whom he had bought oil and vinegar on credit. Olive threatened to bring suit if Nathan did not pay her the money in 30 days. Nathan didn't have the money but was owed $3,000 by Paula and Peter, his best customers. He wrote a(n) ____________________ ordering Paula and Peter to pay Olive $3,000 in 30 days. Nathan was the ____________________, Paula and Peter were the ____________________, and Olive was the ____________________ of the instrument. Because it was payable at a particular time stated in the instrument, it was a(n) ____________________ rather than a(n) ____________________, which is payable when presented for payment to the drawee. Olive presented the instrument to Paula and Peter for ____________________, asking them to agree to pay it when it was due. They did so, making them ____________________ of the instrument. Thirty days later, Paula and Peter borrowed $3,000 from a bank and signed a(n) ____________________, which is

also called a(n) ______________________, promising to pay the money back in two years with interest. Paula was a(n) ______________________ along with Peter, and because two of them existed, they were known as ______________________. The bank was the ______________________. Because the instrument was payable at a particular time, it was called a(n) ______________________ rather than a(n) ______________________ ______________________, which would have been payable on demand. Similarly, because it was to be paid in multiple payments during a period, it was a(n) ______________________ ______________________. Instead of giving them cash, the bank gave them a(n) ______________________, which is the most common kind of draft. It was not a(n) ______________________, because the bank did not guarantee it with special words on its face. Paula and Peter indorsed the instrument "Pay to the Order of Olive" and delivered it to her. This was a(n) ______________________ indorsement, which is sometimes called a(n) ______________________ indorsement. Olive was the ______________________. She was also a(n) ______________________ of the instrument, because she had it in her possession and it was made payable to her. She indorsed it simply by signing her name on the back, which is called a(n) ______________________. On the way to the bank, the instrument blew out of the car window and was picked up by Max. The paper was now ______________________, because of the way it was indorsed, and Max is called a(n) ______________________ as well as a(n) ______________________ of the instrument. He was not a(n) ______________________, because he had not taken the instrument for value; therefore, if he were sued on the instrument, he would be subject to ______________________ or ______________________ defenses in addition to ______________________, ______________________, or ______________________ defenses such as infancy or illegality. Max returned the instrument to Olive, who deposited it in the bank and was given a(n) ______________________ to acknowledge its receipt.

9

PUZZLING OVER WHAT YOU LEARNED

Caveat: Allow squares for spaces between words and punctuation (apostrophes, hyphens, etc.) when filling in crossword.

Across

4. Person who is in possession of an instrument that is payable to bearer.
5. The act by a drawee of writing "accepted" across the face of an instrument.
10. A paper firmly affixed to a negotiable instrument for indorsements.
11. A person who promises to pay money to another on a note.
13 To refuse to accept or pay a negotiable instrument when due.
14. A written order by one person to another person to pay money to a third person.
15. A person named in a draft who is ordered to pay money to the payee.
17. Indorsement that specifies the person to whom it is payable.
19. The signature of an indorser.

Down

1. Instrument that requires the indorsement of the payee to be negotiated.
2. Indorsement that limits the liability of the indorser.
3. A drawee of a draft who signs it on the face, agreeing to pay it.
4. Instrument that requires no indorsement of the payee to be negotiated.
6. A person named in a note or a draft to whom payment is to be made.
7. An indorsement specifying no indorsee; often a mere signature.
8. An indorsement that specifies the person to whom it is payable.
9. Person to whom a negotiable instrument is transferred by indorsement.
12. A person who draws a draft.
16. A draft drawn on a bank and payable upon demand.
18. A written promise by one party to pay money to another party.

PART TEN

TERMS USED IN BUSINESS ORGANIZATION AND BANKRUPTCY

Before opening a business, thought must be given to the type of business organization best suited for that particular enterprise. Similarly, when a business fails or an individual suffers financial loss, consideration must be given to the desirability of filing for bankruptcy. Chapter 41 discusses the principal kinds of business organizations, including the sole proprietorship, the partnership, the corporation, the limited liability company, the joint venture, and the franchise. Chapter 42 explains bankruptcy proceedings generally, pointing out some of the sweeping changes made by the U.S. Congress in 2005. This is followed by a discussion of exemptions provided by the law of bankrupty and an examination of the different types of bankruptcy proceedings.

10

CHAPTER 41

Business Organization

ANTE INTERROGATORY

People who are elected by stockholders to manage a corporation are (A) officers, (B) shareholders, (C) incorporators, (D) directors.

CHAPTER OUTLINE

Sole Proprietorship
Partnership
Corporation
Limited Liability Company
Joint Venture
Franchise

KEY TERMS

articles of organization *(AR·ti·kels ov or·ge·ni·ZAY·shun)*
blue-sky laws
C corporation *(kor·por·AY·shun)*
certificate of incorporation *(ser·TIF·i·ket ov in·kor·por·AY·shun)*
charter *(CHAR·ter)*
close corporation *(klose kor·por·AY·shun)*
common stock *(KOM·on stawk)*
co-partnership *(koh-PART·ner·ship)*
corporation *(kor·por·AY·shun)*
co-venture *(KOH-ven·cher)*
de facto corporation *(de FAK·toh kor·por·AY·shun)*
de jure corporation *(de JOOR·ee kor·por·AY·shun)*
derivative action *(de·RIV·a·tiv AK·shun)*
directors *(de·REK·ters)*
dividends *(DIV·i·denz)*
domestic corporation *(do·MES·tik kor·por·AY·shun)*
dormant partner *(DOR·ment PART·ner)*
double taxation *(DUB·el taks·AY·shun)*
eleemosynary corporation *(el·ee·MOS·en·er·ee kor·por·AY·shun)*
foreign corporation *(FOR·en kor·por·AY·shun)*
franchise *(FRAN·chize)*
franchisee *(fran·chize·EE)*
franchiser *(FRAN·chize·er)*
general partner *(JEN·e·rel PART·ner)*
general partnership *(JEN·e·rel PART·ner·ship)*
incorporators *(in·KOR·por·ay·tors)*
joint enterprise *(joynt EN·ter·prize)*
joint venture *(joynt VEN·cher)*
limited liability company *(LLC) (LIM·i·ted ly·a·BIL·i·tee KUM·pe·nee)*
limited liability limited partnership *(LLLP)*
limited liability partnership *(LLP) (LIM·i·ted ly·a·BIL·i·tee PART·ner·ship)*
limited partner *(LIM·i·ted PART·ner)*
limited partnership *(LIM·i·ted PART·ner·ship)*
liquidate *(LIK·wi·date)*
managers *(MAN·a·jers)*
members *(MEM·bers)*
nominal partner *(NOM·i·nel PART·ner)*
operating agreement *(OP·er·ate·ing a·GREE·ment)*
ostensible partner *(os·TEN·si·bel PART·ner)*
partnership *(PART·ner·ship)*

10

preferred stock *(pre·FERD)*
promoters *(pro·MO·ters)*
S corporation *(kor·por·AY·shun)*
secret partner *(SEE·kret PART·ner)*
shareholders *(SHARE·hold·ers)*
silent partners *(SY·lent PART·ners)*
sole proprietorship *(pro·PRY·e·tor·ship)*
stock certificate *(ser·TIF·i·ket)*
stockholders *(STAWK·hold·ers)*
syndicate *(SIN·de·ket)*
ultra vires act *(UL·tra VY·res)*
unlimited liability *(un·LIM·i·ted ly·a·BIL·i·tee)*
winding-up period *(WINE·ding-up PEER·ee·ed)*

The principal kinds of business organizations are the sole proprietorship, partnership, corporation, and limited liability company. Joint ventures and franchises are also commonly used.

SOLE PROPRIETORSHIP

A **sole proprietorship** is a form of business that is owned and operated by one person. It is the least formal type of business organization, having few requirements for its establishment and being subject to less government regulation than other forms of business ownership. The sole proprietor owns and controls the business and makes all the decisions for its operation. He or she receives all profits and incurs all losses, is taxed personally on business profits, and has unlimited liability for all debts and liabilities incurred from its operation. A sole proprietorship comes to an end at the owner's death, and all business interests pass to the proprietor's heirs.

PARTNERSHIP

Partnership law is based on either the Uniform Partnership Act (UPA), which was adopted by every state except Louisiana, or the Revised Uniform Partnership Act (RUPA), which has been enacted in approximately 35 states.

A **partnership,** sometimes called a **co-partnership,** is an association of two or more persons to carry on as co-owners a business for profit. It may be created by an oral or written agreement of the parties, by an informal arrangement between them, or by their conduct. Simply doing business together with another person is enough to create a partnership whether or not the parties intend such a result.

A **general partnership** is one in which the parties carry on a business for the joint benefit and profit of all partners. In this type of partnership, every partner is an agent of the partnership for business purposes. Similarly, every partner is liable for the debts and wrongdoings caused by every other partner while transacting partnership business. This is known as **unlimited liability** (liability without bounds) and is the principal disadvantage of a partnership.

A **limited partnership** is a partnership formed by two or more persons having as members one or more general partners and one or more limited partners **General partners** manage the business and are personally liable for its debts and obligations. **Limited partners** invest money or other property in the business but are not liable for the debts or obligations of the partnership. They may not participate in the operation of the business, and their surnames may not be used in the partnership name unless it is also the name of a general partner.

WORD WISE

Hyphenated Words

A hyphen is often used to join two words to form a compound word. Some words join together to describe a noun, as in "well-known actress," "winding-up period," "English-speaking people," and "blue-sky laws."

A hyphen usually separates a prefix from a capital letter as in "un-American" or "non-European." Some prefixes, such as "self-," "all-," and "ex-," always require hyphens, as in "self-control," "all-inclusive," and "ex-parte foreign divorce."

A hyphen facilitates reading when the same vowels appear together, as in "de-emphasize" rather than "deemphasize," and helps to clarify meaning when a prefix causes confusion, as in "recreation" (a pleasurable activity) and "re-creation" (a new creation).

A type of partnership that removes the aspect of unlimited liability—the chief disadvantage of a general partnership—is popular. A **limited liability partnership (LLP),** sometimes called a *registered limited liability partnership (RLLP),* is a general partnership in which only the partnership as a whole, and not the individual partners, is liable for the *tort* liabilities of the partnership. In some states, only the partnership as a whole, and not the individual partners, is liable for the *contractual* liabilities of the partnership as well. This type of partnership is established by filing a simple registration form and paying a filing fee to the appropriate state office. The combination of a limited partnership and a limited liability partnership is called a **limited liability limited partnership (LLLP).**

Nominal partners, also called **ostensible partners,** are partners in name only. Their names appear in some way in connection with the business to make it appear that they are partners, but they have no real interest in the partnership. **Silent partners** are ones who may be known to the public as partners but who take no active part in the business. **Dormant partners** are not known to the public as partners and take no active part in the business. **Secret partners** take an active part in the business but are not known to the public as partners.

When a partnership is dissolved, a **winding-up period** first occurs. During this time, the partnership assets are **liquidated** (turned into cash), debts are paid, an accounting is made, and any remaining assets are distributed among the partners or the heirs of deceased partners according to the terms of the partnership agreement. At the conclusion of the winding-up period, the partnership is said to be terminated.

Partners cannot transfer their interest in the partnership to other people without the consent of all other partners, and the death of a partner, other than a limited partner, causes a partnership to come to an end. In addition, any partner may end a partnership at any time by withdrawing from it. Under the Revised Uniform Partnership Act, the withdrawal of a partner (called a *dissociation*) often results in a buyout of the withdrawing partner's interest rather than a winding up of the entire business.

CORPORATION

A **corporation** is a legal entity created under state law with the power to conduct its affairs as though it were a natural person. It comes into existence when the state government issues a **certificate of incorporation** (sometimes called **articles of organization** or **charter**) which is applied for by one or more persons known as **incorporators. Promoters** are people who are used sometimes to begin a corporation by obtaining investors and taking charge up to the time of the corporation's existence.

When a corporation is established in strict compliance with the law, it is called a **de jure corporation.** In contrast, if a defect in its establishment occurs, after being sought in good faith, it is called a **de facto corporation** and exists in fact although not by right, and must be recognized as a valid corporation unless set aside by the state. Any corporate act done outside of its authority as set forth in its charter is called an **ultra vires act** and can be challenged by a stockholder or other affected party. A corporation that is created for charitable and benevolent purposes is known as an **eleemosynary corporation.** A **domestic corporation** is one that is organized in the state in which it is operating. In contrast a **foreign corporation** is a corporation that is organized in a state other than that in which it is operating.

A corporation is owned by people called **stockholders** or **shareholders.** They are not personally responsible for the debts and liabilities of the corporation and can lose only the amount they paid for the stock. This rule of law is a principal advantage of the corporate form of business organization. When stockholders die, their shares of stock pass to their heirs, and the corporation continues in existence. Shares of stock may be sold or given away to other people by stockholders at any time unless the corporation is a **close corporation,** which has restrictions on the transfer of shares. In a close corporation, a stockholder who wishes to sell stock to someone else must first offer to sell it to the corporation. In this way, the ownership of the corporation can be kept within a limited group of people.

Because the income that a corporation earns is taxed directly by the federal government, and because dividends earned by stockholders are also taxed, corporate income is taxed twice, a process referred to as **double taxation.** A corporation that is taxed in this manner is called a **C corporation,** which is a corporation governed by Subchapter C of the Internal Revenue Code. To avoid double taxation, small corporations can elect to be treated as S corporations. An **S corporation** is a corporation governed by Subchapter S of the Internal Revenue Code, which stipulates that the income of the corporation will be taxed directly to the shareholders rather than to the corporation itself.

Each stockholder is issued a **stock certificate,** which evidences ownership of stock in the corporation. **Common stock** is stock with no preferences. Common stockholders have the right to vote, the right to receive profits (called **dividends**) if they are declared by the board of directors, and the right to receive a proportionate share of capital when the corporation is dissolved. **Preferred stock** is stock that has a superior right to dividends and to capital when the corporation is dissolved. Preferred stockholders usually have no voting rights.

Directors, elected by the stockholders at their annual meeting, manage the corporation. Officers, including a president, clerk, and treasurer, are appointed by the board of directors and are responsible for the daily operation of the corporate business.

When directors refuse to bring a lawsuit on behalf of the corporation against a third party to which it is entitled, a stockholder can bring a derivative action to enforce the right of the corporation. A **derivative action** is a suit by a stockholder to enforce a corporate cause of action.

The sale of stock of corporations over a certain size is regulated by both state and federal laws. State laws designed to protect the public from the sale of worthless stocks are known as **blue-sky laws.**

LIMITED LIABILITY COMPANY

A new type of business organization has developed in recent years that is neither a partnership nor a corporation but that combines some aspects of both. A **limited liability company (LLC)** is a nonpartnership form of business organization that has the tax benefits of a partnership and the limited liability benefits of a corporation. Owners of a limited liability company are called **members.** Rather than having bylaws, a limited liability company has an **operating agreement,** which sets forth the rights and obligations of the members and establishes the rules of operation. In place of officers to run the company, the LLC is managed either by its members or by **managers,** who are people designated by the members to manage the LLC. Like stockholders of a corporation, members of an LLC are not liable for the contractual or tort liabilities of the business. A limited liability company is established by filing articles of organization with the secretary of state's office and paying a filing fee.

JOINT VENTURE

A **joint venture,** also called a **joint enterprise, co-venture,** or **syndicate,** is a relationship in which two or more people combine their labor or property for a single business undertaking. It differs from a partnership in that it involves only one undertaking and comes to an end at the completion of the undertaking. Like partners, joint venturers have unlimited liability. Each is responsible for the others' wrongdoings conducted within the scope of the joint venture.

FRANCHISE

A **franchise** is an arrangement in which the owner of a trademark, trade name, or copyright licenses others, under special conditions or limitations, to use the trademark, trade name, or copyright in purveying goods or services. Many fast-food chains use the franchise method of conducting business. The **franchiser** (person who gives a franchise to another) and the **franchisee** (person to whom a franchise is given) are considered to be independent contractors, and their respective rights and duties are governed by the contract between them as regulated by state and federal laws.

REVIEWING WHAT YOU LEARNED

After studying the text, write the answers to each of the following questions.

1. Describe what happens to a sole proprietorship when the owner dies.
2. In what ways may a partnership be created?
3. What is the principal disadvantage of a partnership?
4. What is the difference between a general partner and a limited partner?
5. In what way do silent partners, dormant partners, and secret partners differ?
6. Describe the procedure that occurs when a partnership is dissolved.
7. When does a corporation come into existence?
8. What is a principal advantage of the corporate form of business organization?
9. Compare what happens to a corporation when a stockholder dies with what happens to a partnership when a partner dies.
10. In a close corporation, what must a stockholder do before selling stock to someone else?
11. What is the difference between common stock and preferred stock?
12. Compare the duties of the directors of a corporation with the duties of the officers of a corporation.
13. How does a joint venture differ from a partnership?

UNDERSTANDING LEGAL CONCEPTS

Indicate whether each statement is true or false. Then, change the italicized word or phrase of each *false* statement to make it true.

Answers

_______________ **1.** A sole proprietorship is the *most* formal type of business organization.

_______________ **2.** A partnership *may only be* created by a written agreement.

_______________ **3.** In a general partnership, *every partner* is an agent of the partnership for business purposes.

_______________ **4.** Limited partners *are liable* for the debts or obligations of the partnership.

_______________ **5.** Dormant partners take *an active* part in the business and are not known to the public as partners.

_______________ **6.** When a corporation is established in strict compliance with the law, it is called a *de facto* corporation.

_______________ **7.** Stockholders of a corporation *are not* personally responsible for the debts and liabilities of the corporation and can lose only the amount they paid for the stock.

_______________ **8.** *Preferred* stockholders usually have no voting rights.

_______________ **9.** A joint venture differs from a *partnership* in that it involves only one undertaking and comes to an end at the completion of the undertaking.

_______________ **10.** Franchisers and franchisees are considered to be *independent contractors.*

CHECKING TERMINOLOGY (PART A)

From the list of legal terms that follows, select the one that matches each definition.

a. articles of organization
b. blue-sky laws
c. C corporation
d. certificate of incorporation
e. charter
f. close corporation
g. common stock co-partnership
h. corporation
i. co-venture
j. de facto corporation
k. de jure corporation
l. derivative action
m. directors
n. dividends

Answers

____ **1.** Profits distributed to the stockholders of a corporation.

____ **2.** An arrangement in which the owner of a trademark, trade name, or copyright licenses others, under special conditions or limitations, to use the trademark, trade name, or copyright in purveying goods or services.

____ **3.** A legal entity created under state law with the power to conduct its affairs as though it were a natural person.

____ **4.** A person who gives a franchise to another.

____ **5.** A document that gives authority to an organization to do business as a corporation (select three answers).

____ **6.** Taxes on a corporation's income and on the dividends earned by the corporation's stockholders.

____ **7.** People who are elected by stockholders to manage a corporation.

____ **8.** A corporation that is organized in a state other than that in which it is operating.

____ **9.** People who organize a corporation by filing articles of organization with the state government.

____ **10.** State laws designed to protect the public from the sale of worthless stocks.

____ **11.** A partner who manages the business and is personally liable for its debts and obligations.

10

o. domestic corporation
p. dormant partner
q. double taxation
r. eleemosynary corporation
s. foreign corporation
t. franchise
u. franchisee
v. franchiser
w. general partner
x. general partnership
y. incorporators
z. joint enterprise
aa. joint venture
bb. syndicate

_____12. A partner who is not known to the public as a partner and who takes no active part in the business.
_____13. A corporation that is established in strict compliance with the law.
_____14. A relationship in which two or more people combine their labor or property for a single business undertaking (select four answers).
_____15. A corporation that is governed by Subchapter C of the Internal Revenue Code and that pays corporate taxes on its income.
_____16. A partnership in which the parties carry on a business for the joint benefit and profit of all partners.
_____17. A corporation that is created for charitable and benevolent purposes.
_____18. A corporation that has a defect in its establishment but that must be recognized as a valid corporation unless set aside by the state.
_____19. A corporation that has restrictions on the transfer of shares.
_____20. A corporation that is organized in the state in which it is operating.
_____21. Stock that has no preferences but that gives the owner the right to vote.
_____22. A suit by a stockholder to enforce a corporate cause of action.

CHECKING TERMINOLOGY (PART B)

From the list of legal terms that follows, select the one that matches each definition.

a. co-partnership
b. limited liability company (LLC)
c. limited liability limited partnership (LLLP)
d. limited liability partnership (LLP)
e. limited partner
f. limited partnership
g. liquidate
h. managers
i. members
j. nominal partner
k. operating agreement
l. ostensible partner
m. partnership
n. preferred stock

Answers

_____ 1. Stock that has a superior right to dividends and capital when the corporation is dissolved.
_____ 2. A partner in name only, who has no real interest in the partnership (select two answers).
_____ 3. A form of business that is owned and operated by one person.
_____ 4. A general partnership in which only the partnership, and not the individual partners, is liable for the tort liabilities of the partnership.
_____ 5. People who are designated by its members to manage a limited liability company.
_____ 6. A partner who takes an active part in the business but is not known to the public as a partner.
_____ 7. A partner who invests money or other property in the business but who is not liable for the debts or obligations of the partnership.
_____ 8. Liability that has no bounds.
_____ 9. A document that evidences ownership of stock in a corporation.
_____10. An association of two or more persons to carry on as co-owners a business for profit (select two answers).
_____11. Partners who may be known to the public as partners but who take no active part in the business.

o. promoters
p. S corporation
q. secret partner
r. shareholders
s. silent partner
t. sole proprietorship
u. stock certificate
v. stockholders
w. ultra vires act
x. unlimited liability
y. winding-up period

____**12.** A corporation governed by Subchapter S of the Internal Revenue Code in which the income of the corporation is taxed directly to the shareholders rather than to the corporation itself.

____**13.** Turn into cash.

____**14.** A partnership formed by two or more persons having as members one or more general partners and one or more limited partners.

____**15.** Owners of a limited liability company.

____**16.** A period of time during which partnership assets are liquidated, debts are paid, an accounting is made, and any remaining assets are distributed among the partners.

____**17.** People who own shares in a corporation (select two answers).

____**18.** A nonpartnership form of business organization that has the tax benefits of a partnership and the limited liability benefits of a corporation.

____**19.** A corporate act committed outside of the corporation's authority.

____**20.** An agreement that sets forth the rights and obligations of the members and establishes the rules for operating a limited liability company.

____**21.** People who begin a corporation by obtaining investors and taking charge up to the time of the corporation's existence.

SHARPENING YOUR LATIN SKILLS

In the space provided, write the definition of each of the following legal terms, referring to the glossary when necessary:

de facto ____________________

de jure ____________________

ex parte ____________________

pendente lite ____________________

ultra vires ____________________

UNRAVELING LEGALESE

Use simple, non-legal terms, with the help of the glossary, to write the definitions of each of the underlined terms in the following excerpt from the Revised Uniform Limited Partnership Act (RULPA).

> RULPA Section 403(b) provides that a general partner of a limited partnership "has the liabilities of a partner in a partnership without limited partners." Thus limited partnership law expressly references general partnership law for general partner liability and does not separately consider the liability of such partners. The liability of a general partner of a limited partnership that becomes a LLLP would therefore be the liability of a general partner in an LLP and would be governed by Section 306. The liability of a limited partner in a LLLP is a more complicated matter.

USING LEGAL LANGUAGE

Read the following story and fill in the blank lines with legal terms taken from the list of terms at the beginning of this chapter.

Julio and Juan became good friends while working for the Señor Tacos restaurant chain. The chain used a(n) ____________________ method of operation, because its owner licensed others to use its trade name in making and selling tacos. Julio and Juan worked under the direction of Carmen, the ____________________, who had the license to operate the business, given to her by Señor Tacos, the ____________________. Every evening after work, Julio and Juan spent their time together inventing a greaseless taco fryer. Because this relationship involved two people combining their labor and property for a single business undertaking, it was known as a(n) ____________________, which is also called a(n) ____________________, a(n) ____________________, or a(n) ____________________. When the fryer was completed, Juan left his job with Carmen and opened a taco shop of his own. It was a(n) ____________________, because Juan owned and operated it himself. The business thrived, and although he had no further money to invest, Juan felt it necessary to expand. His friend Julio offered to invest money in the business but did not want to be liable for its debts or obligations. The two formed a(n) ____________________, making Juan a(n) ____________________ partner and Julio a(n) ____________________ partner. Because she was well-known in the trade, Carmen lent her name to the business, but because she had no real interest in it, she was a(n) ____________________ or ____________________ partner. Soon it became necessary to expand again, and Juan and Julio decided to establish a(n) ____________________, which is a legal entity created under state law with the power to conduct its affairs as though it were a natural person. Juan and Julio were the ____________________, because they applied for the ____________________, which is also called ____________________ or ____________________. The organization was established in strict compliance with the law; therefore, it was a(n) ____________________. Miguel, a friend of Juan and Julio, invested in the business, and all three became ____________________, which are also known as ____________________. Because restrictions were placed on the transfer of shares, the business was a(n) ____________________. Miguel, Juan, and Julio received ____________________ as evidence of their ownership in the business. The stock they received was ____________________, which had no preferences and gave each owner the right to vote. All three were elected as ____________________ to manage the business.

10

PUZZLING OVER WHAT YOU LEARNED

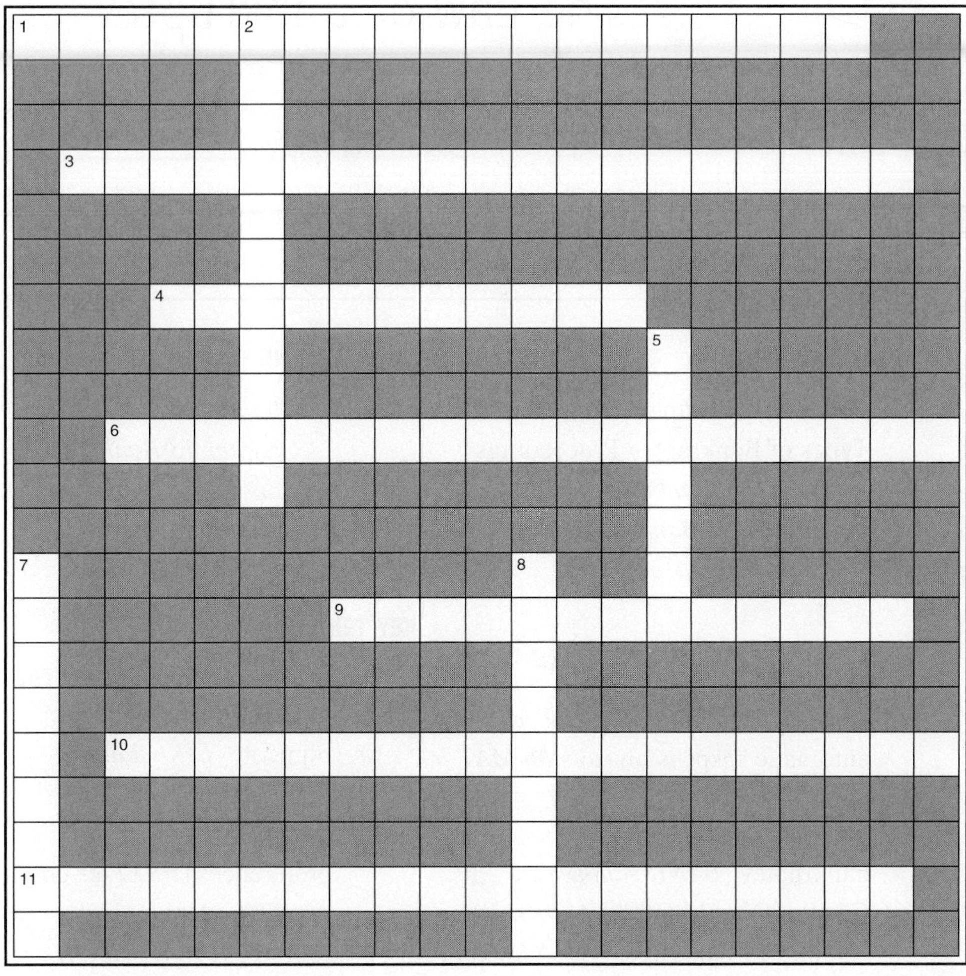

Caveat: Allow squares for spaces between words and punctuation (apostrophes, hyphens, etc.) when filling in crossword.

Across

1. A form of business that is owned and operated by one person.
3. Partnership with one or more general partners and one or more limited partners.
4. Legal entity created under state law with powers of a natural person.
6. Liability that has no bounds.
9. People who organize a corporation.
10. Corporation that is established in compliance with the law.
11. Corporation with a defect in its establishment but recognized as valid.

Down

2. Association of two or more persons to carry on a business.
5. Document that gives authority to a corporation to do business.
7. Profits distributed to the stockholders of a corporation.
8. People who begin a corporation by obtaining investors.

CHAPTER 42

The Law of Bankruptcy

ANTE INTERROGATORY

A method for businesses to reorganize their financial affairs, keep their assets, and remain in business is a (A) Chapter 7 bankruptcy, (B) Chapter 11 bankruptcy, (C) Chapter 12 bankruptcy, (D) Chapter 13 bankruptcy.

CHAPTER OUTLINE

Goals of Bankruptcy Code
Types of Bankruptcy Proceedings
  Chapter 7 Bankruptcy
  Chapter 11 Bankruptcy
  Chapter 12 Bankruptcy
  Chapter 13 Bankruptcy

KEY TERMS

assets *(ASS·ets)*
automatic stay *(aw·toh·MAT·ic)*
automatic suspension *(aw·toh·MAT·ic sus·PEN·shun)*
bankrupt *(BANK·rupt)*
bankruptcy *(BANK·rupt·see)*
Chapter 7 bankruptcy *(BANK·rupt·see)*
Chapter 11 bankruptcy *(BANK·rupt·see)*
Chapter 12 bankruptcy *(BANK·rupt·see)*
Chapter 13 bankruptcy *(BANK·rupt·see)*
claim
creditors *(KRED·et·ers)*
debtor *(DET·er)*
debtor-in-possession *(DET·er in po·SESH·en)*
discharge in bankruptcy *(DIS·charj in BANK·rupt·see)*
exemptions *(eg·ZEMP·shuns)*
homestead exemption *(HOME·sted eg·ZEMP·shun)*
involuntary bankruptcy *(in·VOL·en·ter·ee BANK·rupt·see)*
liquidate *(LIK·wi·date)*
liquidation *(lik·wi·DAY·shun)*
order for relief *(re·LEEF)*
preferences *(PREF·er·en·ses)*
proof of claim
prorated *(pro·RATE·ed)*
reorganization *(re·or·ge·ni·ZAY·shun)*
secured creditors *(se·KYOORD KRED·et·ers)*
straight bankruptcy *(strayt BANK·rupt·see)*
trustee in bankruptcy *(trus·TEE in BANK·rupt·see)*
voluntary bankruptcy *(VOL·en·ter·ee BANK·rupt·see)*
wage earner's plan *(wayj ER·ners)*

10

The United States Bankruptcy Code was enacted by Congress under the authority of Article I of the U.S. Constitution. U.S. Bankruptcy Courts, which decide bankruptcy cases, are attached to district courts within the federal court system. Each state and territory in the United States has at least one federal district court within its boundaries.

In 2005, the U.S. Congress made sweeping changes to the Bankruptcy Code, making it more difficult for people to declare bankruptcy. The discussion that follows includes the new law.

GOALS OF BANKRUPTCY CODE

The goals of the Bankruptcy Code are twofold: (1) to convert the debtor's property into cash and distribute it among **creditors** (people to whom money is owed) and (2) to give the debtor a fresh start by leaving some of his or her **assets** (property) untouched. **Bankruptcy** is the legal process by which the assets of a debtor are sold to pay off creditors so that the debtor can make a fresh start financially. **Bankrupt** means the state of a person (including a business) who is unable to pay debts as they become due. The term **debtor** (one who owes a debt to another) is used in place of the term *bankrupt* in the Bankruptcy Code.

TYPES OF BANKRUPTCY PROCEEDINGS

There are five principal types of bankruptcy proceedings, and they are named after the chapter in the Federal Bankruptcy Code where they are found: Chapter 7 (liquidation), Chapter 9 (municipalities), Chapter 11 (business reorganization), Chapter 12 (family farmers), and Chapter 13 (adjustment of debts of individuals).

Chapter 7 Bankruptcy

Chapter 7 bankruptcy also called **liquidation** or **straight bankruptcy,** is a proceeding designed to **liquidate** (convert to cash) a debtor's property, pay off creditors, and discharge the debtor from most debts. A Chapter 7 bankruptcy may be either voluntary or involuntary.

WORD WISE

"Bankrupt" Replaced by "Debtor"

A person who files for bankruptcy under today's law is called a "debtor." This is a change from earlier law, under which a person who filed for bankruptcy was referred to as the "bankrupt." In 1978, Congress passed the Bankruptcy Reform Act with the aim of giving debtors who are overwhelmed with debt a fresh start. Congress also wanted to reduce the stigma connected with the term "bankrupt" and did so by eliminating the term from the law and replacing it with the word "debtor."

Voluntary Bankruptcy. **Voluntary bankruptcy** is a bankruptcy proceeding that is initiated by the debtor. To be eligible to file for this type of bankruptcy, debtors must

1. Satisfy the *means test;* that is, have income below the debtor's state's median family income for families of that size. If the income is greater, the debtor may be able to file Chapter 13 Bankruptcy, which is discussed in the next section.

2. Meet with an approved nonprofit credit counselor before filing for bankruptcy.
3. Furnish a federal income tax return for the most recent tax year.
4. Take a course in financial management after filing for bankruptcy.

When a debtor files a voluntary bankruptcy petition with the court, an **order for relief** (the acceptance of the case by the bankruptcy court) automatically takes place. At that time, an automatic stay goes into effect. An **automatic stay** (also called an **automatic suspension**) is a self-operating postponement of collection proceedings against the debtor. Creditors must stop all efforts to collect debts except for debts caused by fraud, amounts owed for back taxes, family support, and student loans that do not impose a hardship on the debtor. Creditors, such as credit card companies and lenders of unsecured revolving loans cannot bring suit for what is owed them. Debit cards can no longer be used because any money in the debtor's bank belongs automatically to the bankruptcy trustee.

Involuntary Bankruptcy. **Involuntary bankruptcy** is a bankruptcy proceeding that is initiated by one or more creditors. When there are less than 12 creditors, a single creditor who is owed more than $11,625 may file an involuntary bankruptcy petition. However, when there are 12 or more creditors, at least 3 of them must join in the bankruptcy petition, and the total debt must exceed $11,625. The debtor has 20 days to file an objection in an involuntary case, and if this is done, a hearing is held to determine whether an order for relief will be issued.

Exemptions. As part of the "fresh start" policy of the Bankruptcy Code, some items of property, referred to as **exemptions,** are excepted from bankruptcy proceedings and may be retained by the debtor. Each state has its own list of exemptions. The Federal Bankruptcy Code also has a list of exemptions. Many states require that their state exemptions be taken rather than the federal exemptions. In other states, however, debtors may choose to take either the state or the federal exemptions. The 2005 Bankruptcy Code, nevertheless, requires that a debtor be domiciled in a state for two years for that state's exemption rules to apply.

The **homestead exemption** is the exemption from bankruptcy of one's residence up to a certain amount depending on state or federal law. Except for family farmers, the 2005 Bankruptcy Code limits a state homestead exemption to $125,000 if the property was acquired within the previous 3.3 years from the bankruptcy filing.

State bankruptcy exemptions are too varied to list here. A sampling of the federal exemptions include alimony; child support payments; the homestead exemption to the extent of $18,450; a motor vehicle to the extent of $2,950; household furnishings and personal apparel not exceeding $475 per item and $9,850 total; $1,225 in jewelry; $1,850 in professional books or tools of trade; life insurance policies up to $9,850 in loan value; and $18,450 in awards from personal injury lawsuits.

Trustee in Bankruptcy. When bankruptcy proceedings begin, the court appoints a person, called a **trustee in bankruptcy,** to hold the debtor's non-exempt assets in trust for the benefit of creditors. The trustee's duties are to collect the debtor's property and, with the exception of items that the law allows the debtor to keep, convert it to cash and pay the creditors according to certain priorities established by law. Among other things, the trustee has the power to invalidate **preferences**—that is, transfers made by the debtor to creditors, before the bankruptcy proceeding, enabling them to receive a greater percentage of their claim than they would have otherwise received.

Among the papers filed by the debtor in a bankruptcy proceeding, in addition to a list of assets, is a list of creditors and the amount owed to each. The court notifies them of the time and place of the first meeting of creditors, where they are given an opportunity to examine the debtor under oath. The court also notifies creditors that they must file, within 90 days after the first meeting, a **proof of claim,** which is a written, signed statement setting forth a creditor's claim together with the basis for it. A **claim** is a right to payment or other equitable right, such as the right to receive specific performance of a contract.

Once the debtor's property is collected by the trustee and liquidated, the proceeds are distributed to creditors with allowable claims. **Secured creditors** (those who hold mortgages and other liens) receive payment to the exclusion of other creditors. After they are paid, the remaining non-exempt assets are used to pay administrative expenses and unsecured creditors according to a priority list established by the Bankruptcy Code. Nor-

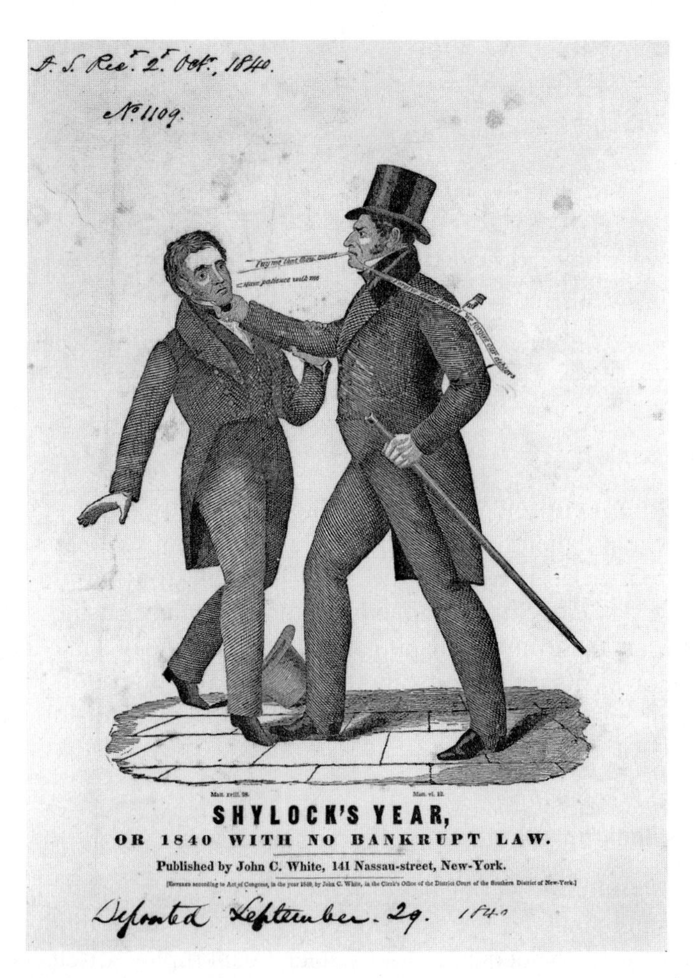

Figure 42-1 This satire was published when Congress failed to pass a national bankruptcy act in 1840. A year later, after the abolishment of debtors' prisons, a bankruptcy act was passed but lasted only two years. In 1867, Congress passed a bankruptcy law that lasted 11 years. The present bankruptcy law began with the Bankruptcy Act of 1898. What types of bankruptcy are available under the current law? (Courtesy of the Library of Congress, Prints and Photographs Division, reproduction number LC-USZ62-91397.)

mally, there is not enough to pay unsecured creditors in full, so their shares are **prorated**—that is, divided proportionately. A **discharge in bankruptcy** releases the debtor from all debts that were proved in the bankruptcy proceeding.

Debtors who file under Chapter 7 must wait at least eight years before filing for bankruptcy again.

Chapter 11 Bankruptcy

Chapter 11 bankruptcy, also called **reorganization,** provides a method for businesses to reorganize their financial affairs, keep their assets, and remain in business. Because the business continues to operate, the debtor in a Chapter 11 bankruptcy case is referred to as a **debtor-in-possession.** Performing the function of a trustee, the debtor develops a reorganization plan, setting forth a method of repaying debts and separating creditors into various classes. To be acceptable by the court, the plan must be feasible and be approved by over half of the creditors in each class. Like Chapter 7, a Chapter 11 bankruptcy may be either voluntary or involuntary.

WEB WISE

Congress can change the federal bankruptcy law at any time. Look for information about the latest bankruptcy law at the following sites:

- **http://www.bankruptcyaction.com**
- **http://www.moranlaw.net**
- **http://www.findlaw.com/01/topics/03bankruptcy/gov_laws.html**

Chapter 12 Bankruptcy

Chapter 12 bankruptcy provides a method for family farmers and also family fishing businesses to adjust their financial affairs while continuing to operate. To qualify, they must receive more than 50 percent of their total income from farming or fishing. Also, if a family farmer, at least 50 percent, and if a family fishing business, at least 80 percent of debt must relate to farming or fishing operations. Total debts may not exceed $3,237,000 for farming or $1,500,000 for fishing. The debtor must develop a reorganization plan as is required in Chapter 11 bankruptcies and serves as a debtor-in-possession, performing the functions of a trustee.

Chapter 13 Bankruptcy

Chapter 13 bankruptcy provides a method for an individual with regular income to pay debts from future income over an extended period of time without being hassled by creditors. Debtors who do not qualify for Chapter 7 bankruptcy (discussed earlier) may be able to file for Chapter 13 Bankruptcy. To be eligible, debtors must first meet with an approved nonprofit credit counselor. Their unsecured debts may not exceed $307,675, and their secured debts may not exceed $922,975. Debtors must make a good faith effort to repay their debts. They must submit a plan, sometimes referred to as a **wage earner's plan,** for the installment payments of outstanding debts, including the eventual payment in full of all claims within three to five years. Chapter 13 Bankruptcy is voluntary. Unlike Chapter 7, there is no waiting period before filing for bankruptcy again.

REVIEWING WHAT YOU LEARNED

After studying the text, write the answers to each of the following questions.

1. What are the goals of the Bankruptcy Code?

2. When do bankruptcy proceedings begin?

3. When may a single creditor file an involuntary bankruptcy petition?

4. Describe the duties of a trustee in bankruptcy.

5. Name some papers filed by a debtor in a bankruptcy proceeding.

6. How are the proceeds from the sale of a debtor's property distributed?

7. List five exemptions under the Federal Bankruptcy Code.

8. How does a Chapter 7 bankruptcy differ from a Chapter 11 bankruptcy?

9. How does a Chapter 13 bankruptcy differ from a Chapter 11 bankruptcy?

10. What is the purpose of a Chapter 12 bankruptcy?

UNDERSTANDING LEGAL CONCEPTS

Indicate whether each statement is true or false. Then, change the italicized word or phrase of each *false* statement to make it true.

Answers

_______________ 1. Bankruptcy proceedings *end* with the filing of a petition with the federal court.

_______________ 2. An order for relief automatically takes place when an *involuntary* bankruptcy petition is filed.

_______________ 3. When there are less than 12 creditors, a single creditor who is owed more than *$3,000* may file an involuntary bankruptcy petition.

_______________ 4. An *order for relief* brings into play an automatic suspension, preventing further efforts by creditors to collect their debts.

_______________ 5. A trustee in bankruptcy has the power, among other things, to *invalidate* preferences.

_______________ 6. The court notifies creditors that they must file, within 90 days after the first meeting, a proof of claim.

_______________ 7. As part of the *nonstop* policy of the Bankruptcy Code, some items of property are exempt from bankruptcy proceedings.

_______________ 8. The federal homestead exemption is one's residence to the extent of $7,500.

_______________ 9. *Chapter 7* bankruptcy provides a method for businesses to reorganize their financial affairs, keep their assets, and remain in business.

_______________ 10. *Chapter 13* bankruptcy provides a method by which an individual with regular income can pay his or her debts from future income over an extended period of time.

CHECKING TERMINOLOGY

From the list of legal terms that follows, select the one that matches each definition.

a. assets
b. automatic stay
c. automatic suspension
d. bankrupt
e. bankruptcy
f. Chapter 7 bankruptcy
g. Chapter 11 bankruptcy
h. Chapter 12 bankruptcy
i. Chapter 13 bankruptcy
j. claim

Answers

____ **1.** People to whom money is owed.

____ **2.** A right to payment.

____ **3.** The legal process by which the assets of a debtor are sold to pay off creditors so that the debtor can make a fresh start financially.

____ **4.** Items of property that are excepted from bankruptcy proceedings and may be retained by the debtor.

____ **5.** Creditors who hold mortgages and other liens.

____ **6.** A self-operating postponement of collection proceedings against a debtor (select two answers).

____ **7.** A bankruptcy proceeding that is initiated by the debtor.

____ **8.** The state of a person (including a business) who is unable to pay debts as they become due.

____ **9.** A proceeding designed to liquidate a debtor's property, pay off creditors, and discharge the debtor from most debts (select three answers).

____ **10.** Divided proportionately.

10

k. creditors
l. debtor
m. debtor-in-possession
n. discharge in bankruptcy
o. exemptions
p. homestead exemption
q. involuntary bankruptcy
r. liquidate
s. liquidation
t. order for relief
u. preferences
v. proof of claim
w. prorated
x. reorganization
y. secured creditors
z. straight bankruptcy
aa. trustee in bankruptcy
bb. voluntary bankruptcy
cc. wage earner's plan

____**11.** A person appointed by a bankruptcy court to hold the debtor's assets in trust for the benefit of creditors.
____**12.** Convert to cash.
____**13.** A method for businesses to reorganize their financial affairs, keep their assets, and remain in business (select two answers).
____**14.** A method for family farmers to adjust their financial affairs while continuing to operate their farms.
____**15.** Property.
____**16.** A bankruptcy proceeding that is initiated by one or more creditors.
____**17.** One who owes a debt to another.
____**18.** Another name for a debtor in Chapter 11, 12, and 13 cases.
____**19.** Transfers made by a debtor to creditors, before a bankruptcy proceeding, enabling them to receive a greater percentage of their claim than they would have otherwise received.
____**20.** A method by which an individual with regular income can pay his or her debts from future income over an extended period of time.
____**21.** A plan for the installment payments of outstanding debts under a Chapter 13 bankruptcy.
____**22.** In bankruptcy, the exemption of one's residence to the extent of $16,150.
____**23.** The acceptance of a case by a bankruptcy court.
____**24.** A signed, written statement setting forth a creditor's claim together with the basis for it.
____**25.** A release of a debtor from all debts that were proved in a bankruptcy proceeding.

UNRAVELING LEGALESE

Use simple, non-legal language, with the help of the glossary, to rewrite this quote from the Bankruptcy Code so that it is shorter and can be understood by a layperson without losing its meaning.

> The definition of "insolvent" in paragraph (26) is adopted from section 1(19) of current law [section 1(19) of former title 11]. An entity is insolvent if its debts are greater than its assets, at a fair valuation, exclusive of property exempted or fraudulently transferred. It is the traditional bankruptcy balance sheet test of insolvency. For a partnership, the definition is modified to account for the liability of a general partner for the partnership's debts. The difference in this definition from that in current law is in the exclusion of exempt property for all purposes in the definition of insolvent.

USING LEGAL LANGUAGE

Read the following story and fill in the blank lines with legal terms taken from the list of terms at the beginning of this chapter:

Valerie worked in a law office that specialized in ______________________—that is, the legal process by which the assets of a(n) ______________________ (one who owes a debt to another) are sold to pay off ______________________ (people to whom money is owed) so that a fresh start can be made financially. Mr. Rodham, a client, had just left, and Attorney Jones had instructed Valerie to prepare the papers for a(n) ________________ bankruptcy, which is also called ________________ or ________________, and is designed to ______________________(covert to cash) Mr. Rodham's property, pay off his debts, and discharge him from most debts. Since the petition will be filed by Mr. Rodham, this will be a(n) ______________________ case, and a(n) ______________________ will automatically take place. When the petition is filed, a(n) ______________________, also called a(n) ______________________________________, occurs, which is a self-operating postponement of collection proceedings against the debtor. A(n) ______________________ will hold Mr. Rodham's assets in trust for the benefit of creditors, some of whom may receive a(n) ______________________share—one that is divided proportionately. Creditors will be required to file a(n) ______________________ within 90 days after their first meeting. The holder of the mortgage on Mr. Rodham's house is known as a(n) ______________________ and will receive payment to the exclusion of other creditors. Any ______________________(earlier transfers resulting in greater percentages to some creditors) that may have occurred will be invalidated. Because of the so-called ______________________, Mr. Rodham may be able to retain an interest in his residence to the extent of $16,150. When the case is finalized, Mr. Rodham will receive a(n) ______________________—that is, a release from all debts that were proved in the proceeding.

10

PUZZLING OVER WHAT YOU LEARNED

Caveat: Do **not** allow squares for spaces between words and punctuation (apostrophes, hyphens, etc.) when filling in crossword.

Across

1. Creditors who hold mortgages and other liens.
5. Another name for a debtor in Chapters 11, 12, and 13 cases.
7. A proceeding designed to liquidate a debtor's property, pay off creditors, and discharge the debtor from most debts.
10. A person appointed by a bankruptcy court to hold the debtor's assets in trust for the benefit of creditors.
12. A proceeding designed to liquidate a debtor's property, pay of creditors, and discharge the debtor from most debts.
16. Convert to cash.
17. A method for businesses to reorganize their financial affairs, keep their assets, and remain in business.

Down

2. Items of property that are excepted from bankruptcy proceedings and may be retained by the debtor.
3. A release of a debtor from all debts that were proved in a bankruptcy proceeding.
4. A bankruptcy proceeding that is initiated by one or more creditors.
6. The legal process by which the assets of a debtor are sold to pay off creditors so that the debtor can make a fresh start financially.
8. The state of a person who is unable to pay debts as they become due.
9. Divided proportionately.
11. Property.
13. People to whom money is owed.
14. A right to payment.
15. One who owes a debt to another.

Glossary of Legal Terms

abortion *(a·BOR·shun)* The act of stopping a pregnancy.

absolute defense *(ab·so·LOOT de·FENSE)* A defense that is good against everyone, including a holder in due course of a negotiable instrument. Also called *real defense* and *universal defense.*

absolute liability *(ab·so·LOOT ly·a·BIL·i·tee)* Liability for an act that causes harm without regard to fault or negligence. Also called *strict liability.*

abstract *(AB·strakt)* To copy in abbreviated form the meaningful parts of an instrument.

abstract of title *(AB·strakt ov TY·tel)* A condensed history of the title to a particular locus.

A–B trust A type of marital deduction trust that reduces the taxation of the second spouse to die by limiting the amount in that person's estate to a sum that is not taxable. Also called *bypass trust, credit-shelter trust,* and *exemption equivalent trust.*

abutter *(a·BUT·er)* A person who owns adjoining land.

acceleration clause *(ak·sel·er·AH·shun)* A clause in a mortgage or note that causes the entire balance of the loan to become due when a default occurs.

acceptance *(ak·SEP·tense)* The assent to the terms of an offer. The act by a drawee of writing "accepted" across the face of a draft and signing it, indicating that he or she agrees to pay it when due.

acceptor *(ak·SEP·tor)* A drawee of a draft who signs it on the face, agreeing to pay it.

accessory after the fact *(ak·SESS·o·ree)* One who receives, relieves, comforts, or assists another with knowledge that the other has committed a felony.

accessory before the fact *(ak·SESS·o·ree)* One who procures, counsels, or commands another to commit a felony but who is not present when the felony is committed.

accomplice *(a·COM·pliss)* Anyone who takes part with another in the commission of a crime.

accord and satisfaction *(a·KORD and sat·is·FAK·shun)* An agreement to perform in a different manner than originally called for, and the completion of that agreed-upon performance.

accretion *(a·KREE·shun)* Any gradual addition to the soil made by nature, such as the gradual accumulation of soil on land next to a stream caused by the action of water. Also called *alluvion.*

acknowledgment *(ak·NAWL·ej·ment)* A formal declaration before an authorized official, by a person who executes an instrument, that it is his or her free act and deed.

acquitted *(a·KWIT·ed)* Discharged from accusation.

action *(AK·shun)* Lawsuit or court proceeding.

actionable *(AK·shun·a·bel)* Furnishing legal ground for a lawsuit.

actual notice *(AK·shoo·el NO·tiss)* Notice actually received.

actus reus *(AHK·tus REE·us)* A voluntary act.

ad damnum *(ahd DAHM·num)* The clause in the complaint stating the damages claimed by the plaintiff.

adeemed ***(a·DEEMD)*** Taken away.

ademption ***(a·DEMP·shun)*** The discharge of a legal obligation by paying a party what is due.

adhesion contract ***(ad·HEE·shen KON·trakt)*** A contract that is drawn by one party to that party's benefit and must be accepted, as is, on a take-it-or-leave-it basis if a contract is to result.

adjudicating ***(a·JOO·di·kay·ting)*** Determining finally by a court.

adjudication ***(a·joo·di·KAY·shun)*** A court judgment.

adjustment of debts of individuals ***(a·JUST·ment ov dets ov in·de·VID·joo·els)*** A method by which an individual with regular income can pay his or her debts from future income over an extended period of time. Also called *Chapter 13 bankruptcy.*

administrator ***(ad·MIN·is·tray·tor)*** A male appointed by the court to administer the estate of an intestate decedent.

administrator ad litem ***(ad LY·tem)*** An administrator appointed by the court to supply a necessary party to a suit in which the estate has an interest.

administrator c.t.a. A person appointed by the court to administer a testate estate in which no executor is nominated or in which the executor has died or for some reason does not settle the estate (c.t.a. is an abbreviation for cum testamento annexo). Also called *administrator with the will annexed* and *administrator w.w.a.*

administrator cum testamento annexo ***(kum tes·ta·MENT·o an·EKS·o)*** A person appointed by the court to administer a testate estate in which no executor is nominated or in which the executor has died or for some reason does not settle the estate. Also called *administrator c.t.a., administrator with the will annexed,* and *administrator w.w.a.*

administrator d.b.n. A person appointed by the court to complete the settlement of an estate in which a previously appointed administrator has died, resigned, or been removed (d.b.n. is an abbreviation for de bonis non).

administrator d.b.n.c.t.a. A person appointed by the court to take the place of a previously appointed executor who has died, resigned, or been removed (d.b.n.c.t.a. is an abbreviation for de bonis non cum testamento annexo).

administrator de bonis non ***(de BO·niss non)*** A person appointed by the court to complete the settlement of an estate in which a previously appointed administrator has died, resigned, or been removed. Also called *administrator d.b.n.*

administrator de bonis non cum testamento annexo A person appointed by the court to take the place of a previously appointed executor who has died, resigned, or been removed. Also called *administrator d.b.n.c.t.a.*

administrator pendente lite ***(pen·DEN·tay LIE·tay)*** A temporary administrator appointed by the court to protect estate assets when there is a will contest.

administrator with the will annexed ***(an·EKSD)*** A person appointed by the court to administer a testate estate in which no executor is nominated or in which the executor has died or for some reason does not settle the estate. Also called *administrator c.t.a., administrator cum testamento annexo,* and *administrator w.w.a.*

administrator w.w.a. A person appointed by the court to administer a testate estate in which no executor is nominated or in which the executor has died or for some reason does not settle the estate (w.w.a. is an abbreviation for with the will annexed). Also called *administrator c.t.a.* and *administrator cum testamento annex.*

administratrix ***(ad·MIN·is·tray·triks)*** A female appointed by the court to administer the estate of an intestate decedent.

admiralty ***(AD·mer·ul·tee)*** Pertaining to the sea.

admissible evidence ***(ad·MISS·e·bel EV·i·dens)*** Evidence that is pertinent and proper to be considered in reaching a decision following specific rules.

adoption ***(a·DOP·shun)*** The legal process in which a child's legal rights and duties toward his or her natural parents are replaced by similar rights and duties toward his or her adopting parents.

adoptive parents ***(a·DOP·tiv)*** Parents who adopt a child.

adultery ***(a·DUL·ter·ee)*** Voluntary sexual intercourse by a married person with someone other than a spouse or by an unmarried person with a married person.

advance directive *(ad·VANS de·REKT·iv)* A written statement specifying whether a person wants life-sustaining medical treatment if he or she becomes desperately ill.

advancement *(ad·VANSE·ment)* The testator's disposing of or giving to a beneficiary, while alive, that which was provided in a will, so as to make it impossible to carry out the will. Also called *satisfaction.*

adverse possession *(AD·verse po·SESH·en)* Title to real property obtained by taking actual possession of it openly, notoriously, exclusively, under a claim of right, and continuously for a period of time set by statute.

affiant *(a·FY·ent)* A person who signs an affidavit. Also called *deponent.*

affidavit *(a·fi·DAY·vit)* A written statement sworn to under oath before a notary public as being true to the affiant's own knowledge, information, and belief.

affiliation proceeding *(a·fil·ee·AY·shun pro·SEED·ing)* A court action to determine whether a person is the father of a child born out of wedlock. Also called *paternity proceeding.*

affinity *(a·FIN·i·tee)* The relationship that one spouse has to the blood relatives of the other.

affirm *(a·FERM)* Approve.

affirmative defense *(a·FERM·a·tiv de·FENSE)* A defense that admits the plaintiff's allegations but introduces another factor that avoids liability. Also called *confession and avoidance.*

agency *(AY·jen·see)* A relationship that exists when one person is authorized to act under the control of another person.

agency by estoppel *(AY·jen·see by es·TOP·el)* Authority that comes about when a principal, through some act, makes it appear that an agent has authority when none actually exists. Also called *apparent authority.*

agency by ratification *(AY·jen·see by rat·i·fi·KAY·shun)* A relationship that occurs when someone performs an act on behalf of another without authority to do so, but the other person later approves of the act.

agent *(AY·jent)* A person authorized to act on behalf of another and subject to the other's control. Also called *surrogate.*

age of consent *(aje ov con·SENT)* The age at which one may be married under state law.

aggravated assault *(AG·ra·va·ted a·SALT)* An assault committed with the intention of committing some additional crime.

aiding and abetting *(a·BET·ing)* Participating in a crime by giving assistance or encouragement.

air rights Rights to the area above the earth's surface.

alderpeople *(AL·der·pee·pel)* People elected to serve as members of the legislative body of a city.

alibi *(AL·i·by)* A defense that places the defendant in a different place than the crime scene, so that it would have been impossible to commit the crime.

alienation of affections *(ale·ee·a·NA·shun ov a·FEK·shuns)* The willful and malicious interference with the marriage relation by a third party without justification or excuse.

alimony *(AL·i·mohn·ee)* An allowance made to a divorced spouse by a former spouse for support and maintenance. Also called *spousal support.*

allegation *(al·e·GAY·shun)* A statement or claim that the party making it expects to prove.

allege *(a·LEJ)* To make an allegation; to assert positively.

alleged *(a·LEJD)* Claimed, asserted, or charged.

allonge *(a·LONJ)* A paper firmly affixed to a negotiable instrument for the writing of indorsements.

alluvion *(a·LOO·vee·en)* Any gradual addition to the soil made by nature, such as the gradual accumulation of soil on land next to a stream caused by the action of water. Also called *accretion.*

alternate jurors *(AL·ter·net JOOR·ors)* Additional jurors impaneled in case of sickness or removal of any of the regular jurors who are deliberating.

alternative dispute resolutions *(al·TERN·a·tiv dis·PYOOT res·o·LOO·shuns)* Procedures for settling disputes by means other than litigation.

ancillary administrator *(AN·sil·a·ree ad·MIN·is·tray·tor)* A person appointed by the court to handle the affairs of a decedent in a foreign state.

animus furandi *(AN·i·mus fer·AN·day)* An intent to steal.

annulment *(a·NUL·ment)* A judicial declaration that no valid marriage ever existed.

answer *(AN·ser)* The main pleading filed by the defendant in a lawsuit in response to the plaintiff's complaint.

antenuptial contract *(an·tee·NUP·shel KON·trakt)* A contract made in contemplation of marriage between prospective spouses setting forth, among other points, the right each spouse will have to property brought into the marriage. Also called *premarital contract* and *prenuptial contract.*

anticipatory breach *(an·TISS·i·pa·tore·ee)* The announcement, before the time for performance, by a party to a contract that he or she is not going to perform.

antilapse statutes *(an·tee·LAPS STAT·shoots)* Laws designed to minimize the effect of lapse.

apparent authority *(a·PAR·ent aw·THAW·ri·tee)* Authority that comes about when a principal, through some act, makes it appear that an agent has authority when none actually exists. Also called *agency by estoppel.*

appeal *(a·PEEL)* A request to a higher court to review the decision of a lower court.

appeal bond A bond often required as security to guarantee the cost of an appeal, especially in civil cases.

appearance *(a·PEER·ens)* The voluntary submission to the court's jurisdiction, either in person or by an agent.

appellant *(a·PEL·ent)* A party bringing an appeal.

appellate courts *(a·PEL·et)* Courts that review the decisions of lower courts. Also called *courts of appeal.*

appellate jurisdiction *(a·PEL·et joo·res·DIK·shen)* The power to hear a case when it is appealed.

appellee *(a·pel·EE)* A party against whom an appeal is brought. Also called *defendant in error* and *respondent.*

appurtenant *(a·PER·ten·ent)* Belonging to; touching and concerning; annexed.

apt words Suitable words.

arbitration *(ar·be·TRAY·shun)* A method of settling disputes in which a neutral third party makes a decision after hearing the arguments on both sides.

arbitrator *(ar·be·TRAY·tor)* A neutral third party in an arbitration session who listens to both sides and makes a decision with regard to the dispute.

arraignment *(a·RAIN·ment)* The act of calling a prisoner before the court to answer an indictment or information.

array *(a·RAY)* The large group of people from which a jury is selected for a trial. Also called *jury panel, jury pool,* and *venire.*

arrest *(a·REST)* To deprive a person of his or her liberty.

arrest warrant *(a·REST WAR·ent)* A written order of the court commanding law enforcement officers to arrest a person and bring him or her before the court.

arson *(AR·sen)* The willful and malicious burning of the dwelling house of another.

articles of organization *(AR·ti·kels ov or·ge·ni·ZAY·shun)* A document that gives authority to an organization to do business as a corporation. Also called *certificate of incorporation* and *charter.*

asportation *(as·por·TA·shun)* The carrying away of goods.

assault *(a·SALT)* The intentional creation of a reasonable apprehension of an imminent battery. An attempt to commit a battery.

assets *(ASS·ets)* Property.

assignee *(ass·en·EE)* One to whom a right is transferred by assignment.

assignment *(a·SINE·ment)* The transfer of a right from one person to another.

assignor *(ass·en·OR)* One who transfers a right by assignment.

assumption of the risk *(a·SUMP·shun)* Plaintiff assumes the consequences of injury; employee agrees that dangers of injury shall be at his or her own risk.

attachment *(a·TACH·ment)* The act of taking or seizing property by the use of a writ, summons, or other judicial order and bringing it into the custody of the court so that it may be applied toward the defendant's debt if the plaintiff wins the case.

attempted arson ***(a·TEMT·ed AR·sen)*** An attempt to commit the crime of arson, falling short of its commission.

attempted larceny ***(a·TEMPT·ed LAR·sen·ee)*** An attempt to commit larceny, falling short of its commission.

attest ***(a·TEST)*** To bear witness to.

attestation clause ***(a·tes·TAY·shun)*** The clause in a will that immediately precedes the witnesses' signatures.

attesting witnesses ***(a·TEST·ing WIT·nes)*** People who witness the signing of a document.

attorney in fact ***(a·TERN·ee)*** An agent who is authorized to act under a power of attorney.

attractive nuisance doctrine ***(a·TRAK·tiv NOO·sens DOK·trin)*** A doctrine establishing property owners' duty to use ordinary care toward trespassing children who might reasonably be attracted to their property.

auction sale ***(AWK·shun)*** A sale of property to the highest bidder.

auction without reserve An auction in which the auctioneer must sell the goods to the highest bidder.

auction with reserve ***(ree·ZERV)*** An auction in which the auctioneer may withdraw the goods without accepting the highest bid.

automatic stay ***(aw·toh·MAT·ic)*** A self-operating postponement of collection proceedings against a debtor. Also called *automatic suspension.*

automatic suspension ***(aw·toh·MAT·ic sus·PEN·shun)*** A self-operating postponement of collection proceedings against a debtor. Also called *automatic stay.*

aver ***(a·VER)*** To make an allegation; to assert positively.

averments ***(a·VER·ments)*** Claims that the party making it expects to prove.

avoid ***(a·VOID)*** To annul, cancel, or make void. To get out of a voidable contract; repudiate. Also called *disaffirm.*

bail Money or property that is left with the court to assure that the person will return to stand trial.

bailee ***(bay·LEE)*** One to whom personal property is given under a bailment contract.

bailment ***(BAYL·ment)*** The relationship that exists when possession (but not ownership) of personal property is transferred to another for a specific purpose.

bailment for the sole benefit of the bailee ***(bay·LEE)*** A gratuitous bailment for the sole benefit of the ***bailee***. (See page 218 for discussion and example.)

bailment for the sole benefit of the bailor ***(bay·LOR)*** A gratuitous bailment benefiting only the bailor.

bailor ***(bay·LOR)*** The owner of personal property that has been temporarily transferred to a bailee under a contract of bailment.

balloon mortgage ***(ba·LOON MORE·gej)*** A mortgage with low fixed payments during the life of the loan, ending with one large final payment.

bankrupt ***(BANK·rupt)*** The state of a person (including a business) who is unable to pay debts as they become due.

bankruptcy ***(BANK·rupt·see)*** A legal process that aims to give debtors who are overwhelmed with debt a "fresh start" and to provide a fair way of distributing a debtor's assets among all creditors.

banns of matrimony ***(MAT·ri·mone·ee)*** Public notice of a marriage contract for a certain number of weeks before the wedding date. Also called *marriage banns.*

bare licensee ***(ly·sen·SEE)*** A person allowed on another's premises by operation of law, such as a firefighter or police officer.

bargain ***(BAR·gen)*** Agreement.

bargain and sale deed ***(BAR·gen)*** A deed that conveys land itself, rather than people's interests therein, and requires consideration.

base lines Horizontal lines running east and west in the United States government survey.

bastards ***(BAS·terds)*** Children born out of wedlock. Also called *illegitimate children* and *nonmarital children.*

battery ***(BAT·er·ee)*** Intentional contact with another person without that person's permission and without justification; the unlawful application of force to another person.

bearer ***(BARE·er)*** A person who is in possession of a negotiable instrument that is payable to bearer, or to cash, or that has been indorsed in blank.

bearer paper ***(BARE·er PAY·per)*** An instrument that requires no indorsement of the payee to be negotiated.

bench trial ***(tryl)*** A trial without a jury. Also called *jury waived trial.*

beneficial title ***(ben·e·FISH·el TY·tel)*** The right to beneficial enjoyment. Also called *equitable title.*

beneficiary ***(ben·e·FISH·ee·air·ee)*** Someone who actually receives a gift under a will; also, one for whose benefit a trust is created. Also called *cestui que trust.*

bequeath ***(be·KWEETH)*** To give personal property in a will.

bequest ***(be·KWEST)*** A gift of personal property in a will.

beyond a reasonable doubt ***(REE·zen·e·bel)*** The fact finder is fully persuaded that the accused has committed the crime.

bidder ***(BID·er)*** Offeror.

bifurcated trial ***(BY·fer·kay·ted tryl)*** A trial that is divided into two parts, providing separate hearings for different issues in the same lawsuit.

bigamy ***(BIG·a·mee)*** The state of a man who has two wives, or of a woman who has two husbands, living at the same time.

bilateral contract ***(by·LAT·er·el KON·trakt)*** A contract containing two promises, one made by each party.

bilateral foreign divorce ***(by·LAT·er·el FOR·en de·VORSE)*** A divorce that occurs when both parties make an appearance in a foreign state or country.

bilateral mistake ***(by·LAT·er·el mis·TAKE)*** When both parties are mistaken about an important aspect of an agreement. Also called *mutual mistake.*

bill of exchange ***(eks·CHANJ)*** A written instrument by which one person orders another person to pay money to a third person. Also called *draft.*

bill of lading ***(LAYD·ing)*** A document issued by a transportation company evidencing the receipt of goods for shipment.

bill of particulars ***(par·TIK·yoo·lars)*** A written statement of the particulars of a complaint showing the details of the amount owed.

bill of sale A signed writing evidencing the transfer of personal property from one person to another.

binding arbitration ***(BINE·ding ar·be·TRAY·shun)*** Arbitration in which the decision of the arbitrator will prevail and must be followed.

blank indorsement ***(in·DORSE·ment)*** An indorsement that specifies no particular indorsee and may consist of a mere signature.

blue-sky laws State laws designed to protect the public from the sale of worthless stocks.

boilerplate ***(BOY·ler·plate)*** Standard language used commonly in documents of the same type.

bond A written instrument promising the payment of a sum of money if certain duties are not performed.

bounds Directions of the boundaries that enclose a parcel of land.

breach of contract ***(KON·trakt)*** The failure of a party to a contract to carry out the terms of the agreement.

breach of promise to marry **(PROM·iss)** Breaking off an engagement to marry.

breaking **(BRAKE·ing)** The putting aside of the dwelling house that is relied on as security against intrusion.

bribery **(BRY·be·ree)** The giving or receiving of a reward to influence any official act.

bulk transfer **(TRANS·fer)** A transfer not in the ordinary course of business in bulk of a major part of the materials, supplies, merchandise, or other inventory of an enterprise.

burden of proof **(BER·den)** The duty of proving a fact.

burglary **(BUR·gler·ee)** At common law, the breaking and entering of a dwelling house of another, in the nighttime, with intent to commit a felony.

business invitee **(BIZ·ness in·vy·TEE)** One invited on the premises for a business or commercial purpose.

bylaw A law enacted by a town.

bypass trust **(BY·pass)** A type of marital deduction trust that reduces the taxation of the second spouse to die by limiting the amount in that person's estate to a sum that is not taxable. Also called *A–B trust, credit-shelter trust,* and *exemption equivalent trust.*

capacity (ka·PAS·e·tee) Legal competency.

capital crime (KAP·i·tel krym) A crime that is punishable by death.

capital criminal case (KAP·i·tel KRIM·i·nel kase) A case in which the death penalty may be inflicted.

carnal knowledge (KAR·nel NOL·ej) Sexual intercourse; the slightest penetration of the sexual organ of the woman by the sexual organ of the man.

case in chief (cheef) The introduction of evidence to prove the allegations that were made in the pleadings and in the opening statement.

castle doctrine (KAS·el DOK·trin) A doctrine that allows people to use all necessary force, without first retreating, to defend themselves when they are in their homes.

causation (kaw·ZAY·shun) The direct and proximate cause of someone's injuries.

cause of action (AK·shun) The ground on which a suit is maintained.

C corporation (kor·por·AY·shun) A corporation governed by Subchapter C of the Internal Revenue Code that pays corporate taxes on its income.

cert. den. (ser·sho·RARE·ee dee·NIDE) Abbreviation meaning certiorari denied.

certificate of deposit (ser·TIF·i·ket ov de·POS·et) An instrument that is given by a bank to acknowledge the receipt of money by a depositor.

certificate of incorporation (ser·TIF·i·ket ov in·kore·per·AY·shen) A document that gives authority to an organization to do business as a corporation. Also called *articles of organization* and *charter.*

certified check (SER·ti·fide) A check that has been accepted, and thus guaranteed, by the bank on which it was drawn and that has been marked to indicate such acceptance.

cestui que trust (SES·twee kay) One for whose benefit a trust is created. Also called *beneficiary.*

chain of title (TY·tel). A series of successive conveyances of real property.

challenge (CHAL·enj) To call or put in question.

challenge for cause (CHAL·enj for kaws) A challenge of a juror made when it is believed that the juror does not stand indifferent.

challenge to the array (CHAL·enj to the a·RAY) A challenge to the entire jury because of some irregularity in the selection of the jury. Also called *motion to quash the array.*

Chapter 7 bankruptcy (BANK·rupt·see) A proceeding designed to liquidate a debtor's property, pay off creditors, and discharge the debtor from most debts. Also called *liquidation* and *straight bankruptcy.*

Chapter 11 bankruptcy (BANK·rupt·see) A method for businesses to reorganize their financial affairs, keep their assets, and remain in business. Also called *reorganization.*

Chapter 12 bankruptcy (BANK·rupt·see) A method for family farmers to adjust their financial affairs while continuing to operate their farms. Also called *family farmer debt adjustment.*

Chapter 13 bankruptcy (BANK·rupt·see) A method by which an individual with regular income can pay his or her debts from future income over an extended period of time. Also called *adjustment of debts of individuals.*

charitable remainder annuity trust (CHAR·i·ta·bel re·MANE·der a·NYOO·i·tee) A trust in which a fixed amount of income is given annually to a beneficiary and the remainder is given to a charity.

charitable remainder trust (CHAR·i·ta·bel re·MANE·der) A trust in which the donor, or a beneficiary, retains the income from the trust for life or other period, after which the trust corpus is given to a charity.

charitable remainder unitrust (CHAR·i·ta·bel re·MANE·der YOO·nee·trust) A trust in which a fixed percentage of income (at least 5 percent of the trust corpus) is given annually to a beneficiary and the remainder is given to a charity.

charitable trust (CHAR·i·ta·bel) A trust established for charitable purposes. Also called *public trust.*

charter (CHAR·ter) A document that gives authority to an organization to do business as a corporation. Also called *articles of organization* and *certificate of incorporation.*

chattels (CHAT·els) Anything that is the subject of ownership other than real property. Also called *personal property* and *personalty.*

check A draft that is drawn on a bank and payable on demand.

Check 21 Act A federal law that authorizes a new negotiable instrument called a substitute check.

child support (su·PORT) The legal obligations of parents to contribute to the economic maintenance and education of their children. Also called *maintenance.*

chose in action (shohz in AK·shun) Evidence of a right to property but not the property itself.

circuits *(SER·kits)* Name given to division of U.S. district courts.

circumstantial evidence (ser·kum·STAN·shel EV·i·dens) Evidence that relates to some fact other than the fact in issue; indirect evidence.

citation *(sy·TAY·shun)* A written order by a judge (or a police officer) commanding a person to appear in court for a particular purpose.

civil action (SIV·el AK·shun) A noncriminal lawsuit.

civil union *(SIV·el YOON·yun)* A relationship in which same-sex couples have the same rights and duties as married couples.

claim A right to payment.

class action *(klas AK·shun)* A lawsuit brought, with the court's permission, by one or more persons on behalf of a very large group of people who have the same interest in the matter.

clear title (TY·tel) Title that is free from any outstanding mortgages, liens, or other encumbrances of record.

close corporation (klose kor·por·AY·shun) A corporation that has restrictions on the transfer of shares.

closing argument (AR·gyoo·ment) Final statement by an attorney summarizing the evidence that has been introduced. Also called *summation.*

code *(KOHD)* A systematic collection of statutes, administrative regulations, and other laws.

codicil (KOD·i·sil) An amendment to a will that must be executed with the same formalities as the will itself.

coercion (ko·ER·shen) Compelling someone to do something by threat or force.

cohabit (koh·HAB·it) Live together.

collateral relatives *(ko·LAT·er·el REL·e·tivs)* Relatives not in a direct line, such as brothers, sisters, nieces, nephews, uncles, aunts, and cousins.

collusion (ke·LOO·shen) An agreement between a husband and wife that one of them will commit a marital offense so that the other may obtain a divorce.

co-maker (KOH-may·ker) A person who, together with someone else, promises to pay money to another on a note.

comity (KOM·i·tee) A doctrine stating that the courts of one jurisdiction will give effect to the laws and judicial decisions of another jurisdiction, not as a matter of obligation but out of deference and respect.

commerce clause (KOM·ers) A clause in the U.S. Constitution giving Congress the power to regulate commerce with foreign nations and among the different states.

common areas (KOM·on AIR·ee·uz) The part of a condominium or apartment building that is owned as tenants in common by all the unit owners.

common law (KOM·on) The case law used in England and the American colonies before the American revolution.

common law marriage (KOM·on law MAHR·ej) A marriage without a formal ceremony.

common law theory of mortgages (KOM·on law THEE·ree ov MORE·ge·jes) The legal theory that a mortgage is a conveyance of title, which becomes void on payment of the obligation. Also called *title theory of mortgages.*

common stock (KOM·on stawk) Stock that has no preferences but that gives the owner the right to vote.

community property (kom·YOON·i·tee PROP·er·tee) Property (other than a gift or inheritance) acquired by a husband or wife during marriage that belongs to both spouses equally.

commutation of sentence (kom·yoo·TAY·shun ov SEN·tense) The changing of a sentence to one that is less severe.

comparative negligence (kom·PAR·e·tiv NEG·li·jens) The proportionate sharing between the plaintiff and the defendant of compensation for injuries, based on the relative negligence of the two.

compensatory damages (kom·PEN·sa·tor·ee DAM·e·jez) Damages that compensate the plaintiff for actual losses resulting from the breach.

complaint (kom·PLAYNT) A formal document containing a short and plain statement of the claim, indicating that the plaintiff is entitled to relief and containing a demand for the relief sought.

compulsory arbitration *(kom·PUL·so·ree ar·be·TRAY·shun)* Arbitration that is required by agreement or by law. Also called *mandatory arbitration.*

computer fraud *(frawd)* Using the computer to obtain money, property, or services by false pretenses.

conciliation *(kon·sil·ee·AY·shun)* An informal process in which a neutral third person listens to both sides and makes suggestions for reaching a solution. Also called *mediation.*

conciliator *(kon·SIL·ee·ay·tor)* A neutral third person in a conciliation session who listens to both sides and makes suggestions for reaching a solution. Also called *mediator.*

concurrent jurisdiction *(kon·KER·ent joo·res·DIK·shen)* The power of two or more courts to decide a particular case.

concurrent ownership *(kon·KER·ent OH·ner·ship)* Owned by more than one person. Also called *co-ownership.*

concurrent sentences *(kon·KER·ent SEN·ten·sez)* Two or more sentences imposed on a defendant to be served at the same time.

condemnation *(kon·dem·NAY·shun)* The process of taking private property for public use through the power of eminent domain.

condition precedent *(kon·DISH·en pree·SEE·dent)* An event that must first occur before an agreement (or deed or will) becomes effective.

condition subsequent *(kon·DISH·en SUB·se·kwent)* A qualification that comes later.

condominium *(kon·de·MIN·ee·um)* A parcel of real property, portions of which are owned separately in fee simple by individual owners and the remainder of which is owned as tenants in common by all the unit owners.

condominium association *(kon·de·MIN·ee·um a·so·see·AY·shun)* A group of people consisting of condominium unit owners that manages and maintains a condominium.

condonation *(kon·do·NAY·shun)* The forgiveness of a matrimonial offense.

confession and avoidance *(kon·FESH·en and a·VOY·dense)* A defense that admits the plaintiff's allegations but introduces another factor that avoids liability. Also called *affirmative defense.*

confidentiality agreement *(kon·fe·den·shee·AL·i·tee a·GREE·ment)* An agreement to refrain from disclosing trade secrets to others. Also called *nondisclosure agreement.*

conforming goods *(kon·FORM·ing)* Goods that are in accordance with the obligations under the contract.

conjugal *(KON·je·gel)* Pertaining to the marriage relationship.

connivance *(ke·NY·vens)* The plaintiff's secret cooperation in the commission of a marital wrong committed by the defendant, which is a common law defense to an action for divorce.

consanguinity *(kon·san·GWIN·i·tee)* Related by blood.

consecutive sentences *(kon·SEK·yoo·tiv SEN·ten·sez)* Two or more sentences imposed on a defendant to be served one after the other. Also called *cumulative sentences.*

consent decree *(kon· SENT de ·KREE)* A decree that is entered by consent of the parties, usually without admitting guilt or wrongdoing.

consequential damages *(kon·se·KWEN·shel DAM·e·jez)* Losses that flow not directly from a breach of contract but from the consequences of it.

conservator *(kon·SER·ve·tor)* One who legally has the care and management of the property, but not the person, of someone who is incompetent.

consideration *(kon·sid·er·AY·shun)* An exchange of benefits and detriments by the parties to an agreement.

consignee *(kon·sine·EE)* One to whom a consignment is made.

consignment *(kon·SINE·ment)* The process of delivering goods to a bailee, called a factor, who attempts to sell them.

consignor ***(kon·sine·OR)*** One who makes a consignment.

consortium ***(kon·SORE·shum)*** The fellowship between a husband and wife.

conspiracy ***(kon·SPIR·a·see)*** The getting together of two or more people to accomplish some criminal or unlawful act.

constructive eviction ***(kon·STRUK·tiv e·VIK·shun)*** Dispossession caused by the landlord doing some act that deprives the tenant of the beneficial enjoyment of the demised premises.

constructively ***(kon·STRUK·tiv·lee)*** Made so by legal interpretation.

constructive notice ***(kon·STRUK·tiv NO·tiss)*** Notice imputed by law.

constructive possession ***(kon·STRUK·tiv po·SESH·en)*** Possession not actual but assumed to exist.

constructive service ***(kon·STRUK·tiv SER·viss)*** A type of service in which the summons and complaint are left at the defendant's last and usual place of abode.

constructive trust ***(kon·STRUK·tiv)*** An implied trust that arises in favor of one who is defrauded when title to property is obtained by fraud.

contract ***(KON·trakt)*** Any agreement that is enforceable in a court of law.

contract implied in fact ***(KON·trakt im·PLIDE)*** A contract that arises from the conduct of the parties rather than from their express statements.

contract implied in law ***(KON·trakt im·PLIDE)*** A contract imposed by law to prevent unjust enrichment. Also called *quasi contract.*

contract to sell ***(KON·trakt)*** A contract under which title to goods is to pass at a future time.

contributory negligence ***(kon·TRIB·u·tor·ee NEG·li·jens)*** Negligence on the part of the plaintiff that contributed to his or her injuries and is a proximate cause of them.

controlled substance ***(kon·TROLED SUB·stanse)*** A drug that is included in any of the five schedules established by the Federal Controlled Substances Act.

conversion ***(kon·VER·shun)*** The wrongful exercise of dominion and control over the personal property in another's possession.

convey ***(kon·VAY)*** To transfer.

conveyance ***(kon·VAY·enss)*** A formal written instrument by which title to real property is transferred from one person to another. Also called *deed.*

conveyance in trust ***(kon·VAY·enss)*** A transfer of legal title to property by the settlor to a trustee to hold for the benefit of a beneficiary.

conveyancing ***(kon·VAY·ens·ing)*** Transferring title to real property.

convicted ***(kon·VICT·ed)*** Found guilty of a crime.

cooperative apartment ***(koh·OP·er·a·tive a·PART·ment)*** A dwelling unit in which the occupants lease individual units and, at the same time, own shares of stock in the corporation that owns the building.

co-ownership ***(koh-OH·ner·ship)*** Owned by more than one person. Also called *concurrent ownership.*

coparceners ***(koh·PAR·se·ners)*** Persons to whom an estate of inheritance descends jointly and by whom it is held as an entire estate (early English law).

co-partnership ***(koh-PART·ner·ship)*** An association of two or more persons to carry on as co-owners of a business for profit. Also called *partnership.*

copulate ***(KOP·yoo·late)*** Engage in sexual intercourse.

copulation ***(kop·yoo·LA·shun)*** Sexual intercourse.

copyright ***(KOP·ee·rite)*** The exclusive right given to an author, composer, artist, or photographer to publish and sell exclusively a work for the life of the author plus 70 years.

copyright infringement ***(KOP·ee·rite in·FRINJ·ment)*** The unauthorized use of copyrighted material.

co-respondent ***(KOH-re·spond·ent)*** The person charged with committing adultery with the defendant in a divorce action.

corporation ***(kor·por·AY·shun)*** A legal entity created under state law with the power to conduct its affairs as though it were a natural person.

corpus ***(KOR·pus)*** The body, principal sum, or capital of a trust. Also called *trust fund, trust principal, trust property,* and *trust res.*

corpus delicti ***(KOR·pus de·LIK·tie)*** A body on which a crime has been committed.

co-tenants *(koh-TEN·entz)* Two or more owners of real property.

counterclaim *(KOWN·ter·klame)* A claim that the defendant has against the plaintiff.

counteroffer *(KOWN·ter·off·er)* A response to an offer in which the terms of the original offer are changed.

court *(KORT)* A body of government organized to administer justice.

court of equity *(EK·wi·tee)* A court that administers justice according to the system of equity.

court of ordinary *(OR·di·ner·ee)* A name given, in some states, to the court that exercises the function of settling decedents' estates.

courts of appeal *(a·PEEL)* Courts that review the decisions of lower courts. Also called *appellate courts.*

covenant *(KOV·e·nent)* A promise or assurance.

covenant marriage *(KOV·e·nent MAHR·ej)* A marriage in which the parties agree to go through counseling before the marriage and also during the marriage to resolve conflicts.

co-venture *(KOH-ven·cher)* A relationship in which two or more people combine their labor or property for a single business undertaking. Also called *joint enterprise, joint venture,* and *syndicate.*

cover *(KUV·er)* The right of a buyer, after breach by a seller, to purchase similar goods from someone else.

coverture *(KUV·er·cher)* Marriage.

creditors *(KRED·et·ers)* People to whom money is owed.

credit-shelter trust *(KRED·et-SHEL·ter)* A type of marital deduction trust that reduces the taxation of the second spouse to die by limiting the amount in that person's estate to a sum that is not taxable. Also called *A–B trust, bypass trust,* and *exemption equivalent trust.*

crime *(krym)* A wrong against society.

crime of moral turpitude *(MOR·el TER·pi·tood)* A crime that is base, vile, and depraved.

criminal complaint *(KRIM·i·nel kom·PLAYNT)* A written statement of the essential facts making up an offense charged in a criminal action.

criminal conversation *(KRIM·i·nel kon·ver·SAY·shun)* A tort action brought by a husband or wife against a third party who committed adultery with the husband or wife's spouse.

criminal fraud *(KRIM·i·nel frawd)* Knowingly and deliberately obtaining the property of another by false pretenses with intent to defraud. Also called *larceny by false pretenses.*

cross claim *(kross klame)* A claim brought by one defendant against another defendant in the same suit.

cross complaint *(kross kom·PLAYNT)* A pleading used in California by a defendant to file a claim against another defendant, a third party, and the plaintiff in the same action.

cross-examination *(kross-eg·zam·in·AY·shun)* The examination of an opposing witness.

cross questions *(kross KWES·chens)* Questions asked by a deponent in response to questions asked at a deposition.

cruelty *(KROO·el·tee)* In a divorce action, personal violence by one spouse that endangers the life, limb, or health of the other spouse.

Crummey powers *(KRUM·ee)* Authority that gives trust beneficiaries the right to withdraw each year the money that is contributed to the trust that year.

culpable negligence *(KUL·pa·bel NEG·li·jens)* The intentional commission of an act that a reasonable person knows would cause injury to another. Also called willful, wanton, and reckless conduct.

cumulative sentences *(KYOOM·yoo·la·tiv SEN·tenses)* Two or more sentences imposed on a defendant to be served one after the other. Also called *consecutive sentences.*

cure *(kyoor)* Correct.

curtesy *(KUR·te·see)* At common law, the right of a widower, if issue of the marriage were born alive, to a life estate in all real property owned by his wife during coverture.

curtilage *(KUR·til·ej)* The enclosed space of ground and buildings immediately surrounding a dwelling house.

custody *(KUS·te·dee)* The care and keeping of anything.

custody of children *(KUS·te·dee)* The care, control, and maintenance of children.

cybercrime ***(SY·ber krym)*** Criminal activity associated with a computer.

cyberlaw ***(SY·ber law)*** The area of law that involves computers and their related problems.

cybertort ***(SY·ber law)*** A tort associated with a computer.

cy pres doctrine ***(sy pray DOK·trin)*** As near as possible.

damages ***(DAM·e·jez)*** The monetary loss suffered by a party as a result of a wrong.

dangerous instrumentalities ***(DAYN·jer·ess in·stroo·men·TAL·i·tees)*** Hazardous items such as explosives and wild animals.

dangerous weapon ***(DAYN·jer·ess WEP·en)*** An item that is, from the way it is used, capable of causing death or serious bodily injury. Also called *deadly weapon.*

deadly weapon ***(DED·lee WEP·en)*** An item that is, from the way it is used, capable of causing death or serious bodily injury. Also called *dangerous weapon.*

debtor ***(DET·er)*** One who owes a debt to another.

debtor-in-possession ***(DET·er-in-po·SESH·en)*** Another name for a debtor in Chapter 11, 12, and 13 cases.

decedent ***(de·SEE·dent)*** A deceased person.

deceit ***(dee·SEET)*** A misrepresentation of a material, existing fact, knowingly made, that causes someone reasonably relying on it to suffer damages. Also called *fraud.*

declaration ***(dek·la·RAY·shun)*** At common law, a formal document containing a short and plain statement of the claim, indicating that the plaintiff is entitled to relief and containing a demand for the relief sought.

declaration of trust ***(dek·la·RAY·shun)*** A written declaration by a settlor that he or she is holding legal title to property as trustee for the benefit of another person.

decree ***(de·KREE)*** The decision of a court of equity.

deed A formal written instrument by which title to real property is transferred from one person to another. Also called *conveyance.*

deed of release ***(re·LEESS)*** A deed releasing property from an encumbrance.

deed of trust An instrument used in some states that replaces a mortgage, by which the legal title to real property is placed in a trustee to secure the repayment of a debt.

deed-poll ***(deed-pole)*** A deed or lease in which only the party making the instrument executes it.

deed without covenants ***(KOV·e·nents)*** A deed to real property in which the grantor transfers only his or her interest, if any, in the property and gives no warranties of title. Also called *fiduciary deed* and *quitclaim deed.*

de facto corporation ***(de FAK·toh kor·por·AY·shun)*** A corporation that has a defect in its establishment but that must be recognized as a valid corporation unless set aside by the state.

defamation ***(de·fa·MAY·shun)*** The wrongful act of damaging another's character or reputation by the use of false statements.

default ***(de·FAWLT)*** A failure to perform a legal duty.

default judgment ***(de·FAWLT JUJ·ment)*** A court decision entered against a party who as failed to plead or defend a lawsuit.

defeasance clause ***(de·FEE·senz)*** A clause in a mortgage providing that the mortgage deed shall be void on payment of the obligation.

defeasible estate ***(de·FEEZ·i·bel es·TATE)*** An estate that can be lost or defeated.

defendant ***(de·FEN·dent)*** A person against whom a legal action is brought.

defendant in error ***(de·FEN·dent in ERR·er)*** A party against whom an appeal is brought. Also called *appellee* and *respondent.*

defense ***(de·FENSE)*** Evidence offered by a defendant to defeat a criminal charge or civil lawsuit.

deficiency judgment ***(de·FISH·en·see JUJ·ment)*** A judgment for the amount remaining due the mortgagee after a foreclosure sale.

degree of kindred ***(de·GREE ov KIN·dred)*** The relationship between a decedent and his or her relatives to determine who are most nearly related by blood.

de jure corporation ***(de JOOR·ee kor·por·AY·shun)*** A corporation that is established in strict compliance with the law.

del credere agent *(del KREH·de·reh AY·jent)* A factor who sells consigned goods on credit and who guarantees to the consignor that the buyer will pay for the goods.

delegation *(del·e·GA·shun)* The transfer of a duty by one person to another.

deliberate *(dee·LIB·e·rate)* To consider slowly and carefully.

demand for bill of particulars *(de·MAND for bill of par·TIK·yoo·lars)* A pleading calling for details of a claim or the separate items of an account.

demand note *(de·MAND)* A note that must be paid whenever the holder demands it.

demise *(de·MIZE)* To lease.

demonstrative legacy *(de·MON·stre·tiv LEG·a·see)* A bequest of a certain sum of money with a direction that it be paid out of a particular fund.

demurrer *(de·MER·er)* A pleading used by the defendant to attack the plaintiff's complaint by raising a point of law, such as the failure of the complaint to state a cause of action.

deponent *(de·PONE·ent)* One who gives testimony under oath. A person who signs an affidavit. Also called *affiant.*

deposition *(dep·e·ZISH·en)* The testimony of a witness, given under oath but not in open court, and later reduced to writing.

deposition on oral examination *(eg·zam·in·AY·shun)* A deposition in which lawyers orally examine and cross-examine a witness.

deposition on written questions *(KWES·chens)* A deposition in which lawyers examine and cross-examine a witness who has received in advance written questions to be answered.

derivative action *(de·RIV·a·tiv AK·shun)* A suit by a stockholder to enforce a corporate cause of action.

derogate *(DEH·ro·gate)* Take away from.

descendants *(de·SEN·dents)* Those who are of the blood stream (including adopted children) of a common ancestor.

descent *(de·SENT)* Succession to the ownership of real property by inheritance (early English law).

desertion *(des·ER·shun)* The voluntary separation of one spouse from the other, for the statutory period, without justification and with the intent of not returning.

destination contract *(des·te·NAY·shun KON·trakt)* A contract that requires the seller to deliver goods to a destination.

determinable fee *(de·TER·min·e·bel)* An estate in real property that is capable of coming to an end automatically because of the happening of some event. Also called *fee simple determinable.*

determine *(de·TER·min)* Coming to an end.

detriment *(DET·ri·ment)* The giving up of a legal right.

devise *(de·VIZE)* A gift of real property in a will.

devisee *(dev·i·ZEE)* A person to whom real property is given by will.

devisor *(dev·i·ZOR)* A person who gives real property by will.

direct evidence *(de·REKT EV·i·dens)* Evidence that directly relates to the fact in issue.

direct examination *(de·REKT eg·zam·in·AY·shun)* The examination of one's own witness.

directive to physicians *(de·REKT·iv to fi·ZI·shens)* A written expression of a person's wishes to be allowed to die a natural death and not be kept alive by heroic or artificial methods. Also called *health care declaration, living will,* and *medical directive.*

directors *(de·REK·ters)* People who are elected by stockholders to manage a corporation.

disaffirm *(dis·a·FERM)* To get out of a voidable contract; repudiate. Also called *avoid.*

discharge in bankruptcy *(DIS·charj in BANK·rupt·see)* A release of a debtor from all debts that were proved in a bankruptcy proceeding.

discovery *(dis·KUV·e·ree)* Methods that allow each party to obtain information from the other party and from witnesses about a case before going to court.

discretion *(dis·KRE·shun)* The power that a judge has to make a decision based on his or her own judgment and conscience.

discretionary trust *(dis·KRE·shun·air·ee)* A trust that allows the trustee to decide how much will be given to each beneficiary in the trustee's discretion. Also called *spray trust* and *sprinkling trust.*

dishonor ***(dis·ON·er)*** To refuse to accept or pay a negotiable instrument when it is presented.

dismissal ***(dis·MISS·el)*** An order disposing of an action without trial of the issues.

dismissal without prejudice A dismissal in which the plaintiff is allowed to correct the error and bring another action on the same claim.

dismissal with prejudice ***(PREJ·e·diss)*** A dismissal in which the plaintiff is barred from bringing another action on the same claim.

dispositive clauses ***(dis·POS·a·tiv)*** The clauses in a will that state exactly what each beneficiary is to receive.

dispossessory warrant proceedings ***(dis·po·SESS·o·ree WAR·ent pro·SEED·ings)*** The legal action used by landlords to evict tenants. Also called *forcible entry and detainer, summary ejectment, summary process,* and *unlawful detainer.*

disseised ***(di·SEEZD)*** Dispossessed.

dissolution of marriage ***(dis·o·LU·shun ov MAHR·ej)*** The act of terminating a valid marriage by a court. Also called *divorce.*

distribution ***(dis·tre·BYOO·shun)*** The apportionment and division of the personal property of an intestate among his or her heirs (early English law).

divested ***(dy·VEST·ed)*** Taken away.

diversity of citizenship ***(dy·VER·sit·ee ov SIT·e·sen·ship)*** A phrase used in connection with the jurisdiction of the federal courts.

divided custody ***(de·VIE·ded KUS·te·dee)*** Custody in which the child will live with each parent part of the year, the other parent usually having visitation rights but not control of the child during that period.

dividends ***(DIV·i·denz)*** Profits distributed to the stockholders of a corporation.

divorce ***(de·VORSE)*** The act of terminating a valid marriage by a court. Also called *dissolution of marriage.*

divorce from bed and board The discontinuance of cohabitation by the spouses. Also called *limited divorce* and *separation of spouses.*

DNA Abbreviation for deoxyribonucleic acid. The double strand of molecules that carries a cell's unique genetic code.

DNA sample Biological evidence of any nature that is utilized to conduct DNA analysis.

docket ***(DOK·et)*** A record of cases that are filed with the court.

docket number ***(DOK·et NUM·ber)*** A number assigned to each case by the clerk of court.

doctrine of charitable immunity ***(DOK·trin ov CHAR·i·ta·bel im·YOO·ni·tee)*** A legal doctrine under which charitable institutions are immune from tort liability.

doctrine of respondeat superior ***(res·PON·dee·at soo·PEER·e·or)*** A legal doctrine under which a master is responsible for the torts of his or her servants that are committed within the scope of employment.

doctrine of sovereign immunity ***(SOV·er·in im·YOO·ni·tee)*** A legal doctrine under which governmental bodies are immune from tort liability.

documentary evidence ***(dok·u·MENT·ta·ree EV·i·dens)*** Evidence consisting of such documents as written contracts, business records, correspondence, wills, and deeds.

Doe defendants ***(de·FEN·dents)*** Reference to defendants whose names are unknown.

domestic bill of exchange ***(do·MES·tik bill ov eks·CHANJ)*** A bill of exchange that is drawn and payable in the United States.

domestic corporation ***(do·MES·tik kor·por·AY·shun)*** A corporation that is organized in the state in which it is operating.

domestic violence ***(do·MES·tik VY·o·lense)*** The abuse of a closely related person such as a present or former spouse or cohabitant.

domicile ***(DOM·i·sile)*** A person's principal place of abode; the place to which, whenever one is absent, one has the present intent of returning.

dominant estate ***(DOM·i·nent es·TATE)*** Land that is benefited by a restriction or easement.

dominant tenement ***(DOM·i·nent TEN·e·ment)*** One who enjoys an easement and to whom it attaches.

donee ***(doh·NEE)*** A person who receives a gift.

donor ***(doh·NOR)*** A person who gives a gift. A person who establishes a trust. Also called *grantor, settlor,* and *trustor.*

dormant partner *(DOR·ment PART·ner)* A partner who is not known to the public as a partner and who takes no active part in the business.

double jeopardy *(DUB·el JEP·er·dee)* Tried twice for the same offense.

double taxation *(DUB·el taks·AY·shun)* Taxes on a corporation's income and on the dividends earned by the corporation's stockholders.

dower *(DOW·er)* At common law, the right of a widow to a life estate in one-third of all real property owned by her husband during coverture.

draft A written instrument by which one person orders another person to pay money to a third person. Also called *bill of exchange.*

drawee *(draw·EE)* A person named in a draft who is ordered to pay money to the payee.

drawer *(draw·ER)* A person who draws a draft.

drugs Chemical substances that have an effect on the body or mind.

drug trafficking *(TRAF·ik·ing)* The unauthorized manufacture or distribution of any controlled substance or the possession of such a substance with the intention of manufacturing or distributing it illegally.

due process clause *(dew PRO·sess)* A clause in the U.S. Constitution requiring that no person shall be deprived of life, liberty, or property without fairness and justice.

durable power of attorney *(DER·e·bel POW·er ov a·TERN·ee)* A document authorizing another person to act on one's behalf with language indicating that it either is to survive one's incapacity or is to become effective when one becomes incapacitated.

duress *(der·ESS)* The overcoming of a person's free will by the use of threat or physical harm.

dwelling house *(DWEL·ing)* A house in which the occupier and family usually reside, including all outbuildings within the curtilage.

easement *(EEZ·ment)* The right to use the land of another for a particular purpose. Also called *right of way.*

easement appurtenant *(EEZ·ment a·PER·ten·ent)* An easement that benefits a particular tract of land.

easement of necessity *(EEZ·ment ov ne·SESS·e·tee)* An easement that is indispensable to the enjoyment of the dominant estate.

easement by prescription *(EEZ·ment by pre·SKRIP·shun)* An easement created by long-continued use of another's property openly, notoriously, continuously, and adversely.

easement in gross *(EEZ·ment in gross)* An easement that is not attached to any parcel of land but is merely a personal right to use the land of another.

e-commerce *(ee-KOM·ers)* Abbreviation for electronic commerce. The buying and selling of goods and services, or the transfer of money, over the Internet.

efficacy *(EF·i·ka·see)* Effectiveness.

ejectment *(e·JEKT·ment)* At common law, the legal action used by landlords to evict tenants.

elective share *(e·LEK·tiv)* A statutory sum given to a surviving spouse who disclaims the provisions made for him or her in a deceased spouse's will. Also called *forced share.*

eleemosynary corporation *(el·ee·MOS·en·er·ee kor·por·AY·shun)* A corporation that is created for charitable and benevolent purposes.

emancipated *(e·MAN·si·pay·ted)* Freed from parental control.

embezzlement *(em·BEZ·ul·ment)* The fraudulent appropriation of property by a person to whom it has been entrusted.

emblements *(EM·ble·ments)* Crops produced annually by labor and industry. Also called *fructus industriales.*

eminent domain *(EM·i·nent doh·MAYN)* The power of the government to take private property for a public purpose.

emotional distress *(e·MO·shun·al dis·TRES)* Emotional suffering caused by the infliction of extreme and outrageous intentional conduct by another.

employee *(em·PLOY·ee)* One who performs services under the direction and control of another.

employer *(em·PLOY·er)* One who employs the services of others in exchange for wages or salaries.

encumbrance *(en·KUM·brens)* A claim that one has against the property of another. A lien, charge, or liability attached to and binding on real property.

enjoin *(en·JOYN)* To require a person to perform or to abstain from some act.

entrapment *(en·TRAP·ment)* A defense that may be used when a police officer induces a person to commit a crime that the person would not have otherwise committed.

equal protection clause *(EE·kwell pro·TEK·shen)* A clause in the U.S. Constitution requiring similarly situated persons to receive similar treatment under the law.

equitable distribution laws *(EK·wit·a·bel dis·tre·BYOO·shun)* Laws that give courts the power to distribute property equitably between the parties upon divorce.

equitable theory of mortgages *(EK·wit·a·bel THEE·ree ov MORE·gejes)* The legal theory that a mortgage is not a conveyance of title but merely a lien against the property. Also called *lien theory of mortgages.*

equitable title *(EK·wit·a·bel TY·tel)* The right to beneficial enjoyment. Also called *beneficial title.*

equity *(EK·wi·tee)* That which is just and fair.

equity of redemption *(EK·wi·tee ov re·DEMP·shun)* The right of a mortgagor to redeem the property any time before the completion of a foreclosure proceeding by paying the amount of the debt, interest, and costs.

erosion *(e·RO·shen)* The gradual eating away of the soil by the operation of currents or tides.

escheat *(es·CHEET)* The reversion of property to the state if the property owner dies without heirs.

escrow *(ES·krow)* An arrangement for completing a real estate transaction by placing the papers and money on a conditional basis with an agent until title is clear and all instruments are recorded.

e-signature *(ee-SIG·na·choor)* Abbreviation for electronic signature, a method of signing an electronic message that identifies the sender and signifies his or her approval of the message's content.

esquire *(ES·kwyr)* A title following the name of an attorney, in place of the prefixes Mr., Mrs., Miss, or Ms. (abbreviated esq.)

establishment clause *(es·TAB·lish·ment)* A clause in the U.S. Constitution that prohibits the government from establishing a state religion.

estate *(es·TATE)* Ownership interest.

estate planning *(es·TATE PLAN·ing)* Arranging a person's assets in a way that maintains and protects the family most effectively both during and after the person's life.

estate pur autre vie *(per OH·tra vee)* An estate that a person holds during the life of another person.

estate tail male A freehold estate restricting ownership to men in the family line.

estate tail special *(SPESH·el)* A freehold estate restricting ownership to a husband and wife and the heirs of their two bodies.

estate tax *(es·TATE)* A tax imposed upon the estate of a deceased person.

et al. *(et ahl)* And another or and others.

et ux. *(et uks)* And wife.

euthanasia *(yooth·e·NAY·zha)* The act of painlessly putting to death someone suffering from an incurable disease as an act of mercy.

eviction *(e·VIK·shun)* The act of depriving a person of the possession of real property either by reentry or by legal process.

exclusionary rule *(eks·KLOO·shun·a·ree)* Evidence obtained by an unconstitutional search or seizure that cannot be used at the trial of a defendant.

exclusive jurisdiction *(eks·KLOO·siv joo·res·DIK·shen)* The power of one court only to hear a particular case to the exclusion of all other courts.

exculpatory clause *(eks·KUL·pa·toh·ree)* A clause that is used in a contract to escape legal responsibility.

excusable homicide *(eks·KYOO·se·bel HOM·i·side)* The taking of a human life when an excuse exists.

execute *(EK·se·kyoot)* To complete, to make, to perform, or to do, such as sign a will.

executed *(EK·se·kyoo·ted)* Carried out or performed.

executor *(eg·ZEK·yoo·tor)* A male nominated in a will of a decedent to carry out the terms of the will; a personal representative of an estate.

executor de son tort *(eg·ZEK·yoo·tor day sown tort)* A person who performs the duties of an executor without authority to do so.

executory ***(eg·ZEK·yoo·tor·ee)*** That which is yet to be executed or performed.

executrix ***(eg·ZEK·yoo·triks)*** A female nominated in a will of a decedent to carry out the terms of the will; a personal representative of an estate.

exemplary damages ***(eg·ZEMP·le·ree DAM·e·jez)*** Damages as a measure of punishment for the defendant's wrongful acts. Also called *punitive damages.*

exemption equivalent trust ***(eg·ZEMP·shun)*** A type of marital deduction trust that reduces the taxation of the second spouse to die by limiting the amount in that person's estate to a sum that is not taxable. Also called *A–B trust, bypass trust,* and *credit-shelter trust.*

exemptions ***(eg·ZEMP·shuns)*** Items of property that are excepted from bankruptcy proceedings and may be retained by the debtor.

exhibits ***(eg·ZIB·its)*** Tangible items that are introduced in evidence.

exordium clause ***(eks·ORD·ee·um)*** The introductory paragraph of a will. Also called *publication clause.*

ex parte ***(eks PAR·tay)*** On one side only.

ex parte foreign divorce ***(eks·PAR·tay FOR·en de·VORSE)*** A divorce that occurs when one spouse appears in a foreign jurisdiction and the other spouse does not appear and fails to respond to the notice of divorce or service of process.

ex post facto ***(eks post FAC·to)*** After the fact.

express authority ***(eks·PRESS aw·THAW·ri·tee)*** Authority that is given explicitly.

express contract ***(eks·PRESS KON·trakt)*** A contract in which the terms are stated or expressed by the parties.

express warranty ***(eks·PRESS WAR·en·tee)*** A statement of fact or promise that goods have certain qualities.

extinction ***(eks·TINK·shun)*** The act of extinguishing or putting to an end.

extortion ***(eks·TOR·shun)*** The corrupt demanding or receiving by a person in office of a fee for services that should be performed gratuitously.

fact finder ***(fakt FINE·der)*** The jury in a jury trial or the judge in a nonjury trial.

factor ***(FAK·ter)*** A bailee to whom goods are consigned for sale.

failure of consideration ***(FAYL·yer ov kon·sid·er·AY·shun)*** A defense available when the consideration provided for in an agreement is not in fact given to the party being sued.

fair-use doctrine ***(DOK·trin)*** A rule stating that the fair use of a copyrighted work for purposes such as criticism, comment, news reporting, teaching, scholarship, or research is not a copyright infringement.

false arrest ***(a·REST)*** The intentional confinement of a person without legal justification. Also called *false imprisonment.*

false imprisonment ***(im·PRIS·on·ment)*** The intentional confinement of a person without legal justification. Also called *false arrest.*

family farmer debt adjustment ***(a·JUST·ment)*** A method for family farmers to adjust their financial affairs while continuing to operate their farms. Also called *Chapter 12 bankruptcy.*

federal question ***(FED·er·ul KWES·chen)*** A matter that involves the U.S. Constitution, acts of Congress, or treason.

fee The largest estate that one can own in land, giving the holder the absolute ownership and power of disposition during life and descending to the owner's heirs at death. Also called *fee simple absolute* and *fee simple estate.*

fee simple absolute ***(SIM·pel ab·so·LOOT)*** The largest estate that one can own in land, giving the holder the absolute ownership and power of disposition during life and descending to the owner's heirs at death. Also called *fee* and *fee simple estate.*

fee simple determinable ***(de·TER·min·e·bel)*** An estate in real property that is capable of coming to an end automatically because of the happening of some event. Also called *determinable fee.*

fee simple estate ***(es·TATE)*** The largest estate that one can own in land, giving the holder the absolute ownership and power of disposition during life and descending to the owner's heirs at death. Also called *fee* and *fee simple absolute.*

fee tail estate ***(es·TATE)*** A freehold estate that restricts ownership of real property to a particular family blood line.

felon ***(FEL·en)*** A person who commits a felony.

felonious homicide ***(fe·LONE·ee·es HOM·i·side)*** Homicide done with the intent to commit a felony.

felony ***(FEL·en·ee)*** A major crime, punishable by imprisonment in a state prison.

felony murder ***(FEL·en·ee MER·der)*** Murder committed while in the commission or attempted commission of a crime punishable with death or imprisonment for life.

feticide ***(FET·e·side)*** Killing a fetus in the womb; abortion.

fiduciary ***(fi·DOO·she·air·ee)*** A person in a position of trust, such as an executor, administrator, guardian, or trustee.

fiduciary capacity ***(fi·DOO·she·air·ee ka·PASS·e·tee)*** A position of trust.

fiduciary deed ***(fi·DOO·she·air·ee)*** A deed to real property in which the grantor transfers only his or her interest, if any, in the property and gives no warranties of title. Also called *deed without covenants* and *quitclaim deed.*

firm offer ***(OFF·er)*** A merchant's written promise to hold an offer open for the sale of goods.

first and final account ***(a·KOWNT)*** An accounting, if it is the only one, presented to the court in final settlement of a decedent's estate.

first-degree murder ***(de·GREE MER·der)*** Murder committed with deliberately premeditated malice aforethought, or with extreme atrocity or cruelty, or while in the commission of a crime punishable by life in prison.

fixed-rate mortgage ***(fiksd-rate MORE·gej)*** A mortgage with an interest rate that does not change during the life of the mortgage.

fixture ***(FIKS·cher)*** Personal property that is physically attached to real property and becomes part of the real property.

flexible-rate mortgage ***(FLEKS·i·bel-rate MORE·gej)*** A mortgage with an interest rate that fluctuates according to changes in an index to which it is connected. Also called *variable-rate mortgage.*

f.o.b. the place of destination ***(des·te·NAY·shun)*** Free on board (no delivery charges) to the place of destination.

f.o.b. the place of shipment ***(SHIP·ment)*** Free on board (no delivery charges) to the place of shipment.

folio ***(FO·lee·oh)*** Page.

forbearance ***(for·BARE·ense)*** Refraining from taking action.

forced heir ***(forssd air)*** A surviving spouse who elects to disclaim the provisions of a deceased spouse's will.

forced share A statutory sum given to a surviving spouse who disclaims the provisions made for him or her in a deceased spouse's will. Also called *elective share.*

forcible entry and detainer ***(FORSS·i·bel EN·tree and de·TAYN·er)*** The legal action used by landlords to evict tenants. Also called *dispossessory warrant proceedings, summary ejectment, summary process,* and *unlawful detainer.*

foreclose ***(for·KLOZE)*** To shut out, bar, or terminate.

foreign corporation ***(FOR·en kor·por·AY·shun)*** A corporation that is organized in a state other than that in which it is operating.

foreign divorce ***(FOR·en de·VORSE)*** A divorce in a state or country other than where the party lives.

foreign jurisdiction ***(FOR·en joo·res·DIK·shen)*** Another state or country.

foreperson ***(FORE·per·son)*** The presiding member of a jury who speaks for the group.

foreseeable ***(fore·SEE·a·bel)*** Known in advance; anticipated.

forgery ***(FOR·jer·ee)*** The fraudulent making or altering of a writing whereby the rights of another might be prejudiced.

fornication ***(for·ni·KA·shun)*** Sexual intercourse between two unmarried persons.

forum ***(FOR·em)*** The place of litigation.

forum non conveniens ***(FOR·em non kon·VEEN·yenz)*** The right of a court to refuse to hear a case if it believes that justice would be better served if the trial were held in a different court.

franchise ***(FRAN·chize)*** An arrangement in which the owner of a trademark, trade name, or copyright licenses others, under special conditions or limitations, to use the trademark, trade name, or copyright in purveying goods or services.

franchisee ***(fran·chize·EE)*** A person to whom a franchise is given.

franchiser ***(FRAN·chize·er)*** A person who gives a franchise to another.

fratricide ***(FRAT·re·side)*** Killing one's brother.

fraud ***(frawd)*** A misrepresentation of a material, existing fact, knowingly made, that causes someone reasonably relying on it to suffer damages. Also called *deceit.*

fraud in esse contractus ***(ESS·ay kon·TRAKT·es)*** Fraud as to the essential nature of the transaction.

fraud in the inducement ***(in·DEWSS·ment)*** Fraud that induces another to enter into a contract.

freedom of assembly ***(FREE·dum ov a·SEM·blee)*** A clause in the U.S. Constitution that guarantees to all persons the right to peaceably associate and assemble with others.

freedom of speech ***(FREE·dum)*** A clause in the U.S. Constitution that guarantees to all persons the right to speak, both orally and in writing.

freedom of the press ***(FREE·dum)*** A clause in the U.S. Constitution that guarantees to all persons the right to publish and circulate their ideas without governmental interference.

free exercise clause ***(EKS·er·size)*** A clause in the U.S. Constitution that guarantees to all persons the right to freely practice their religion.

freehold estate ***(FREE·hold es·TATE)*** An estate in which the holder owns the land for life or forever.

fructus industriales ***(FRUK·tes in·dus·tree·AL·es)*** Crops produced annually by labor and industry. Also called *emblements.*

fructus naturales ***(FRUK·tes nach·er·AL·es)*** Trees and other natural growth.

fruit of the poisonous tree doctrine ***(DOK·trin)*** Evidence generated or derived from an illegal search or seizure that cannot be used at the trial of a defendant.

full age ***(ayj)*** Adulthood.

full covenant and warranty deed ***(KOV·e·nent and WAR·en·tee)*** A deed containing warranties under which the grantor guarantees the property to be free from all encumbrances and to defend the title against the claims of all persons. Also called *general warranty deed.*

full faith and credit clause ***(KRED·et)*** A clause in the U.S. Constitution requiring each state to recognize the laws and court decisions of every other state.

full indorsement ***(in·DORSE·ment)*** An indorsement that specifies the person to whom or to whose order it makes the instrument payable. Also called *special indorsement.*

full warranty ***(WAR·en·tee)*** An express warranty given for consumer goods under which the seller must repair or replace without cost to the buyer defective goods or refund the purchase price.

fungible goods ***(FUN·ji·bel)*** Goods such as grain or oil, of which any unit is the same as any like unit.

future goods ***(FEW·cher)*** Goods that are not yet in existence or under anyone's control.

garnishee ***(gar·nish·EE)*** A third party who holds money or property of a debtor that is subject to a garnishment action.

garnishment ***(GAR·nish·ment)*** A procedure for attaching a defendant's property that is in the hands of a third person.

general agent ***(JEN·e·rel AY·jent)*** An agent who is authorized to conduct all of a principal's activity in connection with a particular business.

general legacy ***(JEN·e·rel LEG·a·see)*** A gift of money out of the general assets of the estate. Also called *general pecuniary legacy.*

general partner ***(JEN·e·rel PART·ner)*** A partner who manages the business and is personally liable for its debts and obligations.

general partnership ***(JEN·e·rel PART·ner·ship)*** A partnership in which the parties carry on a business for the joint benefit and profit of all partners.

general pecuniary legacy ***(JEN·e·rel pee·KYOO·nee·er·ee LEG·a·see)*** A gift of money out of the general assets of the estate. Also called *general legacy.*

general warranty deed ***(JEN·e·rel WAR·en·tee)*** A deed containing warranties under which the grantor guarantees the property to be free from all encumbrances and to defend the title against the claims of all persons. Also called *full covenant and warranty deed.*

generic term ***(jen·ER·ik)*** A term that means relating to or characteristic of a whole group.

genocide ***(JEN·o·side)*** Killing a racial or political group.

gifts causa mortis ***(KAWS·ah MORE·tes)*** Gifts made within three years of the date of death. They are subject to the federal estate tax. Also called *gifts made in contemplation of death.*

gifts made in contemplation of death ***(kon·tem·PLAY·shun)*** Gifts made within three years of the date of death. They are subject to the federal estate tax. Also called *gifts causa mortis.*

gift tax A federal tax that is imposed (with exceptions) on gifts totaling more than $1 million during one's lifetime.

good faith exception to the exclusionary rule ***(ek·SEP·shun)*** Evidence that is discovered by officers acting in good faith but under the mistaken belief that a search was valid and that can be used at the trial of a defendant.

goods Things that are movable.

good samaritan statutes ***(sem·EHR·i·ten STAT·shoots)*** Laws providing that physicians, nurses, and certain other medical personnel will not be liable for negligent acts that occur when they voluntarily, without a fee, render emergency care or treatment outside of the ordinary course of their practice.

government survey system ***(GUV·ern·ment SUR·vey SYS·tem)*** A method of describing real property based on the property's relationship to intersecting lines running east and west (base lines) and lines running north and south (principal or prime meridians). Also called *rectangular survey system.*

graduated-payment mortgage ***(GRAD·yoo·ay·ted MORE·gej)*** A mortgage under which payments increase gradually over the life of the loan.

grand jury ***(JOOR·ee)*** A jury consisting of not more than 23 people who listen to evidence and decide whether or not to charge someone with the commission of a crime.

grand larceny ***(LAR·sen·ee)*** Larceny that is a felony.

grant Conveyance.

grantee ***(gran·TEE)*** A person to whom real property is transferred.

grantee index ***(gran·TEE IN·deks)*** An index that lists by year, in alphabetical order, the names of persons to whom interests in real property are granted.

grantor ***(gran·TOR)*** A person who transfers real property to another. A person who establishes a trust. Also called *donor, settlor,* and *trustor.*

grantor index ***(gran·TOR IN·deks)*** An index that lists by year, in alphabetical order, the names of persons who are named in instruments as conveying away interests in real property.

gratuitous bailment ***(gra·TOO·i·tes BAYL·ment)*** A bailment for the sole benefit of either the bailor or the bailee, in which no consideration is given by one of the parties in exchange for the benefits bestowed by the other.

gratuitous guest ***(gra·TOO·i·tes)*** One invited on the premises for nonbusiness purposes.

gravamen ***(GRAH·va·men)*** The essential basis or gist of a complaint field in a lawsuit.

great pond A pond that is 10 acres or more in size.

gross estate ***(es·TATE)*** All property that the decedent owned at death, including individually and jointly owned property, life insurance, living trusts, and gifts made in contemplation of death.

gross negligence ***(NEG·li·jens)*** Extreme negligence.

guardian ***(GAR·dee·en)*** One who legally has the care and management of the person, property, or both of a minor or incompetent.

guardian ad litem ***(GAR·dee·en ad LY·tem)*** Guardian for the suit. A guardian appointed by a court to protect a minor who brings or defends a lawsuit.

guilty ***(GILL·tee)*** Having committed a crime.

habendum clause ***(ha·BEN·dum)*** The portion of a deed beginning with the words "To have and to hold," which defines the extent of the ownership of the property granted.

half blood Relatives who have one parent in common but not both.

health care declaration ***(dek·la·RAY·shun)*** A written expression of a person's wishes to be allowed to die a natural death and not be kept alive by heroic or artificial methods. Also called *directive to physicians, living will,* and *medical directive.*

health care proxy *(PROK·see)* A written statement authorizing an agent or surrogate to make medical treatment decisions for another in the event of the other's inability to do so.

heart balm statutes *(hart bahm STAT·shoots)* Laws passed in most states abolishing actions for loss of consortium, breach of promise to marry, and alienation of affections.

heir *(air)* A person who inherits property.

heirlooms *(AIR·looms)* Valued possessions with sentimental value passed down through generations within a family.

heirs at law *(airs)* People who would have inherited had a decedent died intestate.

hereditaments *(herr·e·DIT·a·ments)* Things capable of being inherited, including not only lands and everything thereon but also heirlooms.

high treason *(hy TREE·zun)* Acts against the king (under the English common law).

holder *(HOLD·er)* A person who is in possession of a negotiable instrument that has been issued or indorsed to that person's order or to bearer.

holder in due course A holder who has taken a negotiable instrument for value, in good faith, and without any knowledge that it is overdue or that anyone has any claims or defenses to it.

holdover tenant *(HOLD·o·ver TEN·ent)* A tenant who wrongfully remains in possession of the premises after a tenancy has expired. Also called *tenant at sufferance.*

holographic will *(hol·o·GRAF·ik)* A will written entirely in the hand of the testator.

homestead *(HOME·sted)* Property that is beyond the reach of creditors and others' claims as long as the family uses the property as a home.

homestead exemption *(HOME·sted eg·ZEMP·shun)* In bankruptcy, the exemption of one's residence up to a specific amount.

homestead rights *(HOME·sted rites)* Personal rights to the use of the home property free from claims of creditors.

homicide *(HOM·i·side)* The killing of a human being by a human being.

hot pursuit doctrine *(pur·SOOT DOK·trin)* A search warrant is not needed when police pursue a fleeing suspect into a private area.

humanitarian doctrine *(hew·man·i·TAR·ee·en DOK·trin)* A defendant who had the last clear chance to avoid injuring the plaintiff is liable even though the plaintiff was contributorily negligent. Also called *last clear chance doctrine.*

hung jury *(JOOR·ee)* A deadlocked jury; one that cannot agree.

identified goods *(eye·DENT·i·fyd)* Goods that have been selected as the subject matter of a contract.

illegal profiling *(ill·EE·gul PRO·fyl·ing)* A law enforcement action, such as a detention or arrest, based solely on race, religion, national origin, ethnicity, gender, or sexual orientation.

illegitimate children *(il·e·JIT·i·met CHIL·dren)* Children born out of wedlock. Also called *bastards* and *nonmarital children.*

immune *(im·YOON)* Exempt.

impaneled *(im·PAN·eld)* Listed as members of the jury.

impeach *(im·PEECH)* Call in question.

impediment *(im·PED·i·ment)* Disability or hindrance to the making of a contract.

implied authority *(im·PLIDE aw·THAW·ri·tee)* Authority to perform incidental functions that are reasonably and customarily necessary to enable an agent to accomplish the overall purpose of the agency.

implied contract *(im·PLIDE KON·trakt)* A contract in which the terms are not stated or expressed by the parties.

implied trust *(im·PLIDE)* A trust that arises by implication of law from the conduct of the parties.

implied warranty *(im·PLIDE WAR·en·tee)* A warranty that is imposed by law rather than given voluntarily.

impossibility *(im·pos·i·BIL·i·tee)* A method of discharging a contract that is impossible to perform, not merely difficult or costly.

impotency *(IM·pe·ten·see)* The incapacity of either party to consummate a marriage by sexual intercourse because of some physical infirmity or disarrangement.

impute *(im·PEWT)* To charge; to lay the responsibility or blame.

imputed liability *(im·PEW·ted ly·a·BIL·i·tee)* Vicarious responsibility for the torts committed by another person.

inadmissible *(in·ad·MISS·i·bel)* Cannot be received.

incarceration *(in·kar·ser·AY·shun)* Confinement.

incest *(IN·sest)* Sexual intercourse between people who are related by consanguinity or affinity in such a way that they cannot legally marry.

incidental damages *(in·si·DEN·tel DAM·e·jez)* Reasonable expenses that indirectly result from a breach of contract.

incompatibility *(in·kom·pat·e·BIL·i·tee)* Conflicts in personalities and dispositions that are so deep as to be irreconcilable and irremediable and that render it impossible for the parties to continue to live together in a normal marital relationship. Also called *irreconcilable differences* and *irretrievable breakdown.*

incorporation by reference *(in·kore·per·AY·shen by REF·e·renss)* Making a document part of second document by referring to it in the second document and stating the intention of including it.

incorporators *(in·KOR·por·ay·tors)* People who organize a corporation by filing articles of organization with the state government.

indenture *(in·DEN·cher)* A deed or lease to which two or more persons are parties.

independent contractor *(in·de·PEN·dent KON·trak·ter)* One who performs services for others but who is not under the others' control.

indictment *(in·DITE·ment)* A formal written charge of a crime made by a grand jury.

indifferent *(in·DIF·rent)* Impartial, unbiased, and disinterested.

indorsee *(in·dorse·EE)* A person to whom a negotiable instrument is transferred by indorsement.

indorsement *(in·DORSE·ment)* The signature of an indorser, usually on the back of an instrument, for the purpose of transferring the instrument to another.

infancy *(IN·fen·see)* Under the age of majority.

infant *(IN·fent)* The legal name for a minor.

infanticide *(in·FANT·e·side)* Killing an infant soon after birth.

information *(in·for·MA·shun)* A formal written charge of a crime made by a public official rather than by a grand jury.

inheritance tax *(in·HER·i·tense)* A tax imposed on a person who inherits from a decedent's estate.

injunction *(in·JUNK·shun)* An order of a court of equity to do or refrain from doing a particular act.

in pari delicto *(in PAH·ree de·LIK·toh)* In equal fault.

in personam action *(in per·SOH·nem AK·shun)* A lawsuit in which the court has jurisdiction over the person.

personam jurisdiction *(per·SOH·nem joo·res·DIK·shen)* Jurisdiction over the person.

in rem action *(in rem AK·shun)* A lawsuit that is directed against property rather than against a particular person.

insanity *(in·SAN·i·tee)* A defense available to mentally ill defendants who can prove that they did not know the nature and quality of their actions or did not appreciate the criminality of their conduct.

installment note *(in·STALL·ment)* A note that is to be paid in multiple payments during a period.

intangible personal property *(in·TAN·je·bel PER·son·al PROP·er·tee)* Property that is not perceptible to the senses and that cannot be touched.

intellectual property *(in·te·LEK·choo·el PROP·er·tee)* An original work fixed in a tangible medium of expression.

intentional torts *(in·TEN·shun·al)* Torts that are committed intentionally. Also called *willful torts.*

interlocutory decree *(in·ter·LOK·ye·tore·ee de·KREE)* A provisional or temporary decision of a court.

international bill of exchange *(in·ter·NASH·en·el bill ov eks·CHANJ)* A bill of exchange that is drawn in one country and payable in another country.

interrogatories *(in·te·RAW·ga·tore·rees)* A form of discovery in a civil action in which parties are given a series of written questions to be answered under oath.

in terrorem clause ***(in ter·RAW·rem)*** A clause in a will that attempts to disinherit any legatee, devisee, or beneficiary who contests the provisions of the will. Also called *no-contest clause.*

interval ownership ***(IN·ter·vel OH·ner·ship)*** A fee simple ownership of a unit of real property in which the owner can exercise the right of possession for only an interval, such as a week or two, each year. Also called *time-sharing.*

inter vivos ***(IN·ter VY·vose)*** Between the living.

inter vivos trust ***(IN·ter VY·vose)*** A trust that is created by the settlor when he or she is alive. Also called *living trust.*

intestacy ***(in·TESS·te·see)*** The state of dying without having made a valid will.

intestate ***(in·TESS·tate)*** Having made no valid will.

intestate share ***(in·TESS·tate)*** An amount that is inherited when a decedent dies without a will.

intestate succession ***(in·TESS·tate suk·SESH·en)*** The act or process of an heir's becoming beneficially entitled to the property of one who dies without a will.

invasion of privacy ***(in·VA·shun ov PRY·va·see)*** A violation of the right of privacy.

inventory ***(IN·ven·tor·ee)*** A detailed list of articles of property in an estate, made by the executor or administrator thereof.

invitation to deal ***(in·vi·TA·shun)*** A request to an individual or the public to make an offer. Also called *invitation to negotiate.*

invitation to negotiate ***(ne·GO·shee·ate)*** A request to an individual or the public to make an offer. Also called *invitation to deal.*

involuntary bankruptcy ***(in·VOL·en·ter·ee BANK·rupt·see)*** A bankruptcy proceeding that is initiated by one or more creditors.

involuntary manslaughter ***(in·VOL·en·ter·ee MAN·slaw·ter)*** The unintentional killing of another while in the commission of an unlawful act or while in the commission of a reckless act.

irreconcilable differences ***(ir·rek·en·SY·le·bel DIF·ren·sez)*** Conflicts in personalities and dispositions that are so deep as to be irreconcilable and irremediable and that render it impossible for the parties to continue to live together in a normal marital relationship. Also called *incompatibility* and *irretrievable breakdown.*

irretrievable breakdown ***(ir·ree·TREE·ve·bel BRAKE·down)*** Conflicts in personalities and dispositions that are so deep as to be irreconcilable and irremediable and that render it impossible for the parties to continue to live together in a normal marital relationship. Also called *incompatibility* and *irreconcilable differences.*

irrevocable living trust ***(ir·REV·e·ke·bel)*** A trust that may not be rescinded or changed by the settlor at any time during his or her lifetime.

issue ***(ISH·oo)*** All people who have descended from a common ancestor.

joint custody ***(joynt KUS·te·dee)*** Custody in which both parents share the responsibility and authority of child rearing.

joint enterprise ***(joynt EN·ter·prize)*** A relationship in which two or more people combine their labor or property for a single business undertaking. Also called *co-venture, joint venture,* and *syndicate.*

joint liability ***(joynt ly·a·BIL·i·tee)*** Liability under which all joint tortfeasors must be named as defendants in a lawsuit.

joint tenancy ***(TEN·en·see)*** The estate owned by joint tenants. Also called *joint tenancy with the right of survivorship.*

joint tenancy with the right of survivorship ***(ser·VIVE·or·ship)*** The estate owned by joint tenants. Also called *joint tenancy.*

joint tenants ***(TEN·entz)*** Two or more persons holding one and the same interest, accruing by one and the same conveyance, commencing at one and the same time, and held by one and the same undivided possession.

joint tortfeasors ***(tort·FEE·zors)*** Two or more people who participate in the commission of a tort.

joint venture ***(joynt VEN·cher)*** A relationship in which two or more people combine their labor or property for a single business undertaking. Also called *co-venture, joint enterprise,* and *syndicate.*

judgment ***(JUJ·ment)*** The decision of a court of law.

judgment nisi *(JUJ·ment NIE·sie)* A provisional judgment that becomes final at the end of a stated period of time unless a valid reason is shown for not issuing it.

judgment notwithstanding the verdict *(VER·dikt)* A judgment rendered in favor of one party notwithstanding a verdict in favor of the other party. Also called *judgment n.o.v.*

judgment n.o.v. A judgment rendered in favor of one party notwithstanding a verdict in favor of the other party (n.o.v. is the abbreviation for non obstante verdicto, which means notwithstanding a verdict).

judgment on the merits *(MER·its)* A court decision based on the evidence and facts introduced.

judgment on the pleadings *(PLEED·ings)* A judgment rendered without hearing evidence if the court determines that it is clear from the pleadings that one party is entitled to win the case.

junior mortgage *(JOO·nyer MORE·gej)* A mortgage subject to a prior mortgage.

jurisdiction *(joo·res·DIK·shen)* The power or authority that a court has to hear a case.

jurors *(JOOR·ors)* Members of a jury.

jury *(JOOR·ee)* A group of people selected according to law and sworn to determine the facts in a case.

jury charge *(JOOR·ee charj)* Instructions to a jury on matters of law.

jury panel *(JOOR·ee PAN·el)* The large group of people from which a jury is selected for a trial. Also called *array, jury pool,* and *venire.*

jury pool *(JOOR·ee pool)* The large group of people from which a jury is selected for a trial. Also called *array, jury panel,* and *venire.*

jury waived trial *(JOOR·ee waved tryl)* A trial without a jury. Also called *bench trial.*

justice *(JUSS·tis)* The title of an appellate court judge.

justiciable *(jus·TISH·e·bel)* Appropriate for court assessment.

justifiable homicide *(jus·ti·FY·a·bel HOM·i·side)* The taking of a human life when an excuse exists.

kindred *(KIN·dred)* Blood relatives.

lack of consideration *(kon·sid·er·AY·shun)* A defense available to a party being sued when no consideration is contained in the agreement that is sued on.

landlord A person who owns real property and who rents it to another under a lease. Also called *lessor.*

lapsed devise *(lapsd de·VIZE)* A gift of real property in a will that fails because the devisee predeceased the testator.

lapsed legacy *(lapsd LEG·a·see)* A gift of personal property in a will that fails because the legatee predeceased the testator.

larceny *(LAR·sen·ee)* At common law, the wrongful taking and carrying away of personal property of another with the intent to steal.

larceny by false pretenses *(PRE·ten·sez)* Knowingly and deliberately obtaining the property of another by false pretenses with the intent to defraud. Also called *criminal fraud.*

last clear chance doctrine *(DOK·trin)* A defendant who had the last clear chance to avoid injuring the plaintiff is liable even though the plaintiff was contributorily negligent. Also called *humanitarian doctrine.*

lateral support *(LAT·e·rel su·PORT)* To hold up at the side.

leading questions *(LEE·ding)* Questions that suggest to the witness the desired answer.

lease *(leess)* A contract granting the use of certain real property by its owner to another for a specified period in return for the payment of rent.

leasehold estate *(LEESS·hold es·TATE)* An estate that is less than a freehold estate. The interest that is conveyed by a lease.

legacy *(LEG·a·see)* A gift of personal property in a will.

legal fiction *(LEE·gul FIK·shun)* An assumption, for purposes of justice, of a fact that does not exist.

legal issues *(LEE·gul ISH·oos)* Questions of law to be decided by the court in a lawsuit.

legal tender *(LEE·gul TEN·der)* Coin, paper, or other currency that is sufficient under law for the payment of debts.

legal title *(LEE·gul TY·tel)* Full, absolute ownership.

legatee ***(leg·a·TEE)*** A person who receives a gift of personal property under a will.

legator ***(leg·a·TOR)*** A person who makes a gift of personal property by will.

lessee ***(less·EE)*** A person who has temporary possession of and an interest in real property of another under a lease. Also called tenant.

lesser included offense ***(o·FENSE)*** A crime that contains some but not all elements of a greater offense, making it impossible to commit the greater offense without also committing the lesser offense.

lessor ***(less·OR)*** A person who owns real property and who rents it to another under a lease. Also called *landlord.*

letters of administration ***(ad·min·is·TRAY·shun)*** A certificate of appointment as administrator of an estate.

letters testamentary ***(test·e·MEN·ter·ee)*** A certificate of appointment as executor of a will.

levy on execution ***(LEV·ee on ek·se·KYOO·shen)*** To collect a sum of money by putting into effect the judgment of a court.

liability ***(ly·a·BIL·i·tee)*** Legal responsibility, obligation, or duty.

libel ***(LIE·bel)*** Defamation that is communicated by a writing, drawing, photograph, television program, or other means that is directed toward the sense of sight. The initial pleading in a divorce action.

libelant ***(lie·bel·AHNT)*** The plaintiff in a divorce action.

libelee ***(lie·bel·EE)*** The defendant in a divorce action.

license ***(LY·sense)*** A grant or permission to do a particular thing.

licensee ***(ly·sen·SEE)*** A person who has permission to do certain acts.

lien ***(leen)*** A claim or charge on property for the payment of a debt.

lien theory of mortgages ***(leen THEE·ree ov MORE·ge jes)*** The legal theory that a mortgage is not a conveyance of title but merely a lien against the property. Also called *equitable theory of mortgages.*

life estate ***(es·TATE)*** An estate limited in duration to either the life of the owner or the life of another person.

life tenant ***(TEN·ent)*** The owner of a life estate.

limited defense ***(LIM·i·ted de·FENSE)*** A defense that can be used against a holder but not a holder in due course of a negotiable instrument. Also called *personal defense.*

limited divorce ***(LIM·i·ted de·VORSE)*** The discontinuance of cohabitation by the spouses. Also called *divorce from bed and board* and *separation of spouses.*

limited liability company ***(LLC) (LIM·i·ted ly·a·BIL·i·tee KUM·pe·nee)*** A nonpartnership form of business organization that has the tax benefits of a partnership and the limited liability benefits of a corporation.

limited liability limited partnership (LLLP) The combination of a limited partnership and a limited liability partnership.

limited liability partnership ***(LLP) (LIM·i·ted ly·a·BIL·i·tee PART·ner·ship)*** A general partnership in which only the partnership, and not the individual partners, is liable for the tort liabilities of the partnership. Also called *registered limited liability partnership (RLLP)* and *registered partnership having limited liability (RPLL).*

limited partner ***(LIM·i·ted PART·ner)*** A partner who invests money or other property in the business but who is not liable for the debts or obligations of the partnership.

limited partnership ***(LIM·i·ted PART·ner·ship)*** A partnership formed by two or more persons having as members one or more general partners and one or more limited partners.

limited warranty ***(LIM·i·ted WAR·en·tee)*** An express warranty given for consumer goods that is less than a full warranty.

limited warranty deed ***(LIM·i·ted WAR·en·tee)*** A deed containing warranties under which the grantor guarantees that the property is free from all encumbrances made during the time that he or she owned the property and agrees to defend the title only against claims through him or her. Also called *special warranty deed.*

lineal ascendants ***(LIN·ee·el a·SEN·dents)*** People who are in a direct line of ascent (upwards) from the decedent—parents, grandparents, and great grandparents.

lineal descendants ***(LIN·ee·el de·SEN·dents)*** People who are in a direct line of descent (downward) from the decedent—children, grandchildren, and great grandchildren.

liquidate ***(LIK·wi·date)*** Turn into cash.

liquidated damages ***(LIK·wi·day·ted DAM·e·jez)*** Damages that are agreed on by the parties at the time of the execution of a contract in the event of a subsequent breach.

liquidation ***(lik·wi·DAY·shun)*** A proceeding designed to liquidate a debtor's property, pay off creditors, and discharge the debtor from most debts. Also called *Chapter 7 bankruptcy* and *straight bankruptcy.*

lis pendens ***(lis PEN·denz)*** A pending suit.

litigants ***(LIT·i·gants)*** Parties to a lawsuit.

litigation ***(lit·i·GAY·shun)*** A suit at law.

littoral owners ***(LIT·o·rel OH·ners)*** People whose property abuts the ocean or a large lake.

living trust A trust that is created by the settlor when he or she is alive. Also called *inter vivos trust.*

living will A written expression of a person's wishes to be allowed to die a natural death and not be kept alive by heroic or artificial methods. Also called *directive to physicians, health care declaration,* and *medical directive.*

local action ***(LO·kal AK·shun)*** A lawsuit that can occur only in one place.

locus ***(LOH·kus)*** Place; locality.

locus sigilli ***(LOH·kus se·JIL·i)*** Place of the seal.

long-arm statutes ***(STAT·shoots)*** Statutes that allow one state to reach out and obtain personal jurisdiction over a person in another state.

loss of consortium ***(kon·SORE·shum)*** The destruction of fellowship between a husband and wife.

mail fraud ***(frawd)*** Using mail to obtain money, property, or services by false pretenses.

maim ***(maym)*** To cripple or mutilate in any way.

maintenance ***(MAIN·ten·ens)*** The legal obligations of parents to contribute to the economic maintenance and education of their children. Also called *child support.*

majority ***(ma·JAW·ri·tee)*** Full age; adulthood.

maker A person who promises to pay money to another on a note.

mala in se ***(MAL·ah in say)*** Wrong in and of itself.

mala prohibita ***(MAL·ah pro·HIB·i·ta)*** Prohibited wrong.

malefactor ***(mal·e·FAK·ter)*** A person found guilty of a crime.

malfeasance ***(mal·FEE·zense)*** The doing of an act that ought not to be done at all.

malice ***(MAL·iss)*** Evil intent; that state of mind that is reckless of law and of the legal rights of others.

malicious prosecution ***(ma·LISH·us pros·e·KYOO·shun)*** Prosecution begun in malice without probable cause.

malpractice ***(mal·PRAK·tiss)*** Professional misconduct; negligence of a professional.

managers ***(MAN·a·jers)*** People who are designated by the members of a limited liability company to manage the company.

mandatory arbitration ***(MAN·da·tor·ee ar·be·TRAY·shun)*** Arbitration that is required by agreement or by law. Also called *compulsory arbitration.*

mandatory sentence ***(MAN·da·tor·ee SEN·tense)*** A fixed sentence that must be imposed with no room for discretion.

manslaughter ***(MAN·slaw·ter)*** The unlawful killing of one human being by another without malice aforethought.

marital deduction ***(MAR·i·tal de·DUK·shun)*** The amount that passes from a decedent to a surviving spouse and is not taxable under the federal estate tax law.

maritime ***(MER·i·tym)*** Pertaining to the sea.

marriage ***(MAHR·ej)*** Under the laws of the federal government and most states, the union of one man and one woman.

marital deduction trust ***(MAR·i·tal de·DUK·shun)*** A trust that is arranged to make maximum use of the marital deduction that is found in the federal estate tax law.

marriage banns ***(MAHR·ej)*** Public notice of a marriage contract for a certain number of weeks before the wedding date. Also called *banns of matrimony.*

master ***(MAS·ter)*** An employer. A lawyer appointed by the court to hear testimony in a case and report back to the court as to his or her findings or conclusions

master deed ***(MAS·ter deed)*** A deed to a condominium that describes the entire property that is owned by the condominium association.

matricide ***(MAT·ri·side)*** Killing one's mother.

mayhem ***(MAY·hem)*** At common law, violently depriving others of the use of such members as may render them less able in fighting.

mediation ***(mee·dee·AY·shun)*** An informal process in which a neutral third person listens to both sides and makes suggestions for reaching a solution. Also called conciliation.

mediator ***(MEE·dee·ay·tor)*** A neutral third person in a mediation session who listens to both sides and makes suggestions for reaching a solution. Also called *conciliator.*

medical directive ***(MED·i·kel de·REKT·iv)*** A written expression of a person's wishes to be allowed to die a natural death and not be kept alive by heroic or artificial methods. Also called *directive to physicians, health care declaration,* and *living will.*

medical power of attorney ***(MED·ikel POW·er ov a·TERN·ee)*** A written statement authorizing an agent or surrogate to make medical treatment decisions for another in the event of the other's inability to do so.

members ***(MEM·bers)*** Owners of a limited liability company.

memorandum ***(mem·o·RAN·dum)*** The writing that is necessary to satisfy the statute of frauds.

mens rea ***(menz RAY·ah)*** Criminal intent.

merchant ***(MER·chent)*** A person who sells goods of the kind sold in the ordinary course of business or who has knowledge or skills peculiar to those goods.

meridians ***(mer·ID·ee·ens)*** Lines running north and south in the United States government survey. Also called *prime meridians* and *principal meridians.*

metes ***(meets)*** Distances between points.

metes and bounds A system of describing real property by its outer boundaries, with reference to courses, distances, and monuments.

minimum sentence ***(MIN·i·mum SEN·tense)*** The smallest amount of time that a prisoner must serve before being released or placed on parole.

mini-trials ***(tryls)*** Informal trials run by private organizations established for the purpose of settling disputes out of court.

Miranda warnings ***(mer·AN·da)*** The constitutional right given to people who are arrested to be told before being questioned that they have the right to remain silent, that any statements made by them may be used against them, that they have a right to have a lawyer present, and that a lawyer will be provided without cost if they cannot afford one.

miscegenation ***(mis·sej·e·NA·shun)*** Marriage between people of different races.

misdemeanor ***(mis·de·MEEN·er)*** A minor crime; not a felony.

misfeasance ***(mis·FEE·zense)*** The improper doing of an act.

misnomer ***(mis·NO·mer)*** Mistake in name.

misrepresentation ***(mis·rep·rez·en·TA·shun)*** A false or deceptive statement or act.

mistrial ***(MIS·tryl)*** An invalid trial of no consequence.

mitigate ***(MIT·i·gate)*** Lessen; keep as low as possible.

moiety ***(MOY·e·tee)*** A part, portion, or fraction.

monuments ***(MON·yoo·ments)*** Visible marks indicating boundaries.

mortgage ***(MORE·gej)*** A conveyance of real property for the purpose of securing a debt. Also called *mortgage deed.*

mortgage assignment ***(MORE·gej a·SINE·ment)*** The transfer of a mortgagee's interest in a mortgage to another person.

mortgage assumption ***(MORE·gej a·SUMP·shun)*** An agreement by a new owner of real property to pay the former owner's mortgage. Also called *mortgage take-over.*

mortgage deed ***(MORE·gej)*** A conveyance of real property for the purpose of securing a debt. Also called *mortgage.*

mortgage discharge ***(MORE·gej DIS·charj)*** A document stating that a mortgage debt is satisfied.

mortgagee ***(more·gej·EE)*** One who lends money and takes back a mortgage as security for the loan.

mortgagee's foreclosure sale *(more·gej·EES for·KLOH·zher)* A sale of real property that terminates all rights of the mortgagor in the property covered by the mortgage.

mortgage take-over *(MORE·gej)* An agreement by a new owner of real property to pay the former owner's mortgage. Also called *mortgage assumption.*

mortgagor *(more·gej·OR)* One who borrows money and gives a mortgage, that is, pledges property, to the lender as security for the loan.

motion *(MOH·shun)* A written or oral request made to a court for certain action to be taken.

motion for a directed verdict *(de·REK·ted VER·dikt)* In a jury trial, a motion asking the court to find in favor of the moving party as a matter of law, without having the case go to the jury.

motion for a more definite statement *(DEF·e·net STATE·ment)* A motion by a party, when a pleading is vague, asking the court to order the other party to make a more definite statement.

motion for judgment on the pleadings *(JUJ·ment on the PLEED·ings)* A motion by either party for a judgment in that party's favor based solely on information contained in the pleadings.

motion for order compelling discovery *(com·PEL·ing dis·KUV·e·ree)* A motion asking the court to order the other party to produce certain writings, photographs, or other requested items.

motion for recusal *(re·KYOO·zel)* A request that a judge disqualify himself or herself from a case because of bias or prejudice.

motion for summary judgment *(MOH·shun for SUM·er·ee JUJ·ment)* A motion that may be made when all of the papers filed in a case show that there is no genuine issue of fact and that the party making the motion will win the case as a matter of law.

motion in limine *(MOH·shun in LIM·e·nee)* A pretrial motion asking the court to prohibit the introduction of prejudicial evidence by the other party.

motion to dismiss *(dis·MISS)* A motion made by the defendant asking the court to dismiss the case.

motion to quash the array *(MOH·shun to kwash the a·RAY)* A challenge to the entire jury because of some irregularity in the selection of the jury. Also called *challenge to the array.*

motion to strike A motion asking the court to order the other party to remove from a pleading any insufficient defense or any redundant, immaterial, impertinent, or scandalous matter.

murder *(MER·der)* The unlawful killing of a human being by another with malice aforethought.

mutual benefit bailment *(MYOO·choo·el BEN·e·fit BAYL·ment)* A bailment in which both the bailor and the bailee receive some benefit.

mutual mistake *(MYOO·choo·el mis·TAKE)* When both parties are mistaken about an important aspect of an agreement. Also called *bilateral mistake.*

mutuum *(MYOO·choo·um)* A loan of goods, on the agreement that the borrower may consume them, returning to the lender an equivalent in kind and quantity.

navigable airspace *(NAV·i·ga·bel AIR·spays)* The space above 1,000 feet over populated areas and above 500 feet over water and unpopulated areas.

navigable stream *(NAV·i·ga·bel)* A stream that ebbs and flows with the tide or is capable of being navigated by commercial vessels.

necessaries *(NE·se·ser·ees)* Food, clothing, shelter, and medical care that are needed by an infant but not supplied by a parent or guardian.

negligence *(NEG·li·jens)* The failure to use that amount of care and skill that a reasonably prudent person would have used under the same circumstances and conditions.

negotiation *(ne·go·shee·AY·shun)* The transfer of an instrument in such form that the transferee becomes a holder.

next friend One acting for the benefit of an infant in bringing a legal action.

next of kin Those most nearly related by blood.

nighttime The time between one hour after sunset on one day and one hour before sunrise on the next day.

no-contest clause *(no-KON·test)* A clause in a will that attempts to disinherit any legatee, devisee, or beneficiary who contests the provisions of the will. Also called *in terrorem clause.*

no-fault divorce *(de·VORSE)* A dissolution of marriage without regard to fault.

nolo contendere *(NO·lo kon·TEN·de·ray)* A plea in which the defendant neither admits nor denies the charges.

nominal damages *(NOM·i·nel DAM·e·jez)* Damages in name only.

nominal partner *(NOM·i·nel PART·ner)* A partner in name only, who has no real interest in the partnership. Also called *ostensible partner.*

nonbinding arbitration *(non·BIND·ing ar·be·TRAY·shun)* Arbitration in which the arbitrator's decision is simply a recommendation and need not be complied with.

nonconforming goods *(non·kon·FORM·ing)* Goods that are not the same as those called for under the contract.

nonconforming use *(non·kon·FORM·ing)* A use not allowed by the new law but permitted if already being done.

nondisclosure agreement *(non·dis·KLOH·zher a·GREE·ment)* An agreement to refrain from disclosing trade secrets to others. Also called *confidentiality agreement.*

nonfeasance *(non·FEE·zense)* The failure to do an act that ought to be done.

nonmarital children *(non·MAR·i·tel)* Children born out of wedlock. Also called *bastards* and *illegitimate children.*

non obstante verdicto *(non ob·STAN·tee ver·DIK·toh)* Abbreviated n.o.v. Notwithstanding a verdict.

nonsuit *(NON·soot)* The termination of an action that did not adjudicate issues on the merits.

notary public *(NO·te·ree PUB·lik)* A person authorized to administer oaths, attest to and certify documents, take acknowledgments, and perform other official acts.

note A written promise by one party to pay a sum of money to another party. Also called *promissory note.*

novation *(no·VAY·shun)* An agreement whereby an original party to a contract is replaced by a new party.

nudum pactum *(NOO·dum PAK·tum)* Barren promise with no consideration.

nuisance *(NOO·sens)* The use of one's property in a way that causes annoyance, inconvenience, or discomfort to another.

nullity *(NUL·i·tee)* Nothing; as though it had not occurred.

nuncupative will *(NUN·kyoo·pay·tiv)* An oral will.

obscenity *(ob·SEN·i·tee)* Material or conduct that shows or describes some kind of sexual activity and is designed to make people become sexually aroused.

offer *(OFF·er)* A proposal made by an offeror.

offeree *(off·er·EE)* One to whom an offer is made.

offeror *(off·er·OR)* One who makes an offer.

one day—one trial jury system *(JOOR·ee SYS·tem)* A system designed to provide the courts with juries consisting of fair cross sections of the community and to reduce the burden of jury duty on certain classes of citizens.

opening statement *(O·pen·ing STATE·ment)* An attorney's outline to the jury of anticipated proof.

operating agreement *(OP·er·ate·ing a·GREE·ment)* An agreement that sets forth the rights and obligations of the members and establishes the rules for operating a limited liability company.

option contract *(OP·shen KON·trakt)* A binding promise to hold an offer open.

order for relief *(re·LEEF)* The acceptance of a case by a bankruptcy court.

order paper An instrument that requires the indorsement of the payee and delivery to be negotiated.

ordinance *(OR·di·nense)* A law passed by a city council.

ordinary negligence *(OR·di·ner·ee NEG·li·jens)* The want of ordinary care.

original jurisdiction *(o·RIJ·i·nel joo·res·DIK·shen)* The power to hear a case when it first goes to court.

Orphan's Court A name given, in some states, to the court that exercises the function of settling decedents' estates.

ostensible partner *(os·TEN·si·bel PART·ner)* A partner in name only, who has no real interest in the partnership. Also called *nominal partner.*

output contract *(OWT·put KON·trakt)* A contract to sell "all the goods a company manufactures" or "all the crops a farmer grows."

overrule ***(o·ver·ROOL)*** To annul, make void, or refuse to sustain.

pain and suffering ***(SUF·er·ing)*** Physical discomfort and emotional trauma.

pardon ***(PAR·den)*** A setting aside of punishment altogether by a government official.

parole ***(pa·ROLE)*** A conditional release from prison allowing the person to serve the remainder of a sentence outside of prison under specific terms.

parole board A group of people authorized to grant parole. Also called *parole commission.*

parole commission ***(ke·MISH·en)*** A group of people authorized to grant parole. Also called *parole board.*

parolee ***(pa·role·EE)*** A person placed on parole.

parol evidence rule ***(pa·ROLE EV·i·dens)*** Oral evidence of prior or contemporaneous negotiations between the parties is not admissible in court to alter, vary, or contradict the terms of a written agreement.

partial release ***(PAR·shell re·LEESS)*** A document stating that specified parcels of property are released from an encumbrance.

partition ***(par·TI·shun)*** The division of land held by joint tenants or tenants in common into distinct portions so that they may hold them separately.

partnership ***(PART·ner·ship)*** An association of two or more persons to carry on as co-owners of a business for profit. Also called *co-partnership.*

party to a suit ***(PAR·tee)*** A person or organization participating or having a direct interest in a legal proceeding.

patent ***(PAT·ent)*** A grant by the U.S. government of the exclusive right to make, use, and sell an invention for 17 years.

patent infringement ***(PAT·ent in·FRINJ·ment)*** The unauthorized making, using, or selling of a patented invention during the term of the patent.

paternity proceeding ***(pa·TERN·i·tee pro·SEED·ing)*** A court action to determine whether a person is the father of a child born out of wedlock. Also called *affiliation proceeding.*

patricide ***(PAT·ri·side)*** Killing one's father.

payee ***(pay·EE)*** A person named in a note or a draft to whom payment is to be made.

pecuniary gift ***(pee·KYOO·nee·er·ee)*** Gift of money.

penal laws ***(PE·nel)*** Laws that impose a penalty or punishment for a wrong against society.

pendente lite ***(pen·DEN·tay LIE·tay)*** Litigation pending.

per capita ***(per KAP·i·ta)*** Per head.

percolating waters ***(PER·ko·late·ing)*** Waters that pass through the ground beneath the surface of the earth without any definite channel.

peremptory challenge ***(per·EMP·ter·ee CHAL·enj)*** A challenge of a juror for which no reason need be given.

performance ***(per·FORM·ens)*** Discharging a contract by doing that which one agreed to do under the terms of the contract.

periodic tenancy ***(peer·ee·ODD·ik TEN·en·see)*** An estate in real property that continues for successive periods until one of the parties terminates it by giving notice to the other party. Also called *tenancy from year to year.*

perjury ***(PER·jer·ee)*** The giving of false testimony under oath.

per se ***(per say)*** In and of itself; taken alone.

personal covenant ***(PER·son·al KOV·e·nent)*** A promise that is binding on one person only and does not run with the land.

personal defense ***(PER·son·al de·FENSE)*** A defense that can be used against a holder but not a holder in due course of a negotiable instrument. Also called *limited defense.*

personal property ***(PER·son·al PROP·er·tee)*** Anything that is the subject of ownership other than real property. Also called *chattels* and *personalty.*

personal recognizance ***(PER·son·al re·KOG·ni·zense)*** A personal obligation by a person to return to stand trial.

personal representative ***(PER·son·al rep·re·ZEN·ta·tiv)*** The executor or administrator of a deceased person.

personal service ***(PER·son·al SER·viss)*** Delivering a copy of the summons and complaint to the defendant personally.

personalty ***(PER·sen·el·tee)*** Anything that is the subject of ownership other than real property. Also called *chattels* and *personal property.*

per stirpes ***(per STIR·peez)*** By right of representation.

petition ***(pe·TI·shun)*** A written application for a court order.

petitioner ***(pe·TI·shun·er)*** One who presents a petition to a court.

petit jury ***(PET·ee JOOR·ee)*** The ordinary jury of 6 or 12 people used for the trial of a civil or criminal action.

petit larceny ***(PET·ee LAR·sen·ee)*** Larceny that is a misdemeanor rather than a felony. Also called *petty larceny.*

petit treason ***(PET·ee TREE·zan)*** Acts against one's master or lord (under the English common law).

petty larceny ***(PET·ee LAR·sen·ee)*** Larceny that is a misdemeanor rather than a felony. Also called *petit larceny.*

plaintiff ***(PLAIN·tif)*** A person who brings a legal action against another.

plain view doctrine ***(DOK·trin)*** A search warrant is not needed to seize items that are in plain view of a lawfully positioned police officer.

plat A map designating the size and shape of a specific land area. Also called *plat map* and *plot.*

plat book A book that is recorded at the registry of deeds containing plat maps.

plat map A map designating the size and shape of a specific land area. Also called *plat* and *plot.*

plea bargaining ***(plee BAR·gen·ing)*** The working out of a mutually satisfactory disposition of a case by the prosecution and the defense.

pleadings ***(PLEED·ings)*** The written statements of claims and defenses used by the parties in a lawsuit.

plenary jurisdiction ***(PLEN·e·ree joo·res·DIK·shen)*** Complete jurisdiction over both the parties and the subject matter of a lawsuit.

plot A map designating the size and shape of a specific land area. Also called *plat* and *plat map.*

polling the jury ***(POLE·ing)*** A procedure in which individual jurors are asked whether they agree with the verdict given by the jury foreperson.

polygamy ***(po·LIG·a·mee)*** The state of having several wives or husbands at the same time.

pornography ***(por·NAW·graf·ee)*** Material or conduct that shows or describes some kind of sexual activity and is designed to make people become sexually aroused.

possession ***(po·SESH·en)*** The detention and control of anything.

possibility of reverter ***(pos·i·BIL·i·tee ov re·VERT·er)*** An interest in property due to the possibility that an event will occur causing the property to revert to the grantor.

pour-over trust ***(pore-O·ver)*** A provision in a will leaving a bequest or devise to the trustee of an existing living trust.

power of attorney ***(POW·er ov a·TERN·ee)*** A formal writing that authorizes an agent to act for a principal.

power of sale clause ***(POW·er)*** A clause in a mortgage allowing the mortgagee to hold a foreclosure sale without involving the court when a default in payment of the mortgage occurs.

precatory trust ***(PREK·a·tore·ee)*** An express trust that arises from the use of polite, noncommanding language by a testator in a will.

predecease ***(pre·de·SEES)*** Die before.

preferences ***(PREF·er·en·ses)*** Transfers made by a debtor to creditors before a bankruptcy proceeding, enabling them to receive a greater percentage of their claim than they would have otherwise received.

preferred stock ***(pre·FERD)*** Stock that has a superior right to dividends and to capital when the corporation is dissolved.

preliminary hearing ***(pre·LIM·i·ner·ee HEER·ing)*** A hearing before a judge to determine whether there is sufficient evidence to believe that the person has committed a crime. Also called *probable cause hearing.*

preliminary injunction ***(pre·LIM·i·ner·ee in·JUNK·shun)*** An injunction issued by a court before hearing the merits of a case.

premarital contract ***(pre·MAR·i·tel KON·trakt)*** A contract made in contemplation of marriage between prospective spouses setting forth, among other points, the right each spouse will have to property brought into the marriage. Also called *antenuptial contract* and *prenuptial contract.*

premeditated malice aforethought ***(pre·MED·i·tay·ted MAL·iss a·FORE·thawt)*** Thinking over, deliberating on, or weighing in the mind beforehand.

prenuptial contract ***(pre·NUP·shel KON·trakt)*** A contract made in contemplation of marriage between prospective spouses setting forth, among other points, the right each spouse will have to property brought into the marriage. Also called *antenuptial contract* and *premarital contract.*

preponderance of evidence ***(pre·PON·der·ense ov EV·i·dens)*** Evidence of the greater weight.

Prerogative Court ***(pre·ROG·a·tiv)*** A name given in some states to the court that exercises the function of settling decedents' estates.

pretermitted child ***(pre·ter·MIT·ed)*** A child who is omitted by a testator from a will.

pretrial hearing ***(PRE·tryl HEER·ing)*** A hearing before the judge prior to a trial, attended by the attorneys, for the purpose of speeding up the trial.

prima facie case ***(PRY·mah FAY·shee)*** Legally sufficient for proof unless rebutted or contradicted by other evidence.

prime meridians ***(mer·ID·ee·ens)*** Lines running north and south in the United States government survey. Also called *meridians* and *principal meridians.*

primogeniture ***(pry·mo·JEN·e·cher)*** The state of being the first born among several children of the same parents (early English law).

principal ***(PRIN·se·pel)*** One who authorizes another to act on one's behalf.

principal in the first degree ***(de·GREE)*** One who actually commits a felony.

principal in the second degree One who did not commit the act but was present, aiding and abetting another in the commission of a felony.

principal meridians ***(PRIN·se·pel mer·ID·ee·ens)*** Lines running north and south in the United States government survey. Also called *meridians* and *prime meridians.*

prior appropriation doctrine ***(PRY·er a·pro·pree·AY·shun DOK·tren)*** A principle of law allowing the first person who puts water to beneficial use the right to do so even though the flow of water is cut off to other riparian owners.

private nuisance ***(PRV·vet NOO·sens)*** A nuisance that disturbs one neighbor only.

privileges and immunities clause ***(PRIV·i·leg·es and im·YOO·ni·teez)*** A clause in the U.S. Constitution requiring states to give out-of-state citizens the same rights as it gives its own citizens.

privity of contract ***(PRIV·i·tee ov KON·trakt)*** The relationship that exists between contracting parties.

probable cause ***(PROB·a·bel kawz)*** Reasonable grounds for belief that an offense has been committed.

probable cause hearing ***(PROB·a·bel kawz HEER·ing)*** A hearing before a judge to determine whether there is sufficient evidence to believe that the person has committed a crime. Also called *preliminary hearing.*

probate ***(PRO·bate)*** To prove and have allowed by the court.

Probate and Family Court A name given in some states to the court that exercises the function of settling decedents' estates.

proceeding ***(pro·SEED·ing)*** The procedure in California for obtaining a dissolution of marriage.

process ***(PROSS·ess)*** The means of compelling the defendant in an action to appear in court.

process server ***(PROSS·ess SERV·er)*** A person who carries out service of process.

pro-choice ***(pro-choys)*** Favoring legislation that allows abortion.

product liability ***(PROD·ukt ly·a·BIL·i·tee)*** Liability of manufacturers and sellers to compensate people for injuries suffered because of defects in their products.

profit à prendre ***(PROF·et a PRAWN·dra)*** A special type of easement that allows the dominant tenement to remove something, such as sand, gravel, or timber, from the servient property.

pro-life ***(pro-life)*** Favoring legislation that disallows abortion.

promisee ***(prom·i·SEE)*** One to whom a promise is made.

promisor ***(prom·i·SOHR)*** One who makes a promise.

promissory estoppel ***(PROM·i·sore·ee es·TOP·el)*** A doctrine under which no consideration is necessary when someone makes a promise that induces another's action or forbearance, and injustice can be avoided only by enforcing the promise.

promissory note ***(PROM·i·sore·ee)*** A written promise by one party to pay a sum of money to another party. Also called *note.*

promoters ***(pro·MO·ters)*** People who begin a corporation by obtaining investors and taking charge up to the time of the corporation's existence.

proof of claim A signed, written statement setting forth a creditor's claim together with the basis for it.

proponent ***(pro·PO·nent)*** One who proposes or argues in support of something, such as the allowance of a will.

proprietary lease ***(pro·PRY·e·ter·ee)*** A lease to an owner of the property.

prorated ***(pro·RATE·ed)*** Divided proportionately.

prosecute ***(PROS·e·kyoot)*** To proceed against a person criminally.

prosecution ***(pros·e·KYOO·shun)*** A criminal action. The party by whom criminal proceedings are started or conducted; the state.

proximate cause ***(PROK·si·met kaws)*** The dominant or moving cause.

proxy marriage ***(PROK·see MAHR·ej)*** A ceremonial marriage in which one of the parties is absent but represented by an agent who stands in his or her place.

prudent ***(PROO·dent)*** Cautious.

prurient interests ***(PROO·ree·ent IN·trests)*** A shameful or morbid interest in sex.

public administrator ***(PUB·lik ad·MIN· is·tray·tor)*** An official who administers the estate of a person who dies intestate when no relative, heir, or other person appears who is entitled to act as administrator.

publication clause ***(pub·li·KAY·shun)*** The introductory paragraph of a will. Also called *exordium clause.*

public domain ***(PUB·lik doh·MAYN)*** Owned by the public.

public nuisance ***(PUB·lik NOO·sens)*** A nuisance that affects the community at large.

public trust ***(PUB·lik)*** A trust established for charitable purposes. Also called charitable trust.

punitive damages ***(PYOON·i·tiv)*** Damages as a measure of punishment for the defendant's wrongful acts. Also called *exemplary damages.*

qualified indorsement ***(KWAH·li·fide in·DORSE·ment)*** An indorsement that limits the liability of the indorser.

qualified terminable interest property ***(QTIP)*** **trust** ***(KWAH·li·fide TERM·in·a·bel IN·trest PROP·er·tee)*** A marital deduction trust that gives all trust income to a surviving spouse for life, payable at least annually, with the principal passing to someone else upon the spouse's death.

quasi ***(KWAY·zi)*** As if; almost as it were.

quasi contract ***(KWAY·zi KON·trakt)*** A contract imposed by law to prevent unjust enrichment. Also called *contract implied in law.*

quasi in rem action ***(KWAY·zi in rem AK·shun)*** A lawsuit in which the court has jurisdiction over the defendant's property but not over the defendant's person.

questions of fact ***(KWES·chens)*** Questions about the activities that took place between the parties that caused them to go to court.

questions of law Questions relating to the application or interpretation of law.

quiet enjoyment ***(KWY·et en·JOY·ment)*** The right of a tenant to possess the rented property and to be undisturbed in that possession.

quitclaim deed ***(KWIT·klame)*** A deed to real property in which the grantor transfers only his or her interest, if any, in the property and gives no warranties of title. Also called *deed without covenants* and *fiduciary deed.*

racketeering ***(rak·a·TEER·ing)*** Activities of organized criminals who extort money from legitimate businesses.

range ***(rainj)*** A row of townships running north and south in the United States government survey.

rape At common law, the unlawful, forcible carnal knowledge by a man of a woman against her will or without her consent.

rape shield laws ***(sheeld)*** Laws passed to help prevent rape victims from being victimized.

ratify ***(RAT·i·fy)*** Approve; confirm.

real defense ***(de·FENSE)*** A defense that is good against everyone, including a holder in due course of a negotiable instrument. Also called *absolute defense* and *universal defense.*

real estate closing ***(reel es·TATE KLOS·ing)*** The procedure in which title to real property is transferred from a seller to a buyer. Also called *real estate settlement.*

real estate settlement ***(reel es·TATE SET·el·ment)*** The procedure in which title to real property is transferred from a seller to a buyer. Also called *real estate closing.*

real evidence ***(reel EV·i·dens)*** Actual objects that have a bearing on the case, such as an item of clothing, a weapon found at the scene of a crime, a photograph, a chart, or a model.

real property ***(reel PROP·er·tee)*** The ground and anything permanently attached to it, including land, buildings, and growing trees, and the airspace above the ground.

reasonable care ***(REE·zen·e·bel)*** The degree of care that a reasonable person would have used under the circumstances then known.

reasonable doubt ***(REE·zen·e·bel dowt)*** Doubt based on reason.

reasonable time ***(REE·zen·e·bel)*** A time, left to the discretion of the judge, that may be fairly allowed depending on the circumstances.

rebuttal ***(re·BUT·el)*** The introduction of evidence that will destroy the effect of the evidence introduced by the other side.

receiving stolen goods ***(re·SEEV·ing STOH·len)*** The buying, receiving, or aiding in the concealment of stolen or embezzled property, knowing it to have been stolen.

reconciliation ***(rek·on·sil·ee·AY·shun)*** The renewal of amicable relations.

record owner ***(REK·erd)*** One who appears to be the owner of real property according to the records at the registry of deeds.

recrimination ***(re·krim·i·NAY·shun)*** Conduct on the part of the plaintiff that constitutes a ground for divorce, which is a common law defense to an action for divorce.

recross questions ***(RE·kross KWES·chens)*** Further questions asked by a deponent in response to redirect questions.

rectangular survey system ***(rek·TANG·yoo·ler SUR·vey SYS·tem)*** A method of describing real property based on the property's relationship to intersecting lines running east and west (base lines) and lines running north and south (principal or prime meridians). Also called *government survey system.*

recuse ***(re·KYOOZ)*** Disqualify.

redeem ***(re·DEEM)*** Buy back.

redirect questions ***(re·de·REKT KWES·chens)*** Further questions asked by an examiner at a deposition in response to cross questions.

registered land ***(REJ·is·terd)*** Land that is recorded under the Torrens system of land registration, confirming that title to the property is clear except for anything noted on the title certificate.

registered limited liability partnership (RLLP) ***(REJ·is·terd)*** A general partnership in which only the partnership, and not the individual partners, is liable for the tort liabilities of the partnership. Also called *limited liability partnership (LLP)* and *registered partnership having limited liability (RPLL).*

registered partnership having limited liability (RPLL) A general partnership in which only the partnership, and not the individual partners, is liable for the tort liabilities of the partnership. Also called *limited liability partnership (LLP)* and *registered limited liability partnership (RLLP).*

rejection ***(re·JEK·shun)*** The refusal by an offeree of an offer.

relevant evidence ***(REL·e·vent EV·i·dens)*** Evidence tending to prove or disprove an alleged fact.

reliction ***(re·LIK·shun)*** The gradual recession of water, leaving land permanently uncovered.

remainder interest ***(re·MANE·der IN·trest)*** An interest that takes effect after another estate is ended.

remand ***(re·MAND)*** Send back.

rendition ***(ren·DI·shun)*** The return of fugitives to the state where they are accused of having committed a crime by the governor of the state to which they have fled.

reorganization ***(re·or·ge·ni·ZAY·shun)*** A method for businesses to reorganize their financial affairs, keep their assets, and remain in business. Also called *Chapter 11 bankruptcy.*

reply ***(re·PLY)*** The plaintiff's answer to the defendant's counterclaim.

report ***(re·PORT)*** A statement that identifies the locus, names the present owner, gives the dates between which the title was searched, and lists all liens or encumbrances to which the property is subject.

republishing a will ***(re·PUB·lish·ing)*** Reestablishing a will that has been formerly revoked or improperly executed.

requirements contract ***(re·KWIRE·ments KON·trakt)*** A contract to buy "all the fuel (or other goods) needed for one year."

res ***(reyz)*** The property; the thing.

rescind ***(ree·SIND)*** Cancel.

rescission ***(ree·SISH·en)*** Cancellation.

reservation ***(rez·er·VAY·shun)*** The act of keeping back.

residence ***(RES·e·dens)*** A place where a person actually lives.

residuary clause ***(re·ZID·joo·er·ee)*** The clause in a will that disposes of all of the testator's property not otherwise distributed.

residuary estate ***(re·ZID·joo·e·ree es·TATE)*** The estate remaining after individual items have been given out by a will.

res ipsa loquitur ***(reyz IP·sa LO·kwe·ter)*** The thing speaks for itself.

respondeat superior ***(res·PON·dee·at soo·PEER·ee·or)*** A rule of law that makes principals and employers responsible for the torts of their agents and servants committed within the scope of their authority or employment.

respondent ***(re·SPON·dent)*** One who is called on to answer a petition. A party against whom an appeal is brought. Also called *appellee* and *defendant in error.*

response ***(re·SPONS)*** The written answer to a petition filed by a respondent.

restitution ***(res·ti·TEW·shun)*** Restore an injured person to his or her original position prior to a loss.

restraining order ***(re·STRANE·ing)*** An order forbidding a person from doing a particular act.

restrictions ***(re·STRIK·shuns)*** Limitations on the use of real property. Also called *restrictive covenants.*

restrictive covenants ***(re·STRIK·tiv KOV·e·nents)*** Limitations on the use of real property. Also called *restrictions.*

restrictive indorsement ***(re·STRIK·tiv in·DORSE·ment)*** An indorsement that purports to prohibit further transfer of the instrument.

resulting trust ***(re·ZULT·ing)*** An implied trust that arises in favor of the payor when property is transferred to one person after being paid for by another person.

retaliatory eviction ***(re·TAL·ee·a·tore·ee e·VIK·shun)*** The eviction of a tenant for reporting sanitary code or building code violations to the authorities.

reverse ***(re·VERSE)*** Make void. Also called *set aside.*

reversionary interest ***(re·VER·zhen·e·ree IN·trest)*** A right to the future enjoyment of property that one originally owned.

revert ***(re·VERT)*** Go back.

revocable ***(REV·e·ke·bel)*** Capable of being revoked.

revocable living trust ***(REV·e·ke·bel)*** A trust that may be rescinded or changed by the settlor at any time during his or her lifetime.

revocation ***(rev·o·KA·shun)*** The act of revoking. The taking back of an offer by an offeror before it has been accepted.

revoke ***(re·VOKE)*** Cancel or rescind.

RICO ***(REE·coh)*** Acronym for Racketeer Influenced and Corrupt Organizations Act, a federal statute designed to stop organized criminal activity from invading legitimate businesses.

right of contribution ***(kon·tri·BYOO·shun)*** The right to share a loss among joint tortfeasors or other codefendants.

right of privacy ***(PRY·va·see)*** The right to be left alone, the right to be free from uncalled-for publicity, and the right to live without unreasonable interference by the public in private matters.

right of redemption ***(re·DEMP·shun)*** The right to take property back. A statutory right to redeem the property even after a foreclosure sale.

right of way The right to use the land of another for a particular purpose. Also called *easement.*

right-to-die laws Laws allowing dying people to refuse extraordinary treatment to prolong life.

riparian owners ***(ry·PARE·ee·en OH·ners)*** People who own land along the banks of a river or stream.

riparian rights doctrine ***(ry·PARE·ee·en rites DOK·trin)*** A principle of law giving all riparian owners equal rights to the reasonable use of the water that flows past their borders.

ripe for judgment ***(JUJ·ment)*** The stage of a trial when everything has been completed except the court's decision.

ripeness doctrine ***(RIPE·ness DOK·trin)*** A principle under which the court will not hear a case unless there is an actual, present controversy for the court to decide.

risk of loss Responsibility in case of damage or destruction.

robbery ***(ROB·e·ree)*** The wrongful taking and carrying away of the personal property of another from the other's person or personal custody against his or her will by force and violence.

rule against perpetuities ***(per·pe·TYOO·i·teez)*** The principle that no interest in property is good unless it must vest, if at all, not later than 21 years after some life in being, plus the gestation period, at the creation of the interest.

rules of civil procedure ***(SIV·el pro·SEED·jer)*** Regulations that govern the proceedings in civil cases.

rules of criminal procedure ***(KRIM·i·nel pro·SEED·jer)*** Regulations that govern the proceedings in criminal cases.

rundown An examination of the grantor index under the name of each owner in the chain of title during the years that they owned the property.

sale The passing of title from the seller to the buyer for a price.

sale on approval ***(a·PROOV·el)*** A sale of goods that are for the buyer's use rather than for resale, and that may be returned even though they conform to the contract.

sale or return ***(re·TURN)*** A sale of goods that are primarily for resale and that may be returned even though they conform to the contract.

satisfaction ***(sat·is·FAK·shun)*** The testator's disposing of or giving to a beneficiary, while alive, that which was provided in a will, so as to make it impossible to carry out the will. Also called *advancement.*

scienter ***(si·EN·ter)*** Knowingly.

S corporation ***(kor·por·AY·shun)*** A corporation governed by Subchapter S of the Internal Revenue Code, in which the income of the corporation is taxed directly to the shareholders rather than to the corporation itself.

seal A mark, impression, the word "seal," or the letters L.S. placed on a written contract next to a party's signature.

search warrant ***(WAR·ent)*** A written order of the court authorizing law enforcement officers to search and seize certain property.

second-degree murder ***(SEK·end-de·GREE MER·der)*** Murder that is not found to be in the first degree.

second mortgage ***(SEK·end MORE·gej)*** A mortgage subject to a prior mortgage. Also called *junior mortgage.*

secret partner ***(SEE·kret PART·ner)*** A partner who takes an active part in the business but is not known to the public as a partner.

section ***(SEK·shun)*** A square mile of land, containing 640 acres, in the United States government survey.

secured creditors ***(se·KYOORD KRED·et·ers)*** Creditors who hold mortgages and other liens.

security ***(se·KYOOR·i·tee)*** Assurance (usually in the form of a pledge or deposit) given by a debtor to a creditor to make sure a debt is paid.

seisin ***(SEE·zin)*** Possession of a freehold.

selectpeople ***(sel·EKT·pee·pel)*** People elected to serve as the chief administrative authority of a town.

self-defense *(de·FENSE)* An excuse for the use of force in resisting attack, especially for killing an assailant.

self-proving affidavit *(a·fi·DAY·vit)* A clause in a will containing an affidavit that allows the will to be allowed by the court without the testimony of witnesses.

sentence *(SEN·tense)* The judgment of the court imposing punishment when the defendant is found guilty in a criminal case.

separation of spouses *(sep·a·RAY·shun ov SPOW·sez)* The discontinuance of cohabitation by the spouses. Also called *divorce from bed and board* and *limited divorce.*

sequester *(see·KWEST·er)* To set apart; isolate.

servant *(SER·vent)* One who performs services under the direction and control of another; an employee.

servicemark *(SER·viss·mark)* A term used to describe trademark protection for services.

service of process *(SER·viss ov PROSS·ess)* The delivering of summonses or other legal documents to the people who are required to receive them.

servient estate *(SER·vee·ent es·TATE)* Land that bears the burden of a restriction or easement.

servient tenement *(SER·vee·ent TEN·e·ment)* One on whom an easement is imposed.

set aside *(a·SIDE)* Make void. Also called *reverse.*

settlor *(set·LOR)* A person who establishes a trust. Also called *donor, grantor,* and *trustor.*

several *(SEV·er·el)* Separate, individual, and independent.

several liability *(SEV·er·el ly·a·BIL·i·tee)* Liability under which joint tortfeasors may be sued separately in a lawsuit.

severance of actions *(SEV·er·ense ov AK·shuns)* The separation of lawsuits or prosecutions involving multiple parties into separate, independent cases, resulting in separate, final judgments.

sexual assault *(SEKS·yoo·el a·SALT)* Any unwanted sexual contact.

shareholders *(SHARE·hold·ers)* People who own shares in a corporation. Also called *stockholders.*

sheriff's sale *(SHERR·ifs)* A sale of property at public auction conducted by a sheriff.

shipment contract *(SHIP·ment KON·trakt)* A contract under which the seller turns the goods over to a carrier for delivery to a buyer.

sight draft A draft that is payable when it is presented for payment to the drawee.

signature clause *(SIG·na·cher)* The clause in a will that precedes the testator's signature. Also called *testimonium clause.*

silent partners *(SY·lent PART·ners)* Partners who may be known to the public as partners but who take no active part in the business.

simultaneous death *(sy·mul·TAY·nee·us)* The death of two or more people in such a way that it is impossible to determine who died before whom.

slander *(SLAN·der)* Defamation that is communicated by the spoken word.

slayer statutes *(SLAY·er STAT·shoots)* Laws enacted by legislatures stating that murderers cannot inherit from their victims.

small pond A pond that is under 10 acres in size.

sodomy *(SOD·e·mee)* Oral or anal copulation. The act that state statutes often describe as an "abominable and detestable crime against nature."

solemnized *(SAW·lem·nized)* Performed in a ceremonial fashion with witnesses present.

sole proprietorship *(pro·PRY·e·tor·ship)* A form of business that is owned and operated by one person.

sororicide *(so·ROR·i·side)* Killing one's sister.

soundness of mind Sufficient mental ability to make a will.

special administrator *(SPESH·el ad·MIN·is·tray·tor)* A person appointed by the court to handle the affairs of an estate for a limited time only to take care of urgent affairs.

special agent *(SPESH·el AY·jent)* An agent who is authorized to carry out a single transaction or to perform a specified act.

special indorsement *(SPESH·el in·DORSE·ment)* An indorsement that specifies the person to whom or to whose order it makes the instrument payable. Also called *full indorsement.*

special warranty deed *(SPESH·el WAR·en·tee)* A deed containing warranties under which the grantor guarantees that the property is free from all encumbrances made during the time that he or she owned the property and agrees to defend the title only against claims through him or her. Also called *limited warranty deed.*

specific legacy *(spe·SIF·ic LEG·a·see)* A gift by will of a particular article of personal property.

specific performance *(spe·SIF·ic per·FORM·ens)* An order by the court ordering a breaching party to do that which he or she agreed to do under the terms of the contract.

spendthrift *(SPEND·thrift)* One who spends money profusely and improvidently.

spendthrift trust A trust designed to provide a fund for the maintenance of a beneficiary and at the same time to secure it against the beneficiary's improvidence or incapacity.

sponge tax *(spunj taks)* A tax that soaks up money for the state that the estate is being given credit for in any event.

spousal support *(SPOWS·el su·PORT)* An allowance made to a divorced spouse by a former spouse for support and maintenance. Also called *alimony.*

spray trust A trust that allows the trustee to decide how much will be given to each beneficiary in the trustee's discretion. Also called *discretionary trust* and *sprinkling trust.*

springing power *(SPRING·ing POW·er)* A power in a durable power of attorney that does not become effective until the person making it actually becomes incapacitated.

sprinkling trust *(SPRINK·ling)* A trust that allows the trustee to decide how much will be given to each beneficiary in the trustee's discretion. Also called *discretionary trust* and *spray trust.*

stalking *(STAW·king)* The willful, malicious, and repeated following, harassing, and threatening of another person, intending to place the person in fear of death or serious bodily injury.

standing to sue *(STAND·ing to SOO)* A party has a tangible, legally protected interest at stake in a lawsuit.

statute *(STAT·shoot)* A law passed by a legislature.

statute of frauds *(STAT·shoot of frawds)* Certain contracts must be in writing to be enforceable.

statute of limitations *(STAT·shoot ov lim·i·TA·shuns)* A time limit, set by statute, within which suit must be commenced after the cause of action accrues.

statute of repose *(STAT·shoot ov re·POSE)* An absolute time limit for bringing a cause of action regardless of when the cause of action accrues.

statutory arson *(STAT·shoo·tore·ee AR·sen)* The burning of a building other than a dwelling house or the burning of one's own house to collect insurance.

statutory burglary *(STAT·shoo·tore·ee BUR·gler·ee)* Burglary that does not contain all of the elements of common law burglary.

statutory rape *(STAT·shoo·tore·ee)* Sexual intercourse with a child under the age set by state statute regardless of whether the child consented or not. Also called *unlawful sexual intercourse.*

stipulate *(STIP·yoo·late)* Agree.

stipulation *(stip·yoo·LA·shun)* An agreement between the parties to an action regulating any matter relative to the proceedings.

stock certificate *(ser·TIF·i·ket)* A document that evidences ownership of stock in a corporation.

stockholders *(STAWK·hold·ers)* People who own shares in a corporation. Also called *shareholders.*

stop and frisk rule A rule that allows police officers who believe a person is acting suspiciously and could be armed to stop and frisk that person for weapons without a search warrant.

straight bankruptcy *(strayt BANK·rupt·see)* A proceeding designed to liquidate a debtor's property, pay off creditors, and discharge the debtor from most debts. Also called *Chapter 7 bankruptcy* and *liquidation.*

strict liability *(strikt ly·a·BIL·i·tee)* Liability for an act that causes harm without regard to fault or negligence. Also called *absolute liability.*

subjacent support *(sub·JAY·sent)* To hold up from below.

sublease *(SUB·leess)* A lease given by a lessee to a third person conveying the same interest for a shorter term than the period for which the lessee holds it. Also called *underlease.*

subpoena *(suh·PEEN·a)* An order commanding a person to appear and testify in a legal action. Also called *subpoena ad testificandum.*

subpoena ad testificandum *(suh·PEEN·a ad tes·te·fe·KAN·dem)* An order commanding a person to appear and testify in a legal action. Also called *subpoena.*

subpoena duces tecum *(suh·PEEN·a DOO·sess TEK·um)* An order commanding a person to appear and bring certain papers or other materials that are pertinent to a legal action.

subscribe *(sub·SKRIBE)* To sign below or at the end; to write underneath.

substantial performance *(sub·STAN·shel per·FORM·ens)* A doctrine allowing a contracting party to sue the other party for breach even though slight omissions or deviations were made in his or her own performance of the contract.

substitute check *(SUB·ste·toot)* A paper reproduction of an original check that contains an image of the front and back of the original check and can be processed just like the original check.

substituted service *(SUB·sti·tew·ted SER·viss)* A type of service in which the summons and complaint are delivered to the defendant's agent or mailed or published in a newspaper.

subterranean waters *(sub·ter·AYN·ee·en)* Waters that lie wholly beneath the surface of the ground.

successor personal representative *(suk·SESS·or PER·son·al rep·re·ZEN·ta·tiv)* A person appointed to succeed a previously appointed personal representative.

suicide *(SOO·i·side)* Self-destruction.

summarily *(sum·EHR·i·lee)* Quickly.

summary administration *(SUM·e·ree ad·min·is·TRAY·shun)* An informal method used in California to settle estates that do not exceed $30,000.

summary ejectment *(SUM·e·ree e·JEKT·ment)* The legal action used by landlords to evict tenants. Also called *dispossessory warrant proceedings, forcible entry and detainer, summary process,* and *unlawful detainer.*

summary judgment *(SUM·er·ee JUJ·ment)* An immediate decision by the court without going to trial based on the papers filed by the parties.

summary proceeding *(SUM·e·ree pro·SEED·ing)* A short and simple trial.

summary process *(SUM·e·ree PROSS·ess)* The legal action used by landlords to evict tenants. Also called *dispossessory warrant proceedings, forcible entry and detainer, summary ejectment,* and *unlawful detainer.*

summation *(sum·AY·shun)* Final statement by an attorney summarizing the evidence that has been introduced. Also called *closing argument.*

summons *(SUM·ens)* A formal notice to the defendant that a lawsuit has begun and that the defendant must file an answer within the number of days set by state law or lose the case by default.

supervening cause *(su·per·VEEN·ing)* A new occurrence that became the proximate cause of the injury.

supremacy clause *(soo·PREM·i·see)* A clause in the U.S. Constitution making the U.S. Constitution and federal laws the supreme law of the land.

surety *(SHOOR·e·tee)* One who undertakes to stand behind another, that is, pay money or do any other act in the event that his or her principal fails to meet an obligation.

surrogate *(SER·o·get)* A person authorized to act on behalf of another and subject to the other's control. Also called *agent.*

Surrogate's Court *(SER·o·gets)* A name given in some states to the court that exercises the function of settling decedents' estates.

suspended sentence *(sus·PEN·ded SEN·tense)* A sentence that is given formally but not actually served.

sustain *(sus·TANE)* To support.

syndicate *(SIN·de·ket)* A relationship in which two or more people combine their labor or property for a single business undertaking. Also called *co-venture, joint enterprise,* and *joint venture.*

tacking The addition of previous occupants' possession to one's own possession to meet the statutory period for adverse possession.

talesmen and taleswomen ***(TAILZ·men and tailz·WO·men)*** Bystanders or people from the county at large chosen by the court to act as jurors when there are not enough people left on the venire.

tangible personal property ***(TAN·je·bel PER·son·al PROP·er·tee)*** Property that has substance and that can be touched.

temporary custody ***(TEM·po·rare·ee KUS·te·dee)*** Custody of a child awarded to a parent on a temporary basis, pending the outcome of a divorce or separation action.

tenancy at will ***(TEN·en·see)*** An estate in real property for an indefinite period of time.

tenancy by the entirety ***(TEN·en·see by the en·TY·re·tee)*** A type of joint tenancy held by a husband and wife that offers protection against attachment and that cannot be terminated by one spouse alone.

tenancy for years ***(TEN·en·see)*** An estate in real property for a definite or fixed period of time no matter how long or how short.

tenancy from year to year ***(TEN·en·see)*** An estate in real property that continues for successive periods until one of the parties terminates it by giving notice to the other party. Also called *periodic tenancy.*

tenancy in partnership ***(TEN·en·see in PART·ner·ship)*** Ownership in which each person has an interest in partnership property and is a co-owner of such property.

tenant ***(TEN·ent)*** A person who has temporary possession of and an interest in real property of another under a lease. Also called *lessee.*

tenant at sufferance ***(TEN·ent at SUF·er·ense)*** A tenant who wrongfully remains in possession of the premises after a tenancy has expired. Also called *holdover tenant.*

tenants in common ***(TEN·entz in KOM·on)*** Two or more persons holding an undivided interest in property, with each owner's interests going to his or her heirs on death rather than to the surviving co-owners.

tender of payment ***(TEN·der)*** To offer to the other party the money owed under a contract.

tender of performance ***(per·FORM·ens)*** To offer to do that which one has agreed to do under the terms of a contract.

tenements ***(TEN·e·mentz)*** Everything of a permanent nature that may be possessed and, in a more restrictive sense, houses or dwellings.

testament ***(TES·te·ment)*** A legal instrument stating a person's wishes as to the disposition of personal property at death.

testamentary capacity ***(test·e·MEN·ter·ee ca·PASS·i·tee)*** Sufficient mental ability to make a will.

testamentary disposition ***(test·e·MEN·ter·ee dis·po·ZI·shun)*** A gift of property that is not to take effect until the one who makes the gift dies.

testamentary trust ***(test·e·MEN·ter·ee)*** A trust that is created by will and that comes into existence only on the death of the testator.

testate ***(TES·tate)*** The state of a person who has made a will.

testator ***(tes·tay·TOR)*** A man who makes or has made a testament or will.

testatrix ***(tes·tay·TRIX)*** A woman who makes or has made a testament or will.

testimonial evidence ***(tes·ti·MOH·nee·el EV·i·dens)*** Oral testimony of witnesses made under oath in open court.

testimonium clause ***(tes·ti·MOH·nee·um)*** The clause in a will that immediately precedes the testator's signature. Also called*signature clause.*

third party ***(PAR·tee)*** In agency law, one who deals with an agent in making a contract with the agent's principal.

third-party beneficiary ***(ben·e·FISH·ee·air·ee)*** Someone for whose benefit a promise is made but who is not a party to the contract.

time draft A draft that is payable at a particular time stated in the instrument.

time is of the essence ***(ESS·ens)*** Time is critical.

time note A note that is payable at a particular time stated in the instrument.

time-sharing A fee simple ownership of a unit of real property in which the owner can exercise the right of possession for only an interval, such as a week or two, each year. Also called *interval ownership.*

title ***(TY·tel)*** Ownership.

title reference ***(TY·tel REF·e·renss)*** A sentence in a deed indicating from whom the grantor in that deed received the property.

title search ***(TY·tel)*** An examination of all recorded instruments that affect the title to a particular parcel of property for the past 50 or more years.

title theory of mortgages ***(TY·tel THEE·ree ov MORE·ge·jes)*** The legal theory that a mortgage is a conveyance of title, which becomes void on payment of the obligation. Also called *common law theory of mortgages.*

toll ***(tohl)*** To bar, defeat, or take away.

Torrens system ***(TOR·enz SYS·tem)*** A method of land registration that establishes clear title to land. Also called *registered land.*

tort A wrong against an individual.

tortfeasor ***(tort·FEE·zor)*** One who commits a tort.

tortious ***(TOR·shus)*** Wrongful; implying or involving tort.

tortious bailee ***(TOR·shus bay·LEE)*** A person who is wrongfully in possession of another's personal property.

Totten trust ***(TOT·en)*** A bank account in the name of the depositor as trustee for another person.

township ***(TOUN·ship)*** A six-square-mile portion of land in the United States government survey.

tract ***(trakt)*** Parcel.

tract of land ***(trakt)*** A large piece of land.

trade acceptance ***(ak·SEP·tense)*** A draft used with a bill of lading by a seller of goods to extend credit or to be sure that payment for goods is received.

trade fixture ***(FIKS·cher)*** Personal property necessary to carry on a trade or business that is physically attached to real property but does not become part of the real property.

trademark ***(TRADE·mark)*** Any word, name, symbol, or device used by a business to identify goods and distinguish them from those manufactured or sold by others.

trade secret ***(SEE·kret)*** A plan, process, or device that is used in business and is known only to employees who need to know the secret to accomplish their work.

transitory action ***(TRAN·zi·tore·ee AK·shun)*** A lawsuit that may be brought in more than one place as long as the court in which it is heard has proper jurisdiction.

treason ***(TREE·zun)*** Levying war against the United States or giving aid and comfort to its enemies.

trespass ***(TRES·pass)*** The intentional and unauthorized entry on the land of another.

trespass de bonis asportatis ***(de BO·nis as·por·TAH·tis)*** Trespass for goods carried away.

trial docket ***(tryl DOK·et)*** The calendar of cases that are ready for trial. Also called *trial list.*

trial list ***(tryl list)*** The calendar of cases that are ready for trial. Also called *trial docket.*

trust A right of ownership to property held by one person for the benefit of another.

trust deed An instrument that creates a living trust. Also called *trust indenture.*

trustee ***(trus·TEE)*** A person who holds legal title to property in trust for another.

trustee in bankruptcy ***(trus·TEE in BANK·rupt·see)*** A person appointed by a bankruptcy court to hold the debtor's assets in trust for the benefit of creditors.

trustee process ***(trus·TEE PROSS·ess)*** A procedure for attaching the defendant's property that is in the hands of a third person.

trust fund The body, principal sum, or capital of a trust. Also called *corpus, trust property,* and *trust res.*

trust indenture ***(in·DEN·cher)*** An instrument that creates a living trust. Also called *trust deed.*

trustor ***(trus·TOR)*** A person who establishes a trust. Also called *donor, grantor,* and *settlor.*

trust principal ***(PRIN·se·pel)*** The body, principal sum, or capital of a trust. Also called *corpus, trust fund, trust property,* and *trust res.*

trust property ***(PROP·er·tee)*** The body, principal sum, or capital of a trust. Also called *corpus, trust fund, trust principal,* and *trust res.*

trust res *(reyz)* The body, principal sum, or capital of a trust. Also called *corpus, trust fund, trust principal,* and *trust property.*

ultra vires act *(UL·tra VY·rees)* A corporate act committed outside of the corporation's authority.

unconscionable *(un·KON·shun·a·bel)* So harshly one-sided and unfair that the court's conscience is shocked.

underlease *(UN·der·leess)* A lease given by a lessee to a third person conveying the same interest for a shorter term than the period for which the lessee holds it. Also called *sublease.*

undisclosed principal *(un·dis·KLOZED PRIN·se·pel)* One who is not known by a third party to be a principal for an agent.

undue influence *(un·DEW IN·flew·ens)* The overcoming of a person's free will by misusing a position of trust and taking advantage of the other person who is relying on the trust relationship.

unenforceable contract *(un·en·FORS·e·bel KON·trakt)* A contract that cannot be enforced for some legal reason.

Uniform Commercial Code *(UCC) (YOON·i·form ke·MERSH·el kode)* A uniform law, adopted in every state, that governs various commercial transactions.

Uniform Probate Code *(UPC) (YOON·i·form PRO·bate kode)* A law attempting to standardize and modernize laws relating to the affairs of decedents, minors, and certain other people who need protection.

unilateral contract *(yoon·i·LAT·er·el KON·trakt)* A contract containing one promise in exchange for an act.

unilateral mistake *(yoon·i·LAT·er·el mis·TAKE)* A mistake made by only one party to a contract.

unintentional torts *(un·in·TEN·shun·al)* Torts that are committed accidentally.

unit deed *(YOON·it)* A deed to an individual condominium unit being transferred.

units *(YOON·its)* The individual portions of a condominium that are owned separately in fee simple by individual owners.

unity of interest *(YOON·i·tee ov IN·trest)* Equal interest in a property by all owners.

unity of possession *(YOON·i·tee ov po·SESH·en)* Equal rights to possession of the entire property by all owners.

unity of time *(YOON·i·tee)* All owners of a property taking title at the same time.

unity of title *(YOON·i·tee ov TY·tle)* All owners of a property receiving title from the same instrument.

universal defense *(yoon·i·VER·sel de·FENSE)* A defense that is good against everyone, including a holder in due course of a negotiable instrument. Also called *absolute defense* and *real defense.*

unjust enrichment *(un·JUST en·RICH·ment)* Occurs when one person retains money, property, or other benefit that in equity and justice belongs to another.

unlawful detainer *(de·TAYN·er)* The legal action used by landlords to evict tenants. Also called *dispossessory warrant proceedings, forcible entry and detainer, summary ejectment,* and *summary process.*

unlawful sexual intercourse *(un·LAW·ful SEKS·yoo·el IN·ter·kors)* Sexual intercourse with a child under the age set by state statute regardless of whether the child consented or not. Also called *statutory rape.*

unlimited liability *(un·LIM·i·ted ly·a·BIL·i·tee)* Liability that has no bounds.

usufruct *(YOO·se·frukt)* The right to use the profits of property that belongs to another.

usufructuary *(yoo·se·FRUK·shoo·a·ree)* A person who has a usufruct.

usury *(YOO·zer·ee)* The charging of a greater amount of interest than is allowed by law.

uttering *(UT·er·ing)* Offering a forged negotiable instrument to another person, knowing it to be forged and intending to defraud.

uxoricide *(uks·OR·i·side)* Killing one's wife.

vacate *(VA·kate)* Annul.

valid *(VAL·id)* Good; having legal effect.

variable-rate mortgage *(VAR·ee·a·bel-rate MORE·gej)* A mortgage with an interest rate that fluctuates according to changes in an index to which it is connected. Also called *flexible-rate mortgage.*

variance *(VAR·ee·enss)* An exception to the zoning regulation.

vendor *(ven·DOR)* A person who transfers property or goods by sale.

vendee *(ven·DEE)* A purchaser or buyer of property or goods.

venire *(ven·EYE·ree)* The large group of people from whom a jury is selected for a trial. Also called *array, jury panel,* and *jury pool.*

venue *(VEN·yoo)* The place where the trial is held.

verbatim *(ver·BATE·im)* Word for word.

verdict *(VER·dikt)* The decision of a jury.

verdict contrary to law *(KON·trare·ee)* A verdict that is incorrect as a matter of law.

verification *(ver·i·fi·KAY·shun)* A written statement under oath confirming the correctness, truth, or authenticity of a pleading.

vested *(VES·ted)* Fixed or absolute; not contingent.

viable *(VI·a·bel)* Having the appearance of being able to live.

vicarious liability *(vy·KEHR·ee·us)* Liability that is imputed to principals and employers because of the wrongdoings of their agents and employees.

victim's impact statement *(VIK·tems IM·pakt)* A statement to the court, at the time of sentencing, relative to the impact that the crime had on the victim or the victim's family.

void Not good; having no legal effect.

voidable *(VOID·e·bel)* Capable of being disaffirmed or voided.

voir dire *(vwar·deer)* To speak the truth. The examination of jurors by the court to see that they stand indifferent.

volume *(VOL·yoom)* Book.

voluntary administrator *(VOL·en·ter·ee ad·MIN·is·tray·tor)* A person who undertakes the informal administration of a small estate.

voluntary bankruptcy *(VOL·en·ter·ee BANK·rupt·see)* A bankruptcy proceeding that is initiated by the debtor.

voluntary manslaughter *(VOL·en·ter·ee MAN·slaw·ter)* The unlawful killing of another without malice when an intention to kill exists but through the violence of sudden passion.

wage earner's plan *(wayj ER·ners)* A plan for the installment payments of outstanding debts under a Chapter 13 bankruptcy.

waive a spouse's will *(SPOW·sez)* Renounce or disclaim a spouse's will.

warrant *(WAR·ent)* To give assurance.

warranty of fitness for a particular purpose *(WAR·en·tee ov FIT·ness)* An implied warranty, given when a buyer relies on any seller's skill and judgment in selecting goods, that the goods will be fit for a particular purpose.

warranty of habitability *(WAR·en·tee ov hab·i·ta·BIL·i·tee)* An implied warranty by a landlord that the premises are fit for human habitation.

warranty of merchantability *(WAR·en·tee ov mer·chent·a·BIL·e·tee)* An implied warranty, given by merchants in all sales unless excluded, that goods are fit for the ordinary purpose for which such goods are used.

warranty of title *(WAR·en·tee ov TY·tel)* A guarantee that title is good, that the transfer is rightful, and that no unknown liens on the goods exist.

waste The abuse or destructive use of property that is in one's rightful possession.

will Originally, a legal instrument stating a person's wishes as to the disposition of real property at death but now referring to both real and personal property.

will and testament *(TES·te·ment)* Under early English law, a legal instrument that disposed of both real and personal property at death.

will contest A suit over the allowance or disallowance of a will.

willful torts *(WIL·ful)* Torts that are committed intentionally. Also called *intentional torts.*

willful, wanton, and reckless conduct *(WIL·ful WON·ten REK·les KON·dukt)* The intentional commission of an act that a reasonable person knows would cause injury to another. Also called *culpable negligence.*

winding-up period *(WINE·ding-up PEER·ee·ed)* A period of time during which partnership assets are liquidated, debts are paid, an accounting is made, and any remaining assets are distributed among the partners.

wire fraud *(frawd)* Using the wires to obtain money, property, or services by false pretenses.

writ A written order of a court, returnable to the same, commanding the performance or nonperformance of an act.

writ of attachment *(a·TACH·ment)* A written order to the sheriff, commanding the sheriff to attach the real or personal property of the defendant.

writ of certiorari *(ser·sho·RARE·ee)* An order from a higher court to a lower court to deliver its records to the higher court for review.

writ of execution *(ek·se·KYOO·shen)* A written order to the sheriff, commanding the sheriff to enforce a judgment of the court.

writ of garnishment *(GAR·nish·ment)* A written order of a court ordering a garnishee not to give out money or property held for another, but to appear and answer the plaintiff's suit.

writ of venire facias *(ven·EYE·ree FAY·shes)* A written order to cities and towns to provide a designated number of jurors for the next sitting of the court.

wrongful death action *(RONG·ful deth AK·shun)* A suit brought by a decedent's personal representative for the benefit of the decedent's heirs, claiming that death was caused by the defendant's negligent act.

wrongful death statutes *(RONG·ful deth STAT·shoots)* Legislative enactments that govern wrongful death actions.

year-and-a-day rule Death must have occurred within a year and a day after the blow occurred for a defendant to be convicted of homicide.

zoning The process of regulating the use of land by designating specific areas for certain uses.

Index

GLOSSARY OF LATIN TERMS AND PHRASES

a fortiori. with stronger reason; much more — ah for·she·OR·i
a posteriori. from the effect to the cause; from what comes after — ah po·steer·ee·OR·i
a prendre. to take; to seize. — ah PRAWN·dre
a priori. from the cause to the effect; from what comes before — ah pri·OR·i
ab initio. from the beginning — ab in·ish·ee·oh
actio criminalis. a criminal action — AK·shee·oh kri·mi·NAH·lis
actio damni injuria. an action for damages — AK·shee·oh DAM·ni in·JUR·ee·ah
actio ex delicto. an action arising out of fault — AK·shee·oh eks da·lik·toh
ad damnum. to the damage; money loss claimed by the plaintiff — ad DAHM·num
ad hoc. for one special purpose — ad HOK
ad infinitum. indefinitely; forever — ad in·fin·ITE·em
ad litem. for the suit — ad LY·tem
ad respondendum. to make answer — ad ree·spon·DEN·dem
additur. addition by a judge to the amount of damages awarded by a jury — AH·di·toor
amicus curiae. friend of the court — a·MEE·kes KYOOR·ee
animus furandi. intent to steal — AN·i·mus fer·AN·di
animus testandi. intent to make a will — AN·i·mus tes·TAN·di
anno Domini. (A.D.) in the year of our Lord — AN·oh DOM·eh·ni
ante. before — AN·tee
arguendo. in arguing — ar·gyoo·EN·doh
assumpsit. he promised — a·SUMP·sit
bona fide. in good faith — BONE·ah FIDE
caveat. beware — KA·vee·at
caveat emptor. let the buyer beware — KA·vee·at EMP·tor
caveat venditor. let the seller beware — KA·vee·at VEN·de·tor
certiorari. to be informed of; to be assured — ser·sho·RARE·ee
cestui que trust. beneficiary of a trust — SES·twee KAY
compos mentis. sound of mind — KOM·pes MEN·tis
consortium. fellowship of husband and wife — kon·SORE·shum
contra. against — KON·trah
coram. before; in the presence of — KOR·em
corpus delicti. body of the crime — KORE·pus de·LIK·tie
corpus juris. body of law — KORE·pus JOOR·ess
cum testamento annexo. with the will annexed — kum tes·ta·MENT·o an·EKS·o
damnum absque injuria. loss without injury in the legal sense — DAM·num AHB·skwee in·JOO·ree·ah
de facto. in fact; actually — dee FAK·toh
de jure. according to law; rightfully — dee JUR·ee
de minimus. of little importance — dee MIN·e·mes
de novo. anew, afresh, a second time — dee NOH·voh
dictum. unessential statement or remark in a court decision — DIK·tum
doli capaz. capable of criminal intent; able to distinguish between right and wrong — DO·li KAY·paks
duces tecum. bring with you — DOO·sess TEK·um
ergo. therefore; hence — EHR·go
et al. abbreviation for et alii; and others — et AHL
et seq. abbreviation for et sequentia; and the following — et SEK
et ux. abbreviation for et uxor; and wife — et UKS
et vir. and husband — et VEER
ex contractu. out of a contract — eks kon·TRAK·too
ex delicto. out of a tort or wrong — eks de·LIK·toh
ex officio. by virtue of an office — eks oh·FISH·ee·oh
ex parte. apart from; one side only — eks·PAR·tay
ex post facto. after the fact — eks post FAK·toh
forum non conveniens. inconvenient court — for·em non kon·VEEN·yenz
gratis. without reward or consideration — GRAT·is
habeas corpus. you have the body — HAY·bee·ess KORE·pus
habendum. to have thus; clause in a deed that defines extent of ownership — ha·BEN·dum
ibid. abbreviation for ibedim; in the same place — IBid
id. abbreviation for idem; the same — id
in camera. in chambers; in private — in KAM·er·ah
in curia. in court — in KYOOR·ee·ah
in flagrante delicto. in glaring fault; a crime in full light — in flay·GRAN·tee de·LIK·toh
in initio. at the beginning — in i·NISH·ee·o
in litem. during the suit — in LY·tem
in loco. in the place of — in LOH·ko
in loco parentis. in the place of a parent — in LOH·ko pa·REN·tis
in pari delicto. in equal fault — in pah·ree de·LIK·toh
in personam. against or with reference to a person — in per·SOH·nem
in re. in the matter of; concerning — in RAY
in rem. against the thing — in REM
in toto. in the whole; in total — in TOH·toh
infra. below, beneath — IN·frah
injuria absque damno. wrong without damage — in·JUR·ee·ya abs·kwee DAM·no

inter alia. among other things	IN·ter AY·lee·ah
inter vivos. between the living	IN·ter VY·vose.
ipse dixit. he himself says it	IP·see DIK·sit
ipso facto. by the fact itself	IP·soh FAK·toh
juris. of right; of law	JOOR·is
jus habendi. right to have something	jes he·BEN·di
jus tertii. right of a third party	jes ter·SHEE·yi
lis pendens. pending suit	liss PEN·denz
locus sigilli. place of the seal	LOH·kus se·JIL·i
malum in se. wrong in itself	MAL·um in SEH
malum prohibita. wrong because it is prohibited	MAL·um pro·HIB·i·ta
mandamus. we command; order by a court commanding a public official to perform a duty	man·DAY·mus
mens rea. guilty mind	menz RAY·ah
modus operandi. manner of operation	MOH·dus op·er·AN·di
mortis causa. by reason of death	MORE·tis KAW·sa
n.b. abbreviation of nota bene; note well; observe	
nil. contraction of nihil; nothing	nil
nisi. unless	NIE·sie
nolle prosequi. prosection not pursued	NO·lee PROSS·e·kwi
nolo contendere. I will not contest the action	NO·lo kon·TEN·de·ree
non assumpsit. not undertaken or promised	non a·SUMP·sit
non compos mentis. not of sound mind; insane	non KOM·pes MEN·tiss
non obstante verdicto. notwithstanding the verdict	non ob·STAN·tay ver·DIK·toh
non sequitur. it does not follow	non SEK·wi·ter
nudum pactum. naked promise; bare agreement without consideration	NOO·dum PAK·tum
nul tort. no wrong has been done	nul TORT
nulla bona. no goods	null·a·BONE·ah
nunc pro tunc. now for then	nunk pro tunk
obiter dictum. words of a prior decision unnecessary for the decision of the case	OH·bih·ter DIK·tum
onus probandi. burden of proof	OH·nus pro·BAN·di
pendente lite. pending suit	pen·DEN·tay lie·tay
per annum. by the year	per AN·num
per capita. by the head	per KA·pi·tah
per curiam. by the court	KYOO·ree·am
per diem. by the day	per DEE·em
per quod. whereby	per KWOD
per se. by itself; taken alone	per SAY
per stirpes. by representation	per STER·peez
post mortem. after death	post MOR·tem
prima facie. at first sight; on the face of it	PRY·muh FAY·shee
pro bono publico. for the public good	pro BO·no POOB·lek·oh
pro forma. as a matter of form	pro FORM·ah
pro rata. proportionately	pro RAY·ta
pro se. for himself or herself	pro say
pro tanto. for as far as it goes	pro TAHN·tah
pro tempore (pro tem.). temporary; for the time being	pro TEM·po·re
quantum meruit. as much as he or she deserves	KWAN·tum MEHR·oo·it
quasi. as if; almost as it were	KWAY·zie
quasi in rem. as if against the thing	KWAY·zie in REM
quid pro quo. something for something; one thing for another	kwid proh KWOH
res. thing, object	reyz
res gestae. things that have been done	reyz JESS·tee
res ipsa loquitur. thing speaks for itself	res IP·sa LO·kwe·ter
res judicata. thing decided or judged (also res adjudicata)	res joo·di·KAY·ta
respondeat superior. let the superior answer	re·SPOND·ee·yat se·PEER·ee·or
retraxit. he or she has withdrawn	re·TRAK·sit
scienter. knowingly	si·EN·ter
scilicet. to wit; namely; that is to say	SIL·e·set
scintilla. spark	sin·TIL·ah
secundum. according to	se·KUN·dem
seriatim. separately; one by one	see·ree·AH·tem
sic. thus; in such a manner	sik
sigillum. seal	se·JIL·um
simplex obligato. single obligation	SIM·pleks ob·le·GAT·oh
sine qua non. without which, the thing cannot be	SI·nee kway NON
stare decisis. to stand by the decision	STAHR·ee de·SY·sis
sua sponte. of its own motion	SOO·ah SPON·tay
sub curia. under law	sub KURE·ee·ah
sub judice. under judicial consideration	sub JOO·de·say
sub silentio. under silence	sub se·LEN·shee·oh
subpoena. under penalty; a process to cause a witness to appear and give testimony	suh·PEEN·a
subpoena duces tecum. bring with you; a subpoena ordering a witness to produce a paper	suh·PEEN·a DOO·sess TEK·um
sui generis. one of a kind; unique	SOO·ee JEN·e·ris
sue juris. of one's own right; not under guardianship	SOO·ee JOOR·is
supersedeas. writ commanding a stay in the proceedings	soo·per·SEE·dee·es
supra. above; earlier	SOO·prah
ultra vires. beyond the powers	UL·tra VY·res
venire facias. order to the sheriff to bring people to court to serve as jurors	ven·EYE·ree FAY·she·as
versus. against	VER·ses
viz. abbreviation for videlicit; to make more specific that which has been previously stated	viz
volenti non fit injuria. volunteer suffers no wrong	voh·LEN·tie non fit in·JOOR·ee·ah